Concepts and Procedures in Whistleblower Law

Concepts and Procedures in Whistleblower Law

Stephen M. Kohn

QUORUM BOOKS
Westport, Connecticut • London

Library of Congress Cataloging-in-Publication Data

Kohn, Stephen M. (Stephen Martin)
    Concepts and procedures in whistleblower law / Stephen M. Kohn.
        p.   cm.
    Includes bibliographical references and index.
    ISBN 1–56720–354–X (alk. paper)
        1. Employees—Dismissal of—Law and legislation—United States.   2. Discrimination in
    employment—Law and legislation—United States.   3. Whistle blowing—Law and
    legislation—United States.   I. Title.
    KF3471.K638   2001
    344.7301′2596—dc21   00–027073

British Library Cataloguing in Publication Data is available.

Library of Congress Catalog Card Number: 00–027073
ISBN: 1–56720–354–X

First published in 2001

Quorum Books, 88 Post Road West, Westport, CT 06881
An imprint of Greenwood Publishing Group, Inc.
www.quorumbooks.com

Printed in the United States of America

The paper used in this book complies with the
Permanent Paper Standard issued by the National
Information Standards Organization (Z39.48–1984).

10 9 8 7 6 5 4 3 2 1

To my loving children, Nataleigh and Max

Contents

Abbreviations

ADEA	Age Discrimination in Employment Act
AIR 21	Aviation Investment and Reform Act for the 21st Century
ALJ	Administrative Law Judge
APA	Administrative Procedure Act
ARB	Administrative Review Board
BNA	Bureau of National Affairs
CAA	Clean Air Act
CBA	Collective Bargaining Agreement
CEPA	Conscientious Employee Protection Act
CERCLA	Comprehensive Environmental Response, Compensation and Liability Act (Superfund)
CFR	Code of Federal Regulations
COA	Cause of Action
CRA	Civil Rights Act
CSRA	Civil Service Reform Act
D&O	Decision and Order
DFO	Duty of Fair Representation
DOE	Department of Energy
DOL	Department of Labor
EEOC	Equal Employment Opportunity Commission
EPA	Environmental Protection Agency
ERA	Energy Reorganization Act
ERISA	Employment Retirement Income Security Act
FAA	Federal Arbitration Act
FCA	False Claims Act
FDIC	Federal Deposit Insurance Corporation
FIRREA	Financial Institutions Reform, Recovery, and Enforcement Act
FLSA	Fair Labor Standards Act
FMHSA	Federal Mine Health and Safety Act

FMSA	Federal Mine Safety Act
FOIA	Freedom of Information Act
FRCP	Federal Rules of Civil Procedure
FRD	Federal Rules Decision
FSMA	Federal Surface Mining Act
JTPA	Job Training and Partnership Act
LHWCA	Longshoreman's and Harbor Worker's Compensation Act
LMRA	Labor Management Relations Act
MFA	Major Frauds Act
MSPB	Merit Systems Protection Board
NLRA	National Labor Relations Act
NLRB	National Labor Relations Board
NRC	Nuclear Regulatory Commission
OSC	Office of Special Council
OSHA	Occupational Safety and Health Act
RCRA	Resource Conservation and Recovery Act
RICO	Racketeering Influenced and Corrupt Organizations Act
RIF	Reduction in Force
RLA	Railway Labor Act
SDWA	Safe Drinking Water Act
SOL	Secretary of Labor
SWDA	Solid Waste Disposal Act
STAA	Surface Transportation Assistance Act
TSCA	Toxic Substances Control Act
USC	United States Code
WPA	Whistleblower Protection Act
WPCA	Water Pollution Control Act

Acknowledgments

This book was made possible by the support of my wife Leslie, and my law partners, Michael Kohn and David Colapinto. Without the assistance and inspiration of my dedicated staff, legal interns and friends, this book could never have been written. Special thanks are in order for Russell Burchill, Melanie Olsen, Joyce Claro, Heather Cowen Fox, Mary Jane Wilmoth, Judy Perez and Kathleen Westerhoff. I would also like to acknowledge the contributions of Sushmita Srikanth, Juan Villaseñor, Lisa Fabian, Scott Anderson, Christopher Wesser, Mia Gramata-Jones, Eric Valentine, Lynne Goetz, my former law clerks, and the directors of the National Whistleblower Center, Alice Bendheim, Nina Bell, Dennis Brutus, Annette Kronstadt, David Niblack, Mark Toney, Frederic Whitehurst, William Worthy, William Yolton, and Howard Zinn. The encouragement and understanding of my family, Estelle Kohn, Arthur A. Kohn, Ana Maria Ramos–Kohn, Michael Rose, Emily Rose and Sam Rose, were crucial in helping me complete this book. Finally, a special thanks to my mother, Corinne M. Kohn, for her tireless commitment to her children and her unwavering belief that everyone can make a difference.

Chapter 1

Overview of a Whistleblower Claim: A Step-by-Step Approach

Over the past fifty years, a growing national consensus has recognized that whistleblowers positively contribute to society [1] and need protection against retaliation.[2] Despite this consensus, one of the most surprising features in whistleblower law is the absence of a national whistleblower protection statute. Unlike other areas of labor relations, such as age discrimination, race discrimination, and discrimination against union members, there is no uniform national law that protects whistleblowers.[3] Instead of a national law that can be readily understood, there are over thirty separate federal statutes or constitutional provisions governing various types of whistle-blowing, and each state has developed its own common law or statutory approach to whistleblower protection. Given the numerous potential laws that may govern any specific act of whistleblowing, and the radical differences in the protections available under these laws, any analysis of how to properly "blow the whistle" must start with a step-by-step review of the key factors that underlie whistleblower cases.

A STEP-BY-STEP APPROACH

Step 1: Identifying a Remedy

The first step in reviewing a case is to determine what statutes or common law actions may be applicable to the employee's whistleblowing. For example, if an employee working in the private sector blew the whistle in Louisiana on the dumping of toxic waste into the Mississippi River, that

employee would be protected under the federal environmental whistleblower laws[4] and under a Louisiana state environmental whistleblower act.[5] If
the same violation was alleged in California, the federal laws would still
apply, and the whistleblower would also have a tort cause of action under
the state common law for punitive damages.[6] If the employee blew the
whistle on the identical issue but worked for the federal government in
Washington, D.C., the federal environmental statutes would still apply and
she or he would also be covered under the Federal Civil Service Reform
Act/Whistleblower Protection Act but would not have any state cause of
action.[7]

In addition to explicit whistleblower protection laws, employees
may also be protected under traditional tort or contract remedies for damages resulting from retaliation for whistleblowing, including such actions
as intentional infliction of emotional distress,[8] defamation[9] or breach of
contract.[10]

As can be seen, depending upon whom one works for and in which
state one is employed, the nature and scope of whistleblower protection is
varied. Practitioners should review both the state common law and statutory law, as well as federal statutory and constitutional law, to determine
which laws may provide a remedy for the employee. This is an extremely
important threshold process as each separate law has its own unique procedures, its own definitions of adverse actions and protected activity, its own
damages provisions, and its own statute of limitations.

Once the potential causes of action are identified, a plaintiff must
make the difficult choice of under which remedy to file. If only one remedy is available, this selection is easy. However, if multiple remedies are
available, a decision as to which law to use will have a profound impact on
any whistleblower claim. The selection of a remedy will determine how
expensive or risky a particular claim may be, the types of damages that are
recoverable, and the forum in which the case will be adjudicated (i.e.,
federal or state, court or administrative). For example, nuclear whistleblowers are explicitly protected under Section 211 of the Energy Reorganization Act.[11] Section 211 has a 180-day statute of limitations and provides
for a full adversary administrative hearing before the U.S. Department of
Labor.[12] Under Section 211 there is no jury trial, the rules of evidence are
relaxed, and the proceedings are required to be expedited. Although punitive damages are provided for under the statute, employees are entitled to
preliminary reinstatement pending a final decision, reinstatement, full back
pay and benefits, attorney fees, and costs and compensatory damages.
Likewise, Congress altered the burdens of proof in Section 211 cases,
making it easier for an employee to prevail than under most other employ-

ment discrimination laws.

On the other hand, the U.S. Supreme Court has held that Section 211 does not preempt states from also protecting nuclear whistleblowers.[13] In this regard, the Illinois Supreme Court ruled that an employee covered under Section 211 also states a claim under the Illinois public policy exception tort. Thus, in Illinois, an employee could ignore the Section 211 remedy, file a tort action in state court, get around the 180-day statute of limitations, have a jury hear the case, and receive punitive damages.[14] However, under Illinois common law, statutory attorney fees are not available. Moreover, a minority of states refuse to allow employees to utilize common law remedies if statutory remedies also exist.

Some employees have filed for both administrative and common law remedies. Once again, although this approach has been successful, it raises other issues, such as *res judicata* and *collateral estoppel.*

The major questions that should be considered in choosing an appropriate remedy are:

1. What are the benefits, if any, of using a federal statutory remedy versus a state common law or statutory remedy?

2. Is a potential common law action preempted or precluded by a preexisting statutory remedy?

3. How certain is the whistleblower that he or she met the *prima facie* case of any law?

4. What procedure will the adjudicating body utilize in processing a claim (what rules of evidence or discovery are applicable), and who will be the decision maker (i.e., a judge, an administrative agency, or a jury)?

5. Does the case contain facts or issues more suitable for adjudication by an administrative agency, a court, and/or a jury?

6. Is the client willing to underwrite the costs of a long, grueling suit, or are less expensive administrative procedures more practical?

7. How long will a final determination reasonably take in forum?

8. Which forum is most appropriate to review the public policy/public safety concerns raised by the whistleblowing activity?

9. Should simultaneous federal and state actions be filed, and what are the risks of proceeding in multiple forums?

Step 2: Make an Initial Determination of the Strengths and Weaknesses of a Claim

Whistleblower cases—even those with considerable merit—can be difficult to win. Employees who file allegations of wrongdoing are often subject to personal attacks[15] and their credibility is always a central issue.[16] Their employment history, job performance, and motives will be scrutinized. Moreover, the whistleblowers themselves may face unusually harsh adverse actions, that may render them "bitterly regretting that they had spoken out" and "out of work or under employed" for years.[17]

Litigating even the most meritorious claim can be time consuming, exhausting, costly, and prolonged. As one commentator correctly noted: "retaliation cases are not easily resolved and frequently proceed to trial and beyond to appeal. . . . you will find yourself up against a large corporation with a substantial litigation budget."[18]

Consequently, regardless of the legal protections which may be theoretically available to a whistleblower, a number of significant and outcome determinative factors should be weighed at the very initial stages of a case review. These factors should include:

1. *The employee's work history.* Has the employee ever been discharged from a prior position? How long has the employee worked at his or her current job and what type of documented work record exists? Does the employee have a history of nonwhistleblower work-related problems? Are there preexisting conditions (work related or personal), which may surface and impact the employee's credibility?

2. *Has the employee documented his or her allegations?* Almost all commentators recognize the importance of a whistleblower obtaining documented evidence of either the alleged misconduct and/or the alleged retaliation.[19] Has the employee kept a log, made tapes, or otherwise assembled materials that will corroborate the claim. Is there a "smoking gun" memo which demonstrates retaliatory animus? Has the employee diligently assembled exculpatory or inculpatory information?

3. *The nature of the whistleblowing.* On what did the employee "blow the whistle"? Is it a trivial matter or one with readily understandable public impact? Is it possible to prove that the whistleblower's allegations are accurate? Is there an independent review of the allegations and, if so, what are the conclusions?

4. *Is the whistleblower credible?* As one experienced litigator noted: "In employment cases . . . the client's personality and demeanor often become the

focus of the defense. If you do not like the client, it is doubtful the jury will."[20]

Step 3: Insuring That the Claim Is Timely Filed

One major weakness in many statutory whistleblower protection laws is the short statute of limitations. For example, the employee protection provisions of the federal Clean Air Act,[21] the Safe Drinking Water Act,[22] the Water Pollution Act,[23] the Comprehensive Environmental Response, Compensation and Liability Act,[24] the Toxic Substance Control Act,[25] the Surface Mining Control and Reclamation Act,[26] and the Occupational Safety and Health Act (OSHA),[27] all have thirty-day statutes of limitation.

Failure to comply with a statute of limitations is a common defense in whistleblower cases, and the statute is generally held to start running at the time an employee learns that he or she will be retaliated against—not on the last day of employment.[28] Although the U.S. Supreme Court has held that statutes of limitation in employment cases are not normally jurisdictional bars to maintaining a cause of action,[29] practitioners should ensure strict adherence to statutes of limitation. Normally, the very first questions asked in a client interview concern establishing the date in which a statute of limitations commenced running, and thereafter identifying the date in which any complaint must be filed.

If a statute of limitation has been missed, an employee must rely upon the doctrine of *equitable tolling*. This doctrine is narrow. As the U.S. Court of Appeals for the 3rd Circuit stated in *School District of Allentown v. Marshall*: "The restrictions on equitable tolling must be scrupulously observed."[30] The court summarized the general grounds that a complainant must allege in order to obtain equitable relief from the statute of limitations.

1. the defendant has actively misled the plaintiff respecting the cause of action;

2. the plaintiff has in some extraordinary way been prevented from asserting his or her rights; or

3. the plaintiff has raised the precise statutory claim in issue but has mistakenly done so in the wrong forum.[31]

The exact definition of actively misled or fraudulent concealment of an employee's right to file a complaint is analyzed on a case-by-case basis.[32] But an employee's subjective ignorance of the time provisions is not sufficient to invoke equitable modification of the statute of limitations.[33]

If there is a statutory or regulatory duty to post notice of an employee's right to file a discrimination suit under the whistleblower laws, the failure to post such a notice may toll the statute of limitations.[34] Equitable tolling may be available if the employee shows that she or he was lulled into inaction by the assurances of the employer,[35] had no reason to know that he or she was the victim of discrimination until after the statutory period expired,[36] can show the presence of a continuing violation.[37]

Step 4: Establishing a *Prima Facie* Case

Litigation strategy in whistleblower cases centers around proving the required *prima facie* case and rebutting the most typical management defense (i.e., that the employee's discharge was for a legitimate business purpose, not improper retaliation). Once a law is identified as a potentially good remedy (or the only remedy), careful attention must be paid to ensuring that a client can satisfy each element of the *prima facie* case. When a case proceeds into active litigation, a defendant will dissect a claim and, if appropriate, file a motion to dismiss or summary judgment on any element of the *prima facie* case an employee cannot meet.

The following elements run through almost every whistleblower case:

1.   that the plaintiff is an employee or person covered under the specific statutory or common law relied upon for the action;

2.   that the defendant is an employer or person covered under the specific statutory or common law relied upon for the action;

3.   that the plaintiff engaged in protected whistleblower activity covered under the statutory or common law;

4.   that the defendant knew or had knowledge that the plaintiff engaged in such activity;

5.   that retaliation against the employee was motivated, at least in part, by the employee engaging in protected activity;

6.   that plaintiff was subjected to an adverse action cognizable under the statutory remedy, or suffered some other wrong actionable under state common law;

7. where applicable, that plaintiff acted in good faith when he or she engaged in protected activity; and

8. that the defendant cannot demonstrate that he or she would have reached the same decision as to plaintiff's employment in the absence of protected conduct.[38]

The eighth element listed in the *prima facie* case is technically a defense.[39] Employers, however, almost always put forth an alleged legitimate business justification for the adverse action. Practically speaking, if an employee cannot meet this defense, he or she will lose (even if discriminatory motive can be demonstrated).[40]

Step 5: Preserving Evidence and Formulating a Discovery Plan

At the outset of any whistleblower case, a careful review of all potential evidence must be conducted. An employer's rationale for taking whatever adverse action occurred must be reviewed, along with the specific facts for which an employee will build a case. Witnesses can be unreliable, and witnesses who still work for the employer may be intimidated. Thus, interviewing potential witnesses early in a case—and obtaining affidavits if proper—should be seriously considered.

A formal discovery plan should be established. The types of information needed in discovery, and the persons who may need to be deposed, must be evaluated.

In a whistleblower case, discovery can be used to probe into the validity of the original allegations. Simply put, facts concerning the underlying disclosure or misconduct are often extremely relevant for the wrongful discharge case. This prosecutorial use of discovery can be critical for an employee. The underlying misconduct, if documented and fully uncovered, may have a devastating impact on a wrongdoer's credibility.[41]

Courts have recognized the necessity for allowing extensive discovery in employment discrimination cases.[42] In *McDonnell Douglas Corp. v. Green*, the Supreme Court made specific reference to the importance of pretrial discovery in enabling a worker to prove disparate treatment and the pretextual grounds for termination.[43] The necessity for broad discovery, and the importance of carefully developing a discovery plan, is plain and fully recognized in the case law: "[g]enerally, plaintiffs should be permitted a very broad scope of discovery in [discrimination] cases. Since direct evidence of discrimination is rarely obtainable, plaintiffs must rely on circumstantial evidence and statistical data, and evidence of an employer's overall employment practices may be essential to plaintiff's prima facie case."[44]

Typical discovery in a whistleblower claim includes document and interrogatory requests on the following topics:

1. the employee's personnel file and work history;

2. all management investigations, inquiries, evaluations, or documents related to the original whistleblower allegation or concern;

3. all management documents that evaluate the employee and relate to his or her discipline, job performance, or termination;

4. copies of all personnel manuals and work rules;

5. evidence of disparate treatment or evidence that the plaintiff was treated differently or more harshly than other employees who may have committed similar or worse disciplinary infractions;

6. evidence or information regarding federal or state investigations, or legal actions that relate to underlying whistleblower disclosures;

7. all evidence regarding the termination decision, including who participated in it, exactly why it was made, all steps that led to the decision, the alleged reason for the discipline, the exact acts for which the discipline was administered, and who had knowledge of the incident that led to the discipline;

8. evidence and information on each element of the *prima facie* case; and

9. the facts, evidence, and witnesses that the defendant will rely upon to prove its case that the discharge was not retaliatory.

Depositions are also a critical discovery tool. They "rank high in the hierarchy of pretrial, truth-finding mechanisms . . . . Face-to face confrontations prior to trial . . . are a critical component of the tools of justice in civil litigation."[45]

In addition to civil discovery, an employee may also use the federal (5 U.S.C. § 552) or state Freedom of Information Acts (FOIAs) to obtain information from government agencies. Often, various government agencies investigated a whistleblower claim or regulated the area of the employer's business that was the subject of the whistleblowing, and possess relevant information.

Step 6: Demonstrating Causation

The heart of an employment discrimination case is proving that the discrimination arose because the employee engaged in protected activity.[46] Discriminatory motive or other proof of causation can be demonstrated through direct or circumstantial evidence.[47] In rare cases, the employer's conduct is so outrageous as to be "inherently discriminatory" unto itself. The more common case involves subtle discrimination, and requires the employee to carefully demonstrate a variety of circumstances that then give rise to a reasonable inference of discriminatory motive. As described by one court, "Direct evidence of motive rarely exists. Inferences from the evidence almost universally are the only way of determining motive."[48]

The following general categories of facts or circumstances are often used to establish a reasonable inference of discriminatory motive:

1. employer's hostile attitude toward employee's protected conduct;

2. whether the employer is guilty of misconduct upon which the employee blew the whistle;

3. nature of the protected conduct;

4. changes in the treatment of the employee following protected conduct and leading up to discharge;

5. disparate treatment of discharged employee after engaging in protected conduct;

6. previous expressions of satisfaction with work record;

7. disparate treatment of similarly situated employees;

8. termination procedure;

9. timing of discharge; and

10. threats or retaliation against other employees for similar conduct.[49]

Step 7: Formulation of a Theory of the Case

The basic theory to every whistleblower case is premised upon proving that the "employer discharged the employee in retaliation for the employee's activities," and that the discharge was in violation of an antiretaliation statute or in "contravention of a clearly mandated public policy."[50] In demonstrating that the termination or discipline was retaliatory, an employee usually utilizes three major theories: that the adverse personnel action was pretextual, disparate, or taken in direct response against the employee's refusal to perform illegal or hazardous work. These three approaches are not mutually exclusive and can be argued together or in the alternative.

Pretext Theory. A pretext case is based upon proving that the alleged reason given for the discharge did not in fact exist or was not relied upon. In *Wright Line* the National Labor Relations Board (NLRB) defined pretext:

Examination of the evidence may reveal, however, that the asserted justification is a sham in that the purported rule or circumstance advanced by the employer did not exist, or was not, in fact, relied upon. When this occurs, the reason advanced by the employer may be termed pretextual. Since no legitimate business justification for the discipline exists there is, by strict definition, no dual motive.[51]

Demonstrating pretext can be extremely difficult, and the ultimate burden of proof always remains upon the employee to prove pretext.[52]

Dual Motive. Another theory utilized to demonstrate retaliation and overcome the defendant's alleged legitimate business reason for the termination or discipline is the dual motive theory.[53] Dual motive cases differ from pretext cases in that *both* valid and invalid reasons for a discharge exist. The dual motive test can be summarized as follows: The employee must initially establish, by a preponderance of the evidence, a *prima facie* case showing that illegal motives (among other factors) "played some part" in the disciplinary action or discharge.[54] Once the employee meets this burden, the burden of proof or production shifts onto the employer to persuade the court or jury that it would have discharged or disciplined the employee even if the employee had not engaged in protected activity.

If management attempts to meet this burden and demonstrate a "legitimate," nondiscriminatory reason for terminating or disciplining the employee, the primary rebuttal evidence an employee can put forward is proof of "disparate treatment."[55] Disparate treatment simply means that an employee who engages in protected activity was treated differently, or disciplined more harshly, than an employee who committed the same infraction but did not engage in protected activity.[56] It is well settled that "enforcement of an otherwise valid rule only against those engaged in protected activities is discriminatory."[57] In fact, the essence of discrimination is to treat "like cases differently."[58] For example, in an National Labor Relations Act (NLRA) context, where a union organizer and another employee were both caught drinking on the job and the company fired only the union organizer, the court found disparate treatment.[59]

Refusal to Perform Work. Often a discharge is sparked by an explicit refusal by an employee to perform a given task.[60] Although refusal to follow orders is traditionally a valid business reason for a discharge, two limited grounds[61] may exist for an employee to refuse to perform a job assignment. The first is a refusal to perform work that is illegal; the second is a refusal to perform unsafe or immediately hazardous work.

Refusal to work cases are often straightforward, since the act triggering the actual termination is usually not in dispute. The employee, however, has the burden of proving that the requested act was appropriately refused. In an OSHA case, the U.S. Supreme Court articulated the following for use in evaluating a wrongful discharge case on the basis of refusing hazardous work:

[C]ircumstances may sometimes exist in which the employee justifiably believes that the express statutory arrangement does not sufficiently protect him from death or serious injury. Such circumstances will probably not often occur, but such a situation may arise when (1) the employee is ordered by his employer to work under conditions that the employee reasonably believes pose an imminent risk of death or serious bodily injury, and (2) the employee has reason to believe that there is not sufficient time or opportunity either to seek effective redress from his employer or to appraise OSHA of the danger.[62]

This standard has been followed in right to refuse hazardous work cases under other statutes.[63]

Step 8: Understanding the Importance of the Underlying Whistleblower Allegation

Any person involved in a whistleblower case must be sensitive to the subjective importance the initial allegations may have for the employee, the impact these disclosures may have on the employer, and the objective importance the allegations may raise for the public at-large.

For the most part, the validity of the underlying claim is never the focus of a wrongful discharge suit. Most laws protect the whistleblower even if the original disclosure is unproven—it is the act of raising the concerns that is important, not whether the concerns are valid.[64]

Although the validity of the underlying allegation is, for the most part, not a necessary element of proof, attorneys should still aggressively attempt to document the validity of the claim. First, if the underlying allegation was correct, it will help demonstrate that the original allegation was made in good faith and was not frivolous. Second, if the underlying allegation is correct, the credibility of the employee will be enhanced and that of the employer will be diminished. Third, the validity of the underlying claim could provide circumstantial evidence of discriminatory motive (i.e., the employer's intent to cover up the problem).

Step 9: Reviewing Damage Requirements

In selecting a remedy, careful attention must be paid to the damages awardable under the common law or statutory provision. Remedies widely vary in the types of damages awardable. Reinstatement can be the single most important legal remedy, yet it may be unavailable under a common law cause of action. Similarly, entitlement of injunctive relief, punitive damages, compensatory damages, back pay, and attorney fees vary from statute to statute. Moreover, proof of a damage is an element of a *prima facie* case, and the failure to set forth an apparently cognizable claim of damage can be fatal to a claim.[65]

Additionally, some common law remedies do not apply absent an actual discharge,[66] while most statutory remedies allow for corrective action of non-discharge-related adverse actions, such as obtaining relief from a demotion, a retaliatory transfer, or a bad performance review. Obviously, the types of monetary damage for which a client may be entitled will depend on the type of adverse action under review.

Attorney fees are also an important consideration. If a statute provides for the wrongdoer to pay these fees, a client may be able to keep more of his or her reward than in circumstances in which they must pay 40 percent of an award to an attorney. Moreover, if the underlying adverse action will not reasonably result in a large monetary verdict, the only method to properly compensate for attorney fees is through utilizing a law that authorizes such payments.

Finally, actions an employee takes even after discharge can impact damages. Most laws require that the employee "mitigate" his or her damages. That is, an employee must actively and reasonably seek new employment or risk a cut-off in back pay. If a terminated employee cannot find substitute employment, this may provide evidence of reputational loss caused by the illegal discharge. Whistleblowers who are suffering emotional distress or physical ailments related to the retaliatory actions may need to consult with professional health care providers both to document their losses and to recover from the shock that often accompanies a retaliatory discharge.

Step 10: Concurrent Enforcement Actions

Employees are not limited to pursuing their whistleblower case only as a legal action for wrongful discharge. Employees, citizen organizations, and attorneys can also initiate concurrent enforcement actions aimed at remedying the underlying wrongful conduct. For example, if a whistleblower was terminated from a nuclear power plant for blowing the whistle to the Nuclear Regulatory Commission (NRC) about faulty welds, the employee can file a complaint with the NRC regarding the integrity of the welds.[67] Thus, while the attorney and client are pursuing a wrongful discharge case, the NRC is required to investigate the quality of the welds. If the employee works closely with the regulatory authority or investigative body, the regulatory body may vindicate the underlying claim.

Conversely, employees should be leery of putting too much credence in an official, state, local, police, or federal inquiry into the underlying conduct. Government views of whistleblower disclosures are often deficient, compromised, or incomplete.[68] For example, in the famous whistleblower case involving retaliation and wrongful death against Ms. Karen Silkwood, the original NRC investigation vindicated the outrageous actions of the Kerr-McGee Corporation.[69]

Even incomplete or inefficient governmental investigations, however, can be useful for the employee. Employees can obtain access to the closed government investigation files through use of the federal Freedom of Information Act or state FOIAs, and subpoena government records that may relate to their case.[70] Additionally, in cases regarding major issues of public concern, members of the news media and/or representatives from congressional oversight committees may have an interest in investigating a whistleblower case. Such investigations can turn up leads unavailable to the whistleblower, give the whistleblower added credibility, pressure the governmental regulatory agencies to conduct a thorough investigation, and prompt other assistance to a whistleblower.

NOTES

1. The historic contributions of whistleblowers were outlined by Texas Supreme Court Justice Lloyd Doggett in his concurring opinion in *Winters v. Houston Chronicle Pub. Co.*, 795 S.W. 2d 723, 727-733 (Tex. 1990). *See also* Myron Glazer and Penina Glazer, *The Whistleblowers: Exposing Corruption in Government Industry* (New York: Basic Books, 1989) (outlining contributions of whistleblowers in exposing police corruption, nuclear safety hazards, defense contracting and the environment); John F. Kelly & Phillip K. Wearne, *Tainting Evidence: Inside the Scandals at the FBI Crime Lab* (New York: The Free Press,

1998) (whistleblowing in the FBI crime lab); Ernest Fitzgerald, *The High Priests of Waste* (New York: W. W. Norton, 1972) (defense contracting); Alan F. Westin, ed., *Whistle-Blowing! Loyalty and Dissent in the Corporation* (New York: McGraw-Hill, 1980). *See also* Carol M. Bast, "At What Price Silence: Are Confidentiality Agreements Enforceable?" 25 *William Mitchell Law Review* 627, 630 (1999) (suggesting that a tobacco whistleblower's "disclosures served as a catalyst to mobilize anti-tobacco forces and hasten legal liability for the tobacco industry"); Charles S. Clarke, "Whistleblowers," 7 *The CQ Researcher* 1059, 1068-1069 (Congressional Quarterly, Inc., December 7, 1997) (outlining contributions of numerous whistleblowers). The impact one employee's disclosures may have on an employer or society should not be underestimated. For example, one federal employee's documenting conversations in which another employee explained how their boss intended to lie under oath during a federal court proceeding led to the impeachment of a President. H. Rep. 105-830, Report of the House of Representatives Committee on the Judiciary, "The Impeachment of William Jefferson Clinton, President of the United States" (December 16, 1998). In a few areas where the impact of whistleblowing has been the subject to an "objective" review, the results have been very favorable. For example, in a 1997 study of whistleblowing in the nuclear industry, the U.S. General Accounting Office concluded that "actions taken to respond to employee concerns in the past have significantly contributed to improving safety in the nuclear industry." U.S. Govt. Accounting Office, "Nuclear Employee Safety Concerns: Allegation System Offers Better Protection, But Important Issues Remain," at 4 (GAO|HEHS-97-51) (March 1997). *Accord.*, U.S. NRC, "Statement of Policy," 61 *Federal Register* 24336 (May 14, 1996) ("In the past, employees have raised important issues and as a result, the public health and safety has benefitted"). Benefits to taxpayers have also been documented. For example, since 1986, under one law alone (the False Claims Act), the U.S. government recovered over 3.5 billion dollars due to whistleblower provisions. Michael Sniffen, "Government's False Claims Recoveries Rise," *Associated Press* (February 24, 2000).

2. *Management Information Technologies, Inc. v. Alyeska Pipeline Service Co.*, 151 F.R.D. 478, 481-82 (D.D.C. 1993) (collecting authorities); Charles S. Clarke, "Whistleblowers," 7 *The CQ Researcher* 1059, 1065 (Congressional Quarterly, Inc., December 7, 1997) (reproducing survey documenting adverse, stress-related side effects experienced by whistleblowers).

3. Approximately thirty separate federal laws exist that protect whistleblowers. These laws range from the Occupational Safety and Health Act, which contains a thirty-day statute of limitations and no private right of action to the False Claims Act, which contains a six-year statute of limitations. 29 U.S.C. § 660(c) (OSHA statute) and 31 U.S.C. § 3730(h)(FCA statute).

4. 15 U.S.C. § 2622.

5. Bureau of National Affairs (BNA), State Labor Laws 28:203.

6. *Tameny v. Atlantic Richfield Co.*, 164 Cal. Rptr. 839, 610 P.2d 1330 (1980).

7. 5 U.S.C. § 2302.

8. *Agis v. Howard Johnson, Co.*, 355 N.E.2d 315 (Mass. 1976); *Lucas v. Brown & Root, Inc.*, 736 F.2d 1202 (8th Cir. 1984).

9. *Kelly v. Gen. Tel. Co.*, 136 Cal. App. 3d 311, 186 Cal. Rptr. 917 (1981).

10. *Pine River State Bank v. Mettille*, 333 N.W.2d 622 (Minn. 1983); *Arie v. Intentherm*, 648 S.W.2d 142 (Mo. App. 1983); *Morris v. Lutheran Medical Center*, 215 Neb. 677, 340 N.W.2d 388 (1983); *Hammond v. N.D. State Personnel Bd.*, 345 N.W.2d 359 (N.D. 1984); *Langdon v. Saga Corp.*, 569 P.2d 524 (Okla. App. 1976); *Jackson v. Minidoka Irrigation*, 98 Idaho 330, 563 P.2d 54 (1977); *Magnan v. Anaconda Industries, Inc.*, 37 Conn. Supp. 38 (1984); *Terrio v. Millenocket Community Hospital*, 379 A.2d 135 (Me. 1977); *Toussaint v. Blue Cross & Blue Shield*, 408 Mich. 579, 292 N.W.2d 880 (1980).

11. 42 U.S.C. § 5851.

12. 29 C.F.R. Parts 24 and 18.

13. *English v. General Electric*, 496 U.S. 72 (1990).

14. *Caterpillar Tractor Co. v. Wheeler*, 108 Ill. 2d 502, 485 N.E.2d 372 (1985) *cert. denied*, 475 U.S. 1122 (1986).

15. *See Management Information Technologies, Inc. v. Aleyska Pipeline Service Company, et al.* 151 F.R.D. 478, 481 (D.C. 1993). "To their detractors, whistleblowers are viewed as 'snitches', 'stool pigeons', or 'industrial spys' [sic] who are willing to publicly embarrass their co-workers and their companies in order to satisfy their political, ethical, moral, or personal agendas. Such employees not only wish to hurt their companies, their detractors argue, but also wish to keep their jobs. " *Quoting* from Daniel P. Westman, "Whistleblowing: The Law of Retaliatory Discharge" at vii (Washington, D.C.: Bureau of National Affairs, 1991).

16. *See e.g.*, Laura Simoff, "Confusion and Deterrence: The Problems That Arise from a Deficiency in Uniform Laws and Procedures for Environmental Whistleblowers," 8 *Dickinson Law and Policy* 325, 341 (1999) ("Before initiating a whistleblower claim, it is imperative to remember that personal attacks, harassment, termination, or loss of credibility may be the consequences").

17. *Management Information Technologies, supra, quoting* from Sissela Bok, "Secrets: On the Ethics of Concealment and Revelation" at 226 (1982) and Myron Peretz Glazer and Penina Glazer, *The Whistleblowers: Exposing Corruption in Government and Industry* at 231 (New York: Basic Books, 1989).

18. Donald Campbell, "Retaliatory Discharged Injured Workers," *Trial Magazine* (October 1999).

19. *See e.g., Simoff, supra*, at 341 ("The whistleblower should keep a detailed account of all communications and events concerning his claim. . . . it is important to copy all documents necessary to support the claim").

20. Campbell, *supra*.

21. 42 U.S.C. § 7622.

22. 42 U.S.C. § 300j-9.

23. 33 U.S.C. § 1367.

24. 42 U.S.C. § 9610.

25. 15 U.S.C. § 2622.

26. 30 U.S.C. § 1293.

27. 29 U.S.C. § 660(c).

28. *Delaware State College v. Ricks*, 449 U.S. 250 (1982).

29. *Zipes v. Transworld Airlines, Inc.*, 455 U.S. 385 (1982).

30. 657 F.2d 16, 19 (3rd Cir. 1981).

31. 657 F.2d 16, 18 (3rd Cir. 1981); *Dartey v. Zack Co.*, 82-ERA-2, slip op. of the Secretary of Labor (SOL) at 5-6 (April 25, 1983). The Supreme Court has recognized that failure to comply with short employment discrimination filing periods is not a jurisdictional bar to maintaining a cause of action, but instead, the time limits are subject to equitable modification. *Zipes v. Transworld Airlines, Inc.*, 455 U.S. 385, 393 (1982).

32. *See Richards v. Mileski*, 662 F.2d 65, 70 (D.C. Cir. 1981); *Meyer v. Riegal Products Corp.*, 720 F.2d 303, 307-308 (3rd Cir. 1983).

33. *Kocian v. Getty Refining & Marketing Co.*, 707 F.2d 748, 753 (3rd Cir. 1983); *Earnhardt v. Comm. of Puerto Rico*, 691 F.2d 69, 71 (1st Cir. 1982); *Geromette v. General Motors Corp.*, 609 F.2d 1200 (6th Cir. 1979); *Smith v. American President Lines, Ltd.*, 571 F.2d 102, 109 (2nd Cir. 1978); *Martinez v. Orr*, 738 F.2d 1107, 1110 (10th Cir. 1984).

34. *Bonham v. Dresser Industries, Inc.*, 569 F.2d 187, 193 (3rd Cir. 1977) *cert. denied*, 439 U.S. 821 (1978); *Charlier v. S.C. Johnson & Son, Inc.*, 556 F.2d 761 (5th Cir. 1977); *Dartt v. Shell Oil Co.*, 539 F.2d 1256, 1262 (10th Cir. 1976).

35. *Carlile v. South Routt School Dist. RE 3-J*, 652 F.2d 981, 985 (10th Cir. 1981).

36. *Oaxaca v. Roscoe*, 641 F.2d 386 (5th Cir. 1981); *Reeb v. Economic Opportunity Atlanta, Inc.*, 516 F.2d 924 (5th Cir. 1975); *Stoller v. Marsh*, 682 F.2d 971, 974 (D.C. Cir. 1982); *Bickham v. Miller*, 584 F.2d 736 (5th Cir. 1978); *Cooper v. Bell*, 628 F.2d 1208 (9th Cir. 1980).

37. *McKenzie v. Sawyer*, 684 F.2d 62, 72 (D.C. Cir. 1982); *Olson v. Rembrandt Printing Co.*, 511 F.2d 1228, 1234 (8th Cir. 1975). *See also Terry v. Bridgeport Brass Co.*, 519 F.2d 806 (7th Cir. 1975); *Hiscott v. General Elec. Co.*, 521 F.2d 632, 635 (6th Cir. 1975); *Prophet v. Armco Steel Co.*, 575 F.2d 579 (5th Cir. 1978).

38. *Mt. Healthy City School District v. Doyle*, 429 U.S. 274, 286 (1977); *Mackowiak v. University Nuclear Systems, Inc.*, 735 F.2d 1159 (9th Cir. 1984) (Energy Reorganization Act); "Shepard's Causes of Action," 1 COA 273; American Jurisprudence, *Proof of Facts* (2nd), "Proof of Retaliatory Discharge"; *Munsey v. Morton*, 507 F.2d 1202 (D.C. Cir. 1974); (Federal Mine Health and Safety Act) *Cox v. Dardanelle Public School District*, 790 F.2d 668 (8th Cir. 1986) (First Amendment); *Sims v. MME Paulette Dry Cleaners*, 580 F. Supp. 593 (S.D.N.Y. 1984) (Title VII).

39. *Compare Price Waterhouse v. Hopkins*, 490 U.S. 228 (1989), *and St. Mary's Honor Center v. Hicks*, 509 U.S. 502 (1993).

40. *AKA v. Washington Hospital Center*, 156 F.3d 1284 (D.C. Cir. 1998); *Mt. Healthy City School District, supra*, at 285-286.

41. *See* Stephen M. Kohn and Thomas Carpenter, "Nuclear Whistleblower Protection and the Scope of Protected Activity Under Section 210 of the Energy Reorganization Act," 4 *Antioch Law Journal*, 73, 74-77, 94-96 (Summer 1986).

42. *See Mackey v. IBP, Inc.*, 167 F.R.D. 186 (D. Kan. 1996); *Hollander v. American Cyanamid*, 895 F.2d 80, 84-85 (2nd Cir. 1990); *Lyoch v. Anheuser-Busch*, 164 F.R.D. 62, 65 (E.D. Mo. 1995) ("Courts have treated discovery requests in employment cases liberally"); *Graf v. Wackenhut Services*, 98-ERA-37, Order Granting Motion to Compel by ALJ, p. 3 (March 19, 1999) ("Courts have permitted a very broad scope of discovery in discrimination cases").

43. 411 U.S. 792, 804-805 (1973).

44. *Morrison v. City and County of Denver*, 80 F.R.D. 289, 292 (D. Colo. 1978).

45. *Alexander v. FBI*, 186 F.R.D. 113, 121 (D.D.C. 1998), *quoting Founding Church of Scientology v. Webster*, 802 F.2d 1448, 1451 (D.C. Cir. 1986).

46. *U.S. Postal Service v. Atkins*, 460 U.S. 711 (1983); *DeFord v. Secretary of Labor*, 700 F.2d 281, 286 (6th Cir. 1983); *Mackowiak v. University Nuclear Systems, Inc.*, 735 F.2d 1159, 1162 (9th Cir. 1984). Cf. *NLRB v. Mount Desert Island Hosp.*, 695 F.2d 634, 638 (1st Cir. 1984), employer's action construed broadly to prevent intimidation of others in exercise of their rights; *John Hancock Mutual Life Ins. Co. v. NLRB*, 191 F.2d 483, 485 (D.C. Cir. 1951), broad construction necessary to prevent intimidation of prospective complainants and witnesses.

47. *Ellis Fischel State Cancer Hospital v. Marshall*, 629 F.2d 563, 566 (8th Cir. 1980) *cert. denied*, 450 U.S. 1040 (1981). *See also Mackowiak v. University Nuclear Systems, Inc.*, 735 F.2d 1159, 1162 (9th Cir. 1984); *Zoll v. Eastern Allamkee Community School Dist.*, 588 F.2d 246, 250 (8th Cir. 1978); *Rutherford v. American Bank of Commerce*, 565 F.2d 1162, 1164 (10th Cir. 1977).

48. *Donovan v. Zimmer*, 557 F.Supp. 642, 651 (D.S.C. 1982), *quoting Polynesian Cultural Center v. NLRB*, 582 F.2d 467, 473 (9th Cir. 1978).

49. Stephen M. Kohn, *The Whistleblower Litigation Handbook: Environmental, Nuclear, Health and Safety Claims*, pp. 51-55 (John Wiley & Sons, Inc. 1991).

50. *Cosentino v. Price*, 483 N.E.2d 297, 300 (Ill. App. 1 Dist. 1985), *citing from Palmateer v. Int. Harvester Co.*, 85 Ill.2d 124, 134, 421 N.E.2d 876 (1981).

51. *Wright Line*, 251 NLRB 1083 (1980), *aff'd*, 662 F.2d 899 (1st Cir, 1981), *cert. denied*, 455 U.S. 989 (1982); *see also Wittenberg v. Wheels*, 663 F.Supp. 654, 662-63 (N.A. Ill. 1997).

52. *Reeves v. Sanderson Plumbing*, 120 S.Ct. 2097 (2000); *St. Mary's Honor Center v. Hicks*, 509 U.S. 502 (1993); *Texas Dept. of Community Affairs v. Burdine*, 450 U.S. 248 (1981); *McDonnell Douglas Corp. v. Green*, 411 U.S.

792 (1973).

53. *Price Waterhouse v. Hopkins*, 490 U.S. 228 (1989).

54. *Mackowiak v. University Nuclear Systems, Inc.*, 735 F.2d 1159, 1163-64 (9th Cir. 1984).

55. The concept of disparate treatment was defined in the Title VII context in *McDonnell Douglas Corp. v. Green*, 411 U.S. 792, 804 (1973); in an NLRA context in *Wright Line*, 251 NLRB 1083, 1089 (1980), *aff'd sub non. NLRB v. Wright Line*, 662 F.2d 899 (1st Cir. 1981); in a First Amendment context in *Mount Healthy City School Dist. v. Doyle*, 429 U.S. 274, 287 (1977).

56. *Donovan on Behalf of Chacon v. Phelps Dodge Corp.*, 709 F.2d 86, 93 (D.C. Cir. 1983).

57. *Donovan v. Zimmer*, 557 F.Supp. 642, 652 (D.S.C. 1982), *quoting NLRB v. Heck's, Inc.*, 386 F.2d 317, 329 (4th Cir. 1967) (citations omitted).

58. *Donovan v. Zimmer*, 557 F.Supp. 642, 651 (D.S.C. 1982), *quoting Midwest Regional Joint Board v. NLRB*, 564 F.2d 434, 442 (D.C. Cir. 1977).

59. *See NLRB v. Faulkner Hospital*, 691 F.2d 51, 56 (1st Cir. 1982); *NLRB v. Clark Manor Nursing Home Corp.*, 671 F.2d 657, 661-663 (1st Cir. 1982). For some cases where the court failed to find disparate treatment *see Airborne Freight Corp. v. NLRB*, 728 F.2d 357, 358 (6th Cir. 1984); *Viracon, Inc. v. NLRB*, 736 F.2d 1188, 1193 (7th Cir. 1984).

60. *Tameny v. Atlantic Richfield Co.*, 27 Ca.3d 167, 610 P.2d 1330 (1980); *Beasley v. Affiliated Hosp. Products*, 713 S.W.2d 557 (Mo. App. 1986); *Winther v. DEC Intern., Inc.*, 625 F.Supp. 100, 104 (D.C. Col. 1985).

61. *Whirlpool Corp. v. Marshall*, 445 U.S. 1, 10-11 (1980); *Gateway Coal v. U.M.W.A. et al.*, 414 U.S. 368 (1974); *Miller v. Fed. Mine Safety and Health Review Comm'n.*, 687 F.2d 194 (7th Cir. 1982); *Phillips v. Int. Bd. of Mn. Op. App.*, 500 F.2d 772 (D.C. Cir. 1974) *cert. denied*, 420 U.S. 938 (1975); *Blocker v. Dept. of the Army*, 6 MSPB 395 (1981); OSHA Regulation 29 C.F.R. 1977, 12(b)(2); *Wheeler v. Caterpillar Tractor Co.*, 485 N.E.2d 372 (Ill. 1985).

62. *Whirlpool Corp. v. Marshall*,445 U.S. 1, 9-10 (1980).

63. *See Miller v. Federal Mine Safety and Health Act*, 687 F.2d 194 (7th Cir. 1982); *Blocker v. Dept. of the Army*, 6 MSPB 395 (1981); *Pennsyl. v. Catalytic, Inc.*, 1983 Energy Reorganization Act case No. 2, Decision of the U.S. Secretary of Labor (January 13, 1984).

64. Title VII, *Womack v. Munson*, 619 F.2d 1292, 1298 (8th Cir. 1980); NLRA, *Interior Alterations, Inc.*, NLRB, 738 F.2d 373, 376 (10th Cir. 1984);Fair Labor Standards Act (FLSA), *Love v. RE/MAX of America, Inc.*, 738 F.2d 383, 387 (10th Cir. 1984); OSHA, *Donovan v. Hahner Foreman and Harness, Inc.*, 736 F.2d 1421, 1429 (10th Cir. 1984); FMHSA, *Munsey v. Morton*, 507 F.2d 1292 (D.C. Cir. 1974). The controlling rule in environmental cases was set forth by the DOL as "protection predicated on 'proof' that the alleged activity was based on employee's 'active belief' that 'the employer violated the environmental laws' and that such belief was 'reasonable.'" *Melendez v. Exxon*, 93-ERA-6, order of remand by ARB, at 18-19 (July 14, 2000). Once this standard is satisfied, an employee's subjective motivation for becoming a whistleblower is not material.

Id. at 21-22. However, some state laws depart from the rule adopted by the DOL. *Id.* at 22 n. 36.

65. *Taylor v. FDIC*, 132 F.3d 753, 764 (D.C. Cir. 1997).

66. *White v. State*, 929 P.2d 396, 407-408 (Wash. 1997).

67. *See* 10 C.F.R. 2206. The NRC also has concurrent jurisdiction with the U.S. DOL to investigate whistleblower wrongful discharge allegations. *See* 10 C.F.R. 50.7 and Memorandum of Understanding Between NRC and Department of Labor, Employee Protection, 47 Fed. Reg. 54585 (1982).

68. *See generally* Thomas Devine and Donald Aplin, "Abuse of Authority: The Office of the Special Counsel and Whistleblower Protection," 4 *Antioch Law Journal* 5 (Summer 1986). *But see* Thomas M. Devine, "The WPA of 1989: Foundation for the Modern Law of Employment Dissent," 51 *Admin. Law Rev.* 531 (1999).

69. *Silkwood v. Kerr-McGee Corp.*, 464 U.S. 238 (1984).

70. 5 U.S.C. § 552.

Chapter 2

Whistleblower Protection under the Common Law: A State-by-State Review

The overwhelming majority of states, either through judicial modifications to the common law or through legislation (or both), have altered the strict common law *at-will* employment doctrine, which entitled employers to fire employees for any reason or no reason.[1] The common law has been narrowly altered to permit discharge for any reason—except for a reason that violates public policy.[2]

Under the public policy exception, whistleblowers in most states have a tort action for wrongful discharge[3] if they can demonstrate that they were fired for "blowing the whistle" in violation of a clear mandate of public policy. This new tort action altered the standard employment law of "master-servant," which had been accepted in the late nineteenth century.

The origins of the *at-will* doctrine are traced to the publication of *Master and Servant* in 1877 by Horace G. Wood.[4] "Wood's Rule," which provided for the termination of an employee for any reason or no reason, was, in the 1880s and 1890s, uncritically adopted by every state. However, looking backward, "there is now a broad consensus among courts and commentators that the authorities relied on by Wood did not support his thesis."[5]

In the twentieth century, the *at-will* doctrine came under "intense attack from legal scholars,"[6] and it became the "almost unanimous view" from commentators that the rule should be modified, especially in light of "important public policy."[7] For example, as early as 1937 the doctrine was under sharp criticism: "The system of 'free' contract described by nineteenth century theory is now coming to be recognized as a world of fantasy, too orderly, too neatly contrived and too harmonious to correspond with reality."[8]

In addition to the theoretical weaknesses of "Wood's Rule," commentators also noted the insignificant injustices that resulted from strict application of the rule. In his landmark 1967 article on the *at-will* doctrine Professor Lawrence E. Blades catalogued numerous abuses of employees and strongly endorsed judicial modifications to the doctrine:

What is important is that such abuses, however common or uncommon, should not go unremedied. Whether for the sake of providing specific justice for the afflicted individual, deterring a practice which poses an increasingly serious threat to personal freedom generally or instilling into employers a general consciousness of and respect for the individuality of the employee, the law should confront the problem.[9]

Simultaneous with the rising criticism of the *at-will* doctrine developed a public recognition of the "importance of employee-whistleblowers" "in a democratic society":[10]

Whistleblowing is a formal or informal role that arises in and may even be essential to rule systems, for the whistleblower functions to generate information about violations in order that sanctions or feedback to shape human behavior can occur . . . . An institution that seriously intends to prevent . . . misconduct needs to recognize that it is involved in applying rules to human behavior; the institution thus needs the services of the whistleblower to provide information necessary for its rules to be enforced. . . . If the system of institutional rules is to work, the institution needs to utilize the whistleblower's services.[11]

After cataloguing the important societal contributions made by whistleblowers, Texas Supreme Court Justice Lloyd Doggett concluded that the protection of whistleblowers was vital in a "democratic, free enterprise system" and that whistleblowers had made a "lasting contribution to improving our public and private institutions."[12]

As recognized by the North Carolina Court of Appeals, without a prohibition on employer utilization of their economic power to violate the "interests of the public," society as a whole would be severely weakened:

An at will prerogative without limits could be suffered only in an anarchy, and there not for long—it certainly cannot be suffered in a society such as ours without weakening the bond of counter balancing rights and obligations that holds such societies together. Thus, while there may be a right to terminate a contract at will for no reason, or for an arbitrary or irrational reason, there can be no right to terminate such a contract for an unlawful reason or purpose that contravenes public policy.[13]

Thus, the "public policy exception" to the *at-will* doctrine was born and eventually became the rule in a vast majority of common law jurisdictions. California was the first state to recognize an exception to the *at-will* doctrine when, in 1959, it upheld a cause of action by an employee against an employer who had demanded that the employee commit perjury as a condition of continued employment.[14]

The nineteenth century *at-will* doctrine is dead. Today, "the vast majority of states have recognized that an *at-will* employee possesses a tort action when he or she is discharged for performing an act that public policy would encourage, or for refusing to do something that public policy would condemn."[15] The "core value" recognized in the adaptation of whistleblower protection was that the "public welfare" demanded that "employees courageous enough to object to illegal, fraudulent or harmful activity by their employer" be "shielded from retaliation."[16]

Although the public policy exception to the *at-will* doctrine now has "broad acceptance," the definition of what conduct should be protected is strongly debated as courts attempt to "draw the line between claims that genuinely involve matters of public policy and those that concern merely ordinary disputes between employer and employee."[17]

This said, there have been general rules defining the scope of protected activity that are representative of a "majority rule" setting forth the parameters regarding the public policy exception. The vast majority of states, at a minimum, recognized four types of activities under the public policy exception:

(1) employees who refuse to violate a statute, constitutional requirement, or regulation;

(2) employees who perform an obligation required under law;

(3) employees who exercise a legally protected right; and

(4) employees who report a violation of law for the public benefit.[18]

In addition, most states do not absolutely require protected whistleblower disclosures to be directly tied to a violation of criminal law: "While given the importance and general recognition of the 'citizen crime fighter' policy, a court's duty will seldom be clearer than when the violation of a criminal statute is involved."[19]

The majority of states protect employees who "blow the whistle" either to a supervisor or to a governmental authority. The logic behind protecting internal whistleblowing was explained by the New Hampshire Supreme Court when it stated that "giving the employer the first opportunity to correct a violation allows it to avoid harm to its reputation, the burden of undergoing an investigation, preparation for a hearing, etc. Informal resolution of infractions also saves the [government] both time and resources."[20]

Almost every state that protects whistleblower disclosures protects employees who raise the allegations based on a "good faith" belief that a law has been violated or that the public safety is threatened. As explained by the Supreme Court of New Jersey:

[T]he objecting employee must have an objectively reasonable belief, at the time of objection or refusal to participate in the employer's offensive activity, that such activity is either illegal, fraudulent or harmful to the public health, safety or welfare, and that there is a substantial likelihood that the questioned activity is incompatible with a constitutional, statutory or regulatory provision, code of ethics or other recognized source of public policy. Specific knowledge of the precise source of public policy is not required. The object of CEPA [Conscientious Employee Protection Act] is not to make lawyers out of conscientious employees but rather to prevent retaliation against those employees who object to employer conduct that they reasonably believe to be unlawful or indisputably dangerous to the public health, safety or welfare.[21]

The basic four elements of a public policy tort were summarized by Villanova Law Professor Henry Perritt as follows:

1. That clear public policy existed and was manifested in a state or federal constitution, statute or administrative regulation, or in the common law.

2. That dismissing employees under circumstances like those involved in the plaintiff's dismissal would jeopardize the public policy.

3. The plaintiff's dismissal was motivated by conduct related to the public policy.

4. The employer lacked overriding legitimate business justification for the dismissal.[22]

The final major trend in whistleblower protection is the interaction between state law and federal statutory protections. Over the past twenty-five years many states have enacted whistleblower protection statutes.[23] On these issues the U.S. Supreme Court has consistently ruled that federal whistleblower laws do not preempt state common law protections.[24] The state statutes often supplement or supplant common law remedies. Most states have also ruled that common law wrongful discharge claims are not preempted by co-existing state statutory protections, especially if the statutory claims do not provide an "adequate"[25] remedy. However, if the legislature explicitly states that the statutory remedy preempts the common law remedy, then the common law is precluded.[26]

The issue of preclusion has become more significant as a number of state legislatures have passed *bona fide* whistleblower protection laws and employees must determine whether the statutory requirements are exclusive or cumulative.[27] Moreover, two states, Montana and Ohio, have passed statutes that have effectively supplemented the common law remedies. Unfortunately, the laws in these two states have created significant definitional and procedural obstacles to employee protection that did not exist under the common law.

When litigating in state court, employees are not required to limit their cause of action to public policy exceptions.[28] The elements of proof for other potential common law actions are often substantially related to elements of a retaliatory discharge claim. Employers who retaliate against whistleblowers often commit other legally cognizable harms and give rise to other independent claims.[29] Examples of such other causes of action include intentional interference with contracts,[30] breach of contract,[31] an abrogation of an "implied" covenant of good faith and fair dealing,[32] intentional infliction of emotional distress,[33] fraud,[34] negligence,[35] invasion of privacy,[36] defamation,[37] false light[38] or a breach of an implied contract.[39]

Finally, many states have laws that prohibit local government from retaliating against public sector whistleblowers.[40] The importance of state legal protections for public employees has grown over time given recent U.S. Supreme Court decisions that have narrowed the applicability of some federal employment laws to state governmental agencies. For example, in *Kimel v. Florida Board of Regents*,[41] the Supreme Court broadly construed 11th Amendment immunities and found that the federal Age Discrimination in Employment Act did not apply to state employees.[42]

The following is a breakdown of whistleblower causes of action in the fifty states and the District of Columbia.[43]

ALABAMA

Alabama continues to adhere to the traditional *at-will* doctrine.[44] However, in *Harrell v. Reynolds Metals Co.*, the Alabama Supreme Court acknowledged that a wrongful discharge that contravenes public policy may give rise to a tort under "outrageous conduct."[45]

Alabama also has statutorily enacted "certain narrow exceptions" to the *at-will* rule,[46] including a prohibition against discharge for filing a worker's compensation claim or for filing a "written notice of violation of safety rule" under the worker safety statute.[47]

ALASKA

The Supreme Court of Alaska has upheld a cause of action for the public policy exception, as part of a breach of the implied covenant of good faith and fair dealing. The cause of action lies in contract.[48] A retaliatory discharge claim may also be brought upon Alaska's anti-discrimination statute[49] or the Alaska Whistleblower Act.[50]

The tort of intentional interference with another's contract has also been recognized. The following elements must be shown: (1) that a contract existed (or can be implied); (2) that defendant knew of the contract and intended to induce a breach; (3) that the contract was breached; (4) that defendant's wrongful conduct engendered the breach; (5) that the breach caused plaintiff's damages; and (6) that the defendant's conduct was not privileged or justified.[51]

In *Bald v. R.C.A. Alascom*, plaintiff alleged that she was wrongfully discriminated against by both her employer and the union in violation of state antidiscrimination legislation.[52] The Supreme Court of Alaska held that a state cause of action was maintainable and that the National Labor Relations Act did not preempt or deprive state courts from hearing the case.[53]

ARIZONA

The Arizona Supreme Court adopted the public policy exception to the *at-will* doctrine in the case of *Wagenseller v. Scottsdale Memorial Hospital*.[54] The court held that an *at-will* employer may fire an employee for good cause or for no cause, but not for "bad cause" (i.e. that which violates public policy).[55] In *Wagenseller*, the employee was fired for refusing to participate in activities allegedly in violation of the state's indecent exposure statute.[56]

In 1996 the Arizona legislature enacted a statutory definition and procedure for retaliatory discharge claims.[57] The legislature defined public policy and limited the circumstances in which an employee could file a wrongful discharge claim.[58] The statute defined the necessary proof to assert a contract claim based on an employment manual, provided for exclusive coverage for employee claims in which a statute provides a direct remedy, and specifically authorized a *Wagenseller*-style "tort claim for wrongful discharge in violation of the public policy set forth in a statute."[59]

The statute also set forth nine other specific grounds justifying a tort claim, including the "disclosure" by an employee of a violation of state law to a manager who had authority to correct the alleged violation.[60]

Public employees also have statutory protections in Arizona.[61]

ARKANSAS

In *M.B.M. Co. v. Counce*,[62] the Arkansas Supreme Court first recognized an exception to the *at-will* rule if plaintiff had been discharged for exercising a statutory right, for performing a duty required by law or for reasons in violation of some other well-established public policy.[63]

After *Counce*, the Supreme Court held that the public policy cause of action applied to an employee who blew the whistle to appropriate officials on price fixing.[64] However, a state Supreme Court decision extending the public policy exception to worker's compensation cases was statutorily overturned.[65] In Arkansas, the public policy exception arises as a contract claim.[66]

An employee who has been wrongfully discharged may also bring an action in tort for intentional infliction of emotional distress.[67] To be actionable, such a termination must be so extreme and outrageous as to go beyond all possible bounds of decency, and to be atrocious and utterly intolerable in a civilized society.[68] Title VII of the U.S. Civil Rights Act was held not to preempt a state law contract claim.[69]

CALIFORNIA

California was the first state to adopt a public policy–based exception to the *at-will* doctrine in the landmark case of *Petermann v. International Brotherhood of Teamsters,* where an employee was discharged for refusing to commit perjury.[70] Wrongful discharge is a tort.[71]

Since 1980, four major California Supreme Court cases, *Tameny v. Atlantic Richfield Co.,*[72] *Foley v. Interactive Data Corp.,*[73] *Gantt v. Sentry Insurance,*[74] and *Green v. Ralee Engineering Co.,*[75] have defined the contours of whistleblower protection in California. Generally, the court has recognized four categories protected under the public policy exception:

1. employee refusal to violate a statute;

2. employee performance of statutorily mandated obligation;

3. employee exercise of a "constitutional or statutory right or privilege;" and/or

4. employee disclosure or reporting of a "statutory violation for the public's benefit."[76]

The California courts now require that a whistleblower's allegations of misconduct be explicitly "tethered to" a "specific constitutional or statutory authority" and that the concerns be "public" in nature, affecting "society at large."[77] Employees may, in the appropriate circumstances, rely upon both state and federal statutory or regulatory authority to support the "public policy" at issue, and disclosures to both supervisors or governmental authorities are protected.[78] California has acknowledged a cause of action resulting from a wrongful discharge for breach of implied-at-law covenant of good faith and fair dealing,[79] for intentional or negligent infliction of emotional distress,[80] for defamation and invasion of privacy,[81] for fraud,[82] and for interference with contractual relations.[83] In addition, the California Labor Code §1102.5 imposes criminal liability on employers who:

(a) adopt, or enforce any rule, regulation, or policy preventing an employee from disclosing information to a government or law enforcement agency, where the employee has reasonable cause to believe that the information discloses a violation of state or federal statute, or violation or noncompliance with a state or federal regulation.

(b) retaliate against an employee for disclosing information to a government or law enforcement agency, where the employee has reasonable cause to believe that the information discloses a violation of state or federal statute, or violation or noncompliance with a state or federal regulation.[84]

An employee who has been discharged for engaging in any such protected activity can, in addition to filing a civil action, file criminal misdemeanor charges and subject his or her employer to a fine, imprisonment, or both.[85]

Generally, California state courts have not required employees to exhaust administrative remedies prior to filing a wrongful discharge suit.[86] Statutory remedies are generally considered cumulative[87] and do not pre-empt the common law tort.[88] For example, California courts upheld an action for wrongful discharge despite the fact that OSHA also provided a remedy.[89] The administrative remedies created by OSHA were held to be independent of those available under a wrongful discharge action, and the plaintiff was not required to first exhaust his administrative remedies.[90]

COLORADO

Colorado's Supreme Court, "in keeping with the majority of jurisdictions," adopted the tort of wrongful discharge in violation of public policy in 1992.[91] The court held that there was "no reason why the public-policy exception should not apply to the discharge of an employee either because of the employee's performance of an important obligation, or because of the employee's exercise of a statutory right."[92]

In *Corbin v. Sinclair Marketing*,[93] a Colorado state appeals court stated that a public policy exception to the *at-will* doctrine was not available when the statute at issue provided employees with a wrongful discharge remedy.[94] Colorado has specifically enacted legislation to protect public employees[95] from discharge or other coercion for receiving a summons, responding thereto, serving as a juror or attending court for prospective jury service.[96]

CONNECTICUT

The Supreme Court of Connecticut has recognized an exception to the *at-will* doctrine where a termination involves "impropriety . . . derived from some important violation of public policy."[97] A wrongful discharge claim can be framed in either tort or contract.[98] Public policy can be "expressed" in either "explicit statutory or constitutional expressions or judicial decisions."[99] Moreover, the public policy can be based solely on federal law.[100]

In *Magnan v. Anaconda Industries, Inc.*,[101] the Connecticut Supreme Court adopted the implied covenant of good faith and fair dealing as another theory that limits an employer's right to discharge an employee at will.[102] The court held, however, that a breach of such an implied covenant cannot be predicated simply upon the absence of good cause.[103] An employee must prove that the employer was motivated by bad faith or malice or that the employer's actions constituted fraud, deceit or misrepresentations.[104] This cause of action can be defended if the employer "honestly believed" the discharge was for good cause.[105]

Intentional infliction of emotional distress has also been recognized by Connecticut in employment context.[106] It must be shown: (1) that defendant intended to inflict emotional distress or knew, or should have known, that it was likely to result from his or her conduct; (2) that the conduct was extreme and outrageous; (3) that defendant caused plaintiff's distress; and (4) that the emotional distress sustained by plaintiff was severe.[107] The court in *Murray v. Bridgeport Hospital*[108] acknowledged that a claim for tortious interference with contract could also be maintained.[109]

In addition to state common law remedies, the Connecticut legislature has passed a whistleblower protection statute.[110] The statute protects employees in the private sector from retaliation for disclosing an employer's illegal activities.[111] An employee who is discharged or otherwise penalized by his or her employer in violation of this statute may bring a civil action after exhausting all available administrative remedies.[112] The remedies provided by the whistleblower statute include reinstatement of previous job, payment of back wages, reestablishment of employee benefits, costs of litigation, and reasonable attorney's fees.[113] The statute further provides that the rights and remedies created by the statute shall not be construed to diminish or impair the rights of a person under any collective bargaining agreement.[114] However, the law may preclude common law remedies for wrongful discharge prohibited by the statute.[115] The law has a ninety-day statute of limitations.[116]

DELAWARE

Delaware recognizes a "public policy" exception to the *at will* doctrine arising under the general theory of an implied "covenant of good faith" in contractual relations.[117] Under the "covenant" theory, "narrowly defined" exceptions to the *at-will* doctrine, based on a "clear mandate of public policy," can provide protection for employee whistleblowers.[118] Additionally, other employer actions based on "deceit or misrepresentation" are actionable.[119] For example, one court upheld a cause of action based on an employer's creation of "fictitious grounds to terminate" the employee.[120]

Delaware has enacted legislation to protect public employees from being discharged, threatened or otherwise discriminated against for reporting suspected violations of law.[121] Federal courts have "predicted" that the Delaware Supreme Court "would extend the protection of the public policy exception to an employee who 'blew the whistle' on an employer's illegal conduct."[122]

DISTRICT OF COLUMBIA

Since 1991, the District of Columbia has recognized a tort claim for wrongfully discharged whistleblowers. After a series of narrow or conflicting judgments concerning whistleblower protection and the *at will* doctrine,[123] the Court of Appeals for the District of Columbia, sitting *en banc*, fully addressed the issue. Eight of the ten sitting justices, in a *per curiam* decision, applied the public policy exception within the District of Columbia in circumstances beyond those in which an employee refuses to perform an illegal act.[124]

In a concurring opinion, four judges concluded that the court should adjudicate the issue of "public policy" on a "case by case basis" and that the cause of action should be upheld where the employee makes a "clean showing" "based on some identifiable policy" contained in a statute, regulation or the Constitution.[125] Four other judges concurring in the holding advocated a less narrow definition of "public policy," one which recognized some of the First Amendment's purposes in protecting speech.[126]

Other laws in the District of Columbia also protect whistleblowers. For example, D.C. enacted a Whistleblower Protection Act for government employees,[127] a *qui tam* provision under a D.C. version of the False Claims Act,[128] and an antiretaliation provision under its Human Rights Act.[129]

FLORIDA

On June 7, 1991, the Florida Whistleblower's Act became "effective."[130] This law prohibits private sector employers with "ten or more persons" from retaliating against an employee who engages in narrowly defined protected activity. To be protected an employee must have:

1. Disclosed, or threatened to disclose, to any appropriate governmental agency, under oath, in writing, an activity, policy, or practice of the employer that is in violation of a law, rule, or regulation. However, this subsection does not apply unless the employee has, in writing, brought the activity, policy, or practice to the attention of a supervisor or the employer and has afforded the employer a reasonable opportunity to correct the activity, policy, or practice.

2. Provided information to, or testified before, any appropriate governmental agency, person, or entity conducting an investigation, hearing, or inquiry into an alleged violation of a law, rule, or regulation by the employer.

3. Objected to, or refused to participate in, any activity, policy, or practice of the employer that is in violation of a law, rule, or regulation.[131]

If an employee is protected under this statute, he or she is entitled to injunctive relief, reinstatement, back pay and benefits, and "other compensatory damages allowable under law."[132] A court may also award any "prevailing party" its attorney's fees and costs.[133] Prior to the passage of the Whistleblower's Act, the Florida Supreme Court had adopted a narrow public policy exception claim when a statute "confers by implication" such an action.[134]

GEORGIA

Georgia is unique in that it is the only state that adheres to an ironclad interpretation of a statute that codified the *at-will* doctrine.[135] Georgia courts strictly abide by the *at-will* doctrine, even when an employee is terminated in an attempt to cover up illegal activities.[136]

In order for a whistleblower in Georgia to obtain protection, he or she must resort to federal or state statutory protections, or general common law remedies (such as the law of defamation) that may be applicable based on the facts of a given case. Government employees are protected from retaliatory discharge under a narrowly drafted statute.[137]

HAWAII

In 1982, the Hawaii Supreme Court, in *Parnar v. American Hotels, Inc.*,[138] recognized the right of an *at-will* employee to bring an action for retaliatory discharge against her employer. The plaintiff bears the burden of proving that the discharge violated a clear mandate of public policy.[139] The *Parnar* court stated that, in determining whether a clear mandate of public policy is violated, courts should inquire whether the employer's conduct contravenes the letter or purpose of a constitutional, statutory, or regulatory provision or scheme.[140] The employer's motivation for discharging an employee is a material issue subject to jury determination.[141] The public policy exception lies in tort, and an employee can be awarded punitive damages where appropriate.[142] Hawaii also enacted a broad Whistleblower Protection Act.[143]

The Supreme Court refused to impose upon an employer a duty to terminate only in good faith. Wrongful discharge can give rise to a cause of action for intentional infliction of emotional distress.[144] If the legislature passes a specific statute that provides its "own remedy" to vindicate a wrongful discharge, the courts will not apply the *Parnar* common law remedy to that "narrow class" of potential cases.[145] Consequently, the federal district court in Hawaii precluded an employee from proceeding with a *Parnar* cause of action due to the protections afforded under the Hawaii whistleblower statute.[146] The court also dismissed the employee's statutory claim due to failure to comply with the Whistleblower law's ninety-day statute of limitations.[147] However, under the decisions of the Hawaiian Supreme Court, an employee's complaint for unlawful discharge from employment, having its source in a state statute or state common law, will not be automatically preempted by a collective bargaining agreement or federal labor laws.[148]

IDAHO

In 1977 the Supreme Court of Idaho first established the public policy exception. The Supreme Court held that an employee may claim damages for wrongful discharge when the motivation for the firing contravenes public policy.[149] Being terminated for refusing to give false testimony, reporting an injury in order to file for workmen's compensation, refusing to date one's supervisor, and serving on jury duty against the wishes of an employer were all cited as examples of violations of public policy by the Supreme Court of Idaho.[150] Since 1977 the Idaho courts have found that termination based on an employee's "reporting safety code violations," engaging in "legal union activities," or compliance with a subpoena all violated public policy.[151]

ILLINOIS

Illinois joined the growing number of states recognizing the tort of retaliatory discharge with the decision of *Kelsay v. Motorola, Inc.*[152] The Illinois Supreme Court held, "All that is required is that the employer discharge the employee in retaliation for the employee's activities, and that the discharge be in contravention of a clearly mandated public policy."[153] In *Palmateer v. International Harvester Co.*, the court stated that "no public policy was more fundamental than the one favoring the effective protection of the lives and property of citizens."[154] Where, however, no clear mandate of public policy is violated or where only private interests are involved, an employer may discharge an *at-will* employee without liability.[155]

Under the Illinois rule, employees who have publicly criticized unsafe practices of their employer have obtained protection.[156] Employees have also obtained punitive damage awards, in addition to compensatory damages.[157]

The state Supreme Court in 1985 held that the protection of the lives and property of citizens from the hazards of radioactive material was as important and fundamental a public policy as protecting them from crimes of violence.[158] The state common law remedy was not preempted by the federal nuclear whistleblower protection law, Section 210 of the Energy Reorganization Act.[159]

Moreover, a wrongfully discharged employee whose employment is covered by a collective bargaining agreement providing for grievance procedures was not required to exhaust those procedures prior to bringing an action for the tort of retaliatory discharge.[160] A wrongfully discharged employee may be able to sue for intentional infliction of emotional distress.[161] Under Illinois law, a plaintiff seeking recovery for intentional infliction of emotional distress must allege facts showing: (1) that the conduct by defendant was extreme and outrageous; (2) that the plaintiff suffered emotional distress; (3) that the defendant's conduct was intentional, or so reckless that the defendant knew severe emotional distress was substantially certain to result; and (4) that defendant's conduct was the actual and proximate cause of plaintiff's emotional distress.[162]

In 1992 Illinois passed the Whistleblower Reward and Protection Act (WRPA).[163] This law is modeled on the federal False Claims Act and contains a *qui tam* provision that permits employee whistleblowers to obtain significant monetary rewards if they successfully document fraud or other improper billing practices against the State of Illinois. Like the federal law, the WRPA provides that persons who submit false claims to the state must pay triple damages.[164] It provides that "private persons" can initiate actions pursuant to a strict statutory procedure, and if such actions are successful they can obtain 15 percent to 30 percent of the "proceeds of the action or settlement," plus attorney's fees.[165] Finally, as in the federal law, the Illinois law provides for the protection of persons who file said claims or who act in "furtherance" of the False Claims action.[166] Whistleblowers discriminated against in contravention to this law are entitled to double back pay damages, "special damages," and attorney's fees.[167]

INDIANA

In 1973 the revolutionary changes to the *at-will* doctrine were, in part, initiated nation-wide by the Supreme Court of Indiana in the landmark case of *Frampton v. Central Indiana Gas Co.*[168] Indiana's court was one of the first courts to explicitly alter the *at-will* doctrine and create the public policy tort. The Supreme Court, acknowledging that it knew of "no other cases in this or any other jurisdiction" that recognized this tort action, held that "retaliatory discharge" was a "wrongful, unconscionable act and should be actionable in a court of law."[169] The court recognized that the "fear of retaliation for reporting violations" inhibited such reporting and "ultimately undermines a critically important public policy."[170]

Since *Frampton*, the courts have protected employees who have refused to violate state or federal law and when an employee exercised a right protected or granted under law.[171] In one state appeals court ruling, the existence of a federal statutory remedy did not foreclose the application of the tort remedy.[172]

Under *Frampton*, an employee who prevails in a whistleblower action is entitled to be "fully compensated," including an award for lost wages, future wages, compensatory damages and punitive damages.[173]

Indiana has statutorily outlined employment protection provisions for state employees in the State Employees' Bill of Rights.[174] In relevant part, the law provides that no state employee may be dismissed, have benefits withheld, be transferred, or be demoted[175] for reporting in writing the existence of a state, federal, or regulatory violation,[176] or the misuse of public resources.[177]

IOWA

The Iowa Supreme Court recognizes the public policy exception.[178] Employees may rely upon an employee "handbook or policy manual" for a contract-based exception, and the court prohibited the discharge of an employee "where the discharge clearly violates a well-recognized and defined public policy of the state."[179]

KANSAS

In 1988 the Supreme Court of Kansas recognized a "whistleblower exception" to the termination *at-will* doctrine in a case where the employee reported improper medicaid billing practices. The court held that it was the "declared public policy" to "encourage citizens to report infractions of law pertaining to public health."[180] The court provided a tort remedy for employees discharged "in retaliation for the good faith reporting of a coworker's or employer's serious infraction of rules, regulations or law pertaining to public health, safety, and the general welfare."[181]

In Kansas, employees covered under a union contract may also pursue the public policy tort cause of action.[182] Likewise, if a statutory remedy is "inadequate," such as the federal OSHA law, an employee may seek redress through the common law tort remedy, and avoid the problems associated with an inadequate statutory scheme.[183]

KENTUCKY

An exception to the employment-at-will doctrine has been adopted by the Kentucky Supreme Court.[184] A cause of action for retaliatory discharge can lie if the termination was motivated by an employer's desire to punish an employee for seeking benefits to which he or she is entitled by law.[185] The following factors set out the exceptions to the *at-will* doctrine:

1. The discharge must be contrary to a fundamental and well-defined public
    policy as evidenced by existing law.

2. That policy must be evidenced by a constitutional or statutory provision.

3. The decision of whether the public policy asserted meets these criteria is a
    question of law for the court to decide, not a question of fact.[186]

Where a statute both declares the act unlawful and specifies the
civil remedy available, the aggrieved party is limited to the remedy provided by statute.[187]

So far two situations have been found to exist in Kentucky where
grounds for discharging an employee are so contrary to public policy that
they are actionable absent explicit legislative statements prohibiting the
discharge. The first situation exists when an employee is discharged for
refusing to violate a law during the course of employment.[188] The second
situation exists when an employee is discharged as a result of his or her
exercise of a right conferred by a well-established legislative enactment.[189]

Public employees are protected from discharge or other "reprisals"
for reporting "any facts or information" related to a potential violation of
any Kentucky or U.S. law, regulation or mandate to an "appropriate
body."[190]

LOUISIANA

Louisiana, a civil law state, has passed statutes protecting public
sector[191] and private sector[192] employee whistleblowers. Statutes also exist
that protect employees who make disclosures concerning environmental
violations,[193] provide *qui tam* actions regarding fraud in medical assistance
programs,[194] prohibit retaliation against persons who report unlawful discrimination,[195] and prevent retaliation for applying for worker's compensation.[196]

The statutory remedies authorized by the legislature are of mixed
value. For example, the environmental whistleblower law, consistent with
most federal provisions, protects an employee (in either the private or
public sector) who "reports" or "complains about" "possible environmental
violations."[197] Victims of such retaliation are entitled to file a civil action,
collect "triple damages," attorney's fees, and damages for "lost wages,"
"loss of anticipated wages," and "physical or emotional damages." There
is no provision for reverse attorney's fees, and the remedies contained in
the statute are not preclusive of other federal or state remedies.[198]

In juxtaposition with the environmental statute, the general "employee protection" statute requires that an employee first raise the allegation of misconduct with his or her employer.[199] Additionally, provisions exist for a reverse attorney's fee if the employee cannot prove that the "employer's act or practice was not in violation of the law."[200] These two provisions seriously undercut the practical value of the general whistleblower protection statute.

MAINE

Whistleblowers in Maine are protected under the 1983 Whistleblower Protection Act.[201] The WPA equally covers public and private sector employees who make a "good faith" report to either a "public body" or a supervisor of a violation of either state or federal law from discrimination or discharge.[202] However, an employee is initially required to report the suspected violation to his or her employer and allow the employer a "reasonable opportunity to correct the violation," unless the employee has a "specific reason to believe" that the employer will not correct the violation.[203] Jury trials are not available under the WPA.[204]

Claims under the WPA are adjudicated under the analytical framework used by courts under Title VII.[205] Employers must post notice of the WPA, and the WPA may be pursued independent of collective bargaining rights or other common law claims.[206]

A cause of action for breach of an express or implied contract has been recognized when an employee relies on personnel policies, handbooks, manuals and performance review procedures.[207] Punitive damages are available only upon a showing of a willful, independent tort arising from the employer's actions that constitute a breach.[208] Maine's Supreme Court has not recognized the "implied covenant of good faith and fair dealing" cause of action.[209]

MARYLAND

Maryland courts recognize a cause of action for the tort of abusive discharge when the motivation for the termination contravenes public policy.[210] Plaintiffs may rely on both state and federal law as the source of the public policy that would be undermined by refusing an exception to the *at-will* doctrine.[211] Punitive damages are awardable for abusive discharge.[212] In a split decision, the Maryland Court of Appeals held that the public policy tort is not available if the public policy that the employee seeks to vindicate "carries its own remedy for vindicating that public policy."[213]

MASSACHUSETTS

The public policy exception to the *at-will* doctrine has been recognized in Massachusetts.[214] The Supreme Judicial Court has protected under the exception employees who were discharged "for a reason that violates a clear mandate of public policy," including the assertion of a "legal right," performing an act required under law, cooperating with a law enforcement investigation, "enforcing safety laws," refusing to "give false testimony," and reporting wrongdoing to one's employer.[215]

The court protected an employee who, in "good faith" reported suspected criminal conduct to a supervisor, but never reported the allegation to the government. The court reasoned that failing to protect employees who only made disclosures to management would be "illogical."[216]

A covenant of good faith and fair dealing was applied to an *at-will* employment relationship in *Fortune v. National Cash Register Co.*[217] Where the discharge is for a reason contrary to public policy, the courts will find a breach of contract based on the *good faith and fair dealing* doctrine.[218]

In a wrongful discharge claim based on age discrimination before a federal district court in Massachusetts, the court held the action was preempted by a state antidiscrimination statute that provides employees with a statutory remedy.[219] In so holding, however, the court recognized a contrary decision in *McKinney v. National Dairy Council*[220] holding that a discharge motivated by age discrimination was actionable under the implied covenant of good faith and fair dealing.[221]

Public employees are covered under a statutory prohibition against retaliation. Such employees are granted the right to a civil action in "common law tort" and a right to obtain attorney's fees.[222]

MICHIGAN

In 1980, Michigan was one of the first states to pass a Whistleblowers' Protection Act (WPA).[223] This statute equally protects public and private sector employees.[224]

The law protects employees who "report" or are "about to report" a "violation or suspected violation" of state or federal law to a "public body."[225] The "public body" clause requires employees to raise their allegations directly to governmental authorities, such as a law enforcement agency, the "judiciary," or a state "employer, agency, [or] department" of either the state's executive or legislative branch of government.[226] However, merely reporting a violation to a supervisor is not protected under the statute, unless the disclosure could constitute a "threat" to file with a governmental agency under the "about to" clause of the statute.[227]

The statute requires that a civil action be filed "90 days after the occurrence of the alleged" violation and entitles the employee to injunctive relief, actual damages, reinstatement, back pay, and attorney fees and costs.[228] Employers must post notice of employee rights under the WPA.[229]

If an employee is protected under the WPA, the Michigan courts have required the employee to utilize those statutory rights instead of a common law "public policy" claim.[230] Another Michigan statute provides similar protection against retaliatory discharges to employees who file complaints with the Michigan Civil Rights Commission.[231]

The Michigan courts recognized an exception to the *at-will* rule and maintain that an employee cannot be discharged in violation of a clearly articulated, well-accepted public policy.[232] To state a cause of action for wrongful discharge, plaintiff must establish that: (1) he or she was engaged in protected activity;[233] (2) he or she was discharged; and (3) his or her discharge was due to performing the protected activity.[234] In *Sventko v. Kroger Co.*,[235] the court upheld a retaliatory discharge claim because the termination violated an employee's exercise of a right conferred by statute.[236] In addition, refusing to violate a law in the course of employment is protected conduct under the public policy exception.[237] However, as set forth above, the Michigan courts have held that the WPA is the exclusive remedy for claims covered under that law.

MINNESOTA

In 1986, a common law action in tort for wrongful discharge of a whistleblower was upheld by the Minnesota Court of Appeals.[238] Within a year of that decision, Minnesota enacted a whistleblower protection statute, which provided a statutory remedy for employees.[239] This remedy has "displaced" the common law theory of recovery,[240] and whistleblower cases in Minnesota have been adjudicated under that statute.[241]

The state whistleblower statute applies equally to private and public sector employees.[242] It prohibits discrimination or discharge if an employee, "in good faith, reports a violation or suspected violation of any federal or state law . . . to an employer or to any governmental body."[243] It also protects employees who refuse to perform acts that violate state or federal law and protects employees who respond to a "request" by a public body for information or testimony.[244] In 1997 the law was amended to explicitly cover health care whistleblowers who raise concerns about "the quality of health care."[245]

In order to prove a claim under the statute an employee must demonstrate: (1) protected activity; (2) adverse action; and (3) a causal connection between the protected activity and the adverse action.[246] The courts generally follow the *McDonnell Douglas Corp. v. Green* test concerning the allocation of the burden of proof.[247]

Employees are entitled to a jury trial and can collect actual and compensatory damages, including damages for "past and future emotional distress," "lost future earnings," "impairment of reputation," interest, and attorney fees and costs.[248] The law has a two year statute of limitations, which is subject to tolling.[249]

MISSISSIPPI

In 1993 Mississippi joined the majority of states and adopted the "public policy exception to the employment at will" as a common law tort.[250] The Supreme Court of Mississippi found "at least two" forms of protected activity: (1) where an employee refuses to participate in an illegal act; and (2) where a employer reports illegal acts.[251]

MISSOURI

Missouri was a pioneer state in establishing the public policy exception. In a 1963 decision, *Smith v. Arthur Baue Funeral Home*,[252] an employee was fired for asserting his right to be covered by a collective bargaining agreement. The court allowed the wrongful discharge claim, reasoning that the Missouri Constitution created a modified *at-will* doctrine by declaring a right that was violated by the employer.[253]

Smith was a landmark case in that the Supreme Court of Missouri articulated the basic foundation of the public policy exception to the *at-will* doctrine:

[S]ince plaintiff had no contract of employment for any definite term, his employers' right to terminate his employment at any time for any reason was well established by our decisions. However, this right was modified by the adoption of Section 29, Article I, supra, to this extent, namely an employer may not discharge an employee for asserting the constitutional right thereby given him. . . . As between individuals, because it declares a right the violation of which surely is a legal wrong, there is available every appropriate remedy to redress or prevent violation of this right. . . . Thus, plaintiff's discharge, if it was for that reason (and plaintiff had substantial evidence to show that it was), was a wrongful discharge for which he could maintain an action for damages.[254]

Since 1963, four basic exceptions to the *at-will* doctrine have been recognized: (1) refusal to perform an illegal act or action "contrary to a strong mandate of public policy"; (2) "reporting" a "violation of law or public policy" to "superiors or third parties"; (3) "acting in a manner public policy would encourage"; and (4) filing a worker's compensation claim.[255] Warning a wrongdoer to stop his or her misconduct, without reporting the wrongdoer to a higher authority, is not protected activity.[256]

In 1985 the court of appeals analyzed the public policy exception and concluded that employers "are not free to require employees, on pain of losing their jobs, to commit unlawful acts or acts in violation of a clear mandate of public policy expressed in the constitution, statutes, and regulations promulgated pursuant to statute."[257]

Where a collective bargaining agreement provides a grievance procedure for the settlement of disputes between employers and employees, the aggrieved party should, with limited exceptions, exhaust the remedies provided by the agreement before resorting to the courts for redress.[258]

The Missouri Court of Appeals in *Beasley v. Affiliated Hosp. Products*[259] expressly allowed an employee to sue for wrongful termination, and negligent and intentional infliction of emotional distress.[260] The court held that terminating an employee for refusal to violate a law was in clear violation of public policy as announced by both the Missouri and United States legislatures.[261]

MONTANA

Montana is the only state to radically undermine whistleblower protection through the passage of the Wrongful Discharge from Employment Act (WDEA), an antiwhistleblower law that both created statutory roadblocks to setting forth a valid claim and restricted the courts from expanding common law remedies for whistleblowers.[262] The law created "the exclusive remedy" for a whistleblower wrongful discharge case[263] and prohibited the courts from adjudicating other common law remedies in either tort or contract.[264]

Other provisions of the law provided as follows:

1. a narrow definition of protected activity;

2. a one-year statute of limitations; and

3. Limited damages (i.e., back pay was capped at four years and the law *prohibited* courts from awarding compensatory damages and damages for emotional distress).[265]

The WDEA also created procedural roadblocks for filing a claim. Employees were required to exhaust any so-called grievance procedure adopted by the employer.[266] Additionally, a strong arbitration procedure was included, which, if agreed to by the parties, would constitute the exclusive remedy.[267] In order to compel arbitration, if a party declined to arbitrate and thereafter lost its claim in court, this party would be required to pay reverse attorney fees.[268]

Finally, by explicitly preempting state common law claims, the legislature effectively overruled a Montana Supreme Court decision that had broadly interpreted the public policy exception.[269]

NEBRASKA

The traditional common law *at-will* doctrine was changed by the Supreme Court of Nebraska in the 1988 case of *Schriner v. Meginnis Ford Co.*[270] In *Schriner* the court upheld the public policy exception when an *at-will* employee acts in good faith and upon reasonable cause in reporting his employer's suspected violation of the criminal code."[271]

In 1997 the appeals court interpreted *Schriner* as also protecting employees who "are discharged because they refused to commit an act that violates the criminal laws."[272]

NEVADA

Nevada first recognized the public policy exception in 1984.[273] Conduct is against public policy when a state enacts legislation forbidding certain behavior.[274] The failure of the legislature to enact a statute expressly forbidding retaliatory discharge does not preclude the courts from providing a remedy for behavior in violation of public policy. The "tortious discharge" cause of action is "limited to those rare and exceptional cases where the employer's conduct violates strong and compelling public policy."[275]

In order to prevail in a tortious discharge case, the employee must "demonstrate that his protected conduct was the proximate cause of his discharge."[276] Employees need not demonstrate that their employer violated the law, but they do need to demonstrate that they, in "good faith," "reasonably suspected" that their employer was involved in wrongdoing.[277]

As with any intentional tort, punitive damages are may be awarded for the tort of retaliatory discharge where plaintiff can demonstrate malicious, oppressive, or fraudulent conduct on the part of defendant.[278]

Sex or age discrimination was held to fall within the public policy exception to the *at-will* doctrine by a federal district court interpreting Nevada law.[279] The tort of breach of covenant of fair dealing, and damages for humiliation, embarrassment, anxiety, harm to reputation, and health, were also upheld by the district court.[280]

NEW HAMPSHIRE

New Hampshire has adopted the public policy exception to the *at-will* doctrine.[281] The state supreme court in *Monge v. Beebe Rubber Co.* held that "a termination by the employer of a contract of employment at will which is motivated by bad faith or malice or based on retaliation is not in the best interest of the economic system or the public good and constitutes a breach of the employment contract."[282]

The holding in *Monge* has been applied to situations where an employee is discharged because he performed an act that public policy would encourage, or refused to do that which public policy would condemn.[283] To state a claim for wrongful discharge from employment, the plaintiff must show that defendant was motivated by bad faith, malice, or retaliation and demonstrate that the discharge violated public policy.[284] In most cases, whether public policy exists is a question for the jury and can be based on statutory or nonstatutory principles.[285]

In 1987 New Hampshire passed a Whistleblowers' Protection Act.[286] The law, which explicitly did not "impair" rights under the "common law,"[287] created an administrative remedy before the New Hampshire Commissioner of Labor to adjudicate whistleblower claims.[288] The law protects employees who: "report" in "good faith," potential violations of state or federal law; participate in investigations or hearings; and refuse to "execute a directive which in fact violates any law or rule."[289] To be protected, employees must first bring the alleged violation to the attention of a supervisor[290] and provide the employer with a reasonable opportunity" to correct the violation. Internal whistleblowing directly to a supervisor, even if the allegation is not communicated to a public body, is protected.[291]

Other causes of action may also be recognized in the employment context. The tort of intentional infliction of emotional distress and the tort of defamation, for example, were upheld by a federal district court interpreting New Hampshire law.[292]

NEW JERSEY

New Jersey recognizes a common law cause of action for wrongful discharge in both contract and tort.[293] The legislature has also enacted an independent statutory remedy.[294] An action in contract may be predicated on the breach of an implied provision that an employer will not discharge an employee for refusing to perform an act that violated a clear mandate of public policy,[295] whereas a tort action may be based on the employer's duty not to discharge an employee for such reasons.[296] Punitive damages may be awarded in a tort action but not in a contract action.[297] The sources of public policy include legislation (administrative rules, regulations, or decisions) and judicial opinions.[298]

In 1986 the state legislature passed the Conscientious Employee Protection Act (CEPA).[299] The law covers both public and private sector employees[300] who disclose allegations of wrongdoing to a "public body" after they attempted to resolve the matter, if possible, with their supervisor.[301] The CEPA has a one-year statute of limitations[302] and provides for a civil remedy in state court, punitive damages,[303] attorney's fees, and reinstatement with full back pay. Employers found guilty under the CEPA are "strictly liable for equitable relief in the nature of reinstatement, restoration of back pay and the like."[304]

Under the law, an employee need only demonstrate a "reasonable" and "objective" belief that an employer's conduct contravened law or public policy.[305] The CEPA explicitly did not act to waive other common law or statutory remedies that exist in New Jersey,[306] but if an employee utilizes the law, she or he waives the right to pursue other remedies. If utilized, the CEPA is an exclusive remedy for the retaliatory discharge claims, but not other common law claims.[307] Other New Jersey statutes also prohibit employees from wrongful discharge.[308]

The CEPA was intended to "overcome the victimization of employees and to protect those who are especially vulnerable in the workplace from improper or unlawful exercise of authority by employers."[309] The law was passed because "conscientious employees" had been fired or demoted for "calling attention to illegal activity" and to help overcome the "deep-seated fear" of employees that exposing illegal conduct would destroy an employee's "livelihood."[310] The "core value embodied" in the CEPA "is that employees courageous enough to object to illegal, fraudulent or harmful activity by their employers in order to protect the public welfare deserve to be shielded from retaliation by their employers."[311]

Under both the common law and statutory whistleblower protection laws, the issue of what constitutes "a clear mandate of public policy" is a question of law not a jury question.[312] Additionally, an employee is under no obligation to identify or even know the particular statute or other source of public policy at the time he or she blows the whistle. As explained by the New Jersey Supreme Court: "Specific knowledge of the precise source of public policy is not required. The object of CEPA is not to make law-yers out of conscientious employees but rather to prevent retaliation against those employees."[313] Protected activities under the CEPA are broadly construed and cover reports of misconduct by co-employees.[314]

NEW MEXICO

New Mexico first adopted a judicial exception to the *at-will* doc-trine in *Vigil v. Arzola*.[315] Since *Vigil* the state Supreme Court has clarified the tort of retaliatory discharge: "For an employee to recover under this new cause of action, he must demonstrate that he was discharged because he performed an act that public policy has authorized or would encourage, or because he refused to do something required of him by his employer that public policy would condemn."[316]

To prevail in the tort, an employee must show, by a preponderance of evidence, "a causal connection between his actions and the retaliatory discharge by the employer."[317] New Mexico follows the "clear mandate of public policy" standard and has not protected employee conduct absent a public interest basis.[318]

New Mexico has not displaced the common law tort whenever a statutory remedy also exists. Instead, the courts look to the "comprehen-siveness or adequacy" of the statutory alternative: "It is not just 'the pres-ence or absence of a remedy which is significant; rather, the comprehen-siveness, or adequacy, of the remedy provided is a factor which courts and commentators have considered in deciding whether a statute provides the exclusive remedies for retaliatory discharge in violation of public policy."[319]

The legislature has further limited the *at-will* doctrine by prohibit-ing employers from penalizing employees for their participation in jury service;[320] for their particular political opinions or beliefs;[321] or for asserting rights provided in the state workmen's compensation statute.[322]

NEW YORK

New York state courts have rejected establishing a public policy exception.[323] In 1984 New York passed a "Whistleblower Statute." How-ever the inadequacies of the law have led commentators to note that whistleblower protection in New York is all but non-existent.[324] The statute prohibits an employer from taking any retaliatory personnel action[325] against an employee, if such employee does any of the following:

(a) discloses, or threatens to disclose to a supervisor or to a public body an activity, policy or practice of the employer that is violation of law, rule or regulation which violation creates and presents a substantial and specific danger to the public health or safety;

(b) provides information to, or testifies before, any public body conducting an investigation, hearing or inquiry into any such violation of a law, rule or regulation by such employer; or

(c) objects to, or refuses to participate in any such activity, policy or practice in violation of a law, rule or regulation.[326]

The deficiencies in this law are devastating to actual protection of employees. First, the New York courts have interpreted the phrase "in violation of law" to require the showing of an actual violation. Unlike almost all other whistleblower laws, the New York code requires not only a "good faith" and reasonable belief that a "law, rule or regulation" has in fact been violated, but the employee must also demonstrate an actual violation.[327] This requirement not only inhibits the disclosure of potentially improper conduct but creates a very difficult element of proof that could require an employee to retain expensive experts and conduct a technical trial-within-a-trial in order to demonstrate the illegality of the underlying concern.

Additionally, the law only covers one area of whistleblowing (i.e., raising "public health or safety" concerns).[328] Other areas of whistleblowing, such as billing fraud or even violent criminal activity are not included.[329] Even health and safety concerns are not protected unless they rise to the level of a "substantial and specific danger" to the public.[330]

If an employee can meet the strict definition of protected activity contained in the statute, the employee must also meet a number of procedural requirements. For example, an employee must first bring the whistleblower disclosure to the attention of a supervisor[331] and afford the employer a reasonable opportunity to correct its alleged misconduct.[332] The statute of limitations for an action under this statute is one year after the alleged retaliatory personnel action was taken.[333]

Finally, if an employee meets all of these definitional and procedural requirements and prevails on the merits, damages are limited. Employee damages are limited to reinstatement and back pay (with benefits). Compensatory damages are not allowed.[334]

Independent contractors are not protected by the statutory provisions.[335] Furthermore, the fact that the personnel action was predicated upon grounds other than the employee's exercise of any activity protected in the statute will constitute a defense to the action.[336] The statute does not in any way diminish the rights of employees under any other laws, statutes, contracts, or collective bargaining agreements, but institution of an action under the statute will be deemed a waiver of the rights and remedies available under any other contract, collective bargaining agreement, law, rule, or regulation or under the common law.[337]

New York has also statutorily prohibited an employer from discharging or in any way discriminating against an employee for asserting or attempting to assert a worker's compensation claim from such employer.[338] Public employees are also protected under a separate whistleblower law.[339]

NORTH CAROLINA

A claim for wrongful discharge was first recognized in 1985 by the North Carolina Court of Appeals in *Sides v. Duke Hospital,* where an anesthetist was fired for testifying truthfully in a civil action.[340] The court held that no employer in North Carolina has the right to discharge an employee because he refused to testify untruthfully.[341] Actions for intentional infliction of emotional distress, breach of contract, and malicious interference with an employment contract are also recognized.[342] The holding in *Sides* was explicitly adopted by the North Carolina Supreme Court:

[W]hile there may be a right to terminate a contract at will for no reason, or for an arbitrary or irrational reason, there can be no right to terminate such a contract for an unlawful reason or purpose that contravenes public policy. A different interpretation would encourage and sanction lawlessness, which law by its very nature is designed to discourage and prevent.[343]

Punitive damages may be recovered only for tortious conduct.[344] To recover punitive damages, the employee must prove that the employer acted willfully, with malice, or with reckless disregard for the employee's rights.[345]

Actions by employees who have been demoted or discharged in retaliation for instituting a worker's compensation proceeding in good faith, or for testifying in regard to it, are expressly authorized by the General Assembly.[346]

NORTH DAKOTA

The Supreme Court of North Dakota adopted the public policy exception cause of action in a case concerning the discharge of an employee for honoring a subpoena and testifying truthfully in a court of law.[347] The state follows a narrow "clear mandate" standard for defining public policy.[348]

In 1997 the legislature passed a whistleblower law prohibiting discrimination against employees who report "suspected violation(s) of federal or state law" to their employer or a "public body." The law also protects employees who refuse to perform illegal work activities or who participate in investigations when "requested" by a public body."[349]

The law has a ninety-day statute of limitations, limits back pay payments to two years, and provides that a "prevailing party" may obtain attorneys' fees.[350] The law does not explicitly state that it constitutes the exclusive remedy for employee whistleblowers, but, if such an interpretation is given by the courts, whistleblowers will not be properly protected in North Dakota.

OHIO

The Ohio legislature became the second state to pass an antiwhistleblower statute. In 1988 Ohio passed the Whistleblower Statute, which on its face created a remedy for employee whistleblowers, but which, in reality, created procedural impediments that rendered whistleblower protection nearly impossible to obtain.[351]

The law limits what an employee may blow the whistle on (a "criminal offense that is likely to cause an imminent risk of physical harm to persons or a hazard to public health or safety or a felony"), and sets forth a strict procedure that is the "sole acceptable manner in which the employee may 'blow the whistle' to outside authorities."[352] Moreover, if an employee raises a whistleblower-type concern to a supervisor, and the employee did not make a "reasonable and good faith effort to determine the accuracy of any information reported," not only does the employee lose any rights under the so-called Whistleblower Statute, an employer is explicitly granted authority to take "disciplinary action" against the employee, "including suspension or removal."[353] Thus, the statute actually grants an employer the statutory authority to fire an employee who merely raises a concern to his or her supervisor, if the employee did not properly investigate even a simple concern. No other state or federal law has so empowered an employer to explicitly take a preemptive retaliatory action against an employee who merely raises a concern about potential misconduct.

Assuming an employee is willing to risk summary termination for raising a concern, the law then sets forth the mandatory procedural steps to which an employee must adhere. First, the employee *must* orally raise the concern with a management official. Second, the employee *must* file a "written report that provides sufficient detail to identify and describe the violation." Third, the employee must give the employer twenty-four hours to correct the problem. After following these three steps, only then can the employee report the violation to an appropriate authority (these authorities are also limited in scope and spelled out in the statute).[354]

In a decision dismissing an employee's claim for failure to "strictly comply with the dictates" of the statute, the court noted that such failure "prevents the employee from claiming protections" of a whistleblower.[355] In the dissent, one justice noted that Ohio had taken a "backward leap" on whistleblowing into the "world" which "left" whistleblowers "with no rights."[356]

Despite the restrictive nature of the Ohio whistleblower law, employees may still rely upon the state's Supreme Court decision in *Greeley v. Miami Valley Maintenance*[357] to set forth a common law public policy tort.[358] As explained by the Ohio Supreme Court:

> The remedies available pursuant to R.C. 4113.52 are not sufficient to provide the complete relief that would otherwise be available in a Greeley- based cause of action for the tort of wrongful discharge. The statute does not provide for certain compensatory damages and does not specifically authorize recovery of punitive damages. . . . Clearly, the relief available to a whistleblower under a statutory cause of action comes nowhere near the complete relief available in an action based upon the Greeley public-policy exception to the doctrine of employment at will. . . . Thus, we find that the mere existence of statutory remedies for violations of R.C. 4113.52 does not operate as a bar to alternative common-law remedies for wrongful discharge in violation of the public policy embodied in the Whistleblower Statute. [359]

Employees may also rely upon other traditional common law torts to remedy retaliatory conduct.[360]

OKLAHOMA

The Supreme Court of Oklahoma decided to "follow the modern trend and adopt" the public policy exception as an "actionable tort claim."[361] The court adopted the "clear mandate of public policy standard," as recognized under "constitutional, statutory or decisional law."[362]

The courts have upheld the tort action in cases which the employee reported violations of the federal Food, Drug and Cosmetic Act to his supervisors.[363]

A personnel manual can constitute an employment contract, and Oklahoma has some statutory exceptions to the *at-will* doctrine.[364]

OREGON

The state of Oregon recognizes the public policy exception to the *at-will* doctrine as a tort.[365] Damages awardable include, but are not limited to, injunctive relief, reinstatement, back pay,[366] and punitive damages.[367] Oregon courts have provided for the tort act where employees were discharged "exercising a job-related right of important public interest" or for "complying with a public duty."[368] Claims have been upheld for whistleblowers who have reported patient abuse and who have refused to sign false reports.[369]

Oregon has had conflicting opinions concerning whether an employee is precluded from obtaining tort relief on the basis of alternative statutory remedies.[370] One federal court, interpreting the Oregon case law, held that the common law tort would be precluded if either (a) the legislature explicitly held that the statutory remedy was exclusive, or (b) if a preexisting statutory right "adequately protects the public."[371]

Public employees are also protected under a state statute.[372]

PENNSYLVANIA

The Pennsylvania Supreme Court acknowledges a cause of action for wrongful discharge of an *at-will* employee where some recognized facet of public policy is threatened.[373] Public policy can be derived directly from Pennsylvania's Constitution,[374] federal law,[375] or state law.[376] Pennsylvania has rejected the view that "public policy" "is only that which is legislatively enacted," holding that courts have "independent authority" to "discern public policy in the absence of legislation."[377]

The superior courts of Pennsylvania have only recognized public policy claims "in the most limited of circumstances."[378] For example, in a 2-1 decision, a superior court declined to uphold the cause of action because the employee did not have a "statutorily imposed duty" to report the suspected fraud.[379] The "narrow public policy exceptions" "fall into three categories: an employer (1) cannot require an employee to commit a crime, (2) cannot prevent an employee from complying with a statutorily imposed duty, and (3) cannot discharge an employee when specifically prohibited from doing so by statute."[380]

To state a cause of action, an employee must first establish that some public policy[381] was threatened or violated by the discharge.[382] The employee must further prove that she or he was terminated for refusing to perform an illegal act or engaging in an act protected by public policy.[383] However, even if an important public policy is involved, the discharge will be deemed lawful if the employer shows a separate, plausible, and legitimate reason for firing the employee.[384]

Several statutory remedies to protect employees from retaliatory discharges also exist in Pennsylvania,[385] including a Whistleblower Law for public employees.[386]

RHODE ISLAND

In 1995 Rhode Island passed a Whistleblower Protection Act.[387] The law, which has a three-year statute of limitations, protects both public and private sector workers from retaliation on the basis of reporting violations of law to a public body. It provides for reinstatement, back pay, "actual damages," and the "costs of litigation."[388] Employers must post notice of employee whistleblower rights.[389]

The U.S. Court of Appeals for the First Circuit has interpreted this law as protecting employee complaints filed with supervisors.[390]

SOUTH CAROLINA

The state Supreme Court of South Carolina adopted the public policy exception to the *at-will* doctrine in *Ludwick v. Minute of Carolina, Inc.*[391] A retaliatory discharge of an *at-will* employee for refusing to violate the law was held to constitute violation of a clear mandate of public policy.[392] The court in *Ludwick* made no attempt to narrowly define cases involving the public policy exception of refusal to violate the law, and stated that:

An at will prerogative without limits could be suffered only in an anarchy, and there not for long—it certainly cannot be suffered in a society such as ours without weakening the bond of counter balancing rights and obligations that holds such societies together. Thus, while there may be a right to terminate a contract at will for no reason, or for an arbitrary or irrational reason, *there can be no right to terminate such a contract for an unlawful reason or purpose that contravenes public policy.*[393]

The court qualified the exception by ruling that plaintiff has the burden of establishing that the retaliatory discharge contravenes a clear violation of a mandate of public policy.[394]

The court, in a case where a federal statute provided a full remedy to an employee, declined to expand the scope of the public policy tort and required the employee to pursue that remedy.[395] On the other hand, the court permitted a claim to proceed when the federal remedies were clearly inadequate (i.e., when a nuclear worker reported concerns about radioactive contamination to the news media and governmental bodies).[396] Public employees are covered under a whistleblower act.[397]

SOUTH DAKOTA

South Dakota recognized a "contract action" for wrongful discharge in violation of public policy. Under the cause of action, the "employee has the burden of proving that the dismissal violates a clear mandate of public policy." If the employer puts forth a legitimate reason for the discharge, the employee also "must prove by a preponderance of the evidence that the discharge was for an impermissible reason."[398] A wrongful discharge under particularly egregious circumstances may also justify a tort action under the "intentional infliction of emotional distress" theory.[399]

TENNESSEE

In a case concerning the termination of an employee for utilizing her rights under a worker's compensation act, the Supreme Court of Tennessee upheld a public policy wrongful discharge tort, stating that "[a] cause of action for retaliatory discharge, although not explicit, created by the statute, is necessary to enforce the duty of the employer, to secure the rights of the employee and to carry out the intention of the legislature. A statute need not expressly state what is necessarily implied in order to render it effectual."[400]

In 1990 Tennessee passed the Public Protection Act to protect employee whistleblowers who are "terminated solely for refusing to participate in, or refusing to remain silent about, illegal activities."[401] The intent behind this statute was to grant employees "the absolute right to speak out about illegal activities in their workplaces."[402] State employees are covered under this law.[403]

The Public Protection Act does not prevent employees from seeking relief under *both* the common law and the statutory law.[404] This choice of remedy is important because at least one federal court has narrowly interpreted the scope of protection under the Public Protection Act.[405] The court also found that punitive damages were recoverable under a retaliatory discharge tort[406] if an employee demonstrates that the employer acted either "intentionally," "fraudulently," "maliciously," or "recklessly."[407]

TEXAS

Texas has judicially created a public policy exception to the *at-will* doctrine.[408] The exception so far has been narrowly construed to prohibit employers from discharging their employees for refusing to perform an illegal act.[409] The Texas legislature has enacted other exceptions to the *at-will* doctrine,[410] including protections for public employees.[411]

UTAH

In *Hodges v. Gibson Prods. Co.*, the Supreme Court of Utah adopted the "public policy" wrongful discharge cause of action: "When the means used to accomplish a prohibited end, that is, the discharge of an employee, runs counter to public policy, an action for wrongful discharge is the appropriate way to protect both the public interest and the employee from an employer's oppressive use of power."[412]

The courts recognize that the "enforcement of a state's criminal code," the "reporting" of "criminal activity to public authorities," and the "refusal to engage in criminal conduct at the direction of the employer" are all protected under a "clear and substantial" mandate of public policy.[413] However, an employee who discloses allegations of criminal activity to a supervisor may not be protected.[414]

State officers and employees are also statutorily protected against retaliation for reporting governmental violations of law.[415]

VERMONT

In 1986 Vermont adopted the public policy exception to the *termination-at-will* doctrine. The Vermont Supreme Court broadly defined public policy, rejecting the proposition that courts are limited to statutory directives in defining exactly what are protected disclosures or what is protected conduct.[416] Quoting from an old Ohio Supreme Court definition of "public policy" the Vermont court stated: "In substance [public policy] may be said to be the community common sense and common conscience."[417]

The public policy common law tort is not preempted by co-existing statutory remedies. In *Murray v. St. Michael's College*,[418] the Vermont Supreme Court found that a statute granting the Attorney General the authority to seek civil penalties from an employer who violated the prohibition on retaliatory discharge did not preempt the employee seeking a private tort remedy.

VIRGINIA

Virginia's Supreme Court has recognized a "narrow exception to the *at-will* doctrine" by allowing a cause of action in tort for improper discharge.[419] A cause of action for wrongful discharge may also exist where the employer expressly and/or implicitly promised that the employee would only be fired for just cause.[420]

The public policy exception does *not* protect conduct that concerns "only private right."[421] If an employee cannot "identify" a "Virginia statute establishing a public policy," their claim may be dismissed.[422]

WASHINGTON

The Washington Supreme Court recognized a cause of action in tort for wrongful discharge.[423] Under this cause of action, the employee has the burden of proving the dismissal violated a clear mandate of public policy. A cause of action in wrongful discharge exists under any of four circumstances: "(1) where employees are fired for refusing to commit an illegal act; (2) where employees are fired for performing a public duty or obligation, such as serving jury duty; (3) where employees are fired for exercising a legal right or privilege, such as filing workers' compensation claims; and (4) where employees are fired in retaliation for reporting employer misconduct (i.e. whistleblowing)."[424] Once the employee has demonstrated that his or her discharge may have been motivated by reasons that contravene a clear mandate of public policy, the burden shifts to the employer to prove that the dismissal was for reasons other than those alleged by the employee.[425]

Washington's public policy tort is not preempted or precluded by other statutory remedies, unless the legislature explicitly provides for such an exclusion.[426] In *Smith v. Bates Technical College*, the Washington Supreme Court explained the justification for their non-preemption position as follows:

Because the right to be free from wrongful termination in violation of public policy is independent of any underlying contractual agreement or civil service law, we conclude Smith should not be required to exhaust her contractual or administrative remedies.

*   *   *

[The employee's] right to be free from wrongful termination in contravention of public policy may not be altered or waived by private agreement, and is therefore a nonnegotiable right.[427]

The tort is also available to employees covered under a contract for employment and public employees.[428] Additionally, the tort remedy is only available in the context of a wrongful dismissal. Lesser acts, such as a retaliatory job transfer, are not, unto themselves, actionable.[429]

The Washington courts have also held that an *at-will* employment relationship can be modified by provisions found in an employee policy manual.[430] Some limitations on an employer's right to discharge are also based upon state statutes.[431]

WEST VIRGINIA

West Virginia adopted the public policy exception to the *at-will* doctrine in *Harless v. First National Bank in Fairmont*.[432] The court in *Harless* held that where an employer's motivation for the discharge contravenes some substantial public policy principle, the employer may be liable in tort for retaliatory discharge.[433] The public policy contravened was established by the state's legislature protecting credit consumers.[434] The state Supreme Court has since held that substantial public policy exception need not be based on a statute[435] and could be based on the "constitution, legislative enactments, legislatively approved regulations and judicial opinions."[436]

In regard to substantial public policies based on the Constitution, public sector employees are fully protected from a discharge violative of the Constitution, including the First Amendment.[437] Private sector employees, on the other hand, do not enjoy automatic protection under a First Amendment analysis, and establishing a public policy based on a constitutional provision needs to be reviewed "on a case-by-case basis."[438]

A tort for intentional infliction of emotional distress arising from a retaliatory discharge was also recognized in *Harless*.[439] The action was allowed even though there was no impact and no physical injury caused by defendant's wrong. The plaintiff need only show that an emotional or mental disturbance resulted from defendant's intentional or wanton wrongful act.[440]

WISCONSIN

Wisconsin has instituted a narrow contract-based exception to the *at-will* doctrine.[441] The law in Wisconsin prohibits the discharge of an employee for refusing to violate a clear mandate of public policy or for engaging in conduct required by law.[442] The employee must show that the dismissal violated such a public policy. It then becomes the employer's burden to go forward with evidence to show that the firing resulted from just cause and not from refusal to commit an illegal act.[443]

An employee fired for refusing a command to violate public policy does not have to prove that the employer had evil intent in discharging him or her.[444] An employee may, however, be required to exhaust administrative remedies before bringing a state action.[445] Employees are also covered under other potential tort remedies, such as tortious interference wiht employment.[446]

WYOMING

A tort action for retaliatory discharge is available to *at-will* employees in the state of Wyoming.[447] However, this remedy is not available to employees protected under an independent scheme, such as an employment contract or a collective bargaining agreement.[448]

NOTES

1. *See* Robert Vaughn, "State Whistleblower Statutes and the Future of Whistleblower Protection," 51 *Administrative Law Review* 581 (1999); S. Kohn and M. Kohn, "An Overview of Federal and State Whistleblower Protections," 4 *Antioch Law Journal* 99 (1986).

2. *Tameny v. Atlantic Richfield Co.*, 610 P.2d 1330 (Cal. 1980).

3. Unlike most statutory remedies that broadly prohibit various job-related "adverse actions," the public policy tort has primarily been applied in the wrongful discharge context. *See White v. State*, 929 P.2d 396, 407 (Wash. 1997) (declining to apply public policy tort in nondischarge context).

4. *Carl v. Children's Hosp.*, 702 A.2d 159, 175 (D.C. App. 1997) (J. Schwelb concurring).

5. *Id.* at 175.

6. *Id.* at 176.

7. *Smith v. Atlas Off-Shore Boat Serv.*, 653 F.2d 1057, 1061 (5th Cir. 1981).

8. John P. Dawson, "Economic Duress and the Fair Exchange in French and German Law," 11 *Tulane Law Review* 345 (1937).

9. Lawrence Blades, "Employment at Will v. Individual Freedom: On Limiting the Abusive Exercise of Employer Power," 67 *Columbia Law Review* 1404, 1410 (December 1967).

10. *Winters v. Houston Chronicle Pub. Co.*, 795 S.W.2d 723, 728 (Tex. 1990) (concurring opinion of J. Doggett).

11. *Id.* at 728.

12. *Id.* at 723, 730, and 733.

13. *Sides v. Duke University*, 328 S.E.2d 818, 826 (N.C. App. 1985), review denied, 333 S.E.2d 490 (1985).

14. *Petermann v. International Brotherhood of Teamsters*, 344 P.2d 25 (Cal. 1959).

15. *Gantt v. Sentry Ins.*, 824 P.2d 680, 684 (Cal. 1992).

16. *Mehlman v. Mobil Oil*, 707 A.2d 1000, 1016 (N.J. 1998).

17. *Id.*

18. *Green v. Ralee Eng. Co.*, 960 P.2d 1046, 1051 (Cal. 1998); *Gantt, supra*, at 680, 684 (collecting cases); *Carl, supra*, at 182 (J. Schwelb concurring). The *Gantt* court also discussed the different standard applied by a variety of states. *Gantt*, at 684-687.

19. *Stebbings v. University of Chicago*, 726 N.E.2d 1136 (Ill. App. 1 Dist., 2000).

20. *Appeal of Bio Energy Corp.*, 607 A.2d 606, 608 (N.H. 1992). *Contra Faust v. Ryder Commercial Leasing*, 954 S.W.2d 383, 391 (Mo. App. W.D. 1997).

21. *Mehlman, supra*, at 1015-1016. *See Wichita County v. Hart*, 917 S.W.2d 779, 784-786 (Tex. 1996) (discussing employee's motivation for whistle-blowing).

22. *Jamison v. American Showa, Inc.*, 2000 WL 1404 (Ohio App. 5 Dist. 1999) (*quoting* from Professor Perritt).

23. *See* Robert Vaughn, "State Whistleblower Statutes and the Future of Whistleblower Protection," 51 *Administrative Law Review* 581 (1999).

24. *English v. G.E.*, 496 U.S. 72, 74 (1990); *Lingle v. Norge*, 486 U.S. 399 (1988).

25. *Wilmot v. Kaiser Alum.*, 821 P.2d 18 (Wash. 1991) (statutory remedies are cumulative rather than exclusive); *Weidler v. Big J.*, 953 P.2d 1089 (N.M. App. 1997). *But see Draper v. Astoria School Dist.*, 995 F. Supp. 1122 (D. Oregon) (collecting cases from Oregon on conflict between preclusion and nonpreclusion).

26. *Hodges v. S.C. Toof & Co.*, 833 S.W.2d 896, 899 (Tenn. 1992) (If law does "not expressly" state it is "exclusive," then "statutory remedies must be considered cumulative"). Some courts have also precluded common law whistle-blower claims if an employee was covered under a collective bargaining agreement. *See Doll v. U.S. West Communications, Inc.*, 85 F.Supp.2d 1038 (D. Col. 2000).

27. *See* Robert G. Vaughn, "State Whistleblower Statutes and the Future of Whistleblower Protection," 51 Administrative Law Review 581 (1999).

28. *Young v. Schering Corp.*, 660 A.2d 1153, 1161 (N.J. 1995); Lex Larsen, *Unjust Dismissal* (New York: Matthew Bender, 1988), §§ 3-1– 4-10.

29. *Soltani v. Smith*, 812 F. Supp. 1280, 1296-1297 (D. N.H. 1993).

30. *Wagenseller v. Scottsdale Mem. Hosp.*, 710 P.2d 1025, 1041-1044 (Ariz. 1985). *See also Bowman v. State Bank of Keysville*, 311 S.E.2d 797 (Va. 1985); *Stewart v. Ost*, 491 N.E.2d 1306 (Ill. 1986); *Empiregas, Inc. v. Hardy*, 487 So.2d 244 (Ala. 1985).

31. *Pine River State Bank v. Mettille*, 333 N.W.2d 622 (Minn. 1983); *Arie v. Intertherm*, 648 S.W.2d 142 (Mo. App. 1983); *Morris v. Lutheran Medical Center*, 215 Neb. 677, 340 N.W.2d 388 (1983); *Hammond v. N.D. State Personnel Bd.*, 345 N.W.2d 359 (N.D. 1984); *Langdon v. Saga Corp.*, 569 P.2d 524 (Okla. App. 1976); *Jackson v. Minidoka Irrigation*, 98 Idaho 330, 563 P.2d 54 (1977); *Magnan v. Anaconda Industries, Inc.*, 37 Conn.Supp. 38, 479 A.2d 781 (1984); *Terrio v. Millinocket Community Hospital*, 379 A.2d 135 (Me. 1977); *Toussaint v. Blue Cross & Blue Shield*, 408 Mich. 579, 292 N.W.2d 880 (1980).

32. *Mitford v. de Lasala*, 666 P.2d 1000 (Alaska 1983); *Monge v. Beebe Rubber Co.*, 114 N.H. 130, 316 A.2d 549 (1974); *Fortune v. National Cash Register Co.*, 364 N.E.2d 1251 (Mass. 1977); *Cleary v. American Airlines, Inc.*, 111 Cal. App. 3d 443, 168 Cal. Rptr. 722 (1980). Most courts have declined to apply this tort in the employee-employer context..

33. *Bass v. Happy Rest, Inc.*, 507 N.W.2d 317 (S.D. 1993) (upholding intentional infliction claim); *Soltani v. Smith*, 812 F. Supp. 1280 (D. N.H. 1993) (constructive discharge claim may support intentional infliction claim); *Hunger v. Grand Cent.*, 670 A.2d 173 (Pa. Super. 1996) (declining to find intentional infliction claim); *Wagner v. Texas A & M*, 939 F. Supp. 1297 (S.D. Tex. 1996) (employment disputes cannot support intentional infliction claim); *Agis v. Howard Johnson Co.*, 355 N.E.2d 315 (Mass. 1976); *Lucas v. Brown & Root, Inc.*, 736 F.2d 1202 (8th Cir. 1984); *Kelly v. Gen. Tel. Co.*, 136 Cal. App. 3d 278, 186 Cal. Rptr. 184 (1982).

34. *DuSesoi v. United Refining Co.*, 540 F. Supp. 1260 (W.D. Pa. 1982).

35. *Chamberlain v. Bissell, Inc.*, 547 F. Supp. 1067 (W.D. Mich. 1982); *Kelly v. Gen. Tel. Co.*, 136 Cal. App. 3d 278, 186 Cal. Rptr. 184 (1982).

36. *Payton v. City of Santa Clara*, 183 Cal. Rptr. 17, 132 Cal. App. 3d 152.

37. *Mehlman, supra*, at 1000 (remanding defamation claim as distinct from retaliation); *Beck v. Tribert*, 711 A.2d 951 A.2d (N.J. Super. A.D. 1998) (declining to find defamation); *Holewinski v. Children's Hospital*, 649 A.2d 712 (Pa. Super. 1996) (declining to find defamation claim); *Mercer v. City of Cedar Rapids*, 2000 WL 1009698 (N.D. Iowa).

38. *Hart v. Seven Resorts, Inc.*, 947 P.2d 846, 854-855 (Ariz. App. Div.1 1997) (declining to find "false light" tort on basis of termination alone).

39. *Pugh v. See's Candies, Inc.*, 116 Cal. App. 3d 311, 171 Cal. Rptr. 917 (1981).

40. The following states have statutes protecting public sector employee whistleblowers: Alaska Stat. §§ 39.90.100 to 39.90.150; Ariz. Rev. Stat. Ann. §§ 38-532; Cal. Gov't Code §§ 12653; Colo. Rev. Stat. §§ 24-50.5-102 to 24-50.5-105; Conn. Gen. Stat. Ann. 31-51m; Del. Code Ann. tit. 29, §§ 5115; D.C. Code Ann. §§ 1-616.1 to 1-616.3; Fla. Stat. Ann. §§ 112.3187 to 112.31895; Ga. Code Ann. §§ 45-1-4; Haw. Rev. Stat. §§ 378-61 to 378-69; Idaho Code §§ 6-2101 to 6-2109; Ind. Code Ann. §§ 4-15-10-4 and §§ 36-1-8-8; Iowa Code Ann. §§ 70A.28; Ky. Rev. Stat. Ann. §§ 61.101 to 61.103; La. Rev. Stat. Ann. §§ 42:1169; Me. Rev. Stat. Ann. title 26, §§ 831-836; Md. Code Ann., State Pers. &

Pens. §§ 5-301 to 5-313; Mass. Gen. Laws Ann. chapter 149 §§ 185; Mich. Comp. Laws Ann. §§ 15.361 to 15.369; Minn. Stat. Ann. §§ 181.931 to 181.935; Miss. Code Ann. §§ 25-9-171 to 25-9-177; Mo. Ann. Stat. §§ 105.055; Neb. Rev. Stat. §§ 81-2701 to 81-2710; Nev. Rev. Stat. §§ 281.611 to 281.671; N.H. Rev. Stat. Ann. §§ 275-E:1 to 275-E:7; N.J. Stat. Ann. §§ 34:19-1 to 34:19-8; N.Y. Civ. Serv. Law §§ 75-b; N.C. Gen. Stat. §§ 126-84 to 126-88; N.D. Cent. Code 34-11.1-04 to 34-11.1-08; Ohio Rev. Code Ann. §§ 4113.51 to 4113.53; Okla. Stat. Ann. title 74, §§ 840-2.5; Or. Rev. Stat. §§ 659.505 to 659.545; 43 Pa. Cons. Stat. Ann. §§ 1421-1428; R.I. Gen. Laws §§ 28-50-1 to 28-50-9; S.C. Code Ann. §§ 8-27-10 to 8-27-40; S.D. Codified Laws §§ 3-6A-52; Tenn. Code Ann. §§ 50-1-304; Tex. Gov't. Code Ann. §§ 554.001 to 554.010; Utah Code Ann. §§ 67-21-1 to 67-21-9; Wash. Rev. Code Ann. §§ 42.41.010 to 42.41.060; Wash. Rev. Code Ann. §§ 42.40.020 to 42.40.050; W. Va. Code §§ 6C-1-1 to 6C-1-8; Wis. Stat. Ann. §§ 230.80 to 230.89; Wyo. Stat. Ann. §§ 9-11-103. *See generally* Robert Vaughn, "State Whistleblower Statutes and the Future of Whistleblower Protection," 51 *Admin. L. Rev.* 581 (1999).

41. 120 S.Ct. 631 (2000).

42. Even if an employee can escape the 11th Amendment's absolute prohibitions to federal court jurisdiction, the *qualified immunity* doctrine also restricts the liability of state governmental entities and public sector supervisors. *See, e.g., Will v. Michigan Dept. of State Police*, 491 U.S. 58 (1989).

43. Whistleblowers have also been protected in the Virgin Islands and Puerto Rico. *See generally Moore v. Riise Gift Shops*, 659 F. Supp. 1417 (1987); *Negron v. Caleb Brett U.S.A., Inc.*, 2000 WL 655889 (2000).

44. *Howard v. Wolff Broadcasting Corp.*,611 So.2d 307, 309, 312-313 (Ala. 1992); *Meeks v. Opp. Cotton Mills*, 459 So.2d 814 (Ala. 1984); *Hinrichs v. Tranquilaire Hospital*, 352 So.2d 1130 (Ala. 1977).

45. *Harrell v. Reynolds Metals Co.*, 495 So.2d 1381, 1387 (Ala. 1986); *Wood v. Jim Walter Homes, Inc.*, 544 So.2d 1028 (Ala. 1989).

46. *Bird v. Nail Air Freight*, 690 So.2d, 1216, 1217 (Ala. Civ. App. 1996).

47. Ala. Code 1975 § 25-5-11.1; *Twilley v. Daubert*, 536 So.2d 1364, 1369 (Ala. 1988); *Gold Kist v. Griffin*, 657 So.2d 826, 829 (Ala. 1994); *Continental v. Mokrzycki*, 611 So.2d 313 (Ala. 1992).

48. *Knight v. American Guard and Alert, Inc.*, 714 P.2d 788, 791-792 (Alaska 1986); *see also Luedtke v. Nabors Alaska Drilling*, 768 P.2d 1123, 1130 (Alaska 1989).

49. *Veco v. Roesbrock*, 970 P.2d 906, 918 (Alaska 1999).

50. *City of Fairbanks v. Rice*, 2000 WL 283708 (Alaska 2000).

51. *Knight, supra*, at 793.

52. 569 P.2d 1328 (Alaska 1977).

53. *Id.* at 1335 (long distance operator refused to pay union dues because of religious beliefs); *Accord., Eldridge v. Felec*, 920 F.2d 1434 (9th Cir. 1990) (no preemption).

54. 710 P.2d 1025 (Ariz. 1985); *see also Hart v. Seven Resorts, Inc.*, 947 P.2d 846 (Ariz. App. Div. 1 1997) (discussing common law remedies after 1996 Arizona legislative action).

55. *Id.* at 1033.

56. *Id.* at 1035 (employee refused to "moon" co-workers in company skit).

57. A.R.S. § 23-1501 and 1502.

58. *Hart, supra*, at 846, 850, N.7 (discussing relationship between A.R.S. § 23-1501 and *Wagenseller*).

59. A.R.S. § 23-1501(3)(b).

60. A.R.S. § 23-1501(3)(c).

61. A.R.S. §§ 23-1501(3)(d); A.R.S. § 38-531 *et seq. See also Arizona State Board of Regents v. Arizona State Personnel Board*, 985 P.2d 1032 (Ariz. 1999) (*en banc*).

62. 596 S.W.2d 681 (Ark. 1980).

63. *Id.* at 683; the court in *Newton v. Brown & Root*, 658 S.W.2d 370, 371 (1983), also indicated that a public policy exception to the *at-will* doctrine would be recognized. But, because plaintiff was found to have contributed to this termination for violating a safety rule he could not obey, due to his employer's failure to provide safe working conditions, he was denied relief. *See also Scholtes v. Signal Delivery Service, Inc.*, 548 F. Supp. 487, 494 (W.D. Ark. 1982); *Lucas v. Brown & Root, Inc.*, 736 F.2d 1202 (8th Cir. 1984).

64. *Sterling Drug v. Oxford*, 743 S.W.2d 380 (Ark. 1988).

65. Acts of Arkansas, Act 796 § 11-9-107, which overturned *Wal-Mart v. Baysinger*, 812 S.W.2d 643 (Ark. 1991). *Accord., Tackett v. Crain Automotive*, 899 S.W.2d 839 (Ark. 1995).

66. *Wal-Mart* at 463, *overturned on other grounds*; *Tackett* at 839.

67. *Lucas, supra*, at 1206; *M.B.M. Co. v. Counce*, 596 S.W. 2d 681.

68. *Id.* at 687.

69. *Id.* at 1206. Title VII does not "exempt or relieve any person from any liability, duty, penalty, or punishment provided by any present or future law of any state, other than any such law which purports to require or permit the doing of any act which would be an unlawful employment practice under this title." 42 U.S.C. §2000e-7.

70. 344 P.2d 25 (Cal. 1959).

71. *Tameny v. Atlantic Richfield Co.*, 610 P.2d 1330 (Cal. 1980).

72. *Id.*

73. 765 P.2d 376 (Cal. 1988).

74. 824 P.2d 680 (Cal. 1992).

75. 960 P.2d 1046 (Cal. 1998).

76. *Gantt v. Sentry Ins.*, 824 P.2d 680, 684 (Cal. 1992)(collecting cases); *Green v. Ralee Eng. Co.*, 960 P.2d 1046, 1051 (Cal. 1998).

77. *Green* at 1051. *See also Gelini v. Tishgart*, 77 Cal. App. 4th 219 (Cal. App. 1st Dist. 1999) (upholding public policy claim on basis of employee complaint regarding conditions of employment).

78. *Green v. Ralee Eng.*, 960 P.2d 1051-1054 (protecting employee who blew the whistle to supervisor regarding violation of a federal regulation).

79. *Cleary v. American Airlines*, 111 Cal. App. 3d 443, 455 (1980). The court held that the "longevity" of the employee's service, together with the expressed policy of the employer (of adopting specific procedures for adjudicating employee disputes), operates as a form of *estoppel*, precluding any discharge of such an employee by the employer without good cause. *See also Grueberg v. Aetna Ins. Co.*, 510 P.2d 1032 (Cal. 1973); *Comunale v. Traders General Ins.*, 328 P.2d 198 (Cal. 1958).

80. *Lagies v. Copley*, 168 Cal. App. 3d 958 (1980); *Renteria v. County of Orange*, 82 Cal. App. 3d 833 (1978); *Agarwal v. Johnson*, 603 P2d 58 (1959).

81. *See Williams v. Taylor*, 129 Cal. App. 3d 745 (1982); *Kelly v. General Telephone Co.*, 136 Cal. App. 3d 278 (1982); *Deaile v. General Telephone Co.*, 40 Cal. App. 3d 841 (1974).

82. *Childress v. Church's Fried Chicken*, 148 Cal. App. 3d (1983); *Johns Manville Prods. Corp. v. Superior Court*, 612 P.2d 948 (Cal. 1980); *Crocker-Citizen's National Bank v. Control Metals Corp.*, 566 F.2d 631 (9th Cir. 1977).

83. *Seamen's Direct Buying Service v. Standard Oil Co.*, 36 Cal. 3d 752 (1984).

84. Cal. Labor Code §1102.5(a), (b). *See also Green* at 1046, 1052 (Cal. 1998) (statute encourages whistleblowing).

85. Cal. Labor Code §1103.

86. *Flores v. Los Angeles Turf Club*, 361 P.2d 921 (Cal. 1961).

87. *Id. See also S.P. Growers Association v. Rodriguez*, 552 P.2d 721 (Cal. 1976) (holding that a state may impose additional sanctions to those provided by a federal act prohibiting discrimination against a worker and prescribing remedies for such discrimination).

88. *Gantt, supra,* at 680.

89. 188 Cal. App. 3d 290 (1982).

90. *See Hentzel v. Singer Co.*, 138 Cal. App. 3d 290, 188 Cal. Reptr. 159 (1982).

91. *Martin Marietta Corp. v. Lorenz*, 823 P.2d 100, 108 (Colo. 1992).

92. *Id.* at 109 (citations omitted).

93. 684 P.2d 265 (Colo. App. 1984).

94. *Id.* at 267. Nonetheless, the court recognized that handbooks or policy manuals containing specific procedures for termination may give rise to a contractual duty on the part of the employer to comply with such procedures.

95. C.R.S. § 24-50.5-103

96. C.R.S. § 13-71-118.

97. *Sheets v. Teddy's Frosted Foods, Inc.*, 427 A.2d 385, 386-387 (Conn. 1980) (employee was discharged in retaliation for his reporting deviations from food quality standards to his employer). *See also* Thomas Mooney and Jeffrey Pingpank, "Wrongful Discharge: A 'New' Cause of Action?" 54 *Connecticut Bar Journal* 213 (June 1980).

98. *Magnan v. Anaconda Industries, Inc.*, 479 A.2d 781, 789 (Conn. 1984).

99. *Faulkner v. United Technologies*, 693 A.2d 293, 297 (Conn. 1997).

100. *Id.* at 297-298.

101. 479 A.2d 781 (1984).

102. *Id.* at 785.

103. *Id.* at 788.

104. *Id.* at 789-790.

105. *Id.* at 790.

106. *Murray v. Bridgeport Hospital*, 480 A.2d 610 (1984).

107. *Id.* at 614. *See Morris v. Hartford Courant Co.*, 513 A.2d 66 (Conn. 1986) (holding that employee could not sustain claim for intentional emotional distress without asserting risk of illness or bodily harm).

108. 480 A.2d 610 (1984).

109. *Id.* at 613 (the court in *Murray*, however, denied the action because there was no allegation that defendants profited in any way by inducing the alleged breach).

110. Conn. General Statutes § 31-51m (1982). *See LaFond v. General Physics Services*, 50 F.3d 165 (2nd Cir. 1995).

111. *Id.* at § 31-51m(b). No employer shall discharge, discipline, or otherwise penalize any employee because the employee, or a person acting on behalf of the employee, reports, verbally or in writing, a violation or a suspected violation of any state or federal law or regulation or any municipal ordinance or regulation to a public body, or because an employee is requested by a public body to participate in an investigation, hearing, or inquiry held by that public body, or a court action. The provisions of this subsection shall not be applicable when the employee knows that such report is false.

112. *Id.* at § 31-51m(c). An action must be brought within ninety days of the date of the final administrative determination or within ninety days of such violation, whichever is later, in the superior court for the judicial district where the violation is alleged to have occurred, or where the employer has its principal office.

113. *Id.*

114. *Id.* at § 31-51(m)(d).

115. *Burnham v. Karl and Gelb*, 745 A.2d 178 (Conn. 2000). In *Burnham*, the Connecticut Supreme Court not only gave the state's statutory remedy preclusive effect, it also held that the federal OSHA antiretaliation law precluded a state common law remedy.

116. *Id.*

117. *Merrill v. Crothall-American, Inc.*, 606 A.2d 96, 101 (Del. Supr. 1992).

118. *DuPont v. Pressman*, 679 A.2d 436, 441 (Del. 1996).

119. *Id.* at 443.

120. *Id.*

121. 29 Del. Laws, § 5115 (1983).

122. *Paolella v. Browning-Ferris, Inc.*, 158 F.3d 183, 188 (3rd Cir. 1998).

123. *See Ivy v. Army Times Publishing Co.*, 428 A.2d 831 (D.C. App. 1981) (deciding to recognize exemption to *at will* doctrine); *Adams v. George W. Cochran & Co.*, 597 A.2d 28 (D.C. App. 1991)(recognizing narrow public policy exception).

124. *Carl v. Children's Hosp.*, 702 A.2d 159, 160 (D.C. App. 1997)(*en banc*). *See also Fingerhut v. Children's National Medical Center*, 738 A.2d 799 (D.C. 1999); *see also Liberatore v. Melville Corp.*, 168 F.3d 1326 (D.C. Cir. 1999) (holding that complaints to supervisors are protected under D.C. public policy).

125. *Id.* (concurring opinion of J. Terry).

126. *Id.* at 166-189 (concurring opinion of Justices Ferren, Schwelb, and Mack).

127. D.C. Code §§ 1-616.11 *et seq.* (1999). *See also Raphael v. Okyinis* 1999 D.C. App. LEXIS 216.

128. D.C. Act 11-526 (January 3, 1997).

129. D.C. Code § 1-2525(a).

130. *Arrow Air, Inc. v. Walsh*, 645 So.2d 442 (Fla. 1994).

131. Ch. 91-285, §§ 4-8, Laws of Fla., codified at § 448.101-105, Fla. Stat.

132. *Id.* § 448.103(2).

133. *Id.* § 448.104.

134. *Smith v. Piezo Technology & Prof. Admin.*, 427 So.2d 182, 184 (Fla. 1983).

135. Georgia Code §66-101; *Goodroe v. Georgia Power Company*, 251 S.E. 2d 51, 52 (Ga. Ct. App. 1978). Plaintiff alleged that he was fired because he was about to uncover criminal activities within his place of employment. *See also Miles v. Bibb Co.*, 339 S.E.2d 316 (Ga. Ct. App. 1985); *Jacobs v. Georgia-Pacific Corp.*, 323 S.E.2d 238 (Ga. Ct. App. 1984); *Gunn v. Hawaiian Airlines, Inc.*, 291 S.E.2d 779 (Ga. Ct. App. 1982). A state is not required to adopt such a rigorous statutory interpretation of its codified *at-will* doctrine. In California, for example, the courts have adopted an exception to the *at-will* doctrine irrespective of the fact that it was codified in California's Labor Code § 2922; *Robins Federal Credit Union v. Brand*, 507 S.E.2d 185 (Ga. App. 1998).

136. *Taylor v. Foremost-McKesson, Inc.*, 656 F.2d 1029 (1981); *Good roe v. Georgia Power Co.*, 251 S.E.2d 52 (Ga. Ct. App. 1978).

137. *N. Georgia Regional Educational Service Agency v. Weaver*, 2000 WL 25771 (Ga. S.Ct. 2000).

138. *Parnar v. American Hotels, Inc.*, 652 P.2d 625 (1982).

139. *Id.* at 628.

140. *Id.* at 631.

141. *Id.* at 631-632.

142. *Id.* at 629.

143. H.R.S. § 378-63(9).

144. *Lesane v. Hawaiian Airlines*, 75 F. Supp.2d 1113 (D.C. Hawaii 1999).

145. *Ross v. Stouffer Hotel Co.*, 879 P.2d 1037, 1047 (Hawaii 1994); *Takaki v. Allied Machinery*, 951 P.2d 507, 513 (Hawaii App. 1998).

146. *Lesane v. Hawaiian Airlines, supra.*

147. *Id.*

148. *Puchert v. Agsalud*, 677 P.2d 449, 455 (1984); *Norris v. Hawaiian Airlines, Inc.*, 842 P.2d 634 (Hawaii 1992).

149. *Jackson v. Minidoka*, 563 P.2d 54 (Idaho 1977).

150. *Id.* at 57-58.

151. *Ray v. Nampa School Dist. No. 131*, 120 Idaho 117, 814 P.2d 17; *Watson v. Idaho Falls Consol. Hosps. Inc.*, 111 Idaho 44, 720 P.2d 632 (1986); *Hummer v. Evans* 923 P.2d 981, 986-987 (Idaho 1996).

152. 384 N.E.2d 353 (Ill. 1978).

153. *Palmateer v. International Harvester Co.*, 421 N.E.2d 876, 881 (Ill. 1981).

154. *Id.* at 879.   Plaintiff was discharged for informing a local law enforcement agency that a co-worker may have committed a criminal violation.

155. *Cosentino v. Price*, 483 N.E.2d 297 (Ill. App. 1985). *See also Leweling v. Schnading Corp.*, 657 N.E.2d 1107 (Ill. App. 1 Dist. 1995)(discussing elements of claim and collecting cases on protected activity).

156. *Fredrick v. Simmons Airlines, Inc.*, 144 F.3d 500, 504-505 (7th Cir. 1998).

157. *Howard v. Zack*, 637 N.E.2d 1183 (Ill. App. 1 Dist. 1994).

158. *Wheeler v. Caterpillar Tractor Co.*, 485 N.E.2d 372, 377 (1985). *Accord., Stebbings v. University of Chicago*, 726 N.E.2d 1136 (Ill. App. 1st Dist. 2000).

159. *Id.* at 376-377. *See also Layne v. Builders Plumbing*, 596 N.E.2d 1104 (Ill. App. 3 1991)(refusal to work with improperly functioning radioactive machine).

160. *Cosentino* at 297. *Midgett v. Sackett-Chicago, Inc.*, 473 N.E.2d 1280 (Ill. 1984); *Kelsay v. Motorola, Inc.*, 384 N.E.2d 353. *But see Stoecklein v. Illinois Tool Works, Inc.*, 589 F. Supp. 139 (1984); *Ring v. R. J. Reynolds Indus. Inc.*, 597 F. Supp. 1277 (1984).

161. *Payne v. AHFI/Netherlands, B.V.*, 522 F. Supp. 18 (N.D. Ill. 1980). *See also Criscione v. Sears, Roebuck & Co.*, 384 N.E.2d 91 (1st Dist. 1978); *Stoecklein v. Illinois Tool Works, Inc.*, 589 F. Supp. 1277 (1984).

162. *Stoecklein* at 139, 145-146; *Carrillo* v. *Illinois Bell Tel. Co.*, 538 F. Supp. 793 (N.D. Ill. 1982).

163. S.H.A. 740 ILCS 175/1-175/8.

164. 740 ILCS 175/3(a).

165. 740 ILCS 175/4(d).

166. 740 ILCS 175/4(g).

167. *Id.*

168. 297 N.E.2d 425, 428 (Indiana, 1973).

169. *Frampton v. Central Indiana Gas Co.*, 297 N.E.2d 425, 428 (Ind. 1973).

170. *Id.*

171. *Walt's Drive-a-way Service v. Powell*, 638 N.E.2d 857, 858 (Ind. App. 1 Dist. 1994). *See also Orr Westminister Village*, 689 N.E.2d 712 (Ind. 1977).

172. *Walt's, supra. Contra Groce v. Eli Lilly*, 193 F.3d 496 (7th Cir. 1999).

173. *Hass Carriage, Inc. v. Berna*, 651 N.E.2d 284, 289-290 (Ind. App. 1 Dist 1995).

174. Ind. Code 4-15-10-2 (except where otherwise provided by state or federal law).

175. Ind. Code 4-15-10-3.

176. Ind. Code 4-15-10-4.

177. Ind. Code 4-15-10-7.

178. *Fitzgerald v. Salsbury*, 2000 WL 895144 (Iowa 2000). *Huegerich v. IBP, Inc.*, 547 N.W.216, 220 (Iowa 1996).

179. *Id.*; *Fogel v. Trustees*, 446 N.W.2d 451, 455 (Iowa 1989).

180. *Palmer v. Brown*, 752 P.2d 685 (Kan. 1988). Kansas law concerning whistleblower protection was outlined in Worth and Landis, "Fire at Will? The Status of Judicially Created Exceptions to Employment-at-will in Kansas," 64 *J.K.B.A.* 22 (1995).

181. *Flenker v. Willamette Industries, Inc.*, 967 P.2d 295, 298 (Kan. 1998). *See Flenker v. Willamette Industries, Inc.*, 68 F. Supp.2d 1261 (D. Kan. 1999) (explication of proof necessary to sustain a claim).

182. *Coleman v. Safeway Stores, Inc.*, 752 P.2d 645 (Kan. 1988).

183. *Flenker* at 295.

184. *Firestone Textile Co. v. Meadows*, 666 S.W.2d 730 (Ky. 1984); *Pari-Mutuel Clerk's Union v. Ky. Jockey Club*, 551 S.W.2d 801 (Ky. 1977).

185. *Firestone* at 733. *See also Nelson Steel Corp. v. McDaniel*, 898 S.W.2d 66 (Ky. 1995).

186. *Grzyb v. Evans*, 700 S.W.2d 399 (Ky. 1985).

187. *Id.* at 401-402. Sex discrimination and freedom of association claims did not fall within the public policy exception because they lacked a specific constitutional or statutory provision upon which plaintiff could base a claim.

188. *Id.* at 402.

189. *Id.*

190. KRS §§ 61.101-61.103.

191. LSA R.S. § 1169.

192. LSA R.S. § 967.

193. LSA R.S. § 30: 2027. *See also Bartlett v. Reese*, 526 S.2d 475 (La. App. 1 Cir. 1988). The environmental statute protects employees who complain about violations of state or federal law and protects an employee's refusal to participate in illegal and environmentally damaging work. *Cheramie v. J. Wayne*

Plaisance, Inc., 595 So.2d 619 (La. 1992).

194. LSA R.S. § 439.1.

195. LRS 51: 2256(1); *Hailey v. Hickingbottom*, 715 So.2d 647 (La. App. 2 Cir. 1998).

196. LRS 23:1361(B); *Rholdon v. Bio-Medical Applications of Louisiana, Inc.*, 868 F. Supp. 179 (E.D. La. 1994); *Smith v. Holloway Sportswear*, 704 So.2d 470 (La. App. 3 Cir. 1997).

197. LSA R.S. § 30:2027(a).

198. LSA R.S. § 30:2027.

199. LSA R.S. § 967(A).

200. LSA R.S. § 967(D).

201. 26 M.R.S.A. §§ 831-840.

202. 26 M.R.S.A. § 833.

203. 26 M.R.S.A. § 833(2).

204. *DiCentes v. Michaud*, 719 A.2d 509, 513 (Me. 1998); *see also Parks v. City of Brewer*, 56 F. Supp. 2d. 89, 102 (D. 1999).

205. *Dudley v. Augusta School District*, 23 F. Supp.2d 85, 92 (D. Maine 1998).

206. 26 M.R.S.A. §§ 837, 839, 840.

207. *Greene v. Union Mutual Life Ins. Co.*, No. 84-0126-P, slip. op. (D. Me. November 15, 1985).

208. *Id.*

209. *Bard v. Bath Iron Works Corp.*, 590 A.2d 152, 156 (Me. 1991).

210. *Adler v. American Standard Corp.*, 538 F.Supp 572 (D. Md. 1982).

211. *Id.* at 578.

212. *Id.* at 580.

213. *Makovi v. Sherwin-Williams Co.*, 561 A.2d 179, 182 (Md. 1989). *Accord.*, *Gaskins v. Marshall Craft Associates, Inc.*, 678 A.2d 615, 620 (Md. App. 1996).

214. *De Rose v. Putnam Management Co., Inc.*, 496 N.E.2d 428 (1986); *Crews v. Memorex Corp.*, 588 F. Supp. 27, n. 3 at 29 (D. Mass. 1984).

215. *Upton v. JWP Businessland*, 682 N.E.2d 1357, 1358-1359 (Mass. 1997) (collecting cases).

216. *Shea v. Emmanuel College*, 682 N.E.2d 1348, 1350 (Mass. 1997).

217. 364 N.E.2d 1251 (Mass. 1977).

218. *Cort v. Bristol-Myers Co.*, 431 N.E.2d 908 (1982); *Gram v. Liberty Mutual Ins. Co.*, 429 N.E.2d 21 (1981).

219. *Crews, supra*, at 27.

220. 491 F. Supp. 1108 (D. Mass. 1980).

221. *Crews, supra*, at 27 n. 5, 30.

222. M.C.L.A. c.149 § 185.

223. M.S.A. § 17.428 *et seq.*; Schlinker and Szymanski, "Michigan's Whistleblowers Protection Act: A Practitioner's Guide," 74 *Mich. B.J.* 11:1192 (1995); *Roulston v. Tender*, 608 N.W.2d 525 (Mich. App. 2000).

224. M.S.A. § 17.428(1)(a) and (b).

225. M.S.A. § 17.428(2).

226. M.S.A. § 17.428(1)

227. *Shallal v. Catholic Social Services*, 566 N.W.2d 571 (Mich. 1997); *Chandler v. Dowell Schlumberger*, 572 N.W. 210 (Mich. 1998).

228. M.S.A. §§ 17.428(3)(1) and 17.428(4).

229. M.S.A. § 17.428(8).

230. *Driver v. Hanley*, 575 N.W.2d 31, 36 (Mich. App. 1997); *Dudewicz v. Norris Schmid, Inc.*, 503 N.W.2d 645 (Mich. 1993); *Covell v. Spengler*, 366 N.W.2d 76 (Mich. App. 1985).

231. The statute provides that an employer shall not retaliate or discriminate against an employee that has made a charge, filed a complaint, or assisted or participated in an investigation, proceeding, or hearing under the Michigan Elliott-Larsen Civil Rights Act. M.C.L. §37.2701.

232. *Clifford v. Cactus Drilling Corp.*, 353 N.W.2d 469, 474 (Mich. 1984).

233. *Id.*.

234. *Authier v. Ginsberg*, 757 F.2d 796, 798 (1985).

235. *Sventko v. Kroger Co.*, 245 N.W.2d 151 (1976).

236. A claim was maintained against an employer for discharging employee for having filed a workmen's compensation claim: *Goins v. Ford Motor Co.*, 347 N.W.2d 184 (Mich. App. 1983).

237. *Trombetta v. Detroit, T&R Co.*, 265 N.W.2d 385 (Mich. 1978).

238. *Phipps v. Clark Oil & Refining Corp.*, 396 N.W.2d 588 (Minn. App. 1986).

239. *Phipps v. Clark Oil*, 408 N.W.2d 569, 571 (Minn. 1987) (noting that after whistleblower statute was passed court did not have to consider the applicability of the common law public policy exception).

240. *See Williams v. St. Paul Ramsey Medical Center*, 551 N.W.2d 483, 484 (Minn. 1996); *Correll v. Distinctive Dental*, 607 N.W.2d 440 (Minn. 2000).

241. *Bolton v. Department of Human Services*, 527 N.W.2d 149, 154 (Minn. App. 1995); *Hedglin v. City of Willman*, 582 N.W.2d 897, 901 (Minn. 1998).

242. M.S.A. § 181.931.

243. M.S.A. § 181.932(a).

244. M.S.A. § 181.932(b) and (c).

245. M.S.A. § 181.932(d).

246. *Bersch v. Rgnonti & Associates Inc.*, 584 N.W.2d 783, 786 (Minn. App. 1998).

247. *Cox v. Crown Coco, Inc.*, 544 N.W.2d 490, 496 (Minn. App. 1996).

248. *Id.* at 498, 500; *Baufield v. Safelite Glass Corp.*, 831 F. Supp. 713, 719-722 (D. Minn. 1993).

249. *O'Sullivan v. State*, 1999 WL 1058238 (Minn. App. 1999).

250. *McArn v. Allied Bruce-Terminix Co.*, 626 So.2d 603, 607 (Miss. 1993). *See Willard v. Paracelus Health Care Corp.*, 681 So.2d 539 (Miss. 1996) ("Willard I") (public has legitimate interest in seeing that people are not dis-

charged for reporting illegal acts).

251. *McArn, supra. See also Paracelus Health Care Corp. v. Willard,* 1999 WL 1000697 (Miss. 1999) (upholding 1.5 million dollar punitive damage award).

252. 370 S.W.2d 249, 254 (Mo. 1963).

253. *Id.*

254. *Id.* (citations omitted)(quoting in relevant part to *Quinn v. Buchanan,* 298 S.W.2d 413 [Mo. 1957]).

255. *Porter v. Reardon Mach. Co.,* 962 S.W.2d 932, 936-937 (Mo. App. W.D. 1998).

256. *Faust v. Ryder,* 954 S.W.2d 383, 391 (Mo. App. W.D. 1997).

257. *Boyle v. Vista Eyewear, Inc.,* 700 S.W.2d 859 (Mo. App. 1985) (employee was discharged for refusing to violate a Food and Drug Administration regulation).

258. *McKiness v. Western Union Telegraph Co.,* 667 S.W.2d 738, 741. If the arbitration clause is not susceptible to any interpretation that covers the asserted dispute, however, the grievance procedures provided by the collective bargaining agreement need not be exhausted. *See also Cook v. Hussman Corp.,* 852 S.W.2d 342, 344.

259. 713 S.W.2d 557 (Mo. App. 1986).

260. *Id.* at 561 (Plaintiff need only plead the defendant should have realized its conduct involved an unreasonable risk of causing plaintiff's emotional distress and that the distress is "medically diagnosable" and "medically significant").

261. *Id.* at 561. Had plaintiff complied with his employer's demands he would have been subject to criminal prosecution.

262. R.C.M., 39-2-901, *et. seq.*

263. R.C.M. 39-2-902.

264. R.C.M. 39-2-913. Employees were not preempted from pursuing claims under a collective bargaining agreement or state and federal law, provided that these laws provided a "procedure or remedy for contesting the dispute." R.C.M. 39-2-912.

265. R.C.M. 39-2-905.

266. R.C.M. 39-2-911.

267. R.C.M. 39-2-914.

268. R.C.M. 39-2-915.

269. *Keneally v. Orgain,* 606 P.2d 127 (Montana 1980).

270. *Schriner v. Meginnis Ford Co.,* 421 N.W.2d 755 (Neb. 1988).

271. *Id.* at 755, 759.

272. *Simonsen v. Hendricks Sodding,* 558 N.W.2d 825, 829 (Neb. App. 1997).

273. *Hansen v. Harrah's,* 675 P.2d 394 (Nev. 1984) (Recognizing the tort of unlawful discharge in retaliation for filing a workers' compensation claim).

274. *Savage v. Holiday Inn Corp., Inc.,* 603 F. Supp. 311, 313 (D.C. Nev. 1985); *Wolber v. Service Corp. Intern.,* 612 F. Supp. 235, 237 (D.C. Nev.

1985).

275. *Wayment v. Holmes*, 912 P.2d 816, 818 (Nev. 1996).

276. *Allum v. Valley Bank*, 970 P.2d 1062, 1066 (Nev. 1998).

277. *Id.* at 1067.

278. *Hansen* at 394, 397.

279. *Savage, supra*, at 311.

280. *Id.* at 315; *see also Wolber, supra*, at 235.

281. *Monge v. Beebe Rubber Co.*, 316 A.2d 549 (1974).

282. *Id.* at 551.

283. *Howard v. Dorr Woolen Co.*, 414 A.2d 1273 (N.H. 1980). Discharge due to sickness or age does not fall into public policy exception.

284. *Cloutier v. Great Atlantic & Pacific Tea Company*, 436 A.2d 1140 (N.H. 1981).

285. *Lilley v. New Hampshire Ball Bearings, Inc.*, 514 A.2d 818, 821 (N.H. 1986). *See also Short v. School Adm. Unit*, 612 A.2d 364, 370 (N.H. 1992).

286. N.H. R.S.A. § 275-E.

287. N.H. R.S.A. § 275-E:5.

288. *See In re Coffey*, 744 A.2d 603 (N.H. 1999)

289. N.H. R.S.A. §§ 275-E:2 and E:3. *See In re Fred Fuller Oil Co.*, 744 A.2d 1141 (N.H. 2000) (broad definition of term "report").

290. N.H. R.S.A. § 275-E:2(II). *See also In re Fred Fuller Oil Co.*, *supra*, (employee protected if terminated *after* reporting violation but *before* a "reasonable" period of time expired for the employer to correct the violation).

291. *Appeal of Bio. Energy Corp.*, 607 A.2d 606, 608 (N.H. 1992).

292. *Chamberlin v. 101 Realty, Inc.*, 626 F. Supp. 865 (D. N.H. 1985).

293. *Pierce v. Ortho Pharmaceutical Corp.*, 417 A.2d 505, 512 (N.J. 1980).

294. N.J.S.A. § 34:19.

295. *Pierce, supra*, at 512; cf. *Vasquez v. Glassboro Services, Inc.*, 415 A.2d 1156 (N.J. 1980). *See also Schechter v. N.J.*, 743 A.2d 872 (N.J. Super. 2000) (claim dismissed when no public policy at issue).

296. *Id.*

297. *Id.*

298. *Id.* The code of ethics may also provide an expression of public policy.

299. N.J.S.A. § 34:19.

300. In *Barratt v. Cushman & Wakefield*, 675 A.2d 1094 (N.J. 1996), the court held that partnerships are covered under the law.

301. N.J.S.A. § 34:19-4. *See Mehlman v. Mobil Oil*, 707 A.2d 1000, 1008-1010 (N.J. 1998)(collecting cases on protected activity).

302. New Jersey courts have broadly constructed this provision. *Keelan v. Bell Communications*, 674 A.2d 603 (N.J. Super. A.D. 1996).

303. This includes punitive damages against both private sector *and* public sector employers. *Abbamont v. Piscataway Bd. of Ed.*, 650 A.2d 958, 968-971 (N.J. 1994).

304. *Id.* at 958, 964.

305. *Id.* at 958, 967. *But see Roach v. TRW*, 742 A.2d 135 (N.J. Super. 1999).

306. *But see Bleumer v. Parkway Ins.*, 649 A.2d 913 (N.J. Super. L. 1994) (upholding mandatory arbitration).

307. N.J.S.A. § 34:19-8; *Young v. Schering Corp.*, 660 A.2d 1153 (N.J. 1995).

308. *See* the New Jersey Law Against Discrimination, which prohibits employees from discharge due to race and sex. N.J.S.A. § 10:5-1, *et seq.*

309. *Abbamont, supra,* at 958, 964 (N.J. 1994).

310. *Id.* at 964, quoting explanatory statement issued by governor of New Jersey.

311. *Mehlman, supra,* at 1000, 1016.

312. *Id.* at 1000, 1012.

313. *Id.* at 1015.

314. *Higgins v. Pascack Valley Hospital*, 730 A.2d 327 (N.J. 1999). *But see DeLisa v. County of Bergen*, 740 A.2d 648 (N.J. Super. 1999) (narrowly interpreting *Higgins*).

315. 699 P.2d 613 (Ct. App. 1983).

316. *Chavez v. Manville Products Corp.*, 777 P.2d 371, 375 (N.M. 1989), *quoting Vigil*, 699 P.2d at 620.

317. *Shovelin v. Central N.M. Elec.*, 850 P.2d 996, 1006 (N.M. 1993).

318. *Id.* at 1006-1007 (collecting cases).

319. *Michaels v. Anglo American Auto*, 869 P.2d 279, 281 (N.M. 1994), *quoting Wilmont v. Kaiser Aluminum*, 821 P.2d 18, 25 (Wash. 1991) (*en banc*). See also *Weidler v. Big J Enterprises*, 953 P.2d 1089 (N.M. App. 1997) (finding no OSHA preclusion).

320. N.M.S.A. § 38-5-18.

321. N.M.S.A. § 1-20-13.

322. N.M.S.A. §52-1-9. *But see Williams v. Amex Chemical Corp.*, 720 P.2d 1234 (N.M. 1986), holding that a state claim for the tort of retaliatory discharge is pre-empted by the Workmen's Compensation Act, which creates exclusive rights and remedies.

323. *Sabetay v. Sterling Drug Inc.*, 497 N.Y.Supp. 2d 655 (1986); *Salanger v. U.S. Air*, 560 F. Supp. 202 (N.D. N.Y. 1983); *Murphy v. American Home Products Corp.*, 448 N.E.2d 86 (N.Y. Ct. App. 1983). There is indication that New York, while not explicitly adopting a public policy exception, will allow a *prima facie* tort in the employment context. *See McCullough v. Certain Feed Products Corp.*, 417 N.Y.S.2d 353 (1979); *Chin v. American Tel. & Tel. Co.*, 410 N.Y.S.2d 737 (1978).

324. Sandra Mullings, "Is There Whistleblower Protection for Private Employees in New York?" *New York State Bar Journal* (February 1997).

325. § 740(l)(e). Such action includes the discharge, suspension, or demotion of an employee or other adverse employment action taken against an employee in the terms or conditions of employment.

326. § 740(2).

327. *Bordell v. General Electric Co.*, 667 N.E.2d 922 (N.Y. 1996).

328. *Rotwein v. Sunharbor*, 695 N.Y.S. 477 (1999) (claim must present "substantial and specific danger to public health and safety").

329. *Connolly v. Harry Macklowe Real Estate Co.*, 161 A.D. 521, 555 N.Y.S.2d 790 (N.Y. 1st Dept. 1990).

330. *See, e.g., Kern v. DePaul Mental Health Services*, 529 N.Y.S.2d 265 (Sup. Ct. Mon. Co. 1988) (finding reports of sexual abuse of mentally handicapped patients not protected); *Finkelstein v. Cornell University*, 2000 WL 130640 (N.Y. A.D. 1 Dept) (finding disclosure of problems with medical doctor protected).

331. § 740(f), a supervisor means any individual within an employer's organization who has the authority to direct and control the work performance of the affected employee; or who has managerial authority to take corrective action regarding the violation of the law, rule or regulation of which the employee complains.

332. § 740(3).

333. § 740(4)(a).

334. *Scaduto v. Restaurant Assoc. Industries*, 579 N.Y.S.2d 381 (A.D. 1 Dept. 1992).

335. § 740(4)(c).

336. *Id.*

337. § 740(b).

338. Workers' Compensation Law § 120; *Lo Dolce v. Regional Transit Serv., Inc.*, 429 N.Y.S.2d 505 (App. Div. 1980).

339. *Sisson v. Lech*, 697 N.Y.S.2d 805 (N.Y. A.D. 4th 1999).

340. *Sides v. Duke University*, 328 S.E.2d 818 (N.C. Ct. App. 1985)

341. *Sides*, 328 S.E.2d at 826. *See also Lorbacher v. Housing Auth.*, 493 S.E.2d 74, 79 (N.C. App. 1997).

342. *Sides* at 827-28.

343. *Coman v. Thomas Mfg. Co.*, 381 S.E.2d 445, 447 (N.C. 1989), quoting *Sides* at 818, 826.

344. *Fitzgerald v. Wolf*, 252 S.E.2d 523 (N.C. 1979); *Smith v. Ford Motor Co.*, 221 S.E.2d 282 (N.C. 1976).

345. *Sides, supra*, at 830 *citing Hardy v. Toler*, 218 S.E.2d 342 N.C. 1975).

346. *Id.*

347. *Ressler v. Humane Society of Grand Forks*, 480 N.W.2d 429 (N.D. 1992).

348. *Beiswanger v. Northwest Bank of N.D.*, 599 N.W.2d 293 (N.D. 1999).

349. § 34-01-20, N.D.C.C.

350. § 34-01-20-(3).

351. Ohio R.C. § 4113.52. *See e.g., Stanley v. City of Miamisburg*, 2000 WL 84645 (Ohio App. 2nd Dist. 2000); *Poluse v. City of Youngstown*, 1999 WL

1243140 (Ohio App. 7 Dist. 1999).

352. *Contreras v. Ferro Corp.*, 652 N.E. 2d 940, 944 (Ohio, 1995).

353. R.C. 4113.52(c).

354. R.C. 4113.52 (A)(1)(a).

355. *Contreras, supra,* at 940, 946.

356. *Contreras* at 947 (dissenting opinion of Justice Pfeifer).

357. 551 A.2d 981 (Ohio 1990).

358. *Jamison v. American Showa, Inc.*, 2000 WL 1404 (Ohio App. 5 Dist., 1999).

359. *Kulch v. Structural Fibers, Inc.*, 677 N.E.2d 308 (Ohio 1997). *Accord., Berge v. Columbus Community Cable Access*, 1999 Ohio App. LEXIS 6455 (10th App. Dist. 1999) (internal citations omitted).

360. *Bartkowiak v. Pillsbury*, 2000 WL 34359 (Ohio App. 4 Dist. 2000).

361. *Burk v. K-Mart Corp.*, 770 P.2d 24, 28-29 (Okl. 1989).

362. *Id.*

363. *Tyler v. Original Chili Bowl, Inc.*, 934 P.2d 1106 (Ok. Civ. App. Div. 3 1997).

364. *Langdon v. Saga Corp.*, 569 P.2d 524 (Okla. App. 1976). Employers are prohibited from firing employees for serving on juries (Okla. Sta. Ann. 38 § 34). Employers are also prohibited from firing employees who file workers compensation claims in good faith or participate in any workmen's compensation proceeding (Okla. Stat. Ann. 85 § 51). Punitive damages are allowed where employer intended to retaliate when firing employee. *Freeman v. Chicago, Rock Island and Pacific Co.*, 239 F. Supp. 661 (W.D. Okla. 1965); *Hicks v. Tulsa Dynaspan, Inc.*, 695 P.2d 17 (Okla. App. 1985); *Zaragosa v. Oneok, Inc.*, 700 P.2d 662 (1984), cert. denied (1985); *Peabody Galion v. Dollar*, 666 F.2d 1309, 1317 (10th Cir. 1981).

365. *Nees v. Hocks*, 536 P.2d 512 (Or. 1975)(employee was discharged for serving on jury duty). *See also Delaney v. Taco Time*, 681 P.2d 114 (Or. 1984).

366. *Williams v. Waterways Terminal Co.*, 693 P.2d at 1292 (Or. 1985).

367. *Delaney v. Taco Time International, Inc.*, 681 P.2d 114 (Or. 1984).

368. *Draper v. Astoria School Dist.*, 995 F. Supp. 1122, 1127 (D. Or. 1988) (collecting cases).

369. *Id.*

370. *Compare Walsh v. Consolidated Freightways*, 563 P.2d 1205 (Or. 1977) with *Brown v. Transcon Lines*, 588 P.2d 1087 (Or. 1978).

371. *Draper, supra,* at 1122, 1127-1131.

372. O.R.S. §§ 659.510, 659.530.

373. *Geary v. U.S. Steel Corp.*, 319 A.2d 174, 180 (Pa. 1974); *Clay v. Advanced Computer Applications*, 559 A.2d 917 (Pa. 1989); *Shick v. Shirey*, 716 A.2d 1231 (Pa. 1998).

374. *Hunter v. Port Authority of Allegheny County*, 419 A.2d 631 (1980); *Reuther v. Fowler & Williams, Inc.*, 386 A.2d 119, 120 (Pa. Super. 1978). Art. 1, Section 7 of the Pennsylvania Constitution provides that "the free commu-

nication of thought and opinions is one of the invaluable rights of man, and every citizen may freely speak, write and print on any subject, being responsible for the abuse of that liberty."

375. *McNulty v. Borden, Inc.,* 542 F. Supp. 655 (E.D. Pa. 1982). The Robinson-Patman Act, 15 U.S.C. § 13 was alleged to have been violated, but absent finding that act was actually violated by factfinder, without putting forth another public policy consideration, there is no contravention of public policy.

376. *Hansrote v. Amer. Indus. Technologies,* 586 F. Supp. 113 (W.D. Pa. 1984), employee was fired for refusing to violate Pennsylvania law making the acceptance of a commission bribe a criminal offense. *Wolk v. Saks Fifth Ave. Inc.,* 728 F.2d 221 (3rd Cir. 1984); employee was fired in retaliation for the refusal to succumb to sexual advances in violation of Pennsylvania Human Relations Act.

377. *Shick, supra,* at 1231, 1235, 1237.

378. *Smyth v. Pillsbury,* 914 F. Supp. 97, 99 (E.D. Pa. 1996). *See Denton v. Silver Stream Nursing,* 739 A.2d 571 (Pa. Super. 1999).

379. *Spierling v. First American Home Service,* 737 A.2d 1250 (Pa. Super. 1999).

380. *Hennessy v. Santiago,* 708 A.2d 1269, 1273 (Pa. Super. 1998). *Field v. Phil. Elec. Co.,* 565 A.2d 1170 (Pa. Super. 1989)(employee protected for making a required report of a nuclear safety concern); *Hunger v. Grand Cent.,* 670 A.2d 173, 176 (Pa. Super. 1996)(indicating reports of illegal conduct may be protected if actual deliberate violation of law occurred); *Holewinski v. Children's Hospital,* 649 A.2d 712, 715 (Pa. Super. 1994)(threat to report unlawful business practice not protected). *See also Shick, supra,* at 1231 (collecting Superior Court Decisions).

381. *Cisco v. United Parcel Service,* 476 A.2d 1340 (Pa. Super. 1984); *Perks v. Firestone Tire and Rubber Co.,* 611 F.2d 1363 (3rd Cir. 1979) (employee was fired for refusing to take polygraph test contrary to Pennsylvania statute forbidding employers to require test; *Novosel v. Nationwide Ins. Co.,* 721 F.2d 894, 899 (3rd Cir. 1983) (holding that freedom of political expression involves no less a compelling social interest than the fulfillment of jury service or the filing of a workman's compensation claim).

382. *Id.*

383. *McNulty, supra,* at 655, 656; *Perks, supra,* at 1363.

384. *Betts v. Stroehmann Bros.,* 512 A.2d 1280, 1281 (Pa. Super. 1986); *Cisco, supra,* at 1340.

385. The Pennsylvania Human Relations Act, for example, provides in relevant part that:

It shall be an unlawful discriminatory practice, unless based upon a bona fide occupational qualification, or in the case of a fraternal corporation or association, unless based upon membership in such association or corporation, or except where based upon applicable security regulations established by the United States or the Commonwealth of Pennsylvania: (a) For any employer because of the race, color, religious creed, ancestry, age, sex, national origin or non-job related handicap or disability of any individual to refuse to hire or employ, or to bar or to discharge from employment such individual, or to otherwise discriminate against such individual with respect to compensation, hire, tenure, terms, conditions or privileges of employment, if the individual is the best able and most competent to perform the services required.

Clay v. Advanced Computer, 559 A.2d 917 (Pa. 1989) (employees are required to exhaust remedies under the law). State and federal circuit courts have differed on whether an action under this act is exclusive of state action. *Wolk, supra*, at 221, 223, holding act to be exclusive remedy; *contra Ire v. Central Transportation Inc.*, 409 A.2d 2, 4 (1979). *See also Braun v. Kelsey-Hayes Co.*, 635 F. Supp. 75, 80 (E.D. Pa. 1986); and *Kilpatrick v. Delaware County Soc.*, 632 F. Supp. at 548-549 (E.D. Pa. 1986) on issue of whether federal statutory remedies preempt state action.

386. 43 P.S. §§ 1421-1427.

387. R.I. Gen. Law § 28-50-1, *et seq.*

388. R.I. Gen. Law § 28-50-5.

389. R.I. Gen. Law § 28-50-8.

390. *Marques v. Fitzgerald*, 99 F.3d 1, 6 (1st Cir. 1996).

391. *Ludwick v. Imperial Manufacturing Co.*, 337 S.E.2d (1985).

392. *Id.* at 216 (employee was fired for obeying a subpoena).

393. *Id.* at 215, quoting *Sides v. Duke Hospital*, 328 S.E.2d 818 (N.C. 1985).

394. *Id.* at 215. Prior to *Ludwick*, the court articulated its willingness to adopt a public policy exception in *Todd v. South Carolina Farm Bureau Mut. Ins. Co.*, 321 S.E. 2d 602 (Ct. App. 1984), which denied a wrongful discharge claim for firing plaintiff who refused to take a polygraph test because South Carolina had no statute barring polygraph tests as a condition or continuation of employment.

395. *Dockins v. Ingles Markets, Inc.*, 413 S.E.2d 18 (S.C. 1995). *But see Culler v. Blue Ridge Elec.*, 422 S.E.2d 91 (S.C. 1992).

396. *Garner v. Morrison Knudsen Corp.*, 456 S.E.2d 907 (S.C. 1995).

397. 1988 S.C. Act No. 354, S.C. Code Ann. § 8-27-30.

398. *Johnson v. Kreiser's, Inc.*, 433 N.W.2d 225, 227-228 (S.D. 1988). *Accord., Niesent v. Homestake Mining Co.*, 505 N.W.2d 781 (S.D. 1993).

399. *Bass V. Happy Rest, Inc.*, 507 N.W. 317 (S.D. 1993).

400. *Clanton v. Cain-Sloan Co.*, 677 S.W.2d 441, 445 (Tenn. 1984).

401. Tenn. Code § 50-1-304.

402. *Mason v. Seaton*, 942 S.W.2d 470, 476 (Tenn. 1997).

403. *Sinclair v. State*, 1999 WL 807705 (Tenn. Ct. App. 1999).

404. *Id.* at 470, 475. *Accord., Hodges v. S.C. Toof*, 833 S.W.2d 896, 899-900 (Tenn. 1992)("statutory remedies are not exclusive").

405. *Griggs v. Coca-Cola Employees' Credit Union*, 909 F. Supp. 1059 (E.D. Tenn. 1995).

406. *Id.*

407. *Hodges, supra*, at 896, 901.

408. *Sabine Pilots Service v. Hauck*, 687 S.W.2d 733 (Tex. 1985). Employee was discharged for refusing to dump oily bilge water into a river in violation of the federal Water Pollution Control Act.

409. *Winters v. Houston Chronicle Publishing Co.*, 795 S.W.2d 723 (Tex. 1990)(collecting cases); *Austin v. Healthtrust Inc.*, 951 S.W.2d 78, 80 (Tex. App.–Corpus Christi 1997)(Supreme Court did not "foreclose the possibility of a private whistleblower claim, it did not create such an action," with the limiting exception of refusal to commit illegal act).

410. The exceptions include discharges for filing a workers' compensation claim (Tex. Prev. Civ. Stat. Ann. Part. 8307c); discharges based on union membership or nonmembership (Tex. Rev. Civ. Stat. Ann. Art. 5207a); discharges because of active duty in state military services (Tex. Rev. Civ. Stat. Ann. Art. 5765 § 7A); and discharges because of jury service (Tex. Rev. Stat. Ann. Art. 5207b). Employee suing under workmen's compensation statute for wrongful discharge need only prove that her proceeding under the Workmen's Compensation Act was a determining factor. *Azar Nut Co. v. Caille*, 72 S.W.2d 685 (Tex. App. 1986).

The *at-will* doctrine is further modified by the Texas Commission on Human Rights Act, prohibiting discharges based on race, color, handicap, religion, national origin, age or sex (Tex. Rev. Civ. Stat. Ann. Art. 5221k § 1.02). Moreover, legislation exists that expressly protects government employees from retaliatory and discriminatory discharges (*See* Tex. Rev. Civ. Stat. Ann. Art. 6252-16).

411. *Hill v. Texas*, 2000 WL 16436 (N.D. Tex. 2000); *Thompson v. City of Arlington*, 838 F. Supp. 1137, 1153 (N.D. Tex. 1993); *Harris County v. Mc-Dougal*, 2000 WL 190204 (Tex. App. Houston Div. 2000).

412. 881 P.2d 151, 166 (Utah 1991); *see also Barela v. C. R. England and Sons*, 197 F.3d 1313 (10th Cir. 1999).

413. *Fox v. MCI*, 931 P.2d 857, 860-861 (Utah 1997).

414. *Id.*

415. Utah Code Ann. § 74-46-21 (1985); Utah Code Ann. §67-21-1, *et seq.*; *Rose v. Allied Development Co.*, 719 P.2d 83, 85 (Utah 1986) (referring to the Civil Rights Act of 1964, 42 U.S.C. §2000e-2[a][1]). Additionally, the doctrine is limited by state law extending the prohibited reasons for discharge to include age and handicaps. Utah Code Ann. § 34-35-6 (1953); *Rose, supra*, at 85.

416. *Payne v. Rozendall*, 520 A.2d 586, 588 (Vt. 1986).

417. *Id.* at 588.

418. 667 A.2d 294, 298-299 (Vt. 1995).

419. *Bowman v. State Bank of Keysville*, 331 S.E.2d 797, 801 (Va. 1985). The Virginia courts have not recognized a "generalized, common law 'whistleblower' retaliatory discharge claim." *Dray v. New Market Poultry*, 518 S.E.2d 312 (Va. 1999). In *Dray*, the Supreme Court refused to recognize a cause of action when a poultry worker was allegedly discharged for reporting safety concerns to a government inspector.

420. *Frazier v. Colonial Williamsburg Foundation*, 574 F. Supp. 318, 320 (E.D. Va. 1983).

421. *Miller v. SEVAMP, Inc.*, 362 S.E.2d 915, 918 (Va. 1987).

422. *Lawrence Chrysler v. Brooks*, 465 S.E.2d 806, 809 (Va. 1996).

423. *Thompson v. St. Regis Paper Co.*, 685 P.2d 1081 (Wash. 1984); *Roberts v. Dudley*, 993 P.2d 901 (Wash. 2000) (*en banc*).

424. *Warnek v. ABB*, 972 P.2d 453, 458 (Wash. 1999), *citing Gardner v. Loomis Armored*, 913 P.2d 377 (Wash. 1996). *See also e.g., Wilmot v. Kaiser Aluminum*, 821 P.2d 18 (Wash. 1991).

425. *Thompson, supra,* at 1089.

426. *Wilmont v. Kaiser Alum.*, 821 P.2d 18, 21-27 (Wash. 1991); *Smith v. Bates Technical College*, 991 P.2d 1135 (Wash. 2000) (*en banc*).

427. *Smith, supra,* at 1143-1144.

428. *Wilson v. City of Monroe*, 943 F.2d 1134, 1137 (Wash. App. Div. 1 1997); *Smith, supra,* at 1143.

429. *White v. State*, 929 P.2d 396, 407 (Wash. 1997).

430. *Id.*. at 1087-1088.

431. Discharges are prohibited if based on race, color, religion, sex, national origin, or any sensory, mental, or physical handicap (R.C.W. 49.60.030, 49-60.180). Like provisions protecting employees are found in the Industrial Safety and Health Act (R.C.W. 49.46.100) and the Minimum Wage Act (R.C.W. 49.44.090).

432. *Harless v. First Nat. Bank*, 246 S.E.2d 270 (W. Vir. 1978).

433. *Id.* at 275. *See Birthisel v. Tri-Cities Health Services*, 424 S.E.2d 606, 610-612 (W.Va. 1992)(collecting cases).

434. *Harless*, at 276, referring to the West Virginia Consumer Credit and Protection Act, W.Va. Code 46-A-101.

435. *Cordle v. General Hugh Mercer Corp.*, 325 S.E.2d 111 (1984) held that the public policy exception is contravened when employer discharges an *at-will* employee for refusing a polygraph test, advocating the protection of individual privacy.

436. *Williamson v. Greene*, 490 S.E.2d 23, 31 (W.Va. 1997).

437. *Tiernan v. Charleston Area Medical Center*, 506 S.E.2d 578, 585-586 (W.Va. 1998).

438. *Id.* 506 S.E.2d at 587.

439. *Harless, supra,* at 276.

440. *Id.* at 276 (*quoting Monteleone v. Co-Operative Transit Co.*, 36 S.E.2d 475, 478 [1945]).

441. *Brockmeyer v. Dun & Bradstreet*, 335 N.W.2d 834, 838 (Wis. 1983).

442. *Hausman v. St. Croix Care Center*, 571 N.W. 2d 393 (Wis. 1997). *See also Winkelman v. Beloit*, 483 N.W.2d 211 (Wis. 1992).

443. *Brockmeyer, supra,* at 841.

444. *Bushko v. Miller Brewing Co.*, 396 N.W.2d 167 (1986).

445. *See Koehn v. Pabst Brewing Co.*, 763 F.2d 865 (7th Cir. 1985).

446. *MacKenzie v. Miller Brewing Co.*, 2000 WL 199294 (Wis. App. 20000).

447. *Hermreck v. U.P.S.*, 938 P.2d 863, 866 (Wyo. 1997). *See also Dynan v. Rocky Mountain Sav. & Loan*, 792 P.2d 631 (Wyo. 1990).

448. *Hermreck* at 863, 866-867.

Chapter 3

Federal Statutory Protection for Whistleblowers

The failure of Congress to pass comprehensive legislation adequately covering employees who "blow the whistle" on illegal governmental or corporate conduct is the single most remarkable deficiency in the protection of legitimate whistleblower activity. Despite this failure, whistleblowers can obtain legal protection under a host of state and federal remedies. The First Amendment, the Civil Rights Act of 1871, the environmental and nuclear whistleblower statutes, and the False Claims Act all provide relief for employees who are covered under these particular provisions. In addition to these laws, Congress has provided a network of protections for whistleblowers under a host of additional statutes.[1] Although none of these statutes provides comprehensive protection, each of these laws protects employees in specific industries who blow the whistle on specific types of alleged misconduct. Thus, even in the absence of a true federal whistle-blower protection act, employees may find protection.

These statutory remedies cover a significant cross section of the American workforce but are riddled with loopholes. For example, only employees who engage in certain specific whistleblower conduct in certain specifically protected industries are covered under federal law. Each potential whistleblower case must be evaluated on the basis of who the employer is, what the disclosure concerns, and in which state the whistleblowing occurred. On the basis of these variables, an attorney must review various federal laws to determine if the employee is protected and exactly what procedures should be followed in filing a claim for redress.[2]

Each federal statute generally includes its own definition of protect-ed activity, the statute of limitations for filing an action under the law, and its own administrative or judicial rules for adjudication of the claim. Although each statute is different, courts and administrative agencies regularly apply the case law and legal analysis developed under one statute in interpreting other statutes. This has occurred because the basic elements in a retaliatory discharge claim tend to be identical. For example, courts have used case law developed in retaliation cases for exercising First Amendment rights (*i.e.,* the *Mt. Healthy* test) in other retaliation cases— such as wrongful discharge for exercising rights under the National Labor Relations Act.[3] Likewise, Congress has modeled some whistleblower protection statutes after others—for example, the Clean Air Act whistleblower protection statute was modeled after the 1969 Federal Mine Health and Safety Act, and the nuclear whistleblower statute was modeled after the Clean Air Act statute.[4] The interpretive interrelationship between these statutes is highly significant. Often, there is little or no case precedent under one law, and the practitioners must utilize case law from other areas to fill in the gaps. The extensive body of case law dealing with retaliatory discharge under some statutes, such as the NLRA or Title VII, can be extremely useful for analyzing wrongful discharge cases under other less litigated statutes.[5]

This chapter is an overview of federal statutory protections for employee whistleblowers, which are not discussed in other chapters.[6]

AIRLINE SAFETY

On April 5, 2000 President William J. Clinton signed into law the Aviation and Reform Act for the 21st Century. Section 42121 of the Act[7] prohibited air carriers and their contractors and subcontractors from discriminating against employees who disclosed airline safety information either to their employer or the Federal Government. Protected activity includes the disclosure of "information relating to any violation or alleged violation of any order, regulation, or standard of the Federal Aviation Administration or any other provision of federal law relating to air carrier safety."

Congress' intent in passing this legislation was explained by Senator Kerry, the co-sponsor of the initial Senate version of the amendment:

Flight attendants and other airline employees are in the best position to recognize breaches in safety regulations and can be the critical link in ensuring safer air travel. . . . Aviation employees perform an important public service when they choose to report safety concerns. No employee should be put in the position of having to choose between his or her job and reporting violations that threaten the safety of passengers and crew.[8]

Modeled after the environmental and nuclear whistleblower laws,[9] the amendment created an administrative remedy within the Department of Labor. Claims must be filed with the Secretary of Labor within 90 days of an alleged retaliatory action. OSHA is required to conduct a preliminary investigation, and if OSHA determines that the employee was subject to illegal retaliation, a "preliminary order" must be issued providing immediate relief to the employee. Either party may appeal a preliminary finding, and, if appealed, the parities are entitled to a full on-the-record evidentiary hearing. The standards of proof under this law are based on the whistleblower provisions in the Energy Reorganization Act, the Whistleblower Protection Act, and the banking system whistleblower laws.[10]

A prevailing employee is entitled to a full "make whole" remedy, including reinstatement, back pay and benefits, compensatory damages, attorney fees, and costs. If the Secretary of Labor were to determine that the complaint was "frivolous" or filed in "bad faith," the employee could be subject to a maximum sanction of $1000.

Decisions of the DOL are subject to review in the U.S. Court of Appeals and may be enforced in U.S. District Courts.

BANKING SYSTEM EMPLOYEE PROTECTIONS

Congress passed three laws protecting both private sector and federal employees within the banking system. These laws were passed in 1989 to "enhance the regulatory enforcement powers of the depository institution's regulatory agencies to protect against fraud, waste and insider abuse."[11] Consistent with this intent, courts have recognized that "laws protecting whistleblowers are meant to encourage employees to report illegal practices without fear of reprisal" and thus such laws should be "construe[d]" "broadly, in favor of protecting the whistleblower."[12] Moreover, courts should "avoid" "nonsensical result[s]" when interpreting the whistleblower laws.[13] The major law covering the banking sector is the whistleblower provision of the Financial Institutions Reform, Recovery, and Enforcement Act of 1989 (FIRREA), which covers all whistleblowers who work for an "insured depository institution" or a "federal banking agency."[14] An insured depository institution covers most banks, and the law defines a "federal banking agency" as the Federal Deposit Insurance Corporation (FDIC), the Board of Governors of the Federal Reserve System, the Federal Reserve System, the Federal Housing Finance Board, the Comptroller of the Currency, and the Office of Thrift Supervision.[15] In addition to the FIRREA, the Federal Credit Union Act contains a similar provision covering credit unions and the National Credit Union Administration,[16] and a third law covers "financial institutions" involved in "monetary instrument transactions."[17]

The three laws are substantially identical, except for the FIRREA provision, which was amended in 1993 to include a specified burden of proof formulation that overruled the traditional Title VII formula[18] and required FIRREA to follow the more pro-employee formulation set forth in the Whistleblower Protection Act, 5 U.S.C. § 1221(e).[19] Under the 1993 amendment, employees do not have to prove that retaliatory motive was the "motivating" factor in an adverse action. Instead, an employee merely must show that such improper motive was a "contributing factor" in the discharge. Additionally, once an employee meets his or her low burden of proof under the contributing factor test, the burden of proof actually shifts to the employer to demonstrate by "clear and convincing evidence" that the same employment decision would have been reached even if the employee did not engage in protected activity.[20]

Every court that has reviewed the new statutorily mandated burdens of proof under the 1993 amendments has agreed that the new burdens "quite clearly make it easier for the plaintiff to make her case . . . and more difficult for the defendant to avoid liability."[21] As the U.S. Court of Appeals for the Seventh Circuit explained:

[T]he plaintiff, on the one hand, can make out a prima facie case of retaliation, and shift the burden of persuasion to the defendant, with circumstantial evidence that her disclosure was a contributing (not necessarily a substantial or motivating) factor in the adverse personnel action taken against her; and the defendant, once the burden has shifted, must prove not merely by a preponderance but by clear and convincing evidence that it would have taken the same action against the plaintiff even in the absence of her protected disclosure.[22]

Under all three laws, claims are filed in U.S. District Court, and there is a two-year statute of limitations.[23] The laws protect employees who "provide information about violations of the law to the appropriate authorities."[24] Under the monetary transaction provision, protected activity includes providing "information" to the Secretary of Treasury, the Attorney General, and a "Federal supervisory agency."[25] The credit union law protects private sector employees who provide information to the Attorney General or the federal credit union board, and it protects employees of the National Credit Union Administration if they provide information to the Attorney General or the Administration.[26] The law covering "depository institutions" protects disclosures to all Federal banking agencies (including the FDIC, the Attorney General, and the Federal Reserve).[27]

The laws prohibit not only wrongful discharge but discrimination in the "conditions" of employment.[28] In order to obtain protection, employees need not demonstrate that there was an actual violation of the banking laws.[29] However, if the employee "deliberately" caused the violation at issue in a case, or if the employee "knowingly or recklessly provides false information" to the regulatory authorities, the "protections" afforded the employee under the whistleblower law "shall not apply."[30] If an employee prevails in his or her claim, he or she is entitled to reinstatement, compensatory damages, and "other appropriate actions to remedy any past discrimination."[31] Courts have also held that the language of the acts permits, in the appropriate case, punitive damages.[32] These damages can be significant. For example in *Haley v. Retsinas*, the Court of Appeals for the 8th Circuit affirmed an award of $723,533 in back pay, future loss of income, and compensatory damages to a bank examiner employed by the Office of Thrift Supervision.[33]

CIVIL RIGHTS LAWS: PROTECTIONS UNDER TITLE VII, THE FAMILY AND MEDICAL LEAVE ACT, THE AGE DISCRIMINATION IN EMPLOYMENT ACT, AND THE AMERICANS WITH DISABILITIES ACT

The major federal civil rights laws, including Title VII of the Civil Rights Act of 1964, the Age Discrimination in Employment Act, the Americans with Disabilities Act, the Equal Pay Act, and the Family and Medical Leave Act, all contain antiretaliation provisions that protect employees who blow the whistle on potential violations of these laws.[34] The laws prohibit discrimination against employees who testify or file charges concerning potential civil rights violations.

Title VII of the Civil Rights Act of 1964,[35] along with the other civil rights employment discrimination laws, contains broad language protecting employees who object to discriminatory practices or who file a complaint against such discrimination.[36] In relevant part, the statute reads:

It shall be an unlawful employment practice for an employer to discriminate against any . . . [employee] because he has opposed any practice made an unlawful employment practice by this subchapter, or because he has made a charge, testified, assisted, or participated in any manner in an investigation, proceeding, or hearing under this subchapter.[37]

This clause protects two distinct types of potential whistleblowing activity. It protects conduct under the "opposition" clause and under the "participation" clause of the law. The standard of conduct under each of these clauses is very different.[38]

Under the "participation" clause employees are entitled to "exceptionally broad protection,"[39] and "the scope of protection for activity falling under the participation clause is broader than for activity falling under the opposition clause."[40] The "participation" clause protects conduct such as filing a "charge" of discrimination, testifying in administrative or court proceedings, "assisting" another employee in his or her case, and, in a catch-all fashion, "participating in any manner" in proceedings under the anti discrimination provision.[41]

It is well established that "participatory activities are vigorously protected."[42] In interpreting the participation clause, the concept of "participate" is given a very "expansive meaning" and protects employees who "involuntarily" testify in Title VII discovery depositions and very "reluctantly" provide information.[43] Likewise, protection under that clause does "not turn on the substance of an employee's testimony regardless of how unreasonable that testimony may be."[44]

Although courts are required to "liberally construe the provisions" of the opposition clause,[45] that clause is more narrowly construed than the participation clause. Conduct protected under the opposition clause has been described as follows: "Opposition activity encompasses utilizing informal grievance procedures as well as staging informal protests and voicing one's opinions in order to bring attention to an employer's discriminatory practices."[46] The heart of an opposition clause case involves a "balancing test" between the interests of an employee in engaging in oppositionist activities and the interests of an employer in the "harmonious and efficient operation" of its business:

We have previously adopted a balancing test for determining whether an employee's conduct constitutes "protected activity" under Title VII. . . . The court must balance the purpose of the Act to protect persons engaging reasonably in activities opposing . . . discrimination, against Congress' equally manifest desire not to tie the hands of employers in the objective selection and control of personnel. An employee's opposition activity is protected only if it is reasonable in view of the employer's interest in maintaining a harmonious and efficient operation.[47]

The law protects all employees—white and black, men and women —who oppose, disclose, or testify about discriminatory practices. For example, a white employee who discloses that black employees are being subjected to discrimination is protected under Title VII,[48] as are employees who "witness" discrimination and blow the whistle on such practices.[49] Under the participation clause, an employee who admitted that he engaged in sexual harassment in a deposition could not be discharged solely on the basis of his deposition testimony, due to the law's strict prohibition against taking any adverse action against any employee due to his or her testimony.[50] However, such admissions would not prohibit an employer from taking adverse action against an employee for reasons other than the content of his testimony: "The employer may take adverse action against [an employee who engaged in sexual harassment] because of a feeling that justice demands it, or for the more parochial reason of minimizing future liability, but not because the employee 'testified, assisted, or participated in any manner' in another employee's Title VII proceeding."[51]

Another example of whistleblower activity under these laws includes providing "evidence" of "discrimination" to an attorney. In that case the court reasoned that the employee had a "legitimate interest in preserving evidence of [his employer's] unlawful employment practices."[52] Given the facts of a particular case, other oppositionist conduct has been prohibited, including stealing confidential company documents that evidence discrimination.[53] It is "black letter law" that "illegal" conduct is not protected under the opposition clause.[54] An employee alleging discrimination under Title VII, and most of the other civil rights antiretaliation laws,[55] must file a timely complaint with the Equal Employment Opportunity Commission (EEOC).[56] In order to contest a discharge under Title VII in federal court, an employee must file a complaint with the court within ninety days of receiving a "right to sue" letter from the EEOC.[57]

The Age Discrimination in Employment Act (ADEA) contains a whistleblower protection clause nearly identical to that found in Title VII.[58] Under the ADEA employees are entitled to jury trials on "any issue of fact."[59] The Equal Pay provision of the Fair Labor Standards Act[60] protects employees who disclose that an employer pays different wages to employees of the opposite sex for equal work.[61] Such disclosures are protected in most federal judicial circuits even if they are "unofficial" "complaints at work."[62] Remedies under the Equal Pay Act are similar to Title VII, but the employee is also entitled to liquidated damages.[63] Additionally, the Family and Medical Leave Act, [64] the Rehabilitation Act,[65] and the Americans with Disabilities Act[66] both contain provisions that protect employees who blow the whistle, file charges, or testify regarding violations of these acts.

In order to set forth a *prima facie* case of retaliation under Title VII/ADEA (and the other laws), an employee must demonstrate: (1) that she or he engaged in protected activity; (2) that an adverse action occurred; and (3) that there was a causal connection between the protected activity and the adverse employment action.[67] Proof that the decision maker was aware of the employee's protected activity is essential in order for an employee to demonstrate the required causal connection.[68] Retaliation claims are adjudicated in a manner identical to discrimination claims.[69] Employees must demonstrate their cases by a preponderance of the evidence under the legal framework set forth by the U.S. Supreme Court in a number of decisions, most notably *McDonnell Douglas v. Green*, 411 U.S. 792 (1973) (setting forth requirements for *prima facie* cases and the respective burdens of proof and production); *U.S. Postal Service v. Aikens*, 460 U.S. 711 (1983) (finding it improper to require employees to produce direct evidence of discrimination in order to prove intent); *Price Waterhouse v. Hopkins*, 490 U.S. 228 (1989) (if discriminatory animus can be demonstrated by direct evidence the burden of proof shifts to employer to persuade court that the employee would have been discharged had discriminatory purpose not existed); *St. Mary's Honor Center v. Hicks*, 509 U.S. 502 (1993) (employee retains the ultimate burden of persuading the trier of fact of intentional discrimination in pretext cases); *Reeves v. Sanderson Plumbing*, 120 S. Ct. 2097 (2000) (burdens of proof in circumstantial evidence cases).[70]

EMPLOYEE RETIREMENT INCOME SECURITY ACT (ERISA)

It is against federal law to retaliate against any person for participating in an ERISA retirement or benefit plan.[71] This includes retaliation against persons who give information or testify concerning ERISA or the Welfare and Pension Plans Disclosure Act.[72] As the U.S. Court of Appeals for the 9th Circuit recognized, the antiretaliation provision "clearly" was intended "to protect whistleblowers."[73]

A whistleblower complaint under ERISA should be filed in federal district court, and a copy of the complaint should be served on the Secretary of Labor and the Secretary of Treasury.[74] Some courts have required ERISA plaintiffs to exhaust their administrative remedies prior to filing a suit in federal court.[75] A whistleblower claim can still be maintained even if the employer terminated the retirement plan at issue in the case.[76]

ENVIRONMENTAL AND NUCLEAR EMPLOYEE PROTECTION

See Chapter 5.

FAIR LABOR STANDARDS ACT

The Fair Labor Standards Act (FLSA) whistleblower provisions protect all employees covered under the FLSA from retaliation for complaining, testifying, or filing charges regarding a violation of the FLSA.[77]

This includes the FLSA's provision concerning child labor, minimum wage, and sex discrimination under the Equal Pay Act.[78] Most circuits protect "informal" complaints and internal complaints raised directly with an employee's supervisor.[79] Likewise, courts have protected employees from retaliation "based on their employer's mistaken belief that they reported violations of law to the authorities."[80]

The FLSA is a "remedial and humanitarian" law that cannot be interpreted in a "narrow, grudging manner."[81] As such, the statute's antiretaliation provisions must be broadly construed to effectuate Congress' intent to "provide an incentive for employees to report wage and hour violations of their employers."[82] In addition, courts have warned against permitting employer conduct that may cause a "chilling effect" on an employee's assertion of his or her rights under the FLSA:[83] "Courts have therefore not hesitated to apply the protection of [the antiretaliation provisions] to activities less directly connected to formal proceedings where retaliatory conduct has a similar chilling effect on employees' assertion of rights."[84]

A complaint must be filed within two years of when the employee learns about the alleged retaliatory action[85] and may be filed with the U.S. Department of Labor or in federal or state court with competent jurisdiction.[86]

In evaluating a claim under this law, courts apply the evidentiary framework applicable in Title VII cases.[87] Remedies include reinstatement, back pay, liquidated damages, appropriate equitable relief, and a reasonable attorney's fee.[88] In addition, compensatory and punitive damages[89] and prejudgment/postjudgment interest[90] may also be awarded to a prevailing employee. The U.S. Department of Labor has special regulations concerning child labor protection under the FLSA.[91]

FALSE CLAIMS ACT

See Chapter 6.

FIRST AMENDMENT/CIVIL RIGHTS ACT OF 1871

See Chapter 4.

IMPLIED FEDERAL CAUSES OF ACTION

Even if a statute has no express provision providing a civil or administrative remedy for the protection of whistleblowers, such a protection may be established through the doctrine of *implied private cause of action*. In *Cort v. Ash*, Supreme Court Justice Brennan outlined the four-step analysis for implying private right of action from a statute:

1. Does the statute create a federal right in favor of the plaintiff?

2. Is there any indication of legislative intent, explicit or implicit, either to create such a remedy or deny one?

3. Is it consistent with the underlying purposes of the legislative scheme to imply such a remedy for the plaintiff?

4. Is the cause of action one traditionally relegated to state law, in an area basically the concern of the States, so that it would be inappropriate to infer a cause of action based solely on federal law?[92]

The Supreme Court modified the *Cort* analysis in one major aspect. In *Thompson v. Thompson*,[93] the court held that unless the "congressional intent" to create a cause of action can be "inferred from the language of the statute, the statutory structure, or some other source, the essential implication for a private remedy simply does not exist." Thus, the second factor in *Cort* was modified and became the most important single factor in an analysis of whether an implied cause of action should be permitted.

If a whistleblower can point to a federal statute that grants his or her class of employees, consistent with the *Cort v. Ash* analysis, the whistleblower may be able to state an implied federal cause of action. Such implied causes of action have been upheld under the Railway Labor Act for the retaliatory discharge of employees for union organizing,[94] and for testifying or furnishing information pursuant to an action under the Federal Employers Liability Act.[95] Private implied causes of action have been rejected under the Occupational Safety and Health Act,[96] the National Defense Authorization Act,[97] the Animal Welfare Act,[98] the Whistleblower Protection Act,[99] the Consumer Credit Protection Act,[100] and the Federal Aviation Act.[101] There are no cases directly interpreting the statutory prohibition against terminating employees who report violations of the Institutionalized Persons Act,[102] but the statutory language and legislative history of that law strongly imply such a right.[103]

JOB TRAINING AND PARTNERSHIP ACT/WIA

The Job Training and Partnership Act (JTPA) and Workforce Investment Act (WIA) prohibit retaliation against employees who allege that a recipient of a JTPA/WIA grant violated federal or state law, or has filed a complaint under JTPA/WIA.[104] Retaliation complaints under the WIA must be filed under the terms of 29 C.F.R. Part 37.[105] After exhausting the local grievance procedure,[106] the employee may file a complaint directly with the Department of Labor.[107] Complaints can also be filed pursuant to 29 C.F.R. § 629.51 and 29 C.F.R. § 37.11.

FEDERAL CONTRACTING/MAJOR FRAUDS ACT

Congress has enacted a number of statutory protections for whistleblowers who expose fraud in government contracting. The most significant such law is the False Claims Act (see Ch. 6). Other provisions protecting whistleblowers on government contracts are contained in the Federal Acquisition Streamlining Act of 1994,[108] and the Department of Defense procurement laws.[109] In addition to these specific provisions, in 1988 Congress passed the Major Frauds Act (MFA).[110] Like the False Claims Act, the MFA was designed to stop fraud in government contracting. The MFA prohibits schemes or attempts to "defraud the United States"[111] or "obtain money or property" from the United States using "false or fraudulent pretenses, representations or promises," in government contracts worth over one million dollars.[112] The law, which is similar to the False Claims Act, contains civil and criminal penalties. It also contains two sections of interest to whistleblowers.

First, the law contains a "reward" provision. It authorizes the Attorney General, in "his or her sole discretion" to pay whistleblowers who "furnish information relating to possible" violations of the MFA a bounty not to "exceed $250,000."[113] To be eligible for this discretionary award, the whistleblower cannot be a government employee, must have first informed his or her management of the potential MFA violation,[114] cannot have participated in the violation, and cannot have based his or her whistleblowing on a "public disclosure."[115]

The law also contains an antiretaliation provision that is nearly identical to the FCA provision.[116] It prohibits adverse action against any "individual" who engaged in the protected activity of assisting in the "investigation," "initiation," or "furtherance" of an MFA case or who testifies or provides "assistance" in the prosecution of such a case. Employees are entitled to "2 times the amount of back pay," "special damages," reinstatement, and attorney fees and costs.[117]

The antiretaliation provision does not contain a statute of limitations. One court applied the six-year limitations period contained in the FCA, due to the similar nature of the FCA and MFA.[118] Given the similari-

ties between the FCA and MFA, employees alleging retaliation for exposing fraud against the U.S. government may consider seeking protection
under both the FCA and MFA antiretaliation provisions. In regard to
awarding a finder's fee, the provisions of the FCA are far more powerful
and potentially effective then the discretionary provisions of the MFA.

MARITIME LAW: FEDERAL COURT JURISDICTION, THE LONGSHOREMAN'S AND HARBOR WORKER'S COMPENSATION ACT, AND THE COAST GUARD PROTECTION ACT

The United States government has jurisdiction over claims involving maritime law. Pursuant to this authority, the federal courts have adopted a "public policy" exception to the *at-will* doctrine that protects whistleblowers in the maritime industry. Additionally, maritime employees who
file or testify in workers compensation claims, raising safety issues or sea
worthiness complaints to the Coast Guard as whistleblowers, are protected
under this statute.

Congress has prohibited any "owner, charterer, managing operator,
agent, master or individual" from firing or "in any other manner" discriminating against any "seaman" who has, in "good faith" reported a "violation"
of maritime laws or regulations to the Coast Guard.[119] A seaman covered
under this law may file a claim in federal district court and, if he or she
prevails, is entitled to reinstatement, back pay, injunctive relief, and any
other "appropriate relief."[120] This statute has been interpreted as requiring
actual (or threatened) reports to the Coast Guard of potential violations.[121]

The U.S. Court of Appeals for the 5th Circuit also recognized that
a seaman could file a maritime tort against his or her employer for retaliating against an employee "seeking legal redress" under the Jones Act, 46
U.S.C. § 688.[122] The court essentially adopted a public policy exception to
the termination *at-will* doctrine, although the 5th Circuit declined to permit
punitive damages under this maritime tort.[123] The public policy claim may
protect employees who have never contacted the Coast Guard. For example, in one case a ship captain was protected for "refusing to pilot" a "vessel
that the captain reasonably believe[d]" was "unseaworthy, posing an undue
risk of death or serious injury to passengers or crew."[124]

The Longshoreman's and Harbor Worker's Compensation Act
(LHWCA) protects from retaliation employees who either claim protection
or compensation under the act or who testify in a proceeding under the act.
Employers who violate the act are subject to a civil fine,[125] and the employee is entitled to reinstatement and back pay.[126] A complaint under this

section should be filed with the U.S. Department of Labor.[127] The LHWCA is a maritime worker's compensation law, which covers employees engaged in maritime employment (including longshoremen, harbor workers, and shipbuilders)[128] when an injury occurs on navigable waters of the United States or upon adjoining piers, wharfs, or other adjoining areas customarily used for loading, building, or unloading a vessel.[129] The act also covers employees of the District of Columbia.[130] Claimants seeking relief under the act have a "light standard of proof in making their claims." This standard is less than the burden of proof "borne by plaintiffs in civil cases."[131]

MIGRANT AND SEASONAL AGRICULTURAL WORKERS PROTECTION ACT

The Migrant and Seasonal Agricultural Workers Protection Act has provisions that protects migrant workers who file a complaint, participate in enforcement proceedings, testify, or exercise rights under the act.[132] An employee who alleges discrimination in violation of this act must file a complaint with the Secretary of Labor within 180 days after the employee first learns of the alleged violation.[133]

Once the employee files the complaint, the Secretary of Labor must conduct an investigation into the allegations. If the Secretary determines that a violation of the law occurred, then the Secretary must file a suit in federal district court on behalf of the employee.[134]

Employees also have a right to initiate a private cause of action against any person who intentionally violates any provision of the Migrant and Seasonal Agricultural Worker Protection Act. Such suits must be filed in federal district court and may be maintained "without regard to exhaustion of any alternative administrative remedies" provided under the act.[135]

MINE HEALTH AND SAFETY ACT

The Federal Mine Health and Safety Act (FMHSA) provides for an administrative remedy for any miner, miner's representative, or applicant for employment in a mine who files or makes a complaint regarding a potential violation of the FMHSA.[136] This whistleblower law recognizes the "key role" miners play in "implementing" the "health and safety goods" of the FMHSA.[137] Congress recognized that miners should serve as part of an "early warning system" in "reporting potential violations" and that "protecting" miners from retaliation is "crucial to the Act's scheme."[138]

Complaints both to management and to governmental authorities are statutorily protected. A complaint must be filed with the U.S. Department of Labor within sixty days of the alleged retaliatory action.[139] Miners also have a qualified right to refuse to work in hazardous conditions, and an employment offer that conditions such employment on working in hazardous conditions is illegal.[140]

The FMHSA broadly covers almost all mining activities, including coal or "other miners"[141] and applicants for employment.[142] Its purpose was to provide broad safety protection to miners: "the first priority and concern of all in the coal and other mining industries must be the health and safety of its most precious resource—the miner."[143] The FMHSA was first passed in 1969, and was significantly strengthened in 1977.[144] Under both the 1969 and 1977 laws, courts have continuously stressed for "liberal construction" on whistleblower protection provisions.[145]

Under the law, the complaining miner "bears the burden of production and proof to establish (1) that he engaged in protected activity, and (2) that the adverse action complained of was motivated in part by that activity."[146] An operator may "rebut the prima facie case by showing either that no protected activity occurred or that the adverse action was in no way motivated by protected activity."[147] Additionally, an operator may defend its action if it can demonstrate that the adverse action was "motivated by the miner's unprotected activity alone."[148]

A miner has the "right to refuse to perform work which he reasonably believes poses a safety hazard."[149] The basic guidelines governing how an employee may invoke this right were set forth by the Court of Appeals in *National Cement Company v. FMSHC*.[150]

Once a complaint is filed, the Department of Labor's Mine Safety and Health Administration and the Federal Mine Safety and Health Review Commission must expeditiously process the complaint. If a determination is made that the complaint was "not frivolously brought," the commission must order the "immediate reinstatement" of the miner "pending" the full adjudication of the complaint.[151] A similar temporary reinstatement provision was found constitutional under the Surface Transportation Assistance Act.[152] If, after an investigation, the Secretary of Labor finds discrimination, the Secretary must file a complaint with the commission, and the commission will hold a full evidentiary hearing.[153] If the Secretary rules against the employee, the employee may file a complaint with the commission on his or her own behalf. Once again, the commission must afford the employee a full evidentiary hearing.[154] Appeals from a decision of the commission must be filed within thirty days of receipt of an adverse decision, to either the U.S. Court of Appeals for the circuit in which the violation arose or to the District of Columbia Circuit.[155] Successful employees are entitled to reinstatement, back pay, costs, and attorney's fees.[156]

NATIONAL LABOR RELATIONS ACT, SECTION 301 OF THE LABOR MANAGEMENT RELATIONS ACT, AND DUTY OF FAIR REPRESENTATION CLAIMS

Among the oldest statutes that protect employees (and supervisors)[157] who engage in protected conduct, which under some circumstances can be classified as whistleblowing, is the National Labor Relations Act (NLRA). The NLRA protects from retaliation employees who testify or file charges alleging a violation of the NLRA. A complaint should be filed with the regional director of the National Labor Relations Board (NLRB) for the region in which the violation allegedly occurred.[158] The statute of limitations for filing an unfair labor practice charge is six months.[159] Claims filed under this clause of the NLRA are prosecuted by the NLRB, the General Counsel, and regional directors of the NLRB as an unfair labor practice.[160]

It is well established that violations of the NLRA's antiretaliation clause "are within the exclusive jurisdiction of the NLRB" and must be pursued in that forum. The major exception to this rule concerns retaliation claims, which also constitute potential violations of a collective bargaining agreement. If retaliation forms the basis of an alleged violation of a collective bargaining agreement, Section 301 of the Labor Management Relations Act (LMRA) permits employees to raise retaliation defenses in other forums permitted under the LMRA.[161]

Extensive case law has been developed under the antiretaliation clause of the NLRA.[162] Courts regularly apply principles developed in NLRA retaliation cases to other antiretaliation laws. For example, NLRA case law principles have been applied to whistleblower cases under the Atomic Energy Act[163] and the Federal Mine Health and Safety Act.[164] The NLRA lacks a provision for a private right of action. Employees who seek protection under this act must petition the NLRB to file a claim on their behalf.

Employees who are covered under a collective bargaining agreement (CBA) are protected from retaliatory discharge if such a firing is a violation of the union-management contract. If an employee is terminated in violation of the CBA, the employee must exhaust the contractual grievance procedures, such as arbitration, prior to filing a breach of contract claim under Section 301 of the LMRA, 29 U.S.C. § 185.[165] The statute of limitations for a Section 301 suit is six months.[166]

If a labor union fails to properly utilize the grievance and arbitration machinery on behalf of an employee, then both the union and the employee may be sued under Section 301 pursuant to a judicially created

Duty of Fair Representation (DFR) doctrine. The U.S. Supreme Court established the DFR doctrine due to the special nature of a collective bargaining agreement.[167]

Because of the weakness of these labor law remedies, many employees have chosen to seek protection under state common law or other federal statutes. Under Section 301 of the Labor Management Relations Act, discrimination claims (including tort claims) that arise out of a collective bargaining agreement or require the interpretation of such an agreement are preempted, and an employee must utilize the remedies set forth in the collective bargaining agreement.[168] On the other hand, "if a court can uphold state rights without interpreting the terms of a CBA, the state claim is not necessarily preempted."[169]

OCCUPATIONAL SAFETY AND HEALTH ACT

The Occupational Safety and Health Act (OSHA)[170] protects employees from any form of retaliation for raising complaints concerning workplace health and safety,[171] including a right to refuse hazardous work under certain specified and limited circumstances.[172] However, the failure of the OSHA law to provide for a private right of action has rendered this provision ineffectual.[173] For example, the Supreme Court of Kansas carefully analyzed the OSHA law and held that the law did not provide an "adequate alternative remedy" sufficient to *estop* a state common law tort action.[174]

Employees who believe that they have been discriminated or retaliated against for exercising safety and health rights under OSHA must file a complaint with the local OSHA office within thirty days of the time they learn of the alleged discrimination. The Secretary of Labor (SOL) must investigate the allegation. If the SOL determines that there was a violation under OSHA, the secretary must sue on behalf of the employee to obtain appropriate relief, including reinstatement, back pay,[175] and compensatory and punitive damages.[176] There is no statute of limitations restricting the timeliness of a complaint filed by the Secretary of Labor.[177]

OSHA was enacted to "assure as far as possible every working man and woman in the nation safe and healthful working conditions."[178] The whistleblower protection provisions were designed to "encourage employees' reporting of OSHA violations."[179] Employees have been protected for raising OSHA-related safety complaints to the U.S. Department of Labor and also for reporting such violations to their unions,[180] to management,[181] and to the newspapers.[182] Claims can be proven by circumstantial or direct evidence of employer animus.[183]

Under OSHA, an employee does not have a federal statutory right to initiate his or her own suit for retaliatory discharges.[184] The U.S. Courts of Appeals have uniformly held that OSHA does not authorize an implied private cause of action for wrongful discharge.[185] Consequently, if the U.S. Department of Labor does not initiate an action on behalf of a wrongfully discharged employee, that employee does not have another legal remedy under federal OSHA. The employee may, however, still have an action under state law.[186]

RACKETEER INFLUENCED AND CORRUPT ORGANIZATIONS ACT (CIVIL RICO)

The civil remedies section of the Racketeer Influenced and Corrupt Organizations Act (RICO) entitles all persons "injured" in their "business or property by reason of a violation" of the RICO statute to obtain civil damages.[187] On April 26, 2000 the U.S. Supreme Court held that whistleblowers were not protected under Civil RICO "for injuries caused by an overt act that is not an act of racketeering or otherwise unlawful under the [RICO] statute."[188]

One court upheld a civil RICO claim based on a whistleblower's allegation that his wrongful discharge constituted illegal retaliation in violation of 18 U.S.C. § 1512(b), the federal obstruction of justice statute.[189] This statute broadly prohibits a wide variety of conduct that often underlines a whistleblower case, including the intimidation of a witness and delaying or preventing "communication" with a "law enforcement officer" relating to the "commission or possible commission of a Federal offense." The law also prohibits the intentional harassment of a individual who reports a potential violation of federal law to a judge or law enforcement officer. In that case, the court found RICO standing directly under the obstruction of justice statute, since obstruction of justice is one of the criminal violations explicitly covered under RICO.[190]

RAILWAY LABOR ACT

The Railway Labor Act (RLA) established a "mandatory arbitral mechanism" that would "handle disputes 'growing out of grievances' " in the railroad industry.[191] Under the Federal Railway Safety Act, allegations that an employee was discriminated against due to filing a "complaint" to enforce the Safety Act, or a "good faith" refusal to perform hazardous work, were cognizable under the Railway Labor Act's arbitration provisions.[192] In *Hawaiian Airlines, v. Norris*, the U.S. Supreme Court unanimously held that employee whistleblowers can pursue state statutory or common law whistleblower claims despite the RLA's mandatory arbitration requirements.[193] In that case, the Court refused to preempt a state tort claim for a mechanic who was discharged for reporting safety concerns to the Federal Aviation Administration. After that decision, the Supreme Court in California permitted an airline employee to file a state tort action after being fired for raising safety concerns.[194]

In 1980 the Federal Railroad Safety Act (FRSA) was amended to explicitly protect railroad whistleblowers.[195] In passing the 1980 amendments:

Congress recognized . . . that despite the possible tragic consequences that may result from silence, many employees are paralyzed into silence by fear of retaliation. Therefore considering the substantial public policy reasons and benefits, Congress decided to provide extra protection to railroad whistleblowers beyond the protections that govern the employer-employee relationship.[196]

Whistleblower claims under the FRSA must be administratively processed before the National Railroad Adjustment Board.[197] At least one court has held that the limited administrative remedies afforded employees under the FRSA preempts "state wrongful discharge" claims.[198]

SURFACE MINING CONTROL AND RECLAMATION ACT

This act, which is very similar to other environmental whistleblower laws, protects employees who raise an environmental allegation or allege a violation of the Surface Mining Control and Reclamation Act.[199] An employee must file a complaint within thirty days to the Department of Interior.[200] The law provides for reinstatement, back pay and attorney's fees.[201] Administrative regulations contain a mechanism for temporary relief from discrimination.[202] In *Leber v. Pennsylvania Dept. of Environmental Resources,* the U.S. Court of Appeals for the 3rd Circuit held that states were not prohibited from discriminating against their employees under this act.[203]

SURFACE TRANSPORTATION ASSISTANCE ACT

Section 405 of the Surface Transportation Assistance Act (STAA)[204] protects employee whistleblowers (generally truck drivers) who file complaints, testify, or institute proceedings to enforce commercial motor vehicle safety laws, rules, or standards.[205] It also protects truck drivers from discrimination for refusing to drive their loads when confronted with illegal or unsafe conditions. An employee has the right to refuse to operate a vehicle if, after contacting the employer, the employee has "reasonable apprehension" that operating the vehicle would cause "serious injury to himself or the public."[206] Additionally, an employee also can refuse to operate a vehicle if such operation would constitute a "violation of any federal rules, regulations, standards or orders applicable to commercial motor vehicle safety or health."[207] Finally, the law protects employees who file complaints regarding "transportation of hazardous material by commercial motor carriers."[208]

Attacks on the constitutionality of the STAA, including an attack on an employee's right to prosecute his or her own claim after the OSHA division of the Department of Labor (DOL) declined to pursue a case, have been completely rejected.[209] Consistent with most whistleblower laws, the protection of employees under the STAA is "not dependent upon whether [the employee] was actually successful in proving a violation of a federal safety provision."[210] Likewise, "internal" whistleblowing has been protected.[211] Adjudications under the STAA also follow the traditional requirements regarding proof of a *prima facie* case, the shifting burdens of production and proof, and the Administrative Procedure Act's burden requirement.[212]

In a 1987 decision, the U.S. Supreme Court described the purpose behind these protections: "[Section 405 of the STAA] protects employees in the commercial motor transportation industry from being discharged in retaliation for refusing to operate a motor vehicle that does not comply with applicable state and federal safety regulations or for filing complaints alleging such noncompliance."[213]

A complaint must be filed with the Secretary of Labor[214] within 180 days of the alleged discriminatory act.[215] Within 60 days of filing the complaint the Secretary of Labor must have the allegation investigated.[216] If the results of the investigation indicate that there is "reasonable cause" to find that the "complaint has merit," then the Secretary shall issue a preliminary order in support of the employee. This includes immediate temporary reinstatement pending the outcome of a full evidentiary hearing.[217] Either the employee or the employer can appeal, within 30 days, the preliminary investigative finding. On appeal, the parties are entitled to a full evidentiary hearing before a DOL Administrative Law Judge (ALJ), which must be "expeditiously conducted."[218] The procedures used by the DOL in STAA cases, and the substantive case law, are similar or identical to the procedures and law for environmental whistleblowers as set forth in Chapter 5. If a final order of the Secretary is issued in support of the employee, the employee is entitled to reinstatement, back pay, compensatory damages, costs, and attorney's fees.[219]

Appeals of the Secretary's order must be filed in the U.S. Court of Appeals, for the circuit in which the violation occurred, within sixty days of the issuance of the secretary's order.[220] On appeal, the court must affirm the factual conclusions of the DOL ALJ who presided at the hearing, if those findings are "supported by substantial evidence on the record considered as a whole."[221] Unlike the traditional rule in administrative law, regulations of the DOL require that the Secretary of Labor approve factual findings of the ALJ, if those findings are properly supported. The failure of the Secretary to adopt such findings is reversible error.[222]

The authority of the Secretary of Labor to require respondents to temporarily reinstate employees was unsuccessfully subjected to an employer's constitutional challenge in the U.S. Supreme Court case of *Brock v. Roadway Express, Inc.*[223] In *Brock*, the Court found that Congress, in passing this law, "recognized that employees in the transportation industry are often best able to detect safety violations" but often do not do so "because they may be threatened with discharge."[224] Additionally, the Supreme Court found that Congress "recognized that the employee's protection against having to choose between operating an unsafe vehicle and losing his job would lack practical effectiveness if the employee could not be reinstated pending complete review. The longer a discharged employee remains unemployed, the more devastating are the consequences to his personal financial condition and prospects for re-employment."[225] After *Brock*, the courts have regularly issued injunctions mandating the immediate reinstatement of whistleblowers under the STAA.[226] Settlements of STAA cases must be approved by the DOL.[227]

UNSAFE CONTAINERS

The Safe Containers for International Cargo Act[228] contains a whistleblower protection provision.[229] Any employee who reports a violation of the act or who reports the existence of an unsafe container that will be used in international transport is protected from retaliation. A complaint must be filed with the U.S. Secretary of Labor within sixty days after the alleged violation occurs.[230]

The statute does not provide for a private cause of action. Instead, if the Secretary of Labor, after a thirty-day investigation, determines that a violation of the act occurred, the secretary must file a complaint for "appropriate relief" in federal court.[231] The law contains no provision for compensatory damages or attorney's fees.

WHISTLEBLOWER PROTECTION ACT (COVERAGE OF FEDERAL EMPLOYEES)

Federal law prohibits retaliation against most members of the federal civil service. Laws protecting civil servants from discrimination were originally passed following the murder of President James A. Garfield in 1881. President Garfield was assassinated by a "dissatisfied office seeker."[232]

The first major law protecting whistleblowers in the federal service was the Lloyd-LaFollette Act passed in 1912.[233] This law, which in its modern form is codified as 5 U.S.C. § 7211, protects the "right" of federal employees to "individually or collectively" "petition Congress or a Member of Congress or to furnish information to either House of Congress or to a committee or Member thereof." Given the important oversight role Congress has traditionally played regarding the executive branch of government, and the fact that many federal employee whistleblowers have testified against their employing agencies in Congress, this law remains as a centerpiece in prohibiting agencies from retaliating against federal employee whistleblowers.[234]

When originally passed, the Lloyd-LaFollette Act specifically targeted a "gag rule" that was intended to stop old-fashioned whistleblowing from civil servants to members of Congress. Specifically, Presidents Theodore Roosevelt and William Howard Taft issued Executive Orders that prohibited federal employees from communicating with Congress without the "permission of their supervisors."[235] The supporters of the Lloyd-LaFollette Act vehemently argued against the "gag rule," using words that even today describe the strong feelings often evoked when whistleblowers seek to directly communicate with members of Congress: "[I]t is for the purpose of wiping out the existence of this despicable 'gag rule' that this provision is inserted. The rule is unjust, unfair, and against the provisions of the Constitution of the United States, which provides for the right of appeal and the right of free speech to all its citizens."[236] Opponents of the Lloyd-LaFollette Act argued that allowing federal employees to "go over the head" of their "superior" in order to pursue their "own selfish interest, would be detrimental" to the federal civil service and "absolutely destroy the discipline necessary for good service."[237] However, these criticisms "did not prevail,"[238] and Congress passed protections, for employees who contact Congress, that are currently codified as 5 U.S.C. § 7211.

After 1912 Congress and the federal executive, through either Executive Order or legislation, enacted a complex and "elaborate remedial system" governing the employment of federal civil servants. This system has survived broad constitutional challenges under both the "due process" clause of the Constitution and the First Amendment.[239] Currently, the primary legislation protecting federal employees (and employee whistleblowers) is the Civil Service Reform Act (CSRA) of 1978[240] and major amendments to that law, known as the Whistleblower Protection Act (WPA) of 1989.[241]

Federal employees are also protected under a handful of other federal antiretaliation statutes, such as the environmental whistleblower laws, the antiretaliation provisions of Title VII, and the banking whistleblower laws.[242]

Some of these provisions, such as Title VII or the banking laws, provide for federal court review of a whistleblower case.[243] Others, such as the whistleblower provisions of the Clean Air Act, permit federal employees to pursue claims within the DOL.[244] Congress also passed a law protecting whistleblowers in the armed services who file allegations directly with Congress or an Inspector General.[245] This military whistleblower law does not provide for a private cause of action, and its procedures are cumbersome, if not unworkable.

Federal employees may also seek nonmonetary injunctive relief concerning violations of their First Amendment whistleblower rights directly in federal court.[246] Such federal jurisdiction is available only if the claim for declaratory or injunctive relief "stands independently" of any claim requesting a remedy to an actual adverse action.[247] Federal employees are not entitled to a constitutional tort remedy as a "Bivens claim" for damage.[248]

The WPA prohibits a federal agency from taking an adverse "personnel action" against most civil servants in retaliation for a variety of whistleblowing activities.[249] The basic definition of protected whistleblower activity in the CSRA/WPA is found at 5 U.S.C. § 2302(b)(8) as follows: "a disclosure of information by an employee or applicant which the employee or applicant reasonably believes evidences, (i) a violation of any law, rule or regulation, (ii) gross mismanagement, a gross waste of funds, an abuse of authority, or a substantial and specific danger to public health or safety."[250] As can be seen from this definition, some of the terms used in the CSRA are ambiguous. For example, instead of protecting employees who raise "public health or safety" concerns, the law requires that the concern also be "substantial and specific."[251] Similarly, the law protects employee's who make "disclosures," yet the term "disclosure" is undefined. Consequently, the case law under the WPA has been tortured,[252] and Congress has been forced on a number of occasions to pass specific amendments to the whistleblower law in order to overturn prior decisions of the U.S. Court of Appeals for the Federal Circuit (the only circuit court of appeals with jurisdiction over Merit Systems Protection Board [MSPB] appeals).[253] Congress, often with no result, has repeatedly stated that the CSRA/WPA should be interpreted to encourage employee whistleblowing: "The Committee intends that disclosures be encouraged. The OSC [Office of Special Counsel], the Board and the courts should not erect barriers to disclosures which will limit the necessary flow of information from employees who have knowledge of government wrongdoing."[254]

Despite congressional warnings, the interpretations of the CSRA/WPA continue to be narrow and hypertechnical. For example, in recent decisions by the Federal Circuit, employees have had their claims dismissed for raising concerns with supervisors who were accused of being the "wrongdoers themselves."[255] The Federal Circuit also upheld the existence of a "presumption that Government officials act in good faith."[256] Given this presumption, an employee is faced with a contradictory choice. If you act on the "good faith" assumption and bring a concern directly to an official whom the employee believes may have engaged in wrongdoing, the employee whistleblower can be fired and completely stripped of protection under the WPA. On the other hand, if the employee fails to act on the "presumption" of "good faith," they risk judicial criticism by violating that presumption. In addition, the Federal Circuit continues to apply a narrow view of protected activity.[257]

Another example of judicial narrowing concerns the use of "timing" to support an inference of discriminating motive. In response to the Federal Circuit's rejection of a timing-causation method as proof, Congress amended the WPA to mandate a finding of causation if timing could be established.[258] Despite this amendment, the court continues to narrowly construe the timing-motive analysis and has continued to reject the use of timing as evidence of improper motive in certain cases.[259]

These rulings have resulted in harsh congressional criticisms of the Federal Circuit's decision making. On September 24, 1999, Senator Charles Grassley, the principal sponsor of the WPA, pointed to a number of court rulings as the "judicial equivalent of contempt of Congress."[260]

WPA cases must be filed either with the Office of Special Counsel (OSC) (in an original action) or directly with the MSPB (if an allegation of reprisal constitutes an affirmative defense in an adverse personnel action or if the rules permit a direct filing).[261]

To establish MSPB jurisdiction over a whistleblower case, an employee must show, by a preponderance of the evidence, that she or he engaged in activity protected under the Civil Service Reform Act/

Whistleblower Protection Act of 1989[262] and that the governmental agency took, failed to take, or threatened to take a "personnel" action, as defined in the CSRA/WPA.[263] In addition, if the employee files a whistleblower claim with the OSC, the employee must be extremely careful in presenting all of his or her claims and factual supporting material to the OSC. During the hearing stage of the proceeding (*i.e.*, after an appeal is filed from OSC to the MSPB), an employee is required to demonstrate that he or she properly presented his or her claims to the OSC and properly "exhausted" the OSC remedies.[264] The U.S. Court of Appeals for the Federal Circuit has held that employees "must" demonstrate that their "administrative remedies, including those available through the OSC, have been exhausted," as a condition of maintaining a Private Right of Action under the WPA.[265]

Once the employee has demonstrated that she or he engaged in protected activity and that an adverse action occurred, the employee must show that the protected disclosures were a "contributing factor" in the alleged prohibited personnel actions taken by the Agency.[266] A "contributing factor" may be demonstrated by relying on either direct or circumstantial evidence.[267]

In 1994 the WPA was amended in order to clarify Congress' intent to permit employees to rely on circumstantial evidence to meet this element of a whistleblower case.[268] In *Kewley v. Department of Health and Human Services*,[269] the Federal Circuit held that the Whistleblower Protection Act "guarantees" that a federal employee establishes a *prima facie* case simply by meeting the "knowledge/timing test" and that no further nexus need be shown to demonstrate that the protected disclosure was a contributing factor in the alleged personnel action.[270]

Employer "knowledge" that an employee engaged in protected activity may be demonstrated by direct or circumstantial evidence.[271] Likewise, circumstantial evidence may be used to demonstrate the "contributing factor" element of a claim. For example, a number of cases have held that "changing or inconsistent" explanations for a personnel action are evidence of retaliation and pretext.[272]

Once the employee meets his or her burden under the "contributing factor" test, the agency's affirmative defense that it had a legitimate business reason for taking the adverse action must be demonstrated by "clear and convincing evidence."[273] The statutory language itself explicitly raised an agency's burden of proof in order to make it easier for employees to win WPA cases.[274]

Courts have recognized that Congress' use of the "contributing factor" standard and the "clear and convincing evidence" standard in evaluating claims under the WPA was explicitly adopted in order to *reduce* the burden on employees to prove their claims. As the U.S. Court of Appeals for the Federal Circuit explained:

The policy goal behind the WPA was to encourage government personnel to blow the whistle on wasteful, corrupt or illegal government practices without fearing retaliatory action by their supervisors. . . . [S]uch encouragement is guaranteed by the substantially reduced burden that must be carried by the whistleblower to earn the WPA's protection from adverse action. So long as the protected disclosure is a contributing factor to the contested personnel action, and the agency cannot prove its affirmative defense, no harm can come to the whistleblower. We thus view the WPA as a good-government statute.[275]

If an employee wins a WPA case, the employee is entitled to "corrective action, which includes placing the employee, as nearly as possible, in the position she or he would have been in had the prohibited personnel practice not occurred, back pay and related benefits, other reasonable and foreseeable consequential damages, attorneys fees and costs incurred."[276] An agency is obligated to place the employee as nearly as possible in the status quo ante.[277] A prevailing party is entitled to "broad" relief under the WPA in order to make the employee whole.[278] Affirmative relief is also available, usually in the form of notice posting.

The procedures for pursuing a WPA claim are very complex and can result in an employee losing a meritorious claim.[279] Whistleblower cases are generally filed with the OSC. Employees are entitled to a hearing before an Administrative Judge of the MSPB. There is one level of appellate review before the MSPB, and all appeals of the MSPB's final decision must normally be filed in the U.S. Court of Appeals for the Federal Circuit.[280] At each level there are technical rules that must be filed, and the failure to scrupulously follow these rules often results in the dismissal of a potentially meritorious claim.

An example is the complex procedural requirements that harm employees under the WPA rules governing discovery. It is widely recognized that discovery is essential in allowing employees to obtain evidence of discrimination. Under the rules of the MSPB, all discovery requests and motions must be filed within twenty-five days of an initial scheduling order.[281] Failure to meet that deadline can, and often will, result in a cut-off of often essential discovery.

The difficulties federal employees face under the Civil Service Reform Act regulations and requirements were highlighted in a *New York Times* editorial:

The Civil Service Reform Act of 1978 and the Whistle-Blower Protection Act of

1989. . . . prescribe a tortuous and uncertain appeals process that in theory guarantees a whistleblower free speech without fear of retaliation, but in practice is an
exercise in frustration. Despite recent improvements, only a handful of federal
employees, out of some 1,500 who appealed in the last four years, have prevailed
in rulings issued by the Government's administrative tribunal, the Merit System
Protection Board. Overwhelmingly, the rest of the cases were screened out on
technical grounds or were settled informally with token relief.[282]

NOTES

    1. Although this chapter focuses on statutory remedies specifically
enacted to protect whistleblowers, employees subject to retaliation may also be
protected under other federal laws. For example, the Privacy Act places significant restriction on the federal government's ability to smear or undermine the
credibility of whistleblowers through the release of personal or otherwise
confidential information contained in government records. *See, e.g., Alexander
v. F.B.I.* 971 F. Supp. 603 (D.C. Cir. 1997).

    2. *See* Eugene Fidell, *Federal Protection of Private Sector Health and
Safety Whistleblowers: A Report to the Administrative Conference of the United
States* (Washington, D.C.: Administrative Conference of the United States, March
1987), *reprinted in* 2 *Administrative Law Journal* 1 (1988) for a detailed criticism
of the patchwork nature of the federal laws.

    3. *Mackowiak v. University Nuclear Systems, Inc.*, 735 F.2d 1159, 1163-
1164 (9th Cir., 1984).

    4. *See Kansas Gas & Electric v. Brock*, 780 F.2d 1505, 1511-1512 (10th
Cir. 1985).

    5. *See Deford v. Sec'y. of Labor*, 700 F.2d 281, 286 (6th Cir. 1983)
(applied NLRA case-law to nuclear whistleblower case).

    6. Whistleblower protections under the First Amendment, the Civil
Rights Act of 1871, and U.S. Code sections 42 U.S.C. §§ 1983 and 1985 are
discussed in chapter 4. Federal environmental and nuclear whistleblower protections are set forth in chapter 5. Protections under the False Claims Act and a
discussion of the FCA's *qui tam* provisions are set forth in chapter 6. Legal
remedies for blowing the whistle on occupational safety issues are discussed in
chapter 7. Legal principles that apply to most whistleblower cases are set forth
in chapters 8 and 9.

    7. 49 U.S.C. § 42121.

    8. *Congressional Record*, p. S2855 (March 17, 1999).

    9. The adjudicatory procedures set forth in the Aviation Investment and
Reform Act closely mirror those set forth in other Department of Labor administered whistleblower laws. *See* 29 C.F.R. Part 24 and Chapter 5, "Environmental
and Nuclear Whistleblowing."

    10. *See Marano v. Department of Justice*, 2 F.3d 1137, 1140 (Fed. Cir.
1993) (WPA standard of proof); *Frobose v. American Savings & Loan Association*, 152 F.3d 602, 609 (7thCir. 1998) (banking system's standard of proof); *Stone
& Webster v. Herman*, 115 F.3d 1568, 1572 (11th Cir. 1997) (ERA standard of

proof).

11. H.R. Rep. No. 101-54(I), cited in *Simas v. First Citizens' Federal Credit Union*, 170 F.3d 37, 43 (1st Cir. 1999).

12. *Haley v. Retsinas*, 138 F.3d 1245, 1250 (8th Cir. 1998).

13. *Id.*

14. 12 U.S.C. § 1831j.

15. 12 U.S.C. § 1831j(e).

16. 12 U.S.C. § 1790b.

17. 31 U.S.C. § 5328.

18. *Rouse v. Farmers State Bank of Jewell*, 866 F. Supp. 1191, 1208 (N.D. Iowa 1994) (finding *McDonnell Douglas v. Green* Title VII formula for shifting burdens of production and proof "inapplicable" under the FIRREA).

19. *Frobose v. American Savings and Loan*, 152 F.3d 602, 611-612 (7th Cir. 1998).

20. *Id.*

21. *Id.* at 613.

22. *Id.* (collecting cases).

23. 31 U.S.C. § 5328(b), 12 U.S.C. § 1970b(b), and 12 U.S.C. § 1831j (b).

24. *Haley, supra*, at 1251.

25. 31 U.S.C. § 5328(a).

26. 12 U.S.C. § 1790b(a).

27. 12 U.S.C. § 1831j(a).

28. *Simas, supra*, at 48.

29. *Hicks v. RTC*, 767 F. Supp. 167, 172 (N.D. Ill. 1991).

30. *Id.* at 173.

31. 31 U.S.C. § 5328(c), 12 U.S.C. § 1970b(c), and 12 U.S.C. § 1831j (c).

32. *Oldroyd v. Elmira Savings Bank*, 956 F. Supp. 393, 400-401 (W.D. N.Y. 1997).

33. *Haley, supra*, at 1248.

34. Employees who allege intentional discrimination based on membership in a protected class may also be protected under the Equal Protection Act analysis. However, failure to establish a *prima facie* case of discrimination under Title VII is generally fatal to an equal protection analysis under the Reconstruction Era civil rights statutes, *e.g.*, 42 U.S.C. §§ 1981, 1982, and 1985(2). *See Settle v. Baltimore County*, 34 F. Supp.2d 969, 995 (D. Md. 1999).

35. 42 U.S.C. § 2000e *et seq.*

36. 42 U.S.C. § 2000e-4(a). This provision states:

It shall be an unlawful employment practice for an employer to discriminate against any of his employees or applicants for employment, for an employment agency, or joint labor-management committee controlling apprenticeship or other training or retraining, including on-the-job training programs, to discriminate, against any individual, or for a labor organization to discriminate against any member thereof or applicant for membership, because he has opposed any practice made an unlawful employment practice by this title, or because he has made a charge. testified. assisted. or participated in any manner in an investigation. proceeding. or hearing under this title.

See Pettway v. American Cast Iron Pipe Co., 411 F.2d 998 (5th Cir. 1969).

37. 42 U.S.C. § 2000e-3(a).

38. *Kubicko v. Ogden Logistics Services*, 181 F.3d 544 (4th Cir. 1999); *Learned v. City of Bellevue*, 860 F.2d 928, 932 (9th Cir. 1988).

39. *Merritt v. Dillard Paper Co.*, 120 F.3d 1181, 1186 (11th Cir. 1997).

40. *Laughlin v. MWAA*, 149 F.3d 253, 259, n. 4 (4th Cir. 1998).

41. *Id.* at 259.

42. *Id.*

43. *Merritt, supra*, at 1185-1186.

44. *Kubicko, supra. See also Learned, supra,* at 932 ("it is not necessary to prove that underlying discrimination in fact violated Title VII in order to prevail in an action charging unlawful retaliation").

45. *Learned* at 932.

46. *Laughlin, supra,* at 259.

47. *O'Day v. McDonnell Douglas*, 79 F.3d 756, 763 (9th Cir. 1996) (citations and internal quotations omitted).

48. *See Abel v. Bonfant*, 625 F. Supp. 263 (S.D. N.Y. 1985); *Parker v. Baltimore and O.R. Co.*, 652 F.2d 1012 (D.C. Cir. 1981). *See also* under 42 U.S.C. § 1981 white employees who are punished for trying to vindicate the rights of racial minorities are protected. *See Abel v. Bonfant,* at 267; *DeMatteis v. Eastman Kodak Co.*, 511 F.2d 306, *reh'g on other grounds*, 520 F.2d 409 (2nd Cir. 1975).

49. *See E.E.O.C. v. St. Anne's Hospital*, 664 F.2d 128, 132 (7th Cir. 1982).

50. *Merritt, supra,* at 1181.

51. *Id.* at 1188-1189.

52. *Kempcke v. Monsanto Co.*, 132 F.3d 442, 445 (8th Cir. 1998), *quoting from, O'Day v. McDonnell Douglas, supra*, at 763.

53. *Id.* at 446.

54. *Laughlin, supra,* at 259, n. 3.

55. *See Lyles v. Clinton-Ingham-Eaton Community Mental Health Board*, 35 F. Supp.2d 548 (W.D. Mich. 1998) (dismissing age discrimination complaint for failure to "exhaust administrative proceedings").

56. If the state in which the discrimination occurred has no appropriate state or local agency authorized to grant relief, a Title VII charge must be filed with the EEOC within 180 days of the discriminatory act, 42 U.S.C. § 2000e-5(c). If a state has an appropriate agency that can grant relief, the employee must file with the state or local agency before filing with the EEOC, but also must file a complaint with the EEOC within 300 days of the initial discriminatory act, or within 30 days of a notice from the state, that the state either will take no action on behalf of the employee or has denied the complaint—whichever is earlier. 42 U.S.C. § 2000e-5(e). Sixty days after an employee initiates an action with a state

or local agency he or she has standing to file directly to the EEOC, even if the state has not completed its own investigation. *Id.*

57. *See Lynn v. Western Gillette, Inc.*, 564 F.2d 1282 (9th Cir. 1977). *See* Honorable Charles R. Richy, *Manual on Employment Discrimination and Civil Rights Actions in the Federal Courts* (New York: Kluwer Law Book Publishers, Inc., 1985) for a detailed description of the procedure under Title VII and the general substantive and procedural law under all the federal civil rights laws.

58. 29 U.S.C. § 623(d).

59. 29 U.S.C. § 626(c)(2). *See Visser v. Packer Engineering*, 924 F.2d 655, 660 (7th Cir. 1991) (dissenting opinion of J. Flaum).

60. 29 U.S.C. § 206(d).

61. *See Crockwell v. Blackmon-Mooring Steamatic*, 627 F. Supp. 800, 804 (W.D. Tenn. 1985).

62. *EEOC v. Romeo Community Schools*, 976 F.2d 985, 989 (6th Cir. 1992).

63. *Crockwell, supra*, at 805.

64. 29 U.S.C. § 2615.

65. 29 CFR § 1614; *Schneider v. Dalton*, 1999 WL 1079628 (9th Cir. 1999).

66. 42 U.S.C. § 12203.

67. *O'Day, supra*, at 763. *Dorricott v. Fairhill Center for Aging*, 2 F. Supp.2d 982, 988 (N.D. Ohio 1998).

68. *Clover v. Total System Services, Inc.*, 176 F.3d 1346, 1354-1356 (11th Cir. 1999).

69. Congress established a statutory framework in the CRA of 1991, 42 U.S.C. § 2000e-5(g)(2)(B), with respect to the burdens of proof an employee must meet in order to set forth a claim under Title VII. Whether this framework is applicable to retaliation claims has not yet been resolved. *See Borgo v. Goldin* 204 F.3d 251, 255 n. 6 (D.C. Cir. 2000).

70. The respective burdens of proof in Title VII and Age Discrimination Act cases were carefully set forth in *Aka v. Washington Hospital Center*, 156 F.3d 1284 (D.C. Cir. 1998).

71. 29 U.S.C. § 1140.

72. *Id.*

73. *Hashimoto v. Bank of Hawaii*, 999 F.2d 408, 411 (9th Cir. 1993).

74. 29 U.S.C. § 1132; *see also* 29 C.F.R. § 2560.

75. *Kross v. Western Electric Company*, 701 F.2d 1238 (7th Cir. 1983). *But see Zipf v. American Telephone and Telegraph*, 799 F.2d 889 (3rd Cir. 1986).

76. *McBride v. PLM International*, 179 F.3d 737, 743-744 (9th Cir. 1999).

77. 29 U.S.C. § 215.

78. 29 U.S.C. § 206(d). *See EEOC v. Romeo Community Schools*, 976 F.2d 985, 989 (6th Cir. 1992) *and Soto v. Adams Elevator*, 941 F.2d 543 (7th Cir. 1991) (discussing protected activity under Equal Pay Act).

79. *Lambert v. Ackerley,*180 F.3d 997 (9th Cir. 1999), *petition for cert. filed* (1999) (collecting cases). *Contra Lambert v. Genesee Hosp.*, 10 F.3d 46, 55 (2nd Cir. 1993).

80. *Saffels v. Rice,* 40 F.3d 1546, 1548 (8th Cir. 1994).

81. *Tennessee Coal v. Muscoda Local No. 123,* 321 U.S. 590, 597 (1944).

82. *Lambert, supra.*

83. *Saffels, supra.*

84. *Brock v. Casey Truck Sales,* 839 F.2d 872, 879 (2nd Cir. 1988).

85. 29 U.S.C. § 255.

86. 29 U.S.C. § 216.

87. *Wittenberg v. Wheels, Inc.*, 963 F. Supp. 654, 661-663 (N.D. Ill. 1997); *Strickland v. Mica Information Systems,* 800 F. Supp. 1320, 1323 (M.D. N.C. 1992).

88. 29 U.S.C. § 215-216. *See Soto v. Adams Elevator,* 941 F.2d 543 (7th Cir. 1991).

89. *Soto* at 551.

90. *Ford v. Alfaro,* 785 F.2d 835, 842 (9th Cir. 1986).

91. 29 C.F.R. § Part 579.

92. 422 U.S. 66, 78 (1974).

93. 484 U.S. 174, 179 (1988).

94. *See Stepanischen v. Merchants Dispatch Transportation Corp.*, 722 F.2d 922 (1st Cir. 1983); *Brown v. World Airways, Inc.*, 539 F. Supp. 179 (S.D. N.Y. 1982).

95. *Gonzalez v. Southern Pacific Transportation Co.*, 773 F.2d 637 (5th Cir. 1985).

96. *Taylor v. Brighton Corp.*, 616 F.2d 256 (6th Cir. 1980).

97. *Pacheco v. Raytheon Co.*, 777 F. Supp. 1089 (D. R.I. 1991).

98. *Moor-Jankowski v. Nyu,* 1998 WL 474084 (S.D. N.Y. 1998).

99. *Diefenderfer v. MSPB,* 194 F.3d 1275, (Fed Cir. 1999).

100. 15 U.S.C. § 1674(a). *See LeVick v. Skaggs Companies, Inc.*, 701 F.2d 777 (9th Cir. 1983).

101. 49 U.S.C.§ 1301 *et seq.*; *Buethe v. Britt Airlines,* 581 F. Supp. 200 (S.D. Ind. 1984).

102. 42 U.S.C. § 1997d.

103. *See* 1980 *U.S. Code Congress and Administrative News* at 816.

104. 29 U.S.C. § 1574(g).

105. Vol. 64 *Federal Register* 61691 (November 12, 1999).

106. 29 C.F.R. § 636.5

107. 29 C.F.R. § 636.6.

108. 41 U.S.C. § 265, *implemented by*, 48 CFR 3.9 ("Whistleblower Protection for Contractor Employees").

109. 10 U.S.C. § 2409.

110. 18 U.S.C. § 1031.

111. In the context of defense contracts, employees of contractors may also file a claim with the Inspector General (IG) requesting that the IG investigate and take action to remedy antiwhistleblower discrimination. 10 U.S.C. § 2409.

112. 18 U.S.C. § 1031(a). *See U.S. v. Frequency Electronics*, 862 F. Supp. 834 (E.D. N.Y. 1994) (discussing constitutionality and congressional history of MFA); *U.S. v. Brooks*, 111 F.3d 365 (4th Cir. 1997) (discussing the one million dollar jurisdictional limit and the congressional history of the MFA).

113. 18 U.S.C. § 1031(g)(1).

114. The legislative history of the MFA states that Congress wanted to encourage "responsible individuals, when feasible" to first "go to their employers with pertinent information" about potential MFA violations. H. Rep. 101-273, 1989 U.S. Code Congressional & Ad. News 593, 595.

115. 18 U.S.C. § 1031(g)(2).

116. 18 U.S.C. § 1031(h).

117. *Id.*

118. *Kowalski v. Alpha Kappa Alpha Sorority*, 993 F. Supp. 619 (N.D. Ohio 1997).

119. 46 U.S.C. § 2114.

120. 46 U.S.C. § 2114 (b).

121. *Carrie v. Gray, Inc.*, 912 F.2d 808 (5th Cir. 1990).

122. *Smith v. Atlas Off-Shore Boat Service*, 653 F.2d 1057, 1062 (5th Cir. 1981).

123. *Id.* 653 F.2d at 1064. *See also Robinson v. Rebstock Drilling Co., Inc.*, 749 F.2d 1182 (5th Cir. 1985); *Buchanan v. Bott Brothers' Construction Company, Inc.*, 741 F.2d 750 (5th Cir. 1984).

124. *Seymore v. Lake Tahoe Cruises, Inc.*, 888 F. Supp. 1029, 1035 (E.D. Cal. 1995).

125. 33 U.S.C. § 948(a).

126. *Id.*

127. *See* 20 C.F.R. § Ch. VI, Section 702.271 (1985 Edition).

128. 33 U.S.C. § 902(3).

129. 33 U.S.C. § 903(a).

130. *Geddes v. Benefits Review Board U.S. Dept of Labor*, 735 F.2d 1412, 1414, n. 5 (D.C. Cir. 1984); D.C. Code Ann. § 36-501 (1968).

131. *Id.* at 1416. *But see OWCP v. Greenwich Collieries*, 512 U.S. 267 (1994) (clarifying burdens of proof under Administrative Procedure Act and striking down DOL "true doubt" rule).

132. 29 U.S.C. § 1855.

133. 29 C.F.R. § 500.9(b).

134. 29 U.S.C. § 1855(b).

135. 29 U.S.C. § 1854.

136. 30 U.S.C. § 815(c) (1977).

137. *SOL v. Mutual Mining Inc.*, 80 F.3d 110, 115 (4th Cir. 1996).

138. *Id.*

139. *See generally* James A. Broderick and Daniel Minahan, "Employment Discrimination Under the Federal Mine Safety and Health Act," 84 *West Virginia Law Review* 1023 (1982).

140. *Secretary of Labor et al. v. Mullins et al.*, 888 F.2d 1448 (D.C. Cir. 1989).

141. 30 U.S.C. § 802(g).

142. *Secretary of Labor, et al. v. Mullins, et al., supra.*

143. 30 U.S.C. § 801(a).

144. In the 1969 law, the whistleblower provision was codified as 30 U.S.C. § 820(b). After the 1977 amendments, the employee protection provision was codified at 30 U.S.C. § 815(c).

145. *Phillips v. Interior Bd. of Mine Op. App.*, 500 F.2d 772, 782 (D.C. Cir. 1974).

146. *National Cement Company v. FMSHC*, 27 F.3d 526, 532 (11th Cir. 1994) (collecting cases); *Leeco, Inc. v. Hays*, 965 F.2d 1081, 1084 (D.C. Cir. 1992) (collecting cases).

147. *National Cement Company v. FMSHC, supra.*

148. *Id.*

149. *Lecco, supra.*

150. 27 F.3d 526, 532-533 (11th Cir. 1994).

151. 30 U.S.C. § 815 (c)(2).

152. *Brock, supra*, at 252; 107 S.Ct. 1740 (1987).

153. 30 U.S.C. § 815 (c)(2).

154. 30 U.S.C. § 815 (c)(3).

155. 30 U.S.C. § 815 (c)(3); 30 U.S.C. § 816.

156. 30 U.S.C. § 815 (c)(3).

157. *See Automobile Salesmen's Union et al. v. NLRB*, 711 F.2d 383, 385 (D.C. Cir. 1983); *Delling v. NLRB*, 869 F.2d 1397, 1399-1340 (10th Cir. 1989); *NLRB v. Downslope Industries Inc.*, 676 F.2d 1114, 1119 (6th Cir. 1982).

158. 29 C.F.R. § 102.10; *see also* 29 U.S.C. § 158 (a)(4).

159. 29 U.S.C. § 160(b); *Ernst v. Indian Bell Tel. Co., Inc.*, 717 F.2d 1036, 1038 (7th Cir. 1983), *cert. denied* 104 S.Ct. 707 (1984).

160. *See generally* 29 C.F.R. § 101.2-101.16; § 102.9-102.59.

161. *Jurado v. Eleven-Fifty Corp.*, 813 F.2d 1406, 1412 (9th Cir. 1987).

162. *See generally* cases under 42 U.S.C. § 158(a).

163. *See Mackowiak, supra*, at 1159.

164. *See Phillips, supra*, at 772.

165. *See Vaca v. Sipes*, 386 U.S. 171, 183-185 (1967).

166. *Del Costello v. International Brotherhood of Teamsters*, 462 U.S. 151 (1983).

167. *Vaca, supra*, at 177. *See also Ford Motor Co. v. Huffman*, 345 U.S. 330 (1953); *Steele v. Louisville & N.R. Co.*, 323 U.S. 192 (1944); *Agosto v. Correctional Officers*, 2000 WL 1028583 (S.D. N.Y. 2000).

168. *Lingle v. Norge Division of Magic Chef*, 486 U.S. 399 (1988); *Allis-Chalmers Corp. v. Lueck*, 471 U.S. 202 (1985); *Kirton v. Summit Medical Center*,

982 F. Supp. 1381 (N.D. Cal. 1997).

169. *Kirton,* at 1385 (N.D. Cal. 1997). *See Jimeno v. Mobil Oil Corp.,* 66 F.3d 1514, 1522-1528 (9th Cir. 1995).

170. For additional information on workplace whistleblowing under OSHA *see* Chapter 7, "OSHA and Workplace Safety Whistleblowing."

171. 29 U.S.C. § 660(c).

172. *See Whirlpool Corp. v. Marshall,* 445 U.S. 1 (1980). A right to refuse hazardous work was also recognized in certain specific situations under the NLRA, *NLRB v. Washington Aluminum Co.,* 370 U.S. 9 (1962); Section 502 of the LMRA, *Gateway Coal Co. v. United Mine Workers,* 414 U.S. 368 (1974); the Federal Mine Health and Safety Act, *Miller v. Fed. Mine Safety Commission,* 687 F.2d 194 (7th Cir. 1982); Section 210 of the Energy Reorganization Act, *Pennsyl. v. Catalytic, Inc.,* 83 Energy Reorganization Act 2, Opinion of Secretary of Labor (January 13, 1984).

173. *Kennard v. Zimmer,* 632 F. Supp. 635, 637 (E.D. Penn. 1986). If a workplace safety complaint also impacts on the general public health and safety or the environment, an employee may be entitled to a private cause of action under the environmental whistleblower statutes. *See Jones v. EG&G Defense Materials, Inc.,* 95-CAA-3, D&O of ARB, pp. 10-11 (September 29, 1998).

174. *Flenker v. Willanette Industries,* 967 P.2d 295, 303 (Kan. 1998).

175. 29 C.F.R. § 1977.

176. *Reich v. Cambridgeport Air Systems,* 26 F.3d 1187 (1st Cir. 1994).

177. *Donovan v. Square D Co.,* 709 F.2d 335 (5th Cir. 1983).

178. 29 U.S.C. § 651(b).

179. *Donovan v. Square D Co., supra,* at 338.

180. *Donovan v. Diplomat Envelope Corp.,* 587 F. Supp. 1417, 1424-1425 (E.D. N.Y. 1984).

181. *Marshall v. Springville Poultry Farm, Inc.,* 445 F. Supp. 2 (M.D. Pa. 1977).

182. *Donovan v. R. D. Anderson,* 552 F.Supp 249 (D. Kan. 1982).

183. *Martin v. Anslinger, Inc.,* 794 F. Supp. 640, 646 (S.D. Tex. 1992). *See Reich v. Hoy Shoe Co.,* 32 F.3d 361 (8th Cir. 1994).

184. Some courts have used the federal OSHA law as a source of authority for a state public policy tort. *See Kilpatrick v. Delaware County Society for Prevention of Cruelty to Animals (SPCA),* 632 F. Supp. 542, 546 (E.D. Pa. 1986).

185. *Taylor v. Brighton Corp.,* 616 F.2d 256 (6th Cir. 1980); *George v. Aztec Rental Center, Inc.,* 763 F.2d 184, 186 (5th Cir. 1985).

186. *Weidler v. Big J,* 953 P.2d 1089 (N.M. App. 1997); *contra, Burnham v. Carl and Gelb, P.C.,* 745 A.2d 178 (Conn. 2000).

187. 18 U.S.C. § 1964(c).

188. *Beck v. Prupis,* 120 S.Ct. 1608 (2000), slip op. of J. Thomas at 13.

189. *Mnuz v. Caring, Inc.,* 991 F. Supp. 701 (D. N.J. 1998).

190. *Mnuz, supra,* at 715.

191. Railway Labor Act, 45 U.S.C. § 151 *et seq. See Hawaiian Airlines v. Norris,* 512 U.S. 246, 248 (1994).

192. 49 U.S.C. § 20109.

193. *Hawaiian, supra, Contra Raynor v. Smirl,* 873 F.2d 60 (4th Cir. 1989).

194. *Green v. Ralee Engine Co.,* 960 P2d 1046 (Cal. 1998).

195. 49 U.S.C. 20109.

196. *Kelley v. Norfolk and Southern Railway Co.,* 80 F. Supp.2d 587 (S.D. N.Y. 1999); *see also* H. Rep. No. 96-1025, *reprinted in* 1980 U.S. Code Cong. and Admin. News 3830.

197. *Raynor v. Smirl,* 873 F.2d 60, 64 (4th Cir. 1989).

198. *Id.* However, in *Kelley, supra,* the district court did find preemption of a "state wrongful discharge" remedy for a railroad employee who alleged he was discharged for filing an accident report.

199. 30 U.S.C. § 1293; 43 C.F.R. § 4; C.F.R. § 865.

200. *Id.*

201. 30 U.S.C. § 1293(b).

202. 43 C.F.R. § 4.1203.

203. 780 F.2d 372 (3rd Cir. 1986).

204. 49 U.S.C. § 2305. The whistleblower provision of the STAA was originally passed in 1983 and was recodified and reenacted in 1994 "expressly without substantive change." *Clean Harbors Environmental Services v. Herman,* 146 F.3d 12, 20 (1st Cir. 1998).

205. 49 U.S.C. § 2305(a). *See Somerson v. Yellow Freight Systems,* 98-STA-9, D&O of ARB (February 18, 1999) (discussing regulatory overview of STAA).

206. 49 U.S.C. § 2304(b).

207. 49 U.S.C. § 2305(b).

208. *Flor v. U.S. DOE,* 93-TSC-1, D&O of SOL, p. 6 (December 9, 1994).

209. *Yellow Freight System v. Martin,* 983 F.2d 1195, 1200 (2nd Cir. 1993).

210. *Yellow Freight System, Inc. v. Martin,* 954 F.2d 353, 357 (6th Cir. 1992).

211. *Clean Harbors Environmental Services v. Herman, supra,* at 12.

212. *Office of Workers' Compensation Programs, DOL V. Greenwich Collieries,* 512 U.S. 267, 278 (1994); *Yellow Freight System, Inc. v. Reich,* 27 F.3d 1133, 1138 (6th Cir. 1994); *Moon v. Transport Drivers, Inc.,* 836 F.2d 226, 229 (6th Cir. 1987).

213. *Brock v. Roadway Express, Inc.,* 481 U.S. 252, 255 (1987). *Accord., Yellow Freight System, Inc. v. Reich,* at 1133, 1138 (Section 405 was enacted to "encourage employee reporting of noncompliance with safety regulations governing commercial motor vehicles"). *Yellow Freight System v. Martin,* 983 F.2d 1195, 1200 (2nd Cir. 1993) (recognizing the important "public interest" served by protecting "safety on the nation's highways").

214. The offices within the DOL that adjudicate these cases (Office of Administrative Law Judges [ALJ] and Administrative Review Board [ARB]) are

the same offices that hear environmental and nuclear whistleblower cases. Consequently, the case law under the STAA and the environmental statutes are, in most instances, interchangeable.

215. 49 U.S.C. § 2304 (c)(1).

216. The time requirements set forth in the STAA are not jurisdictional but are "directory in nature." The failure of the DOL to follow these requirements is not grounds to have a case dismissed. *Roadway Express, Inc. v. Doyle*, 929 F.2d 1060, 1066 (5th Cir. 1991).

217. 49 U.S.C. § 2305 (c)(2)(A).

218. *Id.*

219. 49 U.S.C. § 2305 (c)(2)(B).

220. 49 U.S.C. § 2305 (d)(1).

221. *Castle Coal & Oil Company v. Reich*, 55 F.3d 41 (2nd Cir. 1995).

222. *BSP v. DOL*, 160 F.3d 38, 46-47 (1st Cir. 1998).

223. 107 S.Ct. 1740 (April 22, 1987).

224. *Id.* at 1745

225. *Id.* at 1745-1746.

226. *Martin v. Yellow Freight System*, 793 F. Supp. 461 (S.D. N.Y. 1992), *affirmed*, 983 F.2d 1201 (2nd Cir. 1993).

227. *Eash v. Roadway Express*, 98-STA-28, D&O of remand by ARB (October 29, 1999).

228. 46 U.S.C. § 1501 *et seq.*

229. 46 U.S.C. § 1506.

230. 46 U.S.C. § 1506(d).

231. 46 U.S.C. § 1506(c) and (d).

232. *Arnett v. Kennedy*, 416 U.S. 134, 148-149 (1974).

233. 37 Stat. 539.

234. Although the Lloyd-LaFollette Act or its contemporary codification is not directly referenced in the current Civil Service Reform Act (CSRA) and Whistleblower Protection Act, discrimination against whistleblowers for providing information to Congress is clearly incorporated into the WPA's core definition of protected activity. Specifically, the WPA defines a prohibited personnel practice as any personnel practice taken in violation of any law. 5 U.S.C. § 2302(b)(11). In this section of the CSRA (which sets forth protected conduct under the WPA), not only is the right to contact Congress under 5 U.S.C. § 7211 implicitly referenced, but Congress explicitly insured that contacts with Congress were not prohibited: "This subsection shall not be construed to authorize the withholding of information from the Congress or the taking of any personnel action against an employee who discloses information to the Congress." 5 U.S.C. § 2302(b)(11). Significantly, although other parts of the CSRA/WPA can also be interpreted as protecting contacts with Congress, the broad language used in 5 U.S.C. § 7211 allows whistleblowers to ensure protection for contacts with Congress, whereas other types of protected activity under other sections of the law have been judicially narrowed. *See e.g., Willis v. Department of Agriculture*, 141 F.3d 1139 (Fed. Cir. 1998).

235. *Bush v. Lucas*, 462 U.S. 367, 382 (1983) (discussing history of civil service laws).

236. 48 Cong. Rec. 4513 (1912) (remarks of Rep. Gregg). *See also Bush* at 383, n. 20 (collecting citations to the Congressional Record).

237. 48 Cong. Rec. 10676 (1912) (remarks of Sen. Bourne).

238. *Bush, supra*, at 384, n. 24.

239. *Arnett, supra*, at 134; and *Bush, supra*, at 367.

240. 5 U.S.C. § 2302. *See also* special provisions covering employees in the foreign service, 22 U.S.C. § 4133.

241. 5 U.S.C. § 1221. For a detailed review of the complex laws and regulations governing federal employee whistleblowing *see* Peter Broida, *A Guide to Merit Systems Board Law and Practice* (Arlington, Va.: Dewey Publications, 1997); Passman and Kaplan, *Federal Employees Legal Survival Guide* (Cincinnati, Ohio: National Employee Rights Institute, 1999); *or* Robert Vaughn, "Merit Systems Protection Board: Rights and Remedies," Law Journal Seminars Press (New York: 1984).

242. *See Marcus v. EPA*, 92-TSC-5, Decision of Secretary of Labor (February 7, 1994) (holding federal employees covered under four environmental whistleblower laws); *Conley v. McClellan Air Force Base*, 84-WPC-1, Decision of Secretary of Labor (September 7, 1993) (holding defense department employees covered under environmental whistleblower laws); 12 U.S.C. § 1831j(2) (coverage of Federal Reserve Board, FDIC, and Office of Thrift Supervision employees under banking whistleblower law); the Civil Rights Act of 1964, 42 U.S.C. § 2000e 16; the Age Discrimination in Employment Act, 29 U.S.C. § 631; the Fair Labor Standards Act, 29 U.S.C. § 206(d); the Rehabilitation Act of 1973; 29 U.S.C. § 791.

243. *See Black v. Reno*, 2000 WL 37991 (S.D. N.Y. 2000) (discussing federal court jurisdiction over mixed Title VII and other MSPB claims).

244. *See Berkman v. Coast Guard Academy*, 97-CAA-2, D&O of ARB (February 29, 2000).

245. 10 U.S.C. § 1034.

246. *Sanjour v. EPA*, 56 F.3d 85 (D.C. Cir. 1995) (*en banc*); *Weaver v. USIA*, 87 F.3d 1429 1434-1435 (D.C. Cir. 1996).

247. *Weaver* at 1429,1434-35.

248. *Bush, supra*; *see also Madden v. Runyon*, 899 F. Supp. 217, 225 (E.D. Penn. 1995).

249. The Civil Service Reform Act of 1978, 5 U.S.C. § 2302(b)(8), defines protected activity as:

(A) a disclosure of information by an employee or applicant which the employee or applicant reasonably believes evidences—
    (i)   a violation of any law, rule or regulation,
    (ii) mismanagement, a gross waste of funds, an abuse of authority, or a substantial and specific danger to public health or safety if such disclosure is not specifically prohibited by law and if such information is not specifically required by Executive order to be kept secret in the interest of national defense or the con-

duct of foreign affairs; or
(B) a disclosure to the Special Counsel of the Merit Systems Protection Board, or to the Inspector General of an agency or another employee designated by the head of the agency to receive such disclosures, or information which the employee or applicant reasonably believes evidences—
   (i) a violation of any law, rule or regulation, or
   (ii) mismanagement, a gross waste of funds, an abuse of authority, or a substantial and specific danger to public health or safety.

See also Thomas Devine, "The Whistleblower Protection Act of 1989: Foundation for the Modern Law of Employment Dissent," 51 *Administrative Law Review* 531 (1999).

    250. Significantly, section (b) of the CSRA, 5 U.S.C. § 2302, actually contains 11 specified grounds for challenging an adverse action, including section (b)(8), which is quoted, in part, above. Other parts of section (b) also cover whistleblower conduct and should also be used, were applicable. *See* 5 U.S.C. § 2302(b)(3) (coerced political activity); § 2302 (b)(9)(A) (nonretaliation for exercising rights under law); § 2302(b)(9)(B)-(C) (nonretaliation for testifying or disclosing information to an Inspector General or Special Counsel); § 2302(b)(9) (D) (protection for refusing to obey an order which would require the employee to violate law); § 2302(b)(10) (nondiscrimination regarding "conduct that does not adversely affect the performance" of duties); § 2302(b)(11) (non-discrimination if adverse action would violate another law, rule or regulation).

    251. *See Gady v. Department of the Navy*, 38 M.S.P.R. 118 (1988).

    252. *See e.g., Willis v. Department of Agriculture*, 141 F.3d 1139 (Fed. Cir. 1998) (narrow definition of protected disclosure); *LaChance v. White*, 174 F.3d 1378 (Fed. Cir. 1999) (narrow definition of "gross mismanagement").

    253. *See e.g., Horton v. Department of the Navy*, 66 F.3d 279 (Fed. Cir. 1995) (noting congressional overruling of Federal Circuit decision related to employee motivation for blowing the whistle); *Marano v. Department of Justice*, 2 F.3d 1137 (Fed. Cir. 1993) (noting congressional overruling of Federal Circuit decision concerning burden of proof).

    254. S. Rep. No. 413, 100th Cong., 2nd Sess. 12-13 (1988).

    255. *Willis, supra*, at 1143. Continuing its hypertechnical interpretation of the WPA, the Federal Circuit also held that revoking a whistleblowers security clearance was not subject to review under the WPA. *Hesse v. Department of State*, –F.3d–, 2000 WL 892712 (Fed. Cir. 2000).

    256. *LaChance, supra*, at 1381.

    257. *See Herman v. DOJ*, 193 F.3d 1375 (Fed. Cir. 1999) (WPA does not protect reports of "minor or inadvertent miscue").

    258. 5 U.S.C. § 1221(e)(1).

    259. *Veneziano v. DOE*, 189 F.3d 1363, 1368 (Fed. Cir. 1999).

    260. Congressional Record S11446 (September 24, 1999).

    261. 5 U.S.C. § 1221(a) and (b); 5 C.F.R. § 1209.

    262. 5 U.S.C. § 2302(b)(1)-(11).

263. 5 U.S.C. § 2302(a)(2). A "personnel action" means "a decision concerning pay, benefits or awards" and "[a]ny other significant change in duties, responsibilities, or working conditions." 5 U.S.C. § 2302(a)(2)(A); 5 C.F.R. § 1209.4(a).

264. *See Escandon v. Dept. of Veterans Affairs*, 1999 WL 1211863 (Fed. Cir. 1999); *Ward v. MSPB*, 981 F.2d 521 (Fed. Cir. 1992); *Engler v. Department of the Navy*, 69 M.S.P.R. 109, 113 (1995); *White v. Department of the Air Force*, 63 M.S.P.R. 90, 94 (1994); *Geyer v. Department of Justice*, 63 M.S.P.R. 13, 16-17 (1994).

265. *Willis, surpa,* at 1142.

266. 5 U.S.C. § 1221(e).

267. *See Costin v. DHHS*, 72 MSPR 525, 539 (1996) (in IRA whistleblower cases the "fact there is no 'smoking gun' direct evidence of a retaliatory motive is not dispositive"); *Marano v. Dept. of Justice*, 2 F.3d 1137 (Fed. Cir. 1993) ("any" weight given to a protected disclosure, either alone or in combination with other factors, will satisfy the contributing factor test).

268. *See* 5 U.S.C. § 1221(e)(1). The WPA was amended in 1994 to specifically provide that:

The employee may demonstrate that the disclosure was a contributing factor in the personnel action through circumstantial evidence, such as evidence that—
(A) the official taking the personnel action knew of the disclosure; and
(B) the personnel action occurred within a period of time that a reasonable person could conclude that the disclosure was a contributing factor in the personnel action.

269. 153 F.3d 1357 (Fed. Cir. 1998).

270. *But see Veneziano, supra,* at 1368 (Fed. Cir. 1999).

271. *McDaid v. DHUDD*, 46 MSPR 416, 420-424 (1990); *Frazier v. MSPB*, 672 F.2d 150, 166-168 (D.C. Cir. 1982); *Mausser v. Dept. of Army*, 63 M.S.P.R. 41 (1994); *Sirgo v. Dept. of Justice*, 66 M.S.P.R. 261, 265-266 (1995).

272. *See e.g., Edwards v. U.S. Postal Service*, 909 F.2d 320, 324 (8th Cir. 1990); *Thurman v. Yellow Freight Systems, Inc.*, 90 F.3d 1160, 1167 (6th Cir. 1996); *Bechtel Construction Co. v. Secretary of Labor*, 50 F.3d 926, 935 (1995).

273. 5 U.S.C. § 1221(e)(2); *Grant v. Dept. of Air Force*, 61 MSPR 370, 376 (1994).

274. For an excellent summary of the factors relevant to weighing whether an agency can meet its burden under the "clear and convincing" standard, *see Williams-Moore v. Dept. of Veterans Affairs* (Fed. Cir. 2000) (table) (unpublished); *Carr v. Social Security Admin.*, 185 F.3d 1318, 1323 (Fed. Cir. 1999).

275. *Marano, supra,* at 1142.

276. 5 U.S.C. § 1221(g).

277. *Bouggat v. Dept. of the Navy*, 56 M.S.P.R. 402, 413 (1993).

278. *See e.g., In the Matter of Frazier*, 1 M.S.P.R. 280, 282 n. 4 (1979).

279. *See* Broida, *supra, A Guide to Merit Systems Board Law and Practice.*

280. *Bosley v. MSPB*, 162 F.3d 665 (Fed. Cir. 1998). *See* 5 U.S.C. § 7703(b) (1) ("a petition to review a final order or final decision of the [MSPB] shall be filed in the United States Court of Appeals for the Federal Circuit"). However, where a case raises a nonfrivolous allegation of discrimination based on both civil rights type claims and an appeal of a whistleblower case, an employee may appeal an MSPB decision to a federal district court. 5 U.S.C. § 7703(b)(2). *See Mack v. U.S. Postal Service*, 1998 WL 546624 (E.D. N.Y. 1998).

281. 5 C.F.R. § 1201.73(d) ("Parties who wish to make discovery requests or motions must serve their initial requests or motions within 25 days after the date on which the judge issues an order to the respondent agency to produce the agency file and response").

282. Editorial, "Helping Whistle-Blowers Survive," *New York Times* (May 1, 1999).

Chapter 4

Whistleblower Protection under the First Amendment and the Civil Rights Act of 1871

The First Amendment to the U.S. Constitution protects the speech of federal, state, and local government-employee whistleblowers.[1] The amendment allows federal employees to seek prospective injunctive relief against policies or conduct that violates the First Amendment rights of federal employees.[2] The First Amendment, as applied through the Fourteenth Amendment[3] and the Civil Rights Act of 1871,[4] allows employees of state and local governments[5] to obtain injunctive[6] and monetary relief if they are discriminated against on the basis of First-Amendment-protected whistleblowing.[7] First Amendment protections also apply to *at-will* government contractors[8] and non-civil service and non tenured government employees.[9]

In 1968 the Supreme Court held that the First Amendment protects government employees who engage in speech on matters of public concern.[10] The First Amendment protects employees who blow the whistle either publicly or privately to their supervisors.[11] Whether any specific speech or disclosure of wrongdoing is protected under the First Amendment depends upon a case-by-case analysis under the rule pronounced in *Pickering v. Board of Education*: "absent proof of false statements knowingly or recklessly made . . . [the] exercise of his right to speak on issues of public importance may not furnish the basis for his dismissal from public employment."[12]

In order for a public employee's speech to be protected, it must pass a two-prong test. First, a court must determine whether the speech can be "fairly characterized as constituting speech on a matter of public concern" and not just a matter of "personal interest."[13] Second, the court must balance "the interest of the [employee] as a citizen, in commenting upon matters of public concern and the interests of the state, as an employer, in promoting the efficiency of the public service it performs through its employees."[14]

Beginning with *Pickering*, courts have recognized that the speech of government employees must be protected, even if it includes direct criticisms of their employing agencies.[15] Courts have frequently recognized that "an employee's First Amendment interest is entitled to more weight where he is acting as a whistleblower exposing government corruption."[16] As the Supreme Court noted, government employee speech on matters of public concern often occupies the "highest rung" in the "hierarchy of First Amendment values" and is "entitled to special protection."[17]

Even if the employee's speech was subject to constitutional protection, the employee still must state a claim sufficient to meet the *Mt. Healthy* test.[18] Under *Mt. Healthy* an employee has the initial burden to demonstrate that the protected speech or conduct was a "motivating factor" in the adverse employment decision. Once this is demonstrated, the burden shifts to the employer to demonstrate, "by a preponderance of the evidence," that it "would have" taken the same action absent the employee's protected conduct. The *Mt. Healthy* test has been applied to analyzing the legality of employer actions under other wrongful discharge statutes.[19]

In *Walters v. Churchill*, the Supreme Court recognized that a public employer may need to "make a substantial showing" that employee-speech is "disruptive," especially in the context of whistleblowing: "Government employees are often in the best position to know what ails the agencies for which they work; public debate may gain much from their informed opinions. . . . [a] government employee, like any citizen, may have a strong, legitimate interest in speaking out on public matters."[20]

Because government whistleblowing arises in the context of the employee-employer relationship, the government has "broader powers" to control this speech than in other First Amendment contexts.[21] This rule was summarized by the Court in *U.S. v. National Treasury Employees Union*:

Congress may impose restraints on the job-related speech of public employees that would be plainly unconstitutional if applied to the public at large. When a court is required to determine the validity of such a restraint, it must arrive at a balance between the interests of the [employee], as a citizen, in commenting upon matters of public concern and the interest of the State, as an employer.[22]

Even with these additional powers, the government still "bears the burden of justifying" "adverse employment action" in cases involving speech on matters of "public concern."[23] Likewise, the Supreme Court has rejected government attempts to require whistleblowers to prove their case-in-chief by clear and convincing evidence,[24] and has similarly rejected any requirement that initial complaints be subjected to a "heightened pleading standard."[25]

In adjudication of a free speech retaliatory discharge case, courts have applied a basic four-part test:

First, the court must determine whether plaintiff's speech involved a matter of public concern. Second, the court must balance the interests of plaintiff in making the statement against defendants' interests in the effective and efficient fulfillment of their responsibilities to the public. Third, if the balance tips in favor of plaintiff, then he must show that the protected speech was a "motivating factor" in the decision. Finally, if plaintiff makes this showing, then the burden shifts to defendants to show by a preponderance of evidence that they would have reached the same decision in the absence of the protected activity.[26]

The scope of protected activities under the First Amendment is broad. It ranges from raising a concern with a supervisor[27] to filing allegations directly with the news media.[28] But to be protected, the speech must be on matters of "public concern." Speech related only to private employment matters is not protected.[29] For example, it is now a matter of "settled" law that a "public employee's expression of grievances concerning his own employment is not a matter of public concern."[30] The issue of whether any particular speech is on a "matter of public concern" is a question of law that is decided by the court.[31]

Courts regularly find whistleblower-type speech fully protected. For example, complaints about conflicts of interest within municipal government, "disclosures" regarding an "alleged abuse of public office" by an elected official, complaints about wasted resources and violations of safety regulations, and exposures of violations of municipal ordinances have all been protected.[32]

FEDERAL EMPLOYEE PROTECTION AND INJUNCTIVE RELIEF

Although protected under the First Amendment, federal employee whistleblowers who suffer adverse personnel actions may not file a First Amendment claim in federal court for monetary damages. In *Bush v. Lucas*[33] the Supreme Court unanimously ruled that federal employees cannot maintain an implied cause of action under the First Amendment for damages but instead must utilize the statutory remedy created by Congress for their protection. Unless Congress has provided an alternative statutory remedy, federal employees are required to seek monetary compensation for illegal discrimination through the Civil Service Reform Act/Whistleblower Protection Act.[34]

Despite this bar on claims demanding monetary relief, federal employees are permitted to seek preenforcement injunctive relief directly in federal court in order to prevent the violation of First Amendment rights,[35] including the right to blow the whistle on his or her federal employer.[36] Laws or regulations that directly or indirectly restrict public employee speech may be challenged by employees whose speech is "chilled"[37] or impeded.[38] To have "standing" to seek prospective injunctive relief, an employee must demonstrate that the feared harms are "actual or imminent, not conjectural or hypothetical."[39]

In such cases there is no need to exhaust administrative procedures in order to "attack" the constitutionality of the "regulation restricting employee speech."[40] Significantly, the government's burden of proof in justifying laws, procedures, or rules which restrict First Amendment speech are much higher than the burden it bears in justifying individual disciplinary action:

unlike an adverse action taken in response to actual speech, this ban chills potential speech before it happens. . . . For these reasons, the Government's burden is greater with respect to this statutory restriction on expression than with respect to an isolated disciplinary action. The Government must show that the interests of both potential audiences and a vast group of present and future employees in a broad range of present and future expression are outweighed by that expression's necessary impact on the actual operation of the Government.[41]

In order to meet this burden the government must show that the harms they seek to prevent are "real" and "not merely conjectural."[42] Simply stated, a preenforcement burden on speech required a "justification far stronger than mere speculation about serious harms."[43]

FIRST AMENDMENT PROTECTIONS FOR EMPLOYEES OF STATE AND LOCAL GOVERNMENTS UNDER 42 U.S.C. § 1983

Employee whistleblowers of state and local governments enjoy protection under Section 1 of the Civil Rights Act of 1871,[44] 42 U.S.C. § 1983. This law, which prohibits the violation of constitutional rights under "color of law,"[45] provides for a tort-styled remedy for wrongfully discharged whistleblowers. Specifically, § 1983 created a "species of tort liability,"[46] allowing a person to be "compensated fairly for injuries caused by the violation of his legal rights."[47]

Under § 1983, government employees alleging adverse action in retaliation for protected speech are entitled to a jury trial,[48] the full array of tort damages (including compensatory and punitive damages),[49] and attorney fees.[50] They are also entitled to injunctive relief,[51] including the same type of broad preenforcement injunction relief available to federal employees.[52]

Section 1983 does not require a plaintiff to exhaust administrative remedies.[53] However, most states have implemented statutory protections for public-employee whistleblowers.[54] Many of these state laws have explicitly waived sovereign immunity and allow whistleblowers to sue directly the state or municipal entities for which they worked, without having to litigate Eleventh Amendment or sovereign immunity issues. Also, given the strength of some of the state remedies, it is not uncommon for plaintiffs to rely upon both § 1983 and the applicable state whistleblower protection statute when filing a suit.[55]

One of the biggest roadblocks to monetary damage awards under § 1983 centers on the issue of immunity.[56] Under the Eleventh Amendment, a citizen cannot sue a state in federal court for monetary damages[57] without the consent of the state.[58] Consequently, § 1983 suits focus on identifying and naming individual wrongdoers, suing these persons in their personal capacity[59] and demonstrating that the conduct of these persons should not be immunized. Municipalities and government corporations may be subject to liability under § 1983,[60] but the federal courts apply state law in determining whether such liability may be established and do not apply principles of *respondent superior* in establishing municipal liability.[61]

Once an individual wrongdoer is named in a suit, that wrongdoer usually will allege an "affirmative defense" of "qualified immunity." This defense may constitute a complete bar to an action, and a trial court's denying a qualified immunity defense is subject to immediate appeal.[62] Discovery is usually stayed until the qualified immunity issue is resolved. In order to overcome a qualified immunity defense, an employee must demonstrate that the conduct at issue violated "clearly established statutory or constitutional rights" and that a "reasonable person" in the position of the alleged wrongdoer "would have known" of this violation. As the Supreme Court stated in its seminal case on qualified immunity:

bare allegations of malice should not suffice to subject government officials either to the costs of trial or the burdens of broad-reaching discovery. We therefore hold that government officials performing discretionary functions generally are shielded from liability for civil damages insofar as their conduct does not violate clearly established statutory or constitutional rights of which a reasonable person would have known.[63]

In most instances employees alleging violations of § 1983 on the basis of whistleblower-related speech should be able to overcome the qualified immunity standard. The "general rule" that the "First Amendment bars retaliation for protected speech" by a whistleblower has been "clearly established."[64] Although questions may arise as to whether any "reasonable" state official would have known that the subject matter of the whistleblowing implicated "matters of public concern,"[65] qualified immunity defenses have been regularly rejected in the context relevant to whistleblower speech:

[R]easonably competent public official[s] . . . would have understood that the First Amendment protection of public employee expression . . . not only protects public employees who engage in protected First Amendment expression from being discharged for such expression, but also protects such employees from being subjected to conduct of harassment in retaliation for such expression.[66]

Retaliatory discharge claims under § 1983 are adjudicated under the principles set forth in *Pickering, Mt. Healthy,* and their progeny.[67] The definition of adverse action is broad.[68] Retaliation claims may be cognizable under the First Amendment even when the conduct does "not deprive a claimant of 'liberty or property interests.' "[69] There is no federal statute of limitations for § 1983 suits, and federal courts generally apply the state's limitations period applicable to personal injury cases.[70]

THE CIVIL RIGHTS ACT OF 1871: CONSPIRACIES TO INTIMIDATE WITNESSES AND OBSTRUCT JUSTICE IN FEDERAL COURT PROCEEDINGS (42 U.S.C. 1985[2])

Section 2 of the Civil Rights Act of 1871 (CRA) protects a wide variety of whistleblower activities in the *private sector.*[71] Unlike Section 1 of the CRA,[72] which only concerns misconduct "under color of law," Section 2 of the CRA prohibits "private conspiracies."[73] Section 2, passed during the Reconstruction era,[74] contains very broad provisions prohibiting conspiracies[75] to intimidate parties or witnesses in proceedings before courts of the United States:

If two or more persons in any State or Territory conspire to deter, by force, intimidation, or threat, any party or witness in any court of the United States from attending such court, or from testifying for any matter pending therein, freely, fully, and truthfully, or to injure such party or witness in his person or property on account of his having so attended or testified . . . the party so injured or deprived may have an action for the recovery of damages.[76]

Section 2 applies to any conspiracies to interfere with the administration of justice in the United States courts.[77] The intent of Section 2 was to restore civil authority and, according to one of its initial sponsors, allow "good men" to help prevent "the evils they see."[78] The requirement of "racial or class based" invidious discrimination, which the U.S. Supreme Court held was necessary to have a cause of action under other clauses or sections of the CRA,[79] is not applicable to suits regarding retaliation against witnesses or parties in federal court proceedings.[80] The U.S. Supreme Court, in *Kush v. Rutledge* held:

Given the structure of §2 of the 1871 Act, it is clear that Congress did not intend to impose a requirement of class-based animus on persons seeking to prove a violation of their rights under the first clause of §1985 (2). The legislative history supports the conclusion we have drawn from the language of the statute. Protection of the processes of the federal courts was an essential component of Congress' solution to disorder and anarchy in the Southern States. Neither proponents nor opponents of the bill had any doubt that the Constitution gave Congress the power to prohibit intimidation of parties, witnesses, and jurors in federal courts.[81]

In *Haddle v. Garrison*,[82] the Supreme Court upheld a cause of action against private parties who had "conspired" to have an *at-will* employee whistleblower fired, after he obeyed a federal grand jury subpoena. The *Haddle* court upheld the cause of action, despite the fact that the employee never actually testified in the federal court proceeding (he had been subpoenaed and was expected to testify). The court upheld two separate causes of action, one for the conspiracy to "deter him from testifying" and the second, for the conspiracy to retaliate against him after he attended a grand jury proceeding.

The Court also held that a plaintiff under a CRA Section 2 claim need not "suffer an injury to a constitutionally protected property interest" in order to state a claim for relief.[83] The court recognized that Section 2 of the CRA would cover "third-party interference with at-will employment relationships" and any other potential tort that would constitute a common law tort.[84]

Unlike other Reconstruction-era civil rights laws (i.e., 42 U.S.C. 1983), Clause 2 of 1985 does not require any state action. Purely private conspiracies are actionable.[85] However, the courts of appeal are split on the nature of an actionable conspiracy.[86] Some courts apply an antitrust definition of conspiracy, which holds that employees of a single corporation cannot "conspire" among themselves.[87] Others reject this doctrine, known as the *intracorporate conspiracy* doctrine, as "fiction without a purpose" in the context of civil rights enforcement actions.[88] Federal circuit courts that apply the *intracorporate conspiracy* doctrine have "recognized an exception" to that rule when an officer or agent of a company has an "independent personal stake in achieving the corporation's illegal objective."[89]

On March 2, 2000 the U.S. Court of Appeals for the 11th Circuit ruled unanimously, *en banc*, in *McAndrew v. Lockheed Martin Corp.*, that civil conspiracies under 42 U.S.C. § 1985 (2) were not subject the limitations of the *intracorporate conspiracy* doctrine.[90] The court drew an important distinction between conspiracies that are purely civil in nature and those that implicate criminal misconduct. The court noted that intimidating a witness from testifying in a federal court proceeding constituted criminal activity and held that the *intracorporate conspiracy* doctrine was not applicable under such circumstances:

A claim arising under § 1985(2), such as McAndrew's, alleging a conspiracy to deter by force, intimidation, or threat, an individual from testifying in a federal court, necessarily alleges criminal activity in violation of 18 U.S.C. § 1512—the criminal statute prohibiting tampering with a witness—and a criminal conspiracy in violation 18 U.S.C. § 371.

*   *   *

As we have explained, the corporate entity fiction was designed to expand corporate liability by holding the corporation liable for the acts of its agents. The intracorporate conspiracy doctrine shielding corporate employees and the corporation itself from unlawful conspiracy claims was a product of this fiction. However, the fiction was never intended nor used to shield conspiratorial conduct that was criminal in nature.

*   *   *

Moreover, application of the criminal conspiracy exception to a § 1985(2) claim is altogether consonant with the original purpose of that statute. Section 1985 derives from Section 2 of the Ku Klux Klan Act of 1871 also known as the Civil Rights Act of 1871. The Act was passed in response to a rising tide of Klan terrorism against blacks and Union sympathizers and was designed to proscribe conspiracies "having the object or effect of frustrating the constitutional operations of government through assaults on the person, property, and liberties of individuals."

*   *   *

The criminal conspiracy exception to the intracorporate conspiracy doctrine promotes the original purpose of the Act by ensuring that individuals and groups can be prosecuted for their criminal activities regardless of their status of incorporation. The exception ensures that conspiratorial criminal conduct is not shielded from civil liability under § 1985(2) of the Civil Rights Act simply by the expedient of incorporation.[91]

The 11th Circuit's holding in *McAndrew*, if followed by other courts, would prevent the *intracorporate conspiracy* doctrine from defeating otherwise valid whistleblower claims filed under Section 2 of the CRA.

A 42 U.S.C. § 1985 (2) suit is not a wrongful discharge action—the tortious conduct is not the termination, per se, but the conspiracy to intimidate.[92] The requirements necessary to prove a civil conspiracy were outlined in *Hampton v. Hanrahan*:

A civil conspiracy is a combination of two or more persons acting in concert to commit an unlawful act, or to commit a lawful act by unlawful means, the principal element of which is an agreement between the parties to inflict a wrong against or injury upon another, and an overt act that results in damage.

*   *   *

An express agreement among all the conspirators is not a necessary element of a civil conspiracy. The participants in the conspiracy must share the general conspiratorial objective, but they need not know all the details of the plan designed to achieve the objective or possess the same motives for desiring the intended conspiratorial result. To demonstrate the existence of a conspiratorial agreement, it simply must be shown that there was a single plan, the essential nature and general scope of which [was] known to each person who is to be held responsible for its consequences. [93]

Moreover, courts recognize that "conspiracies" are by "their nature usually clandestine" and need not be proven by "direct evidence of a conspiratorial agreement."[94] There is also no heightened pleading standard when setting forth facts necessary to plead a valid complaint.[95]

The tortious conduct includes the conspiracy to intimidate the witness—whether the witness is ever fired is only relevant to prove intimidation or injury. It is the conspiracy, not the discharge, per se, that is the actionable conduct. As the U.S. Supreme Court noted in *Haddle*, "The gist of the wrong at which § 1985 (2) is directed is not deprivation of property, but intimidation or retaliation against witnesses in federal court proceedings."[96] Consequently, the *prima facie* case for a § 1985 (2) action is different from that of a traditional wrongful discharge case.

The U.S. Courts of Appeals have articulated the following *prima facie* case for a § 1985 (2) "deterrence" action: "The essential allegations of a 1985(2) claim of witness intimidation are (1) a conspiracy between two or more persons (2) to deter a witness by force, intimidation or threat from attending court or testifying freely in any pending manner, which (3) results in injury to the plaintiffs."[97]

An identical framework is used by the courts in evaluating § 1985 (2) "retaliation" claims, except that the focus of the conspiracy is not to "deter" a witness from testifying but to "retaliate" against a witness after he or she has testified.[98]

In *Irizarry v. Quiros*,[99] the U.S. Court of Appeals for the First Circuit held that the denial of reemployment (blacklisting) constituted both intimidation and an "injury" sufficient to state a claim under Section 2 of the CRA. The court went on to hold that an action based upon an illegal conspiracy to blacklist was not preempted under labor law and that plaintiffs were entitled to both statutory attorney fees under 42 U.S.C. § 1988 and punitive damages.[100]

Protection for Whistleblowers under the Uncodified Provisions of the Civil Rights Act of 1871

The Civil Rights Act of 1871, as originally enacted into law on April 20, 1871, was a long and complex statute, containing seven separate sections and covering a wide variety of conduct.[101] Most of the protections contained in the original CRA have been codified in the official United States Code, which most attorneys utilize as their primary source in identifying federal laws.

Given the complex nature of the CRA, a phrase critical for the protection of whistleblowers was accidently overlooked when the original text of the law was codified.[102] This phrase expands the prohibition against civil rights conspiracies not only to persons who are witnesses or parties in federal court proceedings (i.e., those persons covered under 42 U.S.C. § 1985 [2]), but also to persons who have engaged in what today is often referred to as whistleblower-type conduct. The original text of the statute prohibited private conspiracies "to prevent, hinder, or delay the execution of any law of the United States."[103]

Read in the context of the full text of the CRA, the uncodified clause should be integrated into the statute as follows[104]:

That if two or more persons . . . shall conspire together to . . . by force, intimidation, or threat to prevent, hinder or delay the execution of any law of the United States . . . each and every person so offending shall be deemed guilty of a high crime. . . . And if any one or more persons engaged in any such conspiracy shall do, or cause to be done, any act in furtherance of the object of such conspiracy, whereby any person shall be injured in his person or property, or deprived of having and exercising any right or privilege of a citizen of the United States, the person so injured or deprived of such rights and privileges may have and maintain an action for the recovery of damages occasioned by such injury or deprivation of rights and privileges against any one or more of the persons engaged in such conspiracy.[105]

Whistleblowers often contact federal administrative or law enforcement agencies in order to assist in the execution of U.S. laws, such as environmental protection laws, civil rights laws, and anticrime laws. Conspiracies to "prevent, hinder or delay" should be fully protected under the uncodified clause of the CRA.

During the debates on the CRA of 1871, Senator Oliver P. Morton of Indiana explicitly identified that the law would protect conduct that is now referred to as whistleblowing:

The best remedy for these evils is their full and complete exposure, that they may be known, understood, and execrated by all men, so that a public opinion may be created which shall have power for their ultimate suppression. To remain silent from any cause is to approve of these crimes, is to encourage their continuance, is to give their perpetrators security and impunity.[106]

Because this clause was never codified, no court has ever ruled on its scope or application. However, the Supreme Court recognized in *Kush v. Rutledge*, a leading decision interpreting the meaning of Section 2 of the CRA of 1871, that "when Congress passed legislation in 1874 to consolidate and collect all federal statutes . . . it expressed no intention to change the meaning of the laws."[107] The Court in *Kush* also recognized Congress' intent in passing the first clauses of Section 2 of the CRA was to combat "disorder and anarchy" by protecting the "process of the federal courts."[108] Congress intended to combat "disorder" by prohibiting conspiracies to "prevent, hinder, or delay" the "execution" of federal laws.[109]

NOTES

1. *Pickering v. Board of Education*, 391 U.S. 563 (1968); *U.S. v. National Treasury Employees Union*, 513 U.S. 454 (1995). *Also see* Chapter 11, Endnote 53 regarding Fourteenth Amendment protections.

2. *See Weaver v. USIA*, 87 F.3d 1429, 1433-1435 (D.C. Cir. 1996) (discussing circumstances in which federal employees may avoid the requirement to exhaust administrative remedies and seek injunctive relief directly in federal court); *Sanjour v. Environmental Protection Agency*, 56 F.3d 85 (D.C. Cir. 1995) (*en banc*) (granting nationwide injunctive relief on behalf of federal employee whistleblowers).

3. It is well settled that the First Amendment free speech protections apply to state and local governments through the Due Process Clause of the Fourteenth Amendment. *Colson v. Grohman*, 174 F.3d 498, 506 (5th Cir. 1999), *citing De Jonge v. Oregon*, 299 U.S. 353, 364 (1937).

4. Civil Rights Act of 1871, partially codified as 42 U.S.C. §§ 1983, 1985 and 1986. Attorney fees are available under these laws pursuant to 42 U.S.C. § 1988.

5. Private sector employers may be subject to First Amendment requirements under the "public function" test, the "symbiotic relationship" test, or the "close nexus" test. *See Hennessy v. Santiago*, 708 A.2d 1269, 1276 (Pa. Super. 1998) (collecting and evaluating cases). *See also Tierhan v. Charleston Area Medical Center*, 506 S.E.2d 578 (W.Va. 1998) (collecting cases and rejecting private sector employee's attempt to use the state's free speech constitutional protections as basis for a "public policy exception" wrongful discharge tort).

6. *Housing Works, Inc. v. City of New York*, 1999 WL 1034752 (S.D. N.Y. 1999) (standards for obtaining preliminary injunction to protect whistleblower in a § 1983 action) (granting motion and rejecting request to abstain). *See also Bery v. City of New York*, 97 F.3d 689, 691 (2nd Cir. 1996).

7. *Mt. Healthy City Board of Education v. Doyle*, 429 U.S. 274 (1977).

8. *Board of County Commissioners v. Umbehr*, 518 U.S. 668 (1996).

9. *Perry v. Sindermann*, 408 U.S. 593 (1972) (nontenured public servant); *Rutan v. Republican Party of Illinois*, 497 U.S. 62 (1990) (patronage political appointee).

10. *Pickering, supra.*

11. *Givhan v. Western Line Consolidated School District*, 439 U.S. 410 (1979).

12. *Pickering* at 574.

13. *Connick v. Myers*, 461 U.S. 138, 147 (1983); *Rankin v. McPherson*, 483 U.S. 378; 107 S. Ct. 2891 (1987) (slip op. at 6). In *Connick* the court articulated the prong as follows:

We hold that when a public employee speaks not as a citizen upon matters of public concern, but instead as an employee upon matter of personal interest, absent the most unusual circumstances, a federal court is not the appropriate forum in which to review the wisdom of a personnel decision taken by a public agency allegedly in reaction to the employee's behavior. Cf. *Bishop v. Wood, supra,* at 349-350. Our responsibility is to ensure that citizens are not deprived of fundamental rights by virtue of working for the government: this does not require a grant of immunity for employee grievances not afforded by the First Amendment to those who do not work for the State. Whether an employee's speech addresses a matter of public concern must be determined by the content, form, and context of a given statement, as revealed by the whole record. (*Connick* at 147-148).

The First Amendment also prohibits some discharges based solely on political beliefs. *Branti v. Finkel,* 445 U.S. 507 (1980).

14. *Pickering, supra; Rankin, supra,* at 395 (slip op. at 9); *Cox v. Dardanelle Public School Dist.,* 790 F.2d 668, 672 (8th Cir. 1986). *Cox* outlines the *prima facie* case for a First Amendment action.

15. *Pickering, supra* ("Statements by public officials on matters of public concern must be accorded First Amendment protection despite the fact that the statements are directed at their nominal superiors").

16. *Brockell v. Norton,* 688 F.2d 588, 593 (8th Cir. 1982); *Brockell v. Norton* (2nd Appeal), 732 F.2d 664, 668 (8th Cir. 1984). *See also Orange v. District of Columbia,* 59 F.3d 1267, 1272-1273 (D.C. Cir. 1995) ("As several of our sister circuits have recognized, employees who expose government fraud or corruption engage in First Amendment protected activities") (collecting cases).

17. *Connick, supra,* at 145 (internal quotation marks omitted). In *Goodman v. City of Kansas City,* 906 F. Supp. 537 (W.D. Missouri, 1995), the court summarized the large amount of materials that support this holding: "Numerous courts and commentators have observed that this interest is great because government employees are in a position to offer the public important insights both into the workings of government generally and into their areas of specialization." *Sanjour, supra,* at 91; *see e.g., Pieczynski v. Duffy,* 875 F. 2d 1331 (7th Cir. 1989) ("[P]ublic employees have valuable insights and information about the operation of the government to convey").

18. *Mt. Healthy, supra,* at 287.

19. *See NLRB v. Transportation Management Corp.,* 462 U.S. 393 (1983); *Mackowiak v. University Nuclear Systems,* 735 F.2d 1159, 1163-1164 (9th Cir. 1984).

20. *Walters v. Churchill,* 511 U.S. 611, 674 (1994) (plurality opinion of Justice O'Connor).

21. *Id.* at 671 (plurality opinion of Justice O'Connor).

22. *U.S. v. National Treasury Employees Union, supra,* at 465-466 (citations and internal quotation marks omitted).

23. *Id.* at 466.

24. *Crawford-El v. Britton,* 523 U.S. 574 (1998) ("Neither the text of § 1983 or any other federal statute . . . provides any support for imposing the clear and convincing burden of proof on plaintiffs either at the summary judgment stage or in the trial itself").

25. *Leatherman v. Tarrant County,* 507 U.S. 163 (1993).

26. *Merkel v. Leavenworth County Emergency Medical Services*, 2000 WL 127266 (D. Kan. 2000), *citing Bisbee v. Bey*, 39 F.3d 1096, 1100 (10th Cir. 1994) and *Butler v. City of Prairie Village*, 172 F.3d 736, 745-746 (10th Cir. 1999).

27. *Givhan v. Western Line Consolidated School District*, 439 U.S. 410 (1979).

28. *Pickering, supra.*

29. *Connick, supra,* at 146.

30. *Huang v. Board of Governors*, 902 F.2d 1134, 1140 (4th Cir. 1990).

31. *Id.*

32. *Parks v. City of Brewer*, 56 F. Supp.2d 89, 98-99 (D. Maine 1999) (collecting cases). *See also Board of County Commissioners, supra,* 674-675 (collecting cases defining scope of "public concern").

33. 462 U.S. 367 (1983).

34. *U.S. v. Fausto*, 484 U.S. 439 (1988); *Steadman v. Governor, United States Soldiers' & Airmen's Home*, 918 F.2d 963, 967 (D.C. Cir. 1990); *Suzal v. Director, USIA*, 32 F.3d 574, 578-582 (D.C. Cir. 1994).

35. *U.S. v. National Treasury Employees Union*, 513 U.S. 454 (1995).

36. *Sanjour, supra (en banc).*

37. *U.S. v. National Treasury Employees Union*, 513 U.S. 454, 468 (1995) (noting the ban at issue "chills potential speech before it happens").

38. *Id.* at 467. *See also Van Ee v. EPA*, 202 F.3d 296 (D.C. Cir. 2000).

39. *Lujan v. Defenders of Wildlife*, 504 U.S. 555, 560 (1992). *See Latino Officers Association v. Safir*, 170 F.3d 167, 1999 WL 111498 (2nd Cir. 1999) (collecting cases and setting forth standard for "standing" under a First Amendment injunction analysis).

40. *Weaver, supra,* at 1434.

41. *U.S. v. National Treasury Employees Union, supra* (internal quotations omitted).

42. *Id.* at 475, *quoting Turner Broadcasting System v. FCC*, 512 U.S. 662, 664 (1994).

43. *Id.*

44. 42 U.S.C. 1983. *See also* 42 § 1986 which holds a person liable under the CRA for failing to "assist" or "protect" victims of §§ 1983 and 1984 violations.

45. 42 U.S.C. 1983 reads in part, "Every person who, under color of any statute . . . subjects or causes to be subjected, any citizen . . . to the deprivation of any rights, privileges or immunities secured by the constitution under laws, shall be liable to the party injured in an action at law, suit in equity, or other proper proceeding for redress."

46. *See City of Monterey v. Del Monte Dunes*, 526 U.S. 687, 119 S.Ct. 1624, 1638 (1999) ("there can be no doubt that claims brought pursuant to § 1983 sound in tort"). *See also* concurring opinion of Justice Scalia, 119 S.Ct. 1647-48 (collecting cases).

47. *Heck v. Humphrey*, 512 U.S. 477, 483 (1994). *See also Carey v. Piphus*, 435 U.S. 247, 257-58 (1978).

48. *City of Monterey, supra* at 1638. In a concurring opinion, Justice Scalia summarized the respective role of judge and jury in § 1983 retaliatory discharge cases: "[I]n cases alleging retaliatory discharge of a public employee in violation of the First Amendment, judges determine whether the speech that motivated the termination was constitutionally protected speech, while juries find whether the discharge was caused by that speech" (119 S.Ct. at 1649).

49. *Carey, supra,* at 257-58.

50. 42 U.S.C. § 1988.

51. *See American Postal Workers Union v. U.S. Postal Service*, 595 F. Supp. 403 (D. Conn. 1984); *Fujiwara v. Clark*, 703 F.2d 357 (9th Cir. 1983).

52. *Harman v. City of New York*, 140 F.3d 111 (2nd Cir. 1998); *Castle v. Colonial School District*, 933 F. Supp. 458 (E.D. Penn. 1996); *Will v. Michigan Department of State Police*, 491 U.S. 58, 71 n. 10 (1989); *Board of County Comm'rs. v. Brown*, 520 U.S. 397, 403-404 (1997) (municipality may be liable if "policy" or "custom" caused plaintiff's injury).

53. *Heck, supra,* at 483, *citing Patsy v. Board of Regents*, 457 U.S. 496, 501 (1982).

54. *See e.g.,* Alaska (Alaska Stat. S. 39.90.100); Arizona (A.R.S. S. 38-532); California (Cal. Gov. Code S. 12653); Colorado (C.R.S. 24-50.5-103); Connecticut (1999 Ct. ALS 46); District of Columbia (D.C. Code S. 1-616.12); Georgia (O.C.G.A. S. 45-1-4); Hawaii (HRS S. 378-61); Illinois (820 ILCS 130/11b); Indiana (Burns Ind. Code Ann. S. 22-8-1.1-38.1); Kansas (K.S.A. S. 75-2973); Louisiana (La. R.S. 46:440.3); Maine (26 M.R.S. S. 831); Maryland (Md. State Personnel and Pensions Code Ann. S. 5-301); Massachusetts (Mass. Ann. Laws ch. 149, S. 185); Michigan (MCL S. 324.6532); New Hampshire (RSA 275-E:2); New Mexico (N.M. Stat. Ann. S. 50-9-25); New York (N.Y. C.L.S. Labor S. 740); North Carolina (N.C. Gen. Stat. S. 126-85); Ohio (O.R.C. Ann. 4113.52); Pennsylvania (43 P.S. S.1423); Rhode Island (R.I. Gen. Laws S. 28-50-4); South Carolina (S.C. Code Ann. S. 8-27-30); Texas (Tex. Gov't. Code S. 554.010); Tennessee (Tenn. Code Ann. S. 50-6-108); Virgin Islands (10 V.I.C. S. 123); Washington (Rev. Code Wash. [A.R.C.W.] S. 42.41.040); West Virginia (W.Va. Code S. 6C-1-3).

55. *See e.g., Bowles v. City of Camden*, 993 F. Supp. 225 (D. N.J. 1998) (claim based on both § 1983 and New Jersey whistleblower protection statute); *Dudley v. Augusta School Dept.*, 23 *Id.*2d 85 (D. Maine) (claim based on both § 1983 and Maine Whistleblowers' Protection Act); *Draper v. Astoria School District*, 995 *Id.* 1122 (D. Or. 1998) ("As a general rule, a § 1983 remedy supplements, rather than supplants, any available state law remedies").

56. *See Nixon v. Fitzgerald*, 457 U.S. 731 (1982) (president given complete immunity for official actions taken while in office); *Harlow v. Fitzgerald*, 457 U.S. 800 (1982) (lower level government officials entitled to qualified immunity); U.S. Constitution, Eleventh Amendment (states cannot be sued, without their consent, by individuals in federal court). *See also Edelman v.*

Jordan, 415 U.S. 651 (1974); *Moor v. County of Alameda*, 411 U.S. 693, 717-721 (1973).

57. Under *Ex parte Young*, 209 U.S. 123 (1908), a federal court has jurisdiction over a suit against a state official to enjoin official actions violating federal law, even if the state itself may be immune from suit. *See Quern v. Jordan*, 440 U.S. 332, 337 (1979). Under the *Ex parte Young* doctrine, state officials can be sued for prospective injunctive relief, despite the Eleventh Amendment bar to suits against the state itself, in order to "vindicate" the "federal interest" in ending "continuing violation[s] of federal law." *Green v. Mansour*, 474 U.S. 64, 68 (1985). *See also Will v. Michigan Department of State Police*, 491 U.S. 58 (1989); C. Wright, *Law of Federal Courts*, 4th ed. p. 292 (1983) (*Ex parte Young* doctrine is "indispensable to the establishment of constitutional government and the rule of law").

58. *Seminole Tribe v. Florida*, 517 U.S. 44 (1996). *See also Alden v. Maine*, 119 S.Ct. 2240 (1999) (individual claims based on federal law cannot be litigated in state court without the consent of the state); *Will v. Michigan*, 491 U.S. 58, 65 (1989) ("Section 1983 provides a federal forum to remedy many deprivations of civil liberties, but it does not provide a federal forum for litigants who seek a remedy against a State for alleged deprivations of civil liberties. The Eleventh Amendment bars such suits unless the State has waived its immunity").

59. An individual state employee or officer cannot be sued for monetary damages in his or her "official" capacity. *Will* at 71 ("a suit against a state official in his or her *official* capacity is not a suit against the official but rather is a suit against the official's office," and thus is "no different from a suit against the State itself") (emphasis added). State officials can be sued in their official capacity if the only relief a party seeks is prospective injunctive relief. *Will* at 71, n. 10 (collecting cases). In order to obtain monetary relief from a state employee, that employee must be sued in his or her *individual* capacity.

60. *See Board of County Comm'rs. v. supra*, at 406-407:

Claims involving an allegation that the municipal action itself violated federal law, or directed or authorized the deprivation of federal rights, present much more difficult problems of proof. That the plaintiff has suffered a deprivation of federal rights at the hands of a municipal employee will not alone permit an inference of municipal culpability and causation: the plaintiff will simply have shown that the employee acted culpably.

61. Injunctive relief is also available to enjoin adverse employment actions. *See DeNovellis v. Shalala*, 135 F.3d 58 (1st Cir. 1998); *Gately v. Comm'r. of Mass.*, 2 F.3d 1221 (1st Cir. 1993). *See also Pembaur v. City of Cincinnati*, 475 U.S. 469, 478 (1986) (holding that "local government units could be made liable under § 1983 for deprivations of federal rights," but that a "municipality cannot be made liable by application of the doctrine of *respondeat superior*"). In *City of St. Louis v. Praprotnik*, 485 U.S. 112, 121-122 (1988), quoting from *Monell v. New York*, 436 U.S. 658, 690 (1978), the Court explained that municipal liability for constitutional torts was dependent upon proof that the violation occurred through a "policy, statement, ordinance, regulation or decision

officially adopted and promulgated by that body's officers." In rejecting the
respondeat superior doctrine, the court also held that municipal liability was
dependent upon proof that the decision in question was made by a government's
"lawmakers or by those whose edicts or acts may fairly be said to represent
official policy." *Id.* An unconstitutional government policy can be "inferred from
a single decision taken by the highest officials responsible for setting policy in
that area of the government's business." *Id.* at 123. Identifying who has the final
decision making role "is a question of state law." *Id.* at 123-128.

  62. *Samuel v. Holmes*, 138 F.3d 173, 175 (5th Cir. 1998); *Huskey v. City
of San Jose*, 204 F.3d 893 (9th Cir. 2000). In addition to "qualified immunity,"
some government officials are also entitled to "absolute immunity," i.e., a local
legislator who is sued in a personal capacity for "legislative activities." *Morris
v. Lindau*, 196 F.3d 102, 110 (2nd Cir. 1999). *See also Bogan v. Scott-Harris*,
523 U.S. 44 (1998).

  63. *Harlow v. Fitzgerald*, 457 U.S. 800, 817-818 (1982). More recently,
the Supreme Court has explained the reasons for setting forth this test for adjudicating a qualified immunity issue:

Two reasons that are explicit in our opinion in *Harlow*, together with a third that is
implicit in the holding, amply justified *Harlow*'s reformulation of the qualified immunity
defense. First, there is a strong public interest in protecting public officials from the costs
associated with the defense of damages actions. That interest is best served by a defense
that permits insubstantial lawsuits to be quickly terminated. Second, allegations of
subjective motivation might have been used as to shield baseless lawsuits from summary
judgment. The objective standard, in contrast, raises questions concerning the state of the
law at the time of the challenged conduct—questions that normally can be resolved on
summary judgment. Third, focusing on the "objective legal reasonableness of an official's
acts", avoids the unfairness of imposing liability on a defendant who "could not reasonably be expected to anticipate subsequent legal developments, nor . . . fairly be said to
'know' that the law forbade conduct not previously identified as unlawful." That unfairness may be present even when the official conduct is motivated, in part, by hostility to
the plaintiff.

Crawford-El v. Britton, 523 U.S. 574, 590-591 (1998) (internal citations omitted); *see
also, Conn v. Gabbart*, 526 U.S. 286 (1999).

  64. *Id.* at 592.

  65. *Id.*

  66. *Soltani v. Smith*, 812 F. Supp. 1280, 1301 (D. N.H. 1993). *Accord.,
Parks v. City of Brewer*, 56 *Id.* 89, 100-101 (D. Maine 1999) (qualified immunity
defense rejected where alleged retaliatory action concerned speech exposing
violation of an ordinance); *Wagner v. Texas A&M University*, 939 F. Supp. 1297,
1321 (S.D. Tex. 1996) (right to free speech was "clearly established by 1992"
within the 5th Circuit); *Draper, supra,* at 1136.

  67. *See Board of County Comm'rs.* 674-676 (1996) (collecting cases).

  68. *Wagner, supra,* at 1314 ("Retaliation by way of demotion, transfer,
or reassignment undermines the ability of public employees to speak or testify
truthfully without fear of reprisal").

69. *Id.*

70. *Hardin v. Straub*, 490 U.S. 536, 538 (1989); *Wagner* at 1316-1317 (S.D. Tex. 1996) (federal courts "look to the law of the state in which the action arose to determine the appropriate limitations period, usually borrowing the state's general personal injury limitations period").

71. *Brever v. Rockwell International Corp.*, 40 F.3d 1119 (10th Cir. 1994) (protecting whistleblowers at a nuclear weapons facility who cooperated with FBI and testified before grand jury on possible environmental crimes).

72. 42 U.S.C. § 1983.

73. 42 U.S.C. § 1985(2).

74. *McCord v. Bailey*, 636 F.2d 606, 615 (D.C. Cir. 1980) ("According to the Supreme Court, the Reconstruction civil rights acts are to be accorded a sweep as broad as their language") (internal quotes omitted).

75. *Brever, supra,* at 1126-1128 (collecting cases and discussing meaning of conspiracy under § 1985[2]). *See also* Janet A. Barbiere, "Conspiracies to Obstruct Justice in the Federal Courts: Defining the Scope of Section 1985 (2)," 50 *Fordham Law Review* 1210 (1982).

76. 42 U.S.C. § 1985(2).

77. *Graves v. U.S.*, 961 F. Supp. 314, 319 (D.D.C. 1997). The issue of standing under 42 U.S.C. § 1985(2) has not been resolved. Conflicting court decisions exist regarding whether § 1985(2) is available only to a "party" in a federal court action, or whether witnesses are likewise covered. *Haddle v. Garrison*, 525 U.S. 121 n. 3 (1998). Although there is split authority on this issue, given the original language of the CRA of 1871 and the congressional intent of the statute, actual or potential witnesses in federal court proceedings should be fully protected. *See Heffernan v. Hunter*, 189 F.3d 405, 409-411 (3rd Cir. 1999); *Silverman v. Newspaper and Mail* (S.D. N.Y. 1999). *Contra, Rylewicz v. Beaton Services*, 888 F.2d 1175, 1180 (7th Cir. 1989).

78. *McCord v. Bailey*, 636 F.2d 606, 615 (D.C. Cir. 1980).

79. *See Griffin v. Breckenridge*, 403 U.S. 88, 102 (1971), which held that actionable conspiracies under 42 U.S.C. § 1985(3) must be motivated by "racial, or perhaps otherwise class-based, invidiously discriminatory animus."

80. *Kush v. Rutledge*, 460 U.S. 719 (1983). Retaliation for participation in administrative proceedings has not yet been protected under 42 U.S.C. § 1985(2). *See Soltani, supra,* at 1294.

81. *Kush* at 726-727.

82. 525 U.S. 121, 119 S.Ct. 489 (1998).

83. *Id.* at 492.

84. *Id.* at 492-93.

85. *Id.*

86. *Portman v. County of Santa Clara*, 995 F.2d 898, 910 (9th Cir. 1993) (collecting cases); *Brever, supra,* at 1126-1127 (collecting cases ruling on the *intracorporate conspiracy* doctrine).

87. This doctrine was summarized *McAndrew v. Lockheed Martin Corp.*, 206 F.3d 1031, (11th Cir. 2000) (*en banc*) as follows: "The intracorporate conspir-

acy doctrine holds that acts of corporate agents are attributed to the corporation itself, thereby negating the multiplicity of actors necessary for the formation of a conspiracy. Simply put, under the doctrine, a corporation cannot conspire with its employees, and its employees, when acting in the scope of their employment, cannot conspire among themselves." The doctrine was first applied to the CRA in claims arising under 42 U.S.C. § 1985(3) in *Dombrowski v. Dowling*, 459 F.2d 190 (7th Cir. 1972). A majority of courts of appeals have applied *Dombrowski* in cases under § 1985(3)—which concerns "equal protection" claims—not under witness intimidation claims. *See Dickerson v. Alachua County*, 200 F.3d 761 (11th Cir. 2000). However, because of the distinct differences between 42 U.S.C. § 1985(3) and § 1985(2), even courts which apply the *intracorporate conspiracy* doctrine to § 1985(3) cases have recently rejected the doctrine in § 1985(2) cases. *McAndrew, supra*.

88. *Brever, supra; Stathos v. Bowden*, 728 F.2d 15, 21 (1st Cir. 1984); *Novotny v. Great American Federal Savings and Loan Ass'n*, 584 F.2d 1235, 1256-1259 (3rd Cir. 1978), *vacated on other grounds*, 442 U.S. 366 (1979); *Washington v. Duty Free Shoppers*, 696 F. Supp. 1323, 1327 (N.D. Cal. 1988).

89. *Brever, supra*, at 1127, *quoting Buschi v. Kirven*, 775 F.2d 1240, 1252 (4th Cir. 1985). Thus, even within the circuit courts that broadly apply the *intracorporate conspiracy* doctrine, this exception may be applicable. In *Dickerson, supra*, at 770, the 11th Circuit held: "Similarly, other circuits also have either held or considered holding corporate agents capable of conspiring in civil rights cases when those agents act outside the scope of their employment, have an "independent personal stake" in the corporate action, or engage in a series of discriminatory acts as opposed to a single action." *See Roniger v. McCall*, 72 F.Supp.2d 433, 437-438 (S.D. N.Y. 1999).

90. *McAndrew, supra*.

91. *Id*.

92. *Irizarry v. Quiros*, 722 F.2d 869, 872 (1st Cir. 1983). In *Irizarry*, the court refused to hold that 42 U.S.C. 1985(2) was preempted by other labor laws, such as the Labor Management Relations Act, because 1985(2) was designed to punish conspiracies.

93. *Hampton v. Hanrahan*, 600 F.2d 600, 620-621 (7th Cir. 1979) (internal quotations and citations omitted), *rev'd in part on other grounds*, 446 U.S. 754 (1980). *Accord., Creek v. Village of Westhaven*, 1992 WL 80959 (N.D. Ill. 1992); *Lenard v. Argento*, 699 F.2d 874, 882-883 (7th Cir. 1983); *Mnuz v. Caring Inc.*, 991 F. Supp. 701, 713 n. 19 (D. N.J. 1998) *citing Salinas v. U.S.*, 522 U.S. 52 (1997).

94. *Lewis v. News-Press and Gazette Co.*, 782 F. Supp. 1338, 1344 (W.D. MO. 1992), *citing White v. Walsh*, 649 F.2d 560, 561 (8th Cir. 1981).

95. *Fobbs v. Holy Cross Health System Corp.*, 29 F.3d 1439, 1449 (9th Cir. 1994). Although there is no heightened pleading standard, plaintiff still must set forth sufficient facts that will "give the defendant fair notice of what the plaintiff's claim is and the grounds it rests." *Id., citing Conley v. Gibson*, 355 U.S. 41, 47 (1957). Thus, "complaints containing only conclusory, vague, or

general allegations of a conspiracy will be dismissed." *Brug v. National Coalition For Homeless*, 45 F. Supp.2d 33, 41 (D. D.C. 1999) (internal quotations omitted).

96. *Haddle, supra.*

97. *Chahal v. Paine Webber*, 725 F.2d 20, 23 (2nd Cir. 1984); *Malley-Duff & Associates v. Crown Life Insurance Co.*, 792 F.2d 341, 235 (3rd Cir. 1986); *Brever, supra,* at 1126-1129 (setting forth standards for a "deterrence" claim and a "retaliation" claim under Section 2 of the CRA). *See also Brug, supra* (setting forth elements of an § 1985[3] conspiracy claim).

98. *Brever,* at 1129.

99. 722 F.2d 869 (1st Cir. 1983).

100. *Id.* at 872.

101. *Kush, supra,* at 724. In an appendix to the *Kush* decision, the Court reprinted the original, noncodified version of Section 2 of the CRA of 1871. *Id.* at 727-729.

102. The "prevent, hinder, or delay" clause was not the only law that was erroneously omitted in the Revised Statutes of 1873. In fact, the 1873 revision contained at least sixty-nine material errors, which were discovered right away, and over 180 additional errors that were not discovered until later reviews. *See Third Nat'l Bank v. Impac Ltd.*, 432 U.S. 312, 327; *see also* Dwan and Fiedler, "The Federal Statutes," 22 *Minn. Law Review* 1008, 1014 (1938). As a result of the error-filled codification of 1873, the U.S. Supreme Court has recognized the importance of looking to the original text of the CRA. *Kush v. Rutledge*, 460 U.S. 719. In *Chapman v. Houston Welfare Rights Organization,* 441 U.S. 600, 627 (1979), Justice Powell analyzed the original text of Section 1983—which originated in the CRA of 1866—because he "could not foreclose the possibility that some statutory change attributable solely to the 1874 revision may be accepted at face value. But certainly, the better wisdom is that an insertion of language in the Revised Statutes . . . is not lightly to be read as making a change."

In 1926 Congress again attempted a complete re-codification and enactment into positive law all of the Statutes at Large. At that time, Congress identified the shortcomings and errors contained in the previous attempts to codify the statutes. In order to correct those deficiencies, included in the enabling act new language which made clear that the new codification neither included new law nor repealed old laws. Congress' statement is simple: "the legislation as it appeared in the Statutes at Large should control in the case of conflict." *See* 44 Stat Ch. 12 (June 30, 1926). *See also U.S. v. Ward,* 131 F.3d 335, 339 (3rd Cir. 1997); *American Bank & Trust Co., v. Dallas,* 463 U.S. 855, 864 n. 8 (1983) ("the Statutes at Large prevail over the U.S. Code when the two are inconsistent"); *U.S. v. Welden,* 377 U.S. 95, 98-99 (1963) ("the Code cannot prevail over the Statutes at Large when the two are inconsistent"); *Stephan v. U.S.,* 319 U.S. 423, 426 (1943) ("the very meaning of *prima facie* is that the Code cannot prevail over the Statutes at Large when the two are inconsistent").

103. U.S. Congress, Statutes at Large, Vol. XVII, Ch. 22, Section 2 (Approved, April 20, 1871) 42nd Cong., 1st sess. (Boston: Little, Brown, and Company, 1873).

104. If the omissions and deletions that resulted from errors in the codification process have resulted in an inadvertent repeal of the uncodified clause, the doctrine set forth in *Cort v. Ash,* 422 U.S. 66 (1975), and *Thompson v. Thompson,* 484 U.S. 174 (1988), should permit an "implied cause of action" to be upheld based on the uncodified text. Under *Cort* and *Thompson,* if Congress' "intent" to permit a cause of action "can be inferred from the language of the statute, the statutory structure, or some other source," an implied cause of action may be permitted. *Thompson, supra,* at 179. Based on the actual statutory language of the 1871 act and its legislative history, the uncodified clause provides strong justification for upholding a cause of action.

105. Excerpts from Section 2 of the CRA of 1871, 17 Stat. 13.

106. Marion M. Miller, ed., *Great Debates in American History,* Vol. 8 (Civil Rights: Part Two) (New York: Current Literature Publishing Company, 1913), p. 197.

107. *Kush, supra,* at 724, n. 6.

108. *Id.* at 727.

109. Other cases interpreting Reconstruction Era civil rights laws and other clauses of the CRA of 1871 have held that these laws should be accorded a "sweep as broad as their language." *Griffin, supra* (internal quotes omitted).

Chapter 5

Environmental and Nuclear Whistleblowing

Between 1972 and 1980, Congress passed seven whistleblower protection bills: six environmental and one nuclear. These laws—amendments to the Safe Drinking Water Act (SDWA), the Clean Air Act (CAA), the Energy Reorganization Act (ERA), the Comprehensive Environmental Response, Compensation, and Liability Act (Superfund), the Toxic Substance Control Act (TSCA), the Solid Waste Disposal Act (SWDA, otherwise known as the Resource Conservation and Recovery Act, or RCRA), and the Water Pollution Control Act (WPCA)—protect employees who report violations of environmental or nuclear safety regulations to public authorities.[1]

The categories of employees protected under the whistleblower laws cover the entire panorama of the American workforce. For example, a painter who cooperated with a state investigation into toxic dumping, a teacher who contacted a state Occupational Safety and Health Administration (OSHA) office concerning potential asbestos in the school building, a doctor who complained to the Nuclear Regulatory Commission (NRC) about improper radiation therapy, an inspector who exposed welding deficiencies at a nuclear construction site, and an employee who told a newspaper reporter about the discharge of sludge into the Cedar Rapids were all covered under these laws.

An employee who is terminated, harassed, blacklisted, or in any way discriminated against in retaliation for blowing the whistle on violations of environmental or nuclear safety laws can file a simple complaint within the Department of Labor (DOL)[2] and, if successful, obtain reinstatement, back pay with interest, compensatory damages, damages for pain and suffering and loss of reputation, and other affirmative relief necessary to abate the violation. In addition, if the employee wins the discrimination suit, the Secretary of Labor (SOL) must order reimbursement for all litigation costs and expenses, including attorney fees and expert witness fees.

Two of the laws, the SDWA and TSCA, also have provisions for awarding exemplary damages if the employee wins his or her discrimination suit.

THE LEGISLATIVE HISTORY OF WHISTLEBLOWER PROTECTION LAWS

The first environmental whistleblower protection law, the employee protection provision of the Water Pollution Control Act, was passed in 1972. In discussing the employee protection provision, the Senate Conference Report declared, "Under this section employees and union officials could help assure that employers do not contribute to the degradation of our environment."[3] Congress was looking to workers to help enforce the nation's environmental laws: "The best source of information about what a company is actually doing or not doing is often its own employees, and this amendment would insure that an employee could provide such information without losing his job or otherwise suffering economically from retribution from the polluter."[4]

In addition to protecting employees' jobs, Congress wanted to stop corporations from using the threat of economic retaliation to silence those voicing environmental concerns. Representative William D. Ford, in offering an amendment to the employee protection provision that was pending before the House, declared:

Mr. Chairman, in offering this amendment we are only seeking to protect workers and communities from those very few in industry who refuse to face up to the fact that they are polluting our waterways, and who hope that by pressuring their employees and frightening communities with economic threats, they will gain relief from the requirement of any effluent limitation or abatement order.[5]

After passage of the WPCA whistleblower protection law, Congress passed six other environmental and nuclear whistleblower laws all modeled after the WPCA provision.[6] For example, in 1978, when Congress passed Section 210 of the Energy Reorganization Act,[7] it explicitly stated that Section 210 was "substantially identical" to the whistleblower protections in the WPCA:

This amendment is substantially identical to provisions in the Clean Air Act and the Federal Water Pollution Control Act. The legislative history of those acts indicated that such provisions were patterned after the National Labor Management Act and a similar provision in Public Law 91-173 (FMSA) relating to the health and safety of the nation's coal miners.[8]

The legislative history of these amendments indicates that Congress intended all employees to be covered, whether they were in the private sector or employed by the federal or state governments. Likewise, even if the allegations raised by a worker were unfounded, the worker would still be protected. The Conference Committee report for the Clean Air Act amendment stated that employees would be protected from retaliation:

due to an employee's participation in, or assistance to, the administration, implementation, or enforcement of the Clean Air Act or any requirements promulgated pursuant to it. These requirements would include any State or local requirements which are incorporated in the applicable implementation plan. . . . Retaliatory action by the employer would also be prohibited if it were in response to any employee's exercise of rights under Federal, State, or local Clean Air Act legislation or regulations. This would be the case even if the employee's action was not directed against the employer (e.g., the filing of a citizen suit against the Administrator or against another company). Moreover, as in the Safe Drinking Water Act and the Federal Water Pollution Act, the employer would not have to be proven to be in violation of a Clean Air Act requirement in order for this section to protect the employee's action.[9]

The SOL[10] and the DOL Administrative Review Board (ARB) have reasoned that any interpretation of the environmental law must be read "in conjunction with" these explicit statements of congressional purpose: "[E]mployees must feel secure that any action they may take that furthers that Congressional policy and purpose, especially in the area of public health and safety, will not jeopardize either their current employment or future employment opportunities."[11]

On October 24, 1992, Congress strengthened the nuclear whistleblower law and renamed the provision as Section 211 of the ERA.[12] The amendments were designed to "remove any disincentive to reporting" and to prevent "on-the-job retaliation against employees who report safety violations."[13]

REMEDIAL NATURE OF WHISTLEBLOWER LAWS

The "paramount purpose" of the environmental whistleblower provisions is the "protection of employees."[14] The laws are remedial legislation and should be broadly construed by the Department of Labor and the courts.[15] A "narrow" or "hypertechnical" interpretation of the laws "will do little to effect" the statutes' remedial purposes.[16] The amendments were passed in order to help enforce U. S. environmental laws, enhance environmental quality, and protect public health and safety.[17] Under the laws, employees are encouraged to report violations of the law.[18] In accordance with this underlying philosophy, the DOL "does not simply provide a forum for private parties to litigate their private employment discrimination suits," but also "represents the public interest."[19]

As explained in a nuclear whistleblower case decided by the U.S. Court of Appeals for the 6th Circuit: "Under this anti-discrimination provision [Section 210 of the Energy Reorganization Act, 42 U.S.C. § 5851] . . . the need for broad construction of the statutory purpose can well be characterized as 'necessary to prevent the Nuclear Regulatory Commission's channels of information from being dried up by employer intimidation.' "[20]

Protected whistleblowing "may expose not just private harms but health and safety hazards to the public."[21] The SOL has noted the "magnitude of the potential hazards" implicated in the concerns whistleblowers disclose and the consequential importance of keeping "open the channels of communication regarding potential safety and quality violations."[22]

In a concurring opinion in *Rose v. Secretary of Department of Labor*,[23] 6th Circuit Justice George C. Edwards, Jr., wrote that Congress' intent in passing the nuclear whistleblower protection act,[24] was to "encourage employees" to report "unsafe practices in one of the most dangerous technologies mankind has invented." Justice Edwards identified the remedial scheme behind the whistleblower protection provisions:

If employees are coerced and intimidated into remaining silent when they should speak out, the results can be catastrophic. Recent events here and around the world underscore the realization that such complicated and dangerous technology can never be safe without constant human vigilance. The employee protection provision involved in this case thus serves the dual function of protecting both employees and the public from dangerous radioactive substances.[25]

In *Passaic Valley Sewerage Commissioners v. Department of Labor*, the U.S. Court of Appeals for the 3rd Circuit noted that other courts of appeal "have consistently construed" the environmental and nuclear whistleblower statutes "to lend broad coverage."[26] Likewise, the SOL has continued to recognize the "Congressional intent" behind these laws to "protect public health and safety."[27]

Regulatory agencies, such as the Nuclear Regulatory Commission, also have recognized the broad congressional policies that underscore these

laws.[28] For example, concerning Section 211 of the ERA, 42 U.S.C. §
5851, the NRC commissioners held:

The philosophy underlying the adoption of Section 211 and its implementing
regulations is that any employee of an NRC licensee or of a firm that deals
directly or indirectly with NRC licensees on nuclear-related matters and who is
in a position to have information relating to nuclear safety must feel free to come
to the NRC with that information. Any attempt to "chill" this access to the NRC
by harassing, intimidating, or firing employees who report conditions that could
adversely affect the public health and safety violates section 211.[29]

APPLICATION OF LABOR LAW PRECEDENT

According to the legislative history of the WPCA, the provisions
of the act were modeled after the 1969 Federal Mine Safety Act's (FMSA)
employee protection provision and the National Labor Relations Act
(NLRA).[30] Consequently, the SOL and the courts of appeals have, in the
absence of precedent under the whistleblower laws, used NLRA and mine
safety employment retaliation law and case precedents for guidance in
interpreting the environmental employee protection provisions.[31] The
legislative history of most of the other whistleblower laws indicates that
these laws, like the WPCA, were modeled after the FMSA and NLRA.[32]
Even when the legislative history is silent, courts have applied these labor
law precedents.[33]

Because all seven environmental and nuclear employee protection
acts share similar statutory language and legislative histories, case law
under one of the acts is readily used for interpreting other acts.[34] All of the
laws are administered through one uniform set of Department of Labor
regulations.[35]

PROCEDURAL OVERVIEW OF WHISTLEBLOWER LITIGATION

The Complaint and Investigation

Under the provisions of the six environmental employee protection
laws, the worker (complainant) must file a written complaint with the
Occupational Safety and Health Administration (OSHA) of the Department
of Labor in Washington, D.C., or a local OSHA branch within 30 days of
the discriminatory act.[36] If the employee fails to comply with the 30-day
statute of limitations, his or her complaint will be time barred and dismissed.[37] The nuclear whistleblower law was amended in 1992 to permit
a 180-day filing period.[38]

The limitations period commences to run on the date an employee is informed of a final adverse action.[39] In other words, the "filing period commences" on the date that a complainant receives a "final and unequivocal" notice of the challenged actions rather than at the time the effects of the actions ultimately are felt.[40] Pursuit of other remedies, such as an employee's utilization of an internal grievance or arbitration process, does not extend a filing period.[41]

However, a limitations period is "not jurisdictional" and "may be extended when fairness requires."[42] The grounds for extending a limitations period are "narrowly applied."[43] The basic theories used to enlarge a filing period are *equitable tolling*,[44] *equitable estoppel*[45] or "continuing violation."[46] Even if tolling is justified, an employee still must "bring suit within a reasonable time after he has obtained, or by due diligence could have obtained, the necessary information."[47]

The complaint is deemed filed when mailed.[48] The address for filing a complaint with the Department of Labor is:

> Assistant Secretary for Occupational Safety and Health
> U.S. Department of Labor
> 200 Constitution Avenue, N.W.
> Washington, D.C. 20210[49]

The complaint can be simple and should include a full statement of the acts and omissions, with pertinent dates, that are believed to constitute the violation.[50] A Department of Labor whistleblower complaint need not set forth "every element of a legal cause of action."[51] In *Richter et al. v. Baldwin Associates*,[52] the SOL held that such a complaint is "not a formal pleading setting forth every legal cause of action," but rather is an "informal complaint." Well after a complaint has been filed it may be amended or supplemented to address events that occurred subsequent to the original filing.[53]

Once a complaint is filed, OSHA has thirty days to conduct an investigation of complainant's charges.[54] The complaint must be investigated on a "priority basis,"[55] although an employer need not file a formal answer.[56] Nuclear whistleblower complaints must also be reviewed under a separate provision of the regulation, which mandates that OSHA make a determination even before conducting a formal investigation.[57] The complainant should cooperate and assist with this investigation. In environmental cases, if OSHA fails to conduct an investigation or dismisses a complaint on improper legal grounds prior to the completion of an investigation, the administrative law judge (ALJ) or the SOL can remand the case to OSHA for an investigation.[58] Further, if OSHA fails to complete a timely investigation, a party may (after a reasonable period of time) request a hearing based on the constructive denial of the complaint.[59] Additionally, because of the *de novo* nature of the hearing process, "flaws" in the investigative process are not grounds for either remand or reversal.[60] The OSHA investigator can conduct confidential interviews with the witnesses, but the witnesses must ask for confidentiality.[61] Once the investigation is completed, the complainant can (and should) obtain a copy of the investigatory file through use of the Freedom of Information Act (FOIA) and Privacy Act.[62]

Request for Hearing and Prehearing Procedure

After the investigation is completed, OSHA must decide whether the employee's complaint is valid and issue a formal determination letter.[63] This OSHA finding is nonbinding if either party appeals,[64] and "once a hearing has been requested, the investigated findings . . . carry no weight either before the ALJ or the Board [ARB]."[65] However, the investigation and findings are notable because when the results are forwarded to a Department of Labor administrative law judge, a favorable OSHA determination can facilitate a settlement and give an attorney or representative an idea of the strength of the case.

Each party has only five days from the receipt of the ruling to appeal the OSHA determination.[66] If an appeal is not filed and received by the DOL within the five-day period, the OSHA determination becomes the final decision of the SOL.[67] The appeal of the OSHA determination merely consists of filing a request for a hearing to:

> Chief Administrative Law Judge
> Department of Labor
> 800 K Street, NW, Suite 400
> Washington, D.C. 20001-8002

The hearing request *must* be sent to the DOL Chief ALJ by one of four methods: facsimile, telegram, hand delivery, or next-day delivery service.[68] A copy of the request for hearing *must* also be sent, using one of these methods, to the other parties to the dispute on the same day the request for a hearing is filed with the Chief ALJ.[69] In addition, any party requesting a hearing must send a copy of the hearing request to:

Assistant Secretary for Occupational Safety and Health and
Associate Solicitor Division of Fair Labor Standards
U.S. Department of Labor
Washington, D.C. 20210[70]

Once a request for a hearing is filed, the case is assigned a hearing
officer or administrative law judge, who must set a hearing date within
seven days of receipt of the appeal.[71] No party is required to file an answer
to the request for a hearing.[72] The parties must be given at least five days
notice of the hearing date,[73] and the hearing should be held within sixty
days of the administrative law judge's receipt of the request for a hearing.[74]

All of the time requirements under the employee protection statutes
are extremely short. Both the statutes and the regulations require that the
ARB[75] issue a final decision within ninety days after receipt of a complaint.[76] Thus, a litigator theoretically may have only thirty to sixty days
to conduct all prehearing discovery, respond to or file all prehearing motions, conduct a hearing, file prehearing and post-hearing briefs, and file an
appellate brief with the SOL. Under the rules, continuances are granted
only for "compelling reasons," and administrative law judges have considerable discretion in granting continuances.[77] Likewise, time limits for
responding to motions are short. All motions must be answered within ten
days (if the motion is mailed, five days are added to the answering
period).[78] This includes all responsive motions, motions to quash discovery, and motions for protective orders. Consequently, due to the nature of
the time requirements, complainants often waive their right to an expeditious hearing to obtain more time for discovery and pretrial preparation.[79]

Although the time limits are short, the hearing and the final decision of the SOL are rarely conducted within these constraints. The administrative law judges have held that the short deadlines were designed to
"assure [the] complainant of a speedy decision and may be waived."[80]
Employees' attempts to have a case dismissed due to the Labor Department's failure to comply with the ninety-day deadlines have failed.[81]
Failure of the SOL to abide by the statutory ninety-day requirement to
render a final order does not strip the Secretary of jurisdiction to render a
judgment on behalf of the complainant.[82] The time limits contained in the
statutes and regulations "have been construed as directory, rather than
mandatory or jurisdictional."[83] It is erroneous for an administrative law
judge or the DOL to allow for these time limits to "interfere with the full
and fair presentation" of a case.[84] Parties must also be provided adequate
time for prehearing preparation.[85]

As discussed above, attorneys for the employees often waive their right to an expeditious ninety-day determination in order to allow for adequate pretrial discovery. The administrative law judges frequently grant requests for continuance,[86] especially if the complainant voluntarily waives his or her right to a ninety-day adjudication.[87] Although administrative law judges have discretion on this issue, a "myopic insistence upon expeditiousness in the face of a justifiable request for delay" may violate due process.[88]

It is important to meet all deadlines, as the failure to do so may result in the waiving of certain objections or claims.[89] Allowing a case to drag on can often harm a complainant.[90] Parties may file motions to dismiss and for summary dismissal at least twenty days prior to a hearing.[91] The DOL follows the case-law under FRCP 12 when reviewing motions to dismiss[92] and FRCP 56 when reviewing a motion for summary dismissal.[93] Summary judgment motions are rarely granted in whistleblower proceedings because the central issue, causation, often requires consideration of a person's motive.[94] They may also be denied if discovery is still necessary.[95] However, the failure to file an affidavit or other supporting documentation on the record in opposing summary judgment or a motion to dismiss can be fatal to an employee's case: "Unadorned allegations argued by counsel are not sufficient."[96] The regulations explicitly permit parties to file prehearing briefs.[97] The failure to raise or preserve issues in this brief may result in a waiver of the issues.[98]

Discovery

Prehearing discovery is an integral element of the litigation process, enabling a complainant to obtain the evidence the employer will rely upon to prove its case and assisting the complainant in proving discriminatory motive and disparate treatment.[99] The ARB has noted that an "opportunity for extensive discovery is crucial" for "protecting employees and the public interest." Additionally, "discovery in a whistleblower proceeding may well uncover questionable employment practices" and "safety deficiencies."[100]

Most discovery issues are routinely heard by the presiding administrative law judge, whose rulings will be reversed only if they are "arbitrary or an abuse of discretion."[101] Parties are expected to attempt to informally resolve discovery disputes prior to filing motions to compel or requesting protective orders.[102] The expedited nature of the Department of Labor proceedings affects prehearing discovery.[103] Unless the administrative law judge orders otherwise, a party has thirty days to respond to requests for documents, admissions, or written interrogatories. Depositions may be conducted with only five working days' notice,[104] if the notices are hand served. Protective orders may be requested to keep information confidential.[105] In order to obtain answers to discovery in time for the hearing, discovery requests should be served on a person or party shortly after a request for hearing is filed. Although the discovery process is expedited, the ARB has correctly noted that "requests to extend the time to respond to discovery" are "routinely" granted.[106]

Although the DOL has not been granted explicit subpoena power in environmental whistleblower cases, the DOL maintains the authority to compel parties to produce witnesses withing there control and to respond to discovery requests. Moreover, the labor department maintains its authority to sanction parties for discovery abuses.[107]

Additionally, a party may file a FOIA request to obtain the DOL's initial investigation file with the local OSHA office immediately after the office completes its investigation and issues a finding. FOIA requests can also be filed with any department of the executive branch of government, including the Nuclear Regulatory Commission, the Environmental Protection Agency, the Occupational Safety and Health Administration, and the Department of Labor. Requests should be mailed to both the national office and any regional or local branch of the agency that has files concerning the employee, the corporation, or the allegation raised by the whistleblower.[108]

The Hearing

Department of Labor administrative hearings are conducted as formal adjudicatory proceedings according to the Administrative Procedure Act, 5 U.S.C. § 554.[109] Although similar to courtroom trials, they are not as formal. For example, nonattorneys have the right to represent the parties, and telephonic testimony, where necessary and proper, is permitted.[110] Further, there is never a jury, and one administrative law judge sits as the trier of law and fact. The administrative law judge has wide discretion in admitting testimony into evidence, and the Federal Rules of Evidence are not binding.[111]

During the hearing process the administrative law judge must ensure that each party has a "fair adjudication." Given the complex nature of a whistleblower case, this would include the "full presentation of a broad range of evidence that may prove, or disprove, retaliatory animus."[112]

The hearings are mechanically or stenographically reported and open to the general public.[113] There are specific administrative provisions for taking judicial notice,[114] exchanging and introducing exhibits into evidence,[115] determining the authenticity of documents,[116] obtaining *in camera* inspection of documents, and for protective orders for privileged or sensitive communications.[117]

In conducting the prehearing and hearing process, administrative law judges have "all powers necessary" to conduct a "fair and impartial" proceeding, including the powers to "compel the production of documents and appearance of witnesses in control of the parties," "issue decisions and orders," take any action authorized by the Administrative Procedure Act, and, "where applicable," take "appropriate action" authorized under the FRCP.[118]

The DOL applies three sets of rules in governing whistleblower adjudications. First, 29 C.F.R. § 24 controls the proceedings. When a situation is not controlled by Part 24, the DOL applies the rule set forth under 29 C.F.R. § 18. If both sets of rules are silent on a particular situation, the DOL employs applicable provisions of the FRCP.[119] Moreover, administrative law judges have the discretion to modify the application of Part 18 or the FRCP if "no party will be prejudiced and the ends of justice will be served."[120]

In addition to the employee and employer, other "persons or organizations" that could be "directly and adversely" affected by a final decision have the right to intervene in the case within fifteen days of learning of the proceeding.[121] *Amici* briefs may be filed by interested parties or other federal agencies:[122] the OSHA division of the DOL must be served with copies of all pleadings.[123] The pleadings must be served to:

> Assistant Secretary for Occupational Safety and Health and
> Associate Solicitor Division of Fair Labor Standards
> U.S. Department of Labor
> Washington, D.C. 20210[124]

The Assistant Secretary of OSHA maintains the right to participate as a party or *amicus curiae* at any time and at any stage of the proceeding.[125]

An employee can request that any hearing be held close to his or her home. The DOL "shall," "where possible," conduct the hearing within seventy-five miles of the complainant's home.[126] Additionally, two or more cases can be consolidated if the "same or substantially similar evidence" is relevant to "matters at issue" in each case.[127]

The failure of an administrative law judge to follow basic due process rules,[128] or the hearing requirements of the Administrative Procedure Act, are grounds for reversible error.[129] The standard for procedural due process required in whistleblower cases was outlined by the SOL in *In the Matter of Charles A. Kent:*

Due process in administrative proceedings of a judicial nature has been said generally to be conformity to fair practices of Anglo-Saxon jurisprudence, . . . which is usually equated with adequate notice and a fair hearing. . . . Although strict adherence to the common law rules of evidence at the hearing is not required . . . the parties must generally be allowed an opportunity to know the claims of the opposing party . . . to present evidence to support their contentions . . . and to cross-examine witnesses for the other side. . . . Thus it is not proper to admit *ex parte* evidence, given by witnesses not under oath and not subject to cross-examination by the opposing party.[130]

The administrative law judge is not bound by the formal rules of evidence but should exclude "immaterial, irrelevant, and unduly repetitious evidence."[131] An administrative law judge can commit error by failing to admit into evidence "probative" information.[132] The ARB explained that:

a trial judge who, in the hearing of a non jury case, attempts to make strict rulings on the admissibility of evidence, risks reversal by excluding evidence which is objected to, but which, on review, the appellate body believes should have been admitted. Thus, in a non-jury hearing, it is more efficient for the trier of fact to take under advisement questions regarding the admissibility of evidence than it is to consider arguments concerning the admissibility of evidence at the time that such questions are raised. He or she is then able to sift through that evidence after it has been received to determine what is admissible.[133]

Both parties have the right to call and cross-examine witnesses, introduce documents into evidence, and make opening and closing remarks.[134] Either before or at the commencement of the hearing, the parties must exchange all exhibits they seek to admit into evidence.[135] The parties may also file prehearing briefs.[136] Although the environmental whistleblower statutes do not explicitly provide subpoena power to the DOL,[137] the failure of an administrative law judge to order a party to produce relevant witnesses under its control to testify in a proceeding is an abuse of discretion.[138]

The following is a summary of other basic Department of Labor administrative rules of evidence:

1. Grounds for objecting to evidence:

   a. privilege, 29 C.F.R. § 18.46;

   b. classified or sensitive, 29 C.F.R. § 18.46 (b);

   c. improper use of deposition, 29 C.F.R. § 18.23;

    d.   failure to have produced the information during discovery, 29 C.F.R. § 18.6(d)(2)(iii);

    e.   immaterial, 29 C.F.R. § 24.6(e);

    f.   challenge to the authenticity of a document, 29 C.F.R. §§ 18.44(b) [revised, Department of Labor "Final Rule," 55 Fed. Reg. 13,216 (April 9, 1990)] and 18.50;

    g.   failure to produce a true copy of a record from another criminal or civil proceeding, 29 C.F.R. § 18.48;

    h.   irrelevant, 29 C.F.R. § 24.6(e).

2. Hearsay evidence may be admissible if there are circumstantial indicia of its truthfulness.[139]

3. Judicial notice is permitted.[140]

4. Admission of exhibits:[141]

    a.   all exhibits shall be numbered, marked, and a copy given to both the administrative law judge and the opposing party;

    b.   parties must exchange all exhibits, preferably before the hearing, but no later than the commencement of the hearing. Failure to exchange exhibits in a timely manner can result in the exclusion of the document.[142]

    c.   all documents are presumed authentic unless objected to prior to the hearing.

    d.   "narrow" exception exists for prehearing disclosure of "inconsistent statements by witnesses" used "solely for the purpose of impeachment."[143]

5. True copies of documents, records, or transcripts from other civil or criminal proceedings are admissible into evidence.[144]

6. Parties have the right to submit direct and rebuttal evidence and to conduct reasonable cross-examination.[145]

7. Parties can present oral argument and file pretrial briefs.[146]

8. If the hearings in two or more cases are consolidated, evidence introduced in one case may be considered introduced in the others.[147]

9. Any document that is submitted prior to a hearing is assumed authentic and admissible. Objections to authenticity or admissibility must be filed before the hearing.[148]

10. If a party has relevant information within his or her control, but fails to produce it (this includes both documentary evidence and answering to interrogatories and admissions), the administrative law judge may draw an inference that the evidence is unfavorable to that party.[149]

11. Depositions may be used at the hearing, but their use must conform to 29 C.F.R. § 18.23.

12. Tape recorded conversations are admissible.[150]

13. Settlement offers are not admissible evidence.[151]

14. Nuclear Regulatory Commission reports and decisions may be admitted into evidence.[152] Official notice may be taken of these documents.[153]

15. Findings of an arbitrator are admissible.[154]

16. Fabrication of evidence is potentially criminal and is evidence the offending party has a "weak or unfounded" case, which can result in the exclusion of parties from the proceeding for unethical conduct.[155]

17. Evidence may be admitted into the record after it is closed if such evidence is "new and material" and was not readily available prior to the closing of the record.[156]

18. In a whistleblower case evidence of management's attitude toward safety is highly relevant. An employer's attitude toward the raising of safety issues, such as past instances of "deliberate violations" of safety procedure, may provide evidence of "antagonism" toward environmental regulations and also "provide support" for raising an "inference of retaliatory intent" against the employee.[157]

      The conduct of the Department of Labor hearings and the general rules of evidence are delineated in the Administrative Procedure Act (APA) 5 U.S.C. § 556(d),[158] and hearings are conducted pursuant to the APA, 5 U.S.C. § 554.[159]

The Hearsay Rule

Hearsay evidence may be admissible if it bears "satisfactory indicia of reliability," it is "probative," and its use is "fundamentally fair."[160]

There is no hard and fast rule that determines when hearsay is admissible.[161] Many factors must be considered by the administrative law judge, such as:

whether the statements are signed and sworn to as opposed to anonymous, oral, or unsworn, whether or not the statements are contradicted by direct testimony, whether or not the declarant is available to testify and, if so, whether or not the party objecting to the hearsay statements subpoenas the declarant, or whether the declarant is unavailable and no other evidence is available, the credibility of the declarant if a witness, or of the witness testifying to the hearsay, and finally, whether or not the hearsay is corroborated [citations omitted].[162]

Thus, hearsay evidence cannot be excluded on the grounds that it is an out-of-court statement made to prove the truth of the matter asserted. Hearsay is admissible up to the point of relevancy.[163] An administrative law judge may base his or her decision on hearsay evidence, although "uncorroborated hearsay or rumor" does *not*, unto itself, constitute substantial evidence and cannot be the sole basis for a decision.[164]

Generally, the admissibility of evidence is within the discretion of the administrative law judge.[165] Improper exclusion of evidence by the administrative law judge can provide grounds for reversal and remand of an agency decision by the court of appeals.[166]

Recommended Decision

After the hearing, the administrative law judge, at his or her discretion, can request or grant permission to the parties to file post-hearing briefs.[167] The administrative law judge has twenty days after the termination of the hearing to write a recommended decision. The deadline is usually extended. The recommended decision must be based on the record as a whole and include findings of law and fact (including, where appropriate, determinations of the witnesses' credibility). The recommended decision is subject to review by the Administrative Review Board (ARB) of the DOL (formerly the SOL) if requested in a timely manner (i.e., ten business days from the date of the ALJ order) by any party.[168] The ten-day deadline is subject to tolling.[169]

If the DOL determines that the employee was discriminated against, the DOL shall order "affirmative action to abate the violation," including:

> reinstatement of the complainant to that person's former or substantially equiva-
> lent position, if desired, together with the compensation (including back pay),
> terms, conditions, and privileges of that employment. The Secretary may, where
> deemed appropriate, order the party charged to provide compensatory damages
> to the complainant.[170]

Under the environmental and nuclear whistleblower protection
laws, if the SOL finds illegal discrimination on the part of the employer in
a whistleblower case, the Secretary shall order an abatement of the violation, reinstatement of the employee, all back pay, and full restoration of all
"privileges" of employment. The SOL also has the discretion to award
compensatory damages.[171] Additionally, the DOL may, where appropriate,
award exemplary damages under the Safe Drinking Water Act and the
Toxic Substances Control Act.[172]

If the complainant prevails, attorney fees and all litigation costs
incurred by the employee are recoverable.[173] A successful employee is
"automatically" "entitled" to an award of reasonable attorney fees and
costs, as set by the DOL.[174] Although a complainant is entitled to all
reasonable fees, regardless of the terms of the retainer agreement, if an
attorney agrees to voluntarily limit his or her fees or agrees to a "ceiling on
the award of fees," such a ceiling can act to cut off entitlement to other fees,
even if reasonably incurred.[175] The DOL does not have the discretion to
deny attorney fees and costs to an employee who wins a favorable order.[176]
Applications for fees may be filed after the issuance of a final order.[177]

Any party aggrieved by the DOL's decision, who has sought re-
view before the ARB, has sixty days to file an appeal in the appropriate
U.S. Circuit Court of Appeals. The standard of review is determined by the
Administrative Procedure Act, 5 U.S.C. §§ 701-706. In *Mackowiak v.
University Nuclear Systems, Inc.*, the scope of review was summarized:
"We will set aside the agency decision if it is 'unsupported by substantial
evidence' or 'arbitrary, capricious, an abuse of discretion, or otherwise not
in accordance with law.' "[178]

An appeal will not, unless ordered by the court, act as a stay of the
ARB's order.[179] A stay may be granted if the company shows that it would
suffer "irreparable harm" if it were forced to comply with the order.[180]

Sanctions and Involuntary Dismissals

All persons who appear in a DOL proceeding must "act with integrity and in an ethical manner."[181] Specific provisions exist for the disquali-

fication of counsel[182] and the disqualification of an administrative law judge.[183] Attorneys who have engaged in unethical behavior or "contemptuous misconduct" have been disqualified from appearing in specific proceedings.[184] Disqualification orders may be appealed to the Chief ALJ.[185]

An administrative law judge has the power and responsibility to police the conduct of the parties and sanction parties for misconduct.[186] He or she may dismiss a complaint if a party fails to comply with a lawful order or engages in other misconduct.[187] However, before a complaint may be dismissed, the administrative law judge must issue an order to show cause why dismissal should not be granted.[188] A dismissal with prejudice is a "severe sanction," which must be "tempered by a careful exercise of judicial discretion."[189] Absent "willful or contumacious" misconduct or other aggravated circumstances, a default judgment for misconduct by either party will rarely be justified.[190]

Before a complaint is dismissed, an ALJ must issue a "show cause" order, and afford all parties an opportunity to respond to the order prior to dismissing a claim.[191] Claims have been dismissed against parties for failure to comply with discovery orders,[192] for disrupting a proceeding,[193] abandonment,[194] failure to adhere to a prehearing order,[195] and for failure to comply with an order from an administrative law judge.[196] Simply put, a party is not permitted to "thwart" or "retard" an adjudication by violating an administrative law judge's orders or engaging in misconduct.[197] Attorneys have also been sanctioned for misconduct. Such attorneys have been ordered disqualified and have been subject to nonmonetary sanctions.[198]

The SOL has held that a complainant may not be sanctioned under Rule 11 of the FRCP.[199] The SOL ruled that the sanction available for "conduct which is dilatory, unethical, unreasonable, and in bad faith" is the disqualification of counsel pursuant to DOL rule 29 C.F.R. § 18.36, not FRCP Rule 11 sanctions.[200] Unlike matters tried in federal courts, monetary sanctions are not available in environmental whistleblower actions: "There is no provision for the recovery of costs and attorney's fees by a respondent."[201]

In *Rex v. EBASCO Services, Inc.*, the SOL overturned a $77,000 sanction against a complainant's attorney.[202] The SOL ruled that only an employer can be required to pay attorney fees and costs.[203] Further, the SOL held that 29 C.F.R. § 18.36(b) governed the type of sanction available for "dilatory, unethical, unreasonable or bad faith conduct."[204] Section 18.36(b) provides for the disqualification of counsel.

The SOL interpreted his disqualification authority to allow for the disqualification of attorneys involved in sanctionable conduct in all DOL proceedings:

The Department of Labor is not entirely without recourse where an attorney or the representative of a party abuses the procedures for administrative adjudication of disputes. It is clear that the Secretary has the authority to regulate the admission to practice of those who represent parties in cases arising under the ERA, and to discipline those whose conduct interferes with the carrying out of his responsibilities under the Act.[205]

Other sanctions available to an administrative law judge or the SOL include the refusal to permit a party to testify, taking certain facts to be established, and dismissal of a matter.[206] However, the DOL cannot punish a party for contempt or utilize other sanctions contained in the Federal Rules of Civil Procedure that are not also authorized by the whistleblower laws or administrative regulations.[207]

Although deliberate misconduct by a party may result in the dismissal of a claim,[208] a complainant/employee who provides misleading or false testimony is not automatically barred from obtaining relief under the laws.[209]

Willful Misconduct

All of the environmental whistleblower laws require that the DOL dismiss any complaint where an employee, "acting without direction from his or her employer (or the employer's agent), deliberately causes a violation of any requirement" of the environmental laws.[210] The "willfulness" exception to the applicability of the statutory protections is an "affirmative defense" for which an employer bears the burden of proof "by a preponderance of evidence."[211] The SOL has narrowly construed this defense.[212]

To meet its burden under a "willfulness" defense, an employer must meet a difficult three-part test:

1)   that the act was done without direction from the employer;

2)   that employee deliberately did an act; and

3)   that the act caused a violation of [environmental law] requirements.[213]

In order to establish the first prong of this test, an employer must demonstrate that the employee acted with neither the express nor the implied consent of the employer.[214] To establish the "willfulness" component of the test, an employer must show that the employee had actual "knowledge" that their conduct constituted a violation or that the employee acted with a reckless disregard concerning a violation. The ARB defined the willfulness component as follows: "we find that to establish a valid Section 211(g) defense, a respondent [employer] must show that a complainant [employee] willfully or recklessly caused a violation of the ERA or the Atomic Energy Act, that is, that the complainant acted with knowledge or with reckless disregard of whether his or her act would cause a violation."[215]

Where the defense has been successfully raised, there has usually been an independent finding by a regulatory agency that the employee, in fact, violated an environmental law.[216] But even if an employee engaged in "sloppy practices" that would tend to "cause a violation" of the environmental laws, an employer cannot rely upon this defense unless it can actually demonstrate that the employee "intended to cause a violation or that an actual violation resulted."[217]

ADMINISTRATIVE AND JUDICIAL APPELLATE REVIEW

There are three stages of appellate review in Department of Labor whistleblower cases. The administrative law judge issues a Recommended Decision and Order.[218] This recommended decision will become a final nonreviewable order of the DOL unless a petition for review of the order is filed before the DOL ARB.[219] In order to obtain judicial review of an administrative law judge ruling, parties must exhaust their administrative remedies and seek review of the administrative law judge decision before the ARB.[220]

Requirements of the Administrative Law Judge's Decision

The recommended decision of the administrative law judge becomes part of the official record. Generally, this decision is given substantial weight by the SOL. On appeal, the U.S. courts of appeals also pay close attention to the findings of the administrative law judge.[221]

The administrative law judge is the initial trier of fact and must weigh contradictory evidence, judge the credibility of witnesses, and reach ultimate conclusions as to the facts of the case.[222] The administrative law judge must clearly set forth the rationale for his or her findings. Failure to do so can result in remand of the case by an appellate court.[223] In *Director, Office of Workers' Comp. v. Congleton*, the court stated, "An administrative law judge's conclusory opinion, which does not encompass a discussion of the evidence contrary to his findings, does not warrant affirmance."[224]

The recommended decision must be based upon an analysis of all relevant evidence and should indicate explicitly which evidence has been weighed by the administrative law judge and the weight or credibility he or she assigns to it.[225]

Review by the Administrative Review Board

Under the provisions of the whistleblower protection statutes, the ARB has the sole responsibility to issue a final order if an administrative law judge's decision is appealed.[226] Nevertheless, this decision must be based upon the record that is developed by the administrative law judge and his or her recommended decision.[227]

The ARB is not bound by the decision of the administrative law judge,[228] and has "all the powers" the SOL "would have in making the initial decision."[229] Thus, the ARB is not bound by either the factual findings or the legal conclusions of an ALJ and reviews both *de novo*.[230] However, the ARB will often adopt the recommended decision of the administrative law judge if it is "supported by the evidence in the record," is in "accordance with law," and is "proper."[231] Although the ARB can rule on issues of law, it cannot declare an act of Congress unconstitutional.[232] In addition, the ARB will not normally consider new evidence that was not put into the record established by the administrative law judge, even if the new evidence is "material" to the issues adjudicated.[233] Newly discovered evidence will only be admitted if a party was "excusably ignorant" and had acted with "reasonable diligence" to discover the material prior to trial.[234] For example, the record may be supplemented if a party had attempted to obtain certain documents prior to the hearing but the documents only became available after the hearing record closed,[235] or when new evidence was obtained concerning a witness who was ordered to testify but failed to testify.[236] Impeachment evidence usually will not be admitted after the hearing record is closed.[237]

Seeking review before the ARB is a simple procedure. A petition for review must be filed and received by the ARB within ten business days of the date of the ALJ's Recommended Decision.[238] The petition must be served upon all parties, the Chief ALJ, the Assistant Secretary (OSHA), and the Associate Solicitor, Division of Fair Labor Standards.[239] The address for the ARB is:

Administrative Review Board
U.S. Department of Labor, Rm. S-4309
200 Constitution Ave., N.W.
Washington, D.C. 20210

Once a petition for review is filed, the ARB sets a briefing schedule in which the parties set forth their respective positions.[240] The petition for review is not a substantive document. Briefs filed before the ARB must be served on all parties and the Assistant Secretary (OSHA) and Associate Solicitor, Division of Fair Labor Standards.[241] After the ARB issues a final order, both parties have sixty days to file a petition for review to the appropriate U.S. Court of Appeals.[242] If either party is dissatisfied with the result of the court of appeals, it may file a petition for a *writ of certiorari* to the U.S. Supreme Court.

The scope of the ARB's review of the administrative law judge's initial Recommended Decision is extremely broad and is controlled by 5 U.S.C. § 557 and 29 C.F.R. § 24.6. Briefly, the SOL has "the authority to conduct a *de novo* review of all issues raised in [the] proceeding."[243] After a Final Order has been issued, the ARB has very infrequently granted a motion to reconsider. Although there is authority that suggests that the ARB does not have jurisdiction to grant such a motion,[244] the ARB has upheld its power to grant reconsideration.[245] The filing for a petition for review in the court of appeals can divest the DOL of jurisdiction.[246]

Conflicts Between the Recommended Decision of the Administrative Law Judge and the Final Decision of the ARB

The ARB has the power to reject a factual holding of an administrative law judge.[247] In order to do so, the ARB must point to other evidence on the record that supports this conclusion.[248]

If the ARB and the administrative law judge make contrary findings, an appellate court must defer to the conclusions of the ARB,[249] so long as the ARB's decision is based upon the substantial evidence of the record as a whole. But the administrative law judge's findings must be considered as part of the record and "must be weighed along with other opposing evidence supporting the [ARB's] decision."[250]

The method for analyzing an administrative law judge's findings that are counter to a final Department of Labor determination was outlined by the Supreme Court in *Universal Camera Corp. v. NLRB*.[251] In that case, which dealt with a conflict between the findings of a labor board's trial examiner and the findings of the National Labor Relations Board, the Court recognized that the agency may make the final decision and could reject an administrative law judge's findings even if they were not "clearly erroneous." But the findings of the administrative law judge must be granted reasonable and justifiable deference:

We do not require that the examiner's [i.e., administrative law judge's] findings be given more weight than in reason and in the light of judicial experience they deserve. The "substantial of evidence" standard is not modified in any way when the Board and its examiners disagree. We intend only to recognize that evidence supporting a conclusion may be less substantial when an impartial, experienced examiner who has observed the witnesses and lived with the case has drawn conclusions different from the Board's than when he has reached the same conclusion. The findings of the examiner are to be considered along with the consistency and inherent probability of testimony. The significance of his report, of course, depends largely on the importance of credibility in the particular case. To give it this significance does not seem to us materially more difficult than to heed the other factors which in sum determine whether evidence is "substantial."[252]

Interpreting this Supreme Court decision, the courts of appeals will give weight to the administrative law judge's opinion on issues of credibility of witnesses.[253] In *Pogue v. United States Department of Labor*,[254] the Court of Appeals reversed an order of the SOL in which the SOL had failed to appropriately evaluate an administrative law judge's credibility determinations: "[w]eight is given the [ALJ's] determinations of credibility for the obvious reason that he or she 'sees the witnesses and hears them testify.'"[255] The SOL may reject an administrative law judge's credibility determination if the record does not support the determination.[256] The Secretary may also freely reject credibility findings based on the "substance" of the testimony, as opposed to the "demeanor" of the witness.[257]

If the findings are not based solely on credibility issues or if a finding is based on facts about which no person testified, the ARB's conclusions should be given greater deference.[258] As a general rule, the ARB has deferred to the administrative law judge's credibility determinations.[259] But the ARB has rejected such credibility determinations that were not supported by substantial evidence.[260]

The ARB can also reject an administrative law judge's findings as to "actual motive." Even if the administrative law judge does not find discriminatory motive, the ARB may rely on other evidence, "reasonable and supported by substantial evidence on the record as a whole," and conclude that there was discriminatory motive. The ARB has the discretion to differ with an administrative law judge on the proper inference that can be drawn from the record and the "proper application of the statute."[261]

The ARB has the power to approve, reject, or reformulate the damages awarded to the complainant by the administrative law judge. Again, the ARB's decision must be based upon substantial evidence and the record as a whole.[262] The ARB's determination regarding attorney fees and costs may be set aside only if he or she abused discretion in making that determination.[263]

Interlocutory Appeals from the Administrative Law Judge to the Secretary of Labor

The Department of Labor regulations contain no provision for interlocutory appeals to the ARB of preliminary orders or rulings from the administrative law judges. The ARB has repeatedly refused to accept jurisdiction over interlocutory appeals and has held that such appeals are "disfavored."[264] Likewise, the U.S. courts of appeals have refused to take jurisdiction over interlocutory discovery disputes.[265] Absent an administrative law judge certifying a question for interlocutory review under 28 U.S.C. § 1292(b),[266] it has been suggested that the ARB does not have the discretion to accept a petition for interlocutory review.[267]

Appeal to the U.S. Circuit Courts of Appeals

An appeal of a final order[268] of the ARB must be filed within sixty days of the date of the ARB order.[269] Appellate review of a final decision of the ARB is controlled by 5 U.S.C. §§ 701-706.[270] These sections of the Administrative Procedure Act cover a petitioner's right to review, the actions that are reviewable, methods of obtaining relief pending review, and the scope of review. The whistleblower statutes essentially conform to the basic rules of law that govern judicial review in most administrative contexts. A final order of the SOL may only be reviewed by the U.S. Court of Appeals for the circuit "in which the violation, with respect to which the order was issued, allegedly occurred."[271] This is usually limited to a review of the record on which the Department of Labor's decision was based.[272]

The general rule of appellate review in Department of Labor whistleblower cases was summarized by the 9th Circuit in *Mackowiak v. University Nuclear Systems, Inc.*: "We review the Secretary's decision under the Administrative Procedure Act, 5 U.S.C. § 706. We will set aside the agency decision if it is "unsupported by substantial evidence" or "arbitrary, capricious, an abuse of discretion, or otherwise not in accordance with the law.""[273] This is the same standard of review the circuit courts use when reviewing a decision of the National Labor Relations Board.[274]

Standard of Review

The standard of judicial review of a Final Order of the SOL is set forth in 5 U.S.C. § 706.[275] In its relevant parts, Section 706 states:

To the extent necessary to a decision and when presented, the reviewing court shall decide all relevant questions of law, interpret constitutional and statutory provisions, and determine the meaning or applicability of the terms of an agency action. The reviewing court shall—

(1) compel agency action unlawfully withheld or unreasonably delayed; and

(2) hold unlawful and set aside agency action, findings, and conclusions found to be—

  (A) arbitrary, capricious, an abuse of discretion, or otherwise not in accordance with law;

  (B) contrary to constitutional right, power, privilege, or immunity;

  (C) in excess of statutory jurisdiction, authority, or limitations, or short of statutory right;

  (D) without observance of procedure required by law;

  (E) unsupported by substantial evidence.[276]

In regard to the standard of review for questions of law, the U.S. Court of Appeals for the 3rd Circuit described it as follows:

We exercise plenary review over legal questions concerning the construction of statutes which an agency administers where Congress has unambiguously addressed the question at issue. Federal Administrative Procedures Act, 5 U.S.C. §§ 704, 706. Here, however, we find the facial language of the Clean Water Act's whistleblower protection provision to admit of more than one interpretation, and hence we are compelled to uphold the Secretary's interpretation if it is "based on a permissible construction of the statute."[277]

An argument may be preserved for review even if it was not "forcefully raised" before the DOL.[278] However, an argument is waived if not presented to DOL.[279]

Review of a Legal Conclusion or an Interpretation of Law

While courts may substitute their own judgment when determining questions of law, they usually defer to an agency's interpretation of its own enabling statute.[280] Under the Supreme Court's formulation in *Chevron v. Natural Resources Defense Council*[281] a court must "keep in mind the deference" they must pay to an administrative agency's construction of statutes Congress has "charged" them with administering.[282] In *Udall v. Tallman*, the Supreme Court stated:

When faced with a problem of statutory construction, this Court shows great deference to the interpretation given the statute by the . . . agency charged with its administration. . . . Particularly is this respect due when the administration of a statute by the men charged with the responsibility of making the parts work efficiently . . . while they are yet untried and new [citations omitted].[283]

Applications of law to fact are reviewed under the substantial evidence test.[284]

The failure of the SOL to follow past secretarial precedent may be grounds for reversal. It is a basic tenet of administrative law that "an agency must either conform to its own precedents or explain its departure from them."[285]

When appellate courts review an agency's interpretation of its own regulation, rather than an enabling statute, the agency's construction is given "controlling weight unless it is plainly erroneous or inconsistent with the regulation."[286]

Substantial Evidence Test

If a final order of the SOL is not based upon "substantial evidence," it will be vacated and remanded by the court of appeals.[287] Substantial evidence is a difficult term to define. In a landmark labor case, the Supreme Court interpreted substantial evidence as:

more than a scintilla. It means such relevant evidence as a reasonable mind might accept as adequate to support a conclusion. [Accordingly, it] must do more than create a suspicion of the existence of the fact to be established . . . it must be enough to justify, if the trial were to a jury, a refusal to direct a verdict when the conclusion sought to be drawn from it is one of fact for the jury [citations omitted].[288]

Other definitions include: "Such relevant evidence as a reasonable mind might accept as adequate to support a conclusion."[289]

In its review, the U.S. Court of Appeals must consider the entire record including evidence that detracts from the Secretary's decision, as well as that which upholds it.[290]

The ARB must also review all relevant information in his or her written decision and generally must "indicate explicitly" what "evidence has been weighed and its weight."[291] In *Arnold v. Secretary of H.E.W.*, the

4th Circuit held: "Unless the Secretary has analyzed all evidence and has sufficiently explained the weight he has given to obviously probative exhibits, to say that his decision is supported by substantial evidence approaches an abdication of the court's 'duty to scrutinize the record as a whole to determine whether the conclusions reached are rational.' "[292]

Thus, under 5 U.S.C. § 706, the appeals court will analyze the SOL's decision and determine whether, based on the record as a whole, the decision of the Secretary was reasonable. The court should not substitute its own judgment for that of the Secretary: "In reviewing an agency's decision for substantial evidence, a court may not displace the agency's 'choice between two fairly conflicting views, even though the court would justifiably have made a different choice had the matter been before it *de novo*' " (citations omitted).[293]

The court begins with the Secretary's findings and then determines if the evidence makes those findings reasonable.[294]

"Arbitrary and Capricious" or an "Abuse of Discretion" Decisons

A decision or order of the SOL can be reversed if it is "arbitrary and capricious" or an "abuse of discretion." Under both of these standards the scope of review is narrow. Generally, a decision is not arbitrary and capricious if it is "rational," is "based on consideration of relevant factors," and does not "deviate from the ascertainable legislative intent." In the process of determining these factors, the court of appeals should "engage in a substantial inquiry into the facts," and need not be just a "rubber stamp."[295]

Findings of abuse of discretion are based on an even stricter standard of review. The Secretary can be reversed for abuse of discretion if he or she fails "to apply the appropriate equitable and legal principles to the established or conceded facts and circumstances."[296]

Generally, for an opinion not to be "arbitrary, capricious, an abuse of discretion, or otherwise not in accordance with law,"[297] the court must find that the Secretary's Final Order failed to meet one or more of the following criteria:

1. the Secretary acted within his or her scope of authority;

2. the decision was based on a consideration of relevant factors;

3. there was no clear error of judgment; and

4. the Secretary followed the necessary procedural requirements.[298]

Relief Pending Review—Stays of DOL Final Order

After the SOL issues a Final Order, an aggrieved party can file for a stay of the Secretary's decision pending review. An appeal to the circuit court does not automatically stay an order of the SOL.[299]

Rule 18 of the Federal Rules of Appellate Procedure provides that the application for stay "shall ordinarily be made in the first instance to the agency" (i.e., the SOL). The Secretary will only grant a stay if the petitioner demonstrates four factors: (1) that petitioner will prevail on appeal; (2) that there has been irreparable injury; (3) that a stay will not cause substantial harm to the other interested person; and (4) that a stay would not interfere with the public interest.[300] Merely having to pay a complainant money damages and pay attorney fees pending appeal are not grounds for a stay.[301] If the SOL denies the request or refuses to act upon the request, the aggrieved party may then file for relief pending review with the appropriate U.S. court of appeals. A stay of an agency order is an exercise of judicial discretion and the propriety of its issue depends on the circumstances of the particular case. There is no procedural or statutory right to a stay.[302]

The court of appeals can issue a stay "to prevent irreparable injury."[303] It has been found that retaliatory discrimination or other retaliatory activity may cause a chilling effect that can constitute such irreparable harm.[304] Financial injury alone does not constitute irreparable injury.[305]

The courts consider injunctive relief pending review to be an extraordinary exercise of their authority; as such, the petitioner carries a heavy burden of proof, and there is a strong presumption in favor of an agency decision. In a decision under the nuclear whistleblower law, the seventh Circuit denied an employer's petition for a stay, holding that the employer "had not persuaded us that it would suffer irreparable harm from being forced to continue one weld inspector in its employ for a few months while its petition for review is under consideration by this court."[306]

Thus, an aggrieved party is not entitled, as a matter of right, to a stay of a Department of Labor order pending review of the Secretary's decision. In order to receive such a stay, the aggrieved party must meet the stringent tests put forward in 5 U.S.C. § 705, Rule 18 of the Federal Rules of Appellate Procedure and *Commonwealth-Lord Joint Venture v. Donovan*.[307]

The SOL has repeatedly denied employers' requests for a stay pending the review of a SOL order issued on behalf of an employee[308] and has required employers to pay monetary damages to employees while a case is in appellate review.[309]

Writ of Mandamus

The whistleblower laws permit the aggrieved parties to file a writ of mandamus.[310] A writ of mandamus allows any party to a Department of Labor proceeding to file an action in federal district court to compel the department to perform a nondiscretionary duty imposed by the employee protection statutes or regulations.[311]

Federal mandamus proceedings are controlled by 28 U.S.C. § 1361, which reads, "The district courts shall have original jurisdiction of any action in the nature of mandamus to compel an officer or employee of the United States or any agency thereof to perform a duty owed to the plaintiff."

A writ of mandamus is an extraordinary remedy and is employed only in exceptional circumstances.[312] Before an aggrieved employee can request mandamus relief because of an agency's delay or inaction, the employee must first establish a *prima facie* case to warrant the issuance of a writ. The *prima facie* case is worded differently depending upon the judicial district or circuit in which the case is litigated. Essentially, however, the basic *prima facie* prerequisite may be outlined as follows: "Three elements usually must be satisfied before writ in the nature of mandamus may issue: 1) clear right of plaintiff to relief sought; 2) plainly defined and preemptory duty on defendant's part to do the act in question; and 3) lack of another available remedy."[313]

Writs of mandamus are hardly ever granted. The heavy burden placed on a party seeking such a writ was explicated by the U.S. Court of Appeals for the 5th Circuit when it denied issuing a writ in a nuclear whistleblower case:

Mandamus cannot be used as a substitute for appeal even when hardship may result from delay or from an unnecessary trial. Mandamus is an extraordinary remedy that should be granted only in the clearest and most compelling cases. A party seeking mandamus must show that no other adequate means exist to attain the requested relief and that his right to the issuance of the writ is "clear and indisputable."[314]

ENFORCEMENT PROCEEDINGS

If any person fails to comply with a final order of the SOL, the Secretary (and/or the person on whose behalf the final order was issued) can file a compliance action in federal district court.[315] In such cases, the federal district court is empowered to grant all appropriate relief, including injunctive relief, compensatory damages, and reasonable attorney fees and litigation costs.[316]

The SOL ruled that any request to the DOL for enforcement of a SOL order should be directed to the Solicitor of Labor.[317]

SETTLEMENT OF CLAIMS

Under the environmental employee protection laws, settlement agreements must be submitted to the DOL for review and approval.[318] This review is mandated both by a number of underlying statutes, which require the DOL to "enter into" any agreement reached by the parties, and under DOL case law, which holds that "public policy demands that settlement agreements between the parties . . . be reviewed by the [DOL] to determine whether the terms are fair, adequate, and reasonable."[319] Although "settlements are to be encouraged," the DOL recognizes that if the terms of a settlement are not "fair, adequate, and reasonable," other potential whistleblowers may be discouraged from reporting safety violations.[320] The DOL has held that the review of settlement is mandated by the public interest:

This is not an ordinary lawsuit where a plaintiff's consent to settle a complaint ends the inquiry. The [DOL] does not simply provide a forum for private parties to litigate their private employment discrimination suits such that the parties are free to resolve the case as they choose. Protected whistleblowing may expose not just private harms but health and safety hazards to the public, and the Secretary of Labor has been entrusted by Congress to represent the public interest in keeping channels of information open.[321]

In addition, if a settlement agreement or proposal contains illegal *hush money* restrictions on employee rights to blow the whistle, the agreement or proposal may be void and constitute a separate violation of law for which an employee is entitled to relief.[322] In fact, the mere "offer to pay a complainant to relinquish statutory rights" or the "breaking off" of settlement negotiations because an employee refused to accept *hush money* terms in an agreement constitute independent violations of the environmental and nuclear whistleblower law.[323]

The submission and approval of settlement agreements is a matter of routine procedure in the DOL. The DOL will interpret the agreement— and the conduct of the parties when they negotiated the agreement—in accordance with contract law.[324] Parties must submit the entire agreement to the presiding DOL officer (usually the administrative law judge) for approval.[325] Any "side agreements" related to the whistleblower claims must also be submitted, or the parties to the agreement must certify that there are no other such agreements.[326] The agreement cannot be submitted "under seal,"[327] and the amount of money obtained by the employee, as well as the amount paid for attorney fees, must also be disclosed.[328] In this regard, it is "error" for an administrative law judge to dismiss a complaint on the basis of a settlement without reviewing all of the terms of the agreement.[329] Although the entire agreement must be submitted for approval and placed on the record in a case, a party may, pursuant to DOL Freedom of Information Act (FOIA) regulations codified in 29 C.F.R. § 70.26, designate some or all of the settlement as "confidential business information" and request that the agency not disclose the agreement.[330] However, designating the information as potentially nondisclosable under any FOIA does not automatically protect the confidentiality of the settlement:

The records in this case are agency records which must be made available for public inspection and copying under the FOIA. In the event a request for inspection and copying of the record of this case is made by a member of the public, that request must be responded to as provided in the FOIA. If an exemption is applicable to the record in this case or any specific document in it, the [DOL] would determine at the time the request is made whether to exercise its discretion to claim the exemption and withhold the document. If no exemption were applicable, the document would have to be disclosed.[331]

Despite the prohibitions on *hush money* agreements and the requirement to obtain DOL approval for settlements, the DOL adheres to the principle that "settlements are to be encouraged."[332] Parties regularly execute settlements and submit them to an administrative law judge for approval. The Office of Administrative Law Judges has implemented regulations allowing both for a stay of proceedings (including discovery) in order to provide the parties time to execute agreement and for the appointment of "settlement judges" who can confidentially assist in the voluntary mediation of a dispute.[333] Likewise, under the DOL regulations, if a settlement agreement is approved by a presiding administrative law judge, the agreement may become final if no party files an appeal to the ARB within the ten-day period.[334] If an appeal of the merits decision has been filed with the ARB, then the ARB must approve the settlement.

Settlements can be effective at their execution, and the parties are bound by the contract until the DOL renders a decision.[335] If an employer violates a material term of an agreement during the administrative review process, the DOL may exercise its discretion and "decline" to "enter into" the agreement.[336] A settlement is an enforceable final order of the Secretary,[337] and its construction is governed by principles of contract law.[338] Oral agreements may be binding on the parties.[339]

A settlement can only be approved by the DOL if the complainant consented to it.[340] The settlement should be signed by the complainant individually. If it is not, the complainant should certify in writing to the veracity of the agreement.[341] An "unequivocal agreement and all material terms" can be approved by the DOL even if a party has "second thoughts" about the settlement and attempts to back out of the agreement.[342] However, if the parties did not reach an agreement on all material terms, the SOL will not approve the agreement.[343]

The ARB has jurisdiction to approve only those portions of a settlement that concern environmental whistleblower issues. If a settlement resolves other issues, the Secretary's "approval" of the agreement does not constitute approval of the settlement as it relates to other potentially resolved claims.[344] A settlement agreement may contain the "final terms" of employment for a whistleblower.[345] Consequently, it is fully appropriate for an agreement to contain terms related to employment, such as an agreement that an employer provide "positive references" for an employee.[346]

An order of the DOL rejecting a settlement agreement is not subject to appellate review under the *collateral order* doctrine.[347] Likewise, attempts to require an employee to waive his or her right to file future discrimination claims that may arise after the settlement is executed have been voided.[348]

DISMISSALS WITHOUT PREJUDICE

Under the environmental whistleblower statutes employees often obtain voluntary dismissals without prejudice. Such dismissals are sought for a variety of reasons. Most notably, due to the very short statute of limitations, it is prudent to file a complaint first and conduct the type of factual review that often precedes the filing of a formal complaint, during the OSHA investigation process. Additionally, many employees seek voluntary dismissal in order to pursue their discharge claims under state common law theories.

Regardless of the motive behind seeking a voluntary dismissal, the DOL applies the rule of law outlined in Federal Rule of Civil Procedure 41 in reviewing voluntary dismissals.[349] A complainant is entitled to unilateral and unconditional dismissal of his or her whistleblower complaint if a respondent has not filed the functional equivalent of either an answer to the complaint or a motion for summary judgment.[350] The filing of a telegram request for a hearing constitutes the functional equivalent of an answer.[351]

If the litigation is in an advanced stage and the respondent has expended considerable time and money defending a complaint, an employee is still entitled to a dismissal without prejudice if the respondent was not the party who appealed the determination of the ALJ or if the respondent failed to file a motion for summary judgment.[352] Even if a respondent did file a telegram appeal or a motion to dismiss, a complainant is still generally entitled to a conditional dismissal without prejudice.[353] In *Brown v. Holmes & Narver*, the SOL ruled that:

The ALJ correctly stated the law governing a decision maker's discretion to impose conditions on the grant of a request for dismissal without prejudice. I agree with the ALJ's analysis that to avoid legal harm or prejudice to a respondent as the result of a dismissal without prejudice, a complainant need pay only for items that will not be useful to respondent in defending an anticipated litigation in another forum.[354]

The Chief ALJ's recommended decision in *Brown*, which was explicitly adopted by the SOL, explained the policy reasons behind allowing complainants to withdraw complaints without prejudice:

Alleged whistleblowers should not be discouraged from reporting health and safety hazards or from filing discrimination complaints, and it follows that complainants not be discouraged from pursuing their issues before the Department merely because it may appear at some later date that an action before a state court is an alternative. While this public policy concern is not dispositive of whether attorney's fees should be attached to a given dismissal order, this valid concern does affect the manner in which the parties' arguments have been considered.[355]

Dismissals without prejudice have been granted while a case is on appeal before the ARB.[356]

A dismissal without prejudice allows a complainant to withdraw a DOL complaint and file a new action under state law without fear that a non-final determination of the DOL will prejudice that case:

Respondent accuses complainant of attempting to avoid the consequences of orders that had been previously entered by the ALJ, following a great expenditure of time and money. . . . Procedural tactics employed by the party are not determinative of the legal questions posed here. . . . The effect of Complainant's notice of voluntary dismissal without prejudice was to render the proceeding a nullity and leave the parties as if the action had never been brought.[357]

If a party desires to pursue a DOL whistleblower claim in an alternative forum, a voluntary dismissal is also important to insure that any ruling of the DOL is not afforded *res judicata* effect or acts to otherwise preclude a party from litigating the claim in another forum.[358]

SECTION 211—SPECIAL PROTECTION FOR NUCLEAR WHISTLEBLOWERS

On October 24, 1992, Congress amended Section 210 of the Energy Reorganization Act (ERA), redesignating the new law as Section 211 of the ERA.[359] The amendments, contained as part of the National Energy Policy Act of 1992, were designed to remedy shortcomings in Section 210;[360] to "strengthen the protection of whistleblowers in the nuclear power industry," "extend such protection to workers" in nuclear weapons complexes;[361] and to overturn certain court cases that resulted in a narrow interpretation of Section 210.[362]

Despite the amendments to the nuclear whistleblower statute, the law and procedures governing Section 211 remain, for the most part, identical with environmental case-law. In 1998, the DOL implemented new procedures for the adjudication of nuclear and environmental cases.[363] These regulations explicitly identify which specific rules now apply only to nuclear cases pursuant to the 1992 amendments.[364]

Scope of Protected Activity

Section 211 of the ERA adds three new categories of protected activity to those previously existing under Section 210. The new provisions state that the whistleblower must have:

(A) notified his employer of an alleged violation of this Act or the Atomic Energy Act of 1954 (42 U.S.C. 2011 *et seq.*)

(B) refused to engage in any practice made unlawful by this Act or the Atomic Energy Act of 1954, if the employee has identified the alleged illegality to the employer;

(C) testified before Congress or at any Federal or State proceeding regarding any provision (or proposed provision) of this Act or the Atomic Energy Act of 1954.[365]

These additions specifically overturned the holding of *Brown & Root v. Donovan*,[366] which narrowly interpreted the "old" Section 210 of the ERA. Although these amendments clarify and expand the scope of protected activity, they have little practical effect. Under the "old" Section 210 and the other six environmental whistleblower provisions, the SOL explicitly refused to follow the 5th Circuit precedent in *Brown & Root* and case-law has since held that internal complaints constitute protected activity in every jurisdiction except the 5th Circuit.[367]

For example, in a case under the Federal Water Pollution Control Act (FWPCA) the Secretary held that "the paramount purpose of the whistleblower provisions of the FWPCA, regardless of anything to the contrary in *Brown & Root*, is the protection of employees, a purpose which would be frustrated by failing to protect from retaliatory action employees who report violations internally to their employers."[368] Likewise, every court of appeals that has reviewed the statutory definition of Section 210 of the environmental statute has upheld the Secretary's interpretation that the internal raising of concerns is fully protected.[369]

These amendments codify the broad interpretations of protected activity given by the SOL in *Goldstein v. EBASCO Constructors, Inc.* and *Guttman v. Passaic Valley Sewerage Commissioners* and statutorily overturn the 5th Circuit's decision in *Brown & Root*.

Statute of Limitations

Perhaps the most significant change in the nuclear whistleblower law concerns the statute of limitations. Under Section 210 of the ERA (and under the other six environmental whistleblower provisions), employees had to file a complaint within thirty days of a discriminatory act.[370] Under Section 211 (b)(1), employees have up to 180 days to file a complaint. The other six environmental whistleblower statutes still have the short 30-day limitation period, whereas nuclear whistleblower complaints may now be filed within 180 days of an alleged discriminatory action.

The existing law regarding how to calculate the limitations period, equitable tolling, and continuing violations remains unchanged.

Whistleblower Protection for Department of Energy Contractors

A major loophole in Section 210 of the ERA concerned the coverage of employees who worked at nuclear facilities owned or regulated by the U.S. Department of Energy (DOE). Under Section 210, the SOL and the U.S. Court of Appeals for the 4th Circuit narrowly interpreted the definition of employers covered under the Act. The massive nuclear weapons complexes owned or regulated by the DOE were held to be beyond the protection of Section 210.[371]

Under the new Section 211(a)(1), the definition of "employer" under Section 210 was expanded. Congress explicitly included DOE "contractor or subcontractor" employees in the statutory definition of employers covered under Section 211(a)(2)(D). Congress overturned the narrow judicial construction previously given by the SOL and the 4th Circuit and insured that DOE contract employees at nuclear facilities would have protection. The DOL has ruled that Section 211 does not apply directly to employees of the U.S. Department of Energy, but only applies to DOE contractors.[372]

Investigation

Under the "old" Section 210 the DOL was compelled to investigate any complaint filed under the Act.[373] Section 211 (b)(3) now allows the SOL to decline conducting an investigation if it is determined that a complaint is frivolous.[374] This amendment has little practical impact inasmuch as OSHA regularly refused to investigate complaints deemed frivolous, even without the statutory authority.

An employee whose complaint is not investigated by the DOL may appeal that decision and seek a *de novo* hearing on the merits of the claim before a DOL ALJ.[375]

The new procedures were explained by Congressman Miller, a sponsor and conference manager of the legislation:

I would like to comment on the legislation's whistleblower provisions. Title XXIX of the conference agreement creates a new paragraph (3) in section 210(b) of the Energy Reorganization Act of 1974. Paragraphs (3)(A) and (3)(B) impose a limitation on the investigative authority of the Secretary of Labor in whistleblower cases. If the complainant does not make a prima facie showing that protected activity contributed to the unfavorable personnel action alleged in the complaint, the Secretary must dismiss the complaint and cease the investigation. And if the employer demonstrates by clear and convincing evidence that it would have taken the same unfavorable personnel action in the absence of such behavior, the Secretary must cease the investigation. These limitations apply only to the Secretary's prosecution of the complaint. The complainant is free, as under current law, to pursue the case before the administrative law judge if the Secretary dismisses the complaint. At the administrative law judge hearing and in any subsequent appeal, the complainant's burden of proof will be governed by new section 210 (b)(3)(c) and (d).[376]

If the OSHA decides to conduct an investigation, the investigation must be completed within 30 days under Section 211 (b)(2)(A).

Burden of Proof

In amending Section 210, Congress attempted to "facilitate relief for employees" by explicitly lowering the burden of proof in nuclear whistleblowing cases.[377] This provision, which used language similar to the burdens set forth in the Whistleblower Protection Act of 1989, was intended to eliminate the requirement that employees prove that animus was a "substantial" factor in a discharge.[378] Under the "old" Section 210, the SOL followed the traditional burdens of proof and persuasion set forth in *McDonnell Douglas* and *Mt. Healthy.*[379]

Under Section 211, Congress enacted a "free-standing evidentiary framework" which modified the *McDonnell Douglas/Mt. Healthy* burden:[380]

The Secretary may determine that a violation of subsection (a) of this section has occurred only if the complainant has demonstrated that any behavior described in subparagraphs (A) through (F) of subsection (a)(1) of this section [i.e., protected activities] was a contributing factor in the unfavorable personnel action alleged in the complaint. Relief may not be ordered under paragraph (2) if the employer demonstrates by clear and convincing evidence that it would have taken the same unfavorable personnel action in the absence of such behavior.[381]

This statutorily created standard was also utilized by Congress in the Whistleblower Protection Act of 1989 and the FDIC banking whistleblower law.[382] As explained in a banking case, the new burden of proof was intended to aid whistleblowers:

Those burdens quite clearly make it easier for the plaintiff to make her case under the statute and more difficult for the defendant to avoid liability: the plaintiff on the one hand, can make out a prima facie case of retaliation, and shift the burden of persuasion to the defendant, with circumstantial evidence that her disclosure was a contributing (not necessarily a substantial or motivating) factor in the adverse personnel action taken against her; and the defendant, once the burden has shifted, must prove not merely by a preponderance but by clear and convincing evidence that it would have taken the same action against the plaintiff even in the absence of her personnel disclosure.[383]

Under the new framework an employee still has the initial burden of proof to establish, by a preponderance of the evidence, the standard *prima facie* case.[384] The first significant difference between the standard Title VII evaluation and the new statutory burden concerns the proof of necessary discriminating animus. Employees need not demonstrate that animus was a "significant" or "motivating" factor behind an adverse action.[385] Under the new formulation an employee need only demonstrate, by a preponderance of the evidence, that protected activity was a "contributing factor" in the adverse action.[386]

The new "contributing" factor test completely displaced the

"motivating" factor test:

The words "a contributing factor" . . . [mean] *any factor which, alone or in connection with other factors, tends to affect in any way the outcome of the decision*. This test is specifically intended to over-rule existing law which requires a whistleblower to prove that his protected conduct was a "significant", "motivating", "substantial", or "predominant," factor in personnel action in order to overturn that action [emphasis original].[387]

Once the employee meets the "contributing factor" burden of proof, instead of the traditional burden of *production*, shifting to the employer to articulate a reasonable basis for the adverse action, the burden of proof is now raised to a "clear and convincing" standard,[388] a "higher" standard of proof than the "preponderance of the evidence" standard.[389]

The new standard of proof in Section 211 was summarized by the ARB as follows:

1. whether the complainants establish by a preponderance of the evidence that their protected activity was a contributing factor in [the adverse action], and if so;

2. whether [respondent] demonstrated by clear and convincing evidence that it would have [taken the adverse action] in the absence of their protected activity.[390]

Interim Relief

Section 211 procedurally amended Section 210 of the ERA by authorizing interim relief for employees who prevail in a trial before the DOL Office of ALJs.[391]

Under existing regulations, there are three stages for a whistleblower complaint. First, the OSHA conducts an investigation. Second, either party may appeal the investigative findings by requesting a formal hearing before an ALJ. At this stage of the proceedings, the parties are allowed to conduct discovery and call or cross-examine witnesses. On the basis of the hearing, the ALJ issues a written recommended decision.

The third stage consists of a *de novo* review of the ALJ decision by the ARB. Under the prior statute, an employee was not entitled to any relief until the ARB issued a final decision and order.

The new Section 211 allows for employees who prevail before the ALJ to immediately obtain all ordered relief (except for a compensatory damage award) pending review by the ARB.[392] This procedure was explic-

itly designed to eliminate the long administrative delay that had undermined the effectiveness of the law. As stated by Congressman Ford: "The
conference agreement breaks new ground in the protection of whistleblowers . . . with interim relief that will ensure that successful complainants will
not have to wait years for reinstatement and back pay after prevailing in
their administrative hearing."[393]

The ARB has issued numerous preliminary orders granting interim
relief, including reinstatement, back pay, postings,[394] corrections of performance evaluations, positive references,[395] and expungement of employee
records.[396] Employees are also entitled to preliminary orders for the payment of attorney's fees.[397] But if the ALJ's recommended decision is
reversed, an attorney will be ordered to return the fees and risk debarment
from participation in further DOL adjudication proceedings if he or she
refuses to repay the fees.[398] Employers' requests to obtain a stay of preliminary orders have been rejected.[399]

Federal Preemption

Section 211 of the ERA provides that the federal nuclear whistleblower law does not preempt employees from utilizing state employment
laws to seek redress from wrongful discharge or retaliation. In a new subsection (h), Section 211 states: "This section may not be construed to
expand, diminish or otherwise affect any right otherwise available to an
employee under Federal or State law to redress the employee's discharge
or other discriminatory action taken by the employer against the
employee."[400]

This section codifies the 1990 U.S. Supreme Court decision, which
unanimously held that the old Section 210 of the ERA did not preempt
states from enforcing stricter laws protecting nuclear whistleblowers.[401]

Posting

Section 211 requires all employers covered under the act to prominently post notice of an employee's whistleblower rights in any place of
employment where Section 211 applies.[402]

This statutory requirement mirrored a preexisting regulatory requirement for NRC licensees or contractors.[403] The posting requirement
also impacts on the statute of limitations. Under case law, if an employer
fails to properly post the required notice, an employee may have grounds
for equitable tolling of the statute of limitations.[404]

NOTES

1. 29 C.F.R. § 24. The nuclear whistleblower protection law was amended in 1992. The amended law increased the protections afforded employees under that act. In 1998 the Department of Labor (DOL) issued new regulations concerning the seven environmental and nuclear protection statutes that incorporated the 1992 amendments to the ERA. Office of the Secretary of Labor (SOL), "Procedures for the Handling of Discrimination Complaints Under Federal Employee Protection Statutes," 63 *Federal Register* 6614 (February 9, 1998), codified in 29 C.F.R. § 24 (1999). *See* Stephen M. Kohn, "Protecting Environmental and Nuclear Whistleblowers: A Litigation Manual," Nuclear Information and Resource Service (Washington, DC: 1985).

2. The DOL has exclusive jurisdiction over the adjudication of the seven environmental and nuclear whistleblower statutes. Attempts to enjoin the DOL from exercising this jurisdiction have been denied. *See Martin Marietta Energy Systems v. Martin*, 909 F. Supp. 528 (E.D. Tenn. 1993).

3. S. Rep. No. 414, 92nd Cong., 2nd Sess. at 82, 83, *reprinted in* 1972 U.S. Code Cong. & Admin. News 3668, 3748.

4. Legislative history of WPCA, *cited in* conference report of Clean Air Act, 1977 U.S. Code Cong. & Admin. News 1077, 1404. *See, e.g.,* the legislative history of Section 210 of the Energy Reorganization Act: "Under this section, employees and union officials could help assure that employers do not violate requirements of the Atomic Energy Act." S. Rep. No. 848, 95th Cong., 2nd Sess. at 29, 1978 U.S. Code Cong. & Admin. News 7303, 7304.

5. 118 Cong. Rec. 10,766-768 (1972), *reprinted in* Legislative History of the Water Pollution Control Act Amendments of 1972, at 655.

6. *See* CERCLA, 1980 U.S. Code Cong. & Admin. News 6119; ERA, 1978 U.S. Code Cong. & Admin. News 1077; SWDA, 1976 U.S. Code Cong. & Admin. News 6238; TSCA, 1976 U.S. Code Cong. & Admin. News 4491; SDWA, 1974 U.S. Code Cong. & Admin. News 6454; WPCA, 1972 U.S. Code Cong. & Admin. News 3638.

7. 42 U.S.C. § 5851.

8. 1978 U.S. Code Cong. & Admin. News 7303.

9. 1977 U.S. Code Cong. & Admin. News 1404-1405.

10. In 1996, the SOL delegated authority under the whistleblower laws to a three-member Administrative Review Board (ARB). Secretary's Order 2-96, 61 *Federal Register*, 19978 (May 3, 1996). The SOL mandated that the ARB follow the Code of Federal Regulations (CFR) applicable to the DOL whistleblower proceedings. The SOL also required the ARB to follow all past secretarial precedent, unless they are explicitly reversed. *Id.*

11. *Egenrieder v. Metropolitan Edison Co./G.P.U.*, 85-ERA-23, order of remand by SOL, at 7-8 (April 20, 1987); *see also Stone & Webster Engineering v. Herman*, 115 F.3d 1568 (11th Cir. 1997); *Melendez v. Exxon*, 93-ERA-6, D&O of ARB, at 13-14 (July 14, 2000) (legislative history is useful in understanding scope of protected activity).

12. *Connecticut Light & Power v. SOL*, 85 F.3d 89, 94 (2nd Cir. 1996); *Betchel v. SOL*, 50 F.3d 926, 932 (11th Cir. 1995). The legislative history of the new Section 211 of the ERA can be found in the following locations: H. Rep. 102-474, Part I, Committee on Energy and Commerce, Comprehensive National Energy Policy Act Report (Dingell Report), at 227, 377-378 (March 30, 1992); H. Rep. 102-474, Part 8, Committee on Interior and Insular Affairs, Comprehensive National Energy Policy Act, Report (Miller Report), at 25-26, 78-79 (May 5, 1992), Vol. 138 Congressional Record, No. 142 (October 5, 1992), H 11409 (Miller); H 11412 (Lent); H 11442 (Williams); H 11444 (Ford).

13. *CP&L v. DOL*, 43 F.3d 912, 913 (4th Cir. 1995).

14. *Wagoner v. Technical Products, Inc.*, 87-TSA-4, D&O SOL, at 6 (November 20, 1990), *quoting from English v. General Electric Co.*, 110 S.Ct. 2270, 2277 (1990). *Accord., Guttman v. Passaic Valley Sewerage Commission*, 85-WPC-2, D&O of SOL, at 11 (March 13, 1992), *aff'd*, 992 F. 2d 474 (3rd Cir. 1993).

15. *DeFord v. Secretary of Labor*, 700 F.2d 281, 286 (6th Cir. 1983); *accord., NLRB v. Schrivener*, 405 U.S. 117 (1972).

16. *Kansas Gas & Elec. Co. v. Brock*, 780 F.2d 1505, 1512 (10th Cir. 1985); *Poulos v. Ambassador Fuel Oil Co.*, 86-CAA-1, D&O of remand by SOL, at 6 (April 27, 1987); *contra Brown & Root, Inc. v. Donovan*, 747 F.2d 1029 (5th Cir. 1984).

17. *Chase v. Buncombe County, N.C.*, 85-SWD-4, D&O of remand by SOL, at 4 (November 3, 1986). *See also Faulkner v. Olin Corp.*, 85-SWD-3, Recommended Decision of ALJ, at 5-6 (August 16, 1985), adopted by SOL (November 18, 1985) ("from the legislative history and the court and agency precedents . . . it is clear that Congress intended the 'whistleblower' statutes to be broadly interpreted to achieve the legislative purpose of encouraging employees to report hazards to the public and the environment by offering them protection in their employment"); *Royce v. Bechtel Power Corp.*, 83-ERA-3, slip op. of ALJ, at 2 (November 29, 1983).

18. *English, supra*, at 2270 (slip op. at 8) (June 4, 1990).

19. *Beliveau v. Dept. of Labor*, 170 F.3d 83, 87-88 (1st Cir. 1999), quoting from Decision of the SOL in *Hoffman v. Fuel Econ. Contracting*, 87-ERA-33 (August 4, 1989).

20. *DeFord v. Secretary of Labor*, 700 F.2d 281, 286 (6th Cir. 1983) (citations omitted).

21. *Polizzi v. Gibbs & Hill, Inc.*, 87-ERA-38, Order Rejecting in Part, etc., by SOL, at 2-3 (July 18, 1989).

22. *Hill et al. v. T.V.A.*, 87-ERA-23/24, D&O of remand by SOL, at 4 (May 24, 1989).

23. 800 F.2d 563, 565 (6th Cir. 1986) (J. Edwards concurring).

24. 42 U.S.C. § 5851.

25. 800 F.2d at 565. Justice Edwards' language in *Rose* was adopted by the SOL in *Hill* at 4-5.

26. 992 F.2d 474, 479 (3rd Cir. 1993).

27. *See, e.g., Doyle v. Hydro Nuclear Services*, 89-ERA-22, D&O of SOL, at 6 (March 30, 1994); *accord., Brock v. Richardson*, 812 F.2d 121, 124 (3rd Cir. 1987), *citing Mitchell v. Robert DeMario Jewelry, Inc.*, 361 U.S. 288 (1960).

28. U.S. NRC, "Freedom of Employees in The Nuclear Industry to Raise Safety Concerns With Fear of Retaliation; Policy Statement," 61 *Federal Register* 24336-23440 (May 4, 1996).

29. *In re Five Star Products, Inc.*, 38-NRC-169, slip op. at 12 (October 21, 1993).

30. 1972 U.S. Code Cong. & Admin. News 3668, 3748 ("Section 507 of the bill is patterned after the National Labor Management Act and a similar provision in Public Law 91-173 relating to the health and safety of the nation's coal miners"); 30 U.S.C. § 820(b); *see also* NLRA § 8(a)(4), 29 U.S.C. § 158(a)(4).

31. *See, e.g., Hill, supra*, at 7; *Kansas Gas & Elec. Co., supra*, at 1511-1512; *DeFord supra*, at 286; *Wells v. Kansas Gas & Elec. Co.*, 83-ERA-12, slip op. of ALJ, at 4 (February 27, 1984); *Flanagan v. Bechtel Power Corp.*, 81-ERA-7, slip op. of ALJ, at 8-9 (November 19, 1981). *Contra Brown & Root, supra*, at 1029.

32. *See, e.g.,* 1978 U.S. Code Cong. & Admin. News 7303 (ERA); 1977 U.S. Code Cong. & Admin. News 1077 (CAA); 120 Cong. Rec. 36,393 (1974) (remarks of Sen. Symington) (SDWA).

33. *Faulkner, supra*, at 4-5.

34. *Poulos, supra*, at 5; *Faulkner* at 3-5.

35. 29 C.F.R. §§ 18 and 24. *See also Goldstein v. EBASCO Constructors, Inc.*, 86-ERA-36, D&O of SOL, at 6 (April 7, 1992), *rev'd. on other grounds*, U.S. Court of Appeals for the Fifth Circuit; *Accord., Passaic Valley Sewerage Commissioners v. Department of Labor*, 992 F.2d 474, 479 (3rd Cir. 1993) ("the whistleblower provisions of the Clean Water Act mirrors that of several other federal environmental, safety and energy statutes").

36. 29 C.F.R. § 24.3(b). The statute commences running when an employee has "final and unequivocal notice" that a decision has in fact been made to take adverse action, not on the date the decision is implemented. *See Ross v. FP&L*, 96-ERA-36, D&O of ARB, at 3-5 (March 31, 1999); *McGough v. U.S. Navy*, 86-ERA-18/19/20, at 9-10 (June 30, 1988) (collecting cases); *Rose v. Dole*, 945 F.2d 1331 (6th Cir. 1991). A statute of limitations may be subject to equitable tolling. *See School District of Allentown v. Marshall*, 657 F.2d 16, 18 (3rd Cir. 1981); *Rose v. DOL*, 800 F.2d 563 (6th Cir. 1986). A claim may be timely under a "continuing violation" theory. *See Bruno v. Western Elec. Co.*, 829 F.2d 957, 960-961 (10th Cir. 1987); *Egenrieder v. Met. Ed.*, 85-ERA-23, Order of SOL, at 4 (April 20, 1987).

37. *Pantanizopoulos v. TVA*, 96-ERA-15, D&O of ARB, at 3 (October 20, 1997) ("The Secretary has held that the ERA's limitation period begins running on the date the employee is informed of the challenged employment decision"). The statute runs, not on the date in which the harm or injury would

occur, but on the date in which the employee is informed that a final adverse decision has been made. *Id.* at 3-4; *Accord., Hadden v. Georgia Power Company,* 89-ERA-21, D&O of SOL, at 3-4 (February 9, 1994) ("definite notice" or "final and unequivocal notice" triggers the running of a statute of limitations) .

38. 29 C.F.R. § 24.3(b)(2).

39. *Delaware State College v. Ricks,* 449 U.S. 250, 259 (1980); *English v. Whitfield,* 858 F.2d 957, 961 (4th Cir. 1988). Notice of the decision must be "unequivocal." *Flor v. U.S. Department of Energy,* 93-TSC-1, D&O of Remand by SOL, at 8 (December 9, 1994).

40. *Wagerle v. The Hospital of the University of Pennsylvania,* 93-ERA-1, D&O of SOL, at 3 (March 17, 1995).

41. *International Union v. Robbins & Meyers, Inc.,* 429 U.S. 229, 236-240 (1976); *Prybys v. Seminole Tribe of Florida,* 95-CAA-15, D&O of ARB, at 5 (November 26, 1996).

42. *Hill v. DOL,* 65 F.3d 1331, 1335 (6th Cir. 1995); *Larry v. Detroit Edison,* 86-ERA-32, D&O of SOL, at 12-19 (June 28, 1991); *aff'd sub nom. Detroit Edison v. SOL* (6th Cir. 1992) (unpublished decision); *Hall v. DOL,* 98-9547 (10th Cir. 1999).

43. *Id.* at 1335 (citations and internal quotations omitted).

44. In *Rose, supra,* at 1335, the court delineated five factors to be weighed in determining whether to apply equitable tolling: (1) whether the plaintiff lacked actual notice of the filing requirements; (2) whether the plaintiff lacked constructive notice; (3) the diligence with which the plaintiff pursued his rights; (4) whether there would be prejudice to the defendant if the statute were tolled; and (5) the reasonableness of the plaintiff remaining ignorant of his rights. In *School Dist. of Allentown, supra,* at 19, the court set forth the three basic fact patterns often used in justifying equitable tolling: (1) the defendant has actively misled the plaintiff respecting the cause of action; (2) the plaintiff has in some extraordinary way been prevented from asserting his rights; or (3) the plaintiff has raised the precise statutory claim in issue but has mistakenly done so in the wrong forum. For example, "mental incapacity," *Hall v. EG&G Defense Materials,* 97-SDW-9, D&O of ARB, at 2-3 (September 30, 1998); raising "precise statutory claim . . . mistakenly in wrong forum," *Smith v. American President Lines, LTD,* 571 F.2d 102 (2nd Cir. 1978); or the failure of an employer to post a required notice informing employees of their rights, *Charlier v. S. C. Johnson & Son,* 556 F.2d 761 (10th Cir. 1976); *cf., Hancock v. Nuclear Assurance Corp.,* 91-ERA-33, D&O of SOL, at 6-7 (November 2, 1992). *See also Prybys, supra,* at 4-5.

45. *Prybys, supra,* at 5 ("the doctrine of *equitable tolling* focuses on the question of whether a duly diligent complainant was excusably ignorant of his rights, whereas the principle of *equitable estoppel* focuses on the issue of whether the employer misled the complainant and thus caused the delay in filing the complaint"). *See School Dist. of Allentown, supra,* at 19 (tolling justified if defendant actively misled plaintiff). In *Hill, supra,* at 1335 (citations omitted), the court identified three factors that would be necessary to toll the limitations period based on *fraudulent concealment:* (1) wrongful concealment by the defen-

dants; (2) failure of the plaintiff to discover the operative facts; and (3) plaintiff's due diligence until discovery of the facts.

46. *See, e.g., Vernadore v. SOL*, 141 F.3d 625, 630 (6th Cir. 1998); *OFCCP v. CSX Transportation, Inc.*, 88-OFC-24, D&O of Remand by SOL, at 22-26 (October 13, 1994), *citing Elliott v. Sperry Rand Corp.*, 79 F.R.D. 580, 584-585 (D. Minn. 1978) (setting forth four basic fact patterns used in establishing a continuing violation); *Simmons v. APS*, 93-ERA-5, D&O of Remand by SOL, at 8-9 (May 9, 1995) (finding continuing violation due to a "pattern of discrimination"); *Holden v. Gulf States*, 92-ERA-44, D&O of SOL, at 12-13 (April 14, 1995) (discussing cases finding blacklisting to be a continuing violation); *Thomas v. APS*, 89-ERA-19, D&O of SOL, at 10-16 (September 17, 1993) (denial of promotion held continuing in nature). In *CL&P v. DOL*, 85 F.3d 89, 96 (2nd Cir. 1996) (internal citations omitted), the court set forth the rule governing the application of the continuing violations theory as follows:

> Under the continuing violation standard, a timely charge with respect to any incident of discrimination in furtherance of a policy of discrimination renders claims against other discriminatory actions taken pursuant to that policy timely, even if they would be untimely if standing alone . . . . Thus, in cases where a plaintiff proves i) an underlying discriminatory policy or practice, and ii) an action taken pursuant to that policy during the statutory period preceding the filing of the complaint, the continuing violation rule shelters claims for all other actions taken pursuant to the same policy form the limitations period.

In other words, under the six environmental laws, in order to qualify for coverage under the continuing violation theory, there must be an "allegation of a course of related discriminatory conduct" and the compliant must be "filed within thirty days of the last discriminatory act." *Flor v. U.S. Department of Energy*, 93-TSC-1, D&O of Remand by SOL, at 7 (December 9, 1994) (citations and internal quotations omitted). In order to determine whether alleged discriminatory actions are "related," courts apply a three-part test: "(1) whether the alleged acts involve the same subject matter, (2) whether the alleged acts are recurring or more in the nature of isolated decisions, and (3) the degree of permanence." *Id.* at 7-8 (citations omitted). The continuing violation theory cannot be used to "resurrect" a "time-barred complaint." *Gillilan v. TVA*, 92-ERA-46/50, D&O of SOL, at 4-5 (April 20, 1995).

47. *Bausemer v. TU Electric*, 91-ERA-20, D&O of SOL, at 9 (October 31, 1995). *See also Ross v. FP&L, supra*, at 4 ("statute of limitations begins to run on the date when facts which would support the discrimination complaint were apparent or should have been apparent to a person similarly situated to Complaint with a reasonably prudent regard for his rights") (citations in internal quotations omitted); *Grace v. City of Andalusia*, 95-WPC-6, D&O of ARB, at 2 (September 23, 1996) ("The doctrine of *equitable tolling* is generally inapplicable where a plaintiff is represented by counsel"); *Roberts v. TVA*, 94-ERA-15, D&O of SOL, at 5 (August 18, 1995) (constructive knowledge).

48. 29 C.F.R. § 24.3(b)(1); *see also Sawyers v. Baldwin Union Free School Dist.*, 85-TSC-1, D&O of remand by SOL, at 5 (October 10, 1988).

49. A complaint may also be filed at the local OSHA office, 29 C.F.R. § 24.3(d).

50. 29 C.F.R. § 24.3(c).

51. *Bassett v. Niagara Mohawk Power Co.*, 86-ERA-2, Remand Order of SOL, slip op., at 5 (July 9, 1986); *see also Rudd v. Westinghouse Hanford*, 88-ERA-33, D&O of ARB, at 24, n. 27 (November 10, 1997) (collecting cases).

52. 84-ERA-9-12, D&O of remand by SOL, slip op., at 9-10 (March 12, 1986).

53. *Rudd, supra,* at 22-24 ("Supplementation should be freely permitted absent a showing, by the opposing party, of undue delay, bad faith, dilatory motive, or prejudice").

54. 29 C.F.R. § 24.4(d)(1).

55. 29 C.F.R. § 24.4(b).

56. *English v. General Electric Co.*, 85-ERA-2, D&O of SOL, at 7 (February 13, 1992).

57. 29 C.F.R. § 24.5.

58. *Rex v. EBASCO Servs., Inc.*, No. 87-ERA-6, D&O of remand to the Wage and Hour Administrator by the SOL (April 13, 1987); *Kamin v. Hunter Corp.*, 89-ERA-11, Order of SOL (March 12, 1990). *See Pickett v. TVA*, 99-CAA-25, Order Remanding by ALJ (September 10, 1999) (granting uncontested remand, but recognizing remand not allowed under ERA).

59. *Newton v. State of Alaska*, 96-TSC-10, Order Denying Request for Hearing of the Chief ALJ (October 25, 1996).

60. *Billings v. T.V.A.*, 91-ERA-12, D&O of ARB, at 8-9 (June 26, 1996).

61. 29 C.F.R. § 24.4(c).

62. 5 U.S.C. §§ 552, 552a.

63. 29 C.F.R. § 24.4(d)

64. *Batts v. TVA*, 82-ERA-5, slip op. of ALJ, at 1 (May 3, 1982).

65. *Majors v. Asea Brown Boveri, Inc.*, 96-ERA-33, D&O of ARB, at 1 n. 1, (August 1, 1997).

66. 29 C.F.R. § 24.4(d)(2). *See Staskelunas v. Northeast Utilities*, 98-ERA-7, D&O of ARB, at 2 n. 4, 3 n. 3 (May 4, 1998). The ARB recognizes that all of its administrative deadlines are subject to tolling or modification. *See Garcia v. Wantz Equipment*, Order of ARB, at 2 (February 8, 2000), *citing American Farm Lines v. Black Ball Freight*, 397 U.S. 532, 539 (1970).

67. 29 C.F.R. § 24.4(d)(2).

68. 29 C.F.R. § 24.4(d)(3). Care should be given to ensure strict compliance with this procedural rule. If a technical error does occur in the filing procedure, there is authority supporting "substantial compliance" or "substantial equivalent" test for overcoming such errors. *Daugherty v. General Physics Corp.*, 92-SDW-2, D&O of remand of ALJ, at 3 (December 14, 1992), adopted by SOL (April 19, 1995). *But see Degostin v. Bartlett Nuclear*, 98-ERA-7, D&O of ARB, at 3 (May 4, 1998) ("time limit for filing a request for a hearing has been strictly construed"); *Backen v. Energy Op. Inc.*, 95-ERA-46, D&O of ARB, at 3-4 (June 7, 1996) (time limits for filing a hearing request are "strictly construed").

69. 29 C.F.R. § 24.6(a). However, failing to promptly serve these notices will not be fatal to an appeal. *See Pawlowski v. Hewlett-Packard Co.*, 97-TSC-3, Order of ARB (September 15, 1999).

70. 29 C.F.R. § 24.4(d)(3).

71. 29 C.F.R. § 24.6(a).

72. *English v. General Electric Co.*, 85-ERA-2, D&O of SOL, at 11 n. 5 (February 13, 1992); *contra Allen v. EG&G Defense*, 97-SDW-8 & 10, Order of ALJ (January 26, 1998).

73. 29 C.F.R. § 24.6(a).

74. 29 C.F.R. § 18.42(f).

75. In April 1996, the SOL established the Administrative Review Board *(ARB) (see note 10)* with authority to issue final decisions on behalf of the Secretary in environmental whistleblower cases. The court of appeals has rejected challenge to the ARB's authority. *Varnadore v. SOL*, 141 F.3d 625, 631-632 (6th Cir. 1998).

76. 29 C.F.R. § 24.8(c).

77. 29 C.F.R. § 24.6(a). *See also Malpass v. General Electric Co.*, 85-ERA-38/39, D&O of SOL (March 1, 1994) (discussing cases on granting continuances).

78. 29 C.F.R. §§ 18.4, 18.6(b), 18.24.

79. 29 C.F.R. § 18.1(b); *Young v. E. H. Hinds*, 86-ERA-11, D&O of remand by SOL, at 3 n. 2 (July 8, 1987). *See Forest v. Williams Power Corp.*, 2000-ERA-16/17, D&O of ALJ (April 7, 2000) ("complainant who waives the statutory and regulatory deadline should be allowed time to conduct discovery").

80. *Johnson v. Transco Prods., Inc.*, 85-ERA-7, slip op. of ALJ, at 2 (March 5, 1985); *Bullock v. Rochester Gas & Elec. Corp.*, 84-ERA-22, interim order on motion, slip op. of ALJ, at 2 (1984).

81. *See, e.g., Donovan v. Freeway Construction Co.*, 511 F. Supp. 869, 878 (D. R.I. 1982) ("The defendant may not pervert a statutory provision protecting employees").

82. *Long et al. v. Roadway Express, Inc.*, 88-STA-31, D&O of SOL, at 3-4 (March 9, 1990); *Poulos, supra*, at 12. For authority on this issue, *see also Brock v. Pierce County*, 106 S.Ct. 1834 (1986); *Logan v. Zimmerman Brush Co.*, 455 U.S. 422, 432-437 (1982).

83. *Timmons v. Mattingly Testing Services*, 95-ERA-40, D&O of ARB, at 5 (June 21, 1996).

84. *Id.* at 6.

85. *Id.* at 8.

86. *See Abson v. Kaiser Co.*, 84-ERA-8, slip op. of ALJ, at 2 (January 7, 1985); *Bullock, supra*, decision and interim order on motion of ALJ (continuance ordered to allow *pro se* complainant time to find an attorney); *Guity v. TVA*, 90-ERA-10, Remand Order of SOL (May 3, 1995) (delay due to psychological problems); *Rios-Berrios v. INS*, 776 F.2d 859, 862-863 (9th Cir. 1985); *Lowe v. City of E. Chicago*, 897 F.2d 272 (7th Cir. 1990).

87. *Forest, supra.*

88. *Unger v. Saraflite*, 376 U.S. 575, 589-590 (1964); *see also Administrative Procedure Act*, 5 U.S.C. § 554.

89. The Department of Labor rules for time computation are located at 29 C.F.R. § 18.4.

90. *See, e.g., O'Sullivan et al. v. Northeast Nuclear Energy Co.*, 88-ERA-37/38, recommended D&O of ALJ, at 15-16 (August 18, 1989).

91. 29 C.F.R. §§ 18.40, 18.41.

92. *See, e.g., Studer v. Flowers Baking Co.*, 93-CAA-11, D&O of SOL, at 2 (June 19, 1995); *Varnadure v. Oak Ridge National Laboratory*, 92-CAA-215 & 94-CAA-213, D&O of ARB, at 58 (June 14, 1996).

93. *Gillilan v. TVA*, 91-ERA 31/34, D&O SOL, at 4-5 (August 28, 1995); *Kesterson v. Y-12 Nuclear Weapons Plant*, 95-CAA-12, D&O of ARB, at 5-6 (April 8, 1997).

94. *Richter v. Baldwin Assocs.*, 84-ERA-9/10/11/12, Order of SOL, at 13-14 (March 12, 1986); *Stauffer v. Wal-Mart Stores*, 99-STA-21, D&O of ARB, at 6 (November 30, 1999).

95. *Flor, supra*, at 9-12.

96. *Reid v. Methodist Medical Center*, 93-CAA-4, D&O of SOL, at 32 (April 3, 1995).

97. 29 C.F.R. § 24.6(e)(3).

98. *Ass't Secretary v. Double Trucking, Inc.*, 98-STA-34, D&O of SOL, at 4 (July 16, 1999).

99. *Migliore v. Rhode Island Dept. of Environmental Management*, 98-SWD-3, Order Regarding Discovery Dispute by ALJ, at 3 (October 14, 1998) ("It is clear from the aforementioned regulation and precedent that in determining whether to admit evidence at hearing over an objection of relevance, an ALJ should apply a broad scope of relevance. It logically follows that the scope of discovery is even broader").

100. *See Khandelwal v. Southern California Edison*, 97-ERA-6, D&O of ARB, at 4 (March 31, 1998). *See also Timmons v. Mattingly Testing Services*, 95-ERA-40, D&O of ARB, at 5-6 (June 21, 1996).

101. *Robinson v. Martin Marietta Services*, 94-TSC-7, D&O of ARB, at 4 (September 23, 1996).

102. *Tracanna v. Arctic Slope Inspection Svc.*, 97-WPC-1, D&O of ARB, at 5 n. 6 (November 6, 1997).

103. *Id.*

104. 29 C.F.R. §§ 18.18, 18.19, 18.20.

105. *Johnson v. Oak Ridge Operations*, 95-CAA-201 21/22, D&O of ARB, at 12 (September 30, 1999).

106. *Tracanna, supra*, at 5.

107. *See Immanuel v. DOL*, 139 F.3d 889 (table), unpublished opinion, 1998 WL 129932 (4th Cir. 1998); *Malpass v. General Electric Co., supra*, D&O of SOL, at 20-21 (March 1, 1994); *Ass't. Sec'y. v. Gammon Wire Feeder Corp.*, 87-STA-5, D&O of SOL (September 17, 1987).

108. *See* 5 U.S.C. §§ 552, 552(a). An excellent guide to using the Freedom of Information Act and Privacy Act is Allan Adler, ed., *Litigation Under the Federal Freedom of Information Act and Privacy Act* (American Civil Liberties Union Foundation, 122 Maryland Avenue, N.E., Washington, D.C. 20002, published annually).

109. 29 C.F.R. § 18.26. *See also* SWDA, 42 U.S.C. § 6971 (b); WPCA, 33 U.S.C. § 1367(b); CERCLA, 42 U.S.C. § 9610(b).

110. 29 C.F.R. § 18.34; *See also Seater v. Southern California Edison,* 95-ERA-13, D&O of ARB, at 14-15 (September 27, 1996).

111. 29 C.F.R. § 24.5(e). Application of the Federal Rules of Evidence is contrary to the regulatory mandate applicable to the DOL adjudicatory proceedings. *Melendez v. Exxon,* 93-ERA-6, D&O of ARB, at 24-25 (July 14, 2000).

112. *Timmons, supra,* at 11. *Accord., Seater, supra,* at 5.

113. 29 C.F.R. §§ 18.52, 27.5(e)(2).

114. 29 C.F.R. § 18.45.

115. 29 C.F.R. § 18.47.

116. 29 C.F.R. § 18.50.

117. 29 C.F.R. § 18.46.

118. 29 C.F.R. § 18.29.

119. 29 C.F.R. § 18.1(a).

120. 29 C.F.R. § 18.1(b).

121. 29 C.F.R. § 18.10.

122. 29 C.F.R. § 18.12, § 24.6(g).

123. 29 C.F.R. § 24.6(f)(2).

124. 29 C.F.R. § 24.6(f)(2).

125. 29 C.F.R. § 24.6(f)(1).

126. 29 C.F.R. § 24.6(e).

127. 29 C.F.R. § 24.5(b).

128. *Yellow Freight v. Martin,* 954 F.2d 353, 357 (6th Cir. 1992).

129. *See Matthews v. Eldridge,* 424 U.S. 319 (1976) ("the fundamental requirement of due process is the opportunity to be heard at a meaningful time and in a meaningful manner"); *English v. General Electric Co.,* 85-ERA-2, D&O of SOL, at 7 (February 13, 1992), *quoting Matthews* at 335. See *Melendez, supra,* at 24-25 (parties must be provided a "full and fair opportunity for the presentation of arguments and facts).

130. *In the Matter of Charles A. Kent,* 84-WPC-2, Remand D&O, at 9-10 (April 6, 1987), *quoting from Hornsby v. Allen,* 326 F.2d 605, 608 (5th Cir. 1964). *See also Armstrong v. Manzo,* 380 U.S. 545, 550-552 (1965); *Carson Products Co. v. Califano,* 594 F.2d 453, 459 (5th Cir. 1979); *North Alabama Express, Inc. v. United States,* 585 F.2d 783, 786-787 (5th Cir. 1978); 5 U.S.C. § 554(b) and (c) (1982). *See English v. General Electric Co.,* 85-ERA-2, D&O of SOL, at 7-8 (February 13, 1992) (discussing due process requirements).

131. 29 C.F.R. § 24.6(e)(1).

132. *Frady v. TVA,* 92-ERA-19/34, D&O of SOL, at 7-8 (October 23, 1995); *see also Seater, supra,* at 5-8.

133. *Ass't. Secretary of Labor for Occupational Safety and Health and Anthony Ciotti v. Sysco Foods of Philadelphia*, 97-STA-30, D&O of ARB, at 6 (July 8, 1998).

134. 29 C.F.R. §§ 18.44(b), 24.5(e)(3). Major witnesses should, wherever possible, testify live at the hearing, not through prerecorded depositions. *See Carter v. Electrical District No. 2*, 92-TSC-11, D&O of SOL, at 13 n.1 (July 26, 1995).

135. 29 C.F.R. § 18.47.

136. 29 C.F.R. § 24.6(e)(3).

137. *Oliver v. Hydro-Vac Services, Inc.*, 91-SWD-1, D&O of ARB, at 2 (January 6, 1998). *See* Stephen Smith, "Due process and the subpoena power in federal environmental health and safety whistleblower proceedings," 32 *University of San Francisco Law Review* 533 (1998).

138. *Immanuel v. DOL*, 139 F.3d 889 (table), unpublished opinion, 1998 WL 129932, (4th Cir. 1998).

139. *Richardson v. Perales*, 402 U.S. 389, 410 (1972); *Calhoun v. Bailar*, 626 F.2d 145, 148 (9th Cir. 1980). *See also Ass't. Sec'y. v. Sysco Foods, supra*, at 6.

140. 29 C.F.R. § 18.45.

141. 29 C.F.R. § 18.47.

142. *Seater, supra*, at 16.

143. *Id.* at 17 n. 28.

144. 29 C.F.R. § 18.48.

145. 29 C.F.R. § 18.44(b), *revised*, Department of Labor "Final Rule," 55 Fed. Reg. 13,216 (April 9, 1990).

146. 29 C.F.R. § 24.6(e)(3).

147. 29 C.F.R. § 18.11.

148. 29 C.F.R. § 18.50.

149. 29 C.F.R. § 18.6(d)(2)(i)-(iv). *See also Seater, supra*, at 26; *Rockingham Machine-Lunex v. NLRB*, 665 F.2d 303, 305 (8th Cir. 1981); *International Union (UAW) v. NLRB*, 459 F.2d 1329, 1335-1342 (D.C. Cir. 1972); *Cram v. Pullman-Higgins Co.*, 84-ERA-17, slip op. of ALJ, at 14 (July 24, 1984); *Pulliam v. Worthington Service Corp.*, 81-WPCA-1, slip op. of ALJ, at 3 (May 15, 1981); J. Wigmore, *Evidence*, vol. 2 § 285 (3rd ed. 1940). *But see Fugate v. TVA*, 93-ERA-9, D&O of SOL, at 4 (September 6, 1995) (admitting evidence due to parties' failure to file a timely motion to compel).

150. *Pittman v. Goggin Truck Line*, 96-STA-25, D&O of ARB, at 3 (September 23, 1997); *Vukadinovich v. Zantz*, 995 F.2d 750, 753 (7th Cir. 1993).

151. *Remusat v. Bartlett Nuclear*, 94-ERA-36, D&O of SOL, at 8 (February 26, 1996).

152. *Timmons, supra*, at 15. *See also Mosbaugh v. Georgia Power Co.*, 91-ERA-1/11, D&O of SOL, at 8-10 (November 20, 1995); *Smith v. ESI Corp.*, 93-ERA-16, D&O of SOL, at 11 (March 13, 1996) (admitting internal report).

153. *Creekmore v. ABB Power Systems*, 93-ERA-24, D&O of SOL, at 7 (February 14, 1996).

154. *Straub v. APS*, 94-ERA-37, D&O of SOL, at 4-5 (April 15, 1996). *See also Roadway Express v. Brock*, 830 F.2d 179, 181 (11th Cir. 1987).

155. *Mansour v. Oncology Services*, 94-ERA-41, D&O of ARB, at 4-5 (September 11, 1997).

156. 29 C.F.R. § 18.54(c); *see also Madonia v. Dominicki Finer Food*, 98-STA-2, Order of ARB, at 4 (January 29, 1999); *Foley v. Boston Edison Co.*, 97-ERA-56, Order of ARB, at 4 (February 2, 1999) (admitted before ARB); *Nolan v. AC Express*, 92-STA-37, D&O of SOL, at 3 (January 17, 1995); *Ake v. Ulrich Chemical, Inc.*, 93-STA-41, D&O of SOL, at 3 (March 21, 1994) (denying admission of evidence); *Timmons, supra*, at 3-7 (admitting new evidence and remanding for discovery and new hearing); *Masek v. Cadle Company*, 95-WPC-1, D & O of ARB (April 28, 2000) (denying admission of new evidence); *Vernadore v. Oak Ridge Lab.*, 92-CAA-2/93-CAA-1/3, D&O of ARB (July 14, 2000) (rejecting admission of new evidence under FRCP 60).

157. *Timmons*, at 12; *see e.g., Seater, supra*, at 5-8.

158. The APA, at 5 U.S.C. § 556(d) states:

[a]ny oral or documentary evidence may be received, but the agency as a matter of policy shall provide for the exclusion of irrelevant, immaterial, or unduly repetitious evidence. A sanction may not be imposed or rule or order issued except on consideration of the whole record or those parts thereof cited by a party and supported by and in accordance with the reliable, probative and substantial evidence. . . . A party is entitled to present his case or defense by oral or documentary evidence, to submit rebuttal evidence, and to conduct such cross examination as may be required for a full and true disclosure of the facts. *See also* 29 C.F.R. § 24.5(e).

159. 29 C.F.R. § 18.26; *Melendez, supra*, at 24-25.

160. *Delaney v. DOL*, 69 F.3d 531 (1st Cir. 1995) (unpublished "Table" decision), 1995 WL 648107 (November 6, 1995). *See also Calhoun v. Bailar*, 626 F.2d 145, 148 (9th Cir. 1980); *Hoonsilapa v. Immigration & Naturalization Serv.*, 575 F.2d 735, 738, *modified*, 586 F.2d 755 (9th Cir. 1978); *Marin-Mendoza v. Immigration & Naturalization Serv.*, 499 F.2d 918, 921 (9th Cir. 1974), *cert. denied*, 419 U.S. 1113, *reh'g. denied*, 420 U.S. 984. *See also Richardson v. Perales*, 402 U.S. 389, 407-408 (1971).

161. *See, e.g., Mackowiak v. University Nuclear Systems, Inc.*, 82-ERA-8, D&O of remand by ALJ, at 4 (July 25, 1986).

162. *Calhoun, supra*, at 149, *cert. denied*, 452 U.S. 906 (1986).

163. *Richardson, supra*, at 410.

164. *Consolidated Edison Co. of N.Y. v. NLRB*, 305 U.S. 197, 230 (1938). *But see Richardson, supra*.

165. *Second Taxing District of City of Norwalk v. Federal Energy Regulatory Comm'n.*, 683 F.2d 477, 485 (D.C. Cir. 1982); *National Airlines, Inc. v. Civil Aeronautics Bd.*, 321 F.2d 380, 383 (D.C. Cir. 1963).

166. *Morgan v. United States*, 298 U.S. 468 (1936).

167. 29 C.F.R. § 24.5(e)(3).

168. 29 C.F.R. § 24.

169. *Garcia v. Wantz Equipment*, 99-CAA-11, Order of ARB (February 8, 2000); *Duncan v. Sacramento Met. Air*, 97-CAA-12, Order of ARB (September 1, 1999).

170. 29 C.F.R. § 24.8(d)(1).

171. ERA, 42 U.S.C. § 5851(b)(2)(B); CAA, 42 U.S.C. § 7622(b)(2)(B); SDWA, 42 U.S.C. § 300j-9(i)(2)(B); SWDA, 42 U.S.C. § 6971(b); WPCA, 33 U.S.C. § 1367(b); CERCLA, 42 U.S.C. § 9610(B); TSCA, 15 U.S.C. § 2622(b)(2)(B); *Bassett v. Niagara Mohawk Power Co.*, 86-ERA-2, Remand Order by SOL, at 4 (July 9, 1986).

172. 29 C.F.R. § 24.8(d)(1); 42 U.S.C. § 300j-9(i)(2)(B)(ii); 15 U.S.C. § 2622(b)(2)(B).

173. 29 C.F.R. § 24.8(d)(2).

174. *Pillow v. Bechtel Construction*, 87-ERA-35, Order of ARB, at 3 (September 11, 1997).

175. *McCafferty v. Centerior*, 96-ERA-6, Order of ARB, at 28 (September 24, 1997).

176. *Id.*

177. *Pillow, supra,* at 3.

178. 735 F.2d 1159, 1162 (9th Cir. 1984).

179. 29 C.F.R. § 24.7(a).

180. *Commonwealth-Lord Joint Venture v. Donovan*, 724 F.2d 67, 68 (7th Cir. 1983).

181. 29 C.F.R. § 18.36(a).

182. 29 C.F.R. § 18.36(b). *See Johnson v. Oak Ridge Operations Office*, 95-CAA-20/21/22, Order to Show Cause by ALJ (January 6, 1997). Appeals from an ALJ disqualification order are filed with the Chief ALJ. 29 C.F.R. § 18.36(b); Order Barring Attorney from Appearances, 98-CAA-10/11 (Chief ALJ, October 6, 1998).

183. 29 C.F.R. § 18.36(b). *See Hufstetler v. Roadway Express*, 85-STA-8, SOL Order, at 2 (April 8, 1986) (rejecting motion to reassign ALJ); *Robinson, supra,* at 5; *Flor, supra,* Order of SOL, at 13 (December 9, 1994). ALJs are "presumed to be impartial," and any party seeking their disqualification must meet a "substantial burden." *See Billings v. TVA*, 91-ERA-12, D&O of ALJ, at 5-7 (June 26, 1996).

184. *Johnson v. DOE*, 95-CAA-20/21/22, ALJ (February 4, 1997). *See also Rockefeller v. DOE*, 98-CAA-10/11, Order Barring Counsel from Future Appearances, ALJ (September 28, 1998); *Hasan v. NPS*, 86-ERA-24, ALJ Order of Disqualification (appealed October 21, 1986; settlement reached without concession as to legality of ALJ's decision; joint motion to vacate pursuant to terms of settlement granted) (February 4, 1987).

185. 29 C.F.R. § 18.36(b).

186. *Webb v. CP&L*, 93-ERA-42, D&O of ARB, at 9 (August 26, 1997) ("where the integrity of the department's adjudicative process is at stake, the presiding ALJ should take all appropriate steps to resolve uncertainty surrounding questionable conduct").

187. 29 C.F.R. § 24.6(e)(4)(i)(B); *Young v. CBI Servs., Inc.*, 88-ERA-8, D&O of remand by SOL (August 10, 1988).

188. 29 C.F.R. § 24.6(e)(4)(b)(ii).

189. *Young, supra,* at 2. *See also National Hockey League v. Metropolitan Hockey Club*, 427 U.S. 639 (1976); *Iowa Beef Packers, Inc. v. NLRB*, 331 F.2d 176, 185 (8th Cir. 1964). In *Tracanna, supra,* at 4, the DOL quoted from its basic rule on default judgment: "Dismissal with prejudice is warranted only where there is a clear record of delay or contumacious conduct and a lesser sanction would not better serve the interests of justice."

190. *Young, supra.* 2-3; *Coupar v. DOL*, 105 F.3d 1263, 1267 (9th Cir. 1997) (default denied because respondent had good cause for not appearing at the hearing).

191. 29 C.F.R. § 24.6(e)(4).

192. *Ass't. Sec'y. v. Gammon Wire Feeder Corp.*, 87-STA-5, D&O of SOL (September 17, 1987).

193. *Ridings v. Commonwealth Edison*, 88-ERA-27, recommended order by ALJ, at 14-15 (March 10, 1989).

194. *Ass't. Sec'y. v. Brenner Ice, Inc.*, 94-STA-10, Order of SOL (July 26, 1994).

195. *Billings, supra,* at 9-10.

196. *White v. "Q" Trucking Co., Alliance Trucking and Employment Services of Michigan*, 93-STA-28, Order of SOL (December 2, 1994); *Wellman v. Dipple*, 85-ERA-019, order of dismissal by ALJ, at 3 (November 27, 1985).

197. *Ass't. Sec'y. et al. v. Gammons Wire Feeder Corp., supra,* at 3.

198. *See, e.g., Rex, supra; Hasan v. NPS et al.*, 86-ERA-24, decision of ALJ regarding motion to disqualify (appealed October 21, 1986), settlement reached without concession as to legality of ALJ's decision; joint motion to vacate pursuant to terms of settlement agreement (granted February 4, 1987).

199. *Cable v. Arizona Public Service Co.*, 90-ERA-15, D&O of SOL (November 13, 1992).

200. *Id.,* at 5.

201. *Rogers v. MultiAmp Corp.*, 85-ERA-16, D&O of SOL, at 2 (December 18, 1992). *See also TVA v. Reich*, 25 F.3d 1050 (Table), 1994 WL 236487 (6th Cir. 1994) (upholding DOL denial of costs to a respondent-employer).

202. 87-ERA-6/40, D&O of SOL (March 4, 1994).

203. *Id.,* at 5.

204. *Id.,* at 6.

205. *Rex, supra,* D&O of SOL, at 6 (March 4, 1994). Attorneys who prevail in a debarment are not entitled to counsel fees under the Equal Access to Justice Act. *See id.* D&O of ARB (January 7, 1997).

206. *Malpass v. General Electric Co., supra,* D&O of SOL, at 20-21 (March 1, 1994).

207. *Id.,* at 21-22.

208. *Redings v. Commonwealth Edison,* 88-ERA-27, D&O of SOL (September 20, 1991).

209. *Willy v. Coastal Corp.,* 85-CAA-1, D&O of SOL, at 22 (June 1, 1994); *see also ABF Freight System v. NLRB,* 114 S.Ct. 835 (1994).

210. 29 C.F.R. § 24.9. *See also, e.g.,* 42 U.S.C. § 5851 (2).

211. *Fields v. Florida Power Corp.,* 96-ERA-22, D&O of ARB, at 2 n. 3 (March 13, 1998), *affirmed, sub. nom. Fields v. DOL,* 173 F3d 811 (11th Cir. 1999).

212. *See, e.g., James v. Ketchikan Pulp Co.,* 94-WPC-4, D&O of SOL, at 6-7 (March 15, 1996).

213. *Fields, supra,* at 6.

214. *Id.* at 7-10.

215. *Id.* at 14.

216. *Id.* at 5.

217. *James, supra.*

218. 29 C.F.R. § 24.7.

219. 29 C.F.R. § 24.7(d).

220. 29 C.F.R. § 24.8(a).

221. *Saavedra v. Donovan,* 700 F.2d 496, 498 (9th Cir. 1983) *cert. denied,* 464 U.S. 892; *Director, Office of Workers' Comp. v. Robertson,* 625 F.2d 873, 876 (9th Cir. 1980); *NLRB v. Interboro Contractors, Inc.,* 388 P.2d 495, 499 (2nd Cir. 1967).

222. *Director et al. v. Brandt Airflex Corp.,* 645 F.2d 1053, 1057 (D.C. Cir. 1981).

223. *Director, Office of Workers' Comp. v. Congleton,* 743 F.2d 428, 429-430 (6th Cir. 1984).

224. *Congleton,* at 430.

225. *See, e.g., Peabody Coal Co. v. Helms,* 859 P.2d 486, 492 (7th Cir. 1988); *Burnett v. Bowen,* 830 F.2d 731, 735 (7th Cir. 1987).

226. 29 C.F.R. § 24.8(b).

227. 29 C.F.R. § 24.6(b)(1).

228. 5 U.S.C. § 557(b); *Universal Camera Corp. v. NLRB,* 340 U.S. 474, 492-497 (1951); *Waters v. Transport, Inc.,* 84-STA-8, D&O of SOL, at 3 (October 24, 1984).

229. *Berkman v. U.S. Coast Guard,* 97-CAA-2/9, D&O of ARB, at 15 (February 29, 2000).

230. *Id. Griffith v. Wackenhut Corp.,* 97-ERA-52, D&O of ARB, at 9 (February 29, 2000).

231. *Jaenisch v. Chicago Bridge & Iron Co.,* 81-ERA-5 (June 25, 1981), *reversed on other grounds* (2nd Cir. June 25, 1981).

232. *Hall v. EG&G Defense,* 97-SDW-9, D&O of ARB, at 4 (September 30, 1998).

233. *Ashcraft v. University of Cincinnati,* 83-ERA-7, decision of SOL, at 11 n. 3 (November 1, 1984); 5 U.S.C. § 556(e).

234. *See. e.g.. Boyd v. Belcher Oil Co.*, 87-STA-9, D&O of SOL, at 3 (December 2, 1987); *McDaniel v. Boyd Bros. Transp.*. 86-STA-6, order of dismissal by SOL, at 4 (March 16, 1987).

235. *Thomas v. APS*, 89-ERA-19, D&O of SOL, at 22 n. 10 (September 17, 1993).

236. *Crosby v. Hughes Aircraft Co.*, 85-TSC-2, D&O of SOL, at 14 (August 17, 1993).

237. *Boyd v. Belcher Oil Co., supra*, D&O of Deputy SOL, at 3-4.

238. 29 C.F.R. § 24.8(a). This filing deadline is subject to equitable tolling. *See Gutierrez v. Regents of the University of California*, 98-ERA-19, Order of ARB, at 3-4 (November 8, 1999).

239. *Id. See Pawlowski v. Hewlett-Packard Corp.*, 97-TSC-3, Order of ARB (September 15, 1999).

240. *High v. Lockheed Martin Energy Systems, Inc.*, 96-CAA-8, Order of ARB (October 2, 1998) (giving party "extraordinary" amount of time to file a brief and denying "sixth request" for enlargement).

241. 29 C.F.R. § 24.8(b).

242. ERA, 42 U.S.C. § 5851(c)(1); CAA, 42 U.S.C. § 7622(c)(1); SDWA, 42 U.S.C. § 300j-9(i)(3)(A); SWDA, 42 U.S.C. § 6971(b); WPCA, 33 U.S.C. §§ 1367(b) and 1369(b); CERCLA, 42 U.S.C. § 9610(b); TSCA, 15 U.S.C. § 2622(c)(1). Appeals are filed in the U.S. Court of Appeals, not the District Court. *See Rhode v. City of West Lafayette*, 850 F. Supp. 753 (N.D. Ind. 1993).

243. *Waters v. Transport, Inc.*, 84-STA-8, D&O of SOL, at 3 (October 24, 1984) (*quoting, in part*, from the Administrative Procedure Act, 5 U.S.C. § 557).

244. *See Bartlick v. DOL*, 1994 WL 487174 (6th Cir. 1994), vacated *en banc on other grounds and withdrawn from bound volume*, 34 F.3d 368.

245. *Macktal v. Brown & Root. Inc.*, 86-ERA-23, Order Granting Reconsideration by ARB (November 20, 1998).

246. *Wells v. KG&E*, 85-ERA-22, Order of SOL, at 2 (June 28, 1991).

247. The Court of Appeals must "defer to the inferences" of the ARB, "not to those of the ALJ." *See Varnadore v. SOL*, 141 F.3d 625, 630 (6th Cir. 1998).

248. In *NLRB v. Interboro Contractors, Inc.*, 388 F.2d 495, 499 (2nd Cir. 1967), the appeals court, in a labor board context, summarized the rule of agency review of an administrative law judge's or trial examiner's findings:

Thus the Board may reject the examiner's findings. even though they are not clearly erroneous. if the other evidence provides sufficient support for the Board's decision. But it seems that the Board's supporting evidence. in cases where it rejects the examiner's findings. must be stronger than would be required in cases where the findings are accepted. since in the former cases the supporting evidence must be deemed substantial when measured against the examiner's contrary findings as well as the opposing evidence.

249. *Southwest Sunsites, Inc. v. Federal Trade Commission*, 785 P.2d 1431, 1437 (9th Cir. 1986) ("When the agency and the ALJ disagree, findings of

an ALJ are merely part of the record. . . . The court's deference is to the agency determination, not that of the ALJ").

250. *NLRB v. Brooks Cameras, Inc.*, 691 F.2d 912, 915 (9th Cir. 1982).

251. 340 U.S. 474, 492-497 (1951).

252. *Id.*

253. *See, e.g., Brooks Cameras, Inc., supra*; Penasquitos Village Inc. v. *NLRB*, 565 F.2d 1074, 1078 (9th Cir. 1977), *quoting* 369 U.S. 404, 408 (1982): "Weight is given to the [administrative law judge's] determinations of credibility for the obvious reason that he or she sees the witnesses and hears them testify, while the Board and the reviewing court look only at cold records." *Accord., Jackson v. Ketchikan Pulp Co.*, 93-WPC-718, D&O of SOL, at 6 (March 4, 1996) ("substantial weight" given to ALJ: findings on witness credibility).

If a credibility determination is not based upon the demeanor of the witnesses, but on an analysis of testimony, the opinion of the administrative law judge will deserve "less than the usual deference." *Consolidated Coal Co. v. NLRB*, 669 F.2d 482, 488 (7th Cir. 1982).

254. 940 F.2d 1287 (9th Cir. 1991).

255. *Id. Accord., Simon v. Simmons Industries, Inc.*, 87-TSC-2, D&O of SOL, at 8 (April 4, 1994): "Although I am not bound by the credibility determinations of the ALJ, these findings must be considered in light of 'the consentency [sic] and inherent probability of testimony . . .' and are entitled to weight because the ALJ 'sees the witnesses and hears them testify' (citation omitted).

256. *Bartlik v. TVA*, 88-ERA-15, Final D&O of SOL, at 4-5 (April 7, 1993).

257. *McCafferty v. Centerion*, 96-ERA-6, Order of ARB, at 16 n. 23 (September 24, 1997).

258. *Saavedra, supra*; *Brooks Cameras, Inc., supra*, at 915; *NLRB v. Universal Camera Corp.*, 190 F.2d 429, 432 (2nd Cir. 1951) (J. Frank concurring); *see Simon v. Simmons Foods, Inc.*, 49 F.3d 386, 390 (8th Cir. 1995).

259. *Spencer v. Hatfield Elec. Co.*, 86-ERA-33, D&O of SOL, at 3-4 (October 24, 1988) (*quoting from* the rule laid out in *Beavers v. Secretary of Health*, 577 F.2d 383, 387 [6th Cir. 1978]); *Smith v. Norco Technical Servs., etc.*, 85-ERA-17, D&O of SOL, at 4 (October 2, 1987).

260. *Perez v. Guthmiller Trucking Co., Inc.*, 87-STA-13, D&O of SOL, at 13-14, 27 (December 7, 1988).

261. *NLRB v. Miller Redwood Corp.*, 407 F.2d 1366, 1369 (9th Cir. 1969).

262. *Bangor and A.R. Co. v. ICC*, 574 F.2d 1096, 1110 (1st Cir. 1978).

263. *Plain Dealer Publishing Co. v. City of Lakewood*, 794 F.2d 1139, 1148 (6th Cir. 1986).

264. *See, e.g., Amato v. Assured Transportation*, 96-TSC-6, ARB Order (January 31, 2000); Hasan v. Commonwealth Edison Co., 99-ERA-17, Order of ARB (September 16, 1999); *Shusterman v. EBASCO Services, Inc.*, 87-ERA-27, Order Denying Remand by SOL, at 2 (July 2, 1987); *Plumley v. Federal Bureau*

of Prisons, 86-CAA-6, order denying interlocutory appeal by SOL (April 29, 1987).

265. *See, e.g., In re Willy*, 831 F.2d 545, 549 (5th Cir. 1987).

266. Even in a case in which the ALJ recommended granting interlocutory reviews, the SOL declined the invitation. *See Porter v. Brown & Root*, 91-ERA-4, Order of SOL (September 29, 1993).

267. *Beliveau v. Naval Undersea Warfare Center*, 97-SDW-1/4, Order of ARB (August 14, 1997); *Plumley v. Federal Bureau of Prisons*, 86-CAA-6, order denying interlocutory appeal by SOL, at 2-3 (April 29, 1987).

268. The Eleventh Circuit has held in DOL whistleblower cases that an order establishing liability is not "final" until all issues related to the amount of damages has been decided. *Bechtel v. SOL*, No. 92-5176 (11th Cir. April 8, 1993), citing *Redden v. Director, OWCP*, 825 F.2d 337, 338 (11th Cir. 1987). If the only issue remaining relates to attorney's fees, the order is final and must be appealed. *Fluor Constructors, Inc. v. Reich*, 111 F.3d 94 (11th Cir. 1997)

269. *See, e.g.*, 42 U.S.C. § 5851(c); *Bartlick v. DOL*, 62 F.3d 163 (6th Cir. 1995) (appeal timely if sixtieth day falls on a Saturday, Sunday, or federal holiday and the appeal is docketed on the next business day).

270. ERA, 42 U.S.C. § 5851(c)(1); CAA, 42 U.S.C. § 7622(c)(1); SDWA, 42 U.S.C. § 6971(b); WPCA, 33 U.S.C. § 1367(b); CERCLA, 42 U.S.C. § 9610(b); TSCA, 15 U.S.C. § 2622(c)(1).

271. *See, e.g.*, 42 U.S.C. § 5851(c).

272. For a discussion on what constitutes the administrative record and some of the grounds for a court to go beyond that record *see Thompso, v. DOL*, 885 F.2d 551, 555-556 (9th Cir. 1989).

273. 735 F.2d 1159, 1163 (9th Cir. 1984). *See also Thompson*, at 555.

274. *Universal Camera Corp. v. NLRB*, 340 U.S. 474 (1981).

275. *Mackowiak v. University Nuclear Systems, Inc.*,735 F.2d 1159,1162 (9th Cir. 1984).

276. *See Passaic Valley Sewerage Comm'ns v. DOL*, 992 F.2d 474, 480 (3rd Cir. 1993) (substantial evidence); *Pogue v. DOL*, 940 F.2d 1287, 1289 (9th Cir. 1991) (substantial evidence); *Rose v. Dole*, 945 F.2d 1331, 1334 (6th Cir. 1991) *(de novo* review of relevant questions of law).

277. *Passaic Valley Sewerage Comm'ns v. DOL, supra*, at 478, citing *Chevron, U.S.A., Inc. v. NRDC*, 467 U.S. 837, 843 (1984).

278. *Rose v. Dole*, 945 F.2d 1331, 1334 (6th Cir. 1991).

279. *Id.* at 1335.

280. *Lockert v. DOL*, 867 F.2d 513, 518 (9th Cir. 1989) (review of Secretary's interpretation of whistleblower statute is "deferential").

281. 467 U.S. 837 (1984)

282. *See, e.g., Stone & Webster Engineering v. Herman*, 115 F.3d 1568, 1571 (11th Cir. 1997), citing *Chevron v. NRDC, supra*; *A.N.R. v. DOL*, 134 F.3d 1292, 1294 (6th Cir. 1998) ("defer somewhat to the agency"); *Connecticut Light & Power v. SOL*, 85 F.3d 89, 94 (2nd Cir. 1996) (defer to "permissible construction of the statutory mandate").

283. 380 U.S. 1, 16 (1965). *See also Chevron v. NRDC, supra.*

284. *A.N.R., supra.*

285. *Thompson v. DOL, supra,* at 557. *See also Secretary of Agriculture v. United States,* 347 U.S. 645, 653 (1954).

286. *Talley v. Mathews,* 550 P.2d 911, 919 (4th Cir. 1977).

287. 5 U.S.C. § 706(2)(e); *Couty v. Dole,* 886 F.2d 147, 148-149 (8th Cir. 1989).

288. *Universal Camera Corp., supra,* at 477.

289. *Richardson v. Perales,* 402 U.S. 389, 401 (1971); *Consolidated Edison Co. of N.Y. v. NLRB,* 305 U.S. 197, 229 (1938).

290. *Universal Camera Corp. v. NLRB,* 340 U.S. at 474-94.

291. *Arnold v. Secretary of H.E.W.,* 567 F.2d 258, 259 (4th Cir. 1977). *See also Moon v. U.S. Dep't of Labor,* 727 F.2d 1315, 1318 (D.C. Cir. 1984).

292. *Arnold,* 567 F.2d at 259. *See also Peabody Coal Co. v. Helms,* 859 F.2d 486, 492 (7th Cir. 1988); *Zeigler Coal Co. v. Sieberg,* 839 F.2d 1280, 1283 (7th Cir. 1988).

293. *Lockert v. U.S. DOL, supra,* at 520.

294. *Burnett v. Bowen, supra,* at 734-735; *Janik, Paving & Const., Inc. v. Brock,* 828 F.2d 84, 93 (2nd Cir. 1987).

295. *See, e.g., Ethyl Corp. v. EPA,* 541 F.2d 1, 34-36 (D.C. Cir. 1976).

296. *Home Owners Loan Corp. v. Huffman,* 134 F.2d 314, 317 (8th Cir. 1943). *See also Conway v. Chemical Leaman Tank Lines, Inc.,* 610 F.2d 360, 367 n. 9 (5th Cir. 1980); *NLRB v. Guernsey-Muskingum Electric Co-op, Inc.,* 285 F.2d 8, 11 (6th Cir. 1960).

297. 5 U.S.C. § 706(2)(A).

298. *Citizens to Preserve Overton Park v. Volpe,* 401 U.S. 402, 415-417 (1971); *American Fed'n. of State, City & Municipal Employees v. City of Cleveland,* 484 F.2d 339, 346 (6th Cir. 1973).

299. 5 U.S.C. § 705; Federal Rules of Appellate Procedure, Rule 18; *Commonwealth-Lord Joint Venture, supra,* at 68.

300. *See Virginia Petroleum Jobbers Assn. v. Federal Power Comm'n.,* 259 F.2d 921, 925 (D.C. Cir. 1958); *see, e.g.,* DOL decisions applying the four-factor test in environmental whistleblower proceedings: *Hoffman v. Bossert,* 94-CAA-4, SOL Order (November 20, 1995); *Guttman v. Passaic Valley Sewerage Comm'ns,* 85-WPC-2, SOL Order Denying Stay (June 4, 1992) (compiling cases); *OFCCP v. University of North Carolina,* 84-OFC-20, SOL Order Denying Stay (April 25, 1989).

301. *Rexront v. City of New Albany,* 85-WPC-3, order denying stay by SOL (October 8, 1986).

302. *See also* ERA, 42 U.S.C. § 5851(c)(1); CAA, 42 U.S.C. § 7622(c)(1); SDWA, 42 U.S.C. § 300j-9(i)(3)(A); TSCA, 15 U.S.C. § 2622(c)(1).

303. 5 U.S.C. § 705.

304. *See, e.g., Arcamuzi v. Continental Air Lines, Inc.,* 819 F.2d 935, 938-939 (9th Cir. 1987); *Garcia v. Lawn,* 805 F.2d 1400, 1405 (9th Cir. 1986).

305. *Sampson v. Murray*, 415 U.S. 61, 90 (1974); *Meyers v. Bethlehem Shipbuilding Corp.*, 303 U.S. 41, 51-52 (1938); *Rexront, supra,* at 2-3.

306. *Commonwealth-Lord Joint Venture, supra,* at 68. *See also Rexront* at 2-3.

307. 724 F. 2d 67 (7th Cir. 1983).

308. *Goldstein v. EBASCO Constructors, Inc.*, 86-ERA-36, Order Denying Stay by SOL (August 31, 1992); *Wells v. KG&E Co.*, 85-ERA-22, Order of SOL (June 28, 1991).

309. *Dutkiewicz v. Clean Harbors*, ARB Order Denying Stay (September 23, 1997) (denying stay of "monetary portion" of DOL's final order).

310. 29 C.F.R. § 24.8(c); ERA, 42 U.S.C. § 5851(f); CAA, 42 U.S.C. § 7622; SDWA, 42 U.S.C. § 300j-9(i)(5).

311. For example, 42 U.S.C. § 5851(f) states: "Any nondiscretionary duty imposed by this section shall be enforceable in a mandamus proceeding brought under Section 1361 of Title 28."

312. *Will v. United States*, 389 U.S. 90 (1967); *DeMasi v. Weiss*, 669 F.2d 114 (3rd Cir. 1982).

313. *Food Serv. Dynamics, Inc. v. Bergland*, 465 F. Supp. 1178, 1181 (E.D. N.Y. 1979). *See also Cook v. Arentzen*, 582 F.2d 870 (4th Cir. 1978).

314. *In re Willy*, 831 F.2d 545, 549 (5th Cir. 1987).

315. ERA, 42 U.S.C. § 5851(d), (e); CAA, 42 U.S.C. § 7622(d), (e); SDWA, 42 U.S.C. § 300j-9(i)(4); TSCA, 15 U.S.C. § 2622(d). *See Lockheed Martin*, 19 F.R.D. 449 (E.D. Tenn. 1999).

316. *Id.* An enforcement action is summary in nature, requiring a Court to perform a "ministerial" function in enforcing the DOL's final order. *See Kansas Gas & Elec. Co. v. Brock*, 780 F.2d 1505, 1514-15 (10th Cir. 1985). A district court has no authority to review the merits of the Secretary's order. *See* 42 U.S.C. § 5851(c)(2) ("An order of the Secretary...to which review could have been obtained [in the court of appeals,] shall not be subject to judicial review in any criminal or other civil proceeding."); *Brock*, 780 F.2d at 1515 ("An appeal of the Secretary's decision can lie only with the court of appeals."). For example, the district court in *Brock* held that "[Section 5851(d)] is clear on its face that the district court has jurisdiction to grant appropriate relief through its enforcement of an order by the Secretary. It cannot be interpreted to authorize this court to inquire into the appropriateness of the relief ordered by the Secretary." *Wells v. Kansas Gas & Elec. Co.*, No. 84-2290, slip op. at 2 (D. Kan. Oct. 15, 1984), *aff'd sub nom. Kansas Gas & Elec. Co. v. Brock*, 780 F.2d 1505 (10th Cir. 1985). In an enforcement proceeding, a district court may issue a preliminary injunction mandating the immediate reinstatement of an employee. *See Martin v. Yellow Freight Sys., Inc.*, 793 F. Supp. 461, 473-74 (S.D.N.Y. 1992), *aff'd* 983 F.2d 1201 (2d Cir. 1993) (affirming the district court's order to enforce an order of reinstatement in a Surface Transportation Assistance Act whistleblowing case); *Martin v. Castle Oil Corp.*, No. 92 Civ. 2178, 1992 U.S. Dist. LEXIS 4568, at *14 (S.D.N.Y. 1992) (enforcing the Secretary's order by granting a preliminary injunction), *dismissed on other grounds*, 983 F.2d 1201 (2d Cir. 1993).

317. *Goldstein, supra,* at 3, n. 4.

318. *Thompson v. DOL, supra; Macktal v. SOL,* 923 F.2d 1150, 1153-54 (5th Cir. 1991); *Beliveau v. DOL,* 170 F.3d 83, (1st Cir. 1999). *But see Smith v. Littenberg,* 92-ERA-52, Order of ARB (April 29, 1997), *re.* (DOL authority when a claim settles after a final order and when the case is on appeal).

319. *Faust v. Chemical Leaman Tank Lines,* 92-SWD-2/93-STA-15, D&O of ARB, at 3 (June 13, 1996); *Fuchko, et al. v. Georgia Power Co.,* 89-ERA-9/10, order to submit settlement agreement by SOL, at 2 (March 23, 1989).

320. *Faust, supra,* at 2-3.

321. *McClure v. Interstate Facilities, Inc.,* 92-WPC-2, D&O of SOL, at 3-4 (June 19, 1995); *Beliveau v. Dept. of Labor,* 170 F.3d 83, 88 (1st Cir. 1999).

322. *Connecticut Light & Power v. SOL,* 85 F.3d 89 (2nd Cir. 1996); *Macktal v. Brown & Root, Inc.,* 86-ERA-23, D&O of ARB, at 6-7 (January 6, 1998). *See also High v. Lockheed Martin,* 97-CAA-3, D&O of ARB, at 5 (November 13, 1995) (noting that causes of action based solely on "gag" provisions in a settlement offer are strictly examined); *see also Thompson v. Detroit Edison Co.,* 87-ERA-2, order to show cause by SOL, at 5 (April 26, 1990); *Polizzi v. Gibbs & Hill, Inc.,* 87-ERA-38, order rejecting in part by SOL (July 18, 1988); *Macktal v. Brown & Root, Inc.,* 86-ERA-23, order rejecting in part by SOL (November 14, 1989).

323. *Delcore v. W. J. Barney,* 89-ERA-38, D&O of SOL, at 12-13 (April 19, 1995).

324. *Rudd v. Westinghouse Hanford Co.,* 88-ERA-33, at 11-12 (November 10, 1997).

325. *See, e.g., McDowell v. Doyon Drilling Services,* 96-TSC-8, Order of ARB (August 6, 1997).

326. *Biddy v. Alyeska Pipeline,* 95-TSC-7, Final D&O of ARB, at 3 (December 3, 1996).

327. *Fuchko, supra,* at 2.

328. *Carter v. Electrical District No. 2,* 92-TSC-11, Order of OAA, at 2-3 (April 24, 1996); *Debose v. CP&L,* 92-ERA-14, Order of SOL (February 7, 1994); *McDowell, supra,* D&O of remand of ARB (May 19, 1997); *Goehring v. Koppel Steel Corp.,* 97-ERA-11, Order of ARB (April 10, 1997); *Fuchko, supra,* Order of SOL (June 13, 1994).

329. *McGlynn v. Pulsair, Inc.,* 93-CAA-3, Order of SOL, at 2 (June 28, 1993).

330. *Stephenson v. NASA,* 94-TSC-5, Order of SOL (June 19, 1995).

331. *McDowell, supra,* Order of ARB, (August 6, 1997).

332. *Faust, supra,* at 2.

333. 29 C.F.R. § 18.9.

334. *See, e.g., Marcus v. EPA,* 96-CAA-3/7, Order of ARB (October 29, 1999).

335. *Macktal v. Brown & Root, Inc.,* 86-ERA-23, order rejecting in part by SOL, at 14-16 (November 14, 1989) (vacated on other grounds).

336. *Rudd, supra,* at 18. *But see O'Sullivan v. Northeast Nuclear,* 90-ERA-35/36, Order of Deputy SOL (December 10, 1990).

337. *Williams v. Metzler,* 132 F.3d 937 (3rd Cir. 1997) (enforcement of a settlement must be filed in federal court). *See also Pillow v. Bechtel,* 87-ERA-35, Order of ARB, at 2-3, (September 11, 1997); *O'Sullivan, supra,* (potential new discrimination charge based on employer's post-settlement conduct); *Blanch v. Northeast Nuclear,* 90-ERA-11, Order of SOL at 4 (May 11, 1994) (violation of settlement may constitute a separate, independent violation of the ERA); *Cianfrani v. Public Service Elec. & Gas Co.,* 95-ERA-33, Order of ARB, at 2 (September 19, 1996).

338. *Rudd, supra,* at 11.

339. *O'Sullivan, supra,* at 2-3; *Tankersley v. Triple Crown,* 92-STA-8, D&O of SOL, at 2 (October 17, 1994); *Eash v. Roadway Express,* 98-STA-28, D&O of remand by ARB (October 29, 1999) (rejecting oral agreement).

340. *Thompson v. DOL,* 885 F.2d 551, 556 (9th Cir. 1989).

341. *Hoffman v. Fuel Economy Contracting et al.,* 87-ERA-33, order to submit settlement by SOL (August 10, 1988); *Fuchko, et al., supra,* order to submit settlement by SOL (March 23, 1989).

342. *Tankersley, supra. See also Trice v. Bartlett Nuclear,* 97-ERA-40, Order of ARB, at 3 n. 2 (August 28, 1998) (parties bound by agreement even if one "subsequently believes the agreement is disadvantageous").

343. *Leidigh v. Freightway Corp.,* 87-STA-12, Order of SOL, at 4 (January 22, 1995)

344. *Aurich v. Consolidated Edison Co.,* 86-CAA-2, order approving settlement by SOL (July 29, 1987); *Egenrieder v. Metropolitan Edison Co.,* 85-ERA-23, order approving settlement (April 11, 1988); *Macktal v. Brown & Root, Inc.,* 86-ERA-23, order rejecting in part by SOL, at 16-17 (November 14, 1989).

345. *Connecticut Light & Power v. SOL,* 85 F.3d 89, 95 (2nd Cir. 1996).

346. *Rhyne v. Brand Utilities,* 94-ERA-33/45, Order of SOL, at 2 (June 20, 1995).

347. *Brown & Root v. DOL,* 94-40337 (unpublished decision), (5th Cir. January 11, 1995); *CP&L v. DOL,* 43 F.3d 912 (4th Cir. 1995).

348. *Crider v. Holston Defense Corp., et al.,* 88-CAA-1, order approving settlement by SOL, at 2 (March 1, 1989). *See also Cowan v. Bechtel Constr., Inc.,* 87-ERA-29, D&O of remand by SOL, at 3 (August 9, 1989) ("Settlement of such a prior complaint does not . . . preclude litigation of an alleged separate and distinct act of discrimination after the settlement"); *Smyth v. Regents,* 98-ERA-3, Order of ARB, at 2 (March 13, 1998).

349. *Sylvester v. ABB/Power Systems Energy,* D&O of SOL, 93-ERA-11 (March 21, 1994); *Blevins v. TVA,* 90-ERA-4, D&O of SOL (June 28, 1993); *Mosbaugh v. Georgia Power Co.,* 90-ERA-58, D&O of SOL (September 23, 1992).

350. *Mosbaugh,* D&O of SOL, at 2.

351. *Id.,* at 3-4. *Accord., Carter v. LANL,* 93-CAA-10, D&O of SOL (March 21, 1994).

352. *Mosbaugh,* at 5-6.

353. *See Anderson v. DeKalb Plating Co.,* 97-CER-1, Order of ARB (July 27, 1999) (applying "legal prejudice" standard in evaluating request for dismissal without prejudice).

354. 90-ERA-26, D&O of SOL, at 2 (August 31, 1992).

355. *Brown v. Homes & Narver, Inc.,* 90-ERA-26, D&O of remand of ALJ, at 3 (December 19, 1990) (citations omitted), adopted by SOL (August 31, 1992). *Accord., Young v. CBI Services, Inc.,* 88-ERA-19, D&O of remand of ALJ (April 6, 1993) (case dismissed without prejudice after telegram appeal had been filed by moving party).

356. *Wood v. Lockheed Martin Energy Systems,* 97-ERA-58, ARB Order (May 14, 1998).

357. *Mosbaugh, supra,* at 5-6 n. 4

358. *Billings v. TVA,* 91-ERA-12, D&O of ARB, at 14 (June 26, 1996) (discussing *res judicata* effect of administrative ruling); *Thompson v. DOL,* 885 F.2d 551, 556, 557 (9th Cir. 1989).

359. 42 U.S.C. § 5851 (1993). The legislative history of Section 211 is contained in H. Rep. No. 102-474 (Part I), p. 227; H. Rep. No. 102-474 (Part 8), at 78; Vol. 138 Cong. Rec. H11,409 (Miller); H11,412 (Lent); H11,442 (Williams); H11,444 (Ford) (October 5, 1992).

360. Vol. 138 Cong. Rec. No. 142, H 11442 (Cong. Williams) (October 5, 1992) ("obstacles have been removed that had discouraged employees from bringing to the attention of the public information about potential health and safety problems.").

361. Vol. 138 Cong. Rec. No. 142, H 11409 (October 5, 1992) (remark of Cong. Miller). *Accord.,* H. Rep. 102-474 (Part 8), at 78 (May 5, 1992) ("this title broadens and deepens protections of nuclear whistleblowers against harassment and other retaliatory treatment").

362. *ANRI v. DOL,* 134 F.3d 1292, 1295 n. 3 (6th Cir. 1998).

363. 29 C.F.R. § 24.

364. *Id.*

365. § 210(a)(1)(A)(C).

366. 747 F.2d 1029 (5th Cir. 1984).

367. *Goldstein, supra,* D&O of SOL, at 5-10 (April 7, 1992) *rev'd. on other grounds, EBASCO Construction, Inc. v. Martin,* unpublished opinion of U.S. Court of Appeals for the Fifth Circuit, No. 92-4576 (February 19, 1993) ("I continue to be persuaded that reporting violations of the ERA internally to one's employer is protected activity. . . . I respectfully decline to follow the Fifth Circuit's decision in *Brown & Root*"). *Accord., Jones v. TVA,* 948 F.2d 258, 264 (6th 1991); *Willy v. Coastal Corp.,* 85-CAA-1, D&O of SOL, at 13 (June 1, 1994); *Mandreger v. Detroit Edison Co.,* 88-ERA-17, D&O of SOL, at 13-14 (March 30, 1994); *Croiser v. General Electric Co.,* 91-ERA-2, D&O of SOL, at 6-7 (January 5, 1994); *Pillow v. Bechtel,* 87-ERA-35, D&O of remand by SOL, at 11 (July 19, 1993); *Nichols v. Bechtel Construction, Inc.,* 87-ERA-44, D&O of SOL, at 9 (October 26, 1992); *Adams v. Coastal Production Op., Inc.,* 89-ERA-3,

D&O of SOL, at 8-9 (August 5, 1992); *Guttman v. Passaic Valley Sewerage Commission*, 85-WPC-2, D&O of SOL, at 10-13 (March 13, 1992), *aff'd*, 992 F. 2d 474 (3rd Cir. 1993); *Johnson v. Old Dominion Security*, 86-CAA-3/4/5, D&O of SOL, at 14 (May 29, 1991); *Chavaz v. EBASCO Services, Inc.*, 91-ERA-24, D&O of SOL, at 5 (November 16, 1992).

368. *Guttman, supra.*

369. *Bechtel v. SOL*, 50 F.3d 926, 931 (11th Cir. 1995); *Jones v. TVA, supra; Mackowiak v. UNSI*, 735 F.2d 1159, 1163 (9th Cir. 1984); *Kansas Gas & Elec. v. Brock*, 780 F.2d 1505 (10th Cir. 1985).

370. 29 C.F.R. § 24.3(b).

371. *Wensel v. B. F. Shaw Co.*, 86-ERA-15, 87-ERA-12, 88-ERA-34, SOL Order (March 29, 1990), *aff'd sub nom. Adams v. Dole*, 927 F.2d 711, 776 (4th Cir. 1991).

372. *Teles v. DOE*, 94-ERA-22, D&O of SOL (August 7, 1995).

373. 42 U.S.C. § 5851 (b)(2)(A) (1988).

374. *Trimmer v. DOL*, 174 F.3d 1098 (10th Cir. 1999) (recognizing that Congress was concerned with "stemming frivolous complaints").

375. 29 C.F.R. § 24.5(d); *see also* 29 C.F.R. § 24.7(b).

376. 138 Cong. Rec., No. 142, H11,409 (October 5, 1992), *Accord.*, H11,444 (Ford).

377. *Id.*

378. *Marano v. DOJ*, 2 F.3d 1137, 1140 (Fed. Cir. 1993) (discussing legislative history of WPA); Vol. 138 Cong. Rec. No. 142, H 11,409 (October 5, 1992) (Miller) ("The conferees intend to replace the burden of proof enunciated in *Mt. Healthy v. Doyle*") 11,444 (Ford) ("The conferees intend to replace the complainant's burden of proof enunciated in *Mt. Healthy v. Doyle* . . . in order to facilitate relief for employees").

379. *Darty v. Zack*, 82-ERA-2 D&O of SOL, at 7-8 (April 25, 1983). *See also Carroll v. Bechtel Power*, 91-ERA-46, at 8-12 (February 15, 1995), *affm'd* 78 F.3d 352 (8th Cir. 1996).

380. *Stone & Webster Engineering v. Herman*, 115 F.3d 1568, 1572 (11th Cir. 1997).

381. 42 U.S.C. § 5851(b)(3)(C) and (D).

382. *See, e.g., Frobose v. American Savings and Loan*, 153 F.3d 602, 611-612 (7th Cir. 1998) (FDIC whistleblower law); *Marano v. DOJ*, 2 F.3d 1137 (Fed. Cir. 1993) (WPA); *Rouse v. Farmers State Bank of Jewell*, 866 F. Supp. 1191, 1207-1208 (N.D. Iowa) (comparing Title VII framework with new statutory framework).

383. *Frobose*, at 612; *Accord., Stone & Webster Engineering v. Herman*, 115 F.3d 1568, 1572 (11th Cir. 1997) (ERA case stating: "for employers, this is a tough standard, and not by accident. Congress appears to have intended that companies in the nuclear industry face a difficult time defending themselves"); *Trimmer v. DOL*, 174 F.3d 1098 (10th Cir. 1999) (ERA case: "Congress decided to make it easier for whistleblowers to prevail").

384. *Dysert v. SOL*, 105 F.3d 607, 609-610 (11th Cir. 1997).

385. *Marano v. DOJ*, 2 F.3d 1137, 1140 (Fed. Cir. 1993).

386. *Stone & Webster Engineering v. Herman*, 115 F.3d 1568, 1572 (11th Cir. 1997).

387. *Marano, supra,* at 1140, *quoting* 135 Cong. Rec. 5033 (1989) (WPA Explanatory Statement).

388. *Stone & Webster Engineering v. Herman, supra,* at 1572; *Yule v. Burns International Security*, 93-ERA-12, D&O of SOL, at 7-8 (May 24, 1995) (explains that new burden on employers is higher than "preponderance of evidence" but "less than" "reasonable doubt").

389. *See Zinn v. University of Missouri*, 93-ERA-34/36, D&O of SOL, at 17 (January 18, 1996).

390. *McCafferty v. Centerion*, 96-ERA-6, Order of ARB, at 9 (September 24, 1997).

391. 42 U.S.C. § 5851.

392. 42 U.S.C. § 5851 (b)(2)(A).

393. 138 Cong. Rec., H11,444 (Ford) (October 5, 1992).

394. *Davidson v. Temple University*, 94-ERA-25, Preliminary Order of SOL (August 14, 1995).

395. *McNiece v. Northeast Nuclear Energy Co.*, 95-ERA-18/47, Preliminary Order of SOL (February 21, 1996).

396. *Latorre v. Coriell Institute*, 97-ERA-46, Preliminary Order of ARB (December 17, 1997).

397. *Gaballa v. The Atlantic Group*, 94-ERA-9, Preliminary Order of SOL (June 19, 1995).

398. *Varnadore v. Oak Ridge National Laboratory*, 94-CAA-2/3, Preliminary Order of SOL (September 11, 1995), order rescinded and fees ordered returned (September 6, 1996). *See Lockheed Martin*, 19 F.R.D. 449 (E.D. Tenn. 1999) (federal court order to return fees).

399. *McCafferty v. Centerion*, 96-ERA-6, Order Denying Stay by ARB (October 16, 1996).

400. Sec. 211(h) of the ERA.

401. *English v. General Electric Co.*, 110 S.Ct. 2270 (1990).

402. Sec. 211(i).

403. 10 C.F.R. § 50.7.

404. The DOL has codified the tolling requirement under 29 C.F.R. § 24.2(d)(2).

Chapter 6

The False Claims Act:
Qui Tam Provisions and
Whistleblower Protection

The False Claims Act (FCA)[1] is the major law utilized to "ferret out fraud against the federal government."[2] It was enacted during the Civil War at the "behest" of President Abraham Lincoln to "control fraud in defense contracts" and was subsequently the subject of two important amendments, one in 1943 and the second in 1986.[3] It contains two sections highly relevant to whistleblowers.

First, the law contains a *qui tam*[4] provision which permits private citizens and "original sources" to file suit on behalf of the United States to recover damages incurred by the government as a result of fraud. In return for filing the suit, the whistleblower is entitled to a significant "cut of the judgment proceeds should they prevail."[5] In this manner, a whistleblower can obtain a large monetary award if he or she follow the "complex" procedures set forth in the FCA when seeking to enforce that antifraud law.[6] With mixed results, the constitutionality of various aspects of the *qui tam* provision have been vigorously challenged by the defense bar.[7]

Second, the law also contains an antiretaliation provision that prohibits the discharge or harassment of a whistleblower who makes FCA-protected disclosures or files a *qui tam* suit.[8] Unlike the *qui tam* provisions, which allow the whistleblower to obtain a portion of the recovery obtained by the United States due to a violation of the FCA, the antiretaliation provision was modeled after other federal whistleblower laws and operates under the basic principles underlying employment discrimination cases.

Although the FCA only concerns federal monies or property, a growing number of states have passed their own version of the FCA, usually adopting the federal provisions almost verbatim. California,[9] the District of Columbia,[10] Florida,[11] Illinois[12] and Tennessee[13] have all adopted FCAs to protect state funds.

QUI TAM LITIGATION

Even prior to the passing of the FCA, there existed a long tradition of encouraging private citizens to aid in the enforcement of law. *Qui tam* actions have been "frequently permitted by legislative action" under English and American law for hundreds of years prior to the formation of the United States.[14] As noted by the U.S. Supreme Court in the FCA case of *U.S. ex rel. Marcus v. Hess*:[15] "Statutes providing for actions by a common informer, who himself had no interest whatever in the controversy other than that given by statute, have been in existence for hundreds of years in England, and in this country ever since the foundation of our government."[16]

In addition to the rich history of *qui tam* actions, the government had also historically sought the assistance of its citizens in protecting the federal fisc from fraud. For example, in 1778 the Continental Congress passed the following extraordinary measure:

Resolved, That it is the duty of all persons in the service of the United States, as well as all other inhabitants thereof, to give the earliest information to Congress or any other proper authority of any misconduct, frauds or misdemeanors committed by any persons in the service of these states, which may come to their knowledge.[17]

In 1862 Congress learned of massive fraud that was harming the Civil War effort. The House Committee on Government Contracts carefully reviewed the allegations of fraud and uncovered documentation of "gross mismanagement," "total disregard for the interests of government," and the "total recklessness in the expenditure of the funds of the government."[18] Congress documented fraud both with contractors and with federal employees colluding with these contractors: "[There is] every reason to believe that there was collusion on the part of employees of the government to assist in the robbing of the treasury."[19]

Congress recognized that without the strongest checks on the fraudulent use of federal moneys, by both contractors and civil servants in league, the government itself might go bankrupt:

With such a state of things existing, if officers of the government, who should be imbued with patriotism and integrity enough to have a care of the means of the treasury, are ready to assist speculating contractors to extort upon and defraud the government, where is this system of speculation to end, and how soon may not the finances of the government be reduced to a [woeful] bankruptcy?[20]

The Senate debates on the FCA, published in the *Congressional Globe*,[21] highlight the intent of Congress in passing the FCA. One of the sponsors of the law, Senator Howard,[22] explained how the law was, in part, "based on" the "old-fashioned idea of holding out a temptation and 'setting a rogue to catch a rogue.'" The Senator also explained how the interests of the United States would be served by this "safest and most expeditious" method to bring "rogues to justice"[23] and how the law also could reward "vigilant" civil servants who appropriately filed claims on behalf of the United States.

The goal behind the FCA was to directly appeal to the American citizenry to expose and stop fraud on the government. Instead of relying upon federal employees, many of whom Congress learned were participating in the corruption, the law would provide a generous bounty to any citizen who helped the government expose the fraud. In a sense, the FCA, like other *qui tam* laws, empowered the people with the ability to act on behalf of the sovereign as private attorneys general. By empowering people to directly enforce the law, the FCA was the first major whistleblower law ever passed in the United States and gave meaning to the truism of American democracy identified by Benjamin Franklin in the debates on the U.S. Constitution: "in free governments the rulers are the servants, and the people their superiors and sovereigns."[24]

On March 2, 1863, Congress passed the original FCA.[25] In many ways this law was far more liberal than the current version. Any person could prosecute an FCA claim, and the *qui tam* provision allowed the relator to obtain 50 percent of the fraud recovered from the wrongdoer. The law also provided for double damages and a $2,000 fine per violation.

After the Civil War the FCA was "seldom utilized, until the 1930s and 40s when increased government spending opened up numerous opportunities for unscrupulous government contractors to defraud the government."[26] However, during the New Deal and World War II, the "generous cash bounties" offered under the FCA prompted many citizens to file *qui tam* actions, even if they were not informers and did not materially assist in the detection of the fraud. In fact, the language of the law permitted "piggy-back law suits" in which a relator could merely copy a criminal fraud indictment and rush to the courthouse to beat the government in filing the FCA claim.[27] The government objected to "opportunistic" private *qui tam* suits and the lack of control the Attorney General exercised over the *qui tam* cases. In 1943 the Supreme Court weighed these matters and determined that the law should be strictly applied, and that it was Congress' responsibility to correct any deficiencies in the FCA.[28]

Congress acted, and shortly after the Supreme Court's ruling amended the FCA in 1943. However, the amendments failed to protect the interests of whistleblowers or original sources. Specifically, the Act of December 23, 1943,[29] barred *qui tam* recoveries if the information for which the FCA action was based was already "in the possession of the United States . . . at the time such suit was brought." No provision was made to protect informers, and if a whistleblower/informer had alerted the government to the fraud prior to filing a *qui tam* action, the relator was prohibited from obtaining any monetary award. The 1943 amendment undermined the FCA:

It soon became apparent that by restricting *qui tam* suits by individuals who brought fraudulent activity to the government's attention, Congress had killed the goose that laid the golden egg and eliminated the financial incentive to expose frauds against the government. The use of *qui tam* suits as a weapon for fighting fraud against the government dramatically declined.[30]

The weaknesses in the law were driven home when the state of Wisconsin filed a *qui tam* action to recover monies lost to medicaid fraud. In 1984 the Court of Appeals for the Seventh Circuit dismissed the case solely on the ground that Wisconsin had reported the fraud to the federal government prior to filing the *qui tam* action.[31] This decision highlighted the "perverse logic of the 1943"amendments:

The State of Wisconsin was barred from acting as a *qui tam* plaintiff in a FCA suit . . . because the state had already disclosed the underlying fraud to the government, as required by statute. To make matters worse, the federal government had declined to intervene, leaving no proper plaintiff to pursue patently fraudulent conduct.[32]

In 1986 Congress passed important amendments to the FCA, many of which mitigated the negative impact of the 1943 amendments. The purpose of the 1986 amendments was to "encourage any individual knowing of Government fraud to bring that information forward."[33] The Senate Judiciary Committee noted that "in the face of sophisticated and widespread fraud" "only a coordinated effort of both the Government and the citizenry" will "decrease" the "wave" of fraud facing the government.[34] The committee noted that surveys of government employees uncovered a "great unwillingness to expose illegalities" due to fear of retaliation, and that 69 percent of "those who believed they had direct knowledge of illegalities" still "failed to report" those crimes.[35] The Committee heard from witnesses who reported that even when fraud was disclosed, "no one" was willing to "act on the information," and that whistleblowers regularly faced discharge and "long-term harassment campaign[s]."[36]

Not only was the Judiciary Committee concerned with the hardships facing original sources, they also understood that the government did not allocate sufficient resources to enforce laws against government fraud: "perhaps the most serious problem plaguing effective enforcement is a lack of resources on the part of the Federal enforcement agencies. Unlike most other types of crimes or abuses, fraud against the Federal government can by policed only by one body—the Federal government. State and local law enforcement are normally without jurisdiction where Federal funds are involved."[37]

The Senate Judiciary Committee's report on amendments clarified Congress' intent to "encourage more private enforcement" of the FCA. Congress amended the law to achieve the following goals:

- Insure that "all types of fraud, without qualification, that might result in financial loss to the Government" were included in the definition of false claims.[38]

- Expand the definition of "intent" to defraud to not only include "actual knowledge" that a claim is false, but also to include "gross negligence" of a contractor's obligation to insure that funds are properly spent.[39]

- Establish specific codified procedures *qui tam* relators must follow, including the requirement to file a suit under "seal" and to provide the government with "substantially all material evidence" that supports the claim.[40]

- Permit the *qui tam* relator to actively participate in the suit, even if the government intervenes in the action, as a "check that the Government does not neglect evidence, cause undue delay, or drop the false claims case without legitimate reason."[41]

- Increase the percentage of a FCA recovery the relator would be entitled to, ranging from a low of 15 percent to a high of 30 percent, depending on a number of factors. The amendment also added a statutory attorney fee section that would permit the relator to have all reasonable attorney fees and costs paid by the FCA violator.[42]

- Permit the Attorney General to award rewards to private individuals who provide the government with evidence of fraud but who choose not to file a *qui tam* action.[43]

- Lower the burden of proof for all elements of an FCA case. The amendment overrode some decisions that had created a "clear and convincing evidence" standard and replaced that standard with the "preponderance of the evidence" standard.[44]

- Set forth very liberal venue provisions.[45]

- Establish protections against retaliation for employees who file *qui tam* actions, and assist in investigations of potential FCA violations. The committee wanted to "halt companies and individuals from using the threat of economic retaliation to silence 'whistleblowers,' as well as those who are considering exposing fraud."[46]

The 1986 amendments attempted to strike a "balance between discouraging opportunistic litigation," in which a citizen merely acts on information in the public record, and "encouraging private citizens to come forward with knowledge of fraud."[47] Thus, the 1986 amendments repealed the "government knowledge" bar and replaced it with a two-part formulation.

The first part of the new formulation prohibits *qui tam* suits filed by nonwhistleblowers, if the "allegations or transactions" forming the basis of the suit were the subject of a "public disclosure."[48] However, even if there was a "public disclosure" of the "allegations," an "original source" may proceed with the *qui tam* action if he or she had "direct and independent knowledge of the information on which the allegations" were based *and* "voluntarily provided the information to the government before" filing the *qui tam* action.[49]

The meaning of these two clauses have been hotly contested, and numerous *qui tam* actions have been dismissed under the "public disclosure" clause and the failure of the plaintiff to meet the "original source" definition.[50] The U.S. Court of Appeals for the District of Columbia Circuit described the conflicted state of the law concerning these parts of the FCA when it was noted that "these jurisdictional provisions too have led to extensive litigation and to circuit splits concerning the meaning of the words 'based upon,' 'public disclosure,' 'allegations and transaction,' 'original source,' 'direct and independent knowledge' and 'information.' "[51]

In addition to disputes over a *qui tam* relator's jurisdictional bar, defendants have raised a host of constitutional challenges to the *qui tam* provisions, most of which have been rejected by a vast majority of courts.[52]

For example, in *Vermont of Natural Resources v. U.S. ex rel. Stevens*[53], the U.S. Supreme Court unanimously rejected a constituted attack on the *qui tam* provisions and held that whistleblowers who file *qui tam* suits have "standing" to pursue these claims in federal court.

QUI TAM PROCEDURES

Under the FCA, a whistleblower may be entitled to share in the monies recovered by the United States from contractors who submit "false of fraudulent" claims to the government. The U.S. Supreme Court outlined these *qui tam* provisions as follows:

An FCA action may be commenced in one of two ways. First, the Government itself may bring a civil action against the alleged false claimant. §3730 (a). Second, as is relevant here, a private person (the "relator") may bring a qui tam civil action "for the person and for the United States Government" against the alleged false claimant, "in the name of the Government." §3730(b)(1). If a relator initiates the FCA action, he must deliver a copy of the complaint, and any supporting evidence, to the Government, §3730(b)(2), which then has 60 days to intervene in the action, §§3730(b)(2), (4). If it does so, it assumes primary responsibility for prosecuting the action, §3730(c)(1), though the relator may continue to participate in the litigation and is entitled to a hearing before voluntary dismissal and to a court determination of reasonableness before settlement, §3730(c)(2). If the Government declines to intervene within the 60-day period, the relator has the exclusive right to conduct the action, §3730(b)(4), and the Government may subsequently intervene only on a showing of "good cause," §3730(c)-(3). The relator receives a share of any proceeds from the action—generally ranging from 15 to 25 percent if the Government intervenes (depending upon the relator's contribution to the prosecution), and from 25 to 30 percent if it does not (depending upon the court's assessment of what is reasonable)—plus attorney's fees and costs. §§3730(d)(1)(2).[54]

The FCA imposes on the *qui tam* relator a number of technical and complex substantive and procedural requirements. The failure to meet many of these requirements can result in a "jurisdictional bar" prohibiting the *qui tam* claim from going forward or a mandatory dismissal of a claim, with prejudice.

Simply stated, the FCA imposes civil liability on any person who makes a "false or fraudulent" monetary "claim"[55] to the United States government.[56] False claims are not strictly limited to "legally enforceable claims for amounts supposedly owed by the government, such as inflated invoices," but also include "all attempts" to improperly "cause the Government to pay out sums of money." The "key inquiry" concerns whether the "claim in question has the practical purpose and effect, and poses the attendant risk of, inducing wrongful payment."[57] Under most circumstances, an FCA suit must be filed within six years after the date of the alleged false claim.[58]

Any person who files such a claim is liable to the government for treble damages plus a $5,000 to $10,000 civil penalty for each separate false claim.[59] If a contractor separately files "multiple claims for payment" a court may "impose a separate" $5,000 to $10,000 penalty for "each claim."[60]

Violations of the FCA must be "knowingly" made. But Congress did not require "proof of specific intent to defraud" in order to maintain a valid FCA claim.[61] Although the law was not intended to punish contractors who commit errors based on simple "negligence,"[62] faulty calculations, flawed reasoning,[63] differences of interpretation,[64] or "honest mistakes,"[65] Congress abolished the specific intent requirement and explicitly targeted corporations that engaged in "ostrich-like" conduct in order to shield corporations or their officers from liability: "The express provision that no proof of specific intent was required under the FCA was part and parcel of Congress' attempt to hold large corporations accountable for the fraudulent schemes of high-level executives."[66] Because no direct proof of intent is necessary, some courts have imposed a judicially created "materiality" requirement on the false statements.[67]

Once a federal government contractor's false claim has been identified, the Attorney General may file a civil action against the wrongdoer.[68] Under the *qui tam* provisions of the FCA, a whistleblower or relator may also directly file an FCA case on behalf of the United States. The *qui tam* provisions are set forth in 31 U.S.C. § 3730(b), which contains the specific procedural rules governing these actions. The rules can be generally summarized as follows:

1. *First to File*: The statute allows any *person* to file a *qui tam* action on behalf of the government, and consequently entitles said *person* to obtain the monetary award set forth under the FCA.[69] But the law also encourages the expeditious filing of FCA actions, and, consequently, only the first person to actually file the *qui tam* action may pursue the case.[70] Thus, if two or more whistleblowers file separate FCA claims, only the first claim filed may be maintained. The others will be dismissed.[71] A *qui tam* relator must also file before the federal government files its claims: "In no event may a person bring a [*qui tam*] action based upon allegations or transactions which are the subject of a civil suit or an administrative civil monetary penalty proceeding in which the Government is already a party."[72] Finally, the complaint itself must contain the "requisite specificity" normally needed in pleadings alleging fraud.[73]

2. *Service Requirements*: Unlike standard civil law suits, a *qui tam* action must be filed "under seal" and "in camera" and served only on the Department of Justice (DOJ). In addition to the complaint, the relator must also serve, "in camera," a confidential statement that "substantially" discloses "all material evidence and information" the plaintiff-relator "possesses" that supports the FCA allegations.[74] The failure to follow these "mandatory" procedures may result in a "dismissal of the *qui tam* complaint with prejudice."[75]

3. *Review by DOJ*: Once a complaint is filed under seal in federal district court, the complaint, along with the disclosure statement, must be served on the DOJ. The DOJ has sixty days to review this material and determine whether the federal government will intervene in the suit. This sixty-day period may, with leave of the court, be extended. The complaint may not be served on the defendant until the "court so orders."[76] If the government intervenes, it takes effective control of the case and has "primary responsibility for prosecuting the action."[77] The *qui tam* relator remains a full party to the action, although the court is given the discretion to "limit the *qui tam* relator's role in the litigation upon a showing" of proper cause.[78] If the government intervenes, the relator is still entitled to between 15 percent and 25 percent of the government's recovery.[79] The government also maintains the right to have a claim dismissed or settled, with leave of the court, even if the relator objects to the terms of such conduct.[80] Even if the government does not initially intervene, it may still be granted leave to intervene after the relator serves the complaint.[81] The DOJ also has the authority to request a court to dismiss a potentially meritorious claim.[82] Finally, even when the "government and the relator have litigated a case on the same side," their interests, often "diverge when it comes time to pay the relator's share."[83] Specifically, the DOT may to have a court reduce the relator's share of a judgment at the very end of the case.

4. *Litigation by Relator*: If the government does not intervene in the case, the *qui tam* plaintiff maintains the "right to conduct the action" and fully pursue his or her case against the government contractor.[84] Additionally, if the relator prevails in the action he or she is entitled to a larger portion of the government's recovery, that is, 25 to 30 percent of the total recovery.[85] Even if the government does not intervene, the DOJ still has the right to fully monitor the proceedings,[86] obtain a stay of discovery if the *qui tam* action may interfere with ongoing government investigations or other criminal or civil actions,[87] and the Attorney General must give consent to any dismissal of the case.[88] If a relator pursues the claim independent of DOJ intervention, the relator may be required to pay reverse attorney fees if the court finds that the action was "clearly frivolous, clearly vexatious, or brought primarily for purposes of harassment."[89]

5. *Public Disclosure Jurisdictional Bar:* One of the most common grounds for dismissing a *qui tam* claim concerns the jurisdictional bar related to public disclosure.[90] The provision jurisdictionally bars a court from hearing a *qui tam* case filed by a person who was not the "original source" of the information, if the claim is "based upon"[91] "allegations or transactions"[92] that were publicly disclosed in a "criminal, civil, or administrative hearing, in a congressional, administrative, or Government Accounting Office report, hearing, audit, or investigation, or from the news media."[93] Given the broad interpretation of this jurisdictional bar, and the narrow interpretation given to the definition of "original source," any person seeking to file a *qui tam* action should file an FCA claim, if possible, prior to any "public disclosure." For example, one court applied this bar if "any part" of the *qui tam* allegation was based on publicly disclosed material.[94] Many courts justify their strict construction of this jurisdictional bar on the basis of Congress' intent to encourage "whistleblowers to come forward as soon as possible" and to reward employees who "promptly" "come forward" with "information concerning fraud."[95]

6. *Original Source*: If the "allegations or transactions" that form any part of the factual basis of the *qui tam* action were publicly disclosed, a relator may still go forward with the *qui tam* suit if he or she was an "original source of the information."[96] The FCA defines "original source" as an "individual who has direct and independent knowledge of the information on which the allegations are based and has voluntarily provided the information to the Government before filing an action under this section."[97] This section contains a number of clauses which have been narrowly construed by some courts to defeat *qui tam* cases. For example, the phrase "direct and independent knowledge" has been interpreted to require "first hand" knowledge and would exclude "information" learned from "subordinates."[98] Likewise, the term "voluntarily"[99] has also been narrowly construed to prohibit some employees, such as federal government auditors and managers, from filing *qui tam* actions, based on the purported involuntary nature of the disclosure requirements.[100] The requirement that the information be disclosed to the government prior to the filing of the FCA suit has been interpreted as meaning that the information must be provided to the government even before the first public disclosure.[101] Some courts have gone so far as to require that the relator was both the source to the government and the source of the initial public disclosure.[102] However, a number of courts have rejected this "extra textual requirement" and have not required that the relator also be the "source of the public disclosures."[103]

The statutorily and judicially created procedural impediments to *qui tam* actions, combined with the rigorous defense for which large government contractors mount to defeat such suits, require whistleblowers who allege contractor fraud to carefully proceed in any FCA action. In harmo-

nizing the conflicting results of the strict enforcement of procedural requirements and the goal of the FCA in encouraging whistleblowing, the U.S.
Court of Appeals for the Ninth Circuit reasoned that: "[t]wo of the primary
purposes of the FCA are to alert the government as early as possible to
fraud that is being committed against it and to encourage insiders to come
forward with such information where they would otherwise have little
incentive to do so."[104]

Whistleblowers who want to benefit from the *qui tam* provisions
need to strictly construe the procedural requirements for filing such a claim
and ensure that each action they take complies with each hypertechnical
rule.[105]

FCA WHISTLEBLOWER PROTECTION

In 1986 Congress was concerned that employees would not expose
fraud in government contracting or file FCA *qui tam* claims if they could
be blacklisted or fired in retaliation for such activities. As a result, Congress amended the FCA and added an antiretaliation clause "guided" by
case law developed under the nuclear and environmental whistleblower
statutes.[106] Congress' intent was clear:

The committee recognizes that few individuals will expose fraud if they fear their
disclosures will lead to harassment, demotion, loss of employment, or any other
form of retaliation. . . the Committee seeks to halt companies and individuals
from using the threat of economic retaliation to silence "whistleblowers," as well
as assure those who may be considering exposing fraud that they are legally
protected from retaliatory acts.[107]

The whistleblower provision protects "any employee" "who is
discharged, demoted, suspended, threatened, harassed, or in any other
manner discriminated against in the terms and conditions of employment
by his or her employer because of lawful acts done by the employee on
behalf of the employee or others in furtherance of an action under this
section."[108]

An employee who alleges retaliation under this law may file a
claim against an "employer"[109] in U.S. District Court and seek a full "make
whole" remedy, including, "reinstatement with the same seniority status
such employee would have had but for the discrimination, two times the
amount of back pay, interest on the back pay, and compensation for any
special damages sustained as a result of the discrimination, including
litigation costs and reasonable attorneys' fees."[110]

In order to prevail in a whistleblower case, an employee would not have to prove that there was an actual violation of the FCA.[111] Instead, consistent with the case law developed under the environmental whistleblower laws, an employee must only demonstrate that he or she had a "good faith" belief that such violations may have occurred.[112] A protected employee need not develop a "winning *qui tam* action" in order to be protected from retaliation.[113]

The FCA contains a provision allowing for a six-year statute of limitations for all "civil actions" filed under 31 U.S.C. § 3730.[114] The whistleblower clause is codified as subsection (h) of § 3730.[115] Despite this statutory authority, the courts of appeals are split as to the applicable statute of limitations.

The first court to review this issue applied the six-year statute of limitations,[116] but the 9th Circuit rejected this position and held that there was no uniform federal limitations period for FCA whistleblowers. Instead, it held that employees must identify—without any prior judicial guidance—"the most analogous statute of limitations under" *state* law.[117] In that case, the 9th Circuit applied a one year statute of limitations and dismissed the whistleblower suit as "time-barred."[118]

The problematical nature of the 9th Circuit's ruling is not only evident by the resulting fifty separate statutes of limitations employees must follow, but also by the fact that some states' "analogous" limitations period may be as short as thirty to ninety days.[119]

The basic *prima facie* case under § 3730(h) requires an employee to demonstrate the following factors: "(1) the employee must be engaged in conduct protected by the statute, (2) the employer must know the employee was engaging in such protected conduct, and (3) the employer must have discriminated against the employee because of this protected conduct."[120] According to the legislative history of the act, once an employee proves these three elements "the burden of proof shifts to the employer to prove affirmatively that the same decision would have been made even if the employee had not engaged in the protected activity."[121]

The courts are not in agreement concerning the scope of protected activity under the FCA. For example, one court described the scope of protected activity as "narrow" while another described the scope as "broad."[122] The legislative history explicitly cited to nuclear whistleblower cases which broadly interpreted the scope of protected activity. The Senate Judiciary Committee was clear on this point: "Protected activity should therefore be interpreted broadly."[123] At least one court relied upon these precedents in justifying a liberal interpretation of the law.[124]

In justifying a broad interpretation of the FCA, both the U.S. Courts of Appeals for the 6th and D.C. Circuits have held that the types of conduct explicitly referenced in § 3730(h)—that is, "investigation" of an FCA, "initiation" of such a claim, or testifying or assisting in such a claim—were not inclusive. In this regard the courts have held that Congress gave "no indication" of "examples" of protected conduct.[125]

A majority of courts protect internal investigative-type conduct into potential government fraud issues, even if the employee is unaware of the FCA or that the investigation may "lead to an FCA suit."[126] As explained by the D.C. Circuit Court of Appeals, the law did not presume that whistle-blowers would need to be trained in the law to be protected:

An initial investigation may well further an action under the Act, even though the employee does not know it at the time of the investigation. Were that not the case, only lawyers—or those versed in the law—would be protected by the statute, as only they would know from the outset that what they were investigating could lead to a False Claims Act prosecution. There is no suggestion in the legislative history that Congress meant to extend protection only to lawyers, or to others only after they have consulted with lawyers.[127]

Consistent with the goals of the FCA, the D.C. Circuit concluded that employees can be protected under the whistleblower provision if all their complaints are raised directly to an employer, if there was no actual contact with government officials, and if the employee never directly threatened his or her employer that he would file a *qui tam* action.[128] However, not all "grumbling" is protected:

Nonetheless, a plaintiff still must show that his employer was aware of his activity. Merely grumbling to the employer about job dissatisfaction or regulatory violations does not satisfy the requirement—just as it does not constitute protected activity in the first place. Threatening to file a *qui tam* suit or to make a report to the government, on the other hand, clearly is one way to make an employer aware. But it is not the only way.[129]

In *U.S. ex rel. Yesudian v. Howard University*, the D.C. Circuit held that the employee engaged in protected activity by "repeatedly" telling his supervisor that another employee had "falsified time and attendance records, accepted bribes from vendors, and provided inside information to favored vendors."[130]

In contrast to the *Yesudian* case, the 5th Circuit held that a contract administrator—whose job included investigating fraud–was not protected when he raised allegations of "mischarging" on government contracts to his supervisor.[131] The court reasoned that an employee tasked with investigating fraud within a company was not protected if he or she uncovered such fraud and reported it to the management. In order to be protected such an employee would have to not only identify the "mischarging" but explicitly characterize the "concerns as [also] involving illegal, unlawful, or false claims."[132]

The U.S. Court of Appeals for the 4th Circuit summarized the narrower approach to protecting internal whistleblowers under the FCA as follows:

This court holds that an employee tasked with the internal investigation of fraud against the government cannot bring a section 3730(h) action for retaliation unless the employee puts the employer on notice that a *qui tam* suit under section 3730 is a reasonable possibility. Such notice can be accomplished by expressly stating an intention to bring a *qui tam* suit, but it may also be accomplished by any action which a factfinder reasonably could conclude would put the employer on notice that litigation is a reasonable possibility. Such actions would include, but are not limited to, characterizing the employer's conduct as illegal or fraudulent or recommending that legal conduct become involved. These types of actions are sufficient because they let the employer know, regardless of whether the employee's job duties include investigating potential fraud, that litigation is a reasonable possibility.[133]

Thus, in order to ensure that an employee's conduct will be protected under the FCA antiretaliation clause under any judicial standard, an employee should make his or her employer directly aware that the employee is engaging, or will engage, in conduct set forth explicitly in 31 U.S.C. § 3730(h). Although the legislative history supports a broad interpretation of protected activity, the conflicting judicial interpretations warrant a conservative approach to ensure that a whistleblower be protected.[134]

NOTES

1. 31 U.S.C. §§ 3729-3733.
2. *Lamers v. City of Green Bay*, 998 F. Supp. 971, 977 (E.D. Wis. 1998), *affm'd* 168 F.3d 1013 (1999).
3. *U.S. ex rel. Fine v. MK-Ferguson Co.*, 861 F. Supp. 1544, 1547 (D. N.M. 1994).
4. "*Qui tam*" is an abbreviated Latin phrase of "*qui tam pro domino rege quam pro se ipso in hac parte sequitur*," which means "who pursues this action on our Lord the King's behalf as well as his own." *Vermont Agency of Natural Resources v. U.S. ex rel Stevens*, 120 U.S. 1858 (2000); *U.S. ex rel. Thompson v. Columbia/HCA Healthcare Corp.*, 20 F. Supp.2d 1017, 1045 n. 29 (S.D. Tex. 1998). *See also*, "The History and Development of *Qui Tam*," 1972 *Washington U.L.Q.* at 81, 83.

5. *Lamers, supra,* at 977.

6. *Id.*

7. For example, on May 22, 2000, the U.S. Supreme Court rejected an Article III "standing" challenge to the FCA but also held that the 11th Amendment prohibited *qui tam* actions against states or any state agencies. *Vermont Agency of Natural Resources v. U.S. ex rel Stevens,* 120 U.S. 1858 (2000). *See also, e.g.,* the majority and dissenting opinion in *Riley v. St. Luke's Episcopal Hospital,* 196 F.3d 514 (5th Cir. 1999).

8. 31 U.S.C. § 3730(h).

9. California False Claims Actions, Title 2, Article 9, § 12650, *et seq.*

10. D.C. Act 11-526 (January 3, 1997).

11. Florida False Claims Act, Laws of Florida, Ch. 94-316.

12. Illinois Whistleblower Reward and Protection Act, 740 ILCS 175.

13. Tennessee Health Care False Claims Act, § 56-26-402, *et seq.*

14. *U.S. ex rel. Marcus v. Hess,* 317 U.S. 537, 541 (1943).

15. *Id.* at 541, n. 4.

16. *See, e.g., United States v. Morris,* 23 U.S. 246 (1825). *Accord., Vermont Agency, supra* ("long tradition of *qui tam* actions").

17. *See* Journals of Congress, July 1778, at 732.

18. Report of the House Committee on Government Contracts, H. Rep. No. 2, 37th Congress, p. 69. *But see Vermont Agency, supra,* n. 12 (questioning relevancy report).

19. *Id.*

20. *Id.*

21. *See Hess, supra,* at 544, n. 8.

22. Cong. Globe, 37th Cong. 3d Sess., Feb. 14, 1863 at 952.

23. *Id.* at 956.

24. Benjamin Franklin, in Debates of the Constitutional Convention, July 26, 1787. *Reprinted* in 457 *Formation of the Union: Documents* (Washington, DC: Government Printing Office, 1927).

25. Act of March 2, 1863, Ch. 67, 12 Stat. 696. A history of the FCA is contained in the Senate Judiciary Committee's report on the 1986 FCA amendments. S. Rep. No. 99-345, pp. 8-13.

26. *U.S. ex rel. Findley v. FPC-Boron Employees' Club,* 105 F.3d 675, 679 (D.C. Cir. 1997).

27. *Id.*

28. *Hess, supra,* at 547. Justice Jackson, in a dissenting opinion, articulated many of the policy goals that Congress would eventually try to address in the 1986 amendments:

We should, of course, fully sustain informers in proceedings where Congress has utilized their self-interest as an aid to law enforcement. Informers who disclose law violations even for the worst of motives play an important part in making many laws effective. But there is nothing in the text or history of this statute which indicates to me that Congress intended to enrich a mere busybody who copies a Government's indictment as his own complaint and who brings to light no frauds not already disclosed.

Hess, supra, at 558 (Justice Jackson dissenting).

29. 57 Stat. 608.

30. *Findley, supra,* at 680.

31. *U.S. ex rel. Wisconsin v. Dean,* 729 F.2d 1100 (7th Cir. 1984).

32. *Lamers, supra,* at 977-78.

33. S. Rep. No. 99-345, p. 2, *reprinted in,* 1986 U.S. Code Cong. & Ad. News, pp. 5266-5267.

34. *Id.* at 2.

35. *Id.* at 4.

36. *Id.* at 5.

37. *Id.* at 7.

38. *Id.* at 19.

39. *Id.* at 20.

40. *Id.* at 23-25.

41. *Id.* at 25-27.

42. *Id.* at 27-29.

43. *Id.* at 30.

44. *Id.* at 30-31.

45. *Id.* at 32.

46. *Id.* at 34-35.

47. *Lamers, supra,* at 978.

48. 31 U.S.C. § 3730(e)(4)(A).

49. 31 U.S.C. § 3730(e)(4)(B).

50. *See e.g., U.S. ex rel. Ackley v. IBM Corp.,* 76 F. Supp.2d 654 (D. Md. 1999).

51. *Findley, supra,* at 681.

52. The constitutional grounds for attacking the *qui tam* provisions were spelled out in great detail in the dissenting opinion of Judge Weinstein in *U.S. ex rel. Stevens v. State of Vermont,* 162 F.3d 195, 208-229 (2nd Cir. 1998) (dissenting opinion), *rev'd in part, Vermont Agency of Natural Resources, supra,* and in a district court in Texas, *U.S. ex rel. Riley v. St. Luke's,* 982 F. Supp. 1261 (S.D. Tex. 1997). Most courts have rejected the constitutional attacks on the FCA. *See e.g., U.S. ex rel. El Amin,* 26 F. Supp.2d 162, 165-166 (D.C. Cir. 1998) (rejecting constitutional challenge to "standing") (collecting cases); *U.S. ex rel. Thompson, supra* (detailed analysis rejecting constitutional challenges); *U.S. ex rel. Olloh-Okeke,* 1999 WL 222356 (N.D. Tex.) (citing cases); *U.S. ex rel. Chandler v. Hektoen Institute,* 35 F. Supp.2d 1078 (N.D. Ill. 1999).

53. *Vermont Agency of Natural Resources v. U.S. ex rel Stevens,* 120 U.S. 1858 (2000).

54. *Id.* at 1860-1861.

55. *See Costner v. URS Consultants, Inc.,* 153 F.3d 667, 677 (7th Cir. 1998) for a definition of "claim."

56. The statute, 31 U.S.C. § 3729(a), defines "false claims" and establishes "liability" for any "person" who:

1. knowingly presents. or causes to be presented. to an officer or employee of the United States Government or a member of the Armed Forces of the United States a false or fraudulent claim for payment or approval:
2. knowingly makes. uses. or causes to be made or used. a false record or statement to get a false or fraudulent claim paid or approved by the Government:
3. conspires to defraud the Government by getting a false or fraudulent claim allowed or paid:
4. has possession. custody. or control of property or money used. or to be used. by the Government and. intending to defraud the Government or willfully to conceal the property. delivers. or causes to be delivered. less property than the amount for which the person receives a certificate or receipt:
5. authorized to make or deliver a document certifying receipt of property used, or to be used. by the Government and. intending to defraud the Government. makes or delivers the receipt without completely knowing that the information on the receipt is true:
6. knowingly buys. or receives as a pledge of an obligation or debt. public property from an officer or employee of the Government. or a member of the Armed Forces, who lawfully may not sell or pledge the property: or
7. knowingly makes. uses. or causes to be made or used. a false record or statement to conceal. avoid. or decrease an obligation to pay or transmit money or property to the Government.

57. *Lamers, supra,* at 985. *See, e.g., U.S. ex rel. Schwedt v. Planning Research Corp.*, 59 F.3d 196, 203-204 (D.C. Cir. 1995) (upholding FCA for false statements in program report).

58. 31 U.S.C. § 3731(b) *See U.S. ex rel. Bidani v. Lewis*, 1999 WL 163053 (N.D. Ill. 1999) for a discussion on the various exceptions to the statute of limitations.

59. 31 U.S.C. § 3729(a) ("Any person who [files a false claim] . . . is liable to the United States Government for a civil penalty of not less then $5000 and not more than $10,000, plus 3 times the amount of damages which the government sustains because of the act").

60. *U.S. ex rel. Trim v. McKean*, 31 F. Supp. 2d 1308, 1315 (W.D. Ok. 1998).

61. 31 U.S.C. § 3729(b)(3). In the text of the FCA, 31 U.S.C. § 3729(b), Congress supplied the following definition:

the terms of "knowing" and "knowingly" mean that a person. with respect to informa-tion—
  (1) has actual knowledge of the information:
  (2) acts in deliberate ignorance of the truth or falsity of the information: or,
  (3) acts in a reckless disregard of the truth or falsity of the information, and known proof of specific intent to defraud is required.

62. *Hindo v. University of Health Sciences*, 65 F.3d 608, 613 (7th Cir. 1995).

63. *Wang v. FMC Corp.*, 975 F.2d 1412, 1420 (9th Cir. 1992).

64. *Hagood v. Sonoma County Water Agency*, 81 F.3d 1465, 1477-1478 (9th Cir. 1996).

65. S. Rep. 99-345, p. 7. For example, when a contractor engages in an "open dialogue with government officials" concerning items that may become FCA claims, such a dialogue may "mitigate" against finding the necessary intent to uphold a violation of the FCA. *Lamers, supra,* at 988. Additionally, "not every regulatory violation is tantamount to making a knowingly false statement." *U.S. ex rel. Cantekin v. University of Pittsburgh*, 192 F.3d 402 (3rd Cir. 1999). In this regard, some courts have created a "judicially imposed materiality requirement." *Id.*

66. *Lamers, supra,* at 987.

67. *Cantekin, supra, citing Harrison v. Westinghouse Savannah River Co.*, 176 F.3d 776, 784 (4th Cir. 1999).

68. 31 U.S.C. § 3730(a).

69. 31 U.S.C. § 3730(b)(1).

70. 31 U.S.C. § 3730(b)(5). *See U.S. ex rel. LaCorte v. Smithkline Beecham Clinical Laboratories,* 149 F.3d 227, 232 (3rd Cir. 1998) (this clause "clearly bars claims arising from events that are already the subject of existing suits").

71. *U.S. ex rel. Johnson v. Shell Oil Co.*, 33 F. Supp.2d 528 (E.D. Tex. 1999) (dismissing the "related" actions of other whistleblowers and only allowing the "first filed" claim to go forward).

72. 31 U.S.C. 3730(e)(3).

73. *See U.S. ex rel. Schwedt v. Planning Research Corp.*, 39 F. Supp. 28, 30 (D.C. Cir. 1999). *See also U.S. Ex. Rel. Wilkins v. North American Construction Corp.*, ___ F. Supp.2d ___, 2000 WL 780245 (S. D. Tex. 2000), for a detailed discussion of pleading requirements.

74. 31 U.S.C. § 3730(b)(2). *Qui tam* plaintiffs may also weigh serving the disclosure statement on the proper government official(s) prior to filing the *qui tam* action, in order to ensure meeting the "original source" requirements. *See* 31 U.S.C. § 3730(e)(4)(B) ("original source" must "voluntarily" provide allegations to the "Government before filing" a *qui tam* action).

75. *Stephens, supra,* at 200, *cert. granted on other grounds.*

76. 31 U.S.C. 3730(b)(2) and (3).

77. 31 U.S.C. §§ 3730(b)(4)(A) and (c)(1).

78. *Stephens, supra,* at 200.

79. 31 U.S.C. § 3730(d)(1).

80. 31 U.S.C. § 3730(c)(2)(A) and (B). *See U.S. v. U.S. ex rel. Thornton*, 207 F.3d 769 (5th Cir. 2000).

81. *U.S. ex rel. Sequoia Orange Company v. Baird-Neece Packing Corp.*, 151 F.3d 1139 (9th Cir. 1998).

82. *Id.*

83. *Thornton, supra.*

84. 31 U.S.C. § 3730(b)(4)(B).

85. 31 U.S.C. § 3730(d)(2).

86. 31 U.S.C. § 3730(c)(3).
87. 31 U.S.C. § 3730(c)(4).
88. 31 U.S.C. § 3730(b)(1).
89. 31 U.S.C. § 3730(d)(4).
90. 31 U.S.C. § 3730(e)(4)(A). *See U.S. ex rel. Jones v. Horizon Healthcare Corp.*, 160 F.3d 326, 330-335 (6th Cir. 1999). The FCA's jurisdictional bar states:

No court shall have jurisdiction over an action under this section based upon the public disclosure of allegations or transactions in a criminal, civil, or administrative hearing, in a congressional, administrative, or Government Accounting Office report, hearing, audit, or investigation, or from the news media, unless the action is brought by the Attorney General or the person bringing the action is an original source of the information.

In *Jones,* the 6th Circuit described the basic test for determining whether the "jurisdictional bar" was applicable in any given case as follows:

(A) whether there has been a public disclosure in a criminal, civil, or administrative hearing; or congressional, administrative, or government report, hearing, audit, or investigation; or from the news media; (B) of the allegations or transactions that form the basis of the relator's complaint; and (C) whether the relator's action is "based upon" the publicly disclosed allegations or transactions. If the answer is "no" to any of these questions, the inquiry ends and the *qui tam* action may proceed. If the answer to each of the above questions is "yes" then the final inquiry is (D) whether the relator qualifies as an "original source" under § 3730(e)(4)(B), which also would allow the suit to proceed (160 F.3d at 330).

91. The Courts of Appeal have split concerning the meaning of "based upon." Most courts broadly construe this term to mean merely that a case was "supported by" public disclosures. *See U.S. ex rel. Precision Co. v. Koch Industries,* 971 F.2d 548, 552 (10th Cir. 1992). Under this analysis no "substantial identity" need exist between the information that had been publicly disclosed and the factual basis for the *qui tam* action. *Jones, supra,* at 332. Likewise, the bar would apply even if the plaintiff was unaware of the public disclosure and the public information was not the "actual source" of the "information in the particular complaint." *Findley, supra,* at 682. The U.S. Court of Appeals for the 4th Circuit has rejected this approach and has held that the "based upon" clause only bars suits in which the relator's information actually derived solely from the public record. *U.S. ex rel. Siller v. Becton Dickinson & Co.,* 21 F.3d 1339, 1347-1350 (4th Cir. 1994). *Accord., Jones* at 335-336 (concurring opinion of Judge Gilman).

92. *See U.S. ex rel. Springfield Terminal Railway Co. v. Quinn,* 14 F.3d 645, 654 (D.C. Cir. 1994), in which the court explained that the jurisdictional bar would apply if "either the allegation of fraud or the critical elements of the fraudulent transactions themselves were in the public domain." In this case the

court identified its "X+Y=Z" formulation. Under this formulation, if "X+Y" equals the essential elements of a fraud claim and "Z" equals an explicit statement that a fraud has been alleged, then the public disclosure requirements have been met if the public record contains either "X+Y" or "Z." *Accord., Findley* at 687; *Jones,* at 331 (explaining the "X+Y=Z" formulation).

93. 31 U.S.C. § 3730(e)(4)(A).

94. *U.S. ex rel. McKenzie v. Bellsouth Telecomms. Inc.*, 123 F.3d 935, 940 (6th Cir. 1998).

95. *Jones, supra,* at 335.

96. 31 U.S.C. § 3730(e)(4)(A) and (B).

97. 31 U.S.C. § 3730(e)(4)(B).

98. *Schwedt, supra,* at 35. *Accord., Johnson, supra,* at 541 ("Direct knowledge has been found to mean first-hand knowledge of the material elements of the alleged fraud which the relator has gained through his 'own efforts and not acquired from the labors of others.' ") (collecting cases).

99. *See U.S. ex rel. Biddle v. Stanford University*, 161 F.3d 533, 538-539 (9th Cir. 1998) for a discussion of the "voluntary" standard.

100. *See, e.g., U.S. ex rel. Fine v. Chevron*, 72 F.3d 740, 744 (9th Cir. 1995) (en banc); *Schwedt, supra,* 35-36 (holding that a federal employee who was "duty-bound to disclose" information "concerning alleged fraud" could not have "voluntarily" provided the information to the government). In one case, a district court judge so broadly construed the "voluntary" requirement as to foreclose numerous federal government contractor employee whistleblowers from ever utilizing the FCA provisions. In *U.S. ex rel. Foust v. Group Hospitalization and Medical Services, Inc.*, 26 F. Supp.2d 60, 74 (D.D.C. 1998), the court held that when a government contract required the employee contractors to disclose fraud, those contractors who disclosed the fraud could never meet the "original source" definition.

101. *Jones, supra,* at 335 ("In addition to the requirement that a relator have provided information to the government prior to filing her FCA suit, this Circuit has held that a relator also must provide the government with the information upon which the allegations are based prior to any public disclosure").

102. *U.S. ex rel. Dick v. Long Island Lighting Co.*, 912 F.2d 13, 16-18 (2nd Cir. 1990).

103. *U.S. ex rel. Findley, supra,* at 689-690. *See also Johnson, supra,* at 542 (collecting cases); *U.S. ex rel. Hafter v. Spectrum Emergency Care*, 9 F. Supp.2d 1273, 1279-1281 (D. Kan. 1998) (evaluating differences in circuit opinions); *U.S. ex rel. Hafter D.O. v. Spectrum Emergency Care, Inc.*, 190 F.3d 1156 (10th Cir. 1999) (analyzing "direct and independent knowledge" requirement).

104. Biddle, *supra.*

105. Two excellent texts which comprehensively evaluate the FCA are: John T. Boese, *False Claims Act and Qui Tam Actions* (New York: Aspen, 1998 Supplement) and James B. Helmer, Jr., Ann Lugbill, and Robert C. Neff, Jr., *False Claims Act: Whistleblower Litigation* (Charlottesville: Lexis, 2nd ed. 1999). Additionally, see the non-profit group Taxpayers Against Fraud publica-

tion *False Claims Act and Qui Tam Quarterly Review* (W.I.D.C.)

106. S. Rep. No. 99-345, p. 34, 1986 U.S. Code Cong. & Ad. News 5266, 5299.

107. *Id. See also Luckey v. Baxter Healthcare Corp.*, 2 F. Supp.2d 1034, 1051 (N.D. Ill. 1998); *U.S. ex rel. Garibaldi v. Orleans Parish School Board.*, 21 F. Supp.2d 607, 617 (E.D. La. 1998) ("the whistleblower provision of the FCA encourages employees with 'knowledge' of fraud to come forward by prohibiting retaliation against employees who assist in bringing *qui tam* actions against their employers").

108. 31 U.S.C. § 3730(h).

109. *See Mruz v. Caring, Inc.*, 991 F. Supp. 701, 709 (D. N.J. 1998) (applying Title VII definition of employer and collecting cases).

110. 31 U.S.C. § 3730(h). *Accord., Neal v. Honeywell Inc.*, 191 F.3d 827, 1999 WL 715398 (7th Cir. 1999) (awarding double back pay, upholding $200,000 emotional distress award as part of "special damages," and awarding $1.46 million in attorneys' fees without any reference to "whether or not the winner has an obligation to pay the lawyer that sum"). *See Hammond v. Northland Counseling*, 2000 WL 973545 (8th Cir. 2000).

111. S. Rep. No. 99-55, p. 35.

112. *Id.*

113. *U.S. ex rel. Yesudian v. Howard University*, 153 F.3d 731, 739-740 (D.C. Cir. 1998).

114. 31 U.S.C. § 3731.

115. 31 U.S.C. § 3730(h).

116. *Neal v. Honeywell Inc.*, 33 F.3d 860, 865 (7th Cir. 1994).

117. *U.S. ex rel. Lujan v. Hughes Aircraft Co.*, 162 F.3d 1027, 1035 (9th Cir. 1998).

118. *Id.*

119. For example, in *Kowalski v. Alpha Kappa Alpha*, 993 F. Supp. 619 (N.D. Ohio 1997) the court applied the six-year statute of limitations from the FCA to a whistleblower case arising under the Major Frauds Act. In rejecting the application of an analogous state limitations period, the court noted that under the state law the employee would have had only six months to file a claim.

120. *Luckey, supra,* at 1050 (collecting cases). *Accord., Yesudian, supra,* at 736.

121. S. Rep. No. 99-345, p. 35, *quoted in, Yesudian,* at 736 n. 4. *But see Mann v. Olsten Certified Healthcare Corp.*, 49 F. Supp.2d 1307, 1999 WL 3208-65 (M.D. Ala. 1999) (applying standard Title VII "burden of proof" to FCA).

122. *Compare Luckey, supra,* at 1050 ("protected conduct is interpreted more narrowly when applied to FCA claims than to common or state law retaliatory discharge actions") *with Mann* (FCA "broadly interpreted").

123. S. Rep. No. 99-345, pp. 34-35.

124. *Yesudian, supra,* at 741 n. 9, 742.

125. *Id.* at 741 ("The statute provides examples of the types of activity that are protected, including investigation, initiation of a suit, and testimony, but

these examples are not exclusive and the legislative history indicates '[p]rotected activity should . . . be interpreted broadly' ") (quoting S. Rep. No. 99-345, p. 35, reprinted in 1986 U.S.C.C.A.N. at 5300). *Accord., McKenzie v. Bell South Telephone*, 123 F.3d 935, 944 (6th Cir. 1997).

126. Yesudian, *supra*, at 741 (collecting cases); *Eberhardt v. Integrated Design & Construction*, 167 F.3d 861, 867 (4th Cir. 1999) (collecting cases).

127. *Yesudian*, at 741.

128. *Id.* at 743-744.

129. *Id.*

130. *Id.* at 743.

131. *Robertson v. Bell Helicopter Textron, Inc.*, 32 F.3d 948, 951 (5th Cir. 1994).

132. *Id. Accord S., Zahodnick v. IBM Corp.*, 135 F.3d 911, 914 (4th Cir. 1997) ("[s]imply reporting [the] concern of a mischarging to the government [one's] supervisor does not suffice to establish that [an employee] was acting 'in furtherance of' a *qui tam* action"). *See also, U.S. ex rel. Vallejo*, 2 F. Supp.2d 330, 338-339 (W.D. N.Y. 1998); *Luckey, supra.*

133. *Eberhardt, supra*, at 868.

134. *See*, e.g., *Mann, supra* (the court will look for evidence that the plaintiff, either by words or actions, communicated to the employer that he or she believed that the employer had engaged in illegal or fraudulent conduct involving submission of claims for payment to the government. Such a showing could be made, for example, by evidence that the plaintiff characterized the employer's conduct as illegal or fraudulent or recommended that legal counsel become involved). *See also Garibaldi, supra*, at 617-618 (upholding FCA whistleblower claim); *McKenzie v. BellSouth Telecommunications*, 2000 WL 955746 (6th Cir. 2000) (protected activity must be "reasonably connected" to the FCA").

Chapter 7

OSHA and Workplace Safety Whistleblowing

INTRODUCTION

Many employees work on job sites in which they may be exposed to radioactive, toxic, and other unsafe substances or working conditions. Under a number of whistleblower protection laws, state statutory or common law, the Occupational Safety and Health Act (OSHA), and regulations of the Nuclear Regulatory Commission (NRC), employees are protected from retaliation for exposing occupational hazards and reporting these hazards to the government, the press, or other authorities.[1] These laws provide the right to request a health, safety, or radioactive monitoring inspection; the right to file safety and health grievances; the right to request information from the employer about safety and health hazards; the right to obtain individual radiation exposure data; and, in certain circumstances, the right to refuse unsafe or unhealthful work.[2] Additionally, in certain industries, such as trucking and mining, special whistleblower laws exist that protect employees who expose or protest hazardous working conditions. [3]

The Department of Labor (DOL) enforces OSHA, the most comprehensive workplace safety law. In 1970, while enacting whistleblower protection in OSHA, "Congress recognized employees to be a valuable and knowledgeable source of information regarding work place safety and health hazards. Congress was aware of the shortage of federal and state occupational safety inspectors, and placed great reliance on employee assistance in enforcing the Act."[4] The purpose, consistent with this legislative history was to, "assure so far as possible every working man and woman in the Nation safe and healthful working conditions. [OSHA] is safety legislation that is remedial and preventative in nature and is to be liberally construed to effectuate its congressional purpose."[5] Despite the broad purpose of OSHA, as one of the first antiretaliation laws passed by Congress over thirty years ago, its statutory protections are weak. For example, although the law provides protections for employees who blow the whistle on unsafe working conditions, enforcement of employee rights under that act is vested exclusively in the DOL. There is no private right of action for whistleblowers under OSHA. This has led a number of courts to explicitly criticize that legislation and find that, as a matter of law, the OSHA remedies are "inadequate."

The weaknesses in OSHA's antiretaliation laws are widely recognized. For example, Senator Paul Wellstone (D-MN), while introducing the Safer Workplaces Act of 1999 into the Senate stated the following:

As Assistant Secretary of Labor Charles Jeffress recently testified before the Employment, Safety, and Training Subcommittee, "The provisions in place today in Section 11(c) of the Act are too weak and too cumbersome to discourage employer retaliation or to provide an effective remedy for the victims of retaliation." Many, if not most, employees are simply afraid that they will be punished or fired if they complain. And they have every reason to be afraid. In 1997 the Labor Department's Inspector General, Charles C. Masten, concluded that, "Workers, particularly with small companies, are vulnerable to reprisals by their employers for complaining about unsafe, unhealthy work conditions. The severity of the discrimination is highlighted by the fact that for 653 cases included in our sample, nearly 67 percent of the workers who filed complaints were terminated from their jobs." The IG further found that workers who complain to their employer first—rather than to OSHA—are particularly vulnerable; that workers in small firms are the most vulnerable; that employer retaliation is often severe, most frequently in the form of firing; that OSHA procedures to investigate complaints are inadequate; that there are significant delays in OSHA's decision-making in 11(c) cases; and that the Department is failing to seek effective remedies for employees.[6]

The deficiencies in OSHA have led employees to seek protection under laws that do provide for a private right of action, such as the nuclear and environmental whistleblower laws, the Surface Transportation Assistance Act, the Federal Mine Health and Safety Act, and state public policy tort remedies.

RIGHT TO REQUEST INSPECTIONS

The Occupational Safety and Health Act, 29 U.S.C. § 651 *et seq.,* gives an employee the right to request a DOL Occupational Safety and Health Administration inspection when he or she feels in imminent danger from a hazard that is a violation of an OSHA standard that threatens physical harm. The DOL is required to inform the employee of any action it takes regarding the complaint, and, if requested, will hold an informal review of any decision not to inspect.[7] An OSHA complaint should be in writing and should set forth with reasonable detail the grounds for the investigation. An employee can request that the (DOL) and OSHA keep his or her identity confidential.[8]

OSHA does not have jurisdiction over employees if another federal agency has statutory authority to prescribe or enforce standards or regulations affecting those employees' safety or health, and the other agency is exercising its authority.[9]

RADIATION EXPOSURE AND ON-SITE INSPECTIONS

The regulations of the Nuclear Regulatory Commission provide that all individuals working in or frequenting any potentially radioactive areas must be kept informed of the specific health problems associated with their kind of work and of precautions or procedures to minimize exposure.[10] The employer must keep radiation exposure records and analyses on the employees and, upon request, must provide the employees with access to these records.[11] Radiation reports must be furnished within thirty days of a request. The NRC can inspect these radiation records and consult privately with workers concerning potential overexposure.

Any employee or representative of the employee can request an NRC inspection of potentially hazardous radiological working conditions.[12] The request must be in writing, setting forth the specific grounds that justify an investigation.

RIGHT TO REFUSE HAZARDOUS WORK

In a number of limited circumstances, employees have the right to refuse to perform hazardous work.[13] Specifically, the OSHA regulation states:

However, occasions might arise when an employee is confronted with a choice between not performing assigned tasks or subjecting himself to serious injury or death arising from a hazardous condition at the workplace. If the employee, with no reasonable alternative, refuses in good faith to expose himself to the dangerous condition, he would be protected against subsequent discrimination. The condition causing the employee's apprehension of death or injury must be of such a nature that a reasonable person, under the circumstances then confronting the employee, would conclude that there is a real danger of death or serious injury and that there is insufficient time due to the urgency of the situation, to eliminate the danger through resort to regular statutory enforcement channels. In addition, in such circumstances, the employee, where possible, must also have sought from his employer, and been unable to obtain, a correction of the dangerous condition.[14]

Employees who refuse to perform such work are protected under OSHA from discharge or retaliation, but their rights are limited to situations in which the risk of injury or death is imminent:

Such circumstances will probably not often occur, but such a situation may arise when (1) the employee is ordered by his employer to work under conditions that the employee reasonably believes pose an imminent risk of death or serious bodily injury, and (2) the employee has reason to believe that there is not sufficient time or opportunity either to seek effective redress from his employer or to appraise [sic] OSHA of the danger.[15]

This standard has been applied under other laws, including the Energy Reorganization Act (nuclear work-related hazards), the Surface Transportation Act (hazardous conditions in the trucking industry), and the Federal Mine Safety Act (unsafe mining condition).[16]

In *Pennsylvania. v. Catalytic, Inc.*, the Secretary of Labor held that a nuclear worker who refused to perform hazardous work at an NRC-licensed facility was protected under 42 U.S.C. § 5851. The Secretary outlined the rule for protection under that section:

A worker has a right to refuse to work when he has a good faith, reasonable belief that working conditions are unsafe or unhealthful. Whether the belief is reasonable depends on the knowledge available to a reasonable man in the circumstances with the employee's training and experience. Refusal to work is protected if the [employee] reasonably believed that he confronted a threat to his safety or health. Refusal to work loses its protection after the perceived hazard has been investigated by responsible management officials and government inspectors, if appropriate, and if found safe, adequately explained to the employee [citations omitted].[17]

Refusal to work can become, under certain circumstances, a protected whistleblower activity.[18]

EMPLOYEE PROTECTION AND OSHA

Under OSHA, 29 U.S.C. § 660(c)(1) and 29 C.F.R. Part 1977,

employees have a right to insist upon safety and health on the job without fear of punishment.[19]   The policy concerns behind protecting OSHA whistleblowers are identical to those of other whistleblower statutes, that is, to "promote effective enforcement of the statute by protecting employee communication."[20] The law prohibits employers from punishing or discriminating against workers for exercising rights under OSHA. Protected activities have included:

1. complaining to an employer, union, OSHA, or any other government agency about job safety and health hazards;[21]

2. filing safety or health grievances;

3. participating in a workplace safety and health committee or in union activities concerning job safety and health; and

4. participating in OSHA inspections, conferences, hearings, or other OSHA-related activities.[22]

If an employee is exercising these or other OSHA rights, the employer cannot discriminate against the employee in any way, including firing, demoting, taking away seniority or other benefits earned, transferring the worker to an undesirable job or shift, or threatening or harassing the worker.[23]

Employees who believe they have been discriminated or retaliated against for exercising safety and health rights under OSHA must file a complaint with the local OSHA office within thirty days of the time they learn of the alleged discrimination.[24] A union representative can file the Section 11(c) (i.e., whistleblower) complaint on behalf of the worker. The OSHA thirty-day statute of limitations is subject to equitable tolling.[25] If the charge is filed by the employee with the Labor Department within the thirty-day statute of limitations period, the complaint is deemed timely filed, even if the Department of Labor subsequently waits more than two years—and well past the applicable state statute of limitations—before filing suit in court against the employer.[26] In one case, the district court declined to dismiss an OSHA case in which the employee had waited thirty-nine days to contact the OSHA office. The court held that the defendant had waived its right to a statute of limitations defense.[27]

Once an employee files a Section 11(c) retaliation complaint with OSHA, the Secretary of Labor must investigate the allegation. If the Secretary determines that there was a violation under OSHA, the DOL must sue on behalf of the employee to obtain appropriate relief, including reinstatement, back pay, prejudgment interest, and broad injunctive relief.[28] Employees may rely exclusively on circumstantial evidence to support their claim.[29]

Because employees may confidentially raise workplace safety issues with OSHA, whistleblowers may rely exclusively upon circumstantial evidence in proving that an employer knew the identity of the whistleblower.[30] Retaliation is prohibited even if the employer merely suspects that the employee blew the whistle—even if the suspicion is erroneous.[31] Likewise, circumstantial evidence is sufficient to establish discriminatory motive or causation.[32]

The OSHA whistleblower protection statute is weaker than the environmental and nuclear employee protection acts. First, the OSHA law does not specifically provide for a private right of action.[33] Rather, the employee must rely upon the Secretary of Labor to litigate his or her case. The problems inherent in denying an employee a private cause of action under OSHA have been highlighted by various commentators: "Only OSHA can bring a [whistleblower] action in court. . . . OSHA makes the claim, but if OSHA decides that a case is not meritorious and refuses to proceed on behalf of the employee, that employee does not have the option of pursuing his own claim under the Act. If OSHA does file the suit the employee loses all control over the conduct of the proceedings."[34] OSHA also does not explicitly provide for attorney fees.

OCCUPATIONAL SAFETY AND THE ENVIRONMENTAL AND NUCLEAR WHISTLEBLOWER STATUTES

Unlike OSHA, the environmental and nuclear employee protection statutes do provide for private litigation by an employee. They also have a provision for compensatory damages and attorney fees.[35] For example, workplace safety problems related to radiation are regulated by the Nuclear Regulatory Commission, not OSHA, and whistleblower retaliation complaints in this area are covered under Section 211 of the Energy Reorganization Act,[36] not OSHA. An employee discharged for filing a complaint related to workplace radiation hazards may file a private cause of action under Section 211.[37]

In other areas there is the potential for overlap between an OSHA remedy and a remedy under one of the environmental whistleblower laws. For example, many of the toxic substances that affect occupational safety also impact on the environment. The Secretary of Labor has resolved this tension by requiring administrative law judges to analyze the nature of the employee's whistleblowing activity and make a determination as to which statute should apply on the basis of the alleged protected activity. If an employee raised allegations concerning *public* health and safety or filed complaints regarding compliance with Environmental Protection Agency (EPA) regulations, the environmental whistleblower laws may be utilized. If the allegations relate only to workplace conditions, the employee would be forced to utilize OSHA.[38] In *Aurich v. Consolidated Edison Co.*, the Secretary of Labor reasoned as follows:

If complainant has complained that one or more provisions of these regulations [i.e., the environmental safety regulations] had been violated by Respondent, such complaints would appear to be protected under 42 U.S.C. § 7622 [i.e., the employee protection provision of the Clean Air Act]. On the other hand if complainant's complaint were limited to airborne asbestos as an occupational hazard, the employee protection provision of the CAA would not be triggered. In the converse of the situation in this case, the Occupational Safety and Health Administration has issued regulations which give a broad scope to the employee protection provision of the Occupational Safety and Health Act, 29 U.S.C. Sec. 660(c), protecting complaints with other Federal, state or local agencies regarding occupational safety and health. But "such complaints . . . must relate to conditions at the work place, as distinguished from complaints touching only upon general public safety and health." 29 C.F.R. § 1977.9(b) (1986). I think a complementary approach is applicable to the scope of 42 U.S.C. 7622 [i.e., the CAA employee protection law]. Any complaints regarding effects on public safety and health, or concerning compliance with EPA regulations, under the CAA, are protected under the CAA, but those related only to occupational safety and health are not.[39]

Complaints to OSHA that touch on the public safety and the environment are protected under the Clean Air Act's whistleblower provisions.[40] The substance of the original employee safety complaints determines whether the activity is protected under the environmental whistleblower statutes or OSHA.[41]

OCCUPATIONAL SAFETY AND STATE REMEDIES

OSHA does not preempt employees who blow the whistle on occupational safety concerns from setting forth a retaliatory discharge tort suit under state law.[42] Most states recognize a common law cause of action for wrongful discharge based upon a public policy exception to the *at-will* doctrine.[43] Under this doctrine, the majority of states that have analyzed the OSHA statute have held that OSHA statutes do not preclude the states from permitting employees who were discharged for blowing the whistle on occupational hazards from protection under the public policy exception tort.[44]

The majority of states have also passed laws similar to the federal OSHA law[45] and have passed laws that provide for private remedies and more damages than the federal act.[46]

Given the wide disparity of potential remedies available to employees who blow the whistle on occupational safety and health concerns, any suit concerning OSHA-related allegations must be carefully researched.

NOTES

1. OSHA, 29 U.S.C. § 660(c) and 29 C.F.R. Part 1977. *See also* Gregory G. Sarno, "Liability for Retaliation Against At-Will Employee for Public Complaints or Efforts Relating to Health or Safety," 75 *American Law Reports 4th* 13 (1998); Glenn A. Guarino, "Prohibition of Discrimination Against, or Discharge of, Employee because of Exercise of Right Afforded by OSHA under § 11(c)(1) of the Act," 66 *American Law Reports Fed.* 650 (1998); Robert F. Koets, "What Constitutes Appropriate Relief for Retaliatory Discharge under § 11(c) of OSHA," 134 *American Law Reports Fed.* 629 (1997).

2. In addition, employees who engage in collective activity concerning work-place hazards may be protected under Sections 7 and 8(a) of the National Labor Relations Act, 29 U.S.C. §§ 157 and 158(a)(1).

3. *Eastex, Inc. v. NLRB*, 437 U.S. 5567 (1978); *Ewing v. NLRB*, 861 F.2d 353 (2nd Cir. 1988); *Prill v. NLRB*, 835 F.2d 1481 (D.C. Cir. 1987); the Surface Transportation Act, 42 U.S.C. § 31105 and 29 C.F.R. Part 1978; and the Federal Mine Safety Act, 30 U.S.C. § 815(c).

4. *See Reich v. Hoy Shoe Co.*, 32 F.3d 361, 367 (8th Cir. 1994) (quotations and internal citations omitted).

5. *Id.*

6. Statements on Introduced Bill and Joint Resolutions, Cong. Rec. S2857 (March 17, 1999).

7. *See* 29 U.S.C. § 657.

8. 29 U.S.C. §§ 657(1), 662(d). *See Reich, supra,* at 368.

9. 29 U.S.C. § 653(b)(1). For an analysis of decisions dealing with the limits of OSHA's jurisdiction, *see* 40 *American Law Reports Fed.* 147. *See also Donovan v. Texaco, Inc.*, 535 F. Supp. 641 (E.D. Tex. 1982), *aff'd.*, 720 F.2d 825 (5th Cir. 1983), holding that even Section 11(c) of OSHA can be preempted by another agency.

10. 10 C.F.R. § 19.12.

11. 10 C.F.R. § 19.13.

12. 10 C.F.R. § 19.16(a).

13. This protection is found in the Department of Labor regulations that implement OSHA.

14. 29 C.F.R. § 1977.12(b)(2).

15. *Whirlpool Corp. v. Marshall*, 445 U.S. 1, 10-11 (1980). *See also Gateway Coal Co. v. United Mine Workers of America et al.*, 414 U.S. 368

(1974), where the Court held that a work stoppage called solely to protect employees from immediate danger is authorized by Section 502 of the Labor Management Relations Act, 29 U.S.C. § 143.

16. *Miller v. Federal Mine Safety & Health Review Comm'n.*, 687 F.2d 194 (7th Cir. 1982)(Federal Mine Safety Act, 30 U.S.C. § 815[c]); *Shamel v. Mackey*, No. 85-STA-3, D&O of SOL (August 11, 1985) (Surface Transportation Act, 49 U.S.C. § 2304[b]).

17. *Pennsylvania v. Catalytic, Inc.*, No. 83-ERA-2, slip op. of SOL at 6-7 (January 13, 1984).

18. *See, e.g., Blackburn v. Metric Constructors, Inc.*, 86-ERA-4, D&O of SOL (June 21, 1988) (upholding employee right to refuse to engage in hazardous work); *Smith v. Catalytic, Inc.*, 86-ERA-23, D&O of SOL (March 18, 1988) (upholding discharge because employer had "fulfilled its obligation" to "investigate and explain" why the "perceived safety hazard was not a threat" to the employee).

19. The purposes behind OSHA are very laudable: "OSHA was enacted to 'assure so far as possible every working man and woman in the Nation safe and healthful working conditions and to preserve our human resources." *Donovan v. Square D Company*, 709 F.2d 335, 337 (5th Cir. 1983), *quoting from* 29 U.S.C. § 651(b).

20. *Id.* at 335, 338.

21. *Donovan v. Commercial Sewing, Inc.*, 562 F. Supp. 548 (D. Conn. 1982); *Marshall v. Commonwealth Aquarium*, 469 F. Supp. 690 (D. Mass. 1979), *aff'd.*, 611 F.2d 1 (1st Cir. 1979); *Donovan v. Diplomat Envelope Corp.*, 587 F. Supp. 1417, 1424 (E.D. N.Y 1984) (internal complaints to management protected); *Marshall v. Springville Poultry Farm, Inc.*, 445 F. Supp. 2, 3 (M.D. Pa. 1977); *Dunlop v. Hanover Shoe Farms, Inc.*, 441 F. Supp. 385, 388 (M.D. Pa. 1976); *Donovan v. Freeway Constr. Co.*, 551 F. Supp. 869 (D. R.I. 1982); *Donovan v. Peter Zimmer America, Inc.*, 557 F. Supp. 642 (D. S.C. 1982).

22. For example, communications with the media concerning safety conditions were held to be protected in *Donovan v. R. D. Andersen Constr. Co., Inc.*, 552 F. Supp. 249 (D. Kan. 1982).

23. 29 C.F.R. Part 1977; *Commonwealth Aquarium, supra*, at 690, 692.

24. 29 C.F.R. § 1977.15(d).

25. *Donovan v. Hahner, Foreman & Harness, Inc.*, 736 F.2d 1421, 1427-1428 (10th Cir. 1984).

26. *Donovan v. Square D Co., supra*, at 335.

27. *Donovan v. Diplomat Envelope Corp.*, 587 F. Supp. 1417, 1423 (E.D. N.Y.1984).

28. 29 C.F.R. § 1977.3; *Reich v. Cambridgeport Air Systems*, 26 F.3d 1187 (1st Cir. 1994); *Donovan v. Freeway Constr. Co., supra*, at 879-882; *Donovan v. Commercial Sewing, Inc., supra*, at 554-556; *Donovan v. George Lai Contracting, Ltd.*, 629 F. Supp. 121, 122-124 (W.D. Mo. 1985). *See* Robert F. Koets, "What Constitutes Appropriate Relief for Retaliatory Discharge Under § 11(c) of OSHA," 134 *American Law Reports Federal* 629 (1997).

29. *Reich v. Hoy Shoe Co.*, 32 F.3d 361, 364-368 (8th Cir. 1994).

30. *Reich, supra*, at 368.

31. *Id.*

32. *Id.* at 637.

33. *George v. Aztec Rental Center, Inc.*, 763 F.2d 184 (5th Cir. 1985); *Taylor v. Brighton Corp.*, 616 F.2d 256, 258 (5th Cir. 1980); *Braun v. Kelsey-Hayes Co.*, 635 F. Supp. 75, 80 (E.D. Pa. 1986).

34. Lewis D. Solomon & Terry D. Garcia, "Protecting the Corporate Whistleblower Under Federal Anti-Retaliation Statutes," 5 *The Journal of Corporation Law* 275 (Winter 1980).

35. 29 C.F.R. Part 24. Other federal whistleblower laws also have provisions for private causes of action. *See, e.g.*, STA, 49 U.S.C. § 2305; FMSA, 30 U.S.C. § 815(c); FSMA, 30 U.S.C. § 1293; and other federal laws outlined in Stephen M. Kohn & Michael D. Kohn, *The Labor Lawyer's Guide to the Rights and Responsibilities of Employee Whistleblowers* (New York: Quorum Books, 1988).

36. 42 U.S.C. § 5851.

37. *See, e.g., Pennsylvania v. Catalytic, Inc., supra*, D&O of SOL.

38. *See Post v. Hensel Phelps Construction*, 94-CAA-13, D&O of SOL, at 2 (August 9, 1995) (environmental whistleblower statutes "generally do not protect complaints restricted solely to occupational safety and health, unless the complaints also encompass public safety and health or the environment"); *Tucker v. Morrison & Knudson*, 94-CER-1, D&O of ARB, at 4-5 (February 28, 1996) ("The distinction between complaints about violations of environmental requirements and complaints about violations of occupational safety and health requirements is not a frivolous one. Worker protection for whistleblowing activities related to occupational safety and health is covered by Section 11 of the OSHA. . . . The Secretary has made it clear that there are jurisdictional limits to employee's complaints"); *Roberts v. Rivas Environmental Consultants, Inc.*, 96-CER-1, D&O of ARB (September 17, 1997).

39. 86-CAA-2, remand order of SOL, at 3-4 (April 23, 1987).

40. *Scerbo v. Consolidated Edison of NY*, 89-CAA-2, D&O of SOL, at 4-5 (November 13, 1992). *Accord., Williams v. TIW Fabrication & Machining Inc.*, 88-SWD-3, D&O of SOL, at 8 (June 24, 1992).

41. *Johnson v. Old Dominion Security*, 86-CAA-3, D&O of SOL, at 13-15 (May 29, 1991). *See also Melendez v. Exxon*, 93-ERA-6, D&O of ARB, at 12-17 (July 14, 2000) (relationship between occupational exposure to chemicals and protected activity under TSCA).

42. *Kozar v. AT&T*, 932 F. Supp. 67 (D. N.J. 1996). *See also Lepore v. National Tool and Mfg. Co.*, 540 A.2d 1296, 1306 (N.J. Super. Ct. 1988).

43. *See, e.g., Coman v. Thomas Mfg. Co., Inc.*, 381 S.E.2d 445 (N.C. 1989); *Harless v. First Nat'l Bank*, 162 W. Va. 116, 246 S.E.2d 270 (1978). *See also* Chapter Twelve, *supra*.

44. *See, e.g., Flenker v. Willamette Industries, Inc.*, 68 F. Supp.2d 1261, 1265 (D. Kan. 1999); *Schweiss v. Chrysler Motors Corp.*, 922 F.2d 473 (8th Cir.

1990); *Hentzel v. Singer Co.*, 188 Cal. Rptr. 159 (Cal. Ct. App. 1982); *Brevidk v. Kite Painting, Inc.*, 416 N.W.2d 714 (Minn. 1987); *Cerracchio v. Alden Leeds, Inc.*, 538 A.2d 1292 (N.J. Super. Ct. 1988); *Kilpatrick v. Delaware County Soc.*, 632 F. Supp. 542 (E.D. Pa. 1986). *Contra Burnham v. Karl and Gelb P.C.*, 745 A.2d 178, 183-184 (Conn. 2000) (collecting cases); *Hendrix v. Wainwright Indus.*, 755 S.W.2d 411 (Mo. Ct. App. 1988); *Braun v. Kelsey-Hayes Co.*, 635 F. Supp. 75 (E.D. Pa. 1986).

45. *See, e.g.,* Alaska Stat. § 18.60.089; Ariz. Rev. Stat. Ann. § 230425; Conn. Gen. Stat. § 31-40d *(see also* § 31-51m); Del. Code Ann. Title 16, § 2415, "Hazardous Chemical Information"; Ga. Code Ann. § 45-22-7(L); Haw. Rev. Stat. § 396-6, *et seq.*; Ill. Rev. Stat. ch. 48, para. 1414; Ind. Code § 28-8-1.1.38.1; Iowa Code § 88.9(3); Kan. Stat. Ann. § 44-636(F); Ky. Rev. Stat. Ann. § 338.121 (b); Me. Rev. Stat. Ann. Title 26 § 570; Md. Ann. Code art. 89, § 43; Minn. Stat. § 182.654 *(see also* §§ 181.932 and 181.935); Mont. Code Ann. § 50-78-204; Nev. Rev. Stat. § 618.4451; N.C. Gen. Stat. § 95-130(a); N.H. Rev. Stat. Ann.§ 277-A *(see also* § 275-E:l, *et seq.*); N.M. Stat. Ann. § 50-9-25; N.Y. Lab. Law § 215 *(see also* § 740); Or. Rev. Stat. § 654.062(5); R.I. Gen. Laws §§ 23-1.1-14 and 28-20-21; Tenn. Code Ann. § 50-3-2012; Tex. Rev. Civ. Stat. Ann. art. 5182b; Va. Code Ann. § 40.1-51.2:2; Wash. Rev. Code § 49.17.1670; Wis. Stat. §§ 101.595 and 230.85. *See also Door Co. HWR Dept. v. Dept. of I.L.H.R.*, 404 N.W.2d 548 (Wis. Ct. App. 1987); and Wyo. Stat. § 27-11-109(e).

46. *See, e.g.,* Cal. Lab. Code §§ 6310 and 6312; Fla. Stat. § 442.116; Mich. Comp. Laws § 15.361. *See also Tyrna v. Adams, Inc.*, 407 N.W.2d 47 (Mich. Ct. App. 1987); and N.J. Rev. Stat. §§ 34:5A-17, 34:6A-45, and 34:19-1 *et seq.*

Chapter 8

Legal Principles in Whistleblower Law

Over the past fifty years courts and administrative agencies have been developing a law of whistleblowing. Certain themes reappear in numerous contexts, such as whether internal whistleblowing should be protected, whether federal laws should preempt state laws, whether employees must "blow the whistle" through their chain of command, and what types of proof are necessary in order for an employee to prove discriminatory motive. Of course, many of these issues are resolved on a statute-specific basis. For example, the Whistleblower Protection Act (covering federal employees) sets forth a statutorily mandated burden of proof. But beyond specific statutory mandates, many general legal principles are applicable in most whistleblower cases.

The vast majority of whistleblower statutes are silent on basic jurisprudential issues. Consequently, when facing a new issue under a particular enabling statute, courts and administrative agencies often rely upon established precedent under other whistleblower laws in guiding their interpretations. Moreover, the U.S. Department of Labor (DOL), due to its jurisdiction over nine important and often-used whistleblower laws (including OSHA, the environmental and nuclear whistleblower statutes, and the Surface Transportation Assistance Act), has developed an extensive body of case law carefully interpreting numerous issues that arise in the context of whistleblowing.

This chapter explicates many of the basic legal principles and themes that continuously reappear in whistleblower litigation.

ESTABLISHING A *PRIMA FACIE* CASE

In order to establish a valid whistleblower case under any law, an employee must carefully ensure that he or she can meet the burden of proof in establishing each item of a *prima facie* case. Nearly every whistleblower protection law requires that the employee establish each of the following elements:

1. the party charged with discrimination is an employer subject to the act(s) or is covered as an "employer" under the common law;

2. the complainant was an employee under the act(s) or applicable state common law;

3. the complaining employee was subject to an adverse action cognizable under the statute or common law;

4. the employee engaged in "protected activity" defined in a statute or engaged in conduct protected under common law "public policy";

5. the employer knew or had knowledge that the employee engaged in protected activity; and

6. the retaliation against the employee was motivated, at least in part, by the employee's engaging in protected activity.[1]

A typical summarization of an employee's *prima facie* case was set forth by the Secretary of Labor (SOL) in the nuclear whistleblower case of *Priest v. Baldwin Associates*: "[the employee] established a *prima facie* case of discrimination by showing that he engaged in protected activity of which [the employer] was aware and adverse action . . . was taken against him shortly thereafter [i.e., under circumstances which gave rise to an inference of discriminatory motive]."[2]

Similarly, under a First Amendment analysis, the basic elements of a retaliation claim were set forth as follows:

A plaintiff must show: (i) that [its] conduct was protected by the First Amendment, and (ii) that defendants' conduct was motivated by or substantially caused by [plaintiff's] exercise of free speech. However, defendants may avoid liability if they are able to establish, as an affirmative defense, that . . . they would have . . . [taken the adverse action] even in the absence of plaintiff's protected speech.[3]

However, an employee's establishment of a *prima facie* case merely prevents an employer from prevailing on a motion to dismiss or a motion for summary judgment. Once a *prima facie* case is demonstrated, and a case is heard on the merits, the trier of fact "has before it all the evidence it needs to determine whether 'defendant intentionally discriminated against the plaintiff.' "[4] The central issue that must be adjudicated in all whistleblower cases centers around proving intentional discrimination. As explained in a nuclear whistleblower case:

Logic dictates that once all of the evidence is in, whether a complainant presented a *prima facie* case is unnecessary to the ultimate outcome: If a complainant has not prevailed by a preponderance of the evidence on the ultimate question of liability it matters not at all whether he presented a *prima facie* case. On the other hand, if the complainant has prevailed on the ultimate question of liability, a fortiori he presented a *prima facie* case. In either case the question of real concern is whether the complainant proved by a preponderance of the evidence that he was retaliated against for engaging in protected activity.[5]

Although the heart of a whistleblower case concerns proof of the retaliatory basis of an adverse action, particular care must be given to ensuring that each and every element of the *prima facie* case is established, or a claim will be summarily dismissed.

ESTABLISHING THAT A DEFENDANT IS AN EMPLOYER

Specific definitions of employee and employer are contained either within a particular whistleblower law or are adopted from common law definitions of employee/employer.[6] However, under most whistleblower laws, the definition of "employer" is very broad. For example, under a First Amendment analysis, employer includes entities that obtain services from contractors and independent contractors.[7]

Under the environmental whistleblower statutes, state agencies, Native American Indian Tribes, and the federal government have all been found to be "employers," as well as every private-sector corporation in the United States.[8] In this regard, federal employees are not even required to exhaust their remedies under the Civil Service Reform Act prior to applying for protection under the environmental laws.[9] The Department of Labor and U.S. Courts of Appeals have also rejected state sovereign immunity[10] and Eleventh Amendment defenses under these specific laws.[11]

Employers may also be prohibited from discriminating against "any" employee, even employees who do not directly work for them.[12] Regardless of the "proximate relation of the employer and employee, all employers are prohibited from engaging in discriminatory conduct against any employee, prospective employee, former employee or an employee seeking employment or working for another employer."[13] The SOL, citing established U.S. Supreme Court and U.S. Courts of Appeals precedent under other employment discrimination laws, held that an employer "may violate" the whistleblower laws "with respect to employees other than his own": "For example, a bank which owned a fifty story office building told picketers outside a restaurant, occupying leased space on the 46th floor, to leave the building and threatened them with arrest. The Ninth circuit held that the bank was an employer and had committed an unfair labor practice . . . even though it was not the employer of the picketers."[14]

Separate business entities have been found liable as employers where the interrelation between the company actually employing the worker and the independent corporation was sufficient to qualify the parent company as a "joint employer."[15] Likewise, hiring employees as independent contractors has not necessarily insulated employers from liability.[16]

Some laws do not limit the definition of "employer" to a business entity. Instead, they define employer to include "any person." Under these laws, corporations and individuals may be jointly or individually liable for a discriminatory action.[17]

ESTABLISHING THAT A PLAINTIFF IS AN EMPLOYEE

In order to effectuate the purpose of the whistleblower statutes, the term "employee" has been construed broadly.[18] In the context of environmental whistleblowing, the SOL has reasoned that:

The term "employee" as used in this Act must be given a most liberal interpretation, particularly in view of the evils the Act was designed to prevent. It is obvious the Act is intended to prevent employers from engaging in acts of discrimination, whether it takes the form of termination of employment or simple intimidation. In light of these statutory objectives, the overriding policy considerations involved would compel that the term employee be as inclusive as is rationally possible.[19]

This holding is consistent with the Supreme Court's recent decision in a Title VII case finding that former employees were fully protected under that law's antiretaliation provisions:

According to the EEOC, exclusion of former employees from the protection of [the antiretaliation provision] would undermine the effectiveness of Title VII by allowing the threat of post-employment retaliation to deter victims of discrimination from complaining to EEOC, and would provide a perverse incentive for employers to fire employees who might bring Title VII claims. . . . Those arguments carry persuasive force given their coherence and their consistency with a primary purpose of antiretaliation provisions: Maintaining unfettered access to statutory remedial mechanisms.[20]

Applying case law under the National Labor Relations Act to circumstances directly related to whistleblowing, the Secretary of Labor has interpreted the definition of employee as not limited to "employees of a particular employer." The law's protection may encompass disputes in which there is no "proximate relation" between the employer and employee.[21] An employee is protected from discrimination or harassment from any employer—not just the employer for whom the worker is presently employed or for whom he or she formerly worked.[22] Under a First Amendment analysis, even "volunteer" employees may be subject to protection.[23] Likewise, under the NLRA "supervisors" who engage in certain protected activities are protected from retaliation even though "supervisors" are statutorily excluded from the definition of "employee."[24]

Reasoning that the purpose of the whistleblower laws is to "encourage" employees to report violations, the SOL has consistently applied a broad interpretation of employees covered under the laws: "a broad interpretation of 'employee' is necessary in order to carry out the statutory purpose. . . . Protecting the reporting employee against retaliation only, while that employee is in the employ of the violator has a 'chilling effect' and discourages, rather than encourages, the reporting of safety violations."[25]

"Employee" has been defined to include former employees, contract workers, and probationary or temporary employees;[26] independent contractors;[27] applicants for employment, former employees, and prospective employees;[28] contract job shoppers;[29] representatives of employees[30] and temporary workers.[31] The laws generally protect workers "regardless of their function."[32] Under the nuclear whistleblower act, non-NRC-licensed companies that act as suppliers or vendors for NRC-licensed projects have been found to be employers under the ERA.[33] Individuals engaged as attorneys may also be protected under the whistleblower laws.[34]

DISCRIMINATORY CONDUCT

In the context of labor relations case law, actionable discriminatory conduct includes retaliatory conduct short of an actual discharge. For example, under the First Amendment, the Supreme Court adopted a very broad definition of adverse employer action.[35] In the leading case on this issue, *Rutan v. Republican Party of Illinois*, the Court rejected the argument that adverse actions less severe than dismissal were not actionable under the First Amendment.[36] The Court recognized the "chilling effect" adverse actions may have on an employee's willingness to engage in protected activity.

"Employees who find themselves in dead-end positions due to their [First-Amendment-protected conduct] *are* adversely affected."[37] Discriminatory conduct that negatively impacts "pay or job satisfaction" was found to create "significant penalties" cognizable in a First-Amendment-based employment case.[38]

Most wrongful discharge statutes contain their own definition of discriminatory conduct. Although some statutes narrowly define discrimination, a majority of antiretaliation laws were modeled on the original National Labor Relations Act (NLRA), which broadly prohibited employers from engaging in any conduct, including discharges, which may "otherwise discriminate against an employee."[39] The phrase "otherwise discriminate against" has been liberally construed to include numerous discriminatory actions that fall short of an actual discharge, including discrimination against an employee's spouse or children.[40]

Under the NLRA, all of the following have been held to constitute unlawful discrimination: the refusal to rehire,[41] blacklisting,[42] wage rate discrimination,[43] refusal to grant bonuses,[44] refusal to grant severance pay,[45] reduction of number of work hours,[46] denial of overtime,[47] reprimands,[48] termination of temporary employees,[49] threats of discharge,[50] threats to blacklist,[51] providing unfavorable references,[52] failing to provide letters of reference,[53] harassment,[54] creating an impression that protected activity is being monitored,[55] assignment of an employee to work in unpleasant conditions,[56] layoffs,[57] and discrimination in sick leave policies.[58] Under both the NLRA and the Fair Labor Standards Act (FLSA), the filing of a baseless lawsuit by an employer against an employee with the intent to retaliate is an unfair labor practice.[59]

Modern federal legislation has mirrored the broad approach set forth in the NLRA. For example, the Clean Air Act's whistleblower law defines adverse action as follows: "No employer may discharge any employee or otherwise discriminate against any employee with respect to his compensation, terms, conditions, or privileges of employment."[60] This broad language is also found in the other five environmental whistleblower laws, the nuclear whistleblower law, and the whistleblower laws covering the trucking industry, aviation, asbestos removal, and the banking industry. Consistent with these statutes, the Department of Labor regulation prohibiting the discrimination against environmental whistleblowers broadly defines discriminatory conduct as that which "intimidates, threatens, restrains, coerces, blacklists, discharges, or in any other manner discriminates against any employee (who engages in protected activity)."[61] Moreover, in *Chase v. Buscombe County, N.C. Dept. of Community Improvement*,[62] the SOL held that the purpose of the whistleblower provisions was to "encourage the reporting of violations" and explicitly warned against sanctioning employer practices that may create a "chilling effect" on an employee's rights.

Under the nuclear, trucking, and environmental whistleblower laws, the DOL has "broadly construed" the definition of adverse action to "prevent the intimidation of workers through retaliation."[63] Various employer practices have been held to be illegal discrimination, including the elimination of a position, causing embarrassment and humiliation, transfers, and demotions;[64] "constructive discharge" (or making working conditions so difficult as to force a resignation);[65] blacklisting;[66] issuance of a disciplinary letter;[67] a reassignment to a less desirable position (even if no loss of salary or grade);[68] negative comments in an evaluation;[69] a retaliatory order to undergo a psychological "fitness for duty" examination;[70] denial of unescorted access to a nuclear power plant;[71] suspension of test certifications;[72] denial of promotion;[73] threats;[74] retaliatory harassment[75] or acts constituting "intimidation and coercion;"[76] transfer to position where employee could not perform supervisory duties;[77] circulation of "bad paper" comments and other forms of "bad mouthing;"[78] moving an office and denying parking and access privileges;[79] negative references provided to a reference-checking company;[80] the transfer to a position in which there was "less opportunity to earn overtime pay;"[81] refusal to rehire or denial of employment;[82] layoffs;[83] failure to "recall" an employee back to work;[84] denial of overtime or refusing to let an employee take time off;[85] refusal to refer an employee for work with another employer;[86] forcing an employee to see a doctor during work hours;[87] refusal to provide proper references and job referrals;[88] denial of parking privileges;[89] issuance of a disciplinary letter[90] or a "warning notice;"[91] harassment;[92] offering an employee a "hush money settlement;"[93] violation of a settlement agreement;[94] improperly coercive questioning concerning protected activities;[95] interference with freedom to contact regulatory authorities;[96] or conduct which may create a chilling effect on employee speech.[97] Further, in First Amendment retaliation cases, courts have found campaigns of "petty harassment"[98] retaliation stemming from a policy or "custom" of harassing whistleblowers[99] and "retaliatory harassment," which was "likely to deter a person of ordinary firmness from the exercise of his or her First Amendment rights" to be actionable.[100]

Often, a determination of whether conduct is adverse is *fact specific* and must be reviewed on a case-by-case basis.[101] For example, in one case an employer was ordered to pay the wages for all employees who were subpoenaed to testify.[102] This holding was not based on a rule, but rather was based on the discriminatory practices of one employer. In the case, the defendant paid the pro-defense employee's salaries while they attended the trial but refused to pay the wages for the employees who provided testimony to support the plaintiff.[103]

It is also well settled that "not everything that makes an employee unhappy is actionable adverse action."[104] Speculative harm or conduct that may in fact benefit an employee are not adverse actions.[105] In cases in which evidence of an actual concrete harm does not exist, courts often must "pore over each case to determine whether the challenged employment action reaches the level of 'adverse.' "[106] Hostile work environment cases constitute one of the rare types of adverse-action cases that do not require proof of a "tangible job detriment."[107] Even if the adverse action is temporary or does not result in a concrete harm, liability may still be imposed.[108]

Outside of the context of the First Amendment and federal statutory protections, state courts and legislatures have adopted numerous different approaches to defining adverse action. Some states, such as New Jersey, have enacted laws that mirror the broad federal prohibitions.[109] Others, such as Washington state, have taken a narrow view of retaliatory conduct and have limited the public policy wrongful discharge suit to factual circumstances in which the adverse action rose to the level of an actual or constructive discharge.[110]

Reduction in Force

An employee's lay-off during a reduction in force (RIF) can constitute discriminatory conduct if the decision to include the employee in the RIF was caused, in part, by protected activity.[111] In such circumstances the employer must demonstrate "by a preponderance of the evidence" that "it would have laid off" an employee "even in the absence of the protected conduct."[112]

Hostile Work Environment

Hostile work environment claims have been upheld in the context of retaliation against whistleblowers.[113] Even without suffering from a direct disciplinary action from upper management, an employee can recover from discrimination caused by a "hostile work environment."[114]

The U.S. Supreme Court has identified the following factors to be reviewed in adjudicating a hostile work environment case:

[W]hether an environment is "hostile" or "abusive" can be determined only by looking at all the circumstances. These may include the frequency of the discriminatory conduct; its severity; whether it is physically threatening or humiliating, or a mere offensive utterance; and whether it unreasonably interferes with an employee's work performance. The effect on the employee's psychological well-being is, of course, relevant to determining whether the plaintiff actually found the environment abusive. But while psychological harm, like any other relevant factor, may be taken into account, no single factor is required.[115]

In an environmental whistleblower case, the DOL "tailored" the hostile work environment facts articulated by other courts in the context of Title VII discrimination and set forth six factors that should be "weighed in a hostile work environment" based on antiwhistleblower retaliation:

1. whether the employee "suffered intentional discrimination" because he or she was a member of a "protected class" (i.e., whistleblowers);

2. whether the discrimination was "pervasive and regular";

3. whether the "discrimination detrimentally affected the plaintiff";

4. whether the "discrimination would have detrimentally affected a reasonable person of the same protected class in that position";

5. that the harassment effected a term, condition, or privilege of employment; and

6. whether "*respondeat superior* liability" existed.[116]

In regard to the *respondeat superior* prong of the test, employers are not strictly liable for damages under the "hostile work environment" test. Employer's can "negate" liability if they "adequately and effectively" responded to the harassment or if they never learned of the harassment, despite the existence of a "reasonable avenue" for the employee to raise a complaint.[117] In *Burlington Industries, Inc. v. Ellerth*, the U.S. Supreme Court set forth the standard for finding employer "vicarious liability" for a hostile work environment created by a supervisor:

In order to accommodate the agency principle of vicarious liability for harm caused by misuse of supervisory authority, as well as Title VII's equally basic policies of encouraging forethought by employers and saving action by objecting employees, the Court adopts, in this case and in *Faragher v. Boca Raton*, 524 U.S. 775, 118 S.Ct. 2275, 141 L.Ed.2d 662 (1998), the following holding: An employer is subject to vicarious liability to a victimized employee for an actionable hostile environment created by a supervisor with immediate (or successively higher) authority over the employee. When no tangible employment action is taken, a defending employer may raise an affirmative defense to liability or damages, subject to proof by a preponderance of the evidence, see Fed. Rule. Civ. Proc. 8(c). The defense comprises two necessary elements: (a) that the employer exercised reasonable care to prevent and correct promptly any sexually harassing behavior, and (b) that the plaintiff employee unreasonably failed to take advantage of any preventive or corrective opportunities provided by the employer or to avoid harm otherwise. While proof that an employer had promulgated an antiharassment policy with a complaint procedure is not necessary in every instance as a matter of law, the need for a stated policy suitable to the employment circumstances may appropriately be addressed in any case when litigating the first element of the defense. And while proof that an employee failed to fulfill the corresponding obligation of reasonable care to avoid harm is not limited to showing any unreasonable failure to use any complaint procedure provided by the employer, a demonstration of such failure will normally suffice to satisfy the employer's burden under the second element of the defense. No affirmative defense is available, however, when the supervisor's harassment culminates in a tangible employment action such as discharge, demotion, or undesirable reassignment.[118]

Employees have successfully argued that the continuing violation theory is applicable in some hostile work environment cases.[119]

Refusal to Hire

The Supreme Court has long recognized that discrimination in the hiring process "is twin to discrimination in firing" and that both are prohibited under federal antidiscrimination laws.[120] A refusal to hire may constitute an adverse action. In *Samodurov v. General Physics Corp.*,[121] a nuclear whistleblower case, the DOL applied the analysis used by the U.S. Supreme Court in Title VII refusal to hire cases:

1. An employee must show that he applied and was qualified for a job for which the employer was seeking applicants;

2. Despite his qualifications, he was rejected; and

3. After his rejection the position remained open and the employer continued to seek applications from persons of complainant's qualifications.[122]

A complainant-employee has the burden to demonstrate that the employer "received applications from or hired" a "similarly qualified" person.[123]

Treating Employees Differently

In order to demonstrate adverse action an employee need not always demonstrate that "he was treated differently from other" employees.[124] Quoting from the *DeFord* case, the SOL reasoned:

It has . . . been suggested by [the employer] that [the complainant] should be required to prove that he was treated differently from other similarly situated participants in the NRC investigation, but this contention . . . must be rejected. Inclusion of such a requirement among the elements of a claim would take no account of the possibility that more than one person might be exposed to the same type of discrimination. The statute is aimed at preventing intimidation, and whether the scope of such activity happens to be narrow or broad in a particular case is of no import. An employer should not escape liability upon an otherwise valid claim, for example, solely because it chose to discriminate against three similarly situated employees rather than only one; yet inclusion of the suggested factor as a required element of proof would allow precisely such a result to obtain.[125]

The circumstances set forth in *DeFord* are exceptional. In most cases, proof that an employee was in fact "treated differently than other employees" charged with similar offenses constitutes very important, if not critical, evidence of animus and pretext.[126]

Per Se Violations (Contractual Waivers and Neutral Policies)

Facially neutral polices that directly impact or prohibit protected activity violate whistleblower protection laws, even if the application of the rule in a particular case was not based on an explicit discriminatory motive.[127] A company cannot enforce a policy that has the effect of disciplining employees for engaging in protected activity.[128] A company cannot offer to reemploy an employee on the basis of illegal conditions.[129]

For example, in *Doyle v. Hydro Nuclear Services*,[130] the SOL held that requiring an employee, as a condition of employment, to waive his right to sue former employers who provide reference information constituted a *per se* violation of the whistleblower statutes. The SOL found such waivers void and unenforceable.[131] The failure to hire an employee on the basis of that employee's refusal to execute the release constituted a violation of the ERA:

Requiring Complainant to choose between a job and his rights under the ERA would be equally as destructive of Congressional intent as the waiver in *Brooklyn Bank v. O'Neil*. Employers could refuse to hire those who will not waive their right and hire only those who are willing to waive their right to complain of retaliation. Such employees may reasonably believe they have no protection under the ERA and will be afraid to speak out about safety problems.[132]

The violation of the ERA was upheld even though "all applicants" were required to sign the form.[133] The Secretary has also held that *hush money* settlement agreements, or even the offering of such a settlement agreement to an employee, constitute *per se* violations of the ERA.[134]

EMPLOYER KNOWLEDGE THAT EMPLOYEE ENGAGED IN PROTECTED ACTIVITY

In order to establish a *prima facie* case, the employee must establish that the employer knew he or she engaged in protected activity.[135] An employee must demonstrate that the "officials who made the challenged decision" knew of the employee's protected activities.[136] This can include proof that managers suspected the employee of having engaged in protected activity.[137] The element of "knowledge" may be demonstrated by either direct or circumstantial evidence.[138] But regardless of the method used to prove this element, an employee bears the ultimate burden of persuasion on this issue: "Although knowledge of the protected activity can be shown by circumstantial evidence, that evidence must show that an employee of Respondent with authority to take the complained of action, or an employee with substantial input in that decision, had knowledge of the protected activity."[139]

The Labor Department's administrative law judges have reasoned that there can be no discriminatory motivation without prior knowledge that an employee engaged in protected activity.[140] An employee must prove such employer knowledge through either direct or circumstantial evidence.[141]

An employer cannot insulate itself from liability by creating "layers of bureaucratic 'ignorance' " between a whistleblower's direct line management and the final decision maker.[142] "Constructive knowledge"[143] of the protected activity can be attributed to the employer's final decision maker.[144] In the context of environmental whistleblowing, the SOL reasoned that: "the purpose of the environmental whistleblower statutes [would] be undercut were the discharging official able to hide behind the shield of a lack of actual knowledge where the discharge had, in fact, been effected by a subordinate because of the employee's protected conduct."[145]

Likewise, employer knowledge of protected activity can be inferred from other circumstances, such as the size of the workplace.[146] Also, a deciding official "suspicious" that an employee engaged in protected activity is "sufficient to show" an employer's knowledge.[147]

If an employee with knowledge of the protected activity "contributed heavily" to the decision to take an adverse action against an employee, knowledge on the part of the employer will be inferred, even if the actual decision maker had no knowledge.[148] An employer cannot defend this element of a case by alleging that its "managers did not know" that a concern implicated environmental laws, if the employee's allegations "reasonably" should have been "perceived" as communicating environmental safety issues: "the environmental acts do not require that a complainant articulate each statute or regulation that potentially could be violated because of a defect or safety issue. . . . Rather, a communication about a hazard or defect is sufficient where the *complainant* reasonably has perceived a violation of the environmental acts or regulations."[149]

SCOPE OF PROTECTED ACTIVITY

The vast majority of federal courts have construed the scope of protected activity under the federal antiretaliation laws very broadly.[150] In the leading case under Section 8(a)(4) of the National Labor Relations Act (NLRA), the Supreme Court held that the antiretaliation provision must be broadly construed.[151] Section 8(a)(4) grants protection to employees who have filed charges or given testimony under the Act. In its 1972 decision, the Supreme Court held that the need to protect the flow of employee information to the National Labor Relations Board required broad interpretation of the statute:

This complete freedom is necessary, it has been said, "to prevent the Board's channels of information from being dried up by employer intimidation of prospective complainants and witnesses". . . . Which employees receive statutory protection should not turn on the vagaries of the selection process or on other events that have no relation to the need for protection.[152]

Similar employee protection provisions in the Occupational Safety and Health Act, the Fair Labor Standards Act, the Surface Transportation Assistance Act, the False Claims Act, the Federal Mine Safety Act, the Energy Reorganization Act, and the environmental whistleblower laws have all, for the most part, received similarly broad and liberal interpretations.[153]

The SOL, following judicial precedent, has continuously given a broad interpretation to the scope of protected activity under the environmental and nuclear acts. The Secretary has protected a broad range of employee conduct, including internal complaints to management,[154] contact with citizen intervenor groups,[155] performance of quality control or quality assurance functions,[156] safety-related complaints made by employees who perform supervisory or managerial functions,[157] refusal to perform unsafe work,[158] complaints to union representatives,[159] and refusal to perform work in violation of federal safety standards.[160]

Internal Protected Activity

The issue of whether complaints to management are protected

whistleblowing was first addressed in the case of *Phillips v. Interior Board of Mine Operators*.[161] *Phillips* arose under the 1969 Mine Health and Safety Act which prohibited employment discrimination against any employee who:

(A) has notified the Secretary or his authorized representative of any alleged violation or danger;

(B) has filed, instituted, or caused to be filed or instituted any proceeding under this chapter; or

(C) has testified or is about to testify in any proceeding resulting from the administration or enforcement of the provisions of this chapter.[162]

Based upon that limited statutory definition, the *Phillips* court decided whether a complaint made internally to management—by a miner to a foreman—was protected under the act. Such protection was not explicitly granted under the statute. In a 2-1 decision, Justice Wilkey of the U.S. Court of Appeals for the District of Columbia Circuit held that internal whistleblowing was protected. The court looked at the underlying purpose of the act and the "practicalities" that confront employees, management, and government in attempting to enforce health and safety regulations.[163] Simply put, it is realistic to assume that an employee who discovers a potential problem will first report it to management and that such a disclosure could result in discrimination or possible termination.[164]

The *Phillips* holding has been widely followed by other courts under a host of other federal statutes.[165] It was endorsed by congressional committees when the 1969 Federal Mine Health and Safety Act was amended,[166] and has been upheld by various administrative agencies of the U.S. government.[167]

Departing from this norm, a 5th Circuit case gave a narrow interpretation to the nuclear whistleblower protection statute, holding that the employee was required to have actual contact with the government in order to be protected.[168] The 5th Circuit's decision has been vigorously criticized by the Nuclear Regulatory Commission and every court that has considered the 5th Circuit's holding.[169] In 1992 Congress legislatively overturned the 5th Circuit's narrow interpretation and by statute protected internal whistleblowing.[170]

Another minority view also has limited the scope of internal whistleblowing. Under these cases, blowing the whistle directly to the wrongdoer, as a "courtesy warning" intending to "stop" criminal activity without its being "exposed" is not protected activity. Under this view, "reporting to the wrongdoer" is not, by "definition," whistleblowing.[171] In contrast to this approach, a majority of jurisdictions recognize the benefits of permitting employees to utilize internal mechanisms to informally resolve potential disputes prior to involving governmental authorities:

[It] would [not] be in the interest of law-abiding employers for the statute to force employees to report their concerns outside the corporation in order to gain whistleblower protection. Such a requirement would bypass internal controls and hotlines, damage corporate efforts at self-policing, and make it difficult for corporations and boards of directors to discover and correct [potential problems].[172]

In one case, the DOL directly addressed the tension between an employee's expectation of loyalty to management and an employee's right not to inform potential wrongdoers of facts related to a whistleblower concern: "[D]isciplining an employee for refusing to reveal safety concerns to management when he is about to report his concerns to the [appropriate governmental body] is a violation of the [whistleblower laws]."[173]

In environmental and nuclear whistleblower cases, the SOL adheres to its longstanding doctrine that internal whistleblowing is fully protected.[174] This includes environmental and surface transportation cases arising in the 5th Circuit.[175] In *Passaic Valley Sewerage Commissioners v. United States Department of Labor,* the U.S. Court of Appeals for the 3rd Circuit endorsed the SOL's position:

We believe that the statute's purpose and legislative history allow, and even necessitate, extension of the term "proceeding" to intra-corporate complaints. The whistleblower provision was enacted for the broad remedial purpose of shielding employees from retaliatory actions taken against them by management to discourage or to punish employee efforts to bring the corporation into compliance with the Clean Water Act's safety and quality standards. If the regulatory scheme is to effectuate its substantive goals, employees must be free from threats to their job security in retaliation for their good faith assertions of corporate violations of the statute. Section 507(a)'s protection would be largely hollow if it were restricted to the point of filing a formal complaint with the appropriate external law enforcement agency. Employees should not be discouraged from the normal route of pursuing internal remedies before going public with their good faith allegations. Indeed, it is most appropriate, both in terms of efficiency and economics, as well as congenial with inherent corporate structure, that employees notify management of their observations as to the corporation's failures before formal investigations and litigation are initiated, so as to facilitate prompt voluntary remediation and compliance with the Clean Water Act. Where perceived corporate oversights are a matter of employee misunderstanding, this would afford management the opportunity to justify or clarify its policies.[176]

Consistent with *Phillips*, the overwhelming majority of jurisdictions equally protect internal and external whistleblowing. However, the issue of internal versus external whistleblowing continues to be contested.[177]

Failure to Follow the Chain of Command When Raising Concerns

In raising environmental or nuclear safety concerns, employees are under no obligation to report their concerns to their supervisors.[178] The SOL has adopted the following rule: "[A]n employer may not, with impunity, discipline an employee for failing to follow the chain-of-command, failing to conform to established channels, or circumventing a superior, when the employee raises an environmental health or safety issue."[179] As a matter of law, it is "not permissible to find fault with an employee for failing to observe established channels when making safety complaints."[180] Consequently, taking "adverse action" against an employee merely because the employee "circumvented the chain of command" would constitute a violation of the whistleblower protection statutes.[181]

Under the Atomic Energy Act's whistleblower provision, employees cannot be disciplined for merely refusing to inform management of the concerns they raised with a governmental agency:

An employee who refuses to reveal his safety concerns to management and asserts his right to bypass the "chain of command" to speak directly with the Nuclear Regulatory Commission is protected under the employee protection provision of the Energy Reorganization Act of 1974, as amended (ERA), 42 U.S.C. § 5851 (1988). Covered employers who discipline or discharge an employee for such conduct have violated the ERA.[182]

In this vein, employees are protected even if they go "around established channels" in bringing forward a "safety complain,"[183] go "over" their "supervisor's head" in raising a concern,[184] violate or fail to follow the workforce "chain of command" or normal procedure,[185] or refuse to disclose information they confidentially told the NRC.[186]

Although employees can ignore a mandatory "chain of command" reporting requirement under a number of federal laws, they are not free to participate in protected activities in any manner they so choose. Reasonable restrictions on employee conduct will be sustained, even if the restrictions may impact otherwise protected activities.[187] Thus, an employee who engages in protected activity, still may be discharged for "insubordinate behavior, work refusal, and disruption."[188]

Reporting Violations or Problems Directly to Governmental Sources

The ability of an employee to communicate directly with federal law enforcement or regulatory authority is a critical component to employee whistleblowing. Under a host of federal laws, direct contact with government agencies, federal courts, and Congress is protected. For example, in the context of the environmental whistleblower laws, this includes participation in an on-site government inspection, reporting radiation overexposure to the NRC, writing a letter to the Environmental Protection Agency[189] or providing information to Congress.[190] Similarly, the term "proceeding," which is often used within a statutory definition of protected activity, incorporates protection for "many things," such as filing a federal law suit, assisting in a government investigation, and testifying at a hearing.[191]

Any prohibition on permitting employees to contact federal law enforcement agencies raises issues under the federal obstruction of justice statutes. Under 18 U.S.C. § 1512(b) it is a criminal violation to "knowingly" use "intimidation" or "threat(s)" to "prevent the testimony of any person in an official proceeding" or to "hinder, delay, or prevent the communication to a law enforcement officer" concerning "information relating to the commission or possible commission of a Federal offense." Similarly, it is an illegal obstruction of justice to "harass" any person for "attending or testifying in an official proceeding" or for "reporting to a law enforcement officer" the "possible commission of a Federal offense."[192]

Departing from the federal rule, a number of state whistleblower statutes require an employee to inform management of the potential law violations before reporting the violations to the government. These requirements contradict federal law and make it nearly impossible for an employee to confidentially blow the whistle and remain protected.

Filing a Whistleblower Complaint and Participating in Enforcement Proceedings

Under federal law, employees who "participate" in legal or administrative proceedings related to adjudicating a whistleblower case are entitled to "exceptionally broad protection."[193] The "participation" clauses of most antiretaliation laws protect employees who file charges against the employer, even if management maintains that the allegations are purely "fabricated."[194] The "participation" clauses also protect witnesses who assist in antidiscrimination proceedings, even if these witnesses are "reluctant" or are compelled to testify "involuntarily."[195] Coverage under the "participation" clauses "does not turn on the substance of an employee's testimony," and retaliatory actions are prohibited "regardless of how unreasonable" an employer finds the "testimony."[196]

Filing a nuclear or environmental whistleblower complaint with the U.S. DOL is, unto itself, protected activity.[197] Protected activity also includes meeting with DOL investigators or testifying in a DOL whistleblower proceeding.[198]

Contacts with State or Local Government

Under the environmental whistleblower laws, contacts with state and local agencies are fully protected. Also, the statutory language of the employee protection provisions of the Solid Waste Disposal Act, Safe Drinking Water Act, and Superfund specifically refers to commencing state proceedings or participating in "applicable implementation plan(s)," as part of the protected activity. Likewise, the legislative history of the CAA makes specific reference to the "employee's exercise of rights under federal, state, or local Clean Air Act legislation or regulations."[199]

In *Haney v. North American Car Corp.*, the respondent employer argued that contacting state agencies was not protected under the Resource Conservation and Recovery Act (RCRA). The administrative law judge vigorously disagreed:

Respondent's construction is too narrow to be persuasive of Congressional intent in enacting the statutory provision in issue. RCRA was a broadly conceived remedial statutory scheme in an area which traditionally had been considered the sphere of local responsibility. The purpose of the legislation was to assist cities, counties and the State in solving the nation's discarded materials problem, and to provide nationwide protections against the danger of improper hazardous waste disposal.[200]

An employee's cooperation with "local authorities," such as a fire department or a sheriff's office, is protected conduct under the environmental whistleblower laws.[201]

Threatening or Stating an Intention to Disclose Violations to the Government

Many of the whistleblower statutes make explicit reference to protecting employees who are "about to testify" or "about to commence or cause to be commenced" or "about to assist" a proceeding or action. This language has been interpreted as explicitly protecting employees who threaten to file complaints with federal authorities.[202]

Under the environmental and nuclear whistleblower laws, the SOL has held that employees who are "about to commence or cause to be commenced" a proceeding or action are protected.[203] To be protected, an employee does not have to directly inform management of his or her intention to report disclosures to the government. Instead, circumstantial evidence indicating this intention, including internal complaints to management and the circumstances surrounding the whistleblowing, can indicate an intention to report the violation to the government.[204] The SOL has protected employee activities that may cause an employer to fear that an employee is going to report an alleged violation to the government: "An employer who receives an internal complaint may fear that the complainant is about to cause trouble with the government or cause other employees to create such trouble and act to silence the complainant for those reasons. Employees should be protected against such discrimination."[205]

Taping

Whistleblowers often tape conversations in an attempt to document wrongdoing or retaliation. One-party taping[206] occurs in whistleblower cases due to the individualistic nature of whistleblowing and the difficulty with using less intrusive means to document wrongdoing, especially when the wrongdoing is orally communicated. Under federal law,[207] one-party taping motivated by a desire to "preserve evidence"[208] or to "protect" oneself and to prevent "later distortions" of a conversation is legal.[209] Even before the passage of the federal wiretapping laws, former Chief Justice Earl Warren, while recognizing the "great danger to the privacy of the individual" arising from the misuse of electronic recording devices, upheld the legality of one-party taping in the context of protecting the "credibility" and "reputation" of a government employee who needed to document wrongdoing. Chief Justice Warren found "nothing unfair in this procedure" because an honest employee would otherwise be "defenseless against [the] outright denials" of a wrongdoer.[210] The contents of such tapes are usually admissible evidence.[211]

The Omnibus Crime Control and Safe Streets Act of 1968 (the federal law that places certain restrictions on wiretapping), permits a citizen, under most circumstances, to conduct one-party taping.[212] The legislative history of that law supported citizen one-party taping in order to document illegal conduct: "[The law] would not, however, prohibit [secret one-party taping] when the party records information of criminal activity by the other party with the purpose of taking such information to the police as evidence. Nor does it prohibit such recording in other situations when the party acts out of legitimate desire to protect himself and his own conversations from later distortions."[213] Additionally, placing restrictions on a person's right to record his or her own words may implicate First Amendment and "liberty interest" rights.[214]

The federal wiretapping law permitted states leeway to enact legislation restricting one-party taping. Twenty-three states passed laws mirroring the federal law, and statutorily have permitted one-party tape recording of oral conversations (including telephone calls),[215] and judicial decisions in a number of other states have also permitted one-party taping.[216] Seven states explicitly prohibit surreptitious taping.[217] But even within these seven states, some courts and legislatures have recognized the right to tape one's own conversation under limited circumstances.[218]

In the context of employment law, a number of cases have raised the issue as to whether one-party surreptitious taping in a state that allows such activity is protected activity. In *Heller v. Champion International Corp.*,[219] the U.S. Court of Appeals for the 2nd Circuit, in a 2-1 decision, rejected the argument that employee taping constituted "disloyalty" for which discharge was warranted. The court rejected claims that an employee could "never be justified in tape-recording" on the job and noted that a "range of factors" could justify taping, including the "gathering" of "evidence" to document a "possible claim" of "discrimination."[220] The dissent in *Heller* would have upheld discharging an employee for one-party taping.[221]

Under the environmental whistleblower laws, the SOL held that taping can constitute protected evidence-gathering activity. For example, the SOL upheld the legality of one-party surreptitious taping when the taping was conducted at the request of a government investigator.[222] In *Moshaugh v. Georgia Power Co.*, the SOL held that an employee's "making lawful tape recordings," on his or her own initiative, was protected activity:

I find that [the employee] engaged in protected activity under the ERA by making lawful tape recordings that constituted evidence gathering in support of a nuclear safety complaint. [The employee's] tape recording is analogous to other evidence gathering activities that are protected under employee protection provisions, such as making notes and taking photographs that document environmental or safety complaints.[223]

Additionally, under DOL regulations, taped conversations may be admitted into evidence as "non-hearsay admissions of a party-opponent."[224]

The U.S. Nuclear Regulatory Commission, in formal correspondence to the U.S. Senate Committee on the Environment and Public Works and the Department of Labor,[225] informed these bodies that the Commission believed that one-party taping was, under certain conditions, protected activity:

[T]he NRC believes that legal surreptitious taping by an employee of personal conversations, to which the employee is a party, with the intent of providing the information obtained to the licensee of the NRC, is an activity subject to protection under section 211. . . . [W]hile the commission recognizes that attempts by an employee to gather evidence of safety violations or related discrimination in some respects could have a disruptive effect on the workplace, the mere potential for interruption of routine conduct of operations that may be caused by reasonable whistleblower activities should not be a basis for disciplinary action against an employee. . . . [L]awful taping of conversations to which the employee is a party to obtain safety information, carried out in a limited and reasonable manner, for the purpose of promptly bringing such material to the attention of the licensee or the NRC, should not be a valid basis for terminating an employee.[226]

Contacts with the Media, Trade Unions, or Citizen Environmental Organizations

Whistleblower disclosures to nongovernmental agencies have been protected under federal law. The first cases to weigh this issue arose under the First Amendment, where the courts balanced a public employer's need to control the workforce against the right of an employee to raise allegations with newspaper reports. In *Pickering* the court held that public employees were protected if they raised concerns in the press.[227] Other cases applying the *Pickering* analysis have regularly protected public employees from retaliation for contacting reporters, public interest groups, and for speaking to outside organizations.[228] Employee whistleblowers, even in sensitive government positions, cannot be prohibited access to outside attorneys.[229]

In the private sector, employee whistleblowing to members of the news media has also been protected. For example, under OSHA, courts have protected communications with the press because it was "clear" that an "employee's communication with the media" could result in the initiation of safety proceedings.[230] This holding has been regularly followed in environmental and nuclear whistleblower cases.[231]

Numerous cases have also held that federal whistleblower laws fully protect employee disclosures to other nongovernmental bodies, such as trade unions, attorneys,[232] and environmental organizations. The legislative history of the whistleblower amendments clarifies Congress' intent that trade unions can assist employees in raising allegations. For example, the Senate report on the first nuclear whistleblower law stated: "Under this section employees and union officials could help assure that employers do not violate requirements of the Atomic Energy Act."[233]

In *Cotter v. Consolidated Edison Co. of N.Y.*,[234] the Labor Department found that a member of a union safety committee engaged in protected activity by internally reporting safety problems through the union committee. Many whistleblower laws, including the employee protection provisions of the Solid Waste Disposal Act and the Water Pollution Control Act, make explicit references to "authorized representatives of employees" and state that actions of these representatives are covered under these acts.[235]

Under the nuclear and environmental whistleblower laws, the Department of Labor has protected employee disclosures to "environmental activist(s)" and the news media. In *Wedderspoon v. Milligan*,[236] the administrative law judge wrote:

Complainant's contribution to the institution of these investigations is twofold: (1) to bring the sludge discharge information to the attention of a friend who was an "environmental activist" and could be expected to act on the information as, indeed, he did; (2) to state the information which he had together with his views and charges against the City to a reporter of the *Des Moines Register* (the state's premier newspaper) whom he could expect to publish them (as the Register did over the reporter's by-line) and to bring about a full public airing of the matter. While complainant did not himself ask either the cognizant federal authorities or DEQ (Iowa Dept. of Environment Quality) for an investigation, the causal nexus between what he in fact did and the official action which resulted is so close as to compel the conclusion that complainant "caused to be . . . initiated [a] proceeding under this chapter" [i.e., the Water Pollution Control Act].[237]

The SOL has treated the following types of conduct as protected under the environmental and nuclear whistleblower laws: threat to file an environmental citizen suit,[238] contacting a union representative,[239] contacting a newspaper reporter,[240] threatening to contact the press,[241] causing "negative publicity" in the press,[242] and participating in a television report.[243]

Discussing a safety problem with a member of the "general public," without putting forth evidence that the employee is "about to file a complaint" or participate in a proceeding is "too remote" to be considered protected activity.[244]

Reporting Concerns to Co-employees

Whistleblower disclosures made directly to co-employees have been protected under state and federal law.[245] Under the nuclear whistleblower law the SOL has held that a "complaint to a co-worker may be the first step" in reporting a violation.[246] A "common sense" approach toward protecting complaints made to co-workers was explained by a U.S. District Court for the Eastern District of New York:

The purpose of the statute is to encourage employees to come forward with complaints of health hazards so that remedial action may be taken. In the ordinary course of events, an employee who notices a health hazard will begin by bringing the matter to the attention of those with whom he deals directly in his daily work-life such as the employer, supervisors, *co-workers*, or union official. This is simple common sense. These persons are the ones most likely to be in a position to obtain information regarding the alleged hazard and to take appropriate action.[247]

Mistaken Belief or "Suspicion" That an Employee Engaged in Protected Activity

Most whistleblower laws prohibit employers from discharging employees even if they only "suspect" that the employee engaged in protected conduct.[248] The laws also protect employees who are not personally engaged in protected activity but are believed to be so engaged by their supervisors. The focus of the inquiry is on an employer's perception that an employee engaged in protected activity and whether the employer was motivated by its belief that the employee had engaged in such conduct.[249]

The policy reasons for protecting employees from retaliation under these circumstances was explained by the U.S. Court of Appeals for the 3rd Circuit:

It is evident that the discharge of an employee in the mistaken belief that the employee has engaged in protected activity creates the same atmosphere of intimidation as does the discharge of an employee who did in fact complain of false violations. For that reason, we conclude that a finding that an employer retaliated against an employee because the employer believed the employee complained or engaged in other activity specified in section 15(a)(3) is sufficient to bring the employer's conduct within that section.[250]

In a similar vein, one spouse cannot be subjected to retaliatory conduct based on the protected activities of his or her spouse.[251]

Past Protected Activity

The fact that an employee engaged in protected activity for a significant period of time prior to any alleged retaliation does not, unto itself, defeat a whistleblower claim. Even if the whistleblower allegations were "resolved and dismissed" prior to any alleged retaliation, this does not "transform" the past protected activity "into non-protected conduct" and does not "eliminate the possibility of subsequent retaliatory actions by the employer."[252]

THE MANNER OF ENGAGING IN PROTECTED ACTIVITY

If the manner in which an employee engages in whistleblowing is completely outrageous or improper, the conduct may lose its status as protected activity. Outrageous activity by employees constitutes an independent justification for discipline. Courts have held that where otherwise protected protest activities unjustifiably interfere with an employee's job performance, discipline against such an employee may be proper.[253]

In analyzing whether the manner in which an employee engages in protected activity is so outrageous as to lose protection, the U.S. Supreme Court has drawn a distinction between protected activity that involves speech versus protected activity that involves conduct. Alleged misconduct based solely on the content of employee speech is subject to stricter scrutiny than cases in which employee conduct is at issue.

Content Analysis

Under federal law, if an employee files a charge or complaint against an employer with a government regulatory body, the employee cannot be disciplined, even if the content of the charge is libelous.[254] Disclosures made directly to management or to nongovernmental sources are usually protected.[255] Internal protected speech, whether written or oral, should be protected even if it is "vehement, caustic" or "unpleasantly sharp."[256] In *Linn v. United Plant Guard, Workers of America*, the U.S. Supreme Court applied the *New York Times v. Sullivan* rule to speech issues arising under the NLRA:

The enactment of the NLRA manifests a Congressional intent to encourage free debate on issues dividing labor and management. And, as we stated in another context, cases involving speech are to be considered against the backdrop of a profound . . . commitment to the principle that debate . . . should be uninhibited, robust, and wide-open, and that it may well include vehement, caustic, and sometimes unpleasantly sharp attacks.[257]

Under the *Linn* analysis, speech was protected so long as it did not contain "deliberate or reckless" untruths,[258] was not "grossly disproportionate" to the goal sought,[259] and did not constitute flagrant misconduct.[260] An employee calling the president of the corporation a "son-of-a-bitch";[261] an employee using words such as "m____f____," "damn lies," and "horse's ass";[262] and an employee's circulation of Jack London's statement defining a "scab" as a "two-legged animal with a corkscrew soul, water brain (and) a combination backbone of jelly and glue"[263] were all found to be protected when they occurred within the context of employee activities covered under the NLRA.

The *Linn* rule has been cited to or followed in other contexts—including First Amendment retaliatory discharge cases[264] and environmental whistleblower cases.[265] For example, in a § 1983 anti-retaliation employment case, the U.S. District Court for the Southern District of New York, citing to Supreme Court authority, recognized that a "function of free speech under our system of Government" was to "invite dispute" and create "dissatisfaction with conditions."[266] In this vain, whistleblower speech would be protected even if it "diminish(ed)" the "official reputations" of managers accused of wrongdoing.[267] Case law under Title VII's "participation clause" is also consistent with the *Linn* rule. For example, employee testimony is protected, even if management views it as "unreasonable" or potentially "fabricated."[268]

Employers may place some restrictions on employee speech. For example, employers may prohibit employee speech that improperly por-trays a whistleblower's criticism as an "official" agency position.[269]

Conduct Analysis

When employee conduct transcends speech, a stricter balancing test is applied. An employee who "behaves inappropriately" is not immunized from discipline merely because the "behavior relates to a legitimate safety concern."[270] Alleged protected activity may lose protection if the conduct is indefensible or unduly disruptive.[271] The courts, on a case-by-case basis, consider whether the employer's interest in the "smooth functioning of his business" is outweighed by the employee's interest in internally resolving the discrimination dispute.[272] Under this balancing test, unprotected con-duct included dissemination of false and derogatory accounts of an em-ployer's management practices to nongovernmental sources,[273] the interfer-ence of a company's business relationship with a customer,[274] misuse of a company telephone to call one's attorney,[275] and other conduct that inter-fered with the employee's job performance or disrupted the workplace.[276]

The SOL has recognized that "intemperate language," "impulsive behavior," and even alleged "insubordination" often are associated with protected activity:

In general, employees engaged in statutorily-protected activity may not be disci-plined for insubordination so long as "the activity (claimed to be insubordinate) is lawful and the character of the conduct is not indefensible in its context." The right to engage in statutorily-protected activity permits some leeway for impulsive behavior, which is balanced against the employer's right to maintain order and respect in its business by correcting insubordinate acts. A key inquiry is whether the employee has upset the balance that must be maintained between protected activity and shop discipline. The issue of whether an employee's actions are indefensible under the circumstances turns on the distinctive facts of the case.[277]

If an employee's conduct is extremely disruptive or grossly insubordinate, it will lose protection.[278] In *Dunham v. Brock*, the 5th Circuit held that "abusive or profane language coupled with defiant conduct" may justify discipline of an otherwise protected employee. But the court cautioned that "foul language" and "mere resistance to change" in response to improperly motivated conduct would not be enough to justify discipline.[279] If an employee is provoked into acting insubordinately, he or she may still be protected under the *provoked response* doctrine.[280]

Given the very nature of whistleblowing, employee whistleblowers are often accused of personality problems, criticized for not being able to "get along with" "co-workers,"[281] or attacked for "disloyalty" and for not being a "team player."[282] Relying upon these types of criticisms to justify adverse actions, employers often build a defense on the grounds that they have discretion to set a "wide range of requirements on employees," even if such requirements may be "arbitrary" or "ridiculous."[283] Although an employer may have the discretion to use "loyalty" or an employee's alleged abrasive personality to evaluate or terminate an employee, such seemingly independent criteria cannot be used to interfere with protected activity.[284] Courts have rejected employer reliance upon so-called personality problems when such problems arose as a result or manifestation of protected activity.[285] For example, when criticisms of an employee's "communication style" arose as a result of "auditing work," such conduct is not "indicative of behavior that would negate protection" under whistleblower laws.[286] Likewise, a loss of "trust" arising from protected activity does not justify adverse action.[287] In *Hadley v. Quality Equipment Company*[288] the SOL declined to protect employee conduct that was "beyond the bounds of behavior appropriate to the work place." However, in another case, an employee's "attitude" was not sufficient justification for including an employee in an RIF.[289]

Employees may investigate or file complaints regarding matters which are "outside the course and scope" of their employment. In *Helmstetter v. Pacific Gas & Electric Company*[290] the SOL reasoned that limiting coverage under the whistleblower provisions only to employees who made disclosures related to their "official duties" would "hobble the intended broad protection" afforded employees under the acts. But an employee does not have "carte blanche" authority to "choose the time, place and/or manner" of engaging in protected activity.[291] An employee's on-the-job disobedience in refusing to stop investigating potential wrongdoing on matters that fell outside of his job duties was not protected.[292]

In analyzing whether to protect employee "conduct," courts and administrative agencies regularly apply case law developed under Title VII's "opposition clause."[293] Under this analysis, in retaliation cases courts apply a "balancing test" to determine whether oppositionist activity is "reasonable" in view of an employer's interest in an efficient and harmonious work environment.[294] Cases concerning employee removal of documents often are adjudicated under this clause. On the one hand, if the removal of documents is illegal (i.e., theft under local law), that conduct will almost certainly be found unprotected.[295] On the other hand, copying and disseminating personnel records may be protected if an employee can establish that management would have "destroyed the document had she not taken action to preserve them."[296] Employees who have rummaged through a supervisor's desk attempting to obtain and copy "confidential documents" and show those documents to co-workers have lost protection:

[W]e are loathe to provide employees an incentive to rifle through confidential files looking for evidence that might come in handy in later litigation. The opposition clause protects reasonable attempts to contest an employer's discriminatory practices; it is not an insurance policy, a license to flaunt company rules or an invitation to dishonest behavior.[297]

But under the appropriate set of circumstances, obtaining documents from work is protected conduct. For example, in *Kempcke v. Monsanto Co.*,[298] the U.S. Court of Appeals for the 8th Circuit protected the conduct of an employee who provided company documents to his attorney. The documents at issue had been "innocently acquired" and were not "misused." [299]

Work Refusals

An employee's refusal to perform work is generally not protected. There are, however, exceptions to this rule. First, under a number of anti-retaliation laws, employees can refuse to perform work that they believe, in good faith, would be unsafe or unhealthful.[300] Second, a number of statutes and cases protect employees who have refused to perform illegal work or commit an illegal act.[301] As set forth in chapter seven, work refusals are usually "no longer protected" if the underlying cause of the refusal is "properly investigated, found wanting, and adequately explained."[302]

In *Diaz-Robainas v. Florida Power & Light Company*, an employee was discharged after he refused to submit to a psychological "fitness for duty" examination.[303] The SOL reversed the discharge, reasoning that the employee "did not refuse to perform a particular job function or activity" and that the requirement to be examined by a psychologist was "outside the scope of his normal work requirements." The Secretary cautioned employees that his ruling was based on a finding that the referral to the psychologist was, itself, discriminatory. Had the Secretary found that the employer's referral was nondiscriminatory, Mr. Diaz-Robainas' refusal would have been "at his peril," and Florida Power & Light's decision to discharge him would have been upheld.[304]

GOOD FAITH REQUIREMENT FOR ALLEGATIONS

Under most whistleblower protection laws, an employee is under no obligation to demonstrate the validity of his or her substantive allegations.[305] Although the safety or legal concern that resulted in the initial whistleblower disclosure need only be based on a good faith belief that an actual violation occurred,[306] this "good faith" belief must be based on "reasonably perceived violations" of the applicable law or regulations.[307] Employees are under no duty to demonstrate the underlying veracity or accuracy of their safety allegations.[308] In this vein, allegations remain protected even if facts later demonstrate that the concern was "corrected," that the regulatory agency was "already aware" of the problem,[309] or even if the regulatory authority later rules that the concern was not correct.[310] Even a potentially libelous complaint may be protected.[311]

The rationale for not requiring employees to prove the veracity of their complaints was explained in *DeFord v. Secretary of Labor*, a nuclear whistleblower case.[312] The *DeFord* court expressly rejected any requirement that an employee show "that he disclosed unique evidence." Citing from the Supreme Court case of *NLRB v. Schrivener*,[313] the court stated that one of the purposes of the law was to "prevent employers from discouraging cooperation with NRC investigators, and not merely to prevent employers from inhibiting disclosure of particular facts or types of information."[314]

The legislative history of the whistleblower amendments also supports this conclusion. For example, the House Interstate and Foreign Commerce Committee Report on the Clean Air Act's employee protection provision stated: "Moreover, as in the Safe Drinking Water Act and the Federal Water Pollution Act, the employer would not have to be proven to be in violation of a Clean Air Act requirement in order for this section to protect the employee's action."[315]

An employee's motivation for filing a complaint is, in most jurisdictions, irrelevant, and even if an employer believes that the safety allegations are "trivial," an employee may still be protected.[316] In *Guttman v. Passaic Valley Sewerage Commissioners*,[317] an administrative law judge initially rejected an environmental whistleblower claim, finding that the employee's motivation for blowing the whistle was "job and ego, rather than public pollution protection."[318]

The SOL completely rejected this finding, holding that "it is not complainant's underlying motive" for "reporting violations" that "must be established or considered."[319] The whistleblower law protects an employee's conduct "notwithstanding his motives" for blowing the whistle.[320] The SOL held that it was "Respondent's motivation" that must be placed "under scrutiny," not the motivation of the employee. This holding was affirmed by the U.S. Court of Appeals for the 3rd Circuit. In *Passaic Valley Sewerage Commissioners v. United States Department of Labor*,[321] the court affirmed the SOL's protection of an employee who had filed an "ill-formed" complaint due to being "misguided" or "insufficiently informed." The court explained some of the policy considerations underlying this judgment: "Moreover, an employee's non-frivolous complaint should not have to be guaranteed to withstand the scrutiny of in-house or external review in order to merit protection under § 507(a) for the obvious reason that such a standard would chill employee initiatives in bringing to light perceived discrepancies in the workings of their agency."[322]

The NRC also follows this line of reasoning and has determined that employee safety concerns are protected, "regardless of the accuracy" of the allegation.[323]

However, if an employee's concern is not "grounded in conditions" for which violations of environmental laws could be "reasonably perceived," the employee's allegations may not be protected.[324] In evaluating a nuclear whistleblower case, the U.S. Court of Appeals for the 6th Circuit cautioned that not "every incidental inquiry or superficial suggestion that somehow, in some way, may possibly implicate a safety concern" is protected.[325] To ensure protection, employees need to explain how a concern "definitively and specifically" may "implicate safety."[326]

Usually, courts should not adjudicate the merits of an underlying disclosure, and should refrain from even making findings on these matters. For example, the DOL has reasoned that under various employee-protection laws they lack jurisdiction over substantive safety issues: "[I]t is clear that this office does not have jurisdiction to decide any issues relative to the quality of the construction work in question. Those questions are within the province of other federal regulatory agencies. Therefore, any references to quality in this Decision and Order are not to be construed in any manner as finding in that regard."[327]

Although complaints need only be based on a "good faith" belief that an employer engaged in wrongdoing, proof of the underlying wrongdoing may be highly relevant in evaluating *employer* motive and credibility.[328] For example, demonstrating management "antagonism" toward safety regulations or proving a supervisor disregarded safety procedures is highly relevant evidence of motive.[329]

Many whistleblower or antiretaliation statutes contain a "participation clause" that even further protects employee speech. When engaging
in activities protected under a "participation clause," such as testifying in
a proceeding or providing information to a government investigator, the
scope of employee protections is "exceptionally broad."[330] Under this
clause, "it is not necessary" for an employee to "prove" that the underlying
allegations were accurate.[331] When engaging in whistleblower speech in the
context of participating in a protected proceeding, the public interest in
"maintaining unfettered access to statutory remedial mechanisms" is extremely strong,[332] and Congress intended to "carve out" a "safe harbor from
employer retaliation."[333] Thus, even an employee who is forced, not in
good faith, but against his will, to "participate" in a covered proceeding is
protected from retaliation on the basis of the content of the testimony.[334]

PROOF OF DISCRIMINATORY MOTIVE

The heart of an employment discrimination case often lies in proving that the discrimination arose because the employee engaged in protected
activity.[335] Proof of discrimination (i.e., discriminatory motive) can be
demonstrated through direct or circumstantial evidence, and, in rare cases,
the employer's conduct is so outrageous as to be "inherently discriminatory" unto itself. The more common case involves subtle discrimination,
requiring the employee to carefully demonstrate a variety of circumstances
that give rise to a reasonable inference of discriminatory motive. In fact,
courts recognize that direct proof of discrimination is very rare: "Rarely can
plaintiffs obtain documents or testimony wherein an employer specifically
proclaims his or her desire to retaliate against an employee for engaging in
protected speech."[336]

Direct Evidence of Discrimination

Exactly what constitutes "direct evidence" of animus has been the
subject of a number of differing definitions.[337] It is commonly defined as
evidence which, if believed, "proves the existence" of a disputed fact
"without inference or presumption."[338] In the context of employment
discrimination, "direct evidence" exists where "actions or statements of an
employer reflect a discriminatory or retaliatory attitude correlating to the
discrimination or retaliation complained of by the employee."[339] Put another way, "direct evidence" is "evidence that directly reflects the use of an
illegitimate criterion in the challenged decision," or "actions or remarks"
that tend to "reflect a discriminatory attitude" and are related to the "deci-

sional process."[340] Other courts have defined direct evidence as evidence that "shows that impermissible" factors "played some part in the decision making process,"[341] or evidence that "in and of itself, shows a discriminatory animus."[342]

Despite the different definitions of direct evidence, it is well recognized that obtaining such evidence in an employment case is very difficult. Most employers do not admit to discriminating against employees, and "smoking gun" documents exist only in rare cases.[343] Consequently, as a matter of law, it is "improper to require plaintiffs to produce direct evidence of discriminatory intent in order to prevail at trial" in a whistleblower case.[344]

An employer's statements complaining about protected activity or accusing an employee of filing "unwarranted charges" may constitute direct evidence of animus.[345] In nuclear whistleblower cases, an employer's statement that an employee "uses NRC as a threat" amounted to direct evidence of discrimination.[346] In such a case, merely relying upon a performance rating may not be sufficient to justify complainant's inclusion in an RIF.[347] In other cases, a foreman's becoming angry after an employee raised safety concerns,[348] a reprimand for failing to consult with a supervisor before blowing the whistle,[349] and telling an employee it was wrong to contact the NRC because management could have solved the problem[350] all constituted direct evidence of discriminatory motive. Calling an employee a "troublemaker" for engaging in protected activity is direct evidence of animus.[351]

Under a First Amendment analysis, if an employee can establish direct evidence of discriminatory motive, the burden of proof in a retaliation case shifts to the employer to demonstrate, by a preponderance of the evidence, that the discriminatory motives did not cause the adverse action.[352]

Establishing Discriminatory Motive Through Circumstantial Evidence

In the majority of whistleblower cases, employees rely upon circumstantial evidence to demonstrate discriminatory motive.[353] Circumstantial evidence is "often the only means available to prove retaliation claims.[354]

It is well established that employees do not need direct evidence to prevail in a whistleblower case, and an employee is not required to produce any direct testimony or evidence of discriminatory motive:[355] "Direct evidence of motive rarely exists. Inferences from the evidence almost universally are the only way of determining motive."[356] In *Ellis Fischel State Cancer Hospital v. Marshall*,[357] the court held, "The presence or absence of retaliatory motive is a legal conclusion and is provable by circumstantial evidence even if there is testimony to the contrary by witnesses who perceived lack of such improper motive."[358] In *Richter et al. v. Baldwin Associates*,[359] the SOL held that the presence of a retaliatory motive in environmental and nuclear whistleblower cases usually must be proved by circumstantial evidence and the inferences drawn therefrom. This process requires "careful evaluation of all evidence pertinent to the mind-set of the employer and its agents regarding the protected activity and the adverse action taken."[360] Moreover, evidence that an employer's justification for an adverse action is untrue may itself constitute "persuasive" circumstantial evidence of "intentional discrimination."[361]

Factors that have been used successfully to establish circumstantial evidence of discriminatory motive in whistleblower cases are:[362]

1. high work performance rating prior to engaging in protected activity, and low rating or "problems" thereafter;[363]

2. manner in which the employee was informed of his or her transfer or termination;[364]

3. inadequate investigation of the charge against the employee[365] or the failure to seek input from an employee's immediate supervisor;[366]

4. discipline, transfer, or termination shortly after the employee engaged in protected activity;[367]

5. deviation from routine procedure[368] or an employer's failure to follow its normal procedures;[369]

6. change in attitude of management before and after employee engaged in protected activity,[370] and attitude of supervisors toward whistleblowers;[371]

7. the magnitude of the alleged offense;[372]

8. absence of previous complaints against employee;[373]

9. differences between the way the complainant and other employees were treated;[374]

10. failure of the company to prove allegations of low productivity or to produce relevant documents;[375]

11. determination that the employee was not guilty of violating the work rule under which he or she was charged;[376]

12. charges of "disloyalty" against an employee for engaging in protected activity;[377]

13. employer's remarks concerning the employee's protected activities[378] or criticism of work based on protected activity;[379]

14. absence of warning before termination or transfer;[380]

15. management's "low regard" for corporate environmental personnel (i.e., quality control inspectors);[381]

16. pay increase shortly before termination;[382]

17. willingness to deviate from established procedure;[383]

18. an employer's reference to an employee engaged in protected activity as a "troublemaker"[384] or an otherwise "unfavorable attitude" toward employees who reported violations first to the Nuclear Regulatory Commission rather than discussing them with company personnel;[385]

19. disparate treatment[386] or uneven enforcement of a rule;[387]

20. conflicting reasons as to why disciplinary actions were administered;[388]

21. a pattern of "suspicious circumstances" or a "suspicious sequence of events" surrounding the discipline of an employee;[389]

22. anger, antagonism, or hostility toward complainant's protected conduct;[390]

23. interrogation of employees regarding protected activities;[391]

24. employees being advised not to report safety allegations;[392]

25. removal of employees from inspections after they have reported safety violations;[393]

26. a "pattern of antagonism;"[394]

27. contradictions in an employer's explanation of the purported reasons for the adverse action;[395]

28. "shifting explanations" concerning the reason for taking adverse action;[396]

29. proof that the purported reason for taking an adverse action is not true or believable;[397]

30. evidence that the whistleblower's safety concerns were correct and the poten-
    tial magnitude of the problem identified by the employee;[398] and

31. a supervisor's "disregard of safety procedures" or an employer's "antagonism
    toward" a "regulatory scheme;"[399] and

32. dishonesty regarding a "material fact."[400]

    The above list of factors is not exhaustive. Many cases follow
established patterns, but the circumstances that may potentially give rise to
an inference of retaliatory intent are as diverse as the labor force.

    One of the most common factors used to establish motive is timing:
"Adverse action closely following protected activity is itself evidence of an
illicit motive."[401] The fact that an employer takes disciplinary action shortly after an employee engages in protected activity is, unto itself, usually
"sufficient to raise an inference of causation" and establish that element of
the *prima facie* case.[402] Timing can be relevant not only to support a *prima
facie* case but also as evidence supporting an ultimate finding of discrimination: "Disbelief of the reasons proffered by a respondent [for an adverse
action] together with temporal proximity may be sufficient to establish the
ultimate fact of discrimination."[403]

    In temporal proximity cases, the SOL found that when an em-
ployee's protected activity was followed within two months,[404] six
months,[405] seven to eight months,[406] ten months[407] and one year[408] by disciplinary action, the timing of the two events was sufficiently close to establish a nexus between the protected activity and the discipline. In each case
the nexus was sufficient circumstantial evidence of discriminatory
motive.[409] A four-year interval between the protected activity and disciplinary action negated any such inference.[410] Unquestionably, the less time
between an employer's learning that an employee engaged in protected
activity and the implementation of an adverse action, the stronger the causal
link.

    Proving that the reason given by an employer for taking adverse
action was false can be critical evidence demonstrating discrimination. As
the Supreme Court set forth in *St. Mary's Honor Center v. Hicks*:

The fact finder's disbelief of the reasons put forward by the defendant (particularly if disbelief is accompanied by a suspicion of mendacity) may, together with
the elements of the prima facie case, suffice to show intentional discrimination.
Thus, rejection of the defendant's proffered reasons will permit the trier of fact
to infer the ultimate fact of intentional discrimination.[411]

    Moreover, if an employee can demonstrate that the purported

reason justifying an adverse action is a "lie," that finding constitutes "even stronger evidence of discrimination." In other words, "a lie is evidence of consciousness of guilt."[412]

Evidence of "disparate treatment" is also "highly probative evidence of retaliatory intent."[413] Disparate treatment simply means that an employee who engages in protected activity was treated differently, or disciplined more harshly, than an employee who committed a similar infraction and did not engage in protected activity.[414] For example, in the context of the National Labor Relations Act, where a union organizer and another employee were both caught drinking on the job and the company fired only the union organizer, the court found disparate treatment.[415] Although an employee need not demonstrate "disparate treatment" in order to prevail on the merits,[416] the "essence of discrimination . . . is treating like cases differently."[417]

Where a disciplinary response clearly does not fit with the type of infraction at issue, an inference of discrimination may be demonstrated.[418] However, absent proof of discriminatory motive, courts "do not sit as a super-personnel department" and second-guess employment decisions.[419] Corrective action is warranted only if an employee can demonstrate that discriminatory animus played a role in the decision, regardless of how "medieval" a firm's practices or "mistaken" a manager's decision.[420]

Inherently Discriminatory Conduct

In a rare case, the very nature of the employer's conduct demonstrates discriminatory motive even if the employer acted in "good faith." In cases under the National Labor Relations Act, the Supreme Court has held that where conduct is "inherently discriminatory," the employer must be held to "consequences which forseeably and inescapably flow" from the conduct, even if there is no evidence of illegal or discriminatory intent. In such cases, good faith is not a defense.[421] The Supreme Court outlined this rule:

[T]hat specific proof of intent is unnecessary where employer conduct inherently encourages or discourages union membership is but an application of the common-law rule that a man is held to intend the forseeable consequences of his conduct. Thus an employer's protestation that he did not intend to encourage or discourage must be unavailing where a natural consequence of his action was such encouragement or discouragement. Concluding that encouragement or discouragement will result, it is presumed that he intended such consequence. In such circumstances intent to encourage is sufficiently established [citations omitted].[422]

In the context of environmental and nuclear whistleblowing, the

SOL has held that certain management practices constitute discrimination, regardless of the motive of the employer. The DOL found that requiring an employee to sign a waiver of rights to sue employers for blacklisting under the ERA as a condition of employment constituted discrimination, *per se*.[423] The DOL also found that a "gag" order contained in a settlement agreement constitutes an unlawful adverse action.[424]

Noting in a job reference the fact that an employee had engaged in protected activity constitutes a *per se* violation of the environmental nuclear whistleblower laws.[425] The SOL has also warned against upholding employer action that creates a "chilling effect" or "discourages, rather than encourages, the reporting of safety violations."[426] Finally, uniform job restrictions that interfere with an employee's right to engage in protected activity violate the whistleblower laws.[427]

THE BURDEN OF PROOF—DUAL MOTIVE, PRETEXT, AND CONTRIBUTING FACTOR

Rarely does an employer admit to having engaged in retaliatory conduct. As the Supreme Court noted, eyewitness testimony concerning an "employer's mental processes" seldom exists and questions facing "triers of fact" in discrimination cases are "both sensitive and difficult."[428] Far from admitting to discriminatory animus, in the usual case, the employer comes forward with an alleged valid business reason for the disciplinary action, discrimination, or termination. These cases, usually referred to as "dual motive" and "pretext" cases, involve a number of complex rules concerning the burden of proof and persuasion.[429]

Two recent decisions by the U.S. Supreme Court explain the burden of proof applicable in most whistleblower cases. In *St. Mary's Honor Center v. Hicks*,[430] the Court ruled that an employee always maintains the burden of persuasion that the adverse action was in retaliation for protected activity. But in *Director, Office of Workers' Comp. Programs v. Greenwich Collieries*,[431] the Court explained that once an employee meets the burden of proof under *St. Mary's Honor Center* that discriminatory animus "contributes to the employer's" adverse decision, it would be appropriate to require the employer to have the "burden of persuasion" regarding its "affirmative defense" that it had legitimate reasons to discipline the employee.[432]

Under *St. Mary's Honor Center* and *Director, Office of Workers' Comp. Programs* the following offers of proof are applicable:

(1) The employee must demonstrate a *prima facie* case by a preponderance of the evidence.

(2) The employer must then produce evidence of a legitimate, nondiscriminatory reason for the adverse action.

(3) The employee must demonstrate, by a preponderance of evidence, that the articulated reason for discipline was a "pretext" for "discrimination." In this regard, the employee always has the burden to demonstrate that the adverse action was in retaliation for protected activity.

(4) If an employee demonstrates that discriminatory animus "contributed" to the adverse action (i.e., the adverse action was "motivated by legitimate and prohibited" reasons), then the employer "must show by a preponderance of the evidence that it would have reached the same decision concerning adverse action even in the absence of the protected conduct."[433]

In environmental whistleblower cases, the SOL set forth the following explanation of the burdens of proof:[434]

Under the burdens of persuasion and production in whistleblower proceedings, the complainant first must present a *prima facie* case. . . . The complainant also must present evidence sufficient to raise the inference that the protected activity was the likely reason for the adverse action. . . . The respondent may rebut the complainant's *prima facie* showing by producing evidence that the adverse action was motivated by legitimate, nondiscriminatory reasons. Complainant may counter respondent's evidence by proving that the legitimate reason proffered by respondent is a pretext. In any event, the complainant bears the ultimate burden of proving by a preponderance of the evidence that he was retaliated against in violation of the law. . . . There is only one, limited, variant to this general format. Where an employee proves (*i.e.*, establishes by a preponderance of the evidence) that illegitimate reasons played a part in the employer's decision, the employer then has the burden of proving by a preponderance of the evidence that it would have taken the adverse action against the employee for the legitimate reason alone . . . . Once the respondent has presented his rebuttal evidence, the answer to the question whether the plaintiff presented a *prima facie* case is no longer particularly useful. The trier of fact has before it all the evidence it needs to determine whether the defendant intentionally discriminated against the plaintiff.[435]

If the legitimate business reason for the employer's actions asserted by management did not in fact exist, or was not relied upon, the purported reason for the actions may be deemed "pretextual." In *Wright Line*, the National Labor Relations Board defined "pretext":

Examination of the evidence may reveal, however, that the asserted justification is a sham in that the purported rule or circumstance advanced by the employer did not exist, or was not, in fact, relied upon. When this occurs, the reason advanced by the employer may be termed pretextual. Since no legitimate business justification for the discipline exists, there is, by strict definition, no dual motive.[436]

In a pretext case the court must determine whether substantial evidence supports the finding that no legitimate business reason existed for the termination.[437] But pretext is not established merely by demonstrating that the reason for the adverse action was false. An employee must also demonstrate that the "real reason" for the discipline was discriminatory.[438] One of the major methods of proving pretext is for an employee to demonstrate that the whistleblower was "treated differently than other employees charged with similar offenses."[439]

An employer cannot defend a whistleblower case on the basis of an employee's allegation that the employer may also have violated other anti-discrimination[440] laws or that the employee's protected activity raised concerns beyond the narrow scope of any particular whistleblower protection statute.[441] A defendant cannot defend a whistleblower case by asserting that the alleged animus was caused by hostility toward other antidiscrimination laws: "Public policy considerations preclude" the use of another "potentially unlawful basis" for a discharge as a sufficient justification for firing a whistleblower.[442]

Dual-motive cases differ from pretext cases in that there exist *both* valid and invalid reasons for an employer's disciplinary actions.[443] In such cases, an employee must demonstrate that discriminatory animus was a motivating factor in an adverse action.[444] Once the employee meets this burden and proves that discriminatory animus "contributed to the employer's decision," the "burden of persuasion" may shift to the employer to prove, as a form of an "affirmative defense," that it would have discharged or disciplined the employee even if the protected activity had not occurred:[445]

Under the dual motive analysis, it is not sufficient for an employer to prove that it had good reason to take adverse action against an employee. Rather, the employer must prove by a preponderance of the evidence that it actually would have taken that action, even if the employee had not engaged in protected activity. "[I]t is not a defense to a discrimination case that the plaintiff should have been fired, if he would not have been fired had it not been for discriminatory animus."[446]

The dual motive formulation was first set forth in a First Amendment retaliation case.[447]

CONTRIBUTING FACTOR TEST

Since 1989 Congress has statutorily set forth a new standard for whistleblower cases, referred to as the "contributing factor" test. This test was designed to make it more realistic for employees to demonstrate that they were subject to retaliation.[448] Currently, four federal laws utilize this test, the Whistleblower Protection Act of 1989[449] (governing most federal employee cases), the Energy Reorganization Act[450] (governing nuclear whistleblower cases), the Aviation Whistleblower Protection Provision,[451] and the FDIC whistleblower law[452] (governing most banking related whistleblower cases). In addition, the District of Columbia's public employee whistleblower protection statute[453] also has incorporated the "contributing factor" test.

The "contributing factor" test sets forth a clear statutory mechanism governing the burdens of proof in whistleblower cases. The often conflicting or confusing burdens of proof set forth in numerous judicial decisions have been replaced by a simple statutory formula.[454] This formula can be summarized as follows: First, an employee must demonstrate, by a preponderance of the evidence, that discriminatory animus was a "contributing factor" in an adverse action.[455] To be a "contributing factor," the animus does not have to be the primary reason for the adverse action. Instead, the animus need only play a part in the overall motivation:

The words "a contributing factor" . . . mean any factor which, alone or in connection with other factors, tends to affect in any way the outcome of the decision. This test is specifically intended to overrule existing case law, which requires a whistleblower to prove that his protected conduct was a "significant," "motivating," "substantial," or "predominant" factor in a personnel action.[456]

In order to meet the "contributing factor" test, an employee's burden was "ease(d)." As explained by the U.S. Court of Appeals for the Federal Circuit:

Even though evidence of retaliatory motive would still suffice to establish a violation of the employee's rights . . . a whistleblower need not demonstrate the existence of retaliatory motive on the part of the employee taking the alleged prohibited personnel action in order to establish that her disclosure was a contributing factor to the prohibited action.[457]

Once an employee demonstrates that discriminatory animus was a "contributing factor" to an adverse action,[458] the actual burden of proof shifts to the employer to demonstrate, by "clear and convincing evidence," that the employer would have taken the same adverse action even if the employee had not engaged in whistleblowing activity.[459] The "clear and convincing evidence" test is a "tough standard" for employers.[460]

The precise contours of an employer's burden of persuasion under this test is still developing. One court articulated three factors which need to be evaluated in order to determine if an employer is able to prove by "clear and convincing" evidence that it would have taken the adverse action even in the absence of protected activity:

(1) the strength of the agency's evidence in support of its personnel action;

(2) the existence and strength of any motive to retaliate on the part of the agency officials who were involved in the decision;

(3) any evidence that the agency takes similar action against employees who are not whistleblowers but who are otherwise similarly situated.[461]

DISCOVERY

The necessity for allowing extensive discovery in employment discrimination cases is widely recognized.[462] As a general rule, courts have "consistently allowed extensive discovery in employment discrimination cases"[463] and have repeatedly cited to the maxim that "the public has a right to every man's evidence."[464] Nowhere are these general rules more applicable then in retaliatory discharge cases, where "there will seldom be 'eyewitness' testimony as to the employer's mental processes."[465] As the U.S. Court of Appeals for the Second Circuit correctly noted, "because employers rarely leave a paper trail—or 'smoking gun'—attesting to a discriminatory interest," it is an abuse of discretion in employment cases not to allow broad discovery.[466] The failure of an employer to fully comply with discovery may lead to serious sanctions, adverse inferences and default judgement.[467]

Discovery is not without its limits.[468] Protective orders may be obtained to "protect a party or person from annoyance, embarrassment, oppression, or undue burden or expense."[469] However, objections to discovery must be "specific" and "detailed."[470] A party opposing discovery must show "specifically how" the discovery is "overly broad burdensome or oppressive, by submitting affidavits or offering evidence which reveals the nature of the burden."[471] If a party asserts a privilege, it bears the burden of "conclusively" proving "each element of the privilege."[472] Litigation tactics designed to delay or hide the production of material are highly inappropriate.[473]

Scope of Discovery

In order to obtain discovery, the information requested must be relevant or must lead to information which may be relevant. For the pur-

poses of discovery, the term "relevance" is "broadly construed."[474] The fact
that the information sought may not be introduced at trial does not affect
its relevancy for discovery purposes:[475]

> Certainly, the requirement of relevancy must be construed liberally and with
> common sense rather than measured by the precise issues framed by the pleadings
> or limited by other concepts of narrow legalisms. Thus, discovery should ordi-
> narily be allowed under the concept of relevancy unless it is clear that the infor-
> mation sought can have no possible bearing upon the subject matter of the
> action.[476]

Although discovery disputes are resolved on a case-by-case basis,
a number of disclosure issues frequently arise in whistleblower cases.
Either courts or administrative agencies have permitted discovery of the
following types of information often needed to demonstrate retaliation in
whistleblower cases:

- *Witness statements prepared by government investigators;*[477]

- *Report prepared for and submitted to government agency investigating the employer;*[478]

- *Reports and materials "involuntarily" provided to a regulatory agency;*[479]

- *Documents related to internal company "investigations or reviews" audits,*[480] *management control studies,*[481] *human resource department investigations,*[482] *and reviews conducted by an outside consultant or an attorney;*[483]

- *Employer correspondence with regulatory agency;*[484]

- *Office and laboratory procedures;*[485]

- *Documents related to the substantive safety complaint raised by an employee;*[486]

- *Quality assurance manuals and test results;*[487]

- *Payroll and employment records of other employees;*[488]

- *Company wide requests related to the treatment of other employees;*[489]

- *Production of independent investigation report into the allegations raised by a whistleblower;*[490]

- *An investigators notes containing "candid comments" by co-workers;*[491]

- *Statistical data and evidence of an employer's overall employment practices;*[492]

- *Evidence of disparate treatment;*[493]

- *Evidence of misconduct or a coverup;*[494]

- *Personnel records and performance evaluations of other employees;*[495]

- *Documents pertaining to past treatment or discipline of whistleblowers, the settlement of whistleblower claims*[496] *or prior discrimination suits;*[497]

- *Information evidencing an antagonism toward relevant regulatory schemes;*[498]

- *Confidential tenure*[499] *and peer review files;*[500]

- *Salary information;*[501]

- *Psychiatric counseling data on other employees where plaintiff had been recommended by employer to receive psychiatric counseling;*[502]

- *Names and addresses of third parties who allegedly complained about the plaintiff;*[503]

- *Computer documents, such as a computer's "list screen"*[504] *or information on a hard drive;*[505]

- *Records which show that the "egregious acts" by other employees were "overlooked" while the plaintiff was "disciplined more severely for relatively minor offenses";*[506]

- *Identification of all persons with knowledge of reason(s) an adverse action was taken;*[507]

- *Information contained in a supervisor's personnel file;*[508]

- *Evidence of a pattern of discrimination against other employees;*[509]

- *Documents relating to other discrimination or retaliation claims filed against an employer (including state, federal and administrative claims);*[510]

- *Evidence relevant to expert testimony, including attorney opinion (work product) provided to expert, complete basis for expert opinions, data considered by expert in forming opinions, qualifications of expert, list of all of the expert's publications, the amount of compensation the expert is obtaining from the party to the litigation and a listing of all cases in which the expert testified at trial or in a deposition, are all fully discoverable.*[511]

In addition to the foregoing list, other relevant discovery issues which reoccur in whistleblower cases set forth below:

- *Whistleblowers not required to identify their confidential sources within a company or to turn over documents which may identify their confidential sources;*[512]

- *Most courts will not require an Independent Medical Evaluation ("IME") of an employee merely based on a claim of emotional distress;*[513]

- *Scope of discovery permitted for a "reasonable number of years" prior to alleged act of discrimination;*[514]

- *Protective orders limiting the right of whistleblowers to disclose materials to the press should not be regularly granted;*[515]

- *The so-called "self-critical analysis privilege" does not apply to whistleblower qui tam actions under the False Claims Act,*[516] *and the continued "viability" of the privilege, under any circumstances, is in "serious doubt";*[517]

- *Discovery conducted solely to obtain "after-acquired evidence" may be improper and sanctionable;*[518]

- *Government's "deliberative process privilege" "disappears altogether when there is any reason to believe government misconduct occurred";*[519]

- *"very busy executive" who asserts a lack of knowledge may be compelled to testify at deposition;*[520]

- *Participation of counsel in an investigation or decision does not automatically cloak the investigation/decision in secrecy;*[521]

- *Journalist who discussed confidential documents with a whistleblower shielded from being deposed or disclosing the documents.*[522]

Discovery in DOL Environmental Whistleblower Cases

The DOL, in environmental and nuclear whistleblower cases, follows the general rule that broad discovery must be permitted in employment cases.[523] Moreover, the DOL has mandated that broad discovery is essential in protecting the "public interest."[524] Liberal discovery is appropriate not only to prevent improper retaliation, but also to aid in uncovering "questionable employment practices and nuclear safety deficiencies about which the government should know."[525] The strict time limits set forth in many of the DOL-administered whistleblower provisions can be waived in order to permit broad discovery and provide the parties with an opportunity for the "full and fair presentation" of their cases.[526]

The DOL discovery rules mirror the Federal Rules of Civil Procedure, and permit interrogatories, document requests, requests for admission, physical and mental examinations, physical inspection of land, and depositions.[527] The DOL lacks formal subpoena power under the environmental statutes, but can still order parties to produce witnesses under their control for testimony[528] and sanction parties for discovery abuses.[529]

PREEMPTION

Between 1988 and 1994 the Supreme Court issued three major decisions addressing federal preemption[530] of state law whistleblower remedies. In each case no preemption was found, and the whistleblowers were free to bypass federal statutory remedies and use state law as a source for their protection.

The first case concerned preemption of a state retaliatory discharge tort in the context of a collective bargaining agreement governed under federal law.[531] In *Lingle v. Norge Division of Magic Chef*,[532] a unanimous court held that federal labor law did not preempt a retaliatory discharge tort filed under state law. In *Lingle*, the employee was protected under the "just cause" provisions of a collective bargaining agreement and under the state's tort law for retaliatory discharge in violation of public policy. Applying prior precedent, the court held that because the state tort was "independent" of any rights granted under the collective bargaining agreement, the tort was not preempted. If the *only* source for the cause of action were rights granted by the labor contract, preemption would have applied.[533] But because the state tort remedy existed independent of the labor contract, federal law did not preempt the cause of action.

The second case arose in the context of nuclear power, an area of law in which the courts had applied the *preemption* doctrine in matters directly related to nuclear safety.[534] Again a unanimous court refused to find preemption of a nuclear whistleblower case, even though the allegations raised by the worker directly related to safety and Congress had passed a specific law protecting nuclear whistleblowers.[535] The court held that "the mere existence of a federal regulatory or enforcement scheme, even one as detailed as [the nuclear whistleblower protection law], does not by itself imply preemption of state remedies."[536]

Finally, in 1994 the Supreme Court, again in a unanimous ruling, declined to apply the *preemption* doctrine in a case governed by the mandatory arbitration requirements of the Railway Labor Act.[537] In that case, the Court refused to preempt a state whistleblower claim on the basis of the Railway Labor Act's "mandatory arbitral mechanism."

Read individually or together, this trilogy of cases holds that the Supreme Court will not preempt state whistleblower claims absent clear expression of congressional intent.[538]

In seeking to have a state law case dismissed under a preemption theory, employers often remove a claim filed in state court into a federal court, and then seek to have the federal court dismiss the claim as preempted. But the law is now well settled that an employer's defense of federal preemption, standing alone, does not support the removal of a case from state to federal court.[539] In such circumstances, a case should be remanded to the state court.[540]

MANDATORY ARBITRATION

Prior to 1991 the Supreme Court had weighed the impact of mandatory arbitration agreements in the context of collective bargaining. The Supreme Court held that under federal statutory law, such as Title VII,[541] Fair Labor Standards Act,[542] or the Civil Rights Act of 1871,[543] discrimination claims were not preempted by collective bargaining agreement mandated arbitration—even if the violations of these laws would constitute an unfair labor practice or a breach of a collective bargaining agreement.

The leading case affirming this principle was *Alexander v. Gardner-Denver Co.*[544] In *Alexander,* an employee grieved a termination under a collective bargaining agreement which banned discharge of employees, except if there was "proper cause." The agreement prohibited racial discrimination. Under the labor contract, an arbitrator's decision was "final and binding."[545] The employee lost at arbitration; his termination was upheld.[546] Despite his loss under the collective bargaining agreement, the employee filed a Title VII charge alleging wrongful termination on the basis of racial discrimination. Although two lower courts held that the employee's Title VII claim was precluded, the Supreme Court unanimously disagreed: "In submitting his grievance to arbitration, an employee seeks to vindicate his contractual right under a collective bargaining agreement. By contrast, in filing a lawsuit under Title VII, an employee asserts independent statutory rights accorded by Congress."[547]

There was no preclusion, even though both causes of action arose for the same "factual occurrence."[548] The rights protected by Title VII were not required, as a matter of law, to be arbitrated under the union contract, and the policies behind deferring to labor contract arbitration, so forceful in other aspects of the collective bargaining procedure, did not apply in the Title VII context. The Supreme Court held that antidiscrimination laws did not concern "majoritarian processes" but codified an "individual's right to equal employment opportunities."[549]

In 1991 the Supreme Court decided *Gilmer v. Interstate/Johnson Lane Corp.*[550] The *Gilmer* case called into question the principle that employees did not have to submit federal statutory claims to mandatory arbitration. The case concerned an interpretation of the 1925 Federal Arbitration Act (FAA), a law that placed "arbitration agreements upon the same footing as other contracts," and expressed a federal policy favoring arbitration of disputes.[551] The Court applied FAA case law to the employment context and held that "[i]t is by now clear that statutory claims may be the subject of an arbitration agreement, enforceable pursuant to the FAA."[552] The Court cited to a series of prior FAA precedents requiring arbitration disputes alleging the violation of federal statutes, when the parties had executed a private arbitration agreement. The Court applied these precedents to employment contracts and held that "so long as the prospective litigant effectively may vindicate his or her statutory cause of action in the arbitral forum," arbitration would be compelled.[553]

The Court did note one major issue left undecided by the majority opinion. Specifically, the *Gilmer* case was based on the FAA. However, the FAA itself contained a statutory exclusion concerning employment contracts. The law stated that "nothing herein contained shall apply to contracts of employment . . . of workers engaged in . . . interstate commerce."[554] The majority decision in *Gilmer* recognized that issues related to interpreting this clause had not been raised "below" and that it would be "inappropriate to address" the "scope" of this "exclusion" in the *Gilmer* decision.[555] The dissenting judges in *Gilmer* were not so reluctant to reach the "exclusion" issue and stated that the FAA was not applicable to employment agreements.[556]

After *Gilmer*, the lower courts have split on the issue of FAA applicability to employment agreements. A majority of courts have upheld FAA applicability,[557] while the U.S. Court of Appeals for the 9th Circuit ruled that the FAA does not apply to employment contracts.[558] On May 22, 2000 the U.S. Supreme Court granted *certiorari* in order to resolve this issue.[559]

In 1998 the Supreme Court, in *Wright v. Universal Maritime Service Corp.*, recognized that there was "some tension" in the reasoning behind the *Gardner-Denver* lines of cases and the *Gilmer* line of cases.[560] The Court did not resolve that tension, but instead held that in the context of a collective bargaining agreement, any agreement to arbitrate a statutory right must be "explicitly stated," "clear," and "unmistakable."[561] Because the arbitration agreement at issue in that case was not "clear," the Court did not compel arbitration and did not reach the underlying issue of whether the "waiver," if valid, would have been "enforceable."[562]

Although *Wright* arose in the context of a collective bargaining agreement's mandatory arbitration requirement, some courts have applied the reasoning in *Wright* to require that individual arbitration agreements also set forth a "minimal level of notice to the employee that statutory claims are subject to arbitration."[563]

Until the Supreme Court resolves a number of outstanding issues related to mandatory arbitration, the impact of the *Gilmer* decision on whistleblower cases is unclear. But given the unique legal and factual issues that arise in whistleblower cases, such cases are neither appropriate for mandatory arbitration nor appropriate for any deferral to an arbitration decision. For example, under the whistleblower provisions of the Surface Transportation Assistance Act and the Energy Reorganization Act the Department of Labor is not required to defer to the outcome of an arbitration.[564] Under the STAA, courts have affirmed holdings of the DOL that have differed with the results of arbitrators.[565] In the context of environmental whistleblowing, the DOL case law has vested the ALJs with "discretion to determine the weight to be accorded an arbitral decision with regard to the facts and circumstances of each case."[566] Finally, courts have also upheld the DOL's litigation of a whistleblower complaint under OSHA, even after an arbitrator has issued a determination.[567]

Given the unpopularity of whistleblowers—both with management and co-workers—the "majoritarian" concerns expressed by the Supreme Court in *Alexander v. Gardner-Denver* are fully applicable to whistleblower adjudications. Additionally, it would seem highly inappropriate for arbitrators to determine the "public policy" of a state or adjudicate the scope of protected activity under federal statutes. Thus, the holdings of a number of cases that limit the applicability of *Gilmer* should be weighed in evaluating whether to agree to or to pursue arbitration of a whistleblower case.[568]

NOTES

1. *Uka v. Washington Hospital Center*, 156 F.3d 1284 (D.C. Cir. 1998) (*en banc*) (setting forth burdens of proof in discrimination cases); *Mackowiak v. University Nuclear Systems, Inc.*, 735 F.2d 1159, 1162 (9th Cir. 1984); *DeFord v. Secretary of Labor*, 700 F.2d 281, 286 (6th Cir. 1983); *Kenneway v. Matlack*, 88-STA-20, D&O of SOL, at 4 (June 15, 1989); *Thomas v. APS Co.*, 89-ERA-19, recommended D&O of ALJ, at 2 (April 13, 1989); *Ledford v. Baltimore Gas & Elec. Co.*, 83-ERA-9, slip op. of ALJ at 9 (November 29, 1983), adopted by SOL; *Dartey v. Zack Co.*, 82-ERA-2, D&O of SOL, at 9 (April 25, 1983). *See Sayre v. Alyeska Pipeline Service Co.*, 97-TSC-6, R. D&O of ALJ, at 35-47 (May 18, 1999) (collecting cases on elements of *prima facie* case).

2. 84-ERA-30, D&O of SOL, at 10 (June 11, 1986). *Accord.*, *Couty v. Dole*, 886 F.2d 147, 148 (8th Cir. 1989).

3. *Housing Works, Inc. v. City of New York*, 72 F. Supp.2d 402 (S.D. N.Y. 1999) (internal quotations and citations omitted). *See Board of County Commissioners v. Umbehr.* 518 U.S. 668, 684 (1996); *Mount Healthy v. Doyle*, 429 U.S. 274, 284-285 (1977).

4. *U.S. Postal Service v. Aikens*, 460 U.S. 711, 715 (1983), *quoting from Texas Department of Community Affairs v. Burdine*, 450 U.S. 248, 253 (1981).

5. *Carroll v. Bechtel Power Corp.*, 91-ERA-46, D&O of SOL, at 11 n. 9 (February 15, 1995), *aff'd*, 78 F.3d 352 (8th Cir. 1996).

6. *See Community for Creative Non-Violence v. Reid*, 490 U.S. 730, 751-752 (1989) (using general common law of agency to define employee); *Nationwide Mutual Ins. Co., v. Darden*, 503 U.S. 318 (1992) (applying *Reid* in context of independent contractor liability); *Reid v. Methodist Medical Center*, 93-CAA-4, D&O of SOL, at 8-19 (detailed analysis of "employee" under the environmental whistleblower laws), *aff'd*, *Reid v. Secretary of Labor* (6th Cir. 1996) (unpublished opinion). *But see Coupar v. DOL*, 105 F.3d 1263, 1266-1267 (9th Cir. 1997) (rejecting *Reid* analysis in context of determining whether prisoner can be considered an "employee" under the CAA) .

7. *Umbehr, supra,* at 668; *O'Hare Truck Service, Inc. v. City of Northlake*, 518 U.S. 712 (1996).

8. *Ellis Fischel State Cancer Hosp. v. Marshall*, 629 F.2d 563, 567 (8th Cir. 1980) (state hospital); *Pogue v. U.S. Dept. of Navy*, 87-ERA-21, D&O of SOL (May 10, 1990) (federal government); *Marcus v. U.S. EPA*, 92-TSC-5, D&O of SOL (February 7, 1994) (EPA); *White v. Osage Tribal Council*, 95-SDW-1, D&O of Remand by ARB (August 9, 1997) (Native American Indian Tribe); *Flanagan v. Bechtel Power Corp. et al.*, 81-ERA-7, D&O of SOL, at 4-9 (June 27, 1986) (private sector); *In the Matter of Patrick Wilson*, 77-WPCA-2, slip op. of SOL, at 2 (May 6, 1977) (private sector). *See* H.R. Rep. No. 294, 95th Cong., 2d Sess., *reprinted in* 1977 U.S. Code Cong. & Admin. News 1405 (legislative history of Clean Air Act whistleblower provision) ("This section is applicable, of course, to Federal, state or local employees to the same extent as any employee of a private employer"). *Contra.*, *Kesterson v. Y-12 Nuclear Weapons Plant*, 95-

CAA-12, D&O of ARB, at 2 n. 1 (April 8, 1997) (United States did not waive sovereign immunity under the ERA); *Robinson v. Martin Marietta Services, Inc.*, 94-TSC-7, D&O of ARB, at 6 (September 23, 1996) (United States did not waive sovereign immunity under TSCA). In *Berkman v. U.S. Coast Guard Academy*, 97-CAA-2/9, D&O of ARB, at 11-14 (February 29, 2000), the ARB reviewed the six environmental whistleblower laws and held that the federal government waived its sovereign immunity under Superfund, the Water Pollution Control Act, the Clean Air Act, and the Solid Waste Disposal Act. The ARB found no waiver of federal sovereign immunity under the Toxic Substances Control Act. *See also Johnson et. al v. Oak Ridge Operations Office* 95-CAA-20/21/22, D&O of ARB (September 30, 1999) (waiver of federal sovereign immunity under Safe Drinking Water Act but no waiver under the Atomic Energy Act).

    9. *Marcus, supra*; *Jenkins v. U.S. EPA*, 92-CAA-6, D&O of SOL (May 18, 1994); *Conley v. McClellan Air Force Base*, 84-WPC-1, D&O of SOL (September 7, 1993).

    10. *Osage Tribal Council, supra, aff'd, Osage Tribal Council v. DOL*, 187 F.3d 1174 (10th Cir. 1999).

    11. *Migliore v. R.I. Department of Environmental Management*, 98-SWD-3, 99-SWD-1/2, at 36 (August 13, 1999). Some federal antidiscrimination laws are covered under the Eleventh amendment prohibitions. *See Kimel v. Florida Bd. of Regents*, 120 S.Ct. 631 (U.S. Fla. 2000) (age discrimination law inapplicable to states).

    12. *Hill et al. v. TVA*, 87-ERA-23/24, D&O of Remand by SOL, at 8 (May 24, 1989).

    13. *Id. See also Hudgens v. NLRB*, 424 U.S. 507, 510 n. 3 (1976); *Phelps Dodge Corp. v. NLRB*, 313 U.S. 177, 192 (1941); *Seattle-First National Bank v. NLRB*, 651 F.2d 1272, 1273 n. 2 (9th Cir. 1980), *Sibley Memorial Hosp. v. Wilson*, 488 F.2d 1338, 1341-1342 (D.C. Cir. 1973); *Flanagan v. Bechtel Power Corp., et al.*, 81-ERA-7, decision of SOL (June 27, 1986).

    14. *Hill et al., supra*, at 7-8, *citing Seattle-First Nat'l. Bank v.* at 1273 n.2 (9th Cir. 1980).

    15. *Palmer v. Western Truck Manpower*, 85-STA-6, D&O of Remand by SOL, at 4-5 (January 16, 1987); *Robinson v. Martin Marietta Services, Inc., supra. See also Boire v. Greyhound Corp.*, 376 U.S. 473 (1964); *Tanforan Park Ford v. NLRB*, 656 F.2d 1358, 1360 (9th Cir. 1981).

    16. *See e.g., Hill et al., supra*; *St. Laurent v. Britz, Inc. et al.*, 89-ERA-15, recommended D&O of ALJ, at 6-7 (April 12, 1989); *Faulkner v. Olin Corp.*, 85-SWDA-3, recommended decision of ALJ, at 6-7 (August 16, 1985), adopted by SOL (November 18, 1985).

    17. Use of the term "person" in definition of employer permits findings of individual liability. *Assistant Secretary of Labor v. Bolin Associates*, 91-STA-4, D&O of SOL, 5-6 (December 30, 1991), *citing Donovan v. Diplomat Envelope, Inc.*, 587 F. Supp. 1417, 1425 (E.D. N.Y. 1984). But if statute uses the term "employer" instead of "person," individual liability does not attach. *Varnadore v. Oak Ridge National Laboratory*, 92-CAA-2/5, 93-CAA-2, 94-CAA-2/3, D&O of ARB, at 57 (June 14, 1996).

18. *See Moland v. Bil-Mar Foods*, 994 F. Supp. 1061, 1073 (N.D. Iowa 1998) (finding liability where employer "controls an individual's access to employment opportunities").

19. *Landers v. Commonwealth-Lord Joint Venture*, 83-ERA-5, slip op. of ALJ at 5, adopted by SOL (September 9, 1983).

20. *Robinson v. Shell Oil Co.*, 519 U.S. 843, 848 (1997). *Accord., Umbehr, supra,* (protecting contractors from retaliation under First Amendment); *O'Hare Truck Service, Inc. v. City of Northlake*, 518 U.S. 712 (1996) (protecting independent contractors from retaliation on basis of First Amendment).

21. *Hill et al., supra,* at 7; *Young v. Philadelphia Elec. Co.*, 87-ERA-11/35, 88-ERA-1, order of ALJ, at 4 (February 4, 1988) ("It has long been recognized that . . . [an] employer may violate the Act with respect to employees other than his own").

22. *See Stephenson v. NASA*, 94-TSC-5, D&O of Remand by ARB, at 3 (February 13, 1997) ("A parent company or contracting agency acts in the capacity of an employer establishing, modifying or otherwise interfering with an employee of a subordinate company regarding the employee's compensation, terms, conditions or privileges of employment. For example, the president of a parent company who hires, fires or disciplines an employee of one of its subsidiaries may be deemed an 'employer.' . . . A contracting agency which exercises similar control over the employees of its contractors or subcontractors may be a covered employer").

23. *Ziskend v. O'Leary*, 79 F. Supp.2d 10 (C.D. Mass. 2000); *Hyland v. Wonder*, 972 F.2d 1129, 1135 (9th Cir. 1992).

24. *See Automobile Salesmen's Union et al. v. NLRB*, 711 F.2d 383, 385 (D.C. Cir. 1983); *Delling v. NLRB*, 869 F.2d 1397, 1399-1340 (10th Cir. 1989); *NLRB v. Downslope Industries Inc.*, 676 F.2d 1114, 1119 (6th Cir. 1982).

25. *Chase v. Buncombe County, N.C., etc.*, 85-SWD-4, D&O of Remand by SOL, at 4 (November 3, 1986).

26. *Proud v. Cecos Int'l.*, 83-TSC-1, slip op. of ALJ, at 2 (September 30, 1983), adopted by SOL; *Royce v. Bechtel Power Co.*, 83-ERA-3, slip op. of ALJ, at 3 (March 24, 1983); *Flanagan v. Bechtel Power Corp. et al., supra,* slip op. of ALJ at 7-10 (November 19, 1981), adopted by SOL (June 27, 1986).

27. *Samodurov v. General Physics Corp.*, 89-ERA-20, D&O of SOL, at 5-7 (November 16, 1993); *Cowan v. Bechtel Constr., Inc.*, 87-ERA-24, D&O of Remand by SOL, at 3 (August 8, 1989); *Hill et al., supra; Faulkner v. Olin Corp., supra.*

28. *Hill et al., supra,* at 10; *Chase v. Buncombe County, N.C., etc., supra,* at 2-4; *Flanagan v. Bechtel Power Corp. et al., supra,* decision of SOL (June 27, 1986).

29. *O'Brien v. Stone & Webster Eng. Corp.*, 84-ERA-31, recommended D&O of ALJ, at 12 (February 28, 1985).

30. *Anderson v. Metro Wastewater Reclamation District*, 97-SDW-7, D&O of ARB (March 30, 2000).

31. *Figueroa v. Aponte-Roque*, 864 F.2d 947 (1st Cir. 1989).

32. *Wells v. Kansas Gas & Elec. Co.*, 83-ERA-12, slip op. of ALJ, at 3, adopted and modified by SOL (June 14, 1984).

33. *In re Five Star Products, Inc.*, CLI-93-23, M&O of NRC Commission, 38 NRC 169 (October 21, 1993).

34. *See Willy v. Coastal Corp.*, 85-CAA-1, D&O of SOL, at 14-16 (June 1, 1994).

35. For example, in *Rutan v. Republican Party of Illinois*, 497 U.S. 62, 76 n. 8 (1990), the Court noted that even minor manifestations of retaliation may be prohibited: "[T]he First amendment . . . already protects state employees not only from patronage dismissals but also from 'even an act of retaliation as trivial as failing to hold a birthday party for a public employee . . . when intended to punish her for exercising her free speech rights.' " Despite this dicta in *Rutan*, many courts do recognize that not all "minor adverse actions" would necessary constitute a First Amendment violation. *Colson v. Grohman*, 174 F.3d 498, 510-511 (5th Cir. 1999) (collecting cases).

36. 497 U.S. 62, 71-76 (1990).

37. *Id.* at 73 (emphasis in original).

38. *Id.*

39. 29 U.S.C. § 158(a)(4).

40. *NLRB v. Advertiser's Manufacturing*, 823 F.2d 1086 (7th Cir. 1987).

41. *NLRB v. Lamar Creamery Co.*, 246 F.2d 8 (5th Cir. 1957).

42. *Alaska Salmon Indus., Inc.*, 119 NLRB 612 (1957).

43. *Meyer & Welch, Inc.*, 96 NLRB 236 (1951).

44. *Preston Products Co.*, 169 NLRB 188 (1968).

45. *NLRB v. Darling & Co.*, 420 F.2d 63 (7th Cir. 1970).

46. *Kinter Bros., Inc.*, 167 NLRB 57 (1967).

47. *Capital Elec. Power Ass'n.*, 171 NLRB 262 (1968).

48. *NLRB v. Lifetime Door Co.*, 390 F.2d 272 (4th Cir. 1968).

49. *Figueroa v. Aponte-Roque, supra.*

50. *Fuqua Homes, Inc.*, 211 NLRB 399 (1974).

51. *Peoria Dry Wall, Inc.*, 191 NLRB 434 (1971).

52. *Glover Bottled Gas Corp.*, 255 NLRB No. 11 (1981).

53. *Pantchenko v. C.B. Dolge Co.*, 581 F.2d 1052 (2nd Cir. 1978) (Title VII case); *Sparrow v. Piedmont Health Systems*, 593 F. Supp. 1107 (M.D. N.C. 1984) (Title VII case).

54. *A. Sartorius & Co.*, 40 NLRB 107 (1942).

55. *Electro-Voice, Inc.*, 320 NLRB 134 (1996). *See Seater v. Southern California Edison*, 95-ERA-13, D&O of Remand by ARB, at 10-11 (September 27, 1996) (collecting cases).

56. *Fabric Mart Draperies*, 182 NLRB 390 (1970).

57. *NLRB v. News Syndicate Co.*, 279 F.2d 323 (2nd Cir. 1960), *aff'd*, 365 U.S. 695 (1961).

58. *Fulton Bag & Cotton Mills*, 81 NLRB 1135 (1949). For an excellent detailed compilation of discriminatory conduct, *see* John Ludington, "Employer Discrimination Against Employees for Filing Charges or Giving Testimony Under NLRA," 35 *American Law Reports Fed.* 132, §§ 48-77.

59. *In Bill Johnson's Restaurants, Inc. v. NLRB*, 461 U.S. 731 (1983); *Martin v. Gingerbread House, Inc.*, 977 F.2d 1405 (10th Cir. 1992).

60. 42 U.S.C. § 7622(a).

61. 29 C.F.R. § 24.2(b).

62. 85-SWD-4, D&O of Remand by SOL, at 4 (November 3, 1986).

63. *Boytin v. PP&L*, 94-ERA-32, D&O of Remand by SOL, at 10-11 (October 20, 1995).

64. *DeFord v. Secretary of Labor*, 700 F.2d 281, 283 (6th Cir. 1983); *Ellis Fischel State Cancer Hosp. v. Marshall*, 629 F.2d 563, 566 (9th Cir. 1980); *Wells v. Kansas Gas & Elec. Co.*, 83-ERA-12, slip op. of ALJ at 18, adopted by SOL (June 14, 1984).

65. *Hollis et al. v. Double DD Truck Lines, Inc.*, 84-STA-13, D&O of Undersecretary of Labor, at 8-9 (March 18, 1985). In order to demonstrate a constructive discharge, it is "not necessary to show that the employer intended to force a resignation, only that he intended the employee to work in the intolerable conditions." *Id., citing to Junior v. Texaco, Inc.*, 688 F.2d 377 (5th Cir. 1982). *See also Held v. Gulf Oil Co.*, 684 F.2d 427, 432 (6th Cir. 1982); *Cartwright Hardware Co. v. NLRB*, 600 F.2d 268 (10th Cir. 1979); *Perez v. Guthmiller Trucking Co., Inc.*, 87-STA-13, D&O of SOL, at 24-25 (December 7, 1988); *Talbert v. Washington Public Power Supply System*, 93-ERA-35, D&O of ARB, at 10-11 (September 27, 1996); *Martin v. Department of Army*, 93-SDW-1, D&O of ARB, at 7-9 (July 30, 1999) (discussing circuit split). As noted in *Schafer v. Board of Public Education*, 903 F.2d 243, 248-249 (3rd Cir. 1990), the U.S. Courts of Appeals are split as to the standard for determining what constitutes sufficient adverse action by an employer to warrant a finding of constructive discharge:

> [T]he courts of appeals that have addressed this issue have developed two basic standards for determining constructive discharge, the subjective test and the objective test. The subjective standard requires a finding that the discrimination complained of amounts to an intentional course of conduct calculated to force the victim's resignation. *See Bristow v. Daily Press, Inc.*, 770 F.2d 1251, 1255 (4th Cir. 1985), *cert. denied*, 475 U.S. 1082, 106 S.Ct. 1461, 89 L. Ed. 2d 718 (1986) (a plaintiff must prove "deliberateness of the employer's action, and intolerability of the working conditions" to prove constructive discharge). . . . The objective standard, on the other hand, requires no more than a finding that the conduct complained of would have the foreseeable result of creating working conditions that would be so unpleasant or difficult that a reasonable person in the employee's position would resign. *See Brooms v. Regal Tube Co.*, 881 F.2d 412, 423 (7th Cir. 1989) (affirming district court's application of reasonable person standard); *Watson v. Nationwide Insurance Co.*, 823 F.2d 360, 361 (9th Cir. 1989) ("plaintiff need not show that the employer subjectively intended to force the employee to resign").

The standard for finding a constructive discharge "is a higher one than for finding a hostile work environment," *Berkman v. U.S. Coast Guard*, 97-CAA-2/9, D&O of ARB, at 22 (February 29, 2000). *See also Martin v. Dept. of Army*, 93-SDW-1, D&O of ARB, at 7-8 (July 30, 1999) (discussing restrictive standard applicable in 4th circuit). A demotion to a job with lower status or pay may also justify finding constructive discharge. *James v. Sears & Roebuck Co.*, 21 F.3d 989, 993 (10th Cir. 1994); *Douglas v. Orkin Exterminating*, 2000 WL 667982 (10th Cir. 2000) (collecting cases).

66. *Egenrieder v. Met. Edison Co.*, 85-ERA-23, D&O of Remand by SOL (April 20, 1987); *Simmons v. Florida Power Corp.*, 89-ERA 28/29, R. D&O of ALJ (December 13, 1989); *Gain v. Benchmark Tech.*, 88-ERA-21, D&O of SOL, at 9-11 (September 25, 1990); *Doyle v. Hydro Nuclear Services*, 89-ERA-22, D&O of SOL (March 30, 1994); *Leidigh v. Freightway Corp.*, 87-STA-12, D&O of ARB, at 3-4 (December 18, 1997). *See also Smith v. TVA*, 90-ERA-12, D&O of SOL (April 30, 1992) (declining to find blacklisting and collecting cases).

67. *Helmstetter v. Pacific Gas & Elec. Co.*, 86-SWD-2, D&O of SOL, at 5-6 (September 9, 1992).

68. *Jenkins v. EPA*, 92-CAA-6, R. D&O of ALJ (December 14, 1992); D&O of SOL, at 14-15 (May 18, 1994); *Pogue v. United States Dept. of the Navy*, 87-ERA-21 D&O of SOL, at 51 (May 10, 1990), *Rev'd on other grounds sub nom. Pogue v. United States DOL*, 940 F.2d 1287 (9th Cir. 1991).

69. *Bassett v. Niagara Mohawk Power Corp.*, 85-ERA-34, D&O of SOL, at 4 (September 28, 1993). *See Varnadore v. Oak Ridge National Laboratory*, 92-CAA-2/5, 93-CAA-1, 94-CAA-2/3, Final Consolidated Order of ARB, at 32-33 (June 14, 1996) ("narrative contained in a performance appraisal may constitute adverse action") ("The most useful measure of whether a performance appraisal was given out of retaliatory motive is whether it is a fair and accurate description of an employee's job performance") (collecting cases).

70. *Diaz-Robainas v. Florida Power & Light Co.*, 92-ERA-10, D&O of SOL (January 19, 1996) (finding referral to constitute illegal discrimination); *Mandreger v. Detroit Edison*, 88-ERA-17, D&O of SOL (March 30, 1994) (upholding legality of referral). In fitness-for-duty referral cases, the DOL carefully examines the record to determine if "evidence" of "unusual or threatening behavior" existed sufficient to justify the referral. *Griffin v. Consolidated Freightways*, 97-STA-10/19, at 7 (January 20, 1998).

71. *Id.*

72. *Thomas v. APS*, 89-ERA-19, D&O of SOL, at 17 (September 17, 1993).

73. *Id.*

74. *Varnadore v. SOL*, 141 F.3d 625, 631 (6th Cir. 1998).

75. *Id.*

76. *Nathaniel v. Westinghouse Hanford Co.*, 91-SWD-2, D&O of SOL, at 13-14 (February 1, 1995).

77. *McMahan v. California Water Quality Control Board*, 90-WPC-1, D&O of SOL, at 5 (July 16, 1993).

78. *Bryant v. EBASCO Services, Inc.*, 88-ERA-31, D&O of SOL, at 8 (April 21, 1994). In *Earwood v. Dart Container Corp.*, 93-STA-16, D&O of SOL (December 7, 1994) (internal citations and quotations omitted), the SOL outlined a "prophylactic rule prohibiting improper references," even if the reference did not result in the loss of a job:

The fact that Complainant would not have lost an employment opportunity due to Dart's improper statement should not shield Dart from liability because its statement had a tendency to impede and interfere with Complainant's employment opportunities. I find that effective enforcement of the Act requires a prophylactic rule prohibiting improper references to an employee's protected activity whether or not the employee has suffered damages or loss of employment opportunities as a result.

79. *Hobby v. Georgia Power Co.*, 90-ERA-30, D&O of Remand by SOL, at 27 (August 4, 1995).

80. *Leoville v. New York Air National Guard*, 94-TSC-3/4, D&O of SOL (December 11, 1995) (adverse action in giving bad reference to a "reference checking company that the complainant had hired"); *Gaballa v. The Atlantic Group, Inc.*, 94-ERA-9, D&O of SOL (January 18, 1996) (adverse action by informing a reference-checking company that employee had filed a discrimination complaint); *Marcus v. EPA*, 96- CAA- 3 R. D&O of ALJ (Dec. 15, 1998). *But see Webb v. CP&L*, 93-ERA-42, D&O of ARB, at 11 (August 26, 1997) (informal negative remark to a "colleague" and "friend," standing alone, did not constitute adverse action).

81. *Mandreger v. Detroit Edison Co.*, 88-ERA- 17, D&O of SOL, at 14 (March 30, 1994). *See also House v. TVA*, 91-ERA-42, D&O of SOL (January 13, 1993); *Crosier v. Portland General Electric Corp.*, 91-ERA-2, D&O of SOL, at 8 (January 5, 1994). *See e.g., Helmstetter v. Pacific Gas & Electric Co.*, 91-TSC-1, D&O of SOL (January 13, 1993).

82. *Flanagan v. Bechtel Power Corp. et al.*, *supra*, at 6-7.

83. *Simmons et al. v. Fluor Constructors, Inc.*, 88-ERA-28/30, recommended D&O of ALJ, at 17 (February 8, 1989). *See also NLRB v. News Syndicate Co.*, 279 F.2d 323 (2nd Cir.), *aff'd*, 365 U.S. 695 (1961).

84. *Nolan v. AC Express*, 92-STA-37, D&O of remand by SOL, at 1 (January 17, 1995).

85. *Parkhurst v. L. K. Comstock & Co., Inc.*, 85-ERA-41, recommended D&O of ALJ, at 10 (April 7, 1986).

86. *Hill et al.*, *supra*, at 9; *Artrip v. EBASCO Services*, 89-ERA-23, D&O of SOL (March 21, 1995). *Accord., Sibley Memorial Hospital v. Wilson*, 488 F.2d 1338, 1342-1343 (D.C. Cir. 1973).

87. *Smith v. ESICORP, Inc.*, 93-ERA-16, D&O of Remand by SOL, at 16 (March 13, 1996).

88. *Artrip v. EBASCO Services*, *supra*, at 6-7, 15. In *Artrip* the SOL, citing *Charlton v. Paramus Board of Educ.*, 25 F.3d 194, 202 (3rd Cir. 1994), found that a "defendant's lack of direct authority" for the "ultimate adverse decision does not eliminate" potential liability. 89-ERA-23, at 7.

89. *Bassett v. Niagara Mohawk Power Co.*, 86-ERA-2, order of remand by SOL, at 6 (July 9, 1985).

90. *Helmstetter v. Pacific Gas & Elec. Co.*, 86-SWD-2, D&O of Remand by SOL, at 6-7 (June 15, 1989).

91. *Nolan v. AC Express*, *supra*, at 8.

92. *English v. Whitfield*, 858 F.2d 957, 963 (4th Cir. 1988).

93. *Delcore v. W. J. Barney Corp.*, 89-ERA-38, D&O of SOL (April 19, 1995).

94. *Gillilan v. TVA*, 91-ERA-31/34, D&O of Remand by SOL, at 9 (August 28, 1995). *Contra., Williams v. Metzler*, 132 F.3d 937 (3rd Cir.1997).

95. *Saporito v. FP&L*, 89-ERA-7, D&O of ARB, p.8-9 (August 11, 1998). *Accord., NLRB v. McCullough Environmental Services, Inc.*, 5 F.3d 923, 928 (5th Cir. 1993); *NLRB v. Brookwood Furniture*, 701 F.2d 452, 460-462 (5th Cir. 1983).

96. *Thomas v. A.P.S. Co.*, 89-ERA-19, recommended D&O of ALJ, at 13-14, 16 (April 13, 1989).

97. *Hashimoto v. Dalton*, 118 F.3d 671, 676 (9th Cir. 1997); *Griffith, supra.* (noting that "concrete harm" may arise when employee conduct could have a chilling effect); *Morris v. Lindau*, 196 F.3d 102, (2nd Cir. 1999) (employer policy may constitute prior restraint); *DeGuiseppe v. Village of Bellwood*, 68 F.3d 187, 192 (7th Cir. 1995) ("potential for chilling employee speech").

98. *Bart v. Telford*, 677 F.2d 622, 625 (7th Cir. 1982) ("since there is no justification for harassing people for exercising their constitutional rights [the harassment] need not be great in order to be actionable").

99. *Blair v. City of Pomona*, 206 F.3d 938, (9th Cir. 2000).

100. *Kadetsky v. Egg Harbor Township Bd. of Educ.*, 82 F. Supp.2d 327, (D. N.J. 2000). *Accord., Rodriguez v. Torres*, 60 F. Supp.2d 334, 350 (D. N.J. 1999).

101. *Sanchez v. Denver Public Schools*, 164 F.3d 527, 532-533 (10th Cir. 1998) (adverse action upheld if conduct "adversely affects" status of an employee).

102. *Perdomo v. Sears Roebuck and Co.*, 1999 WL 680149 (M.D. Fla. 1999).

103. *Id.* ("While the Defendant may not be required by law to pay all employees subject to subpoenas, where Defendant pays all employees except those subpoenaed by their adversary, the law has been offended.")

104. *Montandon v. Farmland Industries*, 116 F.3d 355, 359 (8th Cir. 1997). *See Settle v. Baltimore County*, 34 F. Supp.2d 969, 987-989 (D. Md. 1999) (collecting cases and discussing circuit split); *Webb v. CP&L*, 93-ERA-42, D&O of ARB, at 11 (August 26, 1997) (requiring that a "substantial job detriment" be a "predictable and natural outcome" of defendants alleged adverse action); *Griffith v. Wackenhut Corp.*, 97-ERA-52, D&O of ARB, at 12 (February 29, 2000), quoting *Smart and Ball State University*, 89 F.3d 437, 441 (7th Cir. 1996); *Heno v. Sprint/United Management Co.*, 208 F.3d 84 (10th Cir. 2000).

105. *Fortner v. Kansas*, 934 F. Supp. 1252, 1267 (D. Kan. 1996); *Taylor v. FDIC*, 132 F.3d 753, 764 (D.C. Cir. 1997) ("temporary designation" not actionable); *Trimmer v. DOL*, 174 F.3d 1089 (10th Cir. 1999).

106. *Wanamaker v. Columbian Rope Co.*, 108 F.3d 462, 466 (2nd Cir. 1997).

107. *Smith v. ESICORP, Inc.*, 93-ERA-16, D&O of Remand by SOL, at 23 (March 13, 1996).

108. *Hashimoto v. Dalton*, 118 F.3d 671 (9th Cir. 1997) (Noting "that the unlawful personnel action turned out to be inconsequential goes to the issue of damages, not liability"); *Smith v. Sec'y of Navy*, 659 F.2d 1113, 1120 (D.C. Cir. 1981) (liability although no financial loss due to dissemination of retaliating adverse references); *EEOC v. Hacienda Hotel*, 881 F.2d 1504 (9th Cir. 1989); *Haskell v. Anheuser-Busch*, 172 F.3d 876 (9th Cir. 1999) (unpublished). *But see Griffith v. Wackenhut*, 97-ERA-52, D&O of ARB, at 12-15, (February 29, 2000).

109. *See* Chapter 11, which contains a detailed discussion of the New Jersey whistleblower law.

110. *White v. State*, 929 P.2d 396, 407 (Wash. 1997) (collecting cases).

111. *Blake v. Hatfield Elec. Co.*, 87-ERA-4, D&O of SOL, at 4 (January 22, 1992); *McCuistion v. TVA*, 89-ERA-6, D&O of SOL, at 8 (November 13, 1991); *Nichols v. Bechtel Constr. Inc.*, 87-ERA-44, D&O of SOL, at 11 (October 26, 1992).

112. *Goldstein v. EBASCO Constructors, Inc.*, 86-ERA-36, D&O of SOL, at 13 (April 7, 1992), *rev'd on other grounds* (U.S. Court of Appeals for the 5th Cir. 1993). *See also Williams v. TIW Fabrication & Machining, Inc.*, 88-SWD-3, D&O of SOL (June 24, 1992).

113. *Smith v. ESICORP, Inc., supra.* In the context of nuclear whistleblowing, one ALJ awarded an employee $50,000 in emotional distress damages due to a hostile work environment. *Mitchell v. APS/ANPP*, 91-ERA-9, R. D&O of ALJ, at 37 (July 2, 1992). The standards set forth in the *Mitchell* case are consistent with those identified in prior hostile work environment cases. *See Meritor Sav. Bank v. Vinson*, 477 U.S. 57 (1986); *Ellison v. Brady*, 924 F.2d 872 (9th Cir. 1991); *English v. Whitfield, supra. See also House v. TVA*, 92-ERA-9, R. D&O of ALJ, at 8-9 (October 15, 1992).

114. *See e.g., English v. Whitfield*, 858 F.2d 957 (4th Cir. 1988).

115. *Harris v. Forklift Systems, Inc.*, 510 U.S. 17,23 (1993).

116. *Varnadore v. Oak Ridge National Laboratory*, 92-CAA-2/5, 93-CAA-1, 94-CAA-2/3, Final Consolidated D&O of ARB, at 71-72 (June 14, 1996), *citing West v. Philadelphia Electric Co.*, 45 F.3d 744, 753 (3rd Cir. 1995). *Berkman v. U.S. Coast Guard Academy*, D&O of ARB, at 21 (February 29, 2000).

117. *Varnadore v. Oak Ridge National Laboratory, supra*, Final Consolidated D&O of ARB, at 75 (June 14, 1996), *quoting Pierce v. Commonwealth Life Ins.*, 40 F.3d 796, 803 (6th Cir. 1994) *and Karibian v. Columbia University*, 14 F.3d 773, 780 (2nd Cir. 1994).

118. 524 U.S. 742, 745 (1998). *See also Faragher v. Boca Raton*, 524 U.S. 775 (1998).

119. *See Ilgenfritz v. U.S. Coast Guard Academy*, 99-WPC-3, D&O of ALJ, at 39-40 (March 30, 1999) (collecting cases).

120. *Phelps Dodge Corp. v. NLRB*, 313 U.S. 177, 187-188 (1941) ("to differentiate between discrimination in denying employment and in terminating it, would be a differentiation not only without substance but in defiance of that against which the prohibition of discrimination is directed").

121. 89-ERA-20, D&O of SOL, at 9-10 (November 16, 1993).

122. *Id., quoting from McDonnell Douglas Corp. v. Green*, 411 U.S. 792, 802 (1973).

123. *Id.* at 11.

124. *Spearman v. Roadway Express*, 92-STA-1, D&O of SOL, at 13-15 (June 30, 1993), adopting the reasoning of the court in *DeFord v. TVA*, 700 F.2d 281, 286 (6th Cir. 1983). *Cf., Roadway Express v. Dole*, 929 F.2d 1060 (5th Cir. 1991).

125. 700 F.2d 281, 286 (6th Cir. 1983).

126. *Clifton v. UPS*, 94-STA-16, D&O of SOL, p 13 (May 14, 1997).

127. *Ass't. Secretary v. Carolina Freight Carrier*, 91-STA-25, D&O of SOL, at 7 (August 6, 1992) ("To permit an employer to rely on a facially-neutral policy to discipline an employee for engaging in statutorily-protected activity would permit the employer to accomplish what the law prohibits") (collecting cases).

128. *Assistant Secretary v. Sysco Foods of Philadelphia*, 97-STA-30, D&O of ARB, at 8 (July 8, 1998).

129. *Secretary of Labor v. Mullins*, 888 F.2d 1448-1452 (D.C. Cir. 1989); *CL&P v. SOL*, 85 F.3d 89, 95 (2nd Cir. 1996).

130. 89-ERA-22, D&O of SOL (March 30, 1994).

131. *Id.* at 6.

132. *Id.* at 7.

133. *Id.* at 8.

134. *CL&P v. SOL, supra.*

135. *See Clover v. Total System Services, Inc.*, 176 F.3d 1346 (11th Cir. 1999) (Title VII retaliation claim dismissed due to lack of evidence of employer knowledge). In the context of environmental whistleblowing, the SOL has held that employer "knowledge" of the protected conduct is an "essential element of proof." *Miller v. Thermalkem, Inc.*, 94-SWD-1, D&O of SOL, at 3 (November 9, 1995). *Accord., Ertel v. Giroux Bros. Transp., Inc.*, 88-STA-24, D&O of SOL, at 25 n. 16 (February 16, 1989); *Hassel v. Industrial Contractors, Inc.*, 86-CAA-7, D&O of SOL, at 2 (February 13, 1989); *Ledford v. Baltimore Gas & Elec. Co., supra*, at 9-11, adopted by SOL; *Crider v. Pullman Power Prods. Corp.*, 82-ERA-7, slip op. of ALJ, at 2 (October 5, 1982); *Flanagan v. Bechtel Power Corp. et al., supra*, slip op. of ALJ, at 11 (November 19, 1981).

136. *Merriweather v. TVA*, 91-ERA-55, R. D&O of ALJ, at 4-5 (May 21, 1992), *citing to Bartlik v. TVA*, 88-ERA-15, D&O of Remand by SOL, at 7 n. 7 (December 6, 1991). *See also Morris v. The American Inspection Co.*, 92-ERA-5, D&O of SOL, at 6 (December 15, 1992); *Chavez v. EBASCO*, 91-ERA-24, D&O of SOL, at 5 (November 16, 1992); *Young v. Philadelphia Electric Co.*, 88-ERA-1, D&O of SOL, at 6, n. 3 (December 18,1992).

137. *Reich v. Hoy Shoe Co.*, 32 F.3d 361, 368 (8th Cir. 1994) (adverse action based on employer's suspicion of protected activities); *Smith v. ESICORP, Inc.*, 93-ERA-16, D&O of Remand by SOL, at 9-11 (March 13, 1996) (discussing circumstances behind management suspicion that employee engaged in protected activity).

138. *See Flenker v. Williamette Industries, Inc.*, 68 F. Supp.2d 1261, 1266-1267 (D. Kan. 1999) (circumstantial evidence of knowledge).

139. *Bartlik v. TVA, supra*, Final D&O of SOL, at 4, n. 1 (April 7, 1993).

140. *Crider v. Pullman Power Prods. Corp.*, 82-ERA-7, slip op. of ALJ, at 2 (October 5, 1982).

141. *NLRB v. Instrument Corp. of America*, 714 F.2d 324, 328-329 (4th Cir. 1983); *Frazier v. Merit Systems Protection Board*, 672 F.2d 150, 166 (D.C. Cir. 1982); *Larry v. Detroit Edison Co.*, 86-ERA-32, slip op. of ALJ, at 6 (October 17, 1986); *Johnson v. Transco Products., Inc.*, 85-ERA-7 slip op. of ALJ, at 4 (March 5, 1985).

142. *Frazier, supra.*

143. *Wagoner v. Technical Products, Inc.*, 87-TSC-4, D&O of SOL, at 14 n. 8 (November 20, 1990).

144. *Id. See also Larry v. Detroit Edison Co.*, *supra*, D&O of ALJ, at 6.

145. *Id. Accord., Bartlik v. TVA, supra*: "[W]here managerial or supervisory authority is delegated, the official with ultimate responsibility who merely ratifies his subordinates' decisions cannot insulate a respondent from liability by claiming 'bureaucratic' 'ignorance.'"

146. *Ertel v. Giroux Bros. Transp., Inc.*, 88-STA-24, D&O of SOL, at 25 n. 16 (February 16, 1989).

147. *Pillow v. Bechtel Construction, Inc.*, 87-ERA-35, D&O of Remand by SOL (July 19, 1993).

148. *Thompson v. TVA*, 89-ERA-14, D&O of SOL, at 5 (July 19, 1993).

149. *Jones v. EG&G Defense Materials, Inc.*, 95-CAA-3, D&O of ARB, at 15 (September 29, 1998).

150. *Lambert v. Ackerley*, 180 F.3d 997, 1002-1008 (9th Cir. 1999) (*en banc*) (collecting cases and discussing protected activity under various antiretaliation laws).

151. *NLRB v. Scrivener*, 405 U.S. 117, 121-126 (1972).

152. 405 U.S. at 122-24.

153. Fair Labor Standards Act: *Lambert v. Ackerley, supra* (*en banc*) (collecting cases). Surface Transportation Act: *Clean Harbors Environmental Services v. Herman*, 146 F.3d 12 (1st Cir. 1998). 1969 Federal Mine Safety Act: *Baker v. Board of Mine Operations Appeals*, 595 F.2d 746 (D.C. Cir. 1978); *Munsey v. Morton*, 507 F.2d 1202 (D.C. Cir. 1974); *Phillips v. Board of Mine Operations Appeals*, 500 P.2d 772, 781-782 (D.C. Cir. 1974), *cert. denied*, 420 U.S. 938 (1974). OSHA: *Donovan v. Peter Zimmer America, Inc.*, 557 F. Supp 642 (D. S.C. 1982); *Dunlop v. Hanover Shoe Farms Inc.*, 441 F. Supp. 385 (M.D. Pa. 1976). NLRA: *NLRB v. Retail Store Employees' Union*, 570 F.2d 586, 591 (6th Cir. 1978), *cert. denied*, 439 U.S. 819 (1978). 1977 Federal Mine Safety Act: *Donovan v. Stafford Constr. Co.*, 732 F.2d 954, 960-961 (D.C. Cir. 1984). False Claims Act: *U.S. ex rel. Yesudian v. Howard University*, 153 F.3d 731 (D.C. Cir. 1998). Energy Reorganization Act: *Bechtel Construction v. SOL*, 50 F.3d 926, 931-933 (11th Cir. 1995). Clean Water Act: *Passaic Valley Sewerage Commis-*

sioners v. DOL, 992 F.2d 474, 478-479 (3rd Cir. 1993).

154. *Lopez v. West Texas Utilities*, 86-ERA-25, D&O of SOL, at 5-6 (July 26, 1988); *Wilson v. Bechtel Constr., Inc.*, 86-ERA-34, D&O of SOL, at 2-5 (February 9, 1988); *Smith v. Norco Technical Services et al.*, 85-ERA-17, D&O of SOL, at 4 (October 2, 1987) (*see* cases cited therein); *Nunn v. Duke Power Co.*, 84-ERA-27, D&O of Remand by Deputy SOL, at 11-13 (July 13, 1987).

155. *Nunn v. Duke Power Co., supra*, at 13.

156. *Mackowiak v. University Nuclear Systems, supra*, at 1163 ("If the regulatory scheme is to function effectively, inspectors must be free from the threat of retaliatory discharge for identifying safety and quality problems."). *See also Jarvis v. Battelle Pacific Northwest*, 97-ERA-15, D&O of ARB, at 8 (August 27, 1998) ("The protection afforded whistleblowers by the ERA extends to employees who, in the course of their work, must make recommendations regarding how best to serve the interest of nuclear safety, even when they do not allege that the *status quo* is in violation of any specific statutory or regulatory standard"); *Richter et al. v. Baldwin Associates*, 84-ERA-9/10/11/12, D&O of Remand by SOL, at 11-12 (March 12, 1986).

157. *Id.*

158. *Wilson v. Bechtel Constr., Inc., supra.*

159. *Id.; Consolidated Edison Co. of N.Y. v. Donovan*, 673 F.2d 61 (2nd Cir. 1982).

160. *Kenneway v. Matlack, Inc., supra*, at 13.

161. 500 F.2d 772 (D.C. Cir. 1974).

162. 30 U.S.C. 820(b)(1); Federal Coal Mine Health and Safety Act of 1969, Section 110(b)(1).

163. Id. at 779.

164. *Phillips*, 500 F.2d at 778.

165. *See Lambert v. Ackerley, supra*, at 1006 (collecting cases). Banking whistleblower law: *Haley v. Retsinas*, 138 F.3d 1245, 1250-1251 (8th Cir. 1998); Atomic Energy Act cases: *Bechtel Construction v. DOL*, 50 F.3d 926, 931-933 11th Cir. 1995); *Mackowiak v. University Nuclear Systems*, 735 F.2d 1159 (9th Cir. 1984); *Kansas Gas & Electric v. Brock*, 780 F.2d 1505 (10th Cir. 1985); False Claim Act cases: *U.S. ex rel. Yesudian v. Howard University*, 153 F.3d 731, 741-743 (D.C. Cir. 1998) (collecting cases). Fair Labor Act cases: *Love v. Re/Max of America Inc.*, 738 F.2d 383, 387 (10th Cir. 1984); *Marshall v. Parking Co. of America Denver, Inc.*, 670 F.2d 141 (10th Cir. 1982). 1969 Federal Mine Safety Act cases: *Baker v. Board of Mine Operations Appeals*, 595 F.2d 746 (D.C. Cir. 1978). Federal Railroad Safety Act cases: *Rayner v. Smirl*, 873 F.2d 60, 64 (4th Cir. 1989). Clean Water Act cases: *Passaic Valley Sewerage Commissioners v. DOL*, 922 F.2d 474, 478 (3rd Cir, 1993). ERISA cases: *Hashimoto v. Bank of Hawaii*, 999 F.2d 408, 411 (9th Cir. 1993). OSHA cases: *Donovan v. Peter Zimmer America, Inc.*, 557 F. Supp. 642 (D. S.C. 1982). NLRA cases: *NLRB v. Retail Store Employees' Union*, 570 F.2d 586 (6th Cir. 1978), *cert. denied*, 439 U.S. 819 (1978). Surface Transportation Act cases: *Clean Harbors Environmental Services v. Herman*, 146 F.3d 12 (1st Cir. 1998). *See also Givhan v. Western Line Consolidated School District*, 439 U.S. 410 (1979) (upholding

internal whistleblowing under First Amendment). Most state courts also have protected internal whistleblowing. *See e.g.*, *Appeal of Bio Energy Corporation*, 607 A.2d 606 (N.H. 1992). Additionally, the majority of state whistleblower protection laws explicitly protect, encourage, and/or require employees to report wrongdoing to their employers. *See* New Jersey Conscientious Employee Protection Act, N.J.S.A. 34:19. *Contra, Chandler v. Dowell Schlumberger, Inc.*, 572 N.W.2d 210 (Mich. 1998).

166. Senate Report No. 848, 1978 U.S. Code Cong. & Admin. News at 7303; *Kansas Gas & Electric v. Brock*, 780 F.2d 1505, 1511 (10th Cir. 1985).

167. U.S. Secretary of Labor, *see* Decision of the Secretary of Labor, *Lockert v. Pullman Power*, 84-ERA-15 (August 19, 1985); Nuclear Regulatory Commission, *see* Brief of the U.S. Nuclear Regulatory Commission of Americus Curiae in *Kansas Gas & Electric, supra,* at 1505.

168. *Brown & Root, Inc. v. Donovan*, 747 F.2d 1029, 1036 (5th Cir. 1984).

169. *Kansas Gas & Elec.,supra,* at 1505, *cert. denied*, 478 U.S. 1011 (1986); *Wheeler v. Caterpillar Tractor Co.*, 108 Ill. 2d 502, 485 N.E.2d 372 (1985), *cert. denied*, 475 U.S. 1122 (1986). *Accord., Mackowiak, supra,* at 1163.

170. 42 U.S.C. § 5851(a) (1999).

171. *Faust v. Ryder Commercial Leasing*, 954 S.W.2d 383, 391 (Mo. App. 1997). *Accord., Willis v. Department of Agriculture*, 141 F.3d 1139 (Fed. Cir. 1998). *Contra., Passaic Valley Sewerage Comm'rs., supra,* at 478-479 ("Employees should not be discouraged from the normal route of pursuing internal remedies before going public . . . [as this] facilitate[s] prompt voluntary remediation and compliance").

172. *U.S. ex rel. Yesudian, supra,* at 742. *Accord., Zurenda v. J&K Plumbing & Heating*, 97-STA-16, D&O of ARB, at 5 (June 12, 1998).

173. *Saporito v. FP&L*, 89-ERA-7/17, Order of SOL, at 6 (February 16, 1995).

174. *Accord.*, Jones v. *TVA.*, 948 F.2d 258, 264 (6th Cir. 1991); *Willy v. Coastal Corp.*, 85-CAA-1, D&O of SOL, at 13 (June 1, 1994); *Mandreger v. Detroit Edison Co.*, 88-ERA-17, D&O of SOL, at 13-14 (March 30, 1994); *Crosier v. Portland General Electric Co.*, 91-ERA-2, D&O of SOL, at 6-7 (January 5, 1994); *Pillow v. Bechtel Construction*, 87-ERA-35, SOL D&O of Remand, at 11 (July 19, 1993); *Goldstein v. EBASCO Constructors, Inc.*, 86-ERA-36, D&O of SOL, at 5-10 (April 7, 1992), *Rev'd EBASCO Construction, Inc. v. Martin*, unpublished opinion of U.S. Court of Appeals for the Fifth Circuit, No. 92-4576 (February 19, 1993); *Nichols v. Bechtel Construction, Inc.*, 87-ERA-44, D&O of SOL, at 9 (October 26, 1992); *Adams v. Coastal Production Op., Inc.*, 89-ERA-3, D&O of SOL, at 8-9 (August 5, 1992); *Guttman v. Passaic Valley Sewerage Commission*, 85-WPC-2, D&O of SOL, at 10-13 (March 13, 1992), *aff'd* 992 F.2d 474 (3rd Cir. 1993); *Johnson v. Old Dominion Security*, 86-CAA-3/4/5, D&O of SOL, at 14 (May 29, 1991); *Chavez v. EBASCO Services, Inc.*, 91-ERA-24, D&O of SOL, at 5 (November 16, 1992); *Dodd v. Polysar Latex*, 88-SWD-4, D&O of SOL, at 6-7 (September 22, 1994).

175. *Doyle v. Rich Transport*, 93-STA-17, D&O of SOL, at 2 (April 1, 1994); *Hermanson v. Morrison Knudsen Corp.*, 94-CER-2, D&O of ARB, at 5 (June 28, 1996); *Carson v. Tyler Pipe* Co., 93-WPC-11, D&O of SOL, at 7 (March 24, 1995). However, under cases arising under the pre-amended version of the nuclear whistleblower law, the Secretary is adhering to the "controlling" decision of the Fifth Circuit in cases arising within that jurisdiction. *Grover v. Houston Lighting & Power*, 93-ERA-4, D&O of SOL, at 4 (March 16, 1995).

176. 992 F.2d 474, 478-479 (3rd Cir. 1993).

177. *See Lambert v. Ackerley, supra*, at 1006 (*en banc*). For example, the Fifth Circuit still continues to adhere to the *Brown & Root* decision in cases arising under the pre-amended nuclear whistleblower statute. But even that circuit found threats to contact government agencies protected, even if there was no actual communications or contacts with the governmental regulatory authority. *Macktal v. DOL*, 171 F.3d 323 (5th Cir. 1999). Moreover, even within the Fifth Circuit, in a False Claims Act retaliation case, the court found that certain internal whistleblowing would be protected. *See Robertson v. Bell Helicopter Textron, Inc.*, 32 F.3d 948, 952 (5th Cir. 1994).

178. *Fabricius v. Town of Braintree*, 97-CAA-14, D&O of ARB, at 4 (February 9, 1999) (collecting cases); *Talbert v. Washington Public Power Supply System*, 93-ERA-35, D&O of ARB, at 8 (September 27, 1996) ("chain of command" restrictions on reporting concerns would "seriously undermine the purpose of whistleblower laws") (collecting cases); *Pogue v. DOL*, 940 F.2d 1287, 1290 (9th Cir. 1991).

179. *Leoville v. New York Air National Guard*, 94-TSC-3/4, D&O of Remand by SOL, at 16-17 (December 11, 1995) (collecting cases).

180. *West v. Systems Applications International*, 94-CAA-15, D&O of Remand by SOL, at 7 (April 19, 1995).

181. *Dutkiewicz v. Clean Harbors Environmental Services*, 95-STA-34, D&O of ARB, at 7 (August 8, 1997), *aff'd, Clean Harbors Environmental Services v. Herman*, 146 F.3d 12 (1st Cir. 1998). *Contra., Robbins v. Jefferson County School District*, 186 F.3d 1253, 1260 (10th Cir. 1999) (upholding discipline against employee for "making inflammatory, insubordinate comments and disregarding chain of command").

182. *Saporito v. Florida Power & Light Co.*, 89-ERA-7/17, SOL Remand Order, at 1 (June 3, 1994).

183. *Pillow v. Bechtel, supra*, D&O of Remand by SOL, at 23.

184. *Nichols v. Bechtel Constr., Inc., supra*, at 17.

185. *Id.; McMahan v. California Water Quality Control Bd.*, 90-WDC-1, D&O of SOL, at 4 (July 16, 1993); *Brockell v. Norton*, 732 F.2d 664, 668 (8th Cir. 1984).

186. *Saporito v. Florida Power & Light Co., supra*, at 5, n. 4.

187. *Lockert v. Pullman Power Co.*, 867 F.2d 513, 518 (9th Cir. 1989); *Holtzclaw v. Commonwealth of Kentucky*, 95-CAA-7, D&O of ARB, at 5-6 (February 13, 1997).

188. *Saporito v. FP&L, supra*, D&O of ARB, at 8 (August 11, 1998) (internal quotations omitted) (citing cases).

189. *Brown & Root, Inc. v. Donovan*, 747 F.2d 1029, 1036 (5th Cir. 1984). Direct contact with NRC, *DeFord v. Secretary of Labor*, 700 F.2d 281, 283 (6th Cir. 1983); reporting alleged violations to federal authorities, *Ellis Fischel State Cancer Hosp. v. Marshall*, 629 F.2d 563, 564 (9th Cir. 1980); speaking to NRC inspectors regarding radiation exposure, *Jaenisch v. Chicago Bridge & Iron Co.*, 81-ERA-5, slip op. of ALJ, at 2 (May 18, 1981), adopted by SOL (June 25, 1981); writing and signing a letter to the NRC, *Cram v. Puliman-Higgins Co.*, 84-ERA-17, slip op. of ALJ, at 2 (July 24, 1984), adopted in part by SOL (January 14, 1985); contacts with the Department of Transportation concerning STAA violations, *Green v. Creech Brothers Trucking*, 92-STA-4, D&O of SOL, at 12 (December 9, 1992). *Accord., Jenkins v. EPA*, 92-CAA-6, D&O of SOL, at 12 (May 18, 1994).

190. *Tyndall v. EPA*, 93-CAA-6/95-CAA-5, D&O of Remand by ARB, at 6 (June 14, 1996).

191. *McCafferty v. Centerior Energy*, 96-ERA-6, D&O of Remand by ARB, at 9 (September 24, 1997).

192. 18 U.S.C. § 1512(c). *Accord., Mruz v. Caring, Inc.*, 991 F. Supp. 701, 714 (D. N.J. 1998) (upholding civil liability under RICO for harm resulting from violation of § 1512).

193. *Pettway v. American Cast Iron Pipe Co.*, 411 F.2d 998, 1006, n. 18 (5th Cir. 1969).

194. *U.S. v. Glover*, 170 F.3d 411 (4th Cir. 1999).

195. *Merritt v. Dillard Paper Co.*, 120 F.3d 1181, 1184 (11th Cir. 1997). In *Merritt* the court held that an employee who admitted, in testimony, to having participated in discriminatory conduct could not be discharged on the basis of the testimony alone. 120 F. 3d at 1188-1189.

196. *Kubicko v. Ogden Logistics Services*, 181 F.3d 544 (4th Cir. 1999); *U.S. v. Glover*, 170 F.3d 411 (4th Cir. 1999).

197. *Smith v. ESICORP*, 93-ERA-16, D&O of Remand, at 7 (March 13, 1996); *Bryant v. EBASCO Services, Inc.*, 88-ERA-31, D&O of SOL, at 4 (April 21, 1994).

198. *Thompson v. TVA, supra*, D&O of SOL, at 5 (July 19, 1993).

199. *Haney v. North American Car Corp.*, 81-SWD-1, slip op. of ALJ, at 12 (December 15, 1981), adopted by SOL (June 30, 1982); *Hanna v. School District of Allentown*, 79-TSCA-1, slip op. of SOL at 11 (July 28, 1980), *Rev'd on other grounds, School Dist. of Allentown v. Marshall*, 857 F.2d 16 (3rd Cir. 1981); *see also House Interstate and Foreign Commerce Committee*, H.R. Rep. No. 294, 95th Cong., 2d Sess., *reprinted in* 1977 U.S. Code Cong. & Admin. News 1077, 1404.

200. 81-SWD-1, slip op. of ALJ, at 12, adopted by SOL; *see also Fischer v. Town of Steilacoom*, 83-WPC-2, slip op. of ALJ, at 6 (May 2, 1983).

201. *See e.g., Helmstetter v. Pacific Gas & Electric Co., supra*, D&O of SOL, at 5 (January 13, 1993); *Ivory v. Evans Cooperage, Inc.*, 88-WPC-2, D&O of SOL, at 2, 5 (February 22, 1991); *Conley v. McClellan Air Force Base*, 84-WPC-1, D&O of SOL, p.18 (September 7, 1993).

202. *Macktal v. DOL*, 171 F.3d 323 (5th Cir. 1999) (ERA); *Shallal v. Catholic Social Services*, 566 N.W.2d 571 (Mich. 1997). *Accord.*, *Mandreger v. Detroit Edison Co.*, 88-ERA-17, D&O of SOL, at 14 (March 30, 1994) ("threat to report safety issues to the NRC also was a protected activity"). In *Helmstetter v. Pacific Gas & Electric, supra*, D&O of Remand by SOL, at 7 (citations and internal quotations omitted), the SOL explained the reasoning behind protecting such threats: "Concerning Complainant's alleged threat to report the spill to governmental authorities, it is well established that whistleblower provisions protect preliminary steps to commencing or participating in a proceeding when those steps could result in exposure of employer wrongdoing."

203. *Landers v. Commonwealth-Lord Joint Venture*, 83-ERA-5, slip op. of SOL, at 1 (September 9, 1983). *See also Nunn v. Duke Power Co.*, 84-ERA-27, D&O of Remand by Deputy SOL, at 12 (July 30, 1987); *Poulos v. Ambassador Fuel Oil Co., Inc.*, 86-CAA-1, D&O of Remand by SOL, at 6-11 (April 27, 1987); *Hale v. Baldwin Assoc.*, 85-ERA-37, recommended D&O of ALJ, at 17 (October 20, 1986); *Couty v. Arkansas Power & Light Co.*, 87-ERA-10, recommended D&O of ALJ, at 9 (November 16, 1987), adopted by SOL (June 20, 1988), *reversed on other grounds*, 886 F.2d 147 (8th Cir. 1989); *Cram v. Pullman-Higgins Co.*, 84-ERA-17, slip op. of SOL, at 1 (January 14, 1985); *Seraiver v. Bechtel Power Corp.*, 84-ERA-24, slip op. of ALJ, at 7 (July 5, 1984).

204. *Landers v. Commonwealth-Lord Joint Venture*, *supra*, slip op. of ALJ, at 11. *See also Poulos v. Ambassador Fuel Oil Co., Inc.*, *supra*; *Ashcraft v. Univ. of Cincinnati*, 83-ERA-7, slip op. of SOL, at 10 (November 1, 1984).

205. *Poulos v. Ambassador Fuel Oil Co., Inc.*, *supra*, slip op. at 11. In *Francis v. Bogan, Inc.*, 86-ERA-8, recommended decision of ALJ, slip op. at 13, (March 21, 1986), the administrative law judge held that the "about to commence" clause of the Energy Reorganization Act covers threats to report problems to the Nuclear Regulatory Commission, even if no actual complaint was filed. *See also Brown & Root, Inc., v. Donovan, supra*, at 1031 n. 4.

206. One-party surreptitious taping is conducted when one party to a conversation tapes the conversation without telling the other party that such taping is occurring. *See e.g., Heller v. Champion Inter. Corp.*, 891 F.2d 432 (2nd Cir. 1989). One-party taping is legal under federal law and most state laws. However, interception of a conversation without the consent of any party to that conversation is illegal under federal law (and most state laws). In a 2-1 decision, the U.S. Court of Appeals for the District of Columbia Circuit held that a person who disseminates information obtained from an illegal interception of a conversation is not protected under the First Amendment. *Boehner v. McDermott*, 191 F.3d 463 (D.C. Cir. 1999); contra., *Bartnicki v. Vopper*, 200 F.3d 109 (3rd Cir. 1999).

207. A small number of state laws are more restrictive than the federal wiretapping statute and prohibit one-party taping. A listing of state taping laws is set forth in footnote 6 of *Boehner v. McDermott*, 191 F.3d 463 (D.C. Cir. 1999).

208. *Boddie v. A.B.C.*, 731 F.2d 333, 338 (6th Cir. 1984) (citing authorities).

209. *U.S. v. Phillips*, 540 F.2d 319, 325 (8th Cir. 1976). For an over-view of federal law concerning one-party taping, *see Ali v. Douglas Cable*, 929 F. Supp. 1362, 1376-1381 (D. Kan. 1996).

210. *Lopez v. U.S.*, 373 U.S. 427, 442 (1963) (Chief Justice Warren concurring).

211. *Goggin Truck Line Co., Inc. v. ARB* 172 F.3d 872 (Table) (unpub-lished) (6th Cir. 1999); *Accord., U.S. v. Wilkinson*, 53 F.3d 757, 761 (6th Cir. 1995).

212. Title III of the Omnibus Crime Control law, 18 U.S.C. § 2511(2)(d) states as follows: "It shall not be unlawful under this chapter for a person not acting under color of law to intercept a wire or oral communication where such person is a party to the communication or where one of the parties to the commu-nication has given prior consent to such interception unless such communication is intercepted for the purpose of committing any criminal or tortious act." *See also* B. Finberg, "What Constitutes an 'Interception' of a Telephone or Similar Communication Forbidden by the Federal Communications Act [47 U.S.C.A. § 605] or Similar State Statutes," 9 *ALR3d* 423 (1967); M. S. Galinsky, "Eaves-dropping As Violating Right of Privacy," 11 *ALR3d* 1296 (1967); Todd R. Smyth, J.D., "Eavesdropping On Extension Telephone As Invasion of Privacy," 49 *ALR4th* 430 (1986); Eric H. Miller, J.D., "Permissible Surveillance, Under State Communications Interception Statute, By Person Other Than State Or Local Law Enforcement Officer Or One Acting In Concert With Officer," 24 *ALR4th* 1208 (1981). In *United States v. Upton*, 502 F. Supp. 1193, 1198 (D. N.H. 1980) (collecting cases), the court noted that the context of tape recording obtained from one party taping has been held as being admissible in all federal jurisdictions: "In short, every United States Court of Appeals has agreed that intercepted communi-cations where one party thereto has consented are clearly admissible in federal criminal trials."

213. 114 Cong. Rec. 14,694 (1968) (Sen. Hart).

214. *See Bartnicki v. Vopper*, 200 F.3d 109 (3rd Cir. 1999); *Boehner v. McDermott*, 191 F.3d 463 (D.C. Cir. 1999); *Commonwealth v. Goldberg*, 224 A.2d 91 (Pa. Super. 1996) ("paramount right" to make interceptions on one's own phone line) (superceded by statute); *State of Washington v. Faford*, 910 P.2d 447, 451 (Wash. 1996) ("whether a conversation qualifies as private is a question of fact determined by the intent or reasonable expectations of the parties"). Justice Sentelle, in his dissenting opinion in *McDermott*, 191 F.3d at 484, articulated a First Amendment concern over legal prohibitions against the publication of illegally intercepted tapped conversations:

I can envision felonious eavesdroppers . . . obtaining not marginally embarrassing infor-mation . . . but information of critical public importance about, for example, some public officials accepting a bribe or committing perjury or obstruction of justice. Even if those hypothetical felons dumped information of that critical nature not into the hands of politicians but of a newspaper publisher or television news network, the public could never know of the wrongdoing, because under today's ruling, those news media would be barred from further publication of that information.

215. *See* Ala. Code §§ 13A-11-31, 13A-11-35; Ariz. Rev. Stat. Ann. §§ 13-3005, 13-3006; Ark. Code Ann. § 5-60-120(a); Cal. Penal Code §§ 631, 632; Colo. Rev. Stat.§ 18-9-303; Conn. Gen. Stat. §§ 53a-18, 53a-188, 53a-189, 54-41r; Ga. Code Ann. §§ 16-11-62, 16-11-66.1; Haw. Rev. Stat. § 803-42; 720 Ill. Comp. Stat. Ann. 5/14-2; Kan. Stat. Ann. § 21-4002; Ky. Rev. Stat. Ann. §§ 526.020, 526.060; La. Rev. Stat. Ann. §§ 15:1312; Me. Rev. Stat. Ann. title 15, §§ 710, 711; Minn. Stat. Ann. §§ 626A.02, 626A.13; Mo. Rev. Stat. §§ 542.402, 542.418 (1996); Nev. Rev. Stat. §§ 200.620, 200.630, 200.650, 200.690 (1994); N.J. Stat. Ann. §§ 2A-156A-3, 2A-156A-24; N.M. Stat. Ann. §§ 30-12-1, 30-12-11; N.Y. Penal Law §§ 250.05, 250.25; N.D. Cent. Code §§ 12.1-15-02 (1994); Ohio Rev. Code Ann. §§ 2933.52, 2933, 65; Okla. Stat. Ann. title 13, §§ 176.2, 176.5; S. D. Codified laws § 23a-35a-20.

216. *See State v. Reid*, 394 N.W.2d 399, 405 (Iowa Sup. Ct. 1986) (holding party to a conversation may record without other's consent); *Kotrla v. Kotrla*, 718 S. W.2d 853, 855 (Tex. Ct. App. 1986) (holding that a party to a conversation may record without the other's consent); *State v. Waste Management of Wisconsin*, 261 N.W.2d 147,154 (Wis. 1978) (holding that one-party taping lawful); *Baumrind v. Ewing*, 279 SE2d 359 (South Carolina, 1981) (applying 18 U.S.C. § 2511); *Bachlet v. State*, 641 P.2d 200, 208 (Ala. Ct. App. 1997) (one-party taping permissible); *Commonwealth v. Douglas*, 354 Mass. 212, 221-22, 236 N.E.2d 865, 871-72 (1968) (person who speaks incriminating words over the telephone runs the risk that his words may be recorded by his listener); *State v. Ahmadjian*, 432 A.2d 1070, 1081 (R.I. Sup. Ct. 1981) (one-party tapping permissible); *Dickerson v. Raphael*, 222 Mich. App. 185, 198-99, 564 N.W.2d 85, 91 (1997).

217. *See* Fl. Stat. Ann. §§ 934.03 to 934.09; Mont. Code Ann. § 45-8-213; N.H. Rev. Stat. Ann. § 570.A:2; Or. Rev. Stat. §§ 165.540, 165. 543; Pa. Cons. Stat. Ann. §§ 5703, 5725; Wash. Rev. Code Ann. § 9.73.030; Maryland Stat. Ann. § 10-402.

218. *See State v. Inciarrano*, 473 So2d 1272, 1275 (Fla. Sup. Ct. 1985) (no expectation of privacy under the circumstances); *Agnew v. Dupler*, 717 A.2d 519, 522-523 (Pa. 1998) (requirement to demonstrate expectation of privacy); *Commonwealth v. Goldberg*, 224 A.2d 91 (Pa. Sup. 1966) (superceded by statute); *State v. Forrester*, 587 P.2d 179 (1978) (tape recording permissible when one-party consents and there are unlawful requests or demands made over the phone). *See also Moore v. Teflon*, 589 F2d 959, 966 (9th Cir. 1978) (Congress did not intend to prohibit recording a conversation when the purpose of the conversation is to preserve evidence of extortion); *Park v. El Paso Board of Realtors*, 764 F2d 1053, 1066 (5th Cir. 1985) ("Where evidence is obtained in violation, at most, of a local telephone tariff, the public interest in deterrence does not outweigh the benefit of providing the factfinder with all of the relevant testimony."); *Additionally*, in *Meredith v. Gavin*, 446 F2d 794, 799 (8th Cir. 1971), the U.S. Court of Appeals for the Eigth Circuit explained why one-party taping in order to preserve material evidence was justifiable to preserve material evidence of potential perjury:

Surely it could not be contended that the plaintiff was free to make one statement to the defendant Gavin over the phone, and then to make an entirely different one in the compensation proceedings, without fear of contradiction. The defendant Gavin was clearly competent to testify to the contents of the phone conversation, and we think that preserving the contents of the conversation on the recording in the circumstances of this case was not the sort of "injurious act" which the statute condemns.

219. 891 F.2d 432 (2nd Cir. 1989).

220. *Id.* at 436-37.

221. *Id.* at 438 (dissenting opinion of J. Van Graafeiland).

222. *Haney v. North American Car Corp.*, 81-SWDA-1, R. D&O of ALJ (August 10, 1981), *aff'd* by SOL (June 30, 1982).

223. 91-ERA-1/11, D&O of Remand by SOL, at 13 (November 20, 1995). *Accord., Melendez v. Exxon*, 93-ERA-6, D&O of ARB, at 12 (July 14, 2000)

224. *Goggin Truck Line Co., supra.*

225. NRC Public Document Room, Commission Correspondence File, 930B160265/930714.

226. *Id.*

227. *Pickering v. Board of Education*, 391 U.S. 563 (1968).

228. *U.S. v. NTEU*, 513 U.S. 454 (1995); *Sanjour v. EPA*, 56 F.3d 85 (D.C. Cir. 1995) (*en banc*).

229. *Jacobs v. Schiffer*, 204 F.3d 259 (D.C. Cir. 2000); *Matin v. Lauer*, 686 F.2d 24 (D.C. Cir. 1982).

230. *Donovan v. R. D. Anderson Constr. Co.*, 552 F. Supp. 249, 253 (D. Kan. 1982).

231. *Carter v. Electrical District No. 2*, 92-TSC-11, D&O of Remand by SOL, at 21 (July 26, 1995) (collecting cases) (holding that employer criticism of employee for "distributing false information" in the press did not justify adverse action). *See also Trimmer v. LANL*, 93-CAA-9/55, D&O of ARB, at 2-3 (May 8, 1997).

232. *Dunlop v. Hanover Shoe Farms*, 441 F. Supp. 385, 388 (M.D. Pa. 1976) (complaint to attorney covered as hiring attorney constituted first step in the exercise of protected rights). *Accord., Harrison v. Stone & Webster Group*, 93-ERA-44, D&O of SOL, at 12 (August 22, 1995).

233. S. Rep. 848, 95th Cong., 2nd Sess., *reprinted in* 1978 U.S. Code Cong. & Admin. News 7303-7304.

234. 81-ERA-6, slip op. of ALJ, at 2 15-16 (July 7, 1981), *aff'd, Consolidated Edison Co. of N.Y. v. Donovan*, 673 F.2d 61 (2nd Cir. 1982).

235. 42 U.S.C. § 6971(a); 33 U.S.C. § 1367(a); and 42 U.S.C. § 9610(a).

236. 80-WPCA-1, slip op. of ALJ, at 10-11 (July 11, 1980), adopted by SOL (July 28, 1980).

237. *Donovan v. R. D. Andersen Constr. Co.*, 552 F. Supp. 249 (D. Kan. 1982) (contact with the news media is protected activity under OSHA); *Nunn v. Duke Power Co.*, 84-ERA-27, D&O of Remand by Deputy SOL, at 13 (July 30, 1987) (contact with citizen intervener protected).

238. *Crosby v. Hughes Aircraft Co.*, 85-TSC-2, D&O of SOL, at 22-23 (August 17, 1993).

239. *Pillow v. Bechtel Construction, Inc., supra*, D&O of Remand by SOL, at 11; *Mandreger v. Detroit Edison Co.*, 88-ERA-17, D&O of SOL, at 13 (March 30, 1994); *Simon v. Simmons Industries, Inc.*, 87-TSC-2, D&O of SOL, at 4, (April 4, 1994) *citing Legutko v. Local 816, International Brotherhood of Teamsters*, 606 F. Supp. 352, 358-359 (E.D. N.Y. 1985), *aff'd* (2nd Cir. 1988).

240. *Simon v. Simmons Industries, Inc., supra.*

241. *Diaz-Robainas v. FP&L*, 92-ERA-10, D&O of Remand by SOL, at 14 (January 19, 1996).

242. *Hoffman v. W. Max Bossert*, 94-CAA-4, D&O of Remand by SOL, at 8 (September 19, 1995).

243. *Dobreuenaski v. Associated Universities, Inc.*, 96-ERA-44, D&O of ARB, at 9 (June 18, 1998).

244. *Simon v. Simmons Industries, Inc., supra*, at 6.

245. *Higgins v. Pascack Valley Hosp.*, 730 A.2d 327 (N.J. 1999) (collecting state authorities).

246. *Harrison v. Stone & Webster, supra; Stone & Webster v. Herman*, 115 F.3d 1568, 1574-1575 (11th Cir. 1997).

247. *Donovan v. Diplomat Envelope Corp.*, 587 F. Supp. 1417, 1424 (E.D. N.Y. 1984).

248. *Reich v. Hoy Shoe, Inc.*, 32 F.3d 361, 368 (8th Cir. 1994); *Smith v. ESICORP, Inc., supra*, at 9-10.

249. *Willy v. Coastal Corp.*, 85-CAA-1, SOL D&O, at 13-14 (June 1, 1994). *Accord., Ass't. Secretary v. S&S Sand & Gravel, Inc.*, 92-STA-30, D&O of SOL, at 15 (February 5, 1993); *Brock v. Richardson*, 812 F.2d 121, 123-125 (3rd Cir. 1987).

250. *Id. at* 125.

251. *Marshall v. Georgia Southwestern College*, 489 F. Supp. 1322, 1331 (M.D. Georgia, 1980), *aff'd*, 765 F.2d 1026, 1037-1038 (11th Cir. 1985). *Marshall* was cited by the SOL in *Assistant Secretary v. S&S Sand & Gravel, Inc., supra. Accord., Adler v. Pataki*, 185 F.3d 35 (2nd Cir. 1999).

252. *Stack v. Preston Trucking Co.*, 86-STA-22, D&O of SOL, at 3 (February 26, 1987).

253. *Hochstadt v. Worcester Foundation for Experimental Biology*, 545 F.2d 222 (1st Cir. 1976); *EEOC v. Crown Zellerbach Corp.*, 720 F.2d 1008 (9th Cir. 1983); *Wrighten v. Metropolitan Hospitals, Inc.*, 726 F.2d 1346 (9th Cir. 1984).

254. *Pettway v. American Cast Iron Pipe Co.*, 411 F.2d 998 (5th Cir. 1969).

255. *Parker v. Baltimore and O.R. Co.*, 652 F.2d 1012, 1020 (D.C. Cir. 1981).

256. *See Linn v. United Plant Guard, Workers of America*, 383 U.S. 53, 62 (1966); *Montefiore Hospital and Medical Center v. NLRB*, 621 F.2d 510, 517 (2nd Cir. 1980).

257. *Linn*, at 62, *quoting from New York Times v. Sullivan*, 376 U.S. 254 (1964).

258. *NLRB v. Owners Maintenance Corp.*, 581 F.2d 44, 50 (2nd Cir. 1978).

259. *NLRB v. A. Lasaponara Sons, Inc.*, 541 F.2d 992, 998 (2nd Cir. 1976).

260. *American Telephone & Telegraph Co. v. NLRB*, 521 F.2d 1159, 1161 (2nd Cir. 1975).

261. *NLRB v. Cement Transport, Inc.*, 490 F.2d 1024, 1030 (6th Cir. 1974), *cert. denied*, 419 U.S. 828 (1974).

262. *NLRB v. Thor Power Tool Co.*, 351 F.2d 584, 587 (7th Cir. 1965); *Crown Central v. NLRB*, 430 F.2d 724, 726 n. 3 (5th Cir. 1970); *Coors Container Co. v. NLRB*, 628 F.2d 1283, 1285 (10th Cir. 1980).

263. *Old Dominion, etc., v. Austin*, 418 U.S. 264, 268 (1974).

264. *See Pickering v. Board of Education*, 391 U.S. 563, 573 (1968).

265. *Kenneway v. Matlack, Inc.*, 88-STA-20, D&O of SOL, at 6-7, 10-13 (June 15, 1989).

266. *Housing Works, Inc. v. City of New York*, 72 F. Supp.2d 402 (S.D. N.Y., 1999), *quoting Terminiello v. Chicago*, 337 U.S. 1, 4 (1949).

267. *Housing Works, Inc., quoting New York Times v. Sullivan*, 376 U.S. 254, 270-273 (1964).

268. *Kubicko v. Ogden Logistics Services*, 181 F.3d 544 (4th Cir, 1999).

269. *Holtzclaw v. SOL*, 172 F.3d 872 (Table), at 6 (unpublished, 6th Cir. 1999).

270. *American Nuclear Resources, Inc. v. DOL*, 134 F.3d 1292, 1295 (6th Cir. 1998).

271. *See generally Linn, supra*, at 66; *NLRB v. Washington Aluminum Co.*, 370 U.S. 9, 17 (1962); *Wrighten v. Metropolitan Hosps., Inc.*, 726 F.2d 1346, 1355 (9th Cir. 1984); *Hochstadt v. Worcester Found.*, 545 F.2d 222 (1st Cir. 1976).

272. *Parker v. Baltimore & O.R. Co., supra*.

273. *Whatley v. Met. Atlanta Rapid Transit*, 632 F.2d 1325, 1327 (5th Cir. 1980).

274. *Unt v. Aerospace Corp.*, 765 F.2d 1440, 1446 (9th Cir. 1985).

275. *Hochstadt v. Worcester Foundation, Etc.*, 545 F.2d 222, 228 (1st Cir. 1976).

276. *EEOC v. Crown Zellerbach Corp.*, 720 F.2d 1008, 1014-15 (9th Cir. 1983).

277. *Kenneway v. Matlock, Inc., supra*, at 6-7.

278. *Dunham v. Brock*, 794 F.2d 1037 (5th Cir. 1986).

279. 794 F.2d at 1041. *See also Mackowiak, supra*, at 1164-1165.

280. *Melendez, supra*, at 26. *See also NLRB v. Florida Medical Center*, 576 F.2d 666 (5th Cir. 1978); *Kenneway v. Matlock, Inc., supra*, at 2.

281. *Kansas Gas & Elec. Co. v. Brock*, 780 F.2d 1505, 1507 (10th Cir. 1985). *See also Mackowiak, v. University Nuclear Systems, Inc.*, 82-ERA-8, D&O of Remand by ALJ, at 7 (July 25, 1986).

282. *Timmons v. Franklin Electric Cooperative*, 97-SWD-2, D&O of ARB, at 6 (December 1, 1998) (collecting cases).

283. *Id.*, *citing Smith v. Monsanto Chem. Co.*, 770 F.2d 719, 723 n. 3 (8th Cir. 1985) and *Kahn v. SOL*, 64 F.3d 271, 279 (7th Cir. 1995).

284. *Id.*

285. *Passaic Valley Sewerage Commissioners v. DOL*, 992 F.2d 474 (3rd Cir. 1993) (personality problem resulted from whistleblowing); *Mackowiak v. University Nuclear Systems, Inc.*, 735 F.2d 1159 (9th Cir. 1984) (complaint about "bad attitude" arose from persistent protected activity); *Pogue v. DOL*, 940 F.2d 1287, 1290 (9th Cir. 1991) (so-called insubordinate behavior resulted from whistleblowing). *See Dodd v. Polysar Latex*, 88-SWD-4, D&O of SOL, at 15-17 (September 22, 1994) (alleged "insubordinate and negative" behavior did not "upset the balance . . . between protected activity and shop discipline"); *Martin v. Department of the Army*, 93-SDW-1, D&O of Remand by SOL, at 6-7 (July 13, 1995) (alleged unprofessional conduct was not "indefensible under the circumstances").

286. *Jarvis v. Battle Pacific Northwest*, 97-ERA-15, D&O of ARB, at 9, n. 7 (August 27, 1998). *Accord.*, *Carter v. Electrical District No. 2*, 92-TSC-11, D&O of Remand by SOL, at 19-20 (July 26, 1995) (disruption caused by the method employee used to "deliver" his whistleblower speech, combined with the employee's "spontaneous" and "intemperate reactions" were not "indefensible under the circumstances" and remained protected).

287. *Carter v. Electrical District No. 2*, *supra*, at 16.

288. 91-TSC-5, D&O of SOL, at 14 (October 6, 1992)

289. *Blake v. Hatfield Electric Co.*, 87-ERA-4, D&O of SOL, at 9-10 (January 22, 1992).

290. 91-TSC-1, D&O of SOL, at 6-7 (January 13, 1993).

291. *Carter v. Electrical District No. 2*, *supra*, at 20-21.

292. *Lockert v. DOL*, 867 F.2d 513, 519 (9th Cir. 1989).

293. *Office of Federal Contract Compliance Programs v. The Cleveland Clinic Foundation*, 91-OFC-20, D&O of ARB, at 4 n. 6 (July 17, 1996). A major opposition clause case developed under Title VII was *Hochstadt v. Worcester Foundation*, 545 F.2d 222 (1st Cir. 1976). Although this case established many of the principles used in evacuating an "opposition clause" case, the facts in that case are considered "exceptional," and many courts read *Hochstadt* "narrowly lest legitimate activism by employees asserting civil rights be chilled." *Wrighten v. Metropolitan Hospitals, Inc.*, 726 F.2d 1346, 1355 (9th Cir. 1984).

294. *O'Day v. McDonnell Douglas*, 79 F.3d 756, 764 (9th Cir. 1996).

295. *See Laughlin v. Metropolitan Washington Airports Authority*, 149 F.3d 253, 259 n. 3 (4th Cir. 1998) ("It is black letter law that illegal actions are not protected activity under Title VII").

296. *Jefferies v. Harris County Community Action*, 615 F.2d 1025, 1036 (5th Cir. 1980).

297. *O'Day v. McDonnell Douglas*, *supra*, at 763-64. *Accord.*, *Laughlin v. Metropolitan Washington Airports Authority*, *supra*, at 260.

298. 132 F.3d 442, 445-446 (8th Cir. 1998).

299. *Id.* at 446. *See also Grant v. Hazelett Strip-Casting Corp.*, 880 F.2d 1564, 1570 (2nd Cir. 1989) (upholding jury verdict protecting employee who refused to return an incriminating document).

300. In *Whirlpool Corp. v. Marshall*, 445 U.S. 1, 10-11 (1980), the U.S. Supreme Court upheld the legality of OSHA regulations that established a right to refuse work in limited situations where the risk of injury or death is imminent:

Such circumstances will probably not often occur, but such a situation may arise when (1) the employee is ordered by his employer to work under conditions that the employee reasonably believes pose an imminent risk of death or serious bodily injury, and (2) the employee has reason to believe that there is not sufficient time or opportunity either to seek effective redress from his employer or to apprize OSHA of the danger.

450 U.S. at 10-11. *See also Gateway Coal Co. v. United Mine Workers of America*, 414 U.S. 368 (1974), where the Court held that a work stoppage called solely to protect employees from immediate danger is authorized by Section 502 of the Labor Management Relations Act, 29 U.S.C. 143. The right to refuse hazardous work was also recognized under the Federal Mine Safety Act, *Miller v. Fed. Mine Saf. Rev. Comm'n.*, 687 F.2d 194 (7th Cir. 1982), and the Surface Transportation Act, *Somerson v. Yellow Freight System, Inc.*, 98-STA-9, D&O of ARB, at 12 n. 11 (February 18, 1999) (collecting cases concerning refusal to drive due to fatigue or illness); *Sutherland v. Spray Systems*, 95-CAA-1, D&O of SOL, at 4 (February 26, 1996) (work refusal protected under Clean Air Act). Work refusals are also permitted under the Atomic Energy Act's whistleblower law. *See Eltzroth v. Amersham Medi-Physics, Inc.*, 97-ERA-31, D&O of ARB, at 5-6 (April 15, 1999), and the dissenting opinion filed by ARB member Brown, at 12-13, 22-25. Under the nuclear and environmental laws, a work refusal is permitted if an employee has a "good faith, reasonable belief that working conditions are unsafe or unhealthful. Whether the belief is reasonable depends on the knowledge available to a reasonable [person] in the circumstances with the employee's training and experience." *Pennsylvania v. Catalytic, Inc.*, 83-ERA-2, D&O of SOL, at 6-7 (January 13, 1984) (nuclear safety). *Accord., Crow v. Noble Roman's, Inc.*, 95-CAA-8, D&O of SOL, at 2 (February 26, 1996) (Clean Air Act).

301. Examples of such cases are *Brock v. Roadway Express, Inc.*, 481 U.S. 252, 255 (1987) (protecting employee under STAA for "refusing to operate a motor vehicle that does not comply with applicable state and federal safety regulations"); *Petermann v. International Brotherhood of Teamsters Local 396*, 174 Cal. App. 2d 184, 344 P.2d 25 (1959) (for refusing to commit perjury); *Tameny v. Atlantic Richfield Co.*, 27 Cal.3d 167, 610 P.2d 1330, 164 Cal.Rptr. 839 (1980) (for refusing to engage in price-fixing); *Harless v. First National Bank*, 246 S.E.2d 270 (W.Va. 1978) (for refusing to violate a consumer credit code); *O'Sullivan v. Mallon*, 160 N.J. Super. 416, 390 A.2d 149 (1978) (for refusing to practice medicine without a license); *LeBlanc v. Fogleman Truck Lines, Inc.*, 89-STA-8, D&O of Remand by SOL, at 9 (December 20, 1989) (refusal to work based on commission of federal violation). Under the amended nuclear whistleblower statute, an employee was given the right to refuse to

"engage in any practice made unlawful" under the Atomic Energy Act. 42 U.S.C. § 5851(a)(1)(B) (1999); *Harrison v. Stone & Webster, supra*, at 12-13.

302. *Stockdill v. Catalytic Industrial Maintenance*, 90-ERA-43, D&O of SOL, at 3 (1996) (collecting cases under ERA).

303. 92-ERA-10, D&O of Remand by SOL, at 8 (January 19, 1996).

304. *Id.* at 9 n. 6 ("While it might have been more prudent for Diaz-Robainas to comply with the order and then file his claim under the ERA, his assumption of the risk that he would be unable to prove discriminatory motivation in ordering the evaluation does not absolve Florida Power from wrongdoing in imposing the order in violation of the ERA").

305. *Oliver v. Hydro-Vac Services, Inc.*, 91-SWD-1, D&O of Remand by SOL, at 9 (November 1, 1995) (environmental whistleblower law); *Allum v. Valley Bank of Nevada*, 970 P.2d 1062, 1068 (Nev. 1998) (state public policy tort); *Yellow Freight System, Inc. v. Martin*, 954 F.2d 353, 357 (6th Cir. 1992) (STA whistleblower law). *But see Ass't SOL v. West Bank Containers*, 98-STA-30, D&O of ARB, at 10-14 (April 28, 2000) (holding that more than "categorical statements" demonstrating the existence of a real safety issue are necessary in order for an employee to prove a complaint was in fact safety related).

306. *Ashcraft v. Univ. of Cincinnati*, 83-ERA-7, slip op. of ALJ, at 9 (July 1, 1983), adopted by SOL, slip op. at, 10 (November 1, 1984). *See also* the following Title VII cases: *Gifford v. Atchison, Topeka & Santa Fe Ry. Co.*, 685 F.2d 1149, 1156-1157 (9th Cir. 1982); *Peyne v. McLemore's Wholesale & Retail Stores*, 654 F.2d 1130, 1137-1140 (5th Cir. 1981), which used a "reasonable belief" test; *Womack v. Munson*, 619 F.2d 1292, 1298 (8th Cir. 1980).

307. *Johnson v. Oak Ridge Operations Office*, 95-CAA-20/21/22, D&O of ARB, at 8 (September 30, 1999) ("It is well settled that protected activities under the environmental whistleblower provisions are limited to those which are grounded in conditions constituting reasonably perceived violations of the environmental statutes") (collecting cases).

308. *Crosier v. Westinghouse Hanford Co.*, 92-CAA-3, SOL D&O, at 6 (January 12, 1994) ("a complainant under an employee protection provision need not prove an actual violation of the underlying statute"); *Yellow Freight System, Inc. v. Martin, supra*, ("protection is not dependent upon whether [the employee] was *actually* successful in proving a violation of a federal safety provision. The primary consideration is not the outcome of the underlying grievance hearing, but whether the proceeding is based upon possible safety violations").

309. *McCafferty v. Centerior Energy*, 96-ERA-6, Order Denying Stay by ARB, at 4 (October 16, 1996).

310. *Keene v. Ebasco Constructors, Inc.*, 95-ERA-4, D&O of Remand by ARB, at 8 (February 19, 1997) ("An employee's reasonable belief that his employer is violating the ERA's requirements is sufficient, irrespective of after-the-fact determinations regarding the correctness of the employee's belief").

311. *Pettway v. American Cast Iron Pipe Co.*, 411 F.2d 998 (5th Cir. 1969).

312. 700 F.2d 281, 286 (6th Cir. 1983).

313. 405 U.S. 117, 122 (1972).

314. *DeFord v. Secretary of Labor*, 700 F.2d 281, 286 (6th Cir. 1983). *Cf. NLRB v. Mount Desert Island Hosp.*, 695 F.2d 634, 638 (5th Cir. 1984) (employer's action construed broadly to prevent intimidation of others in exercise of their rights); *John Hancock Mutual Life Ins. Co. v. NLRB*, 191 F.2d 483, 485 (D.C. Cir. 1951) (broad construction necessary to prevent intimidation of prospective complainants and witnesses).

315. H.R. Rep. No. 294, 95th Cong., 2nd Sess., *reprinted in* 1977 U.S. Code Cong. & Admin. News 1077.

316. *Goldstein v. EBASCO Constr., Inc.*, 86-ERA-36, recommended D&O of ALJ, at 11 (March 3, 1988); *Sartain v. Bechtel Constr. Corp.*, 87-ERA-37, recommended D&O of ALJ, at 13 (January 14, 1988).

317. 85-WPC-2, D&O of SOL (March 13, 1992), *aff'd*, 992 F.2d 474 (3rd Cir. 1993).

318. *Id.* at 19-20.

319. *Id.* The SOL has also held that employees who are motived by "self-gain" are fully protected:

The Secretary has held that where the complainant has a reasonable belief that the respondent is violating the law, other motives he may have for engaging in protected activity are irrelevant. The purpose of the whistleblower statutes is to encourage employees to come forward with complaints of health hazards so that remedial action may be taken, and if such a course of action furthers the employee's own selfish agenda, so be it. This approach is consistent with case law under other federal statutes.

Oliver v. Hydro-Vac Services, Inc., *supra*, at 14 (internal quotations and citations omitted). *Accord.*, *Nichols v. Gordon Trucking, Inc.*, 97-STA-2, D&O of ARB, at 1 (July 17, 1997) ("A complainant's motivation in making safety complaints has no bearing on whether the complaints are protected"); *Reid v. Scientech, Inc.*, 99-ERA-20, at 1314 (January 28, 2000).

320. 85-WPC-2 at 20.

321. 992 F.2d 474, 478 (3rd Cir. 1993).

322. *Id.* at 479.

323. *In re Five Star Products*, 38 NRC 169, slip op. at 16 n. 6 (October 21, 1993).

324. *Crosby v. Hughes Aircraft Co.*, 85-TSC-2, D&O of SOL, at 26 (August 17, 1993).

325. *American Nuclear Resources, Inc. v. DOL*, 134 F.3d 1292, 1295 (6th Cir. 1998).

326. *Id.* at 1295.

327. *Landers v. Commonwealth-Lord Joint Venture*, 83-ERA-5, slip op. of ALJ, at 3 (May 11, 1983), adopted by SOL (September 9, 1983), *stay denied*, *Commonwealth-Lord Joint Venture v. Donovan*, 724 F.2d 67 (7th Cir. 1983).

328. *Keene v. EBASCO Constructors, Inc.*, *supra*, at 5 ("Most significantly, [the employer] did in fact commit the falsification exactly as alleged by [the whistleblower] and attempted to conceal this wrongdoing . . . all of which

undermines the credibility of [the employer] and lends even more credence to [the whistleblower's] account").

329. *Timmons v. Mattingly Testing Services*, 95-ERA-40, D&O of Remand by ARB, p12 (June 21, 1996) (collecting cases).

330. *U.S. v. Glover*, 170 F.3d 411, 413 (4th Cir. 1999).

331. *Learned v. City of Bellevue*, 860 F.2d 928, 932 (9th Cir. 1988).

332. *U.S. v. Glover, supra*, at 414, *quoting Robinson v. Shell Oil Co.*, 519 U.S. 337 (1997).

333. *Id. Accord., Merritt v. Dillard Paper Co.*, 120 F.3d 1181 (11th Cir. 1997).

334. *Merritt, supra.*

335. *U.S. Postal Service v. Aikens*, 460 U.S. 711, 715 (1983) (the main question at a hearing is whether a plaintiff can prove that the defendant "intentionally discriminated against" him or her); *Carroll v. Bechtel Power Corp.*, 91-ERA-46, D&O of SOL, at 12 (February 15, 1995) (After a case is heard on the merits the "question" that must be resolved is "whether [the employee] proved by a preponderance of the evidence that [the employer] retaliated against him for his alleged safety complaints").

336. *Kane v. Krebser*, 44 F. Supp.2d 542, 547 (S.D. N.Y. 1999).

337. *Tyler v. Bethlehem Steel*, 958 F.2d 1175, 1183-1184 (2nd Cir. 1992) (collecting cases setting forth the various definitions of "direct evidence").

338. *Merritt v. Dillard Paper Co. supra*, at 1189.

339. *Id.* at 1189-1190, *quoting Caban-Wheeler v. Elsea*, 904 F.2d 1549, 1555 (11th Cir. 1990) (collecting cases finding direct evidence of discrimination).

340. *Talbert v. Washington Public Power Supply*, 93-ERA-35, D&O of ARB, at 4 (September 27, 1996). *Accord., Stacks v. Southwestern Bell*, 996 F.2d 200, 202 (8th Cir. 1993).

341. *Barbano v. Madison County*, 922 F.2d 139, 145 (2nd Cir. 1990).

342. *Jackson v. Harvard University*, 900 F.2d 464, 467 (1st Cir. 1990).

343. *Simas v. First Citizens Federal Credit Union*, 170 F.3d 37, 48 (1st Cir. 1999).

344. *Aka v. Washington Hospital Center*, 156 F.3d 1284, 1292 (D.C. Cir. 1998) (*en banc*). *Accord., U.S. Postal Service v. Aikens*, 460 U.S. 711, 714 n. 3, 717 (1983).

345. *Simas v. First Citizens Federal Credit Union, supra.*

346. *Blake v. Hatfield Electric Co.*, 87-ERA-4, D&O of SOL, at 5 (January 22, 1991).

347. *Id.* at 5-6.

348. *Pillow v. Bechtel Constructions, Inc., supra*, at 13.

349. *McMahan v. Calif. Water Quality Control Bd.*, 90-WPC- 1, D&O of SOL, at 4 (July 16, 1993).

350. *Mandreger v. Detroit Edison Co.*, 88-ERA-17, D&O of SOL, at 19 (March 30, 1994).

351. *Stone & Webster v. Herman, supra*, at 1574.

352. *See Mackowiak v. University Nuclear Systems*, 735 F.2d 1159, 1164 (9th Cir. 1984) ("the employer is a wrongdoer; he has acted out of a motive

that is declared illegitimate by the statute. It is fair that they bear the risk that the influence of legal and illegal motives cannot be separated because . . . the risk was created by his own wrongdoing") (citations and internal quotations omitted). *Accord., Caimano v. Brink's Incorporated,* 95-STA-4, D&O of Remand by SOL, at 23-24 (January 26, 1996) ("Where there is direct evidence that the adverse action is motivated, at least in part, by the protected activity, the respondent may avoid liability only by establishing that it would have taken the adverse action in the absence of the protected activity").

353. *Simas v. First Citizens Federal Credit Union,* 170 F.3d 37, 48 (1st Cir. 1999) ("Normally, employers do not leave behind direct evidence of their discriminatory animus . . . Therefore, generally the plaintiff-employee must make do with circumstantial evidence, leaving it to the jury whether to infer from the nature of the materially adverse employment conditions that the defendant-employer harbored a retaliatory animus").

354. *Housing Works, Inc. v. City of New York,* 72 F. Supp.2d 402, 422 (S.D. N.Y. 1999), *citing to Ramseur v. Chase Manhattan Bank,* 865 F.2d 460 (2nd Cir. 1989) ("employers are rarely so cooperative as to include a notation . . . that their actions are motivated by factors expressly forbidden by law").

355. *U.S. Postal Service v. Aikens, supra,* at 714 n. 3, 717.

356. *Donovan v. Zimmer America, Inc.,* 557 F. Supp. 642, 651 (D. S.C. 1982), *quoting from Polynesian Cultural Center, Inc. v. NLRB,* 582 F.2d 467, 473 (9th Cir. 1978).

357. 629 F.2d 563, 566 (8th Cir. 1980), *cert. denied,* 450 U.S. 1040 (1981). *See also Couty v. Dole,* 886 F.2d 147, 148 (8th Cir. 1989) (holding that "temporal proximity is sufficient as a matter of law" to establish discriminatory motive).

358. *See also Mackowiak v. University Nuclear Systems, Inc.,* 735 F.2d 1159, 1162 (9th Cir. 1984); *Zoll v. Eastern Allamkee Community School Dist.,* 588 F.2d 236, 250 (8th Cir. 1978); *Rutherford v. American Bank of Commerce,* 565 F.2d 1162, 1164 (10th Cir. 1977); *Ertel v. Giroux Bros. Transp., Inc.,* 88 STA-24 D&O of SOL, at 24 (February 16, 1989).

359. 84-ERA-9-12, D&O of Remand by SOL, slip op., at 13-14 (March 12, 1986).

360. *Timmons v. Mattingly Testing Services,* 95-ERA-40, D&O of Remand by ARB, at 10 (June 21, 1996).

361. *Reeves v. Sanderson Plumbing,* 120 S. Ct. 2097, 2108 (2000).

362. According to *American Jurisprudence (2nd), Proof of Facts,* "Proof of Retaliatory Termination," Section 7-1, the following general categories of facts or circumstances have been used to establish a reasonable inference of discriminatory motive:

1. employer's hostile attitude toward matter underlying employee's protected conduct;

2. employer's knowledge of protected conduct;

3. nature of protected conduct;

4. special conditions of employment following protected conduct leading up to discharge;

5. disparate treatment of discharged employee prior to protected conduct;

6. previous expressions of satisfaction with work record;

7. disparate treatment of similarly situated employees;

8. termination procedure;

9. timing of discharge; and

10. threats of retaliation against other employees for similar conduct.

363. *Ellis Fischel State Cancer Hosp. v. Marshall* 629 F. 2d 563, 566 (8th Cir. 1980); *Keene v. EBASCO Constructors, Inc., supra,* at 10; *Cram v. Pullman-Higgins Co.,* 84-ERA-17, slip op. of ALJ, at 10 (July 24, 1984), adopted in part by SOL (January 14, 1985); *Hedden v. Conam Inspection Co.,* 82-ERA-3, slip op. of ALJ, at 4 (January 22, 1983), adopted in part by SOL (June 30, 1983). *See also Brown & Root-Northrop,* 174 NLRB 1048, 1050-1051 (1969); *DeFord v. TVA,* 81-ERA-1, slip op. of ALJ, at 6 (January 7, 1981), adopted in part by SOL (March 4, 1981), *aff'd, DeFord v. Secretary of Labor,* 700 F.2d 281 (6th Cir. 1983); *Richter v. Ellis Fischel State Cancer Hosp.,* 79-ERA-1, slip op. of ALJ, at 2-4 (July 6, 1979), adopted by SOL (August 10, 1979).

364. *DeFord v. TVA,* at 6. *See also Landers v. Commonwealth-Lord Joint Venture,* 83-ERA-5, slip op. of ALJ, at 12 (May 11, 1983), adopted by SOL (September 9, 1983), *stay denied, Commonwealth-Lord Joint Venture v. Donovan,* 724 F.2d 67 (7th Cir. 1983).

365. *Landers v. Commonwealth-Lord Joint Venture,* at 12; *Cotter v. Consolidated Edison Co. of N.Y.,* 81-ERA-6, slip op. of ALJ, at 17 (July 7, 1981), adopted by SOL (November 5, 1981), *aff'd, Consolidated Edison Co. of N.Y. v. Donovan,* 673 F.2d 61 (2nd Cir. 1982).

366. *Diaz-Robainas v. FP&L,* 92-ERA-10, D&O of Remand by SOL, at 18 (January 19, 1996).

367. *Moon v. Transportation Drivers, Inc.,* 836 F.2d 226, 229 (6th Cir. 1987); *Couty v. Dole,* 886 F.2d 147, 148 (8th Cir. 1989); *Creekmore v. ABB Power Systems,* 93-ERA-24, D&O of Remand by SOL, at 11 (February 14, 1996); *Wells v. Kansas Gas & Elec. Co.,* 83-ERA-12, slip op., at 6-7 (February 27, 1984), adopted by SOL (June 14, 1984); *Landers v. Commonwealth-Lord Joint Venture, supra; Richter v. Ellis Fischel State Cancer Hosp., supra,* at 3-4. *See also Jim Causley Pontiac v. NLRB,* 620 F.2d 122, 125 (6th Cir. 1980); *Womack v. Munson,* 619 F.2d 1292, 1296 (8th Cir. 1980); *Melchi v. Burns Int'l. Security Servs., Inc.,* 597 F. Supp. 575, 584 (E.D. Mich. 1984); *McCarthy v. Cortland County Community Actions Program,* 487 F. Supp. 333, 340 (N.D. N.Y. 1980); *G & S Metal Prods. Co.,* 199 NLRB 705, 708 (1972), *enforced,* 489 F.2d 441 (6th Cir. 1973). An employee can establish a *prima facie* case of discriminatory

motive by showing that the employee engaged in protected activity and suffered from an adverse action "shortly thereafter." *Priest v. Baldwin Assocs.*, 84-ERA-30, decision of SOL, slip op., at 10 (June 11, 1986).

368. *Wells v. Kansas Gas & Elec. Co.*, *supra*, slip op. of ALJ, at 15; *Hedden v. Conam Inspection Co.*, *supra*, slip op. of ALJ, at 3; *Haney v. North American Car Corp.*, 81-SVTDA-1, slip op. of ALJ, at 17-18 (August 10, 1981), supplemental decision and order (December 15, 1981), adopted by SOL (June 30, 1982).

369. *Johnson v. Old Dominion Security*, 86-CAA-3/4/5, D&O of SOL, at 18 (May 29, 1991).

370. *Simmons v. APS*, 93-ERA-5, D&O of Remand by SOL, at 10 (May 9, 1995).

371. *Hedden v. Conam Inspection Co.*, *supra*, slip op. of ALJ at 4-5; *Cram v. Pullman-Higgins Co.*, 84-ERA-17, slip op. of ALJ, at 16.

372. *Cram v. Pullman-Higgins Co.*; *Fischer v. Town of Steilacoom*, 83-WPC-2, slip op. of ALJ, at 9 (May 2, 1983), settlement approved by SOL (August 22, 1983). *See also NLRB v. Wright Line, A Div. of Wright Line*, 662 F.2d 899, 907-908 (1st Cir. 1981), *cert. denied*, 455 U.S. 989 (1982); *Hedden v. Conam Inspection Co.*, slip op. of ALJ at 4.

373. *Landers v. Commonwealth-Lord Joint Venture*, *supra*. *See also Kendall Co.*, 188 NLRB 805, 809 (1971).

374. *Wells v. Kansas Gas & Elec. Co.*, *supra*, at 11-12. *See also Viracon, Inc. v. NLRB*, 736 F.2d 1188, 1192 (7th Cir. 1984); *M & S Steel Co.*, 148 NLRB 789, 795 (1964), *enforced*, 353 F.2d 80 (5th Cir. 1965).

375. *Cram v. Pullman-Higgins Co.*, *supra*, slip op. of ALJ, at 10.

376. *Lewis Grocer Co. v. Holloway*, 874 F.2d 1008 (5th Cir. 1989). *See also G & S Metal Prods. Co.*, *supra*; *Wedderspoon v. Milligan*, 80-WPC-1, slip op. of ALJ, at 9-10 (July 11, 1980), adopted by SOL (July 28, 1980).

377. *Blake v. Hatfield Elec. Co.*, *supra*, recommended decision of ALJ, at 22 (August 13, 1987); *Fischer v. Town of Steilacoom*, *supra*, slip op. of ALJ, at 8-9; *Haney v. North Am. Car Corp.*, *supra*, slip op. of ALJ, at 17.

378. *Fischer*, slip op. of ALJ, at 18; *Haney*, slip op. of ALJ, at 17.

379. *Bechtel Construction v. SOL*, 50 F.3d 926, 934, 935 (11th Cir. 1995); *Keene v. EBASCO Constructors, Inc.*, 95-ERA-4, D&O of Remand by ARB, at 10 (February 19, 1997).

380. *Haney*, slip op. of ALJ at 18; *DeFord v. TVA*, *supra*, slip op. of ALJ, at 6.

381. *Murphy v. Consolidation Coal Co.*, 83-ERA-4, slip op. of ALJ, at 16 (August 2, 1983), settlement approved by SOL (January 17, 1985).

382. *Id.* at 28.

383. *Francis v. Bogan*, 86-ERA-8, slip op. of ALJ, at 15 (March 21, 1986); *Nix v. NEHI-RC Bottling Co., Inc.*, 84-STA-1, D&O of SOL, at 12 (July 13, 1984) ("inconsistent application of company politics has also been held to be evidence of retaliatory motive").

384. *Stone & Webster v. Herman*, *supra*, at 1574.

385. *Larry v. Detroit Edison Co.*, 86-ERA-32, slip op. of ALJ at 7, (October 17, 1986).

386. *Housing Works, Inc. v. City of New York*, 72 F. Supp.2d 402, 422 (S.D. N.Y. 1999) (collecting cases); *Sumner v. U.S. Postal Service*, 899 F.2d 203, 209 (2nd Cir. 1990) ("The causal connection . . . can be established indirectly with circumstantial evidence, for example . . . through evidence of disparate treatment of employees who engaged in similar conduct"); *O'Brien v. Stone & Webster Eng. Corp.*, 84-ERA-31, slip op. of ALJ, at 19 n. 12 (February 28, 1985); *Clifton v. UPS*, 94-STA-16, D&O of SOL, at 13 (May 9, 1995),

387. *Donovan v. Zimmer America, Inc.*, 557 F. Supp. 642, 652 (D. S.C. 1982), *citing Midwest Regional Joint Board v. NLRB*, 564 F.2d 434, 442 (D.C. Cir. 1977) and *NLRB v. Hecks's Inc.*, 386 F.2d 317, 320 (4th Cir. 1967) ("enforcement of an otherwise valid rule only against those engaged in [protected] activities is discriminatory").

388. *Bechtel Construction v. SOL*, 50 F.3d 926, 935 (11th Cir. 1995); *Hobby v. Georgia Power Co.*, 90-ERA-30, D&O of Remand by SOL, at 20 (August 4, 1995).

389. *Simons v. Simmons Indus., Inc.*, 87-TSC-2, recommended D&O of ALJ, at 5 (July 14, 1988); *Hale v. Baldwin Assocs.*, 85-ERA-37, recommended D&O of ALJ, at 18 (October 20, 1986).

390. *Lewis Grocer Co. v. Holloway*, 874 F.2d 1008 (5th Cir. 1989); *Kenneway v. Matlock, Inc.*, *supra*, at 5; *Thomas v. APS*, 89-ERA-19, recommended D&O of ALJ, at 8 (April 13, 1989); *Zinn v. University of Missouri*, 93-ERA-34/36, D&O of SOL, at 13 (January 18, 1996). In *Timmons v. Mattingly Testing Services*, the Department of Labor noted that "antagonism toward activity that is protected . . . may manifest itself in many ways, *e.g.*, ridicule, openly hostile action or threatening statements, or in the case of a whistleblower who contacts the NRC, simply questioning why the whistleblower did not pursue corrective action through the usual internal channels." 95-ERA-40, D&O of Remand by ARB, at 11 (June 21, 1996).

391. *Dartey v. Zack Co.*, 82-ERA-2, D&O of SOL, at 10 (April 25, 1983).

392. *Id.*

393. *Id.*

394. *Housing Works, Inc. v. City of New York*, *supra*, at 25.

395. *Hobby v. Georgia Power Co.*, *supra*.

396. *James v. Ketchikan Pulp Co.*, 94-WPC-4, D&O of SOL, at 4 (March 15, 1996); *Edwards v. U.S. Postal Service*, 909 F.2d 320, 324 (8th Cir. 1990) ("In light of this record, filled with changing and inconsistent explanations, we can find no legitimate, nondiscriminatory basis for the challenged action that is not mere pretension").

397. *St. Mary's Honor Center v. Hicks*, 509 U.S. 502, 511 (1993); *AKA v. Washington Hospital Center*, 156 F.3d 1284, 1292-1293 (D.C. Cir. 1998).

398. *Seater v. Southern California Edison Co.*, 95-ERA-13, D&O of Remand by ARB, at 4-6 (September 27, 1996).

399. *Timmons v. Mattingly Testing Services*, *supra*, at 12, 14-15.

400. *Reeves v. Sanderson Plumbing*, 120 S. Ct. 2097, 2108 (2000) ("proof that the defendant's explanation is unworthy of credence is simply one form of circumstantial evidence that is probative of intentional discrimination and it might be quite persuasive. . . . In appropriate circumstances, the trier of fact can reasonably infer from the falsity of the explanation that the employer is dissembling to cover up a discriminatory purpose").

401. *Newkirk v. Cypress Trucking Lines, Inc.*, 88-STA-17, D&O of SOL, at 8 (February 13, 1989); *Housing Works, Inc. v. City of New York, supra,* (collecting cases).

402. *Id. See also Bechtel Construction v. SOL*, 50 F.3d 926, 934 (11th Cir. 1995); *Ertel v. Giroux Bros. Transp., Inc.*, 88-STA-24, D&O of SOL, at 24-25 (February 16, 1989); *Priest v. Baldwin Assocs.*, 84-ERA-30, D&O of SOL, at 10 (June 11, 1986). *Accord., Couty v. Dole*, 886 F.2d 147 (8th Cir. 1989). However, the discriminatory inference created by "timing" may be broken by any number of factors. *See Bartlik v. DOL*, 73 F.3d 100, 103 (6th Cir. 1996); *Schulman v. Clean Harbors Environmental Service*, 98-STA-24, D&O of ARB, at 9 (October 18, 1999). For example, in *Carson v. Tyler Pipe Co.*, 93-WPC-11, D&O of SOL, at 10 (March 24, 1995), because the misconduct that precipitated the employee's removal was "wholly unprotected" and "immediately preceded" the discharge, the SOL held that the discharge was not "pretextual."

403. *White v. The Osage Tribal Council*, 95-SDW-1, D&O of Remand by ARB, at 4 (August 9, 1997), *citing Bechtel Construction v. SOL, supra.*

404. *Nichols v. Bechtel Construction, Inc.*, 87-ERA-44, D&O of SOL, at 12 (October 26, 1992).

405. *Helmstetter v. Pacific Gas & Elec.*, 86-SWD-2, D&O of SOL, at 6 (September 9, 1992).

406. *Goldstein v. EBASCO Contractors, Inc.*, 86-ERA-36, D&O of SOL, at 11-12 (April 17, 1992).

407. *Carson v. Tyler Pipe Co.*, 93-WPC-11, D&O of SOL, at 9 (March 24, 1995).

408. *Thomas v. APS*, 89-ERA-19, D&O of SOL, at 19 (September 17, 1993).

409. *Accord., Jenkins v. United States EPA*, 92-CAA-6, D&O of SOL, at 17 (May 18, 1994); *Pillow v. Bechtel Construction, Inc., supra*, at 13.

410. *Shusterman v. EBASCO Services, Inc.*, 87-ERA-27, D&O of SOL, at 8-9 (January 6, 1992). *Also see Young v. Philadelphia Electric Co.*, 88-ERA-1, D&O of SOL, at 7 (December 18, 1992) (when a "significant period of time elapses between the time at which the respondent is aware of the protected activity and the time of the adverse action, the absence of a causal connection between the protected activity and the adverse action may be sufficiently established").

411. 509 U.S 502, 511 (1993). *Accord., Reeves v. Sanderson Plumbing*, 120 S.Ct. 2097 (2000).

412. *AKA v. Washington Hospital Center, supra,* at 1293 (*en banc*). *Accord., Reeves, supra.*

413. *Timmons v. Mattingly Testing Services*, *supra*, D&O of ARB, at 13 (collecting cases).

414. *Donovan on Behalf of Chacon v. Phelps Dodge Corp.*, 709 F.2d 86, 93 (D.C. Cir. 1983).

415. *Borel Restaurant Corp. v. NLRB*, 676 F.2d 190, 192-193 (6th Cir. 1982). *See NLRB v. Faulkner*, 691 F.2d 51, 56 (1st Cir. 1982); *NLRB v.Clark Manor Nursing Home Corp.*, 671 F.2d 657, 661-663 (1st Cir. 1982); *Clifton v. UPS*, 94-STA-16, D&O of SOL, at 13 (May 9, 1995). For some cases where the court failed to find disparate treatment, *see Viracon, Inc. v. NLRB*, 736 F.2d 1188, 1193 (7th Cir. 1984); *Airborne Freight Corp. v. NLRB*, 728 F.2d 357, 358 (6th Cir. 1984).

416. *Timmons v. Mattingly Testing Services*, *supra*, D&O of ARB, at 13 n. 8.

417. *Donovan v. Zimmer America, Inc.*, 557 F. Supp. 642 (D. S.C. 1982), *quoting Midwest Regional Joint Board v. NLRB*, 564 F.2d 434, 442 (D.C. Cir. 1977).

418. *Adams v. Coastal Production Op., Inc.*, 89-ERA-3, D&O of SOL, at 11 (August 5, 1992). *Accord.*, Marcus v. *U.S. EPA*, 92-TSC-5, R. D&O of ALJ, at 26 (December 3, 1992). *Also see Pogue v. U.S. DOL*, 940 F.2d 1287, 1291 (9th Cir. 1991) ("substantially disproportionate" discipline is evidence of retaliation).

419. *McCoy v. WGN Continental Broadcasting Co.*, 957 F.2d 368, 373 (7th Cir. 1992) (citations omitted).

420. *Id. See also Kahn v. SOL*, 64 F.3d 271, 280-281 (7th Cir. 1995); *Abraham v. Lawnwood Regional Medical Center*, 96-ERA-13, D&O of ARB, at 6 (November 25, 1997). Significantly, under this theory of liability, if the decision maker "had a reasonable and good faith belief" that the employee engaged in misconduct, a discharge will be sustained, even if an employee can prove that he or she never committed the misconduct. *Jackson v. Ketchikan Pulp Co.*, 93-WPC-7/8, D&O of SOL, at 7 (March 4, 1996). This "good faith belief" rule is not followed under the NLRA. *See Jackson v. Ketchikan Pulp Co.*, at 7 n. 4, *citing NLRB v. Champ Corp.*, 933 F.2d 688, 700 (9th Cir. 1990).

421. *NLRB v. Erie Resister Corp.*, 373 U.S. 221, 228 (1963); *International Ladies Garment Workers Union v. NLRB*, 366 U.S. 731, 738-739 (1961). *See also Kroger Co. v. NLRB*, 401 F.2d 682, 686 (6th Cir. 1968), *cert. denied*, 395 U.S. 904 (1969).

422. *Radio Officers v. NLRB*, 347 U.S. 17, 45 (1954).

423. *Doyle v. Hydro Nuclear Services*, 89-ERA-22, D&O of SOL (March 30, 1994).

424. *Rudd v. Westinghouse Hanford Co.*, 88-ERA-33, D&O of Remand by ARB, at 8 (November 10, 1997) (employer engages in "unlawful discrimination by restricting complainant's ability to provide regulatory agencies with information; improper 'gag' provision constituted adverse employment action"). *Accord., CL&P v. SOL*, 85 F.3d 89 (2nd Cir. 1996).

425. *Remusat v. Bartlett Nuclear, Inc.*, 94-ERA-36, D&O of SOL, at 9 (February 26, 1996); *Gaballa v. The Atlantic Group*, 94-ERA-9, D&O of SOL, at 3-4 (January 18, 1996); *Earwood v. Dart Container Corp.*, 93-STA-16, D&O of SOL, at 2-6 (December 7, 1994).

426. *Chase v. Buncombe County, N.C., etc.*, 85-SWD-4, D&O of Remand by SOL, at 4 (November 3, 1986).

427. *CL&P v. SOL, supra*, at 95. *Accord., Johnson v. Roadway Express, Inc.*, D&O of ARB, at 10-11 (March 29, 2000); *Ciotti v. Sysco Foods*, 97-STA-30, D&O of ARB, at 8 (July 8, 1998), *aff'd sub nom. Sysco Food Services v. DOL*, No. 98-6265 (3rd Cir. 1999).

428. *Reeves v. Sanderson Plumbing*, 120 S. Ct. 2097, 2105 (2000), (quoting from *U.S. Postal Service v. Aikens*, 460 U.S. 711, 716 (1983).

429. *Reeves v. Sanderson Plumbing*, 120 S. Ct. 2097 (2000).

430. 509 U.S. 502, 422 (1993).

431. 512 U.S. 267, 62 U.S. L.W. 4543 (June 20, 1994).

432. The Court in *Director, Office of Workers' Comp.* overturned the Supreme Court's prior holding in *NLRB v. Transportation Management,* 462 U.S. 393 (1983), inasmuch as that case allowed a finding of discrimination without first requiring that the employee persuade the Court that discriminatory animus ("anti-union sentiment") contributed to the adverse action.

433. *Gallian v. City of Sullivan,* 93-WPC-14, D&O of SOL, at 2-3 (March 28, 1994); *St. Mary's Honor Center v. Hicks,* 509 U.S. 502, 523 (1993); *Director, Office of Workers' Comp. Programs v. Greenwich Collieries*, 512 U.S. 267 (1994). Regarding the *dual motive* doctrine, *see also Mandreger v. Detroit Edison Co.*, 88-ERA-17, D&O of SOL, at 18 (March 30,1994); *Bartlik v. TVA,* 88-ERA-15, Final D&O of SOL, at 4 (April 7, 1993): "Indeed, the order and allocation of burdens of proof and burdens of production in *Dartey v. Zack Co.* are applicable only where circumstantial evidence of discrimination is presented. If direct evidence of discrimination exists, and it is not effectively rebutted, a respondent can avoid liability only by showing it would have taken the same action in the absence of protected activity."

434. *See Dartey v. Zack Co*, 82-ERA-2, D&O of SOL, at 6-9 (April 25, 1983) and David A. Drachsler, "Burdens of Proof in Retaliatory Adverse Action Cases Under Title VII," 35 *Labor Law Journal* 28 (January, 1984) for an explanation of the DOL's application of the burdens of proof in cases prior to the Supreme Court's decisions in *Reeves* and *St. Mary's*, Even after these decisions, the DOL has, for the most part, continued to utilize the methodology set forth in *Dartey v. Zack.* In circumstantial evidence cases, the ARB follows *Reeves. Melendez, supra*, at 31, 32.

435. *Carroll v. Bechtel Power Corp.*, 91-ERA-46, D&O of SOL, at 9-11 (February 15, 1995) (internal citations and quotations omitted), *aff'd, Carroll v. DOL*, 78 F.3d 352, 356 (8th Cir. 1996). The DOL has also held that the "preponderance-of-the-evidence" burden of proof as used by the DOL is required under the Administrative Procedure Act. *See Martin v. Department of Army*, 93-SDW-1, D&O of ARB, at 5 (July 30, 1999). For an explanation of the *dual-motive* test and an analysis of when the burden of proof shifts to the employer, *see e.g., Shannon v. Consolidated Freightways*, 96-STA-15, D&O of ARB, at 6-7 (April 15, 1998).

436. *Wright Line*, 251 NLRB 1083 (1980), aff'd, 662 F.2d 899 (1st Cir. 1981), *cert. denied*, 455 U.S. 989 (1982). *See also Murray v. Henry J. Kaiser*

Co., 84-ERA-4, recommended D&O of ALJ, at 7 (June 22, 1984) ("A 'pretext' in the field of labor relations is a word of art which generally means that 'the purported rule or circumstances advanced by the respondent did not exist, or was not, in fact, relied upon.' "); *Witttenberg v. Wheels, Inc.*, 963 F. Supp. 654, 663 (N.D. Ill. 1997) (pretext is "more than a mistake," it is a "lie" or a "phoney reason").

437. *Republic Die & Tool Co. v. NLRB*, 680 F.2d 463, 465 (6th Cir. 1982). *See also Wells v. Kansas Gas & Elec. Co.*, *supra*, slip op. of ALJ, at 18, adopted and modified by SOL (June 14, 1984).

438. *Reeves v. Sanderson Plumbing*, 120 S. Ct. 2097, 2108 (2000); *St. Mary's Honor Center v. Hick's*, 509 U.S. 502, 515 (1993).

439. *Clifton v. UPS*, 94-STA-16, D&O of SOL, at 13 (May 9, 1995). *See also DeFord v. Secretary of Labor*, 700 F.2d 281, 286 (6th Cir. 1983); *Francis v. Bogan, Inc.*, 86-ERA-8, D&O of SOL, at 5 n. 1 (April 1, 1988).

440. *See Tyndall v. EPA*, 93-CAA-6/95-CAA-5, D&O of Remand by ARB, at 9 (June 14, 1996) ("the allegation of a violation of other statutes does not defeat the claim under the employee protection provision. The Board has authority to rule only upon the CAA claim; it will express no opinion as to violations of the other statutes"). *Accord., Paynes v. Gulf States*, 93-ERA-47, D&O of ARB (August 31, 1999).

441. *Diaz-Robainas*, D&O or Remand by SOL, at 15 n. 9 (January 19, 1996).

442. *Immanuel v. Wyoming Concrete Industries*, 95-WPC-3, D&O of ARB, at 11 n. 10 (May 28, 1997), *reversed on other grounds* (4th cir. 1998); *Paynes, supra.*

443. *Mackowiak v. University Nuclear Systems, Inc.*, 735 F.2d 1159, 1163-1164 (9th Cir. 1984).

444. *Accord v. DOL*, 166 F.3d 1217 (9th Cir. 1999) (unpublished decision) ("dual motive analysis applied only if" the employee "proves that the employer had a retaliatory motive").

445. *Director, Office of Workers' Compensation Programs v. Greenwich Collieries*, 512 U.S. 267, 277-278 (1994). *See also Consolidated Edison Co. of N.Y. v. Donovan*, 673 F.2d 61, 62 (2nd Cir. 1982) (ERA case), and *Mackowiak v. University Nuclear Systems, Inc.*, 735 F.2d 1159 (9th Cir. 1984). *Mackowiak*, an ERA case, articulated the shifting burden rule as: "Once the plaintiff has shown that the protected activity 'played a role' in the employer's decision, the burden shifts to the employer to persuade the court that it would have discharged the plaintiff even if the protected activity had not occurred." 735 F.2d at 1163-1164. *Accord., Guttman v. Passaic Valley Sewerage Comm.*, 85-WPC-2, D&O of SOL, at 19 (March 13, 1992); *Dodd v. Polysar Latex*, 88-SWD-4, recommended decision of ALJ, at 14-15 (November 16, 1989); *Pope v. Transp. Servs., Inc.*, 88-STA-8, recommended D&O of ALJ, at 6 (May 19, 1988), adopted by SOL (September 13, 1988); *Palmer v. Western Truck Manpower*, 85-STA-6, D&O of Remand by SOL at 10 (January 16,1987); *O'Brien v. Stone & Webster Eng. Corp.*, 84-ERA-31, recommended D&O of ALJ, at 19 (February 28, 1985). *See also* the U.S. Supreme Court case of *Price Waterhouse v. Ann B. Hopkins*, 490 U.S. 228 (1989).

446. *Johnson v. Roadway Express, Inc.,* 99-STA-5, D&O of ARB, at 12 (March 29, 2000), *quoting Coco v. Elmwood Care, Inc.,* 128 F.3d 1177, 1180 (7th Cir. 1997).

447. *Mount Healthy City School District v. Doyle,* 429 U.S. 274, 287 (1977).

448. *Rouse v. Farmers State Bank of Jewell,* 866 F. Supp. 1191, 1208 (N.D. Iowa 1994) ("the legislative history reveals that the burden on the plaintiff was intended to be lessened").

449. 5 U.S.C. § 1221(e).

450. 42 U.S.C. § 5851(b)(3)(C) and (D).

451. 49 U.S.C. § 42121.

452. 12 U.S.C. § 1831j.

453. D.C. Code § 1.616.11 (1999).

454. *Rouse, supra,* at 1208 (explaining difference between "contributing factor" test and traditional Title VII formulation). *See also Trimmer v. DOL,* 174 F.3d 1098, 1101 (10th Cir. 1999) (Congress established a "burden-shifting framework distinct from Title VII").

455. *Stone & Webster v. Herman, supra,* at 1572-1573.

456. *Marano v. Department of Justice,* 2 F.3d 1137, 1140 (Fed. Cir. 1993), *citing* 135 Cong. Rec. 5033 (1989) (Explanatory Statement on S. 20). *Accord., Rouse supra,* at 1208.

457. *Kewley v. Department of Health and Human Services,* 153 F.3d 1357, 1362 (Fed. Cir. 1998) (citations and internal quotations omitted).

458. *Rouse, supra,* at 1209 (temporal proximity between the whistleblower disclosures and the adverse action, combined with employer knowledge of the disclosures, is sufficient, standing alone, to meet the "contributing factor" test). *Accord., Kewley* at 1361-1362; *Frobose v. American Savings & Loan Association,* 152 F.3d 602, 609 (7th Cir. 1998).

459. *See* 5 U.S.C. § 1221(e)(2) (Whistleblower Protection Act). The DOL, under the nuclear whistleblower law, summarized the burdens of proof under the "contributing factor" test as follows: "(1) whether [the employee] established by a preponderance of the evidence that their protected activity was a contributing factor in [the employer's adverse action], and if so; (2) whether [the employer] demonstrated by clear and convincing evidence that it would have [taken the adverse action] in the absence of their protected activity." *McCafferty v. Centerior Energy,* 96-ERA-6, D&O of Remand by ARB, at 9 (September 24, 1997).

460. *Stone & Webster v. Herman, supra,* at 1572. *See Grogan v. Garner,* 498 U.S. 297 (1991) (discussing "clear and convincing evidence standard"). The SOL applies the *Grogan* analysis in cases arising under the nuclear whistleblower law. *See Timmons v. Mattingly Testing Services, supra,* D&O of Remand by ARB, at 16.

461. *Williams-Moore v. Dept. of Veterans Affairs,* —F.3d—, 2000 WL 369678 (Table), (unpublished Fed. Cir. April 10, 2000) *quoting Carr v. Social Security,* 185 F.3d 1318, 1323 (Fed. Cir. 1999).

462. Richard Levy, "Discovery: The Plaintiff's Case," 287 PLI/Lit 125 (July 1, 1985) ("Almost invariably plaintiffs complaining of discrimination must rely on discovery to construct major portions of their cases. They rarely have access to the employment files, company records, statistics, etc., which are needed to demonstrate discriminatory conduct"). For example, in *McDonnell Douglas Corp. v. Green*, 411 U.S. 792, 804-05 (1973), the Supreme Court specifically referenced the importance of pretrial discovery in enabling an employee to prove disparate treatment and the pretextual grounds for termination.

463. *Morrison v. City & County of Denver*, 80 F.R.D. 289, 292 (D. Colo. 1978) ("plaintiffs should be permitted a very broad scope of discovery in Title VII cases. Since direct evidence of discrimination is rarely obtainable, plaintiffs must rely on circumstantial evidence and statistical data, and evidence of an employer's overall employment practices").

464. *See, e.g., Holland v. Muscantine General Hospital*, 971 F. Supp. 385, 389 (S.D. Iowa 1997), quoting *University of Pennsylvania v. EEOC*, 493 U.S. 182, 198 (1990).

465. *St. Mary's Honor Center v. Hicks*, 509 U.S. 502 (1993), quoting from *United States Postal Service Bd. v. Aikens*, 460 U.S. 711, 716 (1983).

466. *Hollander v. American Cyanamid Co.*, 895 F.2d 80, 85 (2nd Cir. 1990).

467. *Webb v. Government for the District of Columbia*, 175 F.R.D. 128 (D. D.C. 1997) (default judgment in retaliatory discharge case for discovery abuses and destruction of documents); *International Union (UAW) v. NLRB*, 429 F.2d 1329, 1338 (D.C. Cir. 1972) (setting forth "adverse inference rule").

468. *Rodger v. Electronic Data Systems, Corp.*, 155 F.R.D. 537, 539 (E.D. N.C. 1994).

469. Federal Rule of Civil Procedure 26(c); DOL Rule 29 C.F.R. § 18.15.

470. *Alexander v. FBI*, 2000 WL 351236 (D. D.C. 2000).

471. *Alexander*, 2000 WL 351236 (D. D.C. 2000), *citing Chubb Integrated Systems v. National Bank*, 103 F.R.D. 52, 60-61 (D. D.C. 1984). *See also Harvey v. Eimco Corp.*, 28 F.R.D. 381 (E.D. Penn. 1961) (defendant "can not complain merely because in order to answer the plaintiff's interrogatories it must interrogate its personnel or compile information within its control"); *Alexander v. FBI*, 186 F.R.D. 60, 63 (D. D.C. 1999) (protective orders prohibiting a deposition rarely granted) (citing cases).

472. *Alexander*, 2000 WL 351236 (D. D.C. 2000), *citing In re Lindsey*, 158 F.3d 1263, 1270 (D.C. Cir. 1998). *See, Alexander v. FBI*, 2000 WL 329294 (D. D.C. 2000) (setting forth test to determine if attorney client privilege applies and setting forth "crime-fraud exception" standard for that privilege); *In re Sealed Case*, 737 F.2d 94, 99 (D.C. Cir. 1984) ("when an attorney conveys to his client facts acquired from other persons or sources, those facts are not privileged"). *Alexander v. FBI*, 186 F.R.D. 21, 45 (D. D.C. 1998) (setting forth limits on attorney client privilege). Privileges may be waived. *Alexander v. FBI*, 2000 WL 351221 (D. D.C. 2000), *citing, In re Sealed Case*, 877 F.2d 976, 980-81 (D.C. Cir. 1989). Courts often require the production of a "privilege log" when a party

asserts a privilege. *U.S. v. Western Elec. Co.*, 132 F.R.D. 1, 3 (D. D.C. 1990); *Alexander v. FBI*, 186 F.R.D. 102, 106 (D. D.C. 1998).

473. *Alexander v. FBI*, 186 F.R.D. 6, 9 (D. D.C. 1998) (Court "condemns" discovery response that a party will produce documents "as they are located"); *Alexander v. FBI*, 186 F.R.D. 60, 64 (D. D.C. 1998) (professed "lack of knowledge typically" "insufficient to warrant the quashing of a deposition"); *Alexander v. FBI*, 186 F.R.D. 113 (D. D.C. 1998) (improperly responding to deposition questions with answer that the witness could not "recall" or "remember").

474. *Alexander v. FBI*, 186 F.R.D. 12, 19 (D. D.C. 1998).

475. *See, Fonseca v. Regan*, 98 F.R.D. 694, 700 (E.D. N.Y. 1983); *Roseberg v. Johns-Manville Corp.*, 85 F.R.D. 292, 295-97 (E.D. Pa. 1977).

476. *LaChemise Lacoste v. The Alligator Co.*, 60 F.R.D. 164, 170-71 (D. Del. 1973).

477. The DOL cannot object to producing witness interview statements conducted during the investigative period on the grounds of the informer's privilege, however, the names of confidential informers may be deleted. *Brock v. Panzarino*, 109 F.R.D. 157, 158 (E.D. N.Y. 1986). *See also Malpass, v. General Electric Co.*, 85-ERA-38/39, D&O of SOL, 12-14 (Mar. 1, 1994), which rejected a party's attempt to invoke the informer's privilege concerning the identity of witnesses.

478. *U.S. ex rel. Burns v. Family Practice Associates*, 162 F.R.D. 624, 627 (S.D. Calf. 1995). *See also* Martin A. Schwartz, "Admissibility of Investigatory Reports in Section 1983 Civil Rights Actions—A User's Manual," 79 *Marq. L. Rev.* 453 (1996).

479. *Etienne v. Mitre Corp.*, 146 F.R.D. 145, 148 (E.D. Vir. 1993).

480. *Reich v. Hercules, Inc.*, 857 F. Supp. 367 (D.N.J. 1994); *Spencer v. Sea-Land Service*, 1999 WL 619637 (S.D.N.Y. 1999).

481. *Spencer, supra.*

482. *Barfoot v. The Boeing Co.*, 184 F.R.D. 642, 645 (N.D. Ala. 1999).

483. *Etienne, supra. See also Harding v. Dana Transport, Inc.*, 914 F. Supp. 1084 (D.N.J. 1996) (attorney work product privilege waived when employer relied upon investigation conducted by attorney in defending against allegation of respondeat superior in a hostile work environment case).

484. *Holub v. H. Nash Babcock, Babcock & King, Inc.*,93-ERA-25 Discovery Order of ALJ, at 9 (Mar. 2, 1994).

485. *Id.* at 10-11.

486. *Id.* at 13-14. *See also Lawson v. Fisher-Price, Inc.*, 191 F.R.D. 381 (D. Vt. 1999), *citing Paladino v. Woodloch Pines, Inc.*, 188 F.R.D. 224 (M.D. Pa. 1999) (safety report ordered disclosed).

487. *Id.* at 12-13.

488. *Id.* at 24-27.

489. *Duke v. University of Texas*, 729 F.2d 994 (5th Cir. 1984); *Georgia Power Co., v. EEOC*, 412 F.2d 462, 468 (5th Cir. 1969); *Held v. National R.R. Passenger Corp.*, 101 F.R.D. 420, 425 (D. D.C. 1984). In ordering a company to produce payroll records related to other employees, the ALJ in *Holub* explained

how an employee may use company-wide documentation to demonstrate discrimination:

One of the ways Complainant may accomplish this is to establish the pattern of his compensation *vis-a-vis* other employees, i.e., that his past excellence (according to Complainant) had resulted in monetary rewards. Respondents have countered Complainant's assertion in this regard by stating that all their employees have received raises and or bonuses. Under these circumstances, to deny disclosure of these asserted facts to Complainant would, in effect, deny him the opportunity to prove "indirectly"an intent to discriminate. Clearly, the documents requested are relevant.

Id. at 26. *Also see Hollander v. American Cyanamid Co.*, 895 F.2d 80, 84-85 (2nd Cir. 1990) (upheld company-wide discovery on "similarly situated persons" and "company-wide practices").

490. Following the Supreme Court's decision in *University of Pennsylvania v. EEOC*, 493 U.S. 182 (1990), the SOL refused to extend a discovery privilege to the findings of an "independent investigation" of a whistleblowers safety concerns under the "self-critical analysis" privilege. *Holden v. Gulf States Utilities*, 92-ERA-44, D&O of Remand by SOL, at 7-8 (April 14, 1995). The Secretary reasoned that the "overwhelming public interest in protecting whistleblowers who act to promote nuclear power safety outweighs [the employer's] interest in keeping the [investigative] reports confidential." *Id. Accord., Dowling v. American Hawaii Cruises, Inc.*, 971 F.2d 423, 425-427 (9th Cir. 1992) (narrowly construing the "self-critical analysis" privilege).

491. *Volpe v. U.S. Airways*, 184 F.R.D. 672, 673 (M.D. Fla. 1998).

492. *Morrison v. City and County of Denver*, 80 F.R.D. 289, 292 (D. Colo. 1978).

493. *Hollander v. American Cyanamid Co.*, 895 F.2d 80, 84 (2nd Cir. 1990) ("Evidence relating to company-wide practices may reveal patterns of discrimination against a group of employees, increasing the likelihood that an employer's offered explanation of an employment decision regarding a particular individual masks a discriminatory motive"); *Diaz v. American Tel. & Tel.*, 752 F.2d 1356, 1362-63 (9th Cir. 1985) (holding summary judgment "patently inappropriate" when district court restricts plaintiff's ability to discover evidence necessary to establish disparate treatment prima facie case); *Hollander v. American Cyanamid Co.*, 1997 WL 835057 (D. Conn. 1997) (granting discovery in age discrimination case on every management employee over the age of 40); *Rodger v. Electronic Data Systems Corp.*, 155 F.R.D. 537, 540 (E.D. N.C. 1994) (disparate treatment discovery in areas reasonably related to the circumstances of the alleged discrimination); *Timmons v. Mattingly Testing Services*, 95-ERA-40 (ARB June 21, 1996) ("the past practice of the employer in similar situations is relevant to determining whether there has been disparate treatment, which my provide highly probative evidence of retaliatory intent").

494. *Alexander v. FBI*, 186 F.R.D. 154, 164-66 (D. D.C. 1999) (evidence of potential "cover-up" valid circumstantial evidence of improper motive).

495. *Momah v. Albert Einstein Medical Center,* 164 F.R.D. 412, 417 (E.D. Penn. 1996). *Accord., Coughlin v. Lee,* 946 F.2d 1152, 1159 (5th Cir. 1991) (allowing discovery of records of police officer background check); *Weahkee v. Norton,* 621 F.2d 1080, 1082 (10th Cir. 1980) (allowing discovery of EEOC personnel files); *Griffith v. Wal-Mart Stores,* 163 F.R.D. 4 (E.D. Ky. 1995) (managerial personnel files discoverable); *Watts v. Kimmerly,* 1996 WL 911254 (W.D. Mich. 1996) (no federally recognized privilege for personnel files); *Barfoot v. The Boeing Co.,* 184 F.R.D. 642, 644 (N.D. Ala. 1999).

496.*Graf v. Wackenhut Services,* 98-ERA-37, ALJ Order Granting Motion to Compel, at 4-5 (March 19, 1999).

497. *Rodger v. Electronic Data Systems, Corp.,* 155 F.R.D. 537, 541 (E.D. N.C. 1994).

498. *Timmons v. Mattingly Testing Services,* 95-ERA-40 (ARB June 21, 1996) ("deliberate violations of NRC regulations suggest antagonism toward the NRC regulatory scheme and thus may provide support for an inference of retaliatory intent").

499. *Ibrahim v. American University,* 1999 U.S. Dist. LEXIS 8388 (D. D.C. 1999).

500. *Franzon v. Massena Memorial Hospital,* 189 F.R.D. 220, 224 (N.D. N.Y. 1999).

501. *Lyoch v. Anheuser-Busch,* 164 F.R.D. 62, 67 (E.D. Missouri 1995).

502. *Momah v. Albert Einstein Medical Center, supra.,* at 417.

503. *Id.* at 418.

504. *Id.* at 418.

505. *Alexander v. FBI,* 186 F.R.D. 78, 96-97 (D. D.C. 1998).

506. *Momah, supra,* at 418-19. In *Momah* the defendants objected to the discovery of other wrongful actions committed by other employees stating that the plaintiff was not directly disciplined for these types of misconduct. The court rejected that argument, stating "the issue here, however, is the manner in which Defendants responded to the missteps made by [the employee] vis a vis other [employees]."

507. Lyoch, *supra* at 68-69.

508. *Id.* at 68-69.

509. *Id.* at 70 ("evidence of a pattern and practice of discrimination is relevant to an individual claim of discrimination as well as a class action suit"). *Accord., Barfoot v. The Boeing Co.,* 184 F.R.D. 642, 644 (N.D. Ala. 1999) ("such discovery may reveal the existence of patterns" of discrimination).

510. *Id.* at 69. *Accord., Kern v. University of Notre Dame,* 1997 WL 816518 (N.D. Ind. 1997) ("Notre Dame is directed to produce information as to any charges or complaints filed against the University alleging sex discrimination").

511. *See,* disclosure requirements set forth in FRCP 26(a)(2). *Accord., Smith v. State Farm Fire and Causality Co.,* 164 F.R.D. 49 (S.D.W.V. 1995).

512. *Management Information Technologies, Inc. v. Alyeska Pipeline Service Co.,* 151 F.R.D. 478 (D. D.C. 1993).

513. *Turner v. Imperial Stores*, 161 F.R.D. 89, 95 (S.D. Calf. 1995) ("A number of courts have specifically held that a claim of emotional distress, without more, is not sufficient to place plaintiff's mental condition in controversy"); *Fritsch v. City of Chula Vista*, 187 F.R.D. 614 (S.D. Calf. 1999). This rule was summarized by the Court in *Fox v. The Gates Corporation*, 179 F.R.D. 303, 307 (D. Col. 1998):

The majority of courts, however, will not require a plaintiff to submit to a medical examination unless, in addition to a claim for emotional distress, one or more of the following factors is also present: (1) plaintiff has asserted a specific cause of action for intentional or negligent infliction of emotional distress; (2) plaintiff has alleged a specific mental or psychiatric injury or disorder; (3) plaintiff has claimed unusually severe emotional distress; (4) plaintiff has offered expert testimony in support of her claim for emotional distress damages; and (5) plaintiff concedes that here mental condition is "in controversy."

514. *Miles v. Boeing Co.*, 154 F.R.D. 117, 119 (E.D. Penn. 1994); *McClain v. Mack Trucks, Inc.*, 85 F.R.D. 53, 63 (E.D. Penn. 1979) (discovery permitted five years prior to the plaintiff's termination).

515. *Avirgan v. Hull*, 118 F.R.D. 252 (D. D.C. 1987); *Alexander v. FBI*, 186 F.R.D. 60, 65-66 (D. D.C. 1998) (citing cases). The SOL has also recognized the applicability of the federal court cases holding that, in the absence of a protective order, parities have a first amendment right to disseminate discovery information. *Holden v. Gulf States Utilities*, 92-ERA-44, D&O of Remand by SOL, at 8 (April 14, 1995). Protective orders should not prohibit a party's right to disseminate information obtained outside of the discovery process itself. *Id.* at 9. ALJ's have the authority to issue protective orders and are often asked to impose gag orders on a party's ability to publicly disclose information produced in discovery. Although such orders are often jointly presented to an ALJ for approval, ALJ's have refused to enter such protective orders when they are viewed as to "all-encompassing and draconian" *Scott v. Alyeska Pipeline Service Co.*, 92-TSC-2, ALJ Order Denying Protective Order (January 4, 1992). Once a protective order is issued by an ALJ in an environmental whistleblower case, the ALJ maintains jurisdiction to modify the protective order, even after a case is dismissed. *Holden*, at 6

516. *U.S. ex rel. Falsetti v. Southern Bell*, 915 F. Supp. 308 (N.D. Fla. 1996); *U.S. ex rel. Burns v. Family Practice Associates*, 162 F.R.D. 624 (S.D. Calf. 1995).

517. *Franzon v. Massena Memorial Hospital*, 189 F.R.D. 220, 224 (N.D. N.Y. 1999). *Accord., University of Pennsylvania v. EEOC*, 493 U.S. 182, (1990) (rejecting self critical analysis privilege in context of disclosing confidential "peer review" tenure-related materials); *Lawson v. Fisher-Price, Inc.*, 191 F.R.D. 381 (D. Vt. 1999) (self-critical analysis privilege "rarely found to apply" and some courts have "categorically refused to apply the privilege"); *Federal Trade Commission v. TRW, Inc.*, 628 F.2d 207 (D.C. Cir. 1980) (privilege does not apply to document requests filed by the government). In *Kern v. University of Notre Dame*, 1997 WL 816518 (N.D. Ind. 1997), the court summarized the minimum

criteria a party demonstrate in order obtain protection under that privilege - within the jurisdictions which are still willing to consider the privilege: "(1) the materials must have been prepared for mandatory government reports; (2) the privilege extends only to subjective evaluative materials; (3) the privilege does not extend to objective data in any such reports; and (4) discovery should be denied only where the public policy favoring exclusion clearly outweighs the plaintiff's need." Additionally, such materials must be prepared with an "expectation" that they would be kept confidential, and the materials must in fact have been kept confidential. *Dowling v. American Hawaii Cruises, Inc.*, 971 F.2d 423 (9th Cir. 1992). In regard to the first prong of this test, courts have explicitly held that the privilege does not apply to materials which were required to be produced to the government; *see Etiennne, supra,* and *Lawson, supra.* Still other courts have held that the privilege does not apply to reports conducted for internal use, and which were not mandated by the government. *Paladino v. Woodloch Pines,* 188 F.R.D. 224 (M.D. Pa. 1999). Consequently, it is obvious why many courts have recognized that there are "some doubts about the doctrine's continuing viability." *In the Matter of the Application of Vincenzo NIERI, for Subpoenas,* 2000 WL 60214 (S.D. N.Y. 2000). Finally, in the context of employment discrimination litigation, the privilege may have "no applicability" whatsoever. *Holland v. Muscatine General Hospital,* 971 F. Supp. 385, 390-91 (S.D. Iowa 1997).

518. *McKennon v. Nashville Banner Publishing Co.*, 513 U.S. 352, 363 (1995).

519. *Alexander v. FBI,* 186 F.R.D. 154, 163 (D. D.C. 1999) (citing cases); *Alexander v. FBI,* 186 F.R.D. 200, 206 (D. D.C. 1999).

520. *Less v. Taber Instrument Corp.*, 53 F.R.D. 645 (W.D. N.Y. 1971). *Accord., Alexander v. FBI,* 186 F.R.D. 60, 64 (D. D.C. 1998) ("professed lack of knowledge" and "busy" schedule not sufficient to quash a notice of deposition); *Amherst Leasing Corp. V. Emhart Corp.,* 65 F.R.D. 121 (D. Conn. 1974).

521. *In the Matter of the Application of Vincenzo NIERI, for Subpoenas,* 2000 WL 60214 (S.D. N.Y. 2000), *citing, In re Grand Jury Subpoena,* 599 F.2d 504, 510-11 (2nd Cir. 1979); *Harding v. Dana Transport, Inc.,* 914 F. Supp. 1084 (D.N.J. 1996) (attorney client privilege waived where client relied upon attorneys investigation in defending charge of respondeat superior liability in hostile work environment case); *In re: July 5, 1999 Explosion at Kaiser Aluminum,* 1999 WL 717513 (1999 E.D. La. 1999) (work product privilege not applicable to "documents which have been assembled in the ordinary course of business"); *Reich v. Hercules, Inc.,* 857 F. Supp. 367, 373 (D. N.J. 1994) ("A party may not shield facts from discovery merely by combining them with an attorney's core work product"); *Opthof v. Asland Chemical Company,* 94-CAA-7, ALJ Discovery Order, p. 2 (May 12, 1994) ("The attorney-client privilege does not protect the soliciting or giving business advice").

522. *Management Information Technologies, Inc. v. Alyeska Pipeline Service Co.*, 151 F.R.D. 471 (D. D.C. 1993).

523. *Timmons v. Mattingly Testing Services,* 95-ERA-40, D&O or Remand by ARB, at 5-6 (June 21, 1996); *Migliore v. R.I Department of Environmental Management,* "Order Regarding Discovery" (ALJ, October 14, 1998)

(because rules of admissibility in DOL proceedings are relaxed, the "scope of discovery" broad). *See,* Stephen M. Kohn, "The Whistleblower Litigation Handbook: Environmental, Nuclear, Health and Safety Claims," *Wiley Law Publications* (New York: 1991), at 75-88.

524. *Khandelwal v. Southern California* Edison, 97-ERA-6, ARB No. 97-50, D&O of ARB at 4 (March 31, 1998) ("opportunity for extensive discovery is crucial to serving ERA purposes of protecting employees and public interest"). The DOL ALJs also recognize that "extensive discovery" must be permitted in environmental whistleblower cases. *Mitchell v. APS/ANPP,* 92-ERA-29, Order of ALJ, at 4 (May 3, 1992). *Also see Mulligan v. Vermont Yankee,* 92-ERA-20, Order of ALJ, at 2 (Apr. 17, 1992) ("Plaintiffs in equal employment cases should be permitted a very broad scope of discovery"). For example, in *Holub v. H. Nash Babcock, Babcock & King, Inc.,* 93-ERA-25, Discovery Order of ALJ (Mar. 2, 1994), the ALJ ruled that "the law is well settled regarding the appropriateness of extensive discovery in employment discrimination cases. Further, the courts have held that liberal discovery in these cases is warranted." *Id.* at 6.

525. *Id.*

526. *Timmons, supra.,* at 5-6. The time requirements for responding to discovery are set forth in a administrative regulations. 29 C.F.R. Part 18. An initial request to extend these time limits are "routinely" "granted." *Tracanna v. Arctic Slope Inspection Service,* 97-WPC-1, ARB No. 97-123, D&O of Remand by ARB, at 5 (November 6, 1997). The DOL adjudicatory rules applicable to whistleblower cases permit broad discovery in a manner consistent with the mechanisms available under the Federal Rules of Civil Procedure. *Malpass v. General Electric Co.,* 85-ERA-38/39, D&O of SOL, at 12 (Mar. 1, 1994).

527. *See* 29 C.F.R. §§ 18.14-18.24. In accordance with 29 C.F.R. § 18.14, "parties may obtain discovery regarding any matter, not privileged, which is relevant to the subject matter involved in the proceeding . . . it is not grounds for objection that information sought will not be admissible at the hearing if the information sought appears reasonably calculated to lead to the discovery of admissible evidence." Unlike the federal rules, the DOL rules on discovery do not require that the parties confer prior to the filing of a motion to compel and do not set presumptive limits on the amount of discovery. Although the DOL rules do not require such consultation, the ARB clearly encourages such communications and will evaluate the appropriateness of discovery sanctions in light of whether the party seeking sanctions sought to resolve the discovery dispute with the opposing party. *Tracanna v. Arctic Slope Inspection Service,* 97-WPC-1, ARB No. 97-123, D&O of Remand by ARB, at 5, n. 6 (November 6, 1997) ("we encourage parties to make a good faith attempt to resolve discovery disputes without the intervention of an ALJ").

528. In *Malpass v. General Electric Co.,* the SOL stated that "it seems clear" that the SOL and ALJ have "no power under the ERA to issue subpoenas or to punish for contempt" the "failure to comply with a subpoena." 85-ERA-38/39, D&O of SOL, at 21 (Mar. 1, 1994). The inability of the SOL to issue or enforce subpoenas does not render the DOL powerless to compel discovery. As pointed out in *Malpass,* the DOL "has the authority to impose sanctions for failure

of a party to comply with discovery or other orders under 29 C.F.R. §18.6(d)(2)." *Malpass*, at 19, N.8. These sanctions include applying the adverse inference rule and issuing a default judgment. *Id.*

529. *Assistant SOL, et al. V. Gammons Wire Feeder Corp.*, 87-STA-5, D&O or SOL (September 17, 1987).

530. Federal preemption, which has its roots in the Supremacy Clause of the U.S. Constitution, prohibits states from enacting or enforcing laws that may negate, undermine, or somehow stand as an obstacle to the enforcement of federal law. Congress can explicitly preempt state action, or it can be "implicitly" authorized by a law pursuant to the law's "structure and purpose." *Jones v. Rath Packing Co.*, 97 430 U.S. 519, 525 (1977); *Fidelity Federal Sav. & Loan Ass'n. v. De La Cuesta*, 458 U.S. 141 (1982). State action is implicitly preempted if a federal statutory or regulatory scheme is "so persuasive as to make reasonable the inference that Congress left no room for the states to supplement it." Even if Congress has not "completely displaced" state involvement in a specific area, state laws can be nullified "to the extent that [they] actually conflict[] with federal laws," *Rice v. Santa Fe Elevator Corp.*, 331 U.S. 218 (1947); 67 S.Ct. 1146, 1152 (1947); *Fidelity Federal Sav. & Loan Ass'n. v. De La Cuesta*, 458 U.S. 141, 153 (1982), or where state law "stands as an obstacle to the accomplishment and execution" of federal law. *Hines v. Davidowitz*, 312 U.S. 52 (1941); *Fidelity Fed. Sav. & Loan Ass'n. v. De La Cuesta*, 458 U.S. 141 (1982).

531. The U.S. Supreme Court has articulated a "general rule" that neither state nor federal courts have initial jurisdiction over unfair labor practice suits under the NLRA. *Vaca v. Sipes*, 386 U.S. 171, 179 (1967). The court interpreted Congress' intent in passing the NLRA as giving the National Labor Relations Board broad power to interpret and enforce the NLRA. These powers have been interpreted to be preemptive of state court involvement in unfair labor practice issues. *Garner v. Teamsters Union*, 346 U.S. 485, 490-491 (1953). The Supreme Court also preempted courts from applying state law when interpreting collective bargaining agreements. Instead of using state contract law for interpreting a collective bargaining agreement, the Supreme Court required the application of a federal common law in order to ensure a uniform national approach to interpreting collective bargaining agreements. *See United Steelworkers of America v. Enterprise Wheel and Car Corp.*, 363 U.S. 593, 599 (1960); *Republic Steel Corp. v. Maddox*, 379 U.S. 650 (1965). Despite the strong federal policy of state preemption under labor law, the Court also recognized that federal preemption is not complete. *San Diego Building Trades Council v. Garmon*, 359 U.S. 236, 243-244 (1959). If state law claims did not interfere with the operation of federal labor laws and were not based on rights created by a collective bargaining agreement, the *preemption* doctrine did not apply. For example, the Court has refused to find preemption in cases dealing with trespassing, malicious defamation committed during a labor dispute, intentional infliction of emotional distress, and employer misrepresentations to replacement workers. *Sears, Roebuck & Co. v. San Diego County District Council of Carpenters*, 436 U.S. 180 (1978); *Linn v. United Plant Guard Workers, Local 114*, 383 U.S. 53 (1966); *Farmer v. United Brotherhood of Carpenters, Local 25*, 430 U.S. 290 (1977); *International Union,*

U.A.W. v. Russell, 356 U.S. 634 (1958).

532. *Lingle v. Norge Division of Magic Chef*, 486 U.S. 399 (1988).

533. *See Allis-Chalmers Corp. v. Lueck*, 471 U.S. 202 (1985). *Accord., Cramer v. Consolidated Freightways, Inc.*, 209 F.3d 1122, 2000 WL 485495 (9th Cir. 2000).

534. *Pacific Gas & Electric Co. v. State Energy Resources*, 461 U.S. 190 (1983).

535. *English v. General Electric Co.*, 496 U.S. 72 (1990).

536. *Id.* at 87.

537. *Hawaiian Airlines, Inc. v. Finazzo*, 512 U.S. 246 (1994).

538. *See Espinosa v. Continental Airline*, 80 F. Supp.2d 297 (D. N.J. 2000).

539. *Willy v. Coastal Corp.*, 855 F.2d 1160, 1165 (5th Cir. 1988).

540. *Id.*; *Espinosa v. Continental Airlines*, 80 F. Supp.2d 297 (D. N.J. 2000).

541. *Alexander v. Gardner-Denver Co.*, 415 U.S. 36 (1974).

542. *Barrentine v. Arkansas-Best Freight System, Inc.*, 450 U.S. 728 (1981).

543. *McDonald v. West Branch*, 466 U.S. 284 (1984).

544. 415 U.S. 36 (1974).

545. *Id.* at 38-42.

546. *Id.* at 42.

547. *Id.* at 49-50.

548. *Id.* at 50.

549. *Id.* at 51.

550. 500 U.S. 20 (1991).

551. *Id.* at 24.

552. *Id.* at 26.

553. *Id.* at 28 (internal quotations omitted).

554. 9 U.S.C. § 1.

555. *Gilmer, supra*, at 25 n. 2.

556. *Id.* at 36 (dissenting opinion of Justice Stevens) ("The Court today, in holding that the FAA compels enforcement of arbitration clauses . . . skirts the antecedent question whether the coverage of the Act even extends to arbitration clauses contained in employment contracts. . . . In my opinion, arbitration clauses contained in employment agreements are specifically exempt from coverage of the FAA").

557. *Craft v. Campbell Soup Co.*, 177 F.3d 1083, 1086 n. 6 (9th Cir. 1999) (collecting cases).

558. *Id.* at 1083.

559. *Circuit City Stores Inc. v. Adams*, 194 F.3d 1070 (9th Cir. 1999), *cert. granted*, 2000 WL 217801 (May 22, 2000).

560. *Wright v. Universal Maritime Service Corp.*, 525 U.S. 70, 76 (1998).

561. *Id.* at 396.

562. *Id.* at 397.

563. *Rosenberg v. Merrill Lynch*, 163 F.3d 53, 72-73 (1st Cir. 1998).

564. 29 C.F.R. § 1988.112(c); *Ass't. Secretary of Labor v. Greyhound Bus Lines*, 96-STA-23, D&O of ARB (June 12, 1998). *Paynes, supra*, at 7 (the employee "had a right to file" his "contract claim in the arbitration process." However, "availing himself of separate forums and separate theories seeking redress" for "adverse actions" had no bearing "on ERA claim").

565. *Yellow Freight System, Inc. v. Martin*, 983 F.2d 1195 (2nd Cir. 1993).

566. *Lassin v. Michigan State University*, 93-ERA-31, D&O of SOL, at 6 (June 29, 1995) (recognizing the "strong federal polices" favoring arbitration); *Straub v. APS/ANPP*, 94-ERA-37, D&O of SOL, at 4-5 (April 15, 1996) ("arbitration decisions must be considered during the adjudication of the whistleblower complaint; the probative weight to be accorded such decisions must be determined, based on the adequacy provided the employee's rights in such arbitral proceeding, on an *ad hoc* basis"); *McDonald v. University of Missouri*, 90-ERA-59, D&O of SOL, at 10 (March 21, 1995) (decision of grievance committee "not binding," although it may be "persuasive"); *Smith v. ESICORP, Inc.*, 93-ERA-16, D&O of SOL, at 22 n. 17 (March 13, 1996) ("terms of collective bargaining agreements do not diminish rights afforded to employees under the ERA").

567. *Reich v. Sysco Corp.*, 870 F. Supp. 777 (S.D. Ohio 1994).

568. *Craft v. Campbell Soup Co.*, 177 F.3d 1083 (9th Cir. 1999) (employment agreements not covered under the FAA); *Duffield v. Robertson Stephens & Co.*, 144 F.3d 1182 (9th Cir. 1998) (Civil Rights Act of 1991 precludes compulsory arbitration of civil rights claims); *Gibson v. Neighborhood Health Clinics*, 121 F.3d 1126 (7th Cir. 1997) (arbitration agreement void due to a lack of consideration); *Rosenberg v. Merrill Lynch*, 995 F. Supp. 190 (D. Mass. 1998) (outlining procedural problems with arbitration). *See also Oldroyd v. Elmira Savings Bank*, 956 F. Supp. 393 (W.D. N.Y. 1997) (court weighing various factors to determine whether to require mandatory arbitration).

Chapter 9

Damages, Remedies, and Attorney Fees

The precise amount of damages available to a prevailing employee whistleblower is determined by the specific law relied upon in the underlying claim. That said, there are common reoccurring factual themes and applicable legal rules that both impact and determine how a case should be structured.[1]

The most common relief available under almost all whistleblower laws is a "make whole remedy" in which an employee is entitled to injunctive and monetary compensation with the goal of being made "whole." This generally includes reinstatement, back pay, and a restoration of benefits. A number of federal and state statutes, and most state common law remedies, also allow successful employees to obtain the full array of damage typically available in a tort claim,[2] as well as compensatory and punitive damages.[3] Attorney fees are available only when awardable under a statute.

Potential damages are an important consideration when determining which law to utilize to vindicate an employee's rights. For example, at first blush, a common law whistleblower tort action may appear to be the best remedy. However, the risk of low jury verdicts is substantial. On the other hand, a federal statutory remedy with legislatively mandated back pay, reinstatement, and attorney fees, can reach a valuation far in excess of even a multimillion-dollar jury awarded verdict. In addition, a statutory attorney fee award can both insure that counsel obtain a reasonable fee, regardless of the size of a final judgment, and insure that a whistleblower's award is not unduly burdened by liability for a fee.

"MAKE WHOLE" AWARDS

The vast majority of statutory whistleblower protection laws provide for a standard "make whole" remedy.[4] In *Albermarle Paper Company v. Moody*,[5] the U.S. Supreme Court held that the "purpose" of the damage provisions in Title VII cases was to "make persons whole for injuries suffered on account of unlawful employment discriminations." The court then quoted from an 1867 case defining the "make whole" rule: "[The general rule is, that when a wrong has been done, and the law gives a remedy, the compensation shall be equal to the injury. The latter is the standard by which the former is to be measured. The injured party is to be placed, as near as may be, in the situation he would have occupied if the wrong had not been committed."[6]

"Make whole" relief is justified not only as a logical method for determining amount of damages but also as a necessary tool in vindicating the public policy underlying antidiscrimination laws: "Making the workers whole for losses suffered on account of an unfair labor practice is part of the vindication of the public policy."[7]

Reinstatement

The single most important remedy available to a whistleblower is reinstatement.[8] A job represents a stream of income and benefits, which, over time, can be viewed as a very valuable asset. Given the difficulty many whistleblowers have obtaining comparable employment, reinstatement is often the only realistic method to protect a career. For example, Dr. Penina Glazer, the co-author of a major study on whistleblowing, testified in one case that it was "extremely difficult, if not virtually impossible" for whistleblowers to find "comparable work in the same industry" after blowing the whistle.[9]

Congress, in a number of whistleblower statutes, has expressly used the word "shall" in mandating reinstatement for wrongfully discharged employees.[10] Even where reinstatement is not expressly required under a statute, reinstatement is "normally an integral part of the remedy" and an employee is "presumed" to be entitled to such relief.[11] The rationale behind the presumption of reinstatement was articulated by the late Judge Robert Vance of the U.S. Court of Appeals for the 11th Circuit:

This rule of presumptive reinstatement is justified by reason as well as precedent. When a person loses his job, it is at best disingenuous to say that money damages can suffice to make that person whole. The psychological benefits of work are intangible. yet they are real and cannot be ignored. Yet at the same time, there is a high probability that reinstatement will engender personal friction of one sort or another in almost every case in which a public employee is discharged for a constitutionally infirm reason. Unless we are willing to withhold full relief from all or most successful plaintiffs in discharge cases, and we are not, we cannot allow actual or expected ill-feeling alone to justify nonreinstatement. We also note that reinstatement is an effective deterrent in preventing employer retaliation against employees who exercise their constitutional rights. If an employer's best efforts to remove an employee for unconstitutional reasons are presumptively unlikely to succeed, there is, of course, less incentive to use employment decisions to chill the exercise of constitutional rights.[12]

In whistleblower cases there is often significant animosity between the employee and the person or persons on whom the employee filed his or her whistleblower allegations. Yet even under these circumstances reinstatement is the normal remedy. For example, in a nuclear whistleblower case the Secretary of Labor (SOL) reversed an administrative law judge's (ALJ) order of front pay, and required reinstatement. Articulating a high burden on this issue, the Secretary found that reinstatement would be required absent a showing of the "impossibility of a normal working relationship" or a showing of actual "medical risk" if an employee were reinstated.[13] Other federal courts have also rejected claims that "antagonisms" between an employee and employer should defeat the entitlement to reinstatement: "Enforcement of constitutional rights frequently has disturbing consequences. Relief is not restricted to that which will be pleasing and free of irritation."[14] Indeed, employers' requests to deny reinstatement have been denied when evidence revealed that the employer was "determined to run" the employee "off the job." In that case, granting reinstatement—even in the face of overt "hostility"—was necessary to prevent the wrongdoers from "accomplish[ing] their purpose."[15]

One of the goals of reinstatement is to "restore" the employee "as nearly as possible" to the position he or she would have been in if the discrimination had not occurred. Consequently "unlawfully discharged workers should ordinarily be returned to their original jobs."[16] Reinstatement to the original position sends a message that the "rights" of employees to engage in protected activity "be protected."[17] Employees should be reinstated in a "substantially equivalent" position "only when the original position" is not available.[18] Moreover, an employee may be reinstated to a higher position if the record fully supports a finding that the employee would have received a promotion and has the qualifications for the higher position.[19]

In some cases, both parties will support "front pay" instead of

reinstatement. One court set forth the following factors that can be weighed
in deciding whether such a request can be granted:

Certain factors may counsel against reinstatement in a particular case, including
where the circumstances render it impracticable (the position no longer exists),
where the employee's sincere and rational preference is against reinstatement,
where friction exists between the employer and employee (unrelated to the discrimination), or where the burden of court supervision does not outweigh the
gains achieved from reinstatement.[20]

    Arguments that an employee's position no longer exists, therefore
rendering reinstatement impossible, have been regularly rejected.[21] In such
circumstances courts have ordered employees placed on full-pay status and
instated into "the next available position" or to insure that a comparable
position is opened to the employee "within a reasonable period of time."[22]
In cases under the NLRA employers have been ordered to take extraordinary "affirmative action," such as geographically relocating an improperly
transferred division of a company in order to properly reinstate employees.[23] However, ordering a company to "bump" an existing employee from
his or her current position in order to immediately reinstate an employee is
not a favored remedy.[24] Bumping should be used "sparingly and only when
a careful balancing of the equities indicates" that absent bumping, an employee's "relief will be unjustly inadequate."[25]

Back Pay

    The "legitimacy of back pay as a remedy for unlawful discharge"
is "beyond dispute."[26] Back pay serves to "vindicate the public policy"
behind a wrongful discharge statute, it acts as a "deterrence" to future unfair
labor practices, and it serves to "restore" the injured employee to the same
"status quo" as would have existed "but for the wrongful act."[27]
    The basic black letter law concerning the calculation of back pay
was set forth in a whistleblower case as follows:

The purpose of a back pay award is to make Complainant whole, that is to restore
him to the same position he would have been in but for discrimination by Respondent. Back pay is measured as the difference "between actual earnings for the
period and those she would have earned absent the discrimination by the defendant." Complainant has the burden of establishing the amount of back pay that
Respondent owes. However, because back pay promotes the remedial statutory
purpose of making whole the victims of discrimination, "unrealistic exactitude is
not required" in calculating back pay, and "uncertainties in determining what an
employee would have earned but for the discrimination should be resolved against

the discriminating [party]." The courts permit the construction of a hypothetical employment history for Complainant to determine the appropriate amount of back pay. Complainant is entitled to all promotions and salary increases which he would have obtained, but for the illegal discharge.[28]

Back pay awards are approximate and "uncertainties in determining what an employee would have earned but for the discrimination should be resolved against the discriminating employer."[29] It is fully appropriate when calculating the amount of damage to "recreate the employment history" of the victim and "hypothesize the time and place of each employee's advancement absent the unlawful practice."[30] Thus, sometimes courts must "engage" in this "imprecise process that will necessarily require a certain amount of estimation" in order to make an employee whole.[31]

Back pay awards should continue to "accrue" until an employer fully complies with a damage award, that is, until an employer makes an "unconditional offer of reinstatement."[32] The offer of reinstatement must be to a "comparable" job.[33] If reinstatement is not sought by the employee, back pay generally continues to "accrue until payment" of the damage "award."[34]

Back pay awards are generally calculated on a quarterly basis. Specifically, an employee's interim earnings "in one particular quarter" have "no effect on back pay liability for another quarter."[35]

Other "Make Whole" Remedies

Although reinstatement and back pay are usually the two most significant elements of a "make whole" remedy, courts and administrative agencies are usually authorized to award other damages and award equitable or "affirmative" relief in order to insure that an employee is truly made whole. Often these other aspects of damages can be very significant in ensuring that the impact of an unlawful discharge is remedied. Additionally, in discrimination cases in which retaliatory actions short of a discharge are the basis for a complaint, these other types of damage are central to a complaint.

Other forms of relief awarded employee whistleblowers have included the following: reimbursement for lost overtime;[36] an order to provide complainant with "only good recommendations";[37] front pay;[38] interest on the back pay award;[39] restoration of all pension contributions;[40] restoration of health and welfare benefits;[41] restoration of seniority;[42] the provision of neutral employment references;[43] restoration of parking privileges;[44] the provision of necessary certifications for the employee;[45] prohibition against laying an employee off or terminating an employee in the future except when "good cause" exists;[46] cease and desist orders;[47] prohibition on future employer of "derogatory communications" that would impact future employment;[48] applicable promotions;[49] vacation pay;[50] salary increases;[51] training;[52] compensation for forced sale of assets;[53] job search expenses;[54] expungement of personnel file;[55] benefits;[56] and stock option and employee savings plan.[57] "Presumed damages" may also be available when an injury is "likely to have occurred but difficult to establish."[58] Damages are also fully available in a "refusal to hire" case. A court should conduct a similar analysis when evaluating damages due to a discharge versus damages due to failure to hire: "To differentiate between discrimination in denying employment and in terminating it, would be a differentiation . . . without substance."[59]

An employee must prove at trial each element of damage, including future pain and suffering and future medical expenses.[60] The record can be reopened for damages only if the employee was excusably unaware at the time of the hearing that such future damages would occur.[61]

Front Pay

Most whistleblower protection statutes include reinstatement as one of the explicit remedies in a wrongful discharge case, and consequently an order of reinstatement is the "automatic," "preferred," or "usual" remedy.[62] However, front pay is awardable by juries, courts, or administrative agencies "as a substitute for reinstatement" in circumstances when reinstatement is not possible in order to compensate an employee for loss of future earnings.[63]

Although most statutes do not explicitly reference front pay as a remedy, the courts have created this approach when reinstatement is not feasible.[64] Front pay may be awarded where "irreparable animosity" exists between the employee and employer[65] or where "a productive and amicable working relationship would be impossible."[66] In the context of the environmental whistleblower statute, the DOL permits front pay: "Where the record reflects a sufficient level of hostility between an employer and employee that would cause irreparable damage to the employment relationship, it may be appropriate, at the request of the complainant, to order front pay in lieu of reinstatement."[67]

In *Johnson v. Old Dominion Security*, a Clean Air Act whistleblower case, the SOL held that "[f]ront pay may be awarded prospectively if reinstatement is impractical, impossible, or an inadequate remedy (e.g., reinstatement may not be feasible due to ongoing antagonism between the discriminated person and an employer).["68]

In cases in which reinstatement is not mandated by a statute, front pay is an appropriate method to calculate lost future earnings, and some courts prefer to compensate victims of discrimination through such an award.[69] In federal court, when reinstatement is not mandated by a statute, the judges decide, as a matter of law, whether the equitable remedy of reinstatement should be ordered or whether front pay should be awarded to compensate for loss of future earnings.[70] The judicial circuits are split on determining whether the amount of front pay is a jury question.[71]

COMPENSATORY DAMAGES

Compensatory damages are awardable in jurisdictions that treat whistleblower claims as a tort action and under many state and federal employee protection statutes.[72] These damages are designed to make the injured party completely whole and include compensation for emotional distress, pain and suffering, mental anguish, and lost future earnings.[73] Compensatory damages are also available as compensation for harassment,[74] humiliation, loss of professional reputation,[75] ostracism,[76] depression,[77] "fear" caused by threats,[78] "panic,"[79] and for the "frustration experienced by victims of discrimination."[80] Marital or family problems caused by the retaliation may also be compensable.[81]

Compensatory damages cannot be used to punish the employer. In *Hedden v. Conam Inspection Co.* the administrative law judge held that "compensatory damages, however, are those necessary to make a wronged party whole and no more."[82]

An employee has the burden of proof in establishing compensatory damages with "competent evidence."[83] For example, in a nuclear whistleblower case a DOL judge awarded $250,000 in compensatory damages based not only on the employee's subjective testimony of humiliation but also on the basis of fact—testimony and expert testimony documenting the employee's "unemployment and underemployment" during the course of his unemployment, "inability" to find comparable employment, expert testimony on loss of professional reputation and "negative" "attitude" employers had "toward whistleblowers," and the evidence that the employee would "face significant hostility and lack of professional respect upon his return" to work.[84] Emotional distress injury cannot be presumed, and the employee must demonstrate the existence and magnitude of such injury.[85] It is an error for the court to deny compensatory damages if such damages are supported by substantial evidence.[86] Damages for emotional distress may be awarded even if the employee "did not seek professional counseling and immediately proceeded to other employment."[87] An employee is not required to prove "disabling" emotional distress injuries.[88] Finally, an employee is not required to submit the testimony of medical or psychiatric experts to demonstrate compensatory damages.[89]

The award of compensatory damages is in addition to other remedies in the laws that are designed to restore financial losses.[90] Even if an employee's financial condition is not adversely affected, an employee may still be awarded compensatory damages for intangible damages such as mental anguish.[91]

In *McCuistion v. TVA*[92] the DOL reviewed a number of cases awarding compensatory damages in environmental whistleblower cases. The DOL cited favorably to a series of decisions that upheld compensatory damage awards for the following types of harm: embarrassment and humiliation; symptoms such as insomnia, nightmares, fatigue, and appetite loss; an employee's spouse suffering from tremendous emotional strain, mental suffering caused by an employee's loss of a car and house, and marital problems; a deterioration in health, an exacerbation of preexisting hypertension; and feelings of remorse that the education of the employee's daughter was disrupted.[93] The DOL also uses the amounts of damages awarded in other cases to measure the appropriate range for a specific compensatory injury;[94] however, the department has warned against imposing an "arbitrary upper limit" on the amount of damages and has also warned against allowing the level of damage to become "frozen in time."[95] In *Mitchell v. APS/ANPP*, an ALJ awarded $50,000, in part, because respondent's hostile work environment caused a nuclear whistleblower to become upset and nervous and to suffer from post-traumatic stress disorder.[96]

In setting a compensatory damage award the "severity of the retaliation" is relevant.[97]

EQUITABLE RELIEF AND AFFIRMATIVE ACTION

In addition to the traditional monetary relief available under tort or contract theory, most courts and administrative agencies have also been granted—either explicitly by statute or implicitly under traditional equitable powers—the authority to order nonmonetary or injunctive relief to insure that the wrongful conduct is fully eradicated and/or to insure that any "chilling effect" caused by retaliation is remedied.

The environmental whistleblower laws empower the SOL to order "affirmative action to abate" the violation of the environmental and nuclear employee protection provisions.[98] Under the National Labor Relations Act, the National Labor Relations Board can order affirmative action to effectuate the purposes of the act and to deter future misconduct.[99] These affirmative remedies include ordering collective bargaining, even if a union did not win a representation election; transferring funds from a "company union" to a legitimate union; and nationwide posting requirements.[100]

Similar policy reasons exist for supporting a broad interpretation of "affirmative action" under the environmental and nuclear employee protection laws. The whistleblower laws were passed in order to upgrade enforcement and compliance with environmental laws. Workers were envisioned as playing an important role in this process: "The best source of information about what a company is actually doing or not doing is often its own employees, and this amendment would insure that an employee could provide such information without losing his job or otherwise suffering economically from retribution from the polluter."[101]

The termination of a whistleblower can have a "chilling effect" on the work force.[102] Courts and administrative agencies, such as the Department of Labor, have the remedial power to correct this chilling effect. The SOL and NLRB regularly use this power to require plantwide posting of antidiscrimination orders.[103] Courts, interpreting the Occupational Safety and Health Act (OSHA) protections, have enjoined employers from taking future retaliatory steps and required the posting of explicit notices concerning misconduct and whom to contact if one wants to blow the whistle.[104]

As part of the "affirmative relief" provision of the environmental whistleblower laws, employers have been ordered to issue company-wide statements, prepared with the full participation and consent of a complainant, informing all employees that they must cease and desist from any discrimination against the whistleblower.[105] Consistent with the types of equitable relief available directly from courts, the "discretion" of administrative agencies "to determine what curative measures are needed" to correct violations of employee protection provisions has been regularly affirmed.[106] In exercising this discretion a court can take the "past conduct of the parties" into consideration.[107] Remedies have included requiring the president of a corporation to personally send notices to employees, despite the "ignominy of a forced public reading."[108] Other remedies have included mailing notices signed by a company's president to the home of every employee[109] and publication of notices in newspapers.[110] Employers have also been ordered to provide explicit training to managers regarding the rights of employees to blow the whistle.[111]

PUNITIVE DAMAGES OR LIQUIDATED DAMAGES

Whistleblowers may be entitled to punitive damages under the common law in states that have recognized the "public policy exception" as a tort action[112] or when a statute permits the award of "any other relief."[113] Additionally, such damages are awardable under a number of federal statutes, including the Civil Rights Act of 1871, 42 U.S.C. §§ 1983. For example, in *Smith v. Wade*,[114] the U.S. Supreme Court upheld an award of punitive damages "when the defendant's conduct is shown to be motivated by evil motive or intent, or when it involves reckless or callous indifference to the federally protected rights of others."[115] In a recent case upholding the use of punitive damages under Title VII of the Civil Rights Act of 1964, the Court set limits on when such damages may be imputed onto an employer based on the conduct of a manager.[116] In that case, the Court noted that not all of "intentional discrimination" necessarily "give[s] rise to punitive damage liability."[117] The Court also noted that such damages may not be available if an employer had made "good faith efforts" to comply with the law.[118]

Where permitted, punitive damages may be awarded to punish "unlawful conduct" and deter its "repetition."[119] The "most important indicium of the reasonableness of a punitive damages award is the degree of reprehensibility of the defendant's conduct,"[120] but a "grossly excessive award is clearly impermissible as a matter of constitutional law."[121]

In *Howard v. Zack Company*[122] a state court upheld a $375,000 punitive damage award in a whistleblower case, noting that such awards would have a "deterrent effect" on employer misconduct. In New Mexico, the appeals court explained its justification for affirming a $500,000 punitive damage award for a whistleblower terminated for exposing workplace safety violations:

we believe that discharging an employee for reporting safety concerns is particularly reprehensible. The health and safety of others is put at risk when it is clear that the reporting of safety hazards can cost a person his or her job. Here, where there was evidence of a pattern of threatening employees with their jobs over the raising of safety concerns, the jury could reasonably conclude Big J was engaging in particularly reprehensible conduct. An indifference to or reckless disregard for the health or safety of others is an aggravating factor for punitive damages.[123]

The Supreme Court of Mississippi, in upholding a 1.5 million dollar punitive damage award in a retaliatory discharge case, strongly reinforced the "legitimate interest" of society to ensure that "people are not discharged for reporting illegal acts," and emphasized the important function "of punitive damages in order deter similar future conduct.[124]

Some administratively adjudicated whistleblower laws also provide for punitive or exemplary damages. For example, the employee protection provisions of the Safe Drinking Water Act (SDWA) and the Toxic Substances Control Act (TSCA) contain specific statutory language giving the SOL the discretionary power to award exemplary damages in appropriate situations.[125] Courts have also determined that punitive damages may be awarded under OSHA.[126] The SOL has held that exemplary damages would be appropriate under these laws in order to punish an employee for wanton or reckless conduct in order to deter such conduct in the future.[127] The SOL applied the two-step analysis laid out in the Restatement (Second) of Torts, § 908 (1979) and held:

The threshold inquiry centers on the wrongdoer's state of mind: did the wrongdoer demonstrate reckless or callous indifference to the legally protected rights of others, and did the wrongdoer engage in conscious action in deliberate disregard of those rights? The "state of mind" thus is comprised both of intent and the resolve actually to take action to effect harm. If this state of mind is present, the inquiry proceeds to whether an award is necessary for deterrence.[128]

If an employer merely violates the whistleblower provisions of the TSCA or SDWA, such a violation "generally" is "insufficient to substantiate" an exemplary damage award.[129]

Some statutes mandate "liquidated damages" or double-back-pay awards. The Fair Labor Standards Act, Equal Pay Act, and Age Discrimination Act authorize an award of liquidated damages.[130] The False Claims Act antiretaliation clause also authorizes double-back-pay awards.[131]

INTEREST

Prejudgment interest is awardable under the various whistleblower protection laws. As held by the SOL in a nuclear whistleblower case, although the specific statute at issue did not "expressly provide for interest on back pay," the "make whole" purposes of antidiscrimination laws mandate the award of interest:

Back pay awards are designed to make "whole" the employee who has suffered economic loss as the result of the employer's illegal discrimination. The assessment of prejudgment interest is necessary to achieve this end. *See, Hansard v. Pepsi-Cola Metropolitan Bottling Co.*, 865 F.2d, 1461, 1471 (5th Cir. 1985) ("[t]he primary rationale for this conclusion is that unlawful discrimination deprives an employee of his salary as well as the use of that salary during the interim period") (emphasis in original); *Hunter v. Allis-Chalmers Corp.*, 797 F.2d 1417, 1426 (7th Cir. 1986) ("full compensation requires recognition of the time value of money").[132]

Although courts have discretion in awarding prejudgment interest and setting the rate for such interest,[133] such awards are now a matter of "routine."[134] Given the make-whole purpose of a backpay award, the 2nd Circuit has held that it is "ordinarily an abuse of discretion not to include pre-judgment interest in a backpay award."[135]

Most courts and agencies have followed the lead of the National Labor Relations Board (NLRB) in requiring that prejudgment interest be paid at the rate of interest set forth in the Tax Reform Act of 1986 for the underpayment of federal taxes.[136] The NLRB explained that the policy behind choosing the IRS rate was "to encourage timely compliance with Board orders, discourage the commission of unfair labor practices, and more fully compensate discriminates for their economic losses."[137]

The NLRB also explained the methodology to be employed in calculating the interest:

we shall require that the Respondent pay interest to accrue commencing with the last day of each calendar quarter of the backpay period for the amount due and owing for each quarterly period and continuing until compliance with the Order is achieved, such interest to be computed at the "short-term Federal rate" for the underpayment of taxes as set out in the 1986 amendment to 26 U.S.C. § 6621.[138]

Compounding interest on a quarterly basis is a "widely accepted by the courts."[139] Prejudgment interest is also available on an award of front pay[140] but not on an award of compensatory damages.[141]

Under both the DOL-administered whistleblower laws and the NLRA, the prejudgment interest continues to accrue at the IRS rate for underpayment of taxes until the damages are actually paid.[142] In federal court, postjudgment interest is "mandatory" under 28 U.S.C. § 1961.[143] Postjudgment interest must be awarded on the amount of the "entire" judgment, including prejudgment interest and compensatory and punitive damages.[144]

MITIGATION OF DAMAGES

Employees are required to mitigate damages suffered for retaliation under the whistleblower laws. The underlying justification for mitigation of damages in employment cases was outlined by the U.S. Supreme Court in *Phelps Dodge Corp. v. NLRB*:[145] "Since only actual losses should be made good, it seems fair that deductions should be made not only for actual earnings by the worker but also for losses which were willfully incurred."

The basic rule on mitigation was summarized in an NLRB case:

After the amount of backpay has been established, the burden shifts to the employer to produce evidence that would mitigate its liability. . . . An employer may meet this burden (and thus be entitled to a deduction from gross backpay) by, *inter alia*, establishing that the employee has willfully incurred losses through unjustifiably refusing adequate interim employment. . . . Further, an employer need not establish that the employee would have secured such employment, for the employer meets its burden on the mitigation issue by showing that the employee has withdrawn from the employment market. Accordingly, where the employer demonstrates that an employee did not exercise reasonable diligence in his or her efforts to secure employment, then it has established that the employee has not properly mitigated his or her damages.[146]

An employee is not forced to choose between searching for a job and participating in preparation for his or her whistleblower claim: "An employee who has been the target of an unfair labor practice need not choose between mitigation of damages and the vindication of his statutory rights."[147]

An employer must "affirmatively show" that a backpay award should be reduced due to a willful loss of earnings by the employee.[148] The burden of proof "shifts to defendant to prove facts which would mitigate" liability.[149] However, to meet the burden of proof, an employer must satisfy a two-prong test: "the defendant must demonstrate: 1) there were suitable positions which the plaintiff could have discovered and for which [he or she] was qualified; and 2) the plaintiff failed to use reasonable diligence in seeking such positions."[150]

For example, under the Surface Transportation Assistance Act (STAA) whistleblower provision, an employer must demonstrate that an employee "intentionally or heedlessly failed to protect" his or her interests.[151] An employee "is only required to make reasonable efforts to mitigate damages and is not held to the highest standards of diligence."[152] Additionally, a victim of illegal discrimination "must" be given the "benefit of every doubt" in evaluating his or her efforts to mitigate damages and find alternate employment.[153]

A wrongfully discharged employee "need not go into another line of work, accept a demotion, or take a demeaning position."[154] Comparable alternate employment must provide an employee with equivalent promotional opportunities, compensation, job responsibilities, working conditions, and status as did the position from which the employee was illegally fired.[155]

Although an employee must initially seek comparable employment, after a reasonable period of time the employee can lower his or her sights and accept lesser employment.[156] If an employee is compelled to accept lesser employment, there is "no duty" to continue the search for "more lucrative interim employment."[157]

Although it is very difficult outside a case-by-case analysis to set limits on exactly what constitutes "due diligence"[158] in the context of mitigation, one court found 28 applications submitted over a 1-year period to be sufficient diligence,[159] while the DOL reasoned that an employee who failed to contact employment agencies, answered only 8 of 290 relevant newspaper advertisements, and made only one job application per month "did not exercise reasonable diligence."[160]

If an employer fails to introduce evidence that the damages should be mitigated, the employer may not supplement the record on appeal to forestall a reinstatement or back pay order.[161]

An explicit and unconditional offer of reinstatement can toll back pay liability and can extinguish a right to reinstatement,[162] but the offer must be explicit and must be for "substantially equivalent" employment.[163] The failure to accept an offer of reinstatement does not necessarily "automatically terminate the employer's back pay liability."[164] A court must weigh the circumstances of the offer, the reason given for refusing the offer, and whether the offer was made in good faith.[165]

If an employee voluntarily quits due to unreasonable working conditions, the back pay award is not tolled.[166]

Employer liability for back wages or reinstatement terminates when an employee's employment would have ended for reasons independent of the violations found.[167] If a position would have been eliminated after a discharge, an employee may lose his right to reinstatement.[168] However, even if an employee was terminated after the expiration of a "fixed term contract" or a specific nonpermanent job, if the employee can demonstrate that the "fixed term" contracts of "similarly situated" employees were renewed, then liability for back wages is not extinguished.[169] Evidence that an employer engaged in conduct that interfered with an employee's ability to obtain comparable employment also acts to "continue" liability for back wages, even if the specific job for which the employee had been discharged no longer exists.[170]

An employee's misconduct after discharge may terminate an employer's responsibility to reinstate an employee.[171]

Although the general rule requires interim earnings to be deducted from a backpay award, if an employee can demonstrate that the interim earnings came from "secondary employment," no deduction is required.[172] For example, earnings from a part-time job or a consulting business that existed independent of the main job are not deducted from a backpay award.[173]

Additionally, monies obtained through unemployment compensation are not deducted from a backpay award.[174]

AFTER-ACQUIRED EVIDENCE

The doctrine of *after-acquired evidence* can result in a cutoff of damages.[175] This rule applies when, after an illegal discharge, an employer learns of facts that "would have led to the termination on legitimate grounds had the employer known about it."[176] Typically, the *after-acquired evidence* doctrine applies when, for example. during the discovery phase of an employment case an employer obtains information that absent the discriminatory motive, would have resulted in a lawful dismissal (e.g., information that a school teacher falsified proof of educational background).[177] The general rule in these circumstances is that an employee is entitled to back pay up until the date the employer learned of the *after-acquired evidence*: "Once an employer learns about employee wrongdoing that would lead to a legitimate discharge, we cannot require the employer to ignore the information."[178]

The standard of proof an employer must meet in order to obtain this cutoff of damages is very high.[179] An employer cannot misuse the discovery process in order to obtain such information; also, an employer must prove that the offense in question would in fact have resulted in discharge:

Where an employer seeks to rely upon *after-acquired evidence* of wrongdoing, it must first establish that the wrongdoing was of such severity that the employee in fact would have been terminated on those grounds alone if the employer had known of it at the time of the discharge. The concern that employers might as a routine matter undertake extensive discovery into an employee's background or performance on the job to resist claims under the Act is not an insubstantial one, but we think the authority of the courts to award attorney's fees, mandated under the statute, 29 U.S.C. §§216(b), 626(b), and in appropriate cases to invoke the provisions of Rule 11 of the Federal Rules of Civil Procedure will deter most abuses.[180]

Thus, under the *after-acquired evidence* rule, an employee is still entitled to damages under antidiscrimination laws, and the burden of proof on employers to establish the damage cutoff date is high.[181] Additionally, many courts do not permit *after-acquired evidence* to be introduced in the liability phase of a proceeding and only allow it to be used during the damages phase.[182]

TAX ISSUES RELATED TO DAMAGES AND SETTLEMENT

In prior years, the taxation of damage awards in employment cases was not a major issue. Most courts have determined that damage awards in employment discrimination cases were not taxable. Also, the prior use of "income averaging" mitigated against the harsh impact of obtaining a large lump sum award for back pay accumulated over numerous tax years. Additionally, compensatory damages for emotional distress were non-taxable. However, during the 1990s tax issues in employment law have radically changed.[183] Congress abolished income averaging and amended the tax code to require taxation of compensatory damages paid for emotional distress and punitive damages.[184] In 1995 the Supreme Court held that damages obtained for back pay were taxable as income.[185]

These changes in the tax treatment of employment-related damages have impacted the manner in which employees litigate or settle discrimination cases. Under the current tax code, an employee who prevails in a discrimination case will face the prospect of having to pay a lump sum tax on damages which were incurred over numerous tax years. Such employees find themselves in the position of losing deductions and having to pay taxes at rates far higher than they would have had to pay if the wages had not been obtained in one tax year.[186]

These changes have had a negative impact on the "make whole" requirement, a requirement which underlies the basic methodology most courts utilize in calculating an employment-related damage award.[187] Some employees have sought additional damages from their employer in order to compensate them for the negative tax impact of a large lump sum payment. Authorities on this issue are split.[188]

The Federal Judicial Center's official *Reference Manual on Scientific Evidence* strongly supports taking adverse tax consequences into consideration when calculating damages: "In principle, the calculation of compensation should measure the plaintiff's loss after taxes and then calculate the magnitude of pretax award needed to compensate the plaintiff fully, once taxation of the award is considered."[189] Consistent with the *Manual's* reasoning, the DOL, in environmental and nuclear whistleblower cases, held that employers may be ordered to pay tax-related compensation:

[The] goal of back pay is to make the victims of discrimination whole and restore them to the position they would have occupied in the absence of the unlawful discrimination. . . . Therefore, we agree . . . [with the] contention that a complainant is entitled to an enlargement of the back pay award to reflect the adverse tax consequences of receiving a lump sum payment that represents many years of back pay. . . . As [the employee] states, had he received the pay over the many years involved, he would have been in a lower tax bracket and could have taken advantage of various exemptions available to him. When [the employee] receives the lump sum payment, however, it will place him in the highest tax bracket and he will lose his ability to claim many exemptions.[190]

The DOL also held that an employee seeking compensation for tax-based losses is under a strict obligation to accurately and credibly document the amount of the enhancement.[191]

Another issue which has re-surfaced due to the changes in the tax code concerns how the IRS must treat back wages obtained by an employee in a discrimination suit. In 1946 the Supreme Court, in *Social Security Board v. Nierotko*, held that, for taxing purposes (i.e. Social Security tax), back pay "must be allocated as wages" in the "calendar quarters" of the "year in which the money would have been earned, if the employee had not been wrongfully discharged." The Court reasoned that the purpose of "back pay" in a labor dispute context was for the "protection of the employees and the redress of their grievances" and was thus designed to "make them whole."[192] Justice Frankfurter, in his concurring opinion, clearly set forth the public policy and legal analysis of the Court in reaching its conclusion: "The decisions of this Court leaves no doubt that a man's time may, as a matter of law, be in the service of another, though he be inactive. . . . When the employer is liable for back pay, he is so liable because under the circumstances, though he has illegally discharged the employee, he still absorbs his time. . . . In short, an employer must pay wages although, in violation of law, he has subjected his employee to enforced idleness."[193]

The holding of *Social Security Board* was affirmed by the Sixth Circuit, and expanded to include taxation of wages, along with taxation for Social Security benefits.[194] However, the IRS has refused to follow the Sixth Circuit decision.[195]

One method used by employers and employees to avoid the harsh tax consequences of a lump sum settlement, is for the employer to agree to establish an annuity or deferred compensation plan. These plans spread-out the payment of damages over a number of years, and thus reduce the tax liability for the employee. The requirements for a valid deferred compensation plan/annuity were explicated by the Tax Court in *Childs v. Commissioner of Internal Revenue*.[196] Among the provisions which should be included in a settlement agreement in order to establish a qualified deferred compensation annuity are the following: (1) the annuity should not be secured from the employer's creditors; (2) the employee should have no "right, title or interest" in the annuity; and (3) the employee may be named a revocable beneficiary of the trust or annuity, but may not have any right to accelerate payments.[197]

ATTORNEY FEES AND COSTS

A critical factor in determining which law to utilize in prosecuting a whistleblower claim is the availability of attorney fees. Often the damages in a whistleblower case are modest. Additionally, a wrongfully discharged employee can rarely pay an attorney's standard market rate fee. Indeed, in some cases the whistleblower primarily seeks injunctive-type relief, and monetary damages may be small or nonexistent. If an attorney had to rely upon a standard one-third contingency payment as the sole method of obtaining an attorney fee, many important whistleblower cases would never be filed.

Under the "American Rule," unless attorney fees are explicitly provided for under a statute, a prevailing party is not entitled to court-ordered fees.[198] Consequently, under the public policy exception common law cause of action (be it a tort or contract action), attorney fees are not usually available as an element of damage. Because of the harshness of the "American Rule" Congress passed the Civil Rights Attorney's Fees Awards Act of 1976, codified as 42 U.S.C. § 1988 (commonly referred to as § 1988). Congress intent was spelled out in the legislative history: "[i]f private citizens are to be able to assert their civil rights, and if those who violate the Nation's fundamental laws are not to proceed with impunity, then citizens must have the opportunity to recover what it costs them to vindicate these rights in court."[199] As explained by the U.S. Supreme Court: "The purpose of § 1988 is to ensure effective access to the judicial process; for persons with civil rights grievances."[200] To achieve these goals, the fees awarded under that provision needed to be sufficiently "adequate" to insure that employees could "attract competent counsel."[201] Similarly, in a whistleblower case under the Clean Air Act, the DOL warned against setting a fee "standard that would chill attorneys from taking moderately complicated cases" where an employee "earned modest wages."[202]

The courts have also recognized that, given the nonmonetary aspect of many civil rights cases, attorney fees can be awarded without any direct relationship between the amount of fees and the amount of relief obtained for a client: "[u]nlike most private tort litigants, a civil rights plaintiff seeks to vindicate important civil and constitutional rights that cannot be valued solely in monetary terms. . . . Regardless of the form of relief he actually obtains, a successful civil rights plaintiff often secures important social benefits that are not reflected in nominal or relatively small damages awards."[203]

Section 1988 provides that in a federal civil rights action, "the court, in its discretion, may allow the prevailing party . . . a reasonable attorney's fee as part of costs."[204] Although the statute provides a court with discretion, consistent with the legislative history and subsequent case law, "a prevailing plaintiff should ordinarily recover an attorney's fee unless special circumstances would render such an award unjust."[205] The "prevailing party" concept was a "generous formulation" for plaintiffs and entitled attorneys who attempted to vindicate civil rights claims to prevail, even if they only obtained "partial relief."[206] Not only are attorneys entitled to compensation, but law firms are also entitled to a reasonable fee for paralegal and law clerk time.[207]

Consistent with Section 1988, Congress has passed numerous other statutory attorney fee provisions. Most of the federal whistleblower laws contain a fee shifting provision. In addition, most states have followed Congress' lead and have included fee shifting provisions within their state whistleblower protection statutes. Courts and administrative agencies have applied the case-law developed under Section 1988 when interpreting the various fee provisions contained in the whistleblower protection statutes.

Determining a Reasonable Attorney Fee

In determining a reasonable attorney fee, the basic starting point is the *lodestar* calculation. As defined by the U.S. Supreme Court[208] the *lodestar* calculation is simply the product of multiplying a reasonable attorney fee rate by the number of hours reasonably expended on the litigation. In *Hensley v. Eckerhart*,[209] the U.S. Supreme Court held:

The most useful starting point for determining the amount of a reasonable fee is the number of hours reasonably expended on the litigation multiplied by a reasonable hourly rate. This calculation provides an objective basis on which to make an initial estimate of the value of a lawyer's services.

*   *   *

The product of reasonable hours times a reasonable rate does not end the inquiry. There remain other considerations that may lead the district court to adjust the fee upward or downward, including the important factor of the "results obtained."[210]

Under the *lodestar* method, the first step in determining a reasonable attorney fee is to determine whether the number of hours a complainant's counsel alleges he or she worked on the case and the requested hourly rate are "reasonable for the quantity and quality of the work performed."[211] Next, the reasonable fee would be established by multiplying the number of hours expended on the litigation by the established market hourly rate for attorney time.[212] The fact that an employee did not prevail on every issue does not automatically constitute a valid ground for reducing an attorney fee award,[213] but fees may be reduced when a plaintiff obtains "partial or limited" success.[214]

Once the amount of reasonable hours is determined, the next step is setting a reasonable market rate for each attorney who performed work on the case.[215] In the legislative history of the Civil Rights Attorney's Fee Award Act of 1976, Congress cited with approval twelve factors set forth in the case of *Johnson v. Georgia Highway Express, Inc.*[216] for determining the fair market rate for which an attorney can collect fees.[217] Consequently, most courts use the twelve *"Johnson* factors*"* when evaluating fee petitions.[218] The *Johnson* factors are:

1. the time and labor required;[219]

2. the customary fee;

3. the novelty and difficulty of the questions;

4. the skill requisite to perform the legal service properly;

5. the preclusion of other employment by the attorney due to acceptance of the case;

6. the limitations imposed by the client or the circumstances; priority work that delays the lawyer's other legal work is entitled to some premium;

7. the amount involved and the results obtained;

8. the experience, reputation, and ability of the attorney; if a young attorney demonstrates the skill and ability, he or she should not be penalized merely for being admitted recently to the bar;

9. the "undesirability" of the case;

10. awards in similar cases;

11. whether the fee is fixed or contingent; and

12. the nature and length of the professional relationship with the client.[220]

It is recognized that "the most critical factor in determining a fee award's reasonableness is the degree of success obtained."[221] Additionally, civil rights or employment cases are often viewed as "complex civil litigation," and attorney fee rates must be set in order to "attract competent counsel" to work on such cases.[222]

Other factors may impact on an attorney fee that are not considered either in the lodestar approach or under the *Johnson* factors. For example, attorneys for nonprofit organizations or public interest law firms should be awarded fees at the "prevailing market rates." In cases brought under 42 U.S.C. § 1988, the Supreme Court held that both private and nonprofit attorneys should be paid on the same market rate: "The statute and legislative history establish that 'reasonable fees' under § 1988 are to be calculated according to the prevailing market rates in the relevant community, regardless of whether plaintiff is represented by private or nonprofit counsel."[223]

The complainant is entitled to attorney fees even if the case was resolved through an out-of-court settlement.[224] In a civil rights case, *Maher v. Gagne*, the Supreme Court held that "the fact that respondent prevailed through a settlement rather than through litigation does not weaken her claim to fees."[225]

The Supreme Court has also awarded attorney fees in cases where the plaintiff was only partially successful. The rule for calculating attorney fees in partially successful cases was spelled out in *Hensley v. Eckerhart:*

Where the plaintiff has failed to prevail on a claim that is distinct in all respects from his successful claims, the hours spent on the unsuccessful claim should be excluded in considering the amount of a reasonable fee. Where a lawsuit consists of related claims, a plaintiff who has won substantial relief should not have his attorney's fee reduced simply because the district court did not adopt each contention raised.[226]

If an attorney enters into a contingency fee agreement with a complainant, such an agreement will not automatically bar the attorney from being awarded a statutory fee greater than the contingency fee. Trial judges are not "limited" by any "contractual fee agreement between plaintiff and counsel."[227] But, if a case fully settles for a lump sum, that sum may include both damages for the client and attorney fees.[228]

The "prevailing party" bears the burden for establishing the reasonable hourly rate applicable in any case.[229] This is usually accomplished through affidavits of nonparty attorneys who can attest to the local market rate[230] for attorneys of "comparable skill, expertise and reputation in complex federal litigation."[231] Attorneys are also required to properly document the amount of time spent on a case. If documentation is "inadequate," the fee may be reduced.[232] In *Washington v. Philadelphia County*,[233] the Court of Appeals for the 3rd Circuit upheld the use of "computerized" time records, which set forth the date each activity took place with "sufficient specificity."

Attorneys who represent clients under a contingency fee arrangement are not permitted to obtain a fee enhancement because of the contingency nature of the retainer.[234] However, in complex cases clients are "entitled to retain the most competent counsel available," and a court should be willing to pay counsel its "normal billing rate," even if that rate is higher than the local market fees.[235] Conversely, if a firm reduces its hourly rate in order to represent low income or public interest clients, the firm should still be compensated at normal market rates.[236]

The amount of attorney fees may sometimes be larger than the damage award. In *City of Riverside v. Rivera*,[237] the damage award amounted to $33,350, while the statutory attorney fee was $245,456.25.[238] Due to the significant size of the potential statutory attorney fee, complainants may reduce or waive it as part of a settlement.[239] In some jurisdictions, requiring such a waiver as a precondition to settle may constitute an ethical violation.[240]

In order to compensate for the delay of time between performing legal services and obtaining payment for these services, attorney fee awards are often paid at the rate in effect when awarded, not the rate in effect at the time the services are performed.[241] As the Supreme Court explained in *Missouri v. Jenkins*:

If no compensation were provided for the delay in payment, the prospect of such hardship could well deter otherwise willing attorneys from accepting complex civil rights cases that might offer great benefit to society at large; the result would work to defeat Congress' purpose in enacting § 1988 of "encourag[ing] the enforcement of federal law through lawsuits filed by private persons."[242]

In calculating "current rates," a court should not use an inflation index to merely increase a firm's "historic rate." Instead, the method most often utilized is to pay an attorney fee at the rate the attorney currently charges a client:

Defendants correctly note that plaintiffs offer no evidence concerning the inflation rate during the last four years or how their 1999 rates compare to their rates in prior years as adjusted by inflation. However, plaintiffs have submitted evidence that their attorneys are representing them on a contingency basis. Therefore, payment to plaintiffs' attorneys has been delayed for four years. Such a lengthy delay in payment justifies the use of current rates.[243]

Attorney fees are awardable for "all phases of the litigation," including appeals and for work performed during administrative proceedings.[244] Attorney fees incurred in the preparation of an application for fees are also compensable.[245]

The calculation of a reasonable attorney fee should not result in a "second major litigation," and the fee petition need not "achieve technical perfection."[246] A fee application may be filed after the close of the administrative record.[247] Under the civil rights attorney fee law, applications for attorney fees have been filed after the ten-day period for motions to alter or amend a final judgment.[248]

Costs and Expenses

Most statutory fee provisions permit the prevailing party to be compensated for all costs. In this regard, costs "necessarily include all expenses incident to the litigation that are normally billed to fee-paying clients."[249] In a nuclear whistleblower case, the DOL held that the provision for an employer's payment of costs must be "interpreted broadly."[250]

Like attorney fees, the costs must have been "reasonably incurred" and "sufficiently documented."[251] Recoverable costs have included items such as postage, reproduction, travel, meals,[252] lodging in a "deluxe hotel," paralegal expenses,[253] supplemental secretarial costs, arbitration costs,[254] telephone costs, long distance calls, messengers' fees,[255] certified mailings, gasoline, and parking.[256] The U.S. Supreme Court held in *West Virginia University Hospitals, Inc. v. Casey* that expert witness fees are only available to a prevailing party if they are explicitly authorized in the attorney fees and cost statute.[257] Under this case, if the statutory language authorizing an award for attorney fees and costs does not explicitly reference expert witness fees as an allowable cost, a prevailing party cannot be reimbursed for expert witness fees.

Environmental and Nuclear Whistleblower Laws

All of the environmental and nuclear employee protection laws contain liberal provisions for attorney fees and costs.[258] They provide for compensation for fees at every step of the administrative process, including the OSHA investigation,[259] the hearing process and the appeal before the ARB.[260] In some circumstances, even work performed outside of the formal adjudicatory process may be compensable.[261] In administering these laws, the U.S. Department of Labor generally follows the case law developed under 42 U.S.C. § 1988.

Unlike the other employment discrimination or civil rights attorney fees laws, the whistleblower laws do not give the SOL the discretion to deny reasonable attorney fees.[262] For example, the attorney fee provision in Section 210 of the Energy Reorganization Act states:

If an order is issued under this paragraph, the Secretary, at the request of the complainant shall assess against the person against who the order is issued a sum equal to the aggregate amount of all costs and expenses (including attorneys' fees and expert witness fees) reasonably incurred, as determined by the Secretary, by the complainant for, or in connection with, the bringing of the complaint upon which the order was issued.[263]

The Department of Labor follows the "lodestar" method in determining a reasonable attorney fee: "In calculating attorney fees under these statutes, I employ the lodestar method which requires multiplying the number of hours reasonably expended in bringing the litigation by a reasonable hourly fee."[264]

Only the complainant may obtain reimbursement for expenses and attorney fees.[265] If the respondent (employer) wins, there is no provision for the payment of legal expenses.[266]

The DOL requires an attorney for a prevailing environmental whistleblower to meet the same standards for demonstrating a reasonable attorney fee as do the federal courts under § 1988: "Complainant's attorney's fee petition must include: adequate evidence concerning a reasonable hourly fee for the type of work the attorney performed and consistent for practice in the local geographic area; records indicating date, time and duration necessary to accomplish the specific activity, each activity being identifiable as pertaining to the case; and all claimed costs, specifically identified."[267]

An ALJ can make an initial ruling on attorney fees and costs. As a matter of regulatory authority, the SOL has *de novo* authority to review any such award.[268] The SOL has adopted a considerable deference standard in reviewing attorney fee awards issued by the ALJs. This standard is less stringent than the abuse of discretion standard appellate courts apply when reviewing attorney fee awards issued by the federal district courts, but greater than the *de novo* authority the SOL could have applied.[269]

Attorneys are allowed additional payments to compensate counsel for delays in payment.[270] Specifically, attorneys may recover interest on attorney fees or receive another adjustment to compensate for a delay in obtaining an award.[271]

In calculating a reasonable attorney fee, an attorney's private fee arrangement with a client does not form a ceiling for an award, unless the attorney and client agreed to an explicit cap on attorney's fees. The determining factor is what constitutes a reasonable award.[272] In a nuclear whistleblower case the SOL held: "The fee arrangement between Complainant and his counsel is not controlling. Rather, Complainant has the burden of establishing the reasonableness of the fees. Counsel must submit a fee petition detailing the work performed, the time spent on such work, and the hourly rate of those performing the work. Complainant also must submit itemized costs."[273] The reasonable attorney fee rates are generally established by affidavits from other attorneys regarding the prevailing fees in the community where the attorney practices. However, generalized and conclusory affidavits from friendly attorneys may not be sufficient to establish the prevailing rate of pay.[274]

Attorneys are entitled to compensation for time reasonably spent preparing a fee claim.[275]

The scope of appeal for a final Department of Labor attorney fee award is narrow. The U.S. Court of Appeals may reverse a final fee award only if the SOL abused discretion in calculating the fee.[276]

All of the environmental and nuclear whistleblower laws are silent as to whether attorney fees may be awarded to a prevailing complainant for work performed appealing a claim before the U.S. Court of Appeals. In a split decision, the U.S. Court of Appeals for the 6th Circuit denied a request for attorney fees at the appellate level under Section 210 of the Energy Reorganization Act.[277] However, since that decision another appeals court held that such fees are recoverable, and the DOL subsequently reversed its position on this matter.[278] In *Thompson v. U.S. Department of Labor*,[279] the court held that an employee was entitled to a fee under the Equal Access to Justice Act directly from the U.S. Department of Labor when the Secretary's decision against the employee was "not substantially justified."[280]

NOTES

1. In *Management Information Technologies, Inc. v. Aleyska Pipeline Service Company, et al.* 151 F.R.D. 478, 481 (D.C. 1993), Judge Stanley Sporkin reviewed "academic studies" and other materials which "well document" the types of damage suffered by whistleblowers.

2. *See, e.g., Carey v. Piphus*, 435 U.S. 247, 253 (1978) (§ 1983 remedy creates a "species of tort liability"). *Accord., Memphis Community School District v. Stachura*, 477 U.S. 299 (1986). In whistleblower cases the Secretary of Labor (SOL) has analogized the types of remedies available under § 1983. *Moyer v. Yellow Freight*, 89-STA-7, D&O of SOL, at 32 (August 21, 1995).

3. *See, e.g., Reich v. Cambridgeport Air Systems, Inc.*, 26 F.3d 1187 (1st Cir. 1994) (discussing damages generally available in federal whistleblower claims in which a statute does not limit the type of remedies available).

4. *Nord v. U.S. Steel Corp.*, 758 F.2d 1462, 1470-1471 (11th Cir. 1985) ("It is the duty of the district court, after a finding of discrimination, to place the injured party in the position he or she would have been absent the discriminatory actions").

5. 422 U.S. 405, 418-420 (1975).
6. *Id.* at 418-419, quoting *Wicker v. Hoppock*, 6 Wall. 94, 99 (1867).
7. *Phelps Dodge Corp. v. NLRB*, 313 U.S. 177, 197 (1941).
8. *Reeves v. Claiborne County*, 828 F.2d 1096, 1101 (5th Cir. 1987) ("Reinstatement" is "normally integral part of the remedy for a constitutionally impermissible employment action").
9. *Hobby v. Georgia Power Co.*, 90-ERA-30, R. D&O of ALJ, at 48 (September 17, 1998). *See also* Penina Glazer and Myron Glazer, *The Whistleblowers: Exposing Corruption in Government and Industry* (New York: Basic Books, 1989).
10. *See, e.g.*, 42 U.S.C. 5851(b).
11. *Reeves v. Claiborne County Bd. of Ed.*, 828 F.2d 1096, 1101 (5th Cir. 1987).
12. *Allen v. Autauga County Bd. of Ed.*, 685 F.2d 1302, 1306 (11th Cir. 1982). *Accord., Jackson v. City of Albuquerque*, 890 F.2d 225, 234-235 (10th Cir. 1989); *Reeves v. Claiborne County Bd. of Ed.*, at 1102. *But see McNight v. General Motors Corp.*, 908 F.2d 104 (7th Cir. 1990) (discussing benefits of front pay in lieu of reinstatement).
13. *Creekmore v. ABB Power Systems*, 93-ERA-24, Supplemental Order of Deputy Sec. of Labor, at 3 (April 10, 1996).
14. *Sterzing v. Fort Bend Ind. Sch. Dist.*, 496 F.2d 92, 93 (5th Cir. 1974). *Accord., Donnellon v. Fruehauf Corp.*, 794 F.2d 598, 602 (11th Cir. 1986).
15. *Jackson v. City of Albuquerque, supra*, at 235.
16. *Tualatin Elec., Inc. v. NLRB*, 84 F.3d 1202, 1205 (9th Cir. 1996).
17. *Id.* at 1205-1206.
18. *Id.* at 1206. *Accord., NLRB v. Draper Corp.*, 159 F.2d 294, 297 (1st Cir. 1947); *NLRB v. Jackson Farmers, Inc.*, 457 F.2d 516, 518 (10th Cir. 1972).
19. *Pecker v. Heckler*, 801 F.2d 709, 712-713 (4th Cir. 1986).
20. *Wilson v. A.M. General Corp.*, 979 F. Supp. 800, 802 (N.D. Ind. 1997).
21. *See, e.g., Creekmore v. ABB Power Systems, supra,* (June 20, 1996) (even after sale of a subsidiary the company that retained liability was obligated to reinstate the complainant to a substantially similar position); DeFord v. TVA 81-ERA-1 (Sec'y. August 16, 1984) (the SOL stated that, "[i]f [complainant's] former position no longer exists or there is no vacancy, TVA shall apply to the Administrative Law Judge for approval of the job in which it proposes to place DeFord with an explanation of the duties, functions, responsibilities, physical location and working conditions"); *Hobby v. Georgia Power Co., supra,* at 54-57.
22. *Kuepferle v. Johnson Controls, Inc.*, 713 F. Supp. 171, 173 (M.D. N.C. 1988); *Sennello v. Reserve Life Ins.*, 667 F. Supp. 1498, 1522 (S.D. Fla. 1987).
23. *NLRB v. Taylor Mach. Products*, 136 F.2d 507, 516 (6th Cir. 1998).
24. *Firefighters v. Stotts*, 467 U.S. 561, 579 (1983); *Walsdorf v. Board of Commissioners*, 857 F.2d 1047, 1054 (5th Cir. 1988); *Hicks v. Dothan City Bd. of Ed.*, 814 F. Supp. 1044, 1050 (M.D. Ala. 1993) (equitable power includes

"authority to displace" an "incumbent employee").

25. *Walters v. City of Atlanta*, 803 F.2d 1138, 1149 (11th Cir. 1986).

26. *NLRB v. J. H. Rutter-Rex*, 396 U.S. 258, 263 (1969).

27. *Id.* 396 U.S. at 263-265 (citations omitted).

28. *Hobby v. Georgia Power Co.*, *supra*, at 57 (internal citations omitted). *Accord.*, *Clifton v. U.P.S.*, 94-STA-16, D&O of SOL, at 2 (May 14, 1997) (under Surface Transportation whistleblower provision back pay "is not a matter of discretion but is mandated once it is determined" that the act was violated).

29. *Pettway v. American Cast Iron Pipe Co.*, 494 F.2d 211, 260-261 (5th Cir. 1974); *Clay v. Castle Coal & Oil Company*, 90-STA-37, D&O of SOL at 2 (June 3, 1994) (STA whistleblower case); *Lederhaus v. Donald Paschen*, 91-ERA-13, D&O of SOL, at 9-10 (October 26, 1992) (nuclear whistleblower); *Hoffman v. W. Max Bossert*, 94-CAA-4, D&O of SOL, at 2 (January 22, 1997) (environmental case).

30. *Ross v. Buckeye Cellulose Corp.*, 764 F. Supp. 1543, 1547 (M.D. Ga. 1991) (citations omitted). *See also IBT v. U.S.*, 431 U.S. 324, 372 (1977).

31. *Id. Accord., EEOC v. Korn Industries, Inc.*, 622 F.2d 256, 263 (4th Cir. 1981).

32. *Cook v. Guardian Lubricants*, 95-STA-43, D&O of remand by SOL, at 3 (May 30, 1997); *Creekmore v. ABB Power Systems*, *supra*, D&O of ARB, at 4 (June 20, 1996).

33. *Assistant Secretary of Labor v. T. O. Hass Tire Company*, 94-STA-2, D&O of SOL, at 9 (August 3, 1994).

34. *Dutile v. Tighe Trucking, Inc.*, 93-STA-31, D&O of SOL, at 3-4 (October 31, 1994).

35. *Polgar v. Florida Stage Lines*, 94-STA-46, modified D&O of SOL, at 3 (June 5, 1995).

36. *O'Brien v. Stone & Webster Eng. Corp.*, 84-ERA-31, recommended D&O of ALJ, at 21 (February 28, 1985); *Landers v. Commonwealth-Lord Joint Venture*, 83-ERA-5, slip op. of ALJ, at 16-17, adopted by SOL (1983); *Blackburn v. Martin*, 982 F.2d 125 (4th Cir. 1992).

37. *Fischer v. Town of Steilacoom*, 83-WPC-2, slip op. of ALJ, at 10 (1983); *Tritt v. Fluor Constructors*, 88-ERA-29, D&O of remand by SOL, at 6 (March 16, 1995).

38. In *Fischer*, the employee was awarded $6,554 in lost earnings and expenses and an additional $18,217 for "compensation for a six-month period while complainant seeks employment." *Contra, Goldstein v. EBASCO Constructors, Inc.*, 86-ERA-36, recommended D&O of ALJ, at 13 (March 3, 1988).

39. *Hufstetler v. Roadway Express, Inc.*, 85-STA-8, D&O of SOL, at 58-59 (August 21, 1986). *See, e.g., Donovan v. Freeway Constr. Co.*, 551 P. Supp. 869, 880-881 (D. R.I. 1982).

40. *Id. Blum v. Witco Chemical Corp.*, 829 F.2d 367, 374 (3rd Cir. 1987).

41. *Id. Dutile v. Tighe Trucking, supra*, at 3.

42. *Id. Accord., Sands v. Runyon*, 28 F.3d 1323, 1329 (2nd Cir. 1994); *Bascom v. APT Transportation*, 92-STA-32, D&O of ALJ, at 4 (September 14,

1992), *aff'd* by SOL (November 9, 1992).

43. *Chase v. Buncombe County, N.C.*, 85-SWD-4, D&O of remand by SOL, at 6-7 (November 3, 1986).

44. *Bassett v. Niagara Mohawk Power Co.*, 86-ERA-2, order of remand by SOL, at 4 (July 9, 1986).

45. *Crow v. Noble Roman's Inc.*, 95-CAA-8, D&O of SOL, at 5 (February 26, 1996); *Blake v. Hatfield Elec. Co.*, 87-ERA-4, recommended decision by ALJ, at 23-24 (August 13, 1987).

46. *Id.*

47. *Earwood v. Dart Container*, 93-STA-16, D&O of SOL, at 6 (December 7, 1994).

48. *Cook v. Guardian Lubricants, Inc., supra*, at 13.

49. *Edwards v. Hodel*, 738 F. Supp. 426, 431 (D. Colo. 1990).

50. *Moyer v. Yellow Freight*, 89-STA-7, D&O of SOL, at 17 (August 21, 1995).

51. *Clifton v. UPS, supra*, at 3.

52. *Hoffman v. W. Max Bossert*, 94-CAA-4, D&O of SOL, at 8 (January 22, 1997) (employer ordered to pay for schooling); *Studer v. Flower Baking Company*, 93-CAA-11, D&O of SOL, at 4 (June 19, 1995) (denial of training is adverse action).

53. *Creekmore v. ABB Power*, 93-ERA-24, D&O of remand by SOL, at 26 (February 14, 1996); *Assistant Secretary v. Intermodal*, 94-STA-22, D&O of SOL, at 5 (July 26, 1995).

54. *Creekmore v. ABB Power Systems*, at 27.

55. *Dutile v. Tighe Trucking, supra*, at 6-7.

56. *Creekmore v. ABB Power Systems*, at 21-22; *Hobby v. Georgia Power Co., supra*, at 64-65.

57. *Boytin v. PP&L*, 94-ERA-32, D&O of remand by SOL, at 12 (October 20, 1995).

58. *Memphis Community School District v. Stachura*, 477 U.S. 299 (1986).

59. *Phelps Dodge v. NLRB, supra*, at 188.

60. *Pogue v. United States Dept. of the Navy*, 87-ERA-21, D&O on Remand by SOL, at 7 (April 14, 1994).

61. *Id.*

62. *Nolan v. AC Express*, 92-STA-37, Remand Order of SOL, at 15-16 (January 17, 1995).

63. *Id.*

64. *U.S. v. Burke*, 504 U.S. 229, 119 L.Ed.2d 34, 45 n. 9 (1992).

65. *Blum v. Witco Chem. Corp.*, 829 F.2d 367, 374 (3rd Cir. 1987).

66. *EEOC v. Prudential Federal Sav.*, 763 F.2d 1166, 1172 (10th Cir. 1985).

67. *Clifton v. U.P.S.*, 94-STA-16, D&O of ARB, at 2 (May 14, 1997). *See also Hobby v. Georgia Power Co., supra*, at 54-57, for a discussion of when to order reinstatement or front pay.

68. 86-CAA-3/4/5, D&O of SOL, at 25 (May 29, 1991).

69. *See, e.g., McNight v. General Motors Corp.*, 908 F.2d 104, 115-116 (7th Cir. 1990); *McNeil v. Economics Lab.*, 800 F.2d 111, 118 (7th Cir. 1986).

70. *Dickerson v. Deluxe Check Printers, Inc.*, 703 F.2d 276, 280 (8th Cir. 1983).

71. *See Fite v. First Tennessee Production Credit Ass'n.*, 861 F.2d 884, 893 (6th Cir. 1988); *Maxfield v. Sinclair Int'l.*, 766 F.2d 788, 795-796 (3rd Cir. 1985), *cert. denied*, 474 U.S. 1057, 106 S.Ct. 796, 88 L.Ed.2d 773 (1986); *Cassino v. Reichhold Chemicals, Inc.*, 817 F.2d 1338, 1347 (9th Cir. 1987), *cert. denied*, 484 U.S. 1047, 108 S.Ct. 785, 98 L.Ed.2d 870 (1988); *Coston v. Plitt Theatres, Inc.*, 831 F.2d 1321, 1333 n. 4 (7th Cir.1987), *cert. denied*, 485 U.S. 1007, 108 S.Ct. 1471, 99 L.Ed.2d 700, *vacated and rem. on other grounds*, 486 U.S. 1020, 108 S.Ct. 1990, 100 L.Ed.2d 223 (1988). On the other hand, the 2nd, 4th, and 10th Circuits have held that the amount of front pay is for the judge to decide. *See Dominic v. Consolidated Edison Co.*, 822 F.2d 1249, 1257 (2nd Cir. 1987); *Duke v. Uniroyal, Inc.*, 928 F.2d 1413, 1424 (4th Cir. 1991); *Denison v. Swaco Geolograph Co.*, 941 F.2d 1416 (10th Cir. 1991).

72. *See, e.g., DeFord v. Secretary of Labor*, 700 F.2d 281, 288 (6th Cir. 1983) (explicit reference under ERA); *Soto v. Adams Elevator*, 941 F.2d 543, 551 (7th Cir. 1991) (implicit in Equal Pay Act).

73. *Smith v. Atlas Off-Shore Boat Serv., Inc.*, 653 F.2d 1057, 1064 (5th Cir. 1981).

74. *English v. Whitfield*, 868 F.2d 957 (4th Cir. 1988).

75. *Wieb van der Meer v. Western Kentucky University*, 95-ERA-38, D&O of ARB, at 8-9 (April 20, 1998); *Leveille v. N.Y. Air National Guard*, 94-TSC-3/4, D&O of ARB (October 25, 1999).

76. *Neal v. Honeywell, Inc.*, 995 F. Supp. 889, 895 (E.D. Ill. 1998).

77. *Id.*

78. *Id.*

79. *Creekmore v. ABB Power Systems, supra,* at 24-25.

80. *Walters v. City of Atlanta*, 803 F.2d 1135, 1146 (11th Cir. 1986).

81. *Muldrew v. Anheuser-Busch, Inc.*, 728 F.2d 989, 992, n. 1 (8th Cir. 1984); *Wulf v. City of Wichita*, 883 F.2d 842, 875 (10th Cir. 1989); *Assistant Secretary v. Guaranteed Overnight Delivery*, 95-STA-37, D&O of ARB, at 2-3 (September 5, 1996).

82. 82-ERA-3, slip. op. of ALJ, at 7-8 (1982).

83. *Carey v. Piphus, supra,* at 264 n. 20; *Lederhaus v. Paschen, supra,* at 10.

84. *Hobby v. Georgia Power Co., supra,* at 65-67.

85. *Pogue v. United States Dept. of the Navy, supra,* at 8.

86. *Blackburn v. Martin, supra,* at 132, 133; *Pogue v. United States Dept. of the Navy,* at 13.

87. *Blackburn v. Metric Constructors, Inc.*, 86-ERA-4, Final Order on Compensatory Damages by SOL, at 3 (August 16, 1993).

88. *Id.* at 4.

89. *Lederhaus v. Donald Paschen, et al., supra,* at 11; *Thomas v. APS*, 89-ERA-19, at 27-28 (September 17, 1993).

90. *Blackburn v. Martin, supra,* at 132.

91. *Id. See also Stallworth v. Shuler,* 777 F.2d 1431, 1435 (11th Cir. 1985) (injury may be "intangible" and "need not be financial or physical").

92. 89-ERA-6, D&O of SOL, at 19-20 (November 13, 1991). *See also Smith v. ESICORP, Inc.,* 93-ERA-16, D&O of SOL, at 3-4 (August 27, 1998) (collecting cases).

93. *See, e.g., Thomas v. APS, supra,* D&O of SOL, at 27 ("compensatory damages may be awarded for emotion pain and suffering, mental anguish, embarrassment and humiliation").

94. *Smith v. ESICORP, Inc., supra,* D&O of ARB, at 2. *See also Assistant Secretary v. Guaranteed Overnight Delivery,* 95-STA-37, D&O of ARB, at 3 (September 5, 1996); *EEOC v. AIC Security Investigations,* 55 F.3d 1276, 1285 (7th Cir. 1995).

95. *Leveille v. N.Y. Air National Guard,* 94-TSC-3/4, D&O of ARB, at 5 (October 25, 1999).

96. 91-ERA-9, R. D&O of ALJ, at 45-46 (July 2, 1992).

97. *Smith v. ESICORP, Inc., supra,* at 4. *Accord., U.S. v. Balistrieri,* 981 F.2d 916, 932 (7th Cir. 1993). The amount of compensatory damages can vary widely depending on the circumstances of a case. *See, e.g., Migilore v. R.I. Department of Environmental Management,* 98-SWD-1/2/3, R. D&O of ALJ, at 46-52 (August 13, 1999) (discussing past compensatory damage awards and then awarding $400,000 in damages); *Southwest Forest v. Sutton* 868 F.2d 352 (10th Cir. 1998) (total award of $1,250,000 in actual, compensatory, and punitive damages in retaliatory discharge case not excessive); *Moody v. Pepsi-Cola,* 915 F.2d 201 (6th Cir. 1990) (award of $150,000 for emotional distress not excessive); *Lilley v. BTM Corp.,* 958 F.2d 746, 754 (6th Cir. 1992) (award of $350,000 for mental anguish in discrimination case not excessive); *Purgess v. Sharrock,* 33 F.3d 134, 142 (2nd Cir. 1994) ($3.5 million award not excessive when employee formerly earned $500,000 per year); *Simon v. Shearson Lehman,* 895 F.2d 1304, 1319 (11th Cir. 1990).

98. *See, e.g.,* ERA, 42 U.S.C. § 5851(b)(2)(B).

99. *NLRB v. Gissel Packing Co.,* 395 U.S. 575, 613 (1969); *Virginia Elec. & Power Co. v. NLRB,* 319 U.S. 533, 541 (1943).

100. *See, e.g., NLRB v. Gissell Packing Co.,* at 613-614; *Consolidated Edison Co. of N.Y v. NLRB,* 305 U.S. 197 (1938); *J. P. Stevens Co. v. NLRB,* 380 F.2d 292, 303-304 (2nd Cir. 1967).

101. H.R. Rep. 294, 95th Cong., 2d Sess., *reprinted in* 1977 U.S. Code Cong. & Admin. News 1077.

102. *Chase v. Buncombe County, N.C., supra,* at 4; *Johnson v. Tansco Prods. Inc.,* 85-ERA-7, slip op. of ALJ, at 11 (1985). In *Chase,* the SOL held that the whistleblower laws prohibited some employer action that may have a "chilling effect" or that may "discourage" instead of "encourage" employee reporting of safety violations.

103. *See, e.g., Florida Steel Corp. v. NLRB,* 620 F.2d 79 (5th Cir. 1980); *Wells v. Kansas Gas & Elec. Co.,* 83-ERA-012, slip op. of SOL at 12 (1984); *Tritt v. Fluor Constructors,* 88-ERA-29, D&O of remand by SOL, at 6-7 (March 16,

1995); *Smith v. Richard Littenberg*, 92-ERA-52, D&O of SOL, at 9-10 (September 6, 1995).

104. *Donovan v. Freeway Constr. Co.*, 551 F. Supp. 869, 879-882 (D. R.I. 1982).

105. *Mitchell v. APS/ANPP*, 91-ERA-9, R. D&O of ALJ, at 47 (July 2,1992). *See also Simmons v. Florida Power Corp.*, 81-ERA-28/29, R. D&O of ALJ, at 20 (December 13, 1989) (requiring employer to issue a public retraction of statements adverse to complainants, which had been released to the news media).

106. *Florida Steel Corp. v. NLRB, supra,* at 82.

107. *Id.*

108. *United Food and Commercial Workers Int. Un. v. NLRB*, 852 F.2d 1344, 1348 (D.C. Cir. 1988).

109. *Conair Corp. v. NLRB*, 721 F.2d 1355, 1384 (D.C. Cir. 1983).

110. *Id. See also Smith v. ESICORP, supra,* at 6-7.

111. *Marcus v. EPA*, 96-CAA-3, R. D&O of ALJ (December 15, 1998).

112. *See, e.g., Weidler v. Big J Enterprises, Inc.*, 953 P.2d 1089, 1100-1102 (N.M. App. 1997) (upholding $500,000 punitive damage award).

113. *Veco v. Rosebrock*, 970 P. 2d 906, 922 (Alaska 1999).

114. 461 U.S. 30 (1983).

115. *Id.* at 56.

116. *Kolstad v. American Dental Association*, 527 U.S. 526 (1999).

117. *Id.*

118. *Id.*

119. *BMW v. Gore*, 517 U.S. 559, 568 (1996).

120. *Id.* at 575.

121. *Id.* at 568.

122. 637 N.E.2d 1183, 1194 (Ill. App. 1 Dist. 1994).

123. *Weidler v. Big J Enterprises, supra. See, e.g., Housing Authority v. Lopez*, 955 S.W.2d 152, 160 (Tex. App. 1997) (upholding $100,000 award under Texas law).

124. *Paracelus Health Care Corp. v. Willard* 1999 WL 1000697 (Miss. 1999).

125. SDWA, 42 U.S.C. § 300j-9(i)(2)(B)(ii); TSCA, 15 U.S.C. § 2622 (b)(2)(B).

126. *Reich v. Cambridgeport Air Systems, Inc. supra.*

127. *Johnson v. Old Dominion Security*, 86-CAA-3/4/5, D&O of SOL, at 28 (May 29, 1991).

128. *Id.* at 29. *Accord., Pogue v. United States Dept. of the Navy, supra,* at 15-22 (discussing cases in which punitive damages have been awarded).

129. *Id.* at 30.

130. *Soto v. Adams Elevator*, 941 F.2d 543, 550 (7th Cir. 1991).

131. 31 U.S.C. § 3730(h).

132. *Blackburn v. Metric Constructors, Inc.*, 86-ERA-4, D&O of SOL on Damages, at 18 (October 30, 1991).

133. *Frank v. Relin*, 851 F. Supp. 87, 90-91 (W.D. N.Y. 1994) (setting forth factors that can be weighed in deciding to award interest).

134. *Id.* at 89. *See Donovan v. Freeway Constr. Co.*, *supra*, at 881 (prejudgment instead allowed under OSHA, FLSA, Title VII, and NLRA).

135. *Saulpaugh v. Monroe Community Hosp.*, 4 F.3d 134, 145 (2nd Cir. 1993) (emphasis in original).

136. 26 U.S.C. § 6621. *But see Neal v. Honeywell*, 995 F. Supp. 889, 896-897 (N.D. Ill. 1998) (prime rate compounded annually).

137. *New Horizon for the Retarded*, 283 NLRB 1173 (1987).

138. *Id.* at 1174. *Accord.*, *Clinchfield Coal v. Fed. Mine Safety and H. Com.*, 895 F.2d 773, 780 (D.C. Cir. 1990).

139. *EEOC v. FLC*, 663 F. Supp. 864, 869 (W.D. Va. 1987); *Saulpaugh v. Monroe Community Hosp.*, *supra*; *EEOC v. Kentucky State Police*, 80 F.3d 1086, 1098 (6th Cir. 1996). *See also EEOC v. Guardian Pools, Inc.*, 828 F.2d 1507, 1513 (11th Cir. 1987) (awarding annually compounded interest); *Johnson v. Roadway Express*, 99-STA-5, D&O of ARB (March 29, 2000) (compounded quarterly interest).

140. *Shore v. Federal Express Corp.*, 42 F.3d 373, 380 (6th Cir. 1994); *Doyle v. Hydro Nuclear Services*, 89-ERA-22, R. D&O of ALJ, at 16-17 (December 17, 1998).

141. *Neal v. Honeywell*, *supra*, at 897.

142. *See, e.g., Blackburn v. Metric Constructors*, *supra*, at 26.

143. *Bancamerica v. Mosher Steel*, 103 F.3d 80, 81 (10th Cir. 1986).

144. *Id*; *Lew Wenzel v. London Lith.*, 563 F.2d 1367 (9th Cir. 1977); *Brown v. Petrolite Corp.*, 965 F.2d 38, 51 (5th Cir. 1992).

145. 13 U.S. 177, 197-198 (1941).

146. *Tubari Ltd. v. NLRB*, 959 F.2d 451, 453-454 (3rd Cir. 1992).

147. *NLRB v. Pilot Freight*, 604 F.2d 375, 378 (5th Cir. 1979); *Moyer v. Yellow Freight*, *supra*, at 8; *Hobby v. Georgia Power Co.*, *supra*, at 59.

148. *Hufstetler v. Roadway Express, Inc.*, 85-STA-8, D&O of SOL, at 53, 56 (August 21, 1986).

149. *Lederhaus v. Paschen*, *supra*, at 10. *Accord., Nichols v. Bechtel Construction, Inc.*, 87-ERA-44, D&O of SOL, at 10 (November 18, 1993); *Clay v. Castle Coal & Oil Co.*, *supra*; *Pettway v. American Cast Iron Pipe Co.*, *supra*.

150. *Ali v. City of Clearwater*, 915 F. Supp. 1231, 1242 (M.D. Fla. 1996) (citations omitted).

151. *Assistant Secretary v. Intermodal Cartage Co.*, 94-STA-22, D&O of SOL, at 7 (July 26, 1995).

152. *Rasimas v. Michigan Dept. of Mental Health*, 714 F.2d 614, 624 (6th Cir. 1983).

153. *Moyer v. Yellow Freight*, *supra*, at 14, *quoting in part from EEOC v. Kallir*, 420 F. Supp. 919, 925 (S.D. N.Y. 1976).

154. *Ford Motor Co. v. EEOC*, 458 U.S. 219 (1982).

155. *Rasimas v. Michigan Dept. of Mental Health*, *supra*; *DOL v. Louisville Gas & Elec. Co.*, 88-OFC-12, D&O of DOL, at 4 (January 14, 1992).

156. *NLRB v. Madison Courier, Inc.*, 472 F.2d 1307, 1320 (D.C. Cir. 1972); *Nord v. U.S. Steel*, 758 F.2d 1462, 1471-1472 (11th Cir. 1985).

157. *F. E. Hazard*, 303 NLRB 839 (1991).

158. *Standard Materials v. NLRB*, 862 F.2d 1188, 1192 (5th Cir. 1989) ("no simple test" to determine mitigation).

159. *See Fite v. First Tennessee Production Credit Ass'n.*, *supra*, at 892.

160. *DOL v. Louisville Gas & Elec. Co.*, *supra*, at 7.

161. *Kansas Gas & Elec. Co. v. Brock*, 780 F.2d 1505, 1513-1514 (10th Cir. 1985).

162. *Grocer Co. v. Holloway*, 874 F.2d 1008 (5th Cir. 1989); *Assistant Secretary v. C.A. Express*, 96-STA-5, Remand Order of ARB, at 3 (September 17, 1997).

163. *Francis v. Bogan, Inc.*, 86-ERA-8, D&O of SOL, at 6-7 (April 1, 1988); *Clifton v. UPS*, 94-STA-16, D&O of ARB, at 3-4 (May 14, 1997).

164. *Donovan v. Commercial Sewing, Inc.*, 562 F. Supp. 548, 554 (D. Conn. 1982).

165. *Id.* at 554-55.

166. *Hufstetler v. Roadway Express, Inc.*, *supra*, at 53.

167. *Van Beck v. Daniel Construction Co.*, 86-ERA-26, D&O of remand by SOL, at 9 (August 3, 1993). *Accord., Pillow v. Bechtel Construction, Inc.*, 87-ERA-35, D&O of remand by SOL, at 26 (July 19, 1993); *Blackburn v. Martin*, *supra*, at 129 (employee may only recover damages for the period of time he would have worked but for wrongful termination; he should not recover damages for the time after which his employment would have ended for a nondiscriminatory reason).

168. *Nichols v. Bechtel Construction, Inc.*, *supra*, at 8.

169. *Walker v. Ford Motor Co.*, 684 F.2d 1355, 1362 (11th Cir. 1982); *Doyle v. Hydro Nuclear Services*, 89-ERA-22, D&O of ARB, at 3 (September 6, 1996).

170. *Doyle* at 4.

171. *Willy v. Coastal Corp.*, 85-CAA-1, D&O of SOL, at 26 (June 1, 1994). *See also Williams v. TIW Fabrication & Machining, Inc.*, 88-SWD-3, D&O of SOL, at 10 (June 24, 1992) ("Refusal of an unconditional offer of reinstatement for a substantially equivalent position constitutes a breach of the obligation to mitigate damages").

172. *Behlar v. Smith*, 719 F.2d 950 (8th Cir. 1983).

173. *Marcus v. EPA*, 92-TSC-5, order of remand by SOL, at 2-3 (September 27, 1994).

174. *SOL v. Mutual Mining Award, Inc.*, 80 F.3d 110 (4th Cir. 1996).

175. *Riddle v. Wal-Mart Stores, Inc.*, —P.2d—, 2000 WL 192795 (Kan. App. 2000).

176. *McKennon v. Nashville Banner Publishing Co.*, 513 U.S. 352, 361 (1995).

177. There are strict limits to the application of this doctrine. For example, in *Medlock v. Ortho Biotech, Inc.*, 164 F.3d 545, 555 (10th Cir. 1999), the Appeals Court upheld the trial court's refusal to consider this doctrine as a

result of an employee's post-termination conduct during an unemployment hearing.

178. *Id.*

179. *Sheehan v. Donlen Corp.*, 173 F.3d 1039 (7th Cir. 1999).

180. *McKennon v. Nashville Banner Publishing Co.*, *supra*, at 886-887.

181. The DOL applies the *McKennon* rule in environmental whistleblower cases. *See Smith v. TVA*, 89-ERA-12, Order of SOL, at 4-5 (March 17, 1995); *James v. Ketchikan Pulp Co.*, 94-WPC-4, D&O of SOL, at 8 (March 15, 1996).

182. *Junot v. Maricopa County*, 191 F.3d 460 (9th Cir. 1999).

183. Henry J. Reske, "Taxing Times for Plaintiffs," *ABA Journal*, p. 22 (November, 1996).

184. 26 U.S.C. § 104(a). H. Rep. 104-586, Report of the Committee on Ways and Means of the House of Representatives on H.R. 3448, "Small Business Job Protection Act of 1996," pp. 142-44 (May 20, 1996). President William J. Clinton expressed reservations over these changes to the tax code when he signed the Small Business Job Protection Act of 1996. Statement by the President (August 20, 1996) ("I have reservations about a provision in the Act which makes civil damages based on nonphysical injury or illness taxable. Such damages are paid to compensate for injury, whether physical or not, and are designed to make victims whole, not to enrich them. These damages should not be considered a source of taxable income." The constitutional authority for taxing emotional distress damages as part of "income" has not been tested."); F. Patrick Hubbard, "Making People Whole Again: The Constitutionality of Taxing Compensatory Tort Damages for Emotional Distress," 49 *Florida Law Review* 725 (December 1997).

185. *C.I.R. v. Schleier*, 115 S.Ct. 2159 (1995) (age discrimination damage award taxable); *U.S. v. Burke*, 504 U.S. 229 (1992) (damages awarded under statute which did not provide for compensatory damages were taxable). *See*, David B. Jennings, "The Supreme Court Gets Tough with I.R.C. 104(a)(2) Exclusions: Taxpayer Discrimination Awards Suffer Injury as a Result of Commissioner v. Schleier," 40 *St. Louis Law Journal* 865 (Summer 1996). Most courts consider a contingent fee paid to an attorney on a tort-type claim to be the income of the attorney, and thus non-taxable to a client. *See*, *Estate of Clarks v. U.S.*, 202 F.3d 854 (6th Cir. 2000); *Cotnam v. Commissioner*, 263 F.2d 119 (5th Cir. 1959). *Contra.*, *Alexander v. IRS*, 72 F.3d 938 (1st Cir. 1995) (legal fee incurred in breach of contract claim taxed to client). In order to best insure that an attorney fee will not be taxed to a client, retainer agreements should explicitly state that a contingency contract operates a lien on the recovery. *Estate of Clarks*, *supra.*

186. The unfair nature of these tax requirements have resulted in a number of Congressional proposals to amend to tax code. *See*, H.R. 1997, "Civil Rights Tax Fairness Act of 1999" (introduced by Rep. Deborah Price on May 27, 1999).

187. *Albemarle Paper Company v. Moody*, 95 S.Ct. 2362, 2373 (1975); *NLRB v. J.H. Rutter-Rex*, 90 S.Ct. 417, 421 (1969) ("backpay . . . is also a remedy

designed to restore, so far as possible, the status quo that would have obtained but for the wrongful act"); *Lederhaus v. Donald Baschen*, 91-ERA-13, D&O of SOL, p. 9 (October 26, 1992) ("back pay promotes the remedial statutory purpose of making whole victims of discrimination").

188. The following courts have rejected a "gross-up" on back wages in order to compensate victims of discrimination for the additional tax liability: *Best v. Shell Oil* Company, 4 F.Supp.2d 770, 776 (N.D. Ill. 1998), *Dashnaw v. Pena*, 12 F.3d 1112, 1115 (D.C. Cir. 1994); *Hukkanen v. International Union*, 3 F.3d 281, 287 (8th Cir. 1993); *Johnson v. Harris County*, 869 F.2d 1565, 1580 (5th Cir. 1989). The following cases have indicated that a gross-up may be warranted in order to ensure that an employee is made whole: *Barbour v. Medlantic Management Corp.*, 952 F. Supp. 857, 865 (D.D.C. 1997); *Warren v. Society National Bank*, 905 F.2d 975, 982 (6th Cir. 1990) (ERISA lump-sum distribution case).

189. Robert E. Hall & Victoria A. Lazear, "Estimation of Economic Losses in Damages Awards," *Reference Manual on Scientific Evidence* (Fed. Judicial Ctr. ed., 1994).

190. *Doyle v. Hydro Nuclear Services*, 89-ERA-22, Final D&O on Damages, p. 10 (May 17, 2000).

191. *Id.*, pp. 11-12.

192. *Social Security Board v. Nierotko*, 327 U.S. 358 (1946).

193. *Social Security Board*, 327 U.S. at 371 (Frankfurter concurring).

194. *Bowman v. U.S.*, 824 F.2d 528, 530 (6th Cir. 1987) ("A settlement for back wages should not be allocated [by the taxing authority] to the period when the employer finally pays but should be allocated to the periods when the regular wages were not paid as usual"). *Accord., Johnson v. Harris County Flood Control Dist.*, 869 F.2d 1565, 1581 (5th Cir. 1989) ("plaintiff must pay the taxes due on the wages for the year in which the wages were due").

195. *See, Tungseth v. Mutual of Omaha Ins. Co.*, 43 F.3d 406, 409 (8th Cir. 1994).

196. 103 T.C. 634 (1994). *Accord., Minor v. U.S.*, 772 F.2d 1472 (9th Cir. 1985).

197. Most of these requirements are necessary in order to avoid immediate taxation under the "*constructive receipt*" doctrine. As explained in *Childs*, "under the *constructive receipt* doctrine, a taxpayer recognizes income when the taxpayer has an unqualified, vested right to receive immediate payment. Generally, there must be an amount that is immediately due and owing that the obligor is ready, willing, and able to pay. The amount owed must either be credited to the taxpayer or set aside for the taxpayer so that the taxpayer has an unrestricted right to receive it immediately and the taxpayer being aware of these facts, declines to accept the payment." 103 T.C. at 654 (citations and internal quotations omitted). Thus, language should be incorporated into a settlement agreement which demonstrates that the "income" was "not constructively received" by the taxpayer, and that the taxpayer's "control of its receipt" of the settlement proceeds "is subject to substantial limitations or restrictions." *Id.*

198. *Alyeska Pipeline v. Wilderness Society*, 421 U.S. 240 (1975).

199. S.Rep. 94-1011, at 3 (1976), *reprinted in* 1976 U.S.C.C.A.N. 5908, 5910.

200. *Hensley v. Eckerhart*, 461 U.S. 424, 429 (1983), *quoting, in part*, H.R. Rep. 94-1558, at 1 (1976) (internal quotations omitted).

201. *Blum v. Stenson*, 465 U.S. 886, 897 (1984). *Accord., Valley Disposal v. Central Vermont Solid Waste*, 113 F.3d 357, 361 (2nd Cir. 1997); *Goos v. National Association of Realtors*, 68 F.3d 1380, 1386 (D.C. Cir. 1995) (ability to obtain counsel who will provide "zealous representation").

202. *Hoffman v. W. Max Bossert*, 94-CAA-4, D&O of ARB, at 5 (January 22, 1997).

203. *City of Riverside v. Rivera*, 477 U.S. 561, 574 (1986) (J. Brennan, plurality).

204. 42 U.S.C. § 1988.

205. *Hensley v. Eckerhart, supra* (internal citations omitted).

206. *Id.* at 436-437. *Accord., Phelan v. Bell*, 8 F.3d 369, 373 (6th Cir. 1993).

207. *Missouri v. Jenkins*, 491 U.S. 274 (1989).

208. 478 U.S. 546, 565 (1986).

209. 461 U.S. 424, 433-434 (1983). *Accord., Building Serv. Local 47 Cleaning Contractors Pension Plan v. Grandview Raceway*, 46 F.3d 1392 (6th Cir. 1995); *City of Burlington v. Dague*, 505 U.S. 557 (1992); *Lederhaus v. Paschen et al.*, D&O of SOL (January 13, 1993).

210. 461 U.S. 424, 433-434 (1983).

211. *Hilton v. Glas-Tec Corp.*, 84-STA-6, D&O awarding attorney fees by SOL, at 2-3 (July 15, 1986). *See also Pogue v. U.S. Dept. of Navy, supra*, D&O awarding attorney fees by ALJ (March 24, 1988), *vacated on other grounds by SOL* (May 10, 1990).

212. *Pennsylvania v. Delaware Valley Citizens Council for Clean Air*, 478 U.S. 546, 562 (1986); *Goldstein v. EBASCO Constr., Inc.*, 86-ERA-36, recommended supplemental D&O of ALJ, at 2 (May 17, 1988).

213. *Thurman v. Yellow Freight Systems*, 90 F.3d 1160, 1170 (6th Cir. 1996). In *Thurman*, the plaintiff only partially prevailed in his claims and was *denied* requests for reinstatement, compensatory and punitive damages, prejudgment interest, and front pay. *Id.* at 1164. In addition, the plaintiff was only successful on "two of his original six claims." *Id.* at 1169. Despite this limited success, the Court affirmed a reduction of only 5 percent of the requested fee. *Id.* at 1170.

214. *Hensley v. Eckerhart*, 461 U.S. 424, 436 (1983); *Scott v. Roadway Express, Inc.*, 98-STA-8, D&O of ARB, at 17 (July 28, 1999).

215. The most "appropriate starting point for selecting the proper rate . . . is the community in which the court sits." *National Wildlife Federation v. Hanson*, 859 F.2d 313, 317 (4th Cir. 1988). However, courts will also "entertain circumstances beyond the venue of the location" of the trial court in considering the most applicable markets. *Hoch v. Clark County Health Dept.*, 98-CAA-12, Supplemental Order of ALJ, at 1 (March 15, 2000).

216. 488 F.2d 714, 718 (5th Cir. 1974).

217. *Blanchard v. Bergeron*, 489 U.S. 87, 91-92 (1989).

218. *See, e.g., Hamlin v. Charter Township of Flint*, 165 F.3d 426, 437 (6th Cir. 1999).

219. If more than one attorney is involved, the possibility of duplication of effort along with the proper utilization of time should be scrutinized. It is appropriate to distinguish between legal work, in the strict sense, and investigation, clerical work, compilation of facts and statistics, and other work that can often be accomplished by nonlawyers.

220. *See Johnson v. Georgia Highway Exp., Inc.*, 488 F.2d 714, 717-719 (5th Cir. 1974).

221. *Farrar v. Hobby*, 506 U.S. 103 (1992); 113 S.Ct. 566, 569 (1992).

222. *Covington v. District of Columbia*, 57 F.3d 1101, 1111-1112 (D.C. Cir. 1995).

223. *Blum v. Stenson*, 465 U.S. 886, 894 (1984).

224. *Ashley v. Atlantic Richfield Co.*, 794 F.2d 128 (3rd Cir. 1986).

225. 448 U.S. 122, 129 (1980).

226. 461 U.S. 424, 440 (1983).

227. *Blanchard v. Bergeron*, 489 U.S. 87, 96 (1989).

228. *Marek v. Chesney*, 437 U.S. 1, 6-7 (1985).

229. *Washington v. Philadelphia County*, 89 F.3d 1031, 1035 (3rd Cir. 1996).

230. The local market rate is usually based on rates applied in the geographic area where the trial court is located. However, "rates outside the forum may be used if local counsel was unavailable, either because they were unwilling or unable to perform or because they lack the degree of experience, expertise, or specialization required to handle the case." *Barjon v. Dalton*, 132 F.3d 496, 500 (9th Cir. 1997). *See, e.g., Casey v. City of Cabool, Mo.*, 12 F.3d 799, 805 (3rd Cir. 1993) ("a market for a particular legal specialization may provide the appropriate market"); *Howes v. Medical Components*, 761 F. Supp. 1193, 1195 (E.D. Pa. 1990) (rate paid at attorney's business location, if there is a "good reason"). *Ihler v. Chisholm*, 995 P.2d 439 (Mont. 2000) (out-of-state rates if reasonable).

231. *Laffey v. Northwest Airlines, Inc.*, 572 F. Supp. 354, 371-372 (D. D.C. 1983). *Accord., Blum v. Stenson*, 465 U.S. 886, 896 n. 11 (1984); *Clay v. Castle Coal*, 90-STA-37, D&O of SOL, at 7 (June 3, 1994).

232. *Hensley v. Eckerhart, supra*, at 433.

233. 89 F.3d 1031, 1037-38 (3rd Cir. 1996).

234. *City of Burlington v. Dague*, 505 U.S. 557 (1992). *Accord., Lederhaus v. Donald Paschen, supra*, D&O of SOL. However, in some cases a fee enhancement above the loadstar rate may be available. *Guam Society of Obstetricians v. Ada*, 100 F.3d 691, 697 (9th Cir. 1996).

235. *Howes v. Medical Comp.*, 761 F. Supp. 1193, 1196 (E.D. Pa. 1990).

236. *Hardrick v. Airway Freight Systems*, 2000 WL 263687 (N.D. Ill. 2000), *citing Blum v. Stenson*, 465 U.S. 886 (1984), *Save Our Cumberland Mountains, Inc. v. Hodel*, 857 F.2d 1516 (D.C. Cir. 1988) (*en banc*), and *Barrow v. Falck*, 977 F.2d 1100, 1105 (7th Cir. 1992). *Accord., Goos v. National Ass'n of*

Realtors, 997 F.2d 1565, 1568 (D.C.Cir.1993) ("[A]ttorneys who quote a client a discounted rate to reflect non-economic goals may be compensated at prevailing market rates."); *Central States Pension Fund v. Central States Cartage Co.*, 76 F.3d 114, 117 (7th Cir.1996) (Pension funds are entitled to fees on the basis of prevailing market rate, and not the rate paid to staff counsel, because "the court should make an award representing the cost the victorious litigant would have incurred to buy legal services in the market, no matter how the litigant acquired those services.")

237. 477 U.S. 561 (1986).

238. *Hoffman v. W. Max Bossert, supra*, at 5-6.

239. *Evans v. Jeff D.*, 475 U.S. 717 (1986).

240. *Id.* at 765 (J. Brennan, dissenting). Complainant's counsel may avoid the harshness of this waiver rule by having the client contractually agree not to waive the statutory fee. *Id.* at 766 (J. Brennan, dissenting).

241. *Missouri v. Jenkins*, 491 U.S. 274, 284 (1989); *Barjon v. Dalton*, 132 F.3d 496, 502 (9th Cir. 1997); *Covington v. District of Columbia*, 839 F. Supp. 894, 902 (D. D.C. 1993); *Blackburn v. Metric Constructors, Inc., supra*, Recommended D&O on remand by ALJ, at 7 (February 13, 1989); *Ramos v. Lamm*, 713 F.2d 546, 555 (10th Cir. 1983).

242. 491 U.S. at 283, n. 6 (1989).

243. *Hensley v. Northwest Permanente P.C. Retirement Plan and Trust*, 1999 WL 1271576 (D. Or. 1999).

244. *Blackburn v. Reich*, 79 F.3d 1375 (4th Cir. 1996); *Phelan v. Bell*, 8 F.3d 369, 375 (6th Cir. 1993).

245. *See, e.g., Hernandez v. George*, 793 F.2d 264, 269 (10th Cir. 1986); *Schuenemeyer v. United States*, 776 F.2d 329, 333 (Fed. Cir. 1985); *Tyler Business Servs., Inc. v. NLRB*, 695 F.2d 73, 77 (4th Cir. 1982); *Bond v. Stanton*, 630 F.2d 1231, 1235 (7th Cir. 1980); *Johnson v. State of Mississippi*, 606 F.2d 635, 637-639 (5th Cir. 1979); *Gagne v. Maher*, 594 F.2d 336, 343-344 (2d Cir. 1979), *aff'd* 448 U.S. 122 (1980); *Weisenberger v. Huecker*, 593 F.2d 49, 53-54 (6th Cir. 1979); *Lund v. Affleck*, 587 F.2d 75, 77 (1st Cir. 1978); *Prandini v. National Tea Co.*, 585 F.2d 47, 53-54 (3d Cir. 1978); *Moten v. Bricklayers, Masons, and Plasterers, etc.*, 543 F.2d 224 (D.C. Cir. 1976) (*per curiam*); *Rosenfeld v. Southern Pacific Co.*, 519 F.2d 527, 530-531 (9th Cir. 1975) (*per curiam*); *Blackburn v. Metric Constructors, Inc., supra*, at 7. *But see Hilton v. Glas-Tec Corp., supra*, at 5.

246. *Doyle v. Hydro Nuclear Services*, 89-ERA-22, R. D&O of ALJ, at 2 (July 16, 1996), *aff'd*, ARB Final D&O, at 10 (September 6, 1996). *See also Public Interest Research Group v. Windall*, 51 F.3d 1179, 1190 (3rd Cir. 1995).

247. 29 C.F.R. § 18.54(c); *Williams v. Seiker, et al.*, 88-SWD-3, deferral of consideration of motion for attorney fees by ALJ (August 3, 1989).

248. *White v. New Hampshire Dept. of Employment Security*, 455 U.S. 445 (1982).

249. *Laffey v. Northwest Airlines, Inc., supra*, at 382.

250. *Johnson v. Bechtel Construction*, 95-ERA-11, Supplemental Order of SOL, at 2 (February 26, 1996).

251. *Laffey, supra*, at 382-383.

252. *Id.* at 382.

253. *Goldstein v. EBASCO Constr., Inc., supra*, at 5; *Johnson v. Transco Prods. Inc.*, 85-ERA-7, supp. D&O of ALJ, at 2 (March 29, 1985).

254. *Ass't. Sec'y. v. Freeze*, 98-STA-26, D&O of ARB, at 8 (April 22, 1999).

255. *See, e.g., Spanish Action Committee of Chicago v. Chicago*, 811 F.2d 1129 (7th Cir. 1987); *Northcross v. Board of Ed. of Memphis City Schools*, 611 F.2d 624, 632 (6th Cir. 1979) *cert. denied*, 447 U.S. 911; *Wheeler v. Durham City Bd. of Education*, 585 F.2d 618, 623 (4th Cir. 1978); *Ramos v. Lamm*, 632 F. Supp. 376 (D. Colo. 1986); *Population Servs. Intl. v. Carey*, 476 F. Supp 4, 8 (S.D. N.Y 1979); *Larry v. Detroit Edison Co.*, 86-ERA-32, D&O on Costs by SOL, at 4 (May 19, 1992).

256. *Tritt v. Fluor Constructors*, 88-ERA-29, D&O of SOL, at 5 (March 16, 1995).

257. 499 U.S. 83 (1991).

258. ERA, 42 U.S.C. § 5851(b)(2)(B); CAA, 42 U.S.C. § 7622(b)(2)(B); SDWA, 42 U.S.C. § 300j-9(i)(2)(B)(ii); SWDA, 42 U.S.C. § 6971(c); WPCA, 33 U.S.C. § 1367(c); CERCLA, 42 U.S.C. § 9610(c); TSCA, 15 U.S.C. § 2622(b)(2)(B). *See also* 29 C.F.R. Part 24.

259. *Ishmael v. Calibur Systems*, 96-SWD-2, D&O of ARB, at 2 (October 17, 1997); *Berkman v. U.S. Coast Guard Academy*, 97-CAA-2, D&O of Remand by ARB, at 33 (February 29, 2000).

260. *Goldstein v. EBASCO, supra*, D&O of SOL, at 26-27 (April 7, 1992); *Pittman v. Groggin Truck Line*, 96-STA-25, ARB Order (July 30, 1999).

261. *See Berkman, supra* at 33 (*citing* case in which public relations work was compensable).

262. The Civil Rights Attorney's Fee Act, 42 U.S.C. § 1988, contains weaker language: "[T]he court, in its discretion, may allow the prevailing party, other than the United States, a reasonable attorney's fee as part of the cost."

263. 42 U.S.C. 5851(b)(2)(B).

264. *Jenkins v. U.S. E.P.A.*, 92-CAA-6, Final Decision of the Secretary of Labor, at 2 (December 7, 1994), *citing Hensley v. Eckerhart, supra*. The Administrative Review Board has noted that use of the "lodestar method" of determining the "proper amount of attorney's fees" in "environmental whistle-blower" claims is a "longstanding practice of the Department of Labor." *Wieb van der Meer v. Western Kentucky University, supra*, at 9. *Accord., Berkman, supra*, at 3.

265. *Olsovsky v. Shell Western*, 96-CAA-1, D&O of ARB, at 3 (April 10, 1997). *See also Assistant Secretary v. Florilli Corp.*, 91-STA-7, Order Denying Fee Application of SOL (October 22, 1992) (holding that employer is not entitled to fees under Equal Access to Justice Act).

266. *Abrams v. Roadway Express, Inc.*, 84-STA-2, D&O of SOL (May 25, 1985).

267. *Wieb van der Meer, supra*, at 10.

268. 5 U.S.C. § 557(b); *Goldstein v. EBASCO Constructors, Inc., supra*, D&O of SOL, at 19.

269. *Id.* ("I will give considerable deference to an ALJ's findings, particularly in an area such as competence of counsel, because 'the court saw the attorney's work first hand' ").

270. *Larry v. Detroit Edison Co., supra*, at 2-3.

271. *Johnson v. Old Dominion Security, supra*, at 31.

272. *Id.* at 32, n.21. *See, e.g., Lederhaus v. Donald Paschen, supra*, at 5 ("Respondents are liable only for reasonable attorney fees no matter what amount Complainant may have contracted to pay his attorney").

273. *Delcore v. W. J. Barney Corp.*, 89-ERA-38, D&O of SOL, at 2 (June 9, 1995).

274. *Pogue v. United States Dept. of the Navy, supra*, at 24.

275. *Larry v. Detroit Edison, supra*, at 5. *See also Simmons v. Florida Power Corp.*, 89-ERA-28/29, R. Supplement D&O, at 6-8 (April 11, 1990); *Clay v. Castle Coal and Oil Co., supra*, D&O of SOL, at 14.

276. *Pierce v. Underwood*, 487 U.S. 552, 570-571 (1988); *Hensley v. Eckerhart, supra*, at 437.

277. *DeFord v. Secretary of Labor, supra. Contra Mackowiak v. University Nuclear Systems, Inc.*, 82-ERA-8, D& O on Remand by ALJ (July 28, 1986).

278. *Blackburn v. Reich, supra*, at 1379; *Delcore v. W. J. Barney Corp., supra*, Order of ARB (October 31, 1996). *See also Pittman, supra.*

279. 885 P.2d 551, 558-559 (9th Cir. 1989).

280. *Id.*

Chapter 10

Settlement Agreements and Hush Money

One of the most controversial management practices concerns employer payments to employees in exchange for their agreement not to testify in an administrative or judicial proceeding or to cooperate with federal or state regulatory authorities.[1] Various forms of secrecy agreements, or *hush money* settlements, have been documented in a wide variety of contexts, including tobacco litigation,[2] personal injury cases,[3] and environmental/ nuclear whistleblower disputes.[4]

In a number of cases, employers have insisted upon non-disclosure or settlement agreements that prohibited the employee whistleblower from "voluntarily" testifying in court or regulatory proceedings concerning their former employer.[5] In one settlement, the employee was required to sign agreements obligating him "not to take any action or do anything to encourage or otherwise induce the Nuclear Regulatory Commission" to investigate his claims[6] and not to "interest the news media" in the whistleblower allegation.[7] Another settlement required the employee to "withdraw and forever cease his participation in the NRC and the Public Utilities Commission [PUC] proceedings."[8] Employers have also sought agreements prohibiting employees from assisting in Equal Employment Opportunity Commission (EEOC) investigations,[9] False Claims Act proceedings,[10] and have sought injunctions to prohibit former employees from testifying in court proceedings.[11]

Employer attempts to justify these restrictive agreements have been harshly criticized,[12] and public disclosures of the agreements have been highly embarrassing to the industries involved.[13] In the environmental area, restrictive settlement provisions have not withstood judicial scrutiny.

Various courts, the U.S. Department of Labor (DOL), and the NRC have found clauses restricting an employee's right to make disclosures void under public policy.[14] Courts have also refused to issue injunctions which restrict testimony.[15] Other courts have narrowly construed "non-disclosure agreements" and insisted that such agreements be "carefully scrutinized."[16] In her article "Killing the Messenger," Jodi L. Short described these trends:

Several courts have considered whether an employee bound by a nondisclosure agreement is precluded from providing information arguably covered by that agreement in the context of civil litigation. Although there is some authority to the contrary, the majority of courts to consider the question have permitted the employee to provide both fact and expert testimony. Moreover, to the extent the employer may bar certain portions of the testimony, such as trade secrets and privileged material, courts place the burden on the employer to prove that the information that the employee may reveal by [his or] her testimony is in fact protectable.[17]

The most extensive case law on *hush money* settlements has been developed under the federal environmental and nuclear whistleblower laws. Unlike traditional civil litigation, these federal laws require DOL approval on all settlement agreements.[18] Consequently, settlement practices that ordinarily would remain strictly confidential (unless one of the parties wilfully disclosed the terms of the settlement in violation of an agreement) have been carefully scrutinized by the responsible federal administrative agency and the courts. The case law developed over the last ten years in this controversial area serves as a model in any judicial proceeding in which the legality or enforceability of *hush money* agreements are at issue.[19]

RESTRICTIONS ON TESTIMONY OR CONTACTING AUTHORITIES

In the context of environmental and nuclear whistleblower law, Congress, the courts, and the responsible administrative agencies have recognized that paying an employee "any financial consideration" in exchange for an agreement by that employee not to testify, nor to appear voluntarily as a witness, and/or agree not to communicate safety information, was "illegal and contrary to public policy."[20] For example, in 1989 the U.S. Senate Subcommittee on Nuclear Regulation held public hearings on *hush money* settlements. In a bipartisan manner, both the Democratic and the Republican senators were critical of *hush money* settlements. Senator John Breaux (D-LA), chairman of the Subcommittee, commented at the hearings that:

It is shocking to me that we should even have to hold a hearing on such questions. It seems self-evident that it is wrong to pay witnesses not to testify, regardless of the context. Any judicial procedure becomes a sham if witnesses can be paid to withhold evidence. Yet, we find that in the area of nuclear regulation the practice may be common. . . . I am most surprised that the legality of these payments could even be an issue in light of the substantial body of law that says that agreements of this type are, in fact, illegal. First, basic contract law states that contracts for the suppression of testimony are void as against public policy. Second, section 210 of the Energy Reorganization Act prohibits any NRC licensee, or a contractor, or a subcontractor, from discriminating against any employee for testifying or in any manner assisting or participating in any procedure under the Energy Reorganization Act, or the Atomic Energy Act. Thus, testifying is a protected activity under both the statute and the NRC's regulations implementing that statute.

*   *   *

Third, the Federal Witness Bribery Statute makes it a crime punishable by up to 2 years in prison, to offer to a witness, or for a witness to accept anything of value for that witness to be absent from a procedure before a Federal agency. In addition, the Federal statutes dealing with obstruction of agency proceedings makes it a crime to corruptly interfere with agency procedures.[21]

Senator Alan K. Simpson (R-WI), the ranking minority member of the committee, also condemned *hush money* settlement agreements:

Here we have some poor guy who's a journeyman electrician, who has been engaged by lawyers and ought to be somewhere in this process. This stinks. I think there's some grave deficiencies in these lawyer's conduct. I think there is a crude overreaching, and the next proceeding for those people ought to be a disbarment box somewhere. That's my view about their conduct when I look at it. And so they strapped together this document and put strictly confidential on it. No wonder they did. The Chairman has read some of it; not call [him] as a witness, or join him as a party. We've already heard that phrase, which is repugnant to any lawyer, to resist compulsory process. It's a violation of what we do as lawyers.

*   *   *

I can't believe what I'm seeing. But if anyone believes, in the real world, that after some poor cat signed all this stuff, that he could pick up the phone . . . and call somebody to help him out in the NRC, that strains every bit of common sense that there is in the world. [He] probably went home at night and said, well, I guess I'm going to get $15,000, meanwhile, my attorneys are going to get $20,000 . . . And I better keep my mouth shut. That's what he probably said when he got home. That's called real life at the dinner table.[22]

Members of Congress are not alone in criticizing *hush money* settlements. Courts have held that settlement provisions which require an employee to waive a right to file a charge of discrimination or misconduct with an investigating agency are void as against public policy. In *EEOC v. Cosmair, Inc.,*[23] the 5th Circuit Court of Appeals held that the public policy supporting the settlement of private disputes was outweighed by the public interest insuring that the appropriate federal authority (the EEOC in that case) could obtain information and allegations regarding potential violations of antidiscrimination laws.[24]

This precedent has been followed by both courts and administrative agencies in nuclear whistleblower law. The DOL now regularly voids agreements in which an employee agrees not to file a whistleblower charge.[25] The DOL justified this ruling by pointing out that a federal "investigation" and "ensuing discovery" in a "whistleblower proceeding may well uncover questionable employment practices and nuclear safety deficiencies about which the government should know."[26] In short, the "line of communication" for reporting wrongdoing "cannot be severed through agreement between parties."[27]

SEVERABILITY VS. VOIDING THE AGREEMENT

Once a restrictive clause is identified in the settlement agreement, a court must determine whether to void the entire agreement or to merely sever the illegally restrictive term and approve the remainder of the agreement.

Under traditional common law, agreements to pay consideration in exchange for withholding testimony were fully void.[28] Initially, the DOL attempted to sever restrictive terms for settlement agreements and uphold the remainder of the settlement. But this practice was rejected by the U.S. Court of Appeals, and the DOL now fully voids an entire agreement, even if only one clause is improperly restrictive.[29] A decision to void a settlement agreement and require the parties to proceed with the litigation is not subject to appeal under the *collateral order* doctrine.[30]

RESTRICTIVE SETTLEMENTS: A NEW CAUSE OF ACTION

A *hush money* agreement can be extremely destructive to the public policy behind whistleblowing. Most employees would not risk a breach of contract suit and directly violate the terms of such of a restrictive settlement. In fact, despite having uncovered scores of such agreements in the nuclear industry, to date just one employee, Joseph Macktal, directly breached the secrecy clause of a *hush money* agreement in order to challenge an executed settlement.[31] In the Macktal case, after the DOL voided the agreement, Brown & Root demanded its settlement money back as a condition for Macktal to pursue his case. The DOL rejected this demand and held that employees could keep the proceeds of a restrictive settlement agreement and still pursue their whistleblowing case.[32] Additionally, in another restrictive settlement case, the DOL held that an employee's retention of settlement proceeds did not constitute a "ratification" of an illegal agreement.[33]

The DOL has also evaluated the impact of *hush money* settlements on the legal rights protected under the whistleblower laws. In *Delcore v. Barney Corp. et al.*,[34] the Secretary of Labor (SOL) held that offering an employee a *hush money* settlement constituted a separate violation of the law entitling the employee the relief (i.e. attorney fees incurred for opposing the *hush money* settlement).

The U.S. Court of Appeals for the 2nd Circuit affirmed the Secretary's holding in *Delcore:*

[E]mployees have the right to be free from discriminatory action meant to deprive them of statutory rights. While in this case Delcore may have rejected the settlement, thereby maintaining his prerogative to communicate with the NRC, the behavior of employers to foist such restrictions on the employee's through the guise of a choice does constitute adverse action with respect to an employees rights to communicate with regulatory agencies.[35]

The court concluded that "proffering a settlement agreement containing provisions restricting an employee's access to judicial and administrative agencies violates" the nuclear whistleblower law.[36] After *Delcore*, the DOL has applied this holding to restrictive settlements that an employee executed and subsequently decided to challenge.[37]

Thus, under the environmental and nuclear whistleblower laws, employers who solicit *hush money* settlements face significant legal impediments. Not only are such agreements declared void, but the act of soliciting or executing a *hush money* agreement constitutes a free-standing violation of the law, subjecting an employer to pay attorney fees and other damages. Should other courts follow these precedents, the all too common practice of paying employees not to file charges, blow the whistle, or testify about serious safety problems would be significantly curtailed.

NOTES

1. *See,* Doggett, Lloyd & Michael Mucchetti, "Public Access to Public Courts: Discouraging Secrecy in the Public Interest," 69 *Texas Law Review* 643 (1991); U.S. Senate Subcommittee on Nuclear Regulation, *Hearings on Secret Settlement Agreements Restricting Testimony at Comanche Peak Nuclear Power Plant, etc.*, pp. 131-134, Senate hearing 101-190 (May 4, 1989) (hereinafter U.S. Senate Subcommittee hearings). *See also* Carol M. Bast, "At What Price: Are Confidentiality Agreements Enforceable?," 25 *William Mitchell Law Review* 627, 694-713 (1999); Jodi L. Short, "Killing the Messenger," 60 *University of Pittsburgh Law Review* 1207, 1212-1213 (1999).

2. *See* A. M. Freedman, "The Deposition: Cigarette Defector Says CEO Lied to Congress About View of Nicotine," *Wall Street Journal,* A-1 (January 26, 1996); R. Manelbaum, "Whistle-Blowers; Brown and Williamson v. Wigard," *American Lawyer,* 115 (March 1996); Marie Brenner, "The Man Who Knew Too Much," *Vanity Fair,* 170 (May, 1996).

3. *Baker v. General Motors, Corp.,* 522 U.S. 222 (1998).

4. *Id. See also* Benjamin Weiser,"Lawsuit Spurs a Debate Over Secrets vs. Safety," *The Washington Post,* A1 (July 26, 1994); *Oubre v. Entergy Op., Inc.,* 522 U.S. 422 (1998).

5. Bast, *supra,* (collecting cases); Short, *supra* (collecting cases); *Macktal v. Brown & Root, Inc.,* 86-ERA-23, order rejecting in part and approving in part the settlement, etc., at 10-11 (November 14, 1989).

6. *See* settlement filed on December 27, 1989, in *Bittner v. Fuel Economy Contracting Co. et al.,* 88-ERA-22 (pending before Secretary of Labor).

7. *See* settlement filed in *Hoffman v. Omaha Public Power District, et al.* 88-ERA-13.

8. *See* settlement filed in *Corder v. Bechtel Group Inc.,* 88-ERA-9.

9. *EEOC v. Astra, USA,* 94 F.3d 738 (1st Cir. 1996).

10. *U.S. v. Northrop Corp.,* 59 F.3d 953 (9th Cir. 1995).

11. *Baker v. General Motors Corp., supra; Williams v. General Motors Corp.,* 147 FRD 270, 273 (S.D. Ga. 1993) ("Any interest G.M. might have in silencing [former employee] as to unprivileged or non-trade secret information is outweighed by the public interest in full and fair discovery"); *Anderson v. Cryovac, Inc.,* 805 F.2d 1, 8 (1st Cir. 1986) (order permitting disclosure to governmental authorities); *Chambers v. Capital Cities,* 159 FRD 441, 444 (S.D. N.Y. 1995) ("It has been recognized that . . . agreements obtained by former requiring former employees to remain silent . . . concerning potentially illegal practices . . . can be harmful to the public's ability to rein in improper behavior, and in some contexts, the ability of the United States to police violations of the law"). *Also see Smith*

v. Superior Court, 49 Cal. Rptr. 20 (Cal. Ct. App. 1996); *Ake v. G. M. Corp.*, 942 F. Supp. 869, 880-881(W.D. N.Y. 1996) (citing cases); *Meenach v. G. M. Corp.*, 891 S.W.2d 398 (KY 1995).

12. *See* statement by Senator John Breaux, *reprinted in* 135 Cong. Rec. S15,210 (November 8, 1989).

13. *Id. See also* Wald, Patricia, "NRC Bars Paying Whistleblowers for Silence," *N.Y. Times*, A25 (May 4, 1989); Martin, Read, "Little Big Man," *Dallas Observer* (May 18, 1989); Aronson, Geoffrey, "The Co-opting of CASE," *The Nation*, 678 (December 4, 1989).

14. *See e.g., Restatement (Second) of Contract*, §§ 178 and 179 (public policy) and 208 (unconscionability); *EEOC v. Astra, USA*, 94 F.3d 738 (1st Cir. 1996); *Polizzi v. Gibbs & Hill, Inc.*, 87-ERA-38, Order Rejecting in Part, etc. by SOL (July 18, 1989); *EEOC v. Cosmair, Inc., L'Oreal Hair Care Div.*, 821 F.2d 1085, 1090 (5th Cir. 1987); NRC proposed rule: "Preserving the Free Flow of Information to the Commission," 54 Fed. Reg. 30,049 (July 18, 1989), rule adopted with modifications, 55 Fed. Reg. 10,404 (March 21,1990).

15. *Baker v. General Motors, Corp., supra; Hamad v. Graphic Arts Center, Inc.*, 72 Fair Empl. Prac. Cases (BNA) 1759 (D. Or. January 3, 1997) ("any provision[s] in the settlement agreement which prohibits [former employees] from testifying as required by subpoena are against public policy and therefore void").

16. *Archer Daniels Midland Co. v. Whiteacre*, 60 F.Supp.2d 819 (C.D. Ill. 1999)

17. 60 *University of Pittsburgh Law Review* 1207, 1212-1213 (1999).

18. *See Macktal v. SOL*, 923 F. 2d. 1150 (5th Cir. 1991).

19. Traditional common law rules also provide justification for voiding restrictive or hush money settlements. *See U.S. v. Nixon* 418 U.S. 683, 709 ("Ancient proposition of law" that the "public has a right to every man's evidence"). In his distinguished 1884 *Treatise on Contempt* (§ 22, p. 27 n. 1, New York, 1884), Stewart Rapalje noted that under common law a contempt of court would lie for "any attempt to threaten or intimidate a person from instituting or defending any action." Contempt could also be found if a person acted to "threaten," "intimidate," or coerce a witness to "suppress or withhold the truth." In 1916 the Supreme Court of Arkansas in *Turk v. State* summarized this rule: "It is universally held that intimidating a witness and preventing his appearance at court . . . is a contempt of court." Courts in both England and the United States followed this precedent. *See also Turk v. State*, 123 Ark. 341, 185 S.W. 472 (1916); *Wilson v. Irwin*, 144 Ky. 311, 138 S.W. 373 (1911); *McCarthy v. State*, 89 Tenn. 543, 15 S.W. 736 (1891); *Snow v. Hawkes*, 183 N.C. 365, 111 S.E. 621 (1922); *Sharland v. Sharland*, 1 Times L.R. (Eng., 1885); *Bromilow v. Phillips*, 40 Week Rep. (Eng., 1892); *Smith v. Lakeman*, 2 Jur. N.S. 1202, 26 L.J. Ch. N.S. 305 (Eng. 1856); *Re Muloch*, 10 Jur. N.S. 1188, 33 L.J. Prob. N.S. 205, 13 Week Rep. 278 (Eng., 1864). *See* 23 A.L.R. 183.

20. *Connecticut Light & Power v. SOL*, 85 F.3d 89, 95 (2nd Cir. 1996) (nuclear whistleblower); *see also Martin v. TAO Technical Services*, 94-WPC-

1/2/3, Order Disapproving Settlement by SOL (June 8, 1994) (environmental whistleblower); *Stack v. Preston Trucking Company*, 92-STA-21, Order of Remand by SOL (March 24, 1995) (surface transportation whistleblower); *Macktal v. Brown & Root, Inc.*, 86-ERA-23, D&O of SOL (October 13, 1993) (nuclear whistleblower).

21. *See* Senate Hearing 101-90, Opening Statement of Sen. John Breaux, Chairman, at 2-3 (May 4, 1989).

22. *Id.* at 45.

23. *See EEOC v. Cosmair, Inc., L'Oreal Hair Care Div.*, *supra*, at 1088-1091. *Accord., EEOC v. Astra, USA, supra.*

24. *Shadis v. Beal*, 685 F.2d 824, 833 (3rd Cir. 1982) (stating a contract is not in the interest of the public if it inhibits the public from knowing if safety problems exist at nuclear power plants); *Air Line Stewards v. TWA*, 630 F.2d 1164, 1169 (7th Cir. 1980); *Atlantic Co. v. Broughton*, 146 F.2d 480, 482 (5th Cir. 1944) (holding that a contractual ban on appearing as a witness in an administrative or judicial hearing contravenes and tends to nullify the letter and spirit of an act of Congress); *accord., Jackson Purchase, Etc. v. Local Union 816, Etc.*, 646 F.2d 264, 267 (6th Cir. 1981). *Accord., EEOC v. Astra, USA*, at 744 n. 5 (1st Cir. 1996) (providing testimony is "not a right an employer can purchase from an employee, nor is it a right that an employee can sell to [an] employer").

25. *See Khandelwal v. Southern California Edison*, 97-ERA-6, Order of Remand by ARB (March 31, 1998).

26. *Id.* at 4.

27. *Id.*

28. *See also* Carol M. Bast, "At What Price: Are Confidentiality Agreements Enforceable?," 25 *William Mitchell Law Review* 627, 694-713 (1999).

29. *See Macktal v. SOL, supra; Macktal v. Brown & Root, Inc., supra*, SOL Order Disapproving Settlement (October 13, 1993).

30. *CP&L v. DOL*, 43 F.3d 912 (4th Cir. 1995).

31. *See* administrative record in *Macktal v. Brown & Root, Inc.*, 86-ERA-23 DOL ALJ file.

32. *See Macktal v. Brown & Root, Inc.*, Order of SOL (July 11, 1995) (finding DOL without authority to order employee to return settlement money.)

33. *See Khandelwal v. Southern California Edison, supra*, at 5. *Accord., Oubre v. Entergy Op., Inc., supra.*

34. 89-ERA-38, D&O of SOL (April 19, 1995).

35. *See Connecticut Light & Power v. SOL, supra*, at 95 n. 5.

36. *Id.* at 97.

37. *See Macktal v. Brown & Root, Inc., supra*, at 6-7.

Chapter 11

The Future of Whistleblower Protection: A Model Law

Given the failure of the federal government to act upon legislative proposals to create a uniform national whistleblower protection law, employee
whistleblowers and their attorneys are faced with a difficult problem of
identifying which specific state or federal laws the whistleblower may be
protected under and exactly what they must do to obtain protection. In
many instances, the whistleblower is left with no protection at all.[1] In light
of this national legislative vacuum, persons who have blown the whistle on
federal crimes have often been personally destroyed, both economically and
professionally.[2] This status quo is not acceptable. The federal government
should pass a uniform national whistleblower protection act.[3] In addition,
in the absence of federal action, state legislatures should pass legislation to
insure that whistleblowers are protected.

The current maze of federal whistleblower laws has been widely
and properly criticized. For example, the Administrative Conference of the
United States studied federal whistleblower laws over thirteen years ago.
The conference's report recognized that whistleblowers were completely
unprotected in "potentially important industries such as aviation and
pharmaceuticals" and that the "crazy quilt" of the limited federal remedies
was gravely deficient.[4] Moreover, in many of the areas in which Congress
had passed whistleblower legislation, such as the protection of whistleblowers who disclosed environmental violations, the laws contained thirty-day
statutes of limitations. The Administrative Conference found that such

short statutes of limitation were "unreasonable."[5]

Although the Administrative Conference called for the passage of "omnibus whistleblower legislation" and the closing of the gaps in existing legislation, no such law has passed.[6] Congress' one attempt at creating a uniform national whistleblower law was problematic. In 1990 the Senate Committee on Labor and Human Resources approved, by a one vote margin, the Employee Health and Safety Whistleblower Protection Act.[7] This law, which did not even close the loopholes in existing legislation, was extremely complex and unworkable. The legislation was dead upon arrival. It was never debated or voted upon by the Senate and, since 1990, has not been seriously reintroduced.

At the state level, the effectiveness of whistleblower protection radically varies from jurisdiction to jurisdiction. Although the overwhelming majority of states recognize a cause of action for wrongful discharge,[8] given the state-by-state manner in which these causes of action were adopted, there are radical differences in the nature of protection afforded employee whistleblowers. On the one hand, employees in some states, such as New York and Georgia, lack any meaningful whistleblower protection.[9] On the other hand, some states, such as New Jersey, ensure that whistleblowers have reasonable protections.[10]

Given the fact that there is no national whistleblower protection law that creates a reasonable minimum protection to employee whistleblowers, both Congress and state lawmakers have increasingly proposed or enacted specific whistleblower legislation that has addressed either whistleblower rights within a state or within a specific federally regulated industry.[11] Under the banner of "good government," lawmakers have passed legislation, some of which has enhanced whistleblower protections but some of which has undermined pre-existing state common law protections.[12] Because of the growing trend to address whistleblower protection through statutory action, lawmakers and citizens interested in insuring that whistleblowing is properly protected have a strong need for a constructive legislative model as a basis for future whistleblower legislation.

This chapter discusses what should be contained in a model whistleblower law. The proposed model is equally applicable to both federal or state legislation. It is based on the 1986 New Jersey Conscientious Employee Protection Act (N.J. Code Section 34-19, hereinafter CEPA). The CEPA contains provisions that cover most of the significant legislative terms commonly seen in whistleblower laws. Most of the law was well conceived, and many of its provisions represent a reasonable model for other state legislatures or Congress to follow. Set forth below are each of the statutory provisions of the New Jersey law and a commentary concerning whether that particular provision of the law represents an appropriate national model. The addendum at the end of this chapter contains a final version of a model whistleblower law.[13]

DEFINITION OF EMPLOYER AND EMPLOYEE

Section 34:19-2 (a) and (b) of the CEPA states as follows:

a. "Employer" means any individual, partnership, association, corporation or any person or group of persons acting directly or indirectly on behalf of or in the interest of an employer with the employer's consent and shall include all branches of State Government, or the several counties and municipalities thereof, or any other political subdivision of the State, or a school district, or any special district, or any authority, commission, or board or any other agency or instrumentality thereof.

b. "Employee" means any individual who performs services for and under the control and direction of an employer for wages or other remuneration.

This section provides a realistic framework of employees and employers. Both public sector and private sector employers are covered.[14] This insures that state and private employees receive the same level of protection. Many states have enacted laws that cover only the public or the private sector. The New Jersey law closes this loophole. One potential shortfall exists in the use of the phrase "employer's consent" contained in the definition of "employer." This phrase could be used to undermine the ability of the courts to find corporations liable, if the corporation defended by claiming that the discrimination was conducted without the "employer's consent." However, the Supreme Court of New Jersey has rejected such an interpretation. It is recommended that this phrase be eliminated from future legislation to avoid future confusion.[15] Further, the statutory language should clarify that an employer is also responsible for the actions of its agents, contractors, or subcontractors. Similarly, the statute should explicitly apply to applicants for employment as well as former employees.

DEFINITION OF "PUBLIC BODY" AND "SUPERVISOR"

Section 34:19-2 (c) and (d) contains the following definitions:

c. "Public body" means:

(1) the United States Congress, and State legislature, or any popularly-

elected local governmental body, or any member or employee thereof;

    (2)   any federal, State, or local judiciary, or any member or employee thereof, or any grand or petit jury;

    (3)   any federal, State, or local regulatory, administrative, or public agency or authority, or instrumentality thereof;

    (4)   any federal, State, or local law enforcement agency, prosecutorial office, or police or peace officer;

    (5)   any federal, State or local department of an executive branch of government; or

    (6)   any division, board, bureau, office, committee or commission of any of the public bodies described in the above paragraphs of this subsection.

d.   "Supervisor" means any individual with an employer's organization who has the authority to direct and control the work performance of the affected employee, who has authority to take corrective action regarding the violation of the law, rule or regulation of which the employee complains, or who has been designated by the employer on the notice required under section 7 of this act.

The definition of "public body" is very significant. Under this definition, reports to both federal and state authorities are jointly included. Under the common law case precedents, the issue of whether reports to federal authorities were deemed protected under state law was consistently a matter of costly litigation with almost all jurisdictions protecting contacts with both federal and state officials. Common sense dictates that a whistle-blower may contact a federal authority or a state authority, depending on the nature of the underlying issue. The majority rule covered reports to both federal and state authorities concerning violations of either state or federal law.[16] The New Jersey law also requires employers to "designate" a person to act as a "supervisor" for the purposes of "§ 7." As set forth below, this provision should exist only if requirements of sections 4 and 7 of the CEPA exist.

DEFINITION OF RETALIATION

Section 34:19-2 (e) states:

e.   "Retaliatory action" means the discharge, suspension or demotion of an employee, or other adverse employment action taken against an employee in the terms and conditions of employment.

The definition of "retaliatory action" includes conduct short of an actual discharge. This definition, which is consistent with most federal employment laws,[17] recognizes that discriminatory conduct, such as harassment, demotions, suspensions, and transfers, can have an equally adverse impact on employees. Action short of discharge can ruin an individual's career and discourages other employees from reporting wrongdoing. This aspect of the law is significant, as employee whistleblowers are often subject to a series of escalating adverse actions. Enabling the employee to take action prior to an actual discharge allows both the employer and the employee to identify potentially illegal treatment of the whistleblower and resolve the controversy prior to a full-blown wrongful discharge action.

PATIENT CARE

Section 34:19-2 (f) of the CEPA states:

f.   "Improper quality of patient care" means, with respect to patient care, any practice, procedure, action or failure to act of an employer that is a health care provider which violates any law or any rule, regulation or declaratory ruling adopted pursuant to law, or any professional code of ethics.

The New Jersey law contains an explicit provision insuring that employees who expose health care problems are protected under the law. Although such actions should be fully protected under the more general provisions which exist both in the New Jersey law and other articulations of the "public policy" rule, the failure of at least one court to protect this type of whistleblowing may support the inclusion of this provision into any whistleblower statute.[18]

DEFINITION OF PROTECTED ACTIVITY

Section 34:19-3 of the CEPA defines retaliatory action in the following manner:

An employer shall not take any retaliatory action against an employee because the employee does any of the following:

g.   Discloses, or threatens to disclose to a supervisor or to a public body an activity, policy or practice of the employer or another employer, with whom there is a business relationship, that the employee reasonably believes is in violation of a law, or a rule or regulation promulgated pursuant to law, or, in the case of an employee who is a licensed or certified health care professional, reasonably believes constitutes improper quality of patient care;

h. Provides information to, or testifies before, any public body conducting an investigation, hearing or inquiry into any violation of law, or a rule or regulation promulgated pursuant to law by the employer or another employer, with whom there is a business relationship, or, in the case of an employee who is a licensed or certified health care professional, provides information to, or testifies before, any public body conducting an investigation, hearing or inquiry into the quality of patient care; or

i. Objects to, or refuses to participate in any activity, policy or practice which the employee reasonably believes:

(1) is in violation of a law, or a rule or regulation promulgated pursuant to law or, if the employee is a licensed or certified health care professional, constitutes improper quality of patient care;

(2) is fraudulent or criminal; or

(3) is incompatible with a clear mandate of public policy concerning the public health, safety or welfare or protection of the environment.

This section of the law provides a sound basis for defining protected activity. It covers the range of conduct that most (but not all) state courts have recognized as being within the logical framework of whistleblowing. Significantly, the law contains a specific reference to protecting disclosures or testimony when an employee "reasonably believe(s)" that the law has been violated. This clause has become more important given the restrictive reading some state courts have given to whistleblower legislation. For example, the Court of Appeals of New York, in interpreting the New York whistleblower protection statute which does not contain such a qualifying clause,[19] held that employees not only had to demonstrate wrongful discharge to prevail but also had to demonstrate that the matter in which they originally blew the whistle was, in fact, a "violation of law."[20] This requirement completely undermines whistleblower protection. Almost no whistleblower protection laws contain such a requirement.[21]

The law also provides a limited right to object to performing work that is reasonably perceived as being illegal or a threat to the public health and safety. Again, this type of provision is within the framework of standard court definitions of protected activity.[22]

PRIOR REPORTING TO SUPERVISOR

Section 34:19-4 of the CEPA states as follows:

The protection against retaliatory action provided by this act pertaining to disclosure to a public body shall not apply to an employee who makes a disclosure to a public body unless the employee has brought the activity, policy or practice in violation of a law, or a rule or regulation promulgated pursuant to law to the attention of a supervisor of the employee by written notice and has afforded the employer a reasonable opportunity to correct the activity, policy or practice. Disclosure shall not be required where the employee is reasonably certain that the activity, policy or practice is known to one or more supervisors of the employer or where the employee reasonably fears physical harm as a result of the disclosure provided, however, that the situation is emergency in nature.

This provision of the law requires that, with limited exceptions, most employees first report potential violations of law to their supervisors prior to reporting the violations to public bodies. A similar requirement exists in the provisions of a number of the worst state whistleblower statutes.[23] However, many state statutes have rejected such a requirement and almost all judicial decisions interpreting other statutes or the common law have not mandated such a requirement.[24]

This provision should not exist in whistleblower legislation. Most employees blow the whistle first and only later review the fine language in statutes. As one court correctly noted in rejecting a hyper-technical definition of protected activity, whistleblower laws are not designed only to protect "those versed in the law."[25] The clause provides employers with a defense that does not serve the public interest. Worse, the clause makes it very difficult to blow the whistle confidentially. Because the employee is required to set forth his or her concerns, in writing, to the "supervisor," if similar concerns are ever expressed to a governmental agency, the employee who complained to the supervisor will be "fingerprinted" as the source. Many employers are not hostile to employees who keep their concerns within a company but become very hostile to employees who contact governmental agencies. In addition, employees are often asked questions during governmental audits or other investigations. What happens to the employee who truthfully blows the whistle during such an audit, when he or she had not previously provided the information (in writing) to his or her supervisor? Although the New Jersey statute contains language that mitigates against the harsh application of this provision, other states, such as New York, do not contain such mitigating language. These types of provisions should be vigorously opposed.

As a practical matter, the vast majority of whistleblowers initially disclose their concerns to their supervisors, and the basic legislative intent behind this clause of the New Jersey law will be accomplished even without the statutory provision. Significantly, some courts have actually ruled that disclosures to supervisors are not protected under law and that an employee must have actual contact with a governmental entity in order to be protected.[26] Instead of adding to the confusion concerning the role of reporting allegations of misconduct to supervisors, the best approach is to protect both reports to supervisors and reports to public entities. This "common sense" rule was adopted in a very early whistleblower case under the Federal Mine Health and Safety Act[27] and has been followed by numerous courts.[28]

Statutory restrictions of an employee's right to blow the whistle directly to law enforcement authorities also raises grave issues concerning violations of the "obstruction of justice" criminal laws. It is a serious criminal violation to "hinder" or "delay" any person's communication to federal law enforcement authority. For example, under 18 U.S.C. § 1512 it is a felony:

Whoever knowingly uses intimidation or physical force, threatens, or corruptly persuades another person, or attempts to do so, or engages in misleading conduct towards another person, with intent to–

*   *   *

(3) hinder, delay, or prevent the communication to a law enforcement official or judge of the United States of information relating to the commission or possible commission of a Federal offense

shall be fined under this title or imprisoned not more than ten years, or both.[29]

*   *   *

(c) Whoever intentionally harasses another person and thereby hinders, delays, prevents, or dissuades any person from–

(1) attending or testifying in an official proceeding;

(2) reporting to a law enforcement officer or judge of the United States the commission or possible commission of a federal offense;

shall be fined under this title or imprisoned not more than one year, or both.[30]

Any law that creates an obstacle or impediment to the disclosure of a federal crime is clearly improper. Moreover, any law or regulation which may "hinder" or "delay" the disclosure of criminal violations, itself violates the spirit, if not the letter, of the federal obstruction of justice law. Consequently, state and local laws, which mandate that an employee's disclosure of wrongdoing to their employer (who may be directly involved in the illegal conduct), are, at a minimum, inconsistent with federal law. Worse, an employer who takes adverse action against an employee, who makes a disclosure in reliance upon a state law that requires supervisor pre-notification, may inadvertently commit a violation of federal criminal law.

THE FORUM

The first two sentences of Section 34:19-5 state as follows:

Upon a violation of any of the provisions of this act, an aggrieved employee or former employee may, within one year, institute a civil action in a court of competent jurisdiction. Upon the application of any party, a jury trial shall be directed to try the validity of any claim under this act specified in the suit.

This section allows the whistleblower to file a normal "civil action" in court. Some states (and most federal laws) have established a separate administrative remedy for whistleblowers. Segregating whistleblower actions from other types of tort actions allows governmental agencies to unduly politicize the process. It also discourages attorneys from filing claims due to the time and costs incurred in learning an entirely new administrative area of law. Also, by explicitly allowing for a jury trial, the statute eliminates the ambiguity that some courts have read into whistleblower laws. For example, the New York statute, which also provides for a "civil action in a court of competent jurisdiction," has been interpreted as not allowing for jury trials.[31]

A number of laws provide for administrative adjudication of whistleblower claims. Some of these procedures are very independent and provide inexpensive procedures for accomplishing a fair adjudication of a claim.[32] Because the New Jersey law does not preempt employees from using alternative laws or regulations, the state retains the option of passing specific whistleblower legislation that may contain administrative remedies specifically tailored to the needs of a group of employees and employees can freely choose the best potential forum for adjudicating their case.

The law also sets forth a one-year statute of limitations. One year is a reasonable minimum time period for filing such a claim. Some whistleblower statutes have limitation periods as short as thirty days. As can be imagined, short statutes of limitations result in good cases being dismissed and require employees to file questionable cases prior to a complete factual investigation due to the short nature of the limitations period.

BURDENS OF PROOF

Like most state and federal whistleblower laws, the New Jersey statute is silent concerning the burdens of proof required to prosecute or defend a whistleblower action. The failure of Congress to statutorily set forth these burdens of proof in most employment related legislation has resulted in a series of federal court decisions that attempt to create appropriate burdens on the plaintiff and defendant. These precedents are often complex, contradictory, and unclear.[33] State courts regularly adopt these precedents.[34]

Given the problematic nature of judge-made burdens of proof, the U.S. Congress has, in four recent whistleblower laws, set forth a statutory burden of proof. Congress first established this burden in the 1989 law protecting federal employee whistleblowers.[35] Since then, the burden was written into three other whistleblower laws, the Financial Institutions Reform, Recovery and Enforcement Act of 1989,[36] the Energy Policy Act of 1992 (protecting whistleblowers in the atomic energy area),[37] and the Whistleblower Protection Provision of Wendell H. Ford Aviation Investment and Reform Act for the 21st Century (AIR 21).[38]

This new statutory standard sets forth a two-part test in whistleblower cases. First, the burden of proof is on the whistleblower to demonstrate, by a preponderance of the evidence, that animus toward his or her protected activity was a "contributing factor in the unfavorable personnel action." If the employee meets this burden, the burden of proof shifts to the employer to demonstrate by "clear and convincing evidence that it would have taken the same unfavorable personnel action in the absence of [the whistleblowing]."[39] Thus, even if an employee can demonstrate that animus toward whistleblowing did contribute to the adverse employment action, the employer can still prevail if it can demonstrate that the employee would have been discharged regardless of the whistleblowing. Under this standard, whistleblowers do not obtain immunity from discipline; however, the employer bears the burden of proving that such discipline is warranted.

The "contributing factor" standard has been used in federal laws covering whistleblowers for ten years. There has been no congressional, judicial, or scholarly criticism of this standard. The standards of proof set forth in these recent federal laws should be adopted in future legislation.

REMEDIES

The remaining part of Section 34:19-5 reads as follows:

All remedies available in common law tort actions shall be available to prevailing plaintiffs. These remedies are in addition to any legal or equitable relief provided by this act or any other statute. The court may also order:

a. An injunction to restrain continued violation of this act;

b. The reinstatement of the employee to the same position held before the retaliatory action, or to an equivalent position;

c. The reinstatement of full fringe benefits and seniority rights;

d. The compensation for lost wages, benefits and other remuneration;

e. The payment by the employer of reasonable costs, and attorney's fees;

f. Punitive damages; or

g. An assessment of a civil fine of not more than $1,000.00 for the first violation of the act and not more than $5,000.00 for each subsequent violation, which shall be paid to the State Treasurer for deposit in the General Fund.

The New Jersey law properly sets forth remedies in a whistleblower action. The law authorizes the court to award both tort-type damages (such as damages for emotional distress or loss of reputation) and equitable relief (such as reinstatement, attorney fees and injunctive relief). These provisions are essential.

Most whistleblower laws, including the New Jersey law, allow the employee to obtain payment for attorney fees and costs.[40] Attorney fees are particularly important in whistleblower cases. Most employees cannot afford to pay standard market-rate retainers. Additionally, given the importance to the employee of nonmonetary awards, such as reinstatement, contingency payment plans are often not practicable. In fact, in cases that concern harassment short of discharge, such as a demotion, retaliatory transfer, or hostile work environment case, there may be no actual monetary damages.

REVERSE ATTORNEY FEES

Section 34:19-6 of the New Jersey whistleblower protection law states:

A court, upon notice of motion in accordance with the Rules Governing the
Courts of the State of New Jersey, may also order that reasonable attorneys' fees
and court costs be awarded to an employer if the court determines that an action
brought by an employee under this act was without basis in law or in fact. However, an employee shall not be assessed attorneys' fees under this section if, after
exercising reasonable and diligent efforts after filing a suit, the employee files a
voluntary dismissal concerning the employer, within a reasonable time after
determining that the employer would not be found to be liable for damages.

This section of the law provides for the payment of attorney fees
to employers under a limited number of circumstances. The law essentially
mirrors Rule 11 of the Federal Rules of Civil Procedure. However, many
federal and state whistleblower laws do not contain any provision for
reverse attorney fees. Because of the existence of other sanctions against
attorneys or parties who file frivolous claims, this clause should not be
included in a whistleblower law. Clearly, such a clause would "chill" an
employee from exercising legitimate whistleblower activities.[41] Other
approaches, such as excluding attorney fees or allowing a "prevailing party"
to obtain such fees, should be vigorously opposed as they present a significant impediment to employee whistleblowing.

POSTING NOTICE

Section 34:19-7 of the CEPA states as follows:

An employer shall conspicuously display notices of its employees' protections
and obligations under this act, and use other appropriate means to keep its employees so informed. Each notice posted pursuant to this section shall include the
name of the person or persons the employer has designated to receive written
notifications pursuant to section 4 of this act.

The posting requirement is a very significant provision. Many
employment laws require posting, and there is no justification for not
informing employees of their whistleblower rights, while requiring posting
of other rights, such as minimum wage or child labor laws.[42] Moreover, it
has been documented in the federal area that where posting is not required,
the majority of employees will not learn of their rights, and the strong
public policy the whistleblower laws validate will be undermined.[43]

PREEMPTION AND PRECLUSION

Section 34:19-8 of the New Jersey law states as follows:

Nothing in this act shall be deemed to diminish the rights, privileges, or remedies of any employee under any other federal or State law or regulation or under any collective bargaining agreement or employment contract; except that the institution of an action in accordance with this act shall be deemed a waiver of the rights and remedies available under any other contract, collective bargaining agreement, State law, rule or regulation or under the common law.

This section of the law has become one of the most important provisions in any state whistleblower protection statute. Simply stated, given the large number of federal whistleblower protection statutes and the varying approach of state courts interpreting the common law, it is imperative that state legislation not diminish the preexisting rights available to employee whistleblowers. The failure of a law to contain this form of saving clause may be ground enough, standing alone, to oppose such legislation.[44]

The importance of the nonpreclusion clause was exemplified in the case of Ronald Masters.[45] In that case, the employee was covered by two potential remedies for his wrongful discharge: a federal law and the state public policy tort. However, the federal law had a short statute of limitations (thirty days), did not provide for a jury trial, and had no provision for punitive damages. The employee filed under the state public policy tort. The state court used the existence of the weaker federal remedy to hold that the state would have found the federal remedy "exclusive" and held that Mr. Master's tort claim was "prohibited." This holding had far-reaching negative implications. Many of the old federal whistleblower laws have very short statutes of limitations (at least eight such laws have statutes of limitations of thirty days),[46] and a number of federal laws do not provide an employee with a private right of action. By precluding state tort actions based on these federal laws, the courts have withdrawn protections from extremely significant segments of the economy that have long been recognized as needing whistleblower protection. Consequently, the nonpreclusion clause contained in the New Jersey law is the best manner of insuring that weak statutory remedies enacted at either the state or federal system do not preempt a stronger common law or statutory remedy.

Since the passage of the New Jersey law, a number of courts have adjudicated the issue of whether a preemployment arbitration agreement can waive an employee's right to pursue statutory protections.[47] In order to avoid litigation over this issue and to insure that whistleblower claims

are heard in an objective and fair forum, any law should explicitly allow
employee whistleblowers the right to pursue their statutory remedies,
exclusive of any preemployment arbitration requirement.

The provision of the New Jersey statute requiring an election of
remedies is not needed and should be rejected.[48] The doctrines of *res
judicata* and *collateral estoppel* generally would result in a *de facto* election, even in the absence of a legislative restriction.[49] However, by setting
forth an election requirement, an employee's ability to obtain rights sufficiently unrelated to the whistleblower claim could be defeated. Whistleblower cases often also consist of other violations of law. It would be
inappropriate to prevent (or attempt to prevent) an employee from filing a
whistleblower claim because that employee may also have another cause of
action against an employer (i.e. defamation, breach of contract, etc.).

SETTLEMENT

As set forth in Chapter 10, there has been growing controversy in
employer use of settlement agreements to restrict whistleblower disclosures. Despite a large body of case law which indicates that such settlements are illegal or void, contract-based restrictions on employee whistleblowing are still commonplace. Some regulatory agencies, such as the
Nuclear Regulatory Commission, have enacted rules which prohibit such
agreements,[50] and a number of federal whistleblower laws mandate federal
review of settlement agreements in order to ensure that an agreement does
not restrict legitimate whistleblower disclosures.[51] These statutes, and the
case law interpreting these provisions, provide a solid guide for model
legislation prohibiting improper settlements.

CONCLUSION

The New Jersey whistleblower protection statute represents a good
working model for future legislation on both the federal and the state level.
Current alternatives are inadequate, or worse. Ignorance concerning what
provisions are necessary in order to enact realistic and successful whistleblower laws has resulted in the passage of a number of laws that, in practice, undermine whistleblower protection[52] and potentially run afoul of the
federal obstruction of justice statutes.

Whistleblowers perform a function vital to law enforcement and
public safety. When they expose wrongdoing, or take reasonable steps to
protect themselves from being directly involved in criminal activity, their
conduct must be properly protected. These policy goals are reflected in the

First Amendment's guarantees of speech, the Fifth and Fourteenth Amendments' guarantees of liberty[53] and in common law public policy. The piecemeal approach to drafting whistleblower legislation served a valid purpose during the early development of whistleblower protection. Given the unquestionable contributions of whistleblowers and the retaliation they face,[54] comprehensive whistleblower legislation is needed on the federal and state level.

ADDENDUM:
MODEL WHISTLEBLOWER PROTECTION ACT

§ 1. Short title
This Act may be cited as the "Whistleblower Protection Act."

§ 2. Definitions
(a) "Employer" means any individual, partnership, association, corporation or any person or group of persons acting directly or indirectly on behalf of, and shall also include any public or privately owned corporation, all branches of State Government, or the several counties and municipalities thereof, or any other political subdivision of the State, or a school district, or any special district, or any authority, commission, or board or any other agency or instrumentality thereof. Employer shall also include agents, contractors or subcontractors of an employer.
(b) "Employee" means any individual who performs services for or under the control and direction of an employer for wages or other remuneration. Employee shall also include applicants for employment, former employees or an authorized representative of an employee.
(c) "Public body" means:
   (1) the United States Congress, and State legislature, or any popularly- elected local governmental body, or any member or employee thereof;
   (2) any federal, State, or local judiciary, or any member or employee thereof, or any grand or petit jury;
   (3) any federal, State, or local regulatory, administrative, or public agency or authority, or instrumentality thereof;
   (4) any federal, State, or local law enforcement agency, prosecutorial office, or police or peace officer;
   (5) any federal, State or local department of an executive branch of government; or
   (6) any division, board, bureau, office, committee or commission of any of the public bodies described in the above paragraphs of this subsection.

(d) "Supervisor" means any individual with an employer's organization who has the authority to direct and control the work performance of the affected employee or who has authority to take corrective action regarding the violation of the law, rule or regulation of which the employee complains.

(e) "Retaliatory action" means the discharge, suspension, demotion, harassment, blacklisting or the refusal to hire an employee, or other adverse employment action taken against an employee in the terms and conditions of employment, or other actions which interfere with an employees ability to engage in protected activity set forth in § 3.

(f) "Improper quality of patient care" means, with respect to patient care by an employer that is a health care provider, any practice, procedure, action or failure to act which violates any law or any rule, regulation or declaratory ruling adopted pursuant to law, or any professional code of ethics.

§ 3. Protected activity

An employer shall not take any retaliatory action against an employee because the employee does any of the following:

(a) Discloses, threatens to disclose or is about to disclose to a supervisor or to a public body, an activity, policy or practice of the employer, a co-employee or another employer, that the employee reasonably believes is in violation of a law, or a rule or regulation promulgated pursuant to law, or, in the case of an employee who is a licensed or certified health care professional, reasonably believes constitutes improper quality of patient care;

(b) Provides information to, or testifies before, any public body conducting an investigation, hearing or inquiry into any violation of law, or a rule or regulation promulgated pursuant to law by the employer or another employer, or, in the case of an employee who is a licensed or certified health care professional, provides information to, or testifies before, any public body conducting an investigation, hearing or inquiry into the quality of patient care;

(c) Discloses, threatens to disclose or is about to disclose to a supervisor or to a public body, an activity, policy or practice of the employer, a co-employee or another employer, that the employee reasonably believes is incompatible with a clear mandate of public policy concerning the public health, safety or welfare or protection of the environment;

(d) Assists, or participates in a proceeding to enforce the provisions of this law; or

(e) Objects to, opposes or refuses to participate in any activity, policy or practice which the employee reasonably believes:

(1) is in violation of a law, or a rule or regulation promulgated pursuant to law or, if the employee is a licensed or certified health care professional, constitutes improper quality of patient care;

(2) is fraudulent or criminal; or

(3) is incompatible with a clear mandate of public policy concerning the public health, safety or welfare or protection of the environment.

§ 4. Forum.

Upon a violation of any of the provisions of this act, an aggrieved employee or former employee may, within one year, institute a civil action in a court of competent jurisdiction. Upon the application of any party, a jury trial shall be directed to try the validity of any claim under this act specified in the suit.

§ 5. Burden of proof.

A violation of this statute has occurred only if the employee demonstrates, by a preponderance of the evidence, that any behavior described in § 3 was a contributing factor in the retaliatory action alleged in the complaint by the employee. However, relief may not be ordered under § 6 if the employer demonstrates by clear and convincing evidence that it would have taken the same unfavorable personnel action (retaliatory action) in the absence of such behavior.

§ 6. Remedies

All remedies available in common law tort actions shall be available to prevailing plaintiffs. The court shall also, where appropriate, order:

(a) An injunction to restrain continued violation of this act;

(b) The reinstatement of the employee to the same position held before the retaliatory action, or to an equivalent position;

(c) The reinstatement of full fringe benefits and seniority rights;

(d) The compensation for lost wages, benefits and other remuneration;

(e) The payment by the employer of reasonable costs, expert witness and attorney's fees; and

(f) Compensatory or exemplary damages.

§ 7. Posting

An employer shall conspicuously display notices of its employees' protections and obligations under this act.

§ 8. Preemption

Nothing in this act shall be deemed to diminish the rights, privileges, or remedies of any employee under any other federal or State law or regulation or under any collective bargaining agreement or employment contract. No employee may waive through a private contract any right set forth in this statute, except as set forth in § 9, and no employee may be compelled to adjudicate his or her rights under this statute pursuant to a collective bargaining agreement or any other arbitration agreement.

§ 9. Settlement

The rights afforded employees under this statute may not be waived or modified, except through a court approved settlement agreement reached with the voluntary participation and consent of the employee and employer. An employer may not require an employee to waive, as a condition of settlement, his or her right to reasonably engage in conduct protected under § 3 of this statute.

NOTES

1. Hearing before the Subcommittee on Labor of the Committee on Labor and Human Resources, *Employee Health and Safety Whistleblower Protection Act*, 101st Cong., 1st sess., S. Hrg. 101-147 (March 7, 1989), at 1-2, 46, 119, 131, 197, 250; Eugene R. Fidell, *Federal Protection of Private Sector Health and Safety Whistleblowers: A Report to the Administrative Conference of the United States* (Washington, D.C.: Administrative Conference of the United States, February 1987), *reprinted in* 2 *Administrative Law Journal* 1 (1988).

2. Myron Glazer & Penina Glazer, *The Whistleblowers: Exposing Corruption in Government and Industry* (New York: Basic Books, 1989), at 133-166, 206-237; Soeken and Soeken, "A Survey of Whistleblowers: Their Stressors and Coping Strategies," printed in Senate Committee on Governmental Affairs, Subcommittee on Federal Services, Post Office, and Civil Service, *Hearings on S.508*, 100th Cong., 1st sess. (July 1987), *reprinted in* 2 *The Administrative Law Journal* 1 (1985).

3. Laura Simoff, "Confusion and Deterrence: The Problems That Arise from a Deficiency in Uniform Laws and Procedures for Environmental Whistleblowers," 8 *Dickinson Journal of Environmental Law and Policy* 325, 342 (1999).

4. Fidell, *supra*, at 1.

5. *Id.* at 46.

6. Administrative Conference of the United States, "Recommendation 87-2," *Federal Protection of Private Sector Health and Safety Whistleblowers* (adopted June 11, 1987), 1 C.F.R. § 305.87-2 (1988), at 3.

7. U.S. Senate Committee on Labor and Human Resources, "Report Together with Additional Views," *Employee Health and Safety Whistleblower*

Protection Act, S. Rep. 101-349, 101st Cong. 2d Sess. (June 1990).

8. *See Martin Marietta Energy Systems, Corp. v. Lorenz*, 823 P. 2d 100, 106 n. 3 (Colo. 1991) (citing cases).

9. Sandra J. Mullings, "Is There Whistleblower Protection for Private Employees in New York?" *New York State Bar Journal* (February 1997); *Goodroe v. Georgia Power Company*, 251 S.E. 2d 51 (Ga. Ct. App. 1978).

10. 1986 New Jersey "Conscientious Employee Protection Act" N.J. Code Section 34-19.

11. Tim Barnett, "Overview of State Whistleblower Protection Statutes," 43 *Labor Law Journal* 440 (July 1992). *See also* Mullings, "Is There Whistleblower Protection for Private Employees in New York?" footnote 11(cites to a number of whistleblower laws passed after 1992).

12. Mullings, "Is There Whistleblower Protection for Private Employees in New York?" footnote 11. For a complete overview of state statutory remedies *See* Robert G. Vaughn, "State Whistleblower Statutes and the Future of Whistleblowing Protection" 51 Administrative Law Review 581 (1999).

13. Alternatively, using the administrative procedures enacted into law on April 5, 2000 covering whistleblowers in the airline industry could also serve as an effective model at the federal level. *See* 49 U.S.C. § 42121. This law provides for an effective administrative remedy within the U.S. Department of Labor (DOL) and is modeled after the nuclear whistleblower law. The DOL, including its Office of Administrative Law Judges (ALJ) and the Administrative Review Board (ARB), has obtained substantial experience in adjudicating whistleblower cases. Its current adjudicatory regulations, 29 CFR Part 18, allow parties to engage in extensive discovery and to participate in an evidentiary hearing before an ALJ. However, any federal legislation should explicitly provide that state remedies are *not* preempted and should also provide that private contractual agreements (such as a mandatory preemployment arbitration agreement) do not negate the federal statutory remedy. These provisions are extremely important given the U.S. Supreme Court's decisions enhancing state immunities under the 11th Amendment and its indication that employment agreements may be covered under the Federal Arbitration Act. *See Wright v. Universal Maritime Service Corp.*, 525 U.S. 70 (1998); *Kimel v. Florida Bd. of Regents*, 120 S.Ct. 631(2000).

14. Coverage of public employees under state whistleblower laws was given added impetus by the U.S. Supreme Court in *Kimel, supra*, in a 5-4 decision. In that case, the Court held that the 11th Amendment of the Constitution prevented Congress from prohibiting state governments from discriminating against their employees on the basis of age, thereby making state whistleblower remedies more crucial.

15. *Abbamont v. Piscataway Bd. Ed.*, 650 A.2d 958, 964-965 (N.J. 1994).

16. *Wheeler v. Caterpillar Tractor Co.*, 485 N.E.2d 372 (Ill. 1985).

17. *See, e.g.*, 29 C.F.R. § 24.2 (a) (U.S. Department of Labor regulations defining the scope of retaliatory conduct under seven federal whistleblower laws).

18. *Hinrichs v. Tranquilaire Hospital*, 352 So.2d 1381 (Ala. 1977).

19. McKinney's Labor Law § 740(2)(a).

20. *Bordell v. General Electric Co.*, 667 N.E.2d 922, 923 (N.Y. 1996).

21. *Passaic Valley Sewerage Com'rs v. U.S. DOL*, 992 F.2d 474, 479 (3rd Cir. 1993) ("an employee's non-frivolous complaint should not have to withstand scrutiny of in-house or external review in order to merit protection . . . for the obvious reason that such a standard would chill employee initiatives in bringing to light perceived [violations of law]").

22. *Whirlpool Corp. v. Marshall*, 445 U.S. 1, 10-11 (1980).

23. *See, e.g.*, McKinney's Labor Law § 740 (3) (New York).

24. *See, e.g.*, Hawaii Whistleblower Protection Act, § 378-61-62; Rhode Island Whistleblower Protection Act, § 28-50; *Brockell v. Norton*, 732 F.2d 664, 668 (8th Cir. 1984).

25. *Yesudian v. Howard University*, 153 F.3d 731, 741 (D.C. Cir. 1998).

26. *See, e.g., Brown & Root, Inc. v. Donovan*, 747 F.2d 1029 (5th Cir. 1984).

27. *Phillips v. Board of Mine Operations Appeals*, 500 F.2d 772 (D.C. Cir. 1974). *See also NLRB v. Schrivener*, 405 U.S. 117, 122-124 (1972).

28. *Yesudian, supra*, at 153 F.3d 731, 741-42 (D.C. Cir. 1998) (referencing other cases).

29. 18 U.S.C. § 1512(b)(3), § 1512(c)(1), and §1512(c)(2). *See Mruz v. Caring, Inc.*, 991 F. Supp. 701, 714 (D. N.J. 1998).

30. 18 U.S.C. § 1512(b)(3), § 1512(c)(1), and §1512(c)(2). *See Mruz v. Caring, Inc.*, 991 F. Supp. 701, 714 (D. N.J. 1998).

31. *Scaduto v. Restaurant Associates Industries, Inc.*, 579 N.Y.S. 2d 381 (1st Dept. 1992).

32. *See, e.g.*, 29 C.F.R. Part 18, the U.S. Department of Labor rules governing the adjudication of a number of federal whistleblower protection statutes.

33. *See, e.g., Reeves v. Sanderson Plumbing*, __ U.S. __, 120 S. Ct. 2097, 2105-2106 (2000) (collecting cases); *Mt. Healthy City School District v. Doyle*, 429 U.S. 274 (1977) (burden of proof in First Amendment retaliation cases); *McDonnell-Douglas Corp. v. Green*, 411 U.S. 792 (1973)(burden of proof in Title VII cases); *Texas Dept. of Community Affairs v. Burdine*, 450 U.S. 248, 253 (1981); *St. Mary's Honor Center v. Hicks*, 509 U.S. 502 (1993).

34. *See, e.g., Hubbard v. United Press Intern., Inc.*, 330 N.W.2d 428, 441-442 (Minn. 1983).

35. Whistleblower Protection Act of 1989, 5 U.S.C. § 1221(e); *Marano v. Dept. of Justice*, 2 F.3d 1137, 1140-1141 (Fed. Cir. 1993).

36. 12 U.S.C. § 1831j; *Rouse v. Farmers State Bank of Jewell*, 866 F. Supp. 1191 (D. Iowa 1994).

37. P.L. 102-486, Section 2902(d), codified in the Energy Reorganization Act, 42 U.S.C. § 5851(b)(3)(C) and (D); *Stone & Webster v. Herman*, 115 F.3d 1568 (11th Cir. 1997).

38. 49 U.S.C. 42121.

39. *See, e.g.*, 42 U.S.C. § 5851(b)(3)(C) and (D).

40. *See, e.g.,* McKinney's Labor Law § 740 (5)(e) (New York); Michigan Whistleblower Protection Act, § 17.428(3); Ohio Whistleblower Statute § 4113.52 (b) (3) (E); Hawaii Whistleblower Protection Act § 378-64; federal whistleblower statutes administered by U.S. Department of Labor, 29 C.F.R. § 24.6(b)(3).

41. *McGavock v. Elbar*, 86-STA-5, D&O of SOL (January 25, 1988).

42. *See, e.g.,* Hawaii Whistleblower Protection Act § 378-68; Michigan Whistleblowers' Protection Act § 17.428(8); Rhode Island Whistleblowers' Protection Act § 28-50-8; and the Energy Reorganization Act, 42 U.S.C. § 5851.

43. Stephen M. Kohn, "The Crisis in Environmental Whistleblower Protection: Deficiencies in the Regulations Protecting Employees Who Disclose Violations of Environmental Laws or Testify in 'Citizen Suits,' " 2 *New England Environmental Law Forum* 1, 7-8 (N.E. School of Law, 1995).

44. For example, in Ohio and Montana, the passage of a state Whistleblower Protection Act eliminated the ability of whistleblowers to use preexisting common law remedies. *Contreras v. Ferro Corp.*, 652 N.E.2d 940 (Oh. 1995); Montana Whistleblower Protection Act § 39-2-913. Courts have also relied upon the existence of both federal and state statutory remedies in order to dismiss whistleblower claims under state law. *Cox v. Radiology Consulting Assocs.*, 658 F. Supp. 264 (W.D. Pa. 1987); *Dockins v. Ingles Markets, Inc.*, 413 S.E.2d 18 (S.C. 1992).

45. *Masters v. Daniel International Corporation*, 917 F.2d 455, 457-458 (10th Cir. 1990).

46. *See, e.g.,* 29 C.F.R. § 24.3(b) (thirty-day limitations period for environmental whistleblowers); 29 C.F.R. Part 1977 (thirty day limitations period on health and safety whistleblowers); 30 C.F.R. § 865.12(c) (thirty-day limitations period for surface mining whistleblowers).

47. *Compare, Gilmer v. Interstate/Johnson Lane Corp.*, 500 U.S. 20 (1991) *and Alexander v. Gardner-Denver Co.*, 415 U.S. 36 (1974). *See also Duffield v. Robertson Stephens & Company*, 144 F.3d 1182 (9th Cir. 1998); *Rosenberg v. Merrill Lynch*, 163 F.3d 53 (1st Cir. 1998); *Cole v. Burns International Security*, 105 F.3d 1465 (D.C. Cir. 1997).

48. *Young v. Schering Corp.*, 660 A.2d 1153, 1160 (N.J. 1995).

49. *See Wilkins v. Jakeway*, 993 F. Supp. 635, 644-652 (S.D. Ohio) (precluding First Amendment suit on basis of prior-filed FCA case); *Kosciuk v. Consumers Power Company*, 90-ERA-56, D&O of Remand by SOL (March 31, 1994) (discussing application of *res judicata* in administrative proceeding). *See* Acting Administrator's Brief as Amicus Curiae on the Issue of *res judicata*, filed in *McKinney v. TVA*, 92-ERA-22 (September 11, 1992) (opposing application of *res judicata* in environmental whistleblower case).

50. *See,* 10 C.F.R. § 50.7(g); *In re Texas Utilities Electric Company*, 37 NRC 477 (Directors Decision 1993).

51. *See, e.g. Macktal v. Secretary of Labor*, 923 F.2d 1150 (5th Cir. 1991) (setting forth standard of federal review of whistleblower settlement under the ERA); *Macktal v. Brown & Root*, 86-ERA-23, SOL Order Disapproving

Settlement (October 13, 1993) (setting forth standard for voiding settlement under public policy under ERA); *Martin v. TAD Technical Services*, 94-WPC-1/2/3, SOL Order Disapproving Settlement (June 8, 1994) (setting forth standard for voiding settlement under environmental whistleblower provisions); *CL&P v. SOL*, 85 F.3d 89 (2nd Cir. 1996) (finding the negotiation of hush money settlements improper and actionable).

52. Mullings, "Is There Whisteblower Protection for Private Employees in New York?" footnote 11. See also the Montana Wrongful Discharge from Employment Act § 39-2-901 through 915. This law explicitly prohibited the state courts from adopting any common law remedy for wrongful discharge. The law prohibited damages for "pain and suffering," "emotional distress," and other "compensatory damages" and limited back pay awards. § 39-2-905. The law also contained a very narrow definition of protected activity as well as burdensome and restrictive exhaustion and arbitration requirements, and only covered discharges from employment, not other forms of discrimination. §§ 39-2-903(7), 39-2-904, 39-2-911, and 39-2-914. Given its features, the Montana law is better characterized as an antiwhisteblower law.

53. The 5th and 14th Amendments to the U.S. Constitution protect "individual liberty" from being encroached upon by "certain government actions" regardless to the "fairness of the procedures used to implement" them. These Amendments provide "heightened protection against government interference with certain fundamental rights." *Washington v. Glucksberg*, 521 U.S. 702, 719-20 (1997) (internal citations and quotations omitted). The judicial history regarding these liberty interests were outlined by Justice David Souter in his concurring opinion in *Washington*, 521 U.S. at 756-773. Whistleblowing often impacts fundamental rights. For example, an employee who is threatened with termination for refusing to commit perjury clearly has a fundamental right to expose this employer misconduct and refuse to participate in an illegal conspiracy. *Brown v. Texas A&M University*, 804 F.2d 327, 336-337 (5th Cir. 1986). *See also Roth v. Veteran's Administration*, 856 F.2d 1401 (9th Cir. 1988) (employee whistleblower had "liberty interest" in "good name, reputation, honor" and "integrity"), *quoting Board of Regents v. Roth*, 408 U.S. 564, 573 (1972), *modified by Paul v. David*, 424 U.S. 693 (1976). For a general discussion of the procedural due process rights available to public employees *see Mercer v. City of Cedar Rapids*, 2000 WL 1009698 (N.D. Iowa 2000).

54. *See* Chapter 1, Endnotes 1 & 2.

Appendixes

C. Federal Regulations

APPENDIX A:
U.S. CONSTITUTION AMENDMENTS

Amendment I

Congress shall make no law respecting an establishment of religion, or prohibiting the free exercise thereof; or abridging the freedom of speech, or of the press; or the right of the people peaceably to assemble, and to petition the government for a redress of grievances.

Amendment XIV

Section 1. All persons born or naturalized in the United States, and subject to the jurisdiction thereof, are citizens of the United States and of the state wherein they reside. No state shall make or enforce any law which shall abridge the privileges or immunities of citizens of the United States; nor shall any state deprive any person of life, liberty, or property, without due process of law; nor deny to any person within its jurisdiction the equal protection of the laws.

APPENDIX B:
FEDERAL STATUTES

United States Code
29 U.S.C. § 623(d)
Age Discrimination in Employment Act,
Nonretaliation Provision

§ 623. Prohibition of age discrimination

(d) Opposition to unlawful practices: participation in investigations. proceedings. or litigation. It shall be unlawful for an employer to discriminate against any of his employees or applicants for employment. for an employment agency to discriminate against any individual, or for a labor organization to discriminate against any member thereof or applicant for membership. because such individual. member or applicant for membership has opposed any practice made unlawful by this section. or because such individual. member or applicant for membership has made a charge. testified. assisted. or participated in any manner in an investigation. proceeding. or litigation under this chapter.

United States Code
42 U.S.C. § 12203
Americans With Disabilities Act

§ 12203. Prohibition against retaliation and coercion

(a) *Retaliation.* No person shall discriminate against any individual because such individual has opposed any act or practice made unlawful by this chapter or because such individual made a charge. testified. assisted. or participated in any manner in an investigation. proceeding, or hearing under this chapter.

(b) *Interference. coercion. or intimidation.* It shall be unlawful to coerce. intimidate. threaten. or interfere with any individual in the exercise or enjoyment of. or on account of his or her having exercised or enjoyed. or on account of his or her having aided or encouraged any other individual in the exercise or enjoyment of. any right granted or protected by this chapter.

(c) *Remedies and procedures.* The remedies and procedures available under sections 12117. 12133. and 12188 of this title shall be available to aggrieved persons for violations of subsections (a) and (b) of this section. with respect to subchapter I. subchapter II and subchapter III of this chapter. respectively.

United States Code
20 U.S.C. § 4018
Asbestos School Hazard Abatement,
Whistleblower Provision

§ 4018. Employee protection

No State or local educational agency receiving assistance under this subchapter may discharge any employee or otherwise discriminate against any employee with respect to the employee's compensation. terms. conditions. or privileges of employment because the employee has brought to the attention of the public information concerning any asbestos problem in the school buildings within the jurisdiction of such agency.

United States Code
20 U.S.C. § 3608
Asbestos School Hazard Detection and Control,
Employee Protection Provision

§ 3608. Employee protection

No State or local educational agency receiving assistance under this chapter may discharge any employee or otherwise discriminate against any employee with respect to the employee's compensation, terms, conditions, or privileges of employment because the employee has brought to the attention of the public information concerning any asbestos problem in the school buildings within the jurisdiction of such agency.

United States Code
49 U.S.C. 42121
Whistleblower Protection Provision of Wendell H. Ford
Aviation Investment and Reform Act for the 21st Century
(AIR 21)

§ 42121. Protection of employees providing air safety information

(a) *Discrimination Against Airline Employees.* No air carrier or contractor or subcontractor of an air carrier may discharge an employee or otherwise discriminate against an employee with respect to compensation, terms, conditions, or privileges of employment because the employee (or any person acting pursuant to a request of the employee)

(1) provided, caused to be provided, or is about to provide (with any knowledge of the employer) or cause to be provided to the employer or Federal Government information relating to any violation or alleged violation of any order, regulation, or standard of the Federal Aviation Administration or any other provision of Federal law relating to air carrier safety under this subtitle or any other law of the United States;

(2) has filed, caused to be filed, or is about to file (with any knowledge of the employer) or cause to be filed a proceeding relating to any violation or alleged violation of any order, regulation, or standard of the Federal Aviation Administration or any other provision of Federal law relating to air carrier safety under this subtitle or any other law of the United States;

(3) testified or is about to testify in such a proceeding; or

(4) assisted or participated or is about to assist or participate in such a proceeding.

(b) *Department of Labor Complaint Procedure.* (1) *Filing And Notification.* A person who believes that he or she has been discharged or otherwise discriminated against by any person in violation of subsection (a) may, not later than 90 days after the date on which such violation occurs, file (or have any person file on his or her behalf) a complaint with the Secretary of Labor alleging such discharge or discrimination. Upon receipt of such a complaint, the Secretary of Labor shall notify, in writing, the person named in the complaint and the Administrator of the Federal Aviation Administration of the filing of the complaint, of the allegations contained in the complaint, of the substance of evidence supporting the complaint, and of the opportunities that will be afforded to such person under paragraph (2).

(2) *Investigation; Preliminary Order.* (A) *In General.* Not later than 60 days after the date of receipt of a complaint filed under paragraph (1) and after affording the person named in the complaint an opportunity to submit to the Secretary of Labor a written response to the complaint and an opportunity to meet with a representative of the Secretary to present statements from witnesses, the Secretary of Labor shall conduct an investigation and determine whether there is reasonable cause to believe that the complaint has merit and

notify. in writing. the complainant and the person alleged to have committed a violation of subsection (a) of the Secretary's findings. If the Secretary of Labor concludes that there is a reasonable cause to believe that a violation of subsection (a) has occurred, the Secretary shall accompany the Secretary's findings with a preliminary order providing the relief prescribed by paragraph (3)(B). Not later than 30 days after the date of notification of findings under this paragraph. either the person alleged to have committed the violation or the complainant may file objections to the findings or preliminary order, or both, and request a hearing on the record. The filing of such objections shall not operate to stay any reinstatement remedy contained in the preliminary order. Such hearings shall be conducted expeditiously. If a hearing is not requested in such 30- day period. the preliminary order shall be deemed a final order that is not subject to judicial review.

(B) *Requirements.* (i) *Required Showing by Complainant.* The Secretary of Labor shall dismiss a complaint filed under this subsection and shall not conduct an investigation otherwise required under subparagraph (A) unless the complainant makes a prima facie showing that any behavior described in paragraphs (1) through (4) of subsection (a) was a contributing factor in the unfavorable personnel action alleged in the complaint.

(ii) *Showing by Employer.* Notwithstanding a finding by the Secretary that the complainant has made the showing required under clause (i). no investigation otherwise required under subparagraph (A) shall be conducted if the employer demonstrates, by clear and convincing evidence, that the employer would have taken the same unfavorable personnel action in the absence of that behavior.

(iii) *Criteria For Determination by Secretary.* The Secretary may determine that a violation of subsection (a) has occurred only if the complainant demonstrates that any behavior described in paragraphs (1) through (4) of subsection (a) was a contributing factor in the unfavorable personnel action alleged in the complaint.

(iv) *Prohibition.* Relief may not be ordered under subparagraph (A) if the employer demonstrates by clear and convincing evidence that the employer would have taken the same unfavorable personnel action in the absence of that behavior.

(3) *Final Order.* (A) *Deadline For Issuance; Settlement Agreements.* Not later than 120 days after the date of conclusion of a hearing under paragraph (2). the Secretary of Labor shall issue a final order providing the relief prescribed by this paragraph or denying the complaint. At any time before issuance of a final order. a proceeding under this subsection may be terminated on the basis of a settlement agreement entered into by the Secretary of Labor. the complainant. and the person alleged to have committed the violation.

(B) *Remedy.* If. in response to a complaint filed under paragraph (1). the Secretary of Labor determines that a violation of subsection (a) has occurred. the Secretary of Labor shall order the person who committed such violation to

(i) take affirmative action to abate the violation;

(ii) reinstate the complainant to his or her former position together with the compensation (including back pay) and restore the terms. conditions. and privileges associated with his or her employment; and

(iii) provide compensatory damages to the complainant.

If such an order is issued under this paragraph. the Secretary of Labor. at the request of the complainant. shall assess against the person against whom the order is issued a sum equal to the aggregate amount of all costs and expenses (including attorneys and expert witness fees) reasonably incurred. as determined by the Secretary of Labor. by the complainant for. or in connection with. the bringing the complaint upon which the order was issued.

(C) *Frivolous Complaints.* If the Secretary of Labor finds that a complaint under paragraph (1) is frivolous or has been brought in bad faith. the Secretary of Labor may award to the prevailing employer a reasonable attorneys fee not exceeding $1.000.

(4) *Review*. (A) *Appeal to Court of Appeals*. Any person adversely affected or aggrieved by an order issued under paragraph (3) may obtain review of the order in the United States Court of Appeals for the circuit in which the violation. with respect to which the order was issued. allegedly occurred or the circuit in which the complainant resided on the date of such violation. The petition for review must be filed not later than 60 days after the date of the issuance of the final order of the Secretary of Labor. Review shall conform to chapter 7 of title 5. United States Code. The commencement of proceedings under this subparagraph shall not. unless ordered by the court. operate as a stay of the order.

(B) *Limitation on Collateral Attack*. An order of the Secretary of Labor with respect to which review could have been obtained under subparagraph (A) shall not be subject to judicial review in any criminal or other civil proceeding.

(5) *Enforcement of Order by Secretary of Labor*. Whenever any person has failed to comply with an order issued under paragraph (3). the Secretary of Labor may file a civil action in the United States district court for the district in which the violation was found to occur to enforce such order. In actions brought under this paragraph. the district courts shall have jurisdiction to grant all appropriate relief including. but not limited to. injunctive relief and compensatory damages.

(6) *Enforcement of Order by Parties*. (A) *Commencement of Action*. A person on whose behalf an order was issued under paragraph (3) may commence a civil action against the person to whom such order was issued to require compliance with such order. The appropriate United States district court shall have jurisdiction. without regard to the amount in controversy or the citizenship of the parties. to enforce such order.

(B) *Attorney Fees*. The court. in issuing any final order under this paragraph. may award costs of litigation (including reasonable attorney and expert witness fees) to any party whenever the court determines such award is appropriate.

(C) *Mandamus*. Any nondiscretionary duty imposed by this section shall be enforceable in a mandamus proceeding brought under section 1361 of title 28. United States Code.

(d) *Nonapplicability to Deliberate Violations*. Subsection (a) shall not apply with respect to an employee of an air carrier. contractor. or subcontractor who. acting without direction from such air carrier. contractor. or subcontractor (or such persons agent). deliberately causes a violation of any requirement relating to air carrier safety under this subtitle or any other law of the United States.

(e) *Contractor Defined*. In this section. the term contractor means a company that performs safety-sensitive functions by contract for an air carrier.

United States Code
12 U.S.C. § 1790b
Banking; Credit Union,
Employee Protection Provision

§ 1790b. Credit union employee protection remedy

(a) *In general*. (1) Employees of credit unions. No insured credit union may discharge or otherwise discriminate against any employee with respect to compensation. terms. conditions. or privileges of employment because the employee (or any person acting pursuant to the request of the employee) provided information to the Board or the Attorney General regarding any possible violation of any law or regulation by the credit union or any director. officer. or employee of the credit union.

(2) *Employees of the Administration*. The Administration may not discharge or otherwise

discriminate against any employee (including any employee of the National Credit Union Central Liquidity Facility) with respect to compensation, terms, conditions, or privileges of employment because the employee (or any person acting pursuant to the request of the employee) provided information to the Administration or the Attorney General regarding any possible violation of any law or regulation by—

(A) any credit union or the Administration;

(B) any director, officer, committee member, or employee of any credit union; or

(C) any officer or employee of the Administration.

(b) *Enforcement.* Any employee or former employee who believes he has been discharged or discriminated against in violation of subsection (a) of this section may file a civil action in the appropriate United States district court before the close of the 2-year period beginning on the date of such discharge or discrimination. The complainant shall also file a copy of the complaint initiating such action with the Board.

(c) *Remedies.* If the district court determines that a violation of subsection (a) of this section has occurred, it may order the credit union or the Administration which committed the violation— (1) to reinstate the employee to his former position,

(2) to pay compensatory damages, or

(3) take other appropriate actions to remedy any past discrimination.

(d) *Limitations.* The protections of this section shall not apply to any employee who

(1) deliberately causes or participates in the alleged violation of law or regulation, or

(2) knowingly or recklessly provides substantially false information to such an agency or the Attorney General.

United States Code
12 U.S.C. § 1831j
Banking; FDIC,
Employee Protection Provision

§ 1831j. Depository institution employee protection remedy

(a) *In general.* (1) *Employees of depository institutions.* No insured depository institution may discharge or otherwise discriminate against any employee with respect to compensation, terms, conditions, or privileges of employment because the employee (or any person acting pursuant to the request of the employee) provided information to any Federal banking agency or to the Attorney General regarding—

(A) a possible violation of any law or regulation; or

(B) gross mismanagement, a gross waste of funds, an abuse of authority, or a substantial and specific danger to public health or safety; by the depository institution or any director, officer, or employee of the institution.

(2) *Employees of banking agencies.* No Federal banking agency, Federal home loan bank, Federal reserve bank, or any person who is performing, directly or indirectly, any function or service on behalf of the Corporation may discharge or otherwise discriminate against any employee with respect to compensation, terms, conditions, or privileges of employment because the employee (or any person acting pursuant to the request of the employee) provided information to any such agency or bank or to the Attorney General regarding any possible violation of any law or regulation, gross mismanagement, a gross waste of funds, an abuse of authority, or a substantial and specific danger to public health or safety by—

(A) any depository institution or any such bank or agency;

(B) any director, officer, or employee of any depository institution or any such bank;

(C) any officer or employee of the agency which employs such employee; or

(D) the person, or any officer or employee of the person, who employs such employee.

(b) *Enforcement*. Any employee or former employee who believes he has been discharged or discriminated against in violation of subsection (a) of this section may file a civil action in the appropriate United States district court before the close of the 2-year period beginning on the date of such discharge or discrimination. The complainant shall also file a copy of the complaint initiating such action with the appropriate Federal banking agency.

(c) *Remedies*. If the district court determines that a violation of subsection (a) of this section has occurred, it may order the depository institution, Federal home loan bank, Federal Reserve bank, or Federal banking agency which committed the violation—

(1) to reinstate the employee to his former position;

(2) to pay compensatory damages; or

(3) take other appropriate actions to remedy any past discrimination.

(d) *Limitation*. The protections of this section shall not apply to any employee who—

(1) deliberately causes or participates in the alleged violation of law or regulation; or

(2) knowingly or recklessly provides substantially false information to such an agency or the Attorney General.

(e) "*Federal banking agency*" defined—

For purposes of subsections (a) and (c) of this section, the term "Federal banking agency" means the Corporation, the Board of Governors of the Federal Reserve System, the Federal Housing Finance Board, the Comptroller of the Currency, and the Director of the Office of Thrift Supervision.

(f) *Burdens of proof*. The legal burdens of proof that prevail under subchapter III of chapter 12 of title 5 shall govern adjudication of protected activities under this section.

United States Code
31 U.S.C. § 5328
Banking; Monetary Transactions,
Whistleblower Protections Provision

§ 5328. Whistleblower protections

(a) *Prohibition Against Discrimination*. No financial institution may discharge or otherwise discriminate against any employee with respect to compensation, terms, conditions, or privileges of employment because the employee (or any person acting pursuant to the request of the employee) provided information to the Secretary of the Treasury, the Attorney General, or any Federal supervisory agency regarding a possible violation of any provision of this subchapter or section 1956, 1957, or 1960 of title 18, or any regulation under any such provision, by the financial institution or any director, officer, or employee of the financial institution.

(b) *Enforcement*. Any employee or former employee who believes that such employee has been discharged or discriminated against in violation of subsection (a) may file a civil action in the appropriate United States district court before the end of the 2-year period beginning on the date of such discharge or discrimination.

(c) *Remedies*. If the district court determines that a violation has occurred, the court may order the financial institution which committed the violation to—

(1) reinstate the employee to the employee's former position;

(2) pay compensatory damages; or

(3) take other appropriate actions to remedy any past discrimination.

(d) *Limitation*. The protections of this section shall not apply to any employee who—

(1) deliberately causes or participates in the alleged violation of law or regulation; or

(2) knowingly or recklessly provides substantially false information to the Secretary, the Attorney General, or any Federal supervisory agency.

(e) *Coordination With Other Provisions of Law.* This section shall not apply with respect to any financial institution which is subject to section 33 of the Federal Deposit Insurance Act, section 213 of the Federal Credit Union Act, or section 21A(q) of the Home Owners' Loan Act (as added by section 251(c) of the Federal Deposit Insurance Corporation Improvement Act of 1991).

United States Code
42 U.S.C. § 2000e-3(a)
Civil Rights Act 1964, Title VII,
Nonretaliation Provision
§ 2000e-3. Other unlawful employment practices

(a) Discrimination for making charges, testifying, assisting, or participating in enforcement proceedings. It shall be an unlawful employment practice for an employer to discriminate against any of his employees or applicants for employment, for an employment agency, or joint labor-management committee controlling apprenticeship or other training or retraining, including on the job training programs, to discriminate against any individual or for a labor organization to discriminate against any member thereof or applicant for membership, because he has opposed any practice made an unlawful employment practice by this subchapter, or because he has made a charge, testified, assisted or participate in any manor in an investigation, proceeding, or hearing under this subchapter.

Civil Rights Act of 1871,
Excerpts from Original Statute, § 2

§ 2. That if two or more persons within any States or Territory of the United States shall conspire together to * * * by force, intimidation, or threat to prevent, hinder, or delay the execution of any law of the United States * * * each and every person so offending shall be deemed guilty of a high crime * * *

* * *

And if any one or more persons engaged in any such conspiracy shall do, or cause to be done, any act in furtherance of the object of conspiracy, whereby any person shall be injured in his person or property, or deprived of having and exercising any right or privilege of a citizen of the United States, the person so injured or deprived of such rights and privileges may have and maintain an action for the recovery of damages occasioned by such injury or deprivation of rights and privileges against any one or more of the persons engaged in such conspiracy, such action should be prosecuted in the proper district or circuit court of the United States, with and subject to the same rights of appeal, review upon error, and other remedies provided in like cases in such courts under the provisions of the act of April ninth, eighteen hundred and sixty-six, entitled "An act to protect all persons in the United States in their civil rights, and to furnish the means of their vindication."

United States Code
42 U.S.C. § 1983
Civil Rights Act of 1871
§ 1983. Civil action for deprivation of rights

Every person who, under color of any statute, ordinance, regulation, custom, or usage, of any State or Territory or the District of Columbia, subjects, or causes to be subjected, any citizen of the United States or other person within the jurisdiction thereof to the deprivation of any rights, privileges, or immunities secured by the Constitution and laws, shall be liable to the party injured in an action at law, suit in equity, or other proper proceeding for redress, except that in any action brought against a judicial officer for an act or omission taken in such officer's judicial capacity, injunctive relief shall not be granted unless a declaratory decree was violated or declaratory relief was unavailable. For the purposes of this section, any Act of Congress applicable exclusively to the District of Columbia shall be considered to be a statute of the District of Columbia.

United States Code
42 U.S.C. § 1985(2) and (3)
Civil Rights Act of 1871
§ 1985. Conspiracy to interfere with civil rights

(2) *Obstructing justice; intimidating party, witness, or juror.* If two or more persons in any State or Territory conspire to deter, by force, intimidation, or threat, any party or witness in any court of the United States from attending such court, or from testifying to any matter pending therein, freely, fully, and truthfully, or to injure such party or witness in his person or property on account of his having so attended or testified

* * *

(3) * * * in any case of conspiracy set forth in this section, if one or more persons engaged therein do, or cause to be done, any act in furtherance of the object of such conspiracy, whereby another is injured in his person or property, or deprived of having and exercising any right or privilege of a citizen of the United States, the party so injured or deprived may have an action for the recovery of damages occasioned by such injury or deprivation, against any one or more of the conspirators.

United States Code
5 U.S.C. § 2302
Civil Service Reform Act,
Prohibited Personnel Practices
§ 2302. Prohibited personnel practices

(a)(1) For purposes of this title, "*prohibited personnel practice*" means the following:

(A) Any action described in subsection (b) of this section.

(B) Any action or failure to act that is designated as a prohibited personnel action under section 1599c(a) of title 10.

(2) For the purpose of this section—

(A) "*personnel action*" means—

(i) an appointment; (ii) a promotion; (iii) an action under chapter 75 of this title or other disciplinary or corrective action; (iv) a detail, transfer, or reassignment; (v) a reinstatement; (vi) a restoration; (vii) a re-employment; (viii) a performance evaluation under chapter 43 of this title; (ix) a decision concerning pay, benefits, or awards, concerning education or training if the education or training may reasonably be expected to lead to an appointment, promotion, performance evaluation, or other action described in this subparagraph; (x) a decision to order psychiatric testing or examination; and (xi) any other significant change in duties, responsibilities, or working conditions; with respect to an employee in, or applicant for, a covered position in an agency, and in the case of an alleged prohibited personnel practice described in subsection (b)(8), an employee or applicant for employment in a Government corporation as defined in section 9101 of title 31:

(B) *"covered position"* means, with respect to any personnel action, any position in the competitive service, a career appointee position in the Senior Executive Service, or a position in the excepted service, but does not include any position which is, prior to the personnel action—

(i) excepted from the competitive service because of its confidential, policy-determining, policy-making, or policy-advocating character; or

(ii) excluded from the coverage of this section by the President based on a determination by the President that it is necessary and warranted by conditions of good administration; and

(C) *"agency"* means an Executive agency and the Government Printing Office, but does not include—

(i) a Government corporation, except in the case of an alleged prohibited personnel practice described under subsection (b)(8); (ii) the Federal Bureau of Investigation, the Central Intelligence Agency, the Defense Intelligence Agency, the National Imagery and Mapping Agency, the National Security Agency, and, as determined by the President, any Executive agency or unit thereof the principal function of which is the conduct of foreign intelligence or counterintelligence activities; or (iii) the General Accounting Office.

(b) Any employee who has authority to take, direct others to take, recommend, or approve any personnel action, shall not, with respect to such authority—

(1) discriminate for or against any employee or applicant for employment—

(A) on the basis of race, color, religion, sex, or national origin, as prohibited under section 717 of the Civil Rights Act of 1964 (42 U.S.C. 2000e-16);

(B) on the basis of age, as prohibited under sections 12 and 15 of the Age Discrimination in Employment Act of 1967 (29 U.S.C. 631, 633a);

(C) on the basis of sex, as prohibited under section 6(d) of the Fair Labor Standards Act of 1938 (29 U.S.C. 206(d));

(D) on the basis of handicapping condition, as prohibited under section 501 of the Rehabilitation Act of 1973 (29 U.S.C. 791); or

(E) on the basis of marital status or political affiliation, as prohibited under any law, rule, or regulation;

(2) solicit or consider any recommendation or statement, oral or written, with respect to any individual who requests or is under consideration for any personnel action unless such recommendation or statement is based on the personal knowledge or records of the person furnishing it and consists of—

(A) an evaluation of the work performance, ability, aptitude, or general qualifications of such individual; or

(B) an evaluation of the character, loyalty, or suitability of such individual;

(3) coerce the political activity of any person (including the providing of any political contribution or service), or take any action against any employee or applicant for employment as a reprisal for the refusal of any person to engage in such political activity;

(4) deceive or willfully obstruct any person with respect to such person's right to compete for employment;

(5) influence any person to withdraw from competition for any position for the purpose of improving or injuring the prospects of any other person for employment;

(6) grant any preference or advantage not authorized by law, rule, or regulation to any employee or applicant for employment (including defining the scope or manner of competition or the requirements for any position) for the purpose of improving or injuring the prospects of any particular person for employment;

(7) appoint. employ. promote. advance. or advocate for appointment. employment. promotion. or advancement. in or to a civilian position any individual who is a relative (as defined in section 3110(a)(3) of this title) of such employee if such position is in the agency in which such employee is serving as a public official (as defined in section 3110(a)(2) of this title) or over which such employee exercises jurisdiction or control as such an official:

(8) take or fail to take. or to threaten to take or fail to take. a personnel action with respect to any employee or applicant for employment because of—

(A) any disclosure of information by an employee or applicant which the employee or applicant reasonably believes evidences—

(i) a violation of any law. rule. or regulation. or

(ii) gross mismanagement. a gross waste of funds. an abuse of authority. or a substantial and specific danger to public health or safety. if such disclosure is not specifically prohibited by law and if such information is not specifically required by Executive order to be kept secret in the interest of national defense or the conduct of foreign affairs; or

(B) any disclosure to the Special Counsel. or to the Inspector General of an agency or another employee designated by the head of the agency to receive such disclosures. of information which the employee or applicant reasonably believes evidences—

(i) a violation of any law. rule. or regulation. or

(ii) gross mismanagement. a gross waste of funds. an abuse of authority. or a substantial and specific danger to public health or safety;

(9) take or fail to take. or threaten to take or fail to take, any personnel action against any employee or applicant for employment because of—

(A) the exercise of any appeal. complaint. or grievance right granted by any law, rule, or regulation;

(B) testifying for or otherwise lawfully assisting any individual in the exercise of any right referred to in subparagraph (A);

(C) cooperating with or disclosing information to the Inspector General of an agency, or the Special Counsel. in accordance with applicable provisions of law; or

(D) for refusing to obey an order that would require the individual to violate a law;

(10) discriminate for or against any employee or applicant for employment on the basis of conduct which does not adversely affect the performance of the employee or applicant or the performance of others; except that nothing in this paragraph shall prohibit an agency from taking into account in determining suitability or fitness any conviction of the employee or applicant for any crime under the laws of any State. of the District of Columbia. or of the United States; or (11) take or fail to take any other personnel action if the taking of or failure to take such action violates any law. rule. or regulation implementing. or directly concerning. the merit system principles contained in section 2301 of this title. This subsection shall not be construed to authorize the withholding of information from the Congress or the taking of any personnel action against an employee who discloses information to the Congress.

(c) The head of each agency shall be responsible for the prevention of prohibited personnel practices. for the compliance with and enforcement of applicable civil service laws. rules. and regulations. and other aspects of personnel management. and for ensuring (in consultation with the Office of Special Counsel) that agency employees are informed of the rights and remedies available to them under this chapter and chapter 12 of this title. Any individual to whom the head of an agency delegates authority for personnel management. or for any aspect thereof. shall be similarly responsible within the limits of the delegation.

(d) This section shall not be construed to extinguish or lessen any effort to achieve equal employment opportunity through affirmative action or any right or remedy available to any employee or applicant for employment in the civil service under—

(1) section 717 of the Civil Rights Act of 1964 (42 U.S.C. 2000e-16), prohibiting discrimination on the basis of race, color, religion, sex, or national origin;

(2) sections 12 and 15 of the Age Discrimination in Employment Act of 1967 (29 U.S.C. 631, 633a), prohibiting discrimination on the basis of age;

(3) under section 6(d) of the Fair Labor Standards Act of 1938 (29 U.S.C. 206(d)), prohibiting discrimination on the basis of sex;

(4) section 501 of the Rehabilitation Act of 1973 (29 U.S.C. 791), prohibiting discrimination on the basis of handicapping condition; or

(5) the provisions of any law, rule, or regulation prohibiting discrimination on the basis of marital status or political affiliation.

United States Code
5 U.S.C. § 1221
Civil Service Reform Act
Whistleblower Protection Act,
Individual Right of Action

§ 1221. Individual right of action in certain reprisal cases

(a) Subject to the provisions of subsection (b) of this section and subsection 1214(a) (3), an employee, former employee, or applicant for employment may, with respect to any personnel action taken, or proposed to be taken, against such employee, former employee, or applicant for employment, as a result of a prohibited personnel practice described in section 2302(b)(8), seek corrective action from the Merit Systems Protection Board.

(b) This section may not be construed to prohibit any employee, former employee, or applicant for employment from seeking corrective action from the Merit Systems Protection Board before seeking corrective action from the Special Counsel, if such employee, former employee, or applicant for employment has the right to appeal directly to the Board under any law, rule, or regulation.

(c)(1) Any employee, former employee, or applicant for employment seeking corrective action under subsection (a) may request that the Board order a stay of the personnel action involved.

(2) Any stay requested under paragraph (1) shall be granted within 10 calendar days (excluding Saturdays, Sundays, and legal holidays) after the date the request is made, if the Board determines that such a stay would be appropriate.

(3)(A) The Board shall allow any agency which would be subject to a stay under this subsection to comment to the Board on such stay request.

(B) Except as provided in subparagraph (C), a stay granted under this subsection shall remain in effect for such period as the Board determines to be appropriate.

(C) The Board may modify or dissolve a stay under this subsection at any time, if the Board determines that such a modification or dissolution is appropriate.

(d)(1) At the request of an employee, former employee, or applicant for employment seeking corrective action under subsection (a), the Board shall issue a subpoena for the attendance and testimony of any person or the production of documentary or other evidence from any person if the Board finds that the testimony or production requested is not unduly burdensome and appears reasonably calculated to lead to the discovery of admissible evidence.

(2) A subpoena under this subsection may be issued, and shall be enforced, in the same

manner as applies in the case of subpoenas under section 1204.

(e)(1) Subject to the provisions of paragraph (2). in any case involving an alleged prohibited personnel practice as described under section 2302(b)(8). the Board shall order such corrective action as the Board considers appropriate if the employee. former employee. or applicant for employment has demonstrated that a disclosure described under section 2302(b)(8) was a contributing factor in the personnel action which was taken or is to be taken against such employee. former employee, or applicant. The employee may demonstrate that the disclosure was a contributing factor in the personnel action through circumstantial evidence. such as evidence that—

(A) the official taking the personnel action knew of the disclosure: and

(B) the personnel action occurred within a period of time such that a reasonable person could conclude that the disclosure was a contributing factor in the personnel action.

(2) Corrective action under paragraph (1) may not be ordered if the agency demonstrates by clear and convincing evidence that it would have taken the same personnel action in the absence of such disclosure.

(f)(1) A final order or decision shall be rendered by the Board as soon as practicable after the commencement of any proceeding under this section.

(2) A decision to terminate an investigation under subchapter II may not be considered in any action or other proceeding under this section.

(3) If. based on evidence presented to it under this section, the Merit Systems Protection Board determines that there is reason to believe that a current employee may have committed a prohibited personnel practice. the Board shall refer the matter to the Special Counsel to investigate and take appropriate action under section 1215.

(g)(1)(A) If the Board orders corrective action under this section. such corrective action may include—

(i) that the individual be placed. as nearly as possible, in the position the individual would have been in had the prohibited personnel practice not occurred: and

(ii) back pay and related benefits. medical costs incurred. travel expenses. and any other reasonable and foreseeable consequential changes.

(B) Corrective action shall include attorney's fees and costs as provided for under paragraphs (2) and (3).

(2) If an employee. former employee. or applicant for employment is the prevailing party before the Merit Systems Protection Board. and the decision is based on a finding of a prohibited personnel practice. the agency involved shall be liable to the employee. former employee. or applicant for reasonable attorney's fees and any other reasonable costs incurred.

(3) If an employee. former em[p]loyee. or applicant for employment is the prevailing party in an appeal from the Merit Systems Protection Board. the agency involved shall be liable to the employee. former employee. or applicant for reasonable attorney's fees and any other reasonable costs incurred. regardless of the basis of the decision.

(h)(1) An employee. former employee. or applicant for employment adversely affected or aggrieved by a final order or decision of the Board under this section may obtain judicial review of the order or decision.

(2) A petition for review under this subsection shall be filed with such court. and within such time. as provided for under section 7703(b).

(i) Subsections (a) through (h) shall apply in any proceeding brought under section 7513(d) if. or to the extent that. a prohibited personnel practice as defined in section 2302(b)(8) is alleged.

(j) In determining the appealability of any case involving an allegation made by an individual under the provisions of this chapter, neither the status of an individual under any retirement system established under a Federal statute nor any election made by such individual under any such system may be taken into account.

United States Code
5 U.S.C. § 1214
Civil Service Reform Act
Whistleblower Protection Act,
Office of Special Counsel

§ 1214. Investigation of prohibited personnel practices; corrective action

(a)(1)(A) The Special Counsel shall receive any allegation of a prohibited personnel practice and shall investigate the allegation to the extent necessary to determine whether there are reasonable grounds to believe that a prohibited personnel practice has occurred, exists, or is to be taken.

(B) Within 15 days after the date of receiving an allegation of a prohibited personnel practice under paragraph (1), the Special Counsel shall provide written notice to the person who made the allegation that—

(i) the allegation has been received by the Special Counsel; and

(ii) shall include the name of a person at the Office of Special Counsel who shall serve as a contact with the person making the allegation.

(C) Unless an investigation is terminated under paragraph (2), the Special Counsel shall—

(i) within 90 days after notice is provided under subparagraph (B), notify the person who made the allegation of the status of the investigation and any action taken by the Office of the Special Counsel since the filing of the allegation;

(ii) notify such person of the status of the investigation and any action taken by the Office of the Special Counsel since the last notice, at least every 60 days after notice is given under clause (i); and

(iii) notify such person of the status of the investigation and any action taken by the Special Counsel at such time as determined appropriate by the Special Counsel.

(D) No later than 10 days before the Special Counsel terminates any investigation of a prohibited personnel practice, the Special Counsel shall provide a written status report to the person who made the allegation of the proposed findings of fact and legal conclusions. The person may submit written comments about the report to the Special Counsel. The Special Counsel shall not be required to provide a subsequent written status report under this subparagraph after the submission of such written comments.

(2)(A) If the Special Counsel terminates any investigation under paragraph (1), the Special Counsel shall prepare and transmit to any person on whose allegation the investigation was initiated a written statement notifying the person of—

(i) the termination of the investigation;

(ii) a summary of relevant facts ascertained by the Special Counsel, including the facts that support, and the facts that do not support, the allegations of such person;

(iii) the reasons for terminating the investigation; and

(iv) a response to any comments submitted under paragraph (1)(D).

(B) A written statement under subparagraph (A) may not be admissible as evidence in any judicial or administrative proceeding, without the consent of the person who received such statement under subparagraph (A).

(3) Except in a case in which an employee, former employee, or applicant for employment has the right to appeal directly to the Merit Systems Protection Board under any law, rule, or regulation, any such employee, former employee, or applicant shall seek corrective

action from the Special Counsel before seeking corrective action from the Board. An employee. former employee. or applicant for employment may seek corrective action from the Board under section 1221. if such employee. former employee. or applicant seeks corrective action for a prohibited personnel practice described in section 2302(b)(8) from the Special Counsel and—

(A)(i) the Special Counsel notifies such employee. former employee. or applicant that an investigation concerning such employee. former employee. or applicant has been terminated: and

(ii) no more than 60 days have elapsed since notification was provided to such employee. former employee. or applicant for employment that such investigation was terminated: or

(B) 120 days after seeking corrective action from the Special Counsel. such employee. former employee. or applicant has not been notified by the Special Counsel that the Special Counsel shall seek corrective action on behalf of such employee. former employee. or applicant.

(4) If an employee. former employee. or applicant seeks a corrective action from the Board under section 1221. pursuant to the provisions of paragraph (3)(B). the Special Counsel may continue to seek corrective action personal to such employee. former employee. or applicant only with the consent of such employee. former employee. or applicant.

(5) In addition to any authority granted under paragraph (1). the Special Counsel may. in the absence of an allegation. conduct an investigation for the purpose of determining whether there are reasonable grounds to believe that a prohibited personnel practice (or a pattern of prohibited personnel practices) has occurred. exists. or is to be taken.

(b)(1)(A)(i) The Special Counsel may request any member of the Merit Systems Protection Board to order a stay of any personnel action for 45 days if the Special Counsel determines that there are reasonable grounds to believe that the personnel action was taken. or is to be taken. as a result of a prohibited personnel practice.

(ii) Any member of the Board requested by the Special Counsel to order a stay under clause (i) shall order such stay unless the member determines that. under the facts and circumstances involved. such a stay would not be appropriate.

(iii) Unless denied under clause (ii). any stay under this subparagraph shall be granted within 3 calendar days (excluding Saturdays. Sundays. and legal holidays) after the date of the request for the stay by the Special Counsel.

(B) The Board may extend the period of any stay granted under subparagraph (A) for any period which the Board considers appropriate.

(C) The Board shall allow any agency which is the subject of a stay to comment to the Board on any extension of stay proposed under subparagraph (B).

(D) A stay may be terminated by the Board at any time. except that a stay may not be terminated by the Board—

(i) on its own motion or on the motion of an agency. unless notice and opportunity for oral or written comments are first provided to the Special Counsel and the individual on whose behalf the stay was ordered: or

(ii) on motion of the Special Counsel. unless notice and opportunity for oral or written comments are first provided to the individual on whose behalf the stay was ordered.

(2)(A)(i) Except as provided under clause (ii). no later than 240 days after the date of receiving an allegation of a prohibited personnel practice under paragraph (1). the Special Counsel shall make a determination whether there are reasonable grounds to believe that a prohibited personnel practice has occurred. exists. or is to be taken.

(ii) If the Special Counsel is unable to make the required determination within the 240-day period specified under clause (i) and the person submitting the allegation of a prohibited personnel practice agrees to an extension of time, the determination shall be made within such additional period of time as shall be agreed upon between the Special Counsel and the person submitting the allegation.

(B) If, in connection with any investigation, the Special Counsel determines that there are reasonable grounds to believe that a prohibited personnel practice has occurred, exists, or is to be taken which requires corrective action, the Special Counsel shall report the determination together with any findings or recommendations to the Board, the agency involved and to the Office of Personnel Management, and may report such determination, findings and recommendations to the President. The Special Counsel may include in the report recommendations for corrective action to be taken.

(C) If, after a reasonable period of time, the agency does not act to correct the prohibited personnel practice, the Special Counsel may petition the Board for corrective action.

(D) If the Special Counsel finds, in consultation with the individual subject to the prohibited personnel practice, that the agency has acted to correct the prohibited personnel practice, the Special Counsel shall file such finding with the Board, together with any written comments which the individual may provide.

(E) A determination by the Special Counsel under this paragraph shall not be cited or referred to in any proceeding under this paragraph or any other administrative or judicial proceeding for any purpose, without the consent of the person submitting the allegation of a prohibited personnel practice.

(3) Whenever the Special Counsel petitions the Board for corrective action, the Board shall provide an opportunity for—

(A) oral or written comments by the Special Counsel, the agency involved, and the Office of Personnel Management; and

(B) written comments by any individual who alleges to be the subject of the prohibited personnel practice.

(4)(A) The Board shall order such corrective action as the Board considers appropriate, if the Board determines that the Special Counsel has demonstrated that a prohibited personnel practice, other than one described in section 2302(b)(8), has occurred, exists, or is to be taken.

(B)(i) Subject to the provisions of clause (ii), in any case involving an alleged prohibited personnel practice as described under section 2302(b)(8), the Board shall order such corrective action as the Board considers appropriate if the Special Counsel has demonstrated that a disclosure described under section 2302(b)(8) was a contributing factor in the personnel action which was taken or is to be taken against the individual.

(ii) Corrective action under clause (i) may not be ordered if the agency demonstrates by clear and convincing evidence that it would have taken the same personnel action in the absence of such disclosure.

(c)(1) Judicial review of any final order or decision of the Board under this section may be obtained by any employee, former employee, or applicant for employment adversely affected by such order or decision.

(2) A petition for review under this subsection shall be filed with such court, and within such time, as provided for under section 7703(b).

(d)(1) If, in connection with any investigation under this subchapter, the Special Counsel determines that there is reasonable cause to believe that a criminal violation has occurred, the Special Counsel shall report the determination to the Attorney General and to the head of the agency involved, and shall submit a copy of the report to the Director of the Office of Personnel Management and the Director of the Office of Management and Budget.

(2) In any case in which the Special Counsel determines that there are reasonable grounds to believe that a prohibited personnel practice has occurred, exists, or is to be taken, the Special Counsel shall proceed with any investigation or proceeding unless—

(A) the alleged violation has been reported to the Attorney General; and

(B) the Attorney General is pursuing an investigation, in which case the Special Counsel, after consultation with the Attorney General, has discretion as to whether to proceed.

(e) If, in connection with any investigation under this subchapter, the Special Counsel determines that there is reasonable cause to believe that any violation of any law, rule, or regulation has occurred other than one referred to in subsection (b) or (d), the Special Counsel shall report such violation to the head of the agency involved. The Special Counsel shall require, within 30 days after the receipt of the report by the agency, a certification by the head of the agency which states—

(1) that the head of the agency has personally reviewed the report; and

(2) what action has been or is to be taken, and when the action will be completed.

(f) During any investigation initiated under this subchapter, no disciplinary action shall be taken against any employee for any alleged prohibited activity under investigation or for any related activity without the approval of the Special Counsel.

(g) If the Board orders corrective action under this section, such corrective action may include—

(1) that the individual be placed, as nearly as possible, in the position the individual would have been in had the prohibited personnel practice not occurred; and

(2) reimbursement for attorney's fees, back pay and related benefits, medical costs incurred, travel expenses, and any other reasonable and foreseeable consequential damages.

United States Code
42 U.S.C. § 7622
Clean Air Act,
Employee Protection Provision

§ 7622. Employee protection

(a) *Discharge or discrimination prohibited.* No employer may discharge any employee or otherwise discriminate against any employee with respect to his compensation, terms, conditions, or privileges of employment because the employee (or any person acting pursuant to a request of the employee)—

(1) commenced, caused to be commenced, or is about to commence or cause to be commenced a proceeding under this chapter or a proceeding for the administration or enforcement of any requirement imposed under this chapter or under any applicable implementation plan,

(2) testified or is about to testify in any such proceeding, or

(3) assisted or participated or is about to assist or participate in any manner in such a proceeding or in any other action to carry out the purposes of this chapter.

(b) *Complaint charging unlawful discharge or discrimination; investigation; order*

(1) Any employee who believes that he has been discharged or otherwise discriminated against by any person in violation of subsection (a) of this section may, within thirty days after such violation occurs, file (or have any person file on his behalf) a complaint with the Secretary of Labor (hereinafter in this subsection referred to as the "Secretary") alleging such discharge or discrimination. Upon receipt of such a complaint, the Secretary shall notify the person named in the complaint of the filing of the complaint.

(2)(A) Upon receipt of a complaint filed under paragraph (1), the Secretary shall conduct an investigation of the violation alleged in the complaint. Within thirty days of the receipt of such complaint. the Secretary shall complete such investigation and shall notify in writing the complainant (and any person acting in his behalf) and the person alleged to have committed such violation of the results of the investigation conducted pursuant to this subparagraph. Within ninety days of the receipt of such complaint the Secretary shall. unless the proceeding on the complaint is terminated by the Secretary on the basis of a settlement entered into by the Secretary and the person alleged to have committed such violation. issue an order either providing the relief prescribed by subparagraph (B) or denying the complaint. An order of the Secretary shall be made on the record after notice and opportunity for public hearing. The Secretary may not enter into a settlement terminating a proceeding on a complaint without the participation and consent of the complainant.

(B) If. in response to a complaint filed under paragraph (1). the Secretary determines that a violation of subsection (a) of this section has occurred. the Secretary shall order the person who committed such violation to (i) take affirmative action to abate the violation. and (ii) reinstate the complainant to his former position together with the compensation (including back pay). terms. conditions. and privileges of his employment. and the Secretary may order such person to provide compensatory damages to the complainant. If an order is issued under this paragraph. the Secretary. at the request of the complainant. shall assess against the person against whom the order is issued a sum equal to the aggregate amount of all costs and expenses (including attorneys' and expert witness fees) reasonably incurred. as determined by the Secretary. by the complainant for. or in connection with. the bringing of the complaint upon which the order was issued.

(c) *Review.* (1) Any person adversely affected or aggrieved by an order issued under subsection (b) of this section may obtain review of the order in the United States court of appeals for the circuit in which the violation. with respect to which the order was issued. allegedly occurred. The petition for review must be filed within sixty days from the issuance of the Secretary's order. Review shall conform to chapter 7 of title 5. The commencement of proceedings under this subparagraph shall not. unless ordered by the court. operate as a stay of the Secretary's order.

(2) An order of the Secretary with respect to which review could have been obtained under paragraph (1) shall not be subject to judicial review in any criminal or other civil proceeding.

(d) *Enforcement of order by Secretary.* Whenever a person has failed to comply with an order issued under subsection (b)(2) of this section. the Secretary may file a civil action in the United States district court for the district in which the violation was found to occur to enforce such order. In actions brought under this subsection. the district courts shall have jurisdiction to grant all appropriate relief including. but not limited to. injunctive relief. compensatory. and exemplary damages.

(e) *Enforcement of order by person on whose behalf order was issued.* (1) Any person on whose behalf an order was issued under paragraph (2) of subsection (b) of this section may commence a civil action against the person to whom such order was issued to require compliance with such order. The appropriate United States district court shall have jurisdiction. without regard to the amount in controversy or the citizenship of the parties. to enforce such order.

(2) The court. in issuing any final order under this subsection. may award costs of litigation (including reasonable attorney and expert witness fees) to any party whenever the court determines such award is appropriate.

(f) *Mandamus.* Any nondiscretionary duty imposed by this section shall be enforceable in a mandamus proceeding brought under section 1361 of title 28.

(g) *Deliberate violation by employee.* Subsection (a) of this section shall not apply with respect to any employee who, acting without direction from his employer (or the employer's agent), deliberately causes a violation of any requirement of this chapter.

United States Code
46 U.S.C. § 2114
Coast Guard Whistleblower Protection Provision
§ 2114. Protection of seamen against discrimination

(a) An owner, charterer, managing operator, agent, master, or individual in charge of a vessel may not discharge or in any manner discriminate against a seaman because the seaman in good faith has reported or is about to report to the Coast Guard that the seaman believes that a violation of this subtitle, or a regulation issued under this subtitle, has occurred.

(b) A seaman discharged or otherwise discriminated against in violation of this section may bring an action in an appropriate district court of the United States. In that action, the court may order any appropriate relief, including —

(1) restraining violations of this section; and

(2) reinstatement to the seaman's former position with back pay.

United States Code
42 U.S.C. § 9610
Comprehensive Environmental Response, Compensation and Liability Act ("Superfund"), Employee Protection Provision
§ 9610. Employee protection.

(a) *Activities of employee subject to protection.* No person shall fire or in any other way discriminate against, or cause to be fired or discriminated against, any employee or any authorized representative of employees by reason of the fact that such employee or representative has provided information to a State or to the Federal Government, filed, instituted, or caused to be filed or instituted any proceeding under this chapter, or has testified or is about to testify in any proceeding resulting from the administration or enforcement of the provisions of this chapter.

(b) *Administrative grievance procedure in cases of alleged violations.* Any employee or a representative of employees who believes that he has been fired or otherwise discriminated against by any person in violation of subsection (a) of this section may, within thirty days after such alleged violation occurs, apply to the Secretary of Labor for a review of such firing or alleged discrimination. A copy of the application shall be sent to such person, who shall be the respondent. Upon receipt of such application, the Secretary of Labor shall cause such investigation to be made as he deems appropriate. Such investigation shall provide an opportunity for a public hearing at the request of any party to such review to enable the parties to present information relating to such alleged violation. The parties shall be given written notice of the time and place of the hearing at least five days prior to the hearing. Any such hearing shall be of record and shall be subject to section 554 of title 5. Upon receiving the report of such investigation, the Secretary of Labor shall make findings of fact. If he finds that such violation did occur, he shall issue a decision, incorporating an order therein and his findings, requiring the party committing such violation to take such affirmative action to abate the violation as the Secretary of Labor deems appropriate, including, but not limited to, the rehiring or reinstatement of the employee or representative of employees to his former position with compensation. If he finds that there was no such violation, he shall issue an order denying the application. Such order issued by the Secretary of Labor under this subparagraph shall be subject to judicial review in the same manner as orders and decisions are subject to judicial review under this chapter.

(c) *Assessment of costs and expenses against violator subsequent to issuance of order of abatement.* Whenever an order is issued under this section to abate such violation, at the request of the applicant a sum equal to the aggregate amount of all costs and expenses (including the attorney's fees) determined by the Secretary of Labor to have been reasonably incurred by the applicant for, or in connection with, the institution and prosecution of such proceedings, shall be assessed against the person committing such violation.

(d) *Defenses.* This section shall have no application to any employee who acting without discretion from his employer (or his agent) deliberately violates any requirement of this chapter.

(e) *Presidential evaluations of potential loss of shifts of employment resulting from administration or enforcement of provisions; investigations; procedures applicable, etc.* The President shall conduct continuing evaluations of potential loss of shifts of employment which may result from the administration or enforcement of the provisions of this chapter, including, where appropriate, investigating threatened plant closures or reductions in employment allegedly resulting from such administration or enforcement. Any employee who is discharged, or laid off, threatened with discharge or layoff, or otherwise discriminated against by any person because of the alleged results of such administration or enforcement, or any representative of such employee, may request the President to conduct a full investigation of the matter and, at the request of any party, shall hold public hearings, require the parties, including the employer involved, to present information relating to the actual or potential effect of such administration or enforcement on employment and any alleged discharge, layoff, or other discrimination, and the detailed reasons or justification there[of]. Any such hearing shall be of record and shall be subject to section 554 of title 5. Upon receiving the report of such investigation, the President shall make findings of fact as to the effect of such administration or enforcement on employment and on the alleged discharge, layoff, or discrimination and shall make such recommendations as he deems appropriate. Such report, findings, and recommendations shall be available to the public. Nothing in this subsection shall be construed to require or authorize the President or any State to modify or withdraw any action, standard, limitation, or any other requirement of this chapter.

United States Code
29 U.S.C. § 2002
Employee Polygraph Protection,
Employee Protection Provision

§ 2002. Prohibitions on lie detector use.

Except as provided in sections 2006 and 2007 of this title, it shall be unlawful for any employer engaged in or affecting commerce or in the production of goods for commerce—

(1) directly or indirectly, to require, request, suggest, or cause any employee or prospective employee to take or submit to any lie detector test;

(2) to use, accept, refer to, or inquire concerning the results of any lie detector test of any employee or prospective employee;

(3) to discharge, discipline, discriminate against in any manner, or deny employment or promotion to, or threaten to take any such action against—

(A) any employee or prospective employee who refuses, declines, or fails to take or submit to any lie detector test, or

(B) any employee or prospective employee on the basis of the results of any lie detector test; or

(4) to discharge. discipline. discriminate against in any manner. or deny employment or promotion to. or threaten to take any such action against. any employee or prospective employee because—

(A) such employee or prospective employee has filed any complaint or instituted or caused to be instituted any proceeding under or related to this chapter.

(B) such employee or prospective employee has testified or is about to testify in any such proceeding. or

(C) of the exercise by such employee or prospective employee. on behalf of such employee or another person. of any right afforded by this chapter.

United States Code
42 U.S.C. § 5851
Energy Reorganization Act,
Employee Protection Provision

§ 5851 Employee protection

(a) *Discrimination against employee.* (1) No employer may discharge any employee or otherwise discriminate against any employee with respect to his compensation, terms, conditions, or privileges of employment because the employee (or any person acting pursuant to a request of the employee)—

(A) notified his employer of an alleged violation of this chapter or the Atomic Energy Act of 1954 (42 U.S.C. 2011 et seq.);

(B) refused to engage in any practice made unlawful by this chapter or the Atomic Energy Act of 1954. if the employee has identified the alleged illegality to the employer;

(C) testified before Congress or at any Federal or State proceeding regarding any provision (or proposed provision) of this chapter or the Atomic Energy Act of 1954;

(D) commenced. caused to be commenced. or is about to commence or cause to be commenced a proceeding under this chapter or the Atomic Energy Act of 1954, as amended, or a proceeding for the administration or enforcement of any requirement imposed under this chapter or the Atomic Energy Act of 1954. as amended;

(E) testified or is about to testify in any such proceeding or;

(F) assisted or participated or is about to assist or participate in any manner in such a proceeding or in any other manner in such a proceeding or in any other action to carry out the purposes of this chapter or the Atomic Energy Act of 1954. as amended.

(2) For purposes of this section. the term "*employer*" includes—

(A) a licensee of the Commission or of an agreement State under section 274 of the Atomic Energy Act of 1954 (42 U.S.C. 2021);

(B) an applicant for a license from the Commission or such an agreement State;

(C) a contractor or subcontractor of such a licensee or applicant; and

(D) a contractor or subcontractor of the Department of Energy that is indemnified by the Department under section 170 d. of the Atomic Energy Act of 1954 (42 U.S.C. 2210(d)), but such term shall not include any contractor or subcontractor covered by Executive Order No. 12344.

(b) *Complaint. filing and notification.* (1) Any employee who believes that he has been discharged or otherwise discriminated against by any person in violation of subsection (a) of this section may. within 180 days after such violation occurs. file (or have any person file on his behalf) a complaint with the Secretary of Labor (in this section referred to as the "Secretary") alleging such discharge or discrimination. Upon receipt of such a complaint. the Secretary shall notify the person named in the complaint of the filing of the complaint. the Commission. and the Department of Energy.

(2)(A) Upon receipt of a complaint filed under paragraph (1). the Secretary shall conduct an investigation of the violation alleged in the complaint. Within thirty days of the receipt of such complaint, the Secretary shall complete such investigation and shall notify in writing the complainant (and any person acting in his behalf) and the person alleged to have committed such violation of the results of the investigation conducted pursuant to this subparagraph. Within ninety days of the receipt of such complaint the Secretary shall, unless the proceeding on the complaint is terminated by the Secretary on the basis of a settlement entered into by the Secretary and the person alleged to have committed such violation, issue an order either providing the relief prescribed by subparagraph (B) or denying the complaint. An order of the Secretary shall be made on the record after notice and opportunity for public hearing. Upon the conclusion of such hearing and the issuance of a recommended decision that the complaint has merit, the Secretary shall issue a preliminary order providing the relief prescribed in subparagraph (B), but may not order compensatory damages pending a final order. The Secretary may not enter into a settlement terminating a proceeding on a complaint without the participation and consent of the complainant.

(B) If, in response to a complaint filed under paragraph (1), the Secretary determines that a violation of subsection (a) of this section has occurred, the Secretary shall order the person who committed such violation to

(i) take affirmative action to abate the violation, and

(ii) reinstate the complainant to his former position together with the compensation (including back pay), terms, conditions, and privileges of his employment, and the Secretary may order such person to provide compensatory damages to the complainant. If an order is issued under this paragraph, the Secretary, at the request of the complainant shall assess against the person against whom the order is issued a sum equal to the aggregate amount of all costs and expenses (including attorneys' and expert witness fees) reasonably incurred, as determined by the Secretary, by the complainant for, or in connection with, the bringing of the complaint upon which the order was issued.

(3)(A) The Secretary shall dismiss a complaint filed under paragraph (1), and shall not conduct the investigation required under paragraph (2), unless the complainant has made a prima facie showing that any behavior described in subparagraphs (A) through (F) of subsection (a)(1) of this section was a contributing factor in the unfavorable personnel action alleged in the complaint.

(B) Notwithstanding a finding by the Secretary that the complainant has made the showing required by subparagraph (A), no investigation required under paragraph (2) shall be conducted if the employer demonstrates, by clear and convincing evidence, that it would have taken the same unfavorable personnel action in the absence of such behavior.

(C) The Secretary may determine that a violation of subsection (a) of this section has occurred only if the complainant has demonstrated that any behavior described in subparagraphs (A) through (F) of subsection (a)(1) of this section was a contributing factor in the unfavorable personnel action alleged in the complaint.

(D) Relief may not be ordered under paragraph (2) if the employer demonstrates by clear and convincing evidence that it would have taken the same unfavorable personnel action in the absence of such behavior.

(c) *Review.* (1) Any person adversely affected or aggrieved by an order issued under subsection (b) of this section may obtain review of the order in the United States court of appeals for the circuit in which the violation, with respect to which the order was issued, allegedly occurred. The petition for review must be filed within sixty days from the issuance of the Secretary's order. Review shall conform to chapter 7 of title 5. The commencement of proceedings under this subparagraph shall not, unless ordered by the court, operate as a stay of the Secretary's order.

(2) An order of the Secretary with respect to which review could have been obtained under paragraph (1) shall not be subject to judicial review in any criminal or other civil proceeding.

(d) *Jurisdiction.* Whenever a person has failed to comply with an order issued under subsection (b)(2) of this section, the Secretary may file a civil action in the United States district court for the district in which the violation was found to occur to enforce such order. In actions brought under this subsection, the district courts shall have jurisdiction to grant all appropriate relief including, but not limited to, injunctive relief, compensatory, and exemplary damages.

(e) *Commencement of action.* (1) Any person on whose behalf an order was issued under paragraph (2) of subsection (b) of this section may commence a civil action against the person to whom such order was issued to require compliance with such order. The appropriate United States district court shall have jurisdiction, without regard to the amount in controversy or the citizenship of the parties, to enforce such order.

(2) The court, in issuing any final order under this subsection, may award costs of litigation (including reasonable attorney and expert witness fees) to any party whenever the court determines such award is appropriate.

(f) *Enforcement.* Any nondiscretionary duty imposed by this section shall be enforceable in a mandamus proceeding brought under section 1361 of title 28.

(g) *Deliberate violations.* Subsection (a) of this section shall not apply with respect to any employee who, acting without direction from his or her employer (or the employer's agent), deliberately causes a violation of any requirement of this chapter or of the Atomic Energy Act of 1954, as amended (42 U.S.C. 2011 et seq.).

(h) *Non-preemption.* This section may not be construed to expand, diminish, or otherwise affect any right otherwise available to an employee under Federal or State law to redress the employee's discharge or other discriminatory action taken by the employer against the employee.

(i) *Posting requirement.* The provisions of this section shall be prominently posted in any place of employment to which this section applies.

(j) *Investigation of allegations.* (1) The Commission or the Department of Energy shall not delay taking appropriate action with respect to an allegation of a substantial safety hazard on the basis of—

(A) the filing of a complaint under subsection (b)(1) of this section arising from such allegation; or

(B) any investigation by the Secretary, or other action, under this section in response to such complaint.

(2) A determination by the Secretary under this section that a violation of subsection (a) of this section has not occurred shall not be considered by the Commission or the Department of Energy in its determination of whether a substantial safety hazard exists.

United States Code
29 U.S.C. § 215(a)(3)
Fair Labor Standards Act,
Nonretaliation Provision

§ 215. Prohibited acts; prima facie evidence

(a)After the expiration of one hundred and twenty days from June 25, 1938, it shall be unlawful for any person— * * *

(3) to discharge or in any other manner discriminate against any employee because such employee has filed any complaint or instituted or caused to be instituted any proceeding

under or related to this chapter. or has testified or is about to testify in any such proceeding. or has served or is about to serve on an industry committee.

United States Code
31 U.S.C. § 3729-3732
False Claims Act

§ 3729. False claims

(a) *Liability for Certain Acts.* Any person who—

(1) knowingly presents. or causes to be presented. to an officer or employee of the United States Government or a member of the Armed Forces of the United States a false or fraudulent claim for payment or approval:

(2) knowingly makes. uses. or causes to be made or used. a false record or statement to get a false or fraudulent claim paid or approved by the Government:

(3) conspires to defraud the Government by getting a false or fraudulent claim allowed or paid:

(4) has possession. custody. or control of property or money used. or to be used. by the Government and. intending to defraud the Government or willfully to conceal the property. delivers. or causes to be delivered. less property than the amount for which the person receives a certificate or receipt:

(5) authorized to make or deliver a document certifying receipt of property used. or to be used. by the Government and. intending to defraud the Government. makes or delivers the receipt without completely knowing that the information on the receipt is true:

(6) knowingly buys. or receives as a pledge of an obligation or debt. public property from an officer or employee of the Government. or a member of the Armed Forces. who lawfully may not sell or pledge the property: or

(7) knowingly makes. uses. or causes to be made or used. a false record or statement to conceal. avoid. or decrease an obligation to pay or transmit money or property to the Government. is liable to the United States Government for a civil penalty of not less than $5.000 and not more than $10.000. plus 3 times the amount of damages which the Government sustains because of the act of that person. except that if the court finds that—

(A) the person committing the violation of this subsection furnished officials of the United States responsible for investigating false claims violations with all information known to such person about the violation within 30 days after the date on which the defendant first obtained the information:

(B) such person fully cooperated with any Government investigation of such violation: and

(C) at the time such person furnished the United States with the information about the violation. no criminal prosecution. civil action. or administrative action had commenced under this title with respect to such violation. and the person did not have actual knowledge of the existence of an investigation into such violation: the court may assess not less than 2 times the amount of damages which the Government sustains because of the act of the person. A person violating this subsection shall also be liable to the United States Government for the costs of a civil action brought to recover any such penalty or damages.

(b) *Knowing and Knowingly Defined.* For purposes of this section. the terms "knowing" and "knowingly" mean that a person. with respect to information—

(1) has actual knowledge of the information:

(2) acts in deliberate ignorance of the truth or falsity of the information: or

(3) acts in reckless disregard of the truth or falsity of the information. and no proof of specific intent to defraud is required.

(c) *Claim Defined.* For purposes of this section, "claim" includes any request or demand, whether under a contract or otherwise, for money or property which is made to a contractor, grantee, or other recipient if the United States Government provides any portion of the money or property which is requested or demanded, or if the Government will reimburse such contractor, grantee, or other recipient for any portion of the money or property which is requested or demanded.

(d) *Exemption From Disclosure.* Any information furnished pursuant to subparagraphs (A) through (C) of subsection (a) shall be exempt from disclosure under section 552 of title 5.

(e) *Exclusion.* This section does not apply to claims, records, or statements made under the Internal Revenue Code of 1986.

§ 3730. Civil actions for false claims

(a) *Responsibilities of the Attorney General.* The Attorney General diligently shall investigate a violation under section 3729. If the Attorney General finds that a person has violated or is violating section 3729, the Attorney General may bring a civil action under this section against the person.

(b) *Actions by Private Persons.* (1) A person may bring a civil action for a violation of section 3729 for the person and for the United States Government. The action shall be brought in the name of the Government. The action may be dismissed only if the court and the Attorney General give written consent to the dismissal and their reasons for consenting.

(2) A copy of the complaint and written disclosure of substantially all material evidence and information the person possesses shall be served on the Government pursuant to Rule 4(d)(4) of the Federal Rules of Civil Procedure. The complaint shall be filed in camera, shall remain under seal for at least 60 days, and shall not be served on the defendant until the court so orders. The Government may elect to intervene and proceed with the action within 60 days after it receives both the complaint and the material evidence and information.

(3) The Government may, for good cause shown, move the court for extensions of the time during which the complaint remains under seal under paragraph (2). Any such motions may be supported by affidavits or other submissions in camera. The defendant shall not be required to respond to any complaint filed under this section until 20 days after the complaint is unsealed and served upon the defendant pursuant to Rule 4 of the Federal Rules of Civil Procedure.

(4) Before the expiration of the 60-day period or any extensions obtained under paragraph (3), the Government shall—

(A) proceed with the action, in which case the action shall be conducted by the Government; or

(B) notify the court that it declines to take over the action, in which case the person bringing the action shall have the right to conduct the action.

(5) When a person brings an action under this subsection, no person other than the Government may intervene or bring a related action based on the facts underlying the pending action.

(c) *Rights of the Parties to Qui Tam Actions.* (1) If the Government proceeds with the action, it shall have the primary responsibility for prosecuting the action, and shall not be bound by an act of the person bringing the action. Such person shall have the right to continue as a party to the action, subject to the limitations set forth in paragraph (2).

(2)(A) The Government may dismiss the action notwithstanding the objections of the person initiating the action if the person has been notified by the Government of the filing of the motion and the court has provided the person with an opportunity for a hearing on the motion.

(B) The Government may settle the action with the defendant notwithstanding the objections of the person initiating the action if the court determines, after a hearing, that the proposed settlement is fair, adequate, and reasonable under all the circumstances. Upon a showing of good cause, such hearing may be held in camera.

(C) Upon a showing by the Government that unrestricted participation during the course of the litigation by the person initiating the action would interfere with or unduly delay the Government's prosecution of the case, or would be repetitious, irrelevant, or for purposes of harassment, the court may, in its discretion, impose limitations on the person's participation, such as—

(i) limiting the number of witnesses the person may call; (ii) limiting the length of the testimony of such witnesses; (iii) limiting the person's cross-examination of witnesses; or (iv) otherwise limiting the participation by the person in the litigation.

(D) Upon a showing by the defendant that unrestricted participation during the course of the litigation by the person initiating the action would be for purposes of harassment or would cause the defendant undue burden or unnecessary expense, the court may limit the participation by the person in the litigation.

(3) If the Government elects not to proceed with the action, the person who initiated the action shall have the right to conduct the action. If the Government so requests, it shall be served with copies of all pleadings filed in the action and shall be supplied with copies of all deposition transcripts (at the Government's expense). When a person proceeds with the action, the court, without limiting the status and rights of the person initiating the action, may nevertheless permit the Government to intervene at a later date upon a showing of good cause.

(4) Whether or not the Government proceeds with the action, upon a showing by the Government that certain actions of discovery by the person initiating the action would interfere with the Government's investigation or prosecution of a criminal or civil matter arising out of the same facts, the court may stay such discovery for a period of not more than 60 days. Such a showing shall be conducted in camera. The court may extend the 60-day period upon a further showing in camera that the Government has pursued the criminal or civil investigation or proceedings with reasonable diligence and any proposed discovery in the civil action will interfere with the ongoing criminal or civil investigation or proceedings.

(5) Notwithstanding subsection (b), the Government may elect to pursue its claim through any alternate remedy available to the Government, including any administrative proceeding to determine a civil money penalty. If any such alternate remedy is pursued in another proceeding, the person initiating the action shall have the same rights in such proceeding as such person would have had if the action had continued under this section. Any finding of fact or conclusion of law made in such other proceeding that has become final shall be conclusive on all parties to an action under this section. For purposes of the preceding sentence, a finding or conclusion is final if it has been finally determined on appeal to the appropriate court of the United States, if all time for filing such an appeal with respect to the finding or conclusion has expired, or if the finding or conclusion is not subject to judicial review.

(d) *Award to Qui Tam Plaintiff*. (1) If the Government proceeds with an action brought by a person under subsection (b), such person shall, subject to the second sentence of this paragraph, receive at least 15 percent but not more than 25 percent of the proceeds of the action or settlement of the claim, depending upon the extent to which the person substantially contributed to the prosecution of the action. Where the action is one which the court finds to be based primarily on disclosures of specific information (other than information provided by the person bringing the action) relating to allegations or transactions in a criminal, civil, or administrative hearing, in a congressional, administrative, or Government [*sic*] Accounting Office report, hearing, audit, or investigation, or from the news media, the court may award such sums as it considers appropriate, but in no case more than 10 percent of the proceeds, taking into account the significance of the information and the role of the person bringing the action in advancing the case to litigation. Any payment to a person under the first or second sentence of this paragraph shall be made from the proceeds. Any such person shall also receive an amount for reasonable expenses which the court finds to have been necessarily incurred, plus reasonable attorneys' fees and costs. All such expenses, fees, and costs shall be awarded against the defendant.

(2) If the Government does not proceed with an action under this section, the person bringing the action or settling the claim shall receive an amount which the court decides is reasonable for collecting the civil penalty and damages. The amount shall be not less than 25 percent and not more than 30 percent of the proceeds of the action or settlement and shall be paid out of such proceeds. Such person shall also receive an amount for reasonable expenses which the court finds to have been necessarily incurred, plus reasonable attorneys' fees and costs. All such expenses, fees, and costs shall be awarded against the defendant.

(3) Whether or not the Government proceeds with the action, if the court finds that the action was brought by a person who planned and initiated the violation of section 3729 upon which the action was brought, then the court may, to the extent the court considers appropriate, reduce the share of the proceeds of the action which the person would otherwise receive under paragraph (1) or (2) of this subsection, taking into account the role of that person in advancing the case to litigation and any relevant circumstances pertaining to the violation. If the person bringing the action is convicted of criminal conduct arising from his or her role in the violation of section 3729, that person shall be dismissed from the civil action and shall not receive any share of the proceeds of the action. Such dismissal shall not prejudice the right of the United States to continue the action, represented by the Department of Justice.

(4) If the Government does not proceed with the action and the person bringing the action conducts the action, the court may award to the defendant its reasonable attorneys' fees and expenses if the defendant prevails in the action and the court finds that the claim of the person bringing the action was clearly frivolous, clearly vexatious, or brought primarily for purposes of harassment.

(e) *Certain Actions Barred.* (1) No court shall have jurisdiction over an action brought by a former or present member of the armed forces under subsection (b) of this section against a member of the armed forces arising out of such person's service in the armed forces.

(2)(A) No court shall have jurisdiction over an action brought under subsection (b) against a Member of Congress, a member of the judiciary, or a senior executive branch official if the action is based on evidence or information known to the Government when the action was brought.

(B) For purposes of this paragraph, "*senior executive branch official*" means any officer or employee listed in paragraphs (1) through (8) of section 101(f) of the Ethics in Government Act of 1978 (5 U.S.C. App.).

(3) In no event may a person bring an action under subsection (b) which is based upon allegations or transactions which are the subject of a civil suit or an administrative civil money penalty proceeding in which the Government is already a party.

(4)(A) No court shall have jurisdiction over an action under this section based upon the public disclosure of allegations or transactions in a criminal, civil, or administrative hearing, in a congressional, administrative, or Government [*sic*] Accounting Office report, hearing, audit, or investigation, or from the news media, unless the action is brought by the Attorney General or the person bringing the action is an original source of the information.

(B) For purposes of this paragraph, "*original source*" means an individual who has direct and independent knowledge of the information on which the allegations are based and has voluntarily provided the information to the Government before filing an action under this section which is based on the information.

(f) *Government Not Liable for Certain Expenses.* The Government is not liable for expenses which a person incurs in bringing an action under this section.

(g) *Fees and Expenses to Prevailing Defendant.* In civil actions brought under this section by the United States, the provisions of section 2412(d) of title 28 shall apply.

(h) Any employee who is discharged, demoted, suspended, threatened, harassed, or in any other manner discriminated against in the terms and conditions of employment by his or her employer because of lawful acts done by the employee on behalf of the employee or others in furtherance of an action under this section, including investigation for, initiation of, testimony for, or assistance in an action filed or to be filed under this section, shall be entitled to all relief necessary to make the employee whole. Such relief shall include reinstatement with the same seniority status such employee would have had but for the discrimination, 2 times the amount of back pay, interest on the back pay, and compensation for any special damages sustained as a result of the discrimination, including litigation costs and reasonable attorneys' fees. An employee may bring an action in the appropriate district court of the United States for the relief provided in this subsection.

§ 3731. False claims procedure

(a) A subpoena requiring the attendance of a witness at a trial or hearing conducted under section 3730 of this title may be served at any place in the United States.

(b) A civil action under section 3730 may not be brought—

(1) more than 6 years after the date on which the violation of section 3729 is committed, or

(2) more than 3 years after the date when facts material to the right of action are known or reasonably should have been known by the official of the United States charged with responsibility to act in the circumstances, but in no event more than 10 years after the date on which the violation is committed, whichever occurs last.

(c) In any action brought under section 3730, the United States shall be required to prove all essential elements of the cause of action, including damages, by a preponderance of the evidence.

(d) Notwithstanding any other provision of law, the Federal Rules of Criminal Procedure, or the Federal Rules of Evidence, a final judgment rendered in favor of the United States in any criminal proceeding charging fraud or false statements, whether upon a verdict after trial or upon a plea of guilty or nolo contendere, shall estop the defendant from denying the essential elements of the offense in any action which involves the same transaction as in the criminal proceeding and which is brought under subsection (a) or (b) of section 3730.

§ 3732. False claims jurisdiction.

(a) *Actions Under Section 3730.* Any action under section 3730 may be brought in any judicial district in which the defendant or, in the case of multiple defendants, any one defendant can be found. resides. transacts business. or in which any act proscribed by section 3729 occurred. A summons as required by the Federal Rules of Civil Procedure shall be issued by the appropriate

district court and served at any place within or outside the United States.

(b) *Claims Under State Law*. The district courts shall have jurisdiction over any action brought under the laws of any State for the recovery of funds paid by a State or local government if the action arises from the same transaction or occurrence as an action brought under section 3730.

United States Code
29 U.S.C. §§ 2615(a) and (b), and 2617
Family and Medical Leave Act

§ 2615. Prohibited acts

(a) *Interference with rights*. (1) *Exercise of rights*. It shall be unlawful for any employer to interfere with. restrain. or deny the exercise of or the attempt to exercise.

any right provided under this subchapter.

(2) *Discrimination*. It shall be unlawful for any employer to discharge or in any other manner discriminate against any individual for opposing any practice made unlawful by this subchapter.

(b) *Interference with proceedings or inquiries*. It shall be unlawful for any person to discharge or in any other manner discriminate against any individual because such individual—

(1) has filed any charge. or has instituted or caused to be instituted any proceeding. under or related to this subchapter;

(2) has given. or is about to give. any information in connection with any inquiry or proceeding relating to any right provided under this subchapter; or

(3) has testified. or is about to testify. in any inquiry or proceeding relating to any right provided under this subchapter.

§ 2617. Enforcement

(a) *Civil action by employees*. (1) *Liability*. Any employer who violates section 2615 of this title shall be liable to any eligible employee affected.

(A) for damages equal to—

(i) the amount of—

(I) any wages. salary. employment benefits. or other compensation denied or lost to such employee by reason of the violation; or

(II) in a case in which wages. salary.

employment benefits. or other compensation have not been denied or lost to the employee. any actual monetary losses sustained by the employee as a direct result of the violation. such as the cost of providing care. up to a sum equal to 12 weeks of wages or salary for the employee;

(ii) the interest on the amount described in clause (i) calculated at the prevailing rate; and

(iii) an additional amount as liquidated damages equal to the sum of the amount described in clause (i) and the interest described in clause (ii). except that if an employer who has violated section 2615 of this title proves to the satisfaction of the court that the act or omission which violated section 2615 of this title was in good faith and that the employer had reasonable grounds for believing that the act or omission was not a violation of section 2615 of this title. such court may. in the discretion of the court. reduce the amount of the liability to the amount and interest determined under clauses (i) and (ii). respectively; and

(B) for such equitable relief as may be appropriate, including employment, reinstatement, and promotion.

(2) *Right of action.* An action to recover the damages or equitable relief prescribed in paragraph (1) may be maintained against any employer (including a public agency) in any Federal or State court of competent jurisdiction by any one or more employees for and in behalf of—

(A) the employees; or

(B) the employees and other employees similarly situated.

(3) *Fees and costs.* The court in such an action shall, in addition to any judgment awarded to the plaintiff, allow a reasonable attorney's fee, reasonable expert witness fees, and other costs of the action to be paid by the defendant.

(4) *Limitations.* The right provided by paragraph (2) to bring an action by or on behalf of any employee shall terminate—

(A) on the filing of a complaint by the Secretary in an action under subsection (d) of this section in which restraint is sought of any further delay in the payment of the amount described in paragraph (1)(A) to such employee by an employer responsible under paragraph (1) for the payment; or

(B) on the filing of a complaint by the Secretary in an action under subsection (b) of this section in which a recovery is sought of the damages described in paragraph (1)(A) owing to an eligible employee by an employer liable under paragraph (1), unless the action described in subparagraph (A) or (B) is dismissed without prejudice on motion of the Secretary.

(b) *Action by Secretary.* (1) *Administrative action.* The Secretary shall receive, investigate, and attempt to resolve complaints of violations of section 2615 of this title in the same manner that the Secretary receives, investigates, and attempts to resolve complaints of violations of sections 206 and 207 of this title.

(2) *Civil action.* The Secretary may bring an action in any court of competent jurisdiction to recover the damages described in subsection (a)(1)(A) of this section.

(3) *Sums recovered.* Sums recovered by the Secretary pursuant to paragraph (2) shall be held in a special deposit account and shall be paid, on order of the Secretary, directly to each employee affected. Any such sums not paid to an employee because of inability to do so within a period of 3 years shall be deposited into the Treasury of the United States as miscellaneous receipts.

(c) *Limitation.* (1) In general Except as provided in paragraph (2), an action may be brought under this section not later than 2 years after the date of the last event constituting the alleged violation for which the action is brought.

(2) *Willful violation.* In the case of such action brought for a willful violation of section 2615 of this title, such action may be brought within 3 years of the date of the last event constituting the alleged violation for which such action is brought.

(3) *Commencement.* In determining when an action is commenced by the Secretary under this section for the purposes of this subsection, it shall be considered to be commenced on the date when the complaint is filed.

(d) *Action for injunction by Secretary.* The district courts of the United States shall have jurisdiction, for cause shown, in an action brought by the Secretary—

(1) to restrain violations of section 2615 of this title, including the restraint of any withholding of payment of wages, salary, employment benefits, or other compensation, plus interest, found by the court to be due to eligible employees; or

(2) to award such other equitable relief as may be appropriate,
including employment, reinstatement, and promotion.

(e) *Solicitor of Labor.* The Solicitor of Labor may appear for and represent the Secretary on any litigation brought under this section.

(f) *General Accounting Office and Library of Congress.* In the case of the General Accounting Office and the Library of Congress, the authority of the Secretary of Labor under this subchapter shall be exercised respectively by the Comptroller General of the United States and the Librarian of Congress.

United States Code
29 U.S.C. § 1574(g)
Job Training and Partnership Act,
Nonretaliation Provision
§ 1574. Fiscal controls; sanctions

(g) *Secretary's action against harassment of complainants.* If the Secretary determines that any recipient under this chapter has discharged or in any other manner discriminated against a participant or against any individual in connection with the administration of the program involved, or against any individual because such individual has filed any complaint or instituted or caused to be instituted any proceeding under or related to this chapter, or has testified or is about to testify in any such proceeding or investigation under or related to this chapter, or otherwise unlawfully denied to any individual a benefit to which that individual is entitled under the provisions of this chapter or the Secretary's regulations, the Secretary shall, within thirty days, take such action or order such corrective measures, as necessary, with respect to the recipient or the aggrieved individual, or both.

United States Code
5 U.S.C. § 7211
Lloyd—LaFollette Act
§ 7211. Employee's right to petition Congress

The right of employees, individually or collectively, to petition Congress or a Member of Congress, or to furnish information to either House of Congress, or to a committee or Member thereof, may not be interfered with or denied.

United States Code
33 U.S.C. § 948a
Longshore and Harbor Workers' Compensation Act
§ 948a. Discrimination against employees who bring proceedings; penalties; deposit of payments in special fund; civil actions; entitlement to restoration of employment and compensation, qualifications requirement; liability of employer for penalties and payments; insurance policy exemption from liability

It shall be unlawful for any employer or his duly authorized agent to discharge or in any other manner discriminate against an employee as to his employment because such employee has claimed or attempted to claim compensation from such employer, or because he has testified or is about to testify in a proceeding under this chapter. The discharge or refusal to employ a person who has been adjudicated to have filed a fraudulent claim for compensation is not a violation of this section. Any employer who violates this section shall be liable to a penalty of not less than $1,000 or more than $5,000, as may be determined by the deputy commissioner. All such penalties shall be paid to the deputy commissioner for deposit in the special fund as described in section 944 of this title, and if not paid may be recovered in a civil action brought in the appropriate United States district court. Any employee so discriminated against shall be restored to his employment and shall be compensated by his employer for any loss of wages arising out of such discrimination: Provided, that if such employee shall cease to be qualified to perform the duties of his employment, he shall not be entitled to such restoration and compensation. The employer alone and not his carrier shall be liable for such penalties and payments. Any provision in an insurance policy undertaking to relieve the employer from the liability for such penalties and payments shall be void.

United States Code
29 U.S.C. § 1855
Migrant and Seasonal Agricultural Workers Protection Act, Nonretaliation Provision

§ 1855. Discrimination prohibited

(a) *Prohibited activities.* No person shall intimidate, threaten, restrain, coerce, blacklist, discharge, or in any manner discriminate against any migrant or seasonal agricultural worker because such worker has, with just cause, filed any complaint or instituted, or caused to be instituted, any proceeding under or related to this chapter, or has testified or is about to testify in any such proceedings, or because of the exercise, with just cause, by such worker on behalf of himself or others of any right or protection afforded by this chapter.

(b) *Proceedings for redress of violations.* A migrant or seasonal agricultural worker who believes, with just cause, that he has been discriminated against by any person in violation of this section may, within 180 days after such violation occurs, file a complaint with the Secretary alleging such discrimination. Upon receipt of such complaint, the Secretary shall cause such investigation to be made as he deems appropriate. If upon such investigation, the Secretary determines that the provisions of this section have been violated, the Secretary shall bring an action in any appropriate United States district court against such person. In any such action the United States district courts shall have jurisdiction, for cause shown, to restrain violation of subsection (a) of this section and order all appropriate relief, including rehiring or reinstatement of the worker, with back pay, or damages.

United States Code
30 U.S.C. § 815(c)
Mine Health and Safety Act, Nonretaliation Act

§ 815. Procedure for enforcement

(c) *Discrimination or interference prohibited; complaint; investigation; determination; hearing.*

(1) No person shall discharge or in any manner discriminate against or cause to be discharged or cause discrimination against or otherwise interfere with the exercise of the statutory rights of any miner, representative of miners or applicant for employment in any coal or other mine subject to this chapter because such miner, representative of miners or applicant for employment has filed or made a complaint under or related to this chapter, including a complaint notifying the operator or the operator's agent, or the representative of the miners at the coal or other mine of an alleged danger or safety or health violation in a coal or other mine, or because such miner, representative of miners or applicant for employment is the subject of medical evaluations and potential transfer under a standard published pursuant to section 811 of this title or because such miner, representative of miners or applicant for employment has instituted or caused to be instituted any proceeding under or related to this chapter or has testified or is about to testify in any such proceeding, or because of the exercise by such miner, representative of miners or applicant for employment on behalf of himself or others of any statutory right afforded by this

chapter.

(2) Any miner or applicant for employment or representative of miners who believes that he has been discharged, interfered with, or otherwise discriminated against by any person in violation of this subsection may, within 60 days after such violation occurs, file a complaint with the Secretary alleging such discrimination. Upon receipt of such complaint, the Secretary shall forward a copy of the complaint to the respondent and shall cause such investigation to be made as he deems appropriate. Such investigation shall commence within 15 days of the Secretary's receipt of the complaint, and if the Secretary finds that such complaint was not frivolously brought, the Commission, on an expedited basis upon application of the Secretary, shall order the immediate reinstatement of the miner pending final order on the complaint. If upon such investigation, the Secretary determines that the provisions of this subsection have been violated, he shall immediately file a complaint with the Commission, with service upon the alleged violator and the miner, applicant for employment, or representative of miners alleging such discrimination or interference and propose an order granting appropriate relief. The Commission shall afford an opportunity for a hearing (in accordance with section 554 of title 5 but without regard to subsection (a)(3) of such section) and thereafter shall issue an order, based upon findings of fact, affirming, modifying, or vacating the Secretary's proposed order, or directing other appropriate relief. Such order shall become final 30 days after its issuance. The Commission shall have authority in such proceedings to require a person committing a violation of this subsection to take such affirmative action to abate the violation as the Commission deems appropriate, including, but not limited to, the rehiring or reinstatement of the miner to his former position with back pay and interest. The complaining miner, applicant, or representative of miners may present additional evidence on his own behalf during any hearing held pursuant to [t]his paragraph.

(3) Within 90 days of the receipt of a complaint filed under paragraph (2), the Secretary shall notify, in writing, the miner, applicant for employment, or representative of miners of his determination whether a violation has occurred. If the Secretary, upon investigation, determines that the provisions of this subsection have not been violated, the complainant shall have the right, within 30 days of notice of the Secretary's determination, to file an action in his own behalf before the Commission, charging discrimination or interference in violation of paragraph (1). The Commission shall afford an opportunity for a hearing (in accordance with section 554 of title 5 but without regard to subsection (a)(3) of such section), and thereafter shall issue an order, based upon findings of fact, dismissing or sustaining the complainant's charges and, if the charges are sustained, granting such relief as it deems appropriate, including, but not limited to, an order requiring the rehiring or reinstatement of the miner to his former position with back pay and interest or such remedy as may be appropriate. Such order shall become final 30 days after its issuance. Whenever an order is issued sustaining the complainant's charges under this subsection, a sum equal to the aggregate amount of all costs and expenses (including attorney's fees) as determined by the Commission to have been reasonably incurred by the miner, applicant for employment or representative of miners for, or in connection with, the institution and prosecution of such proceedings shall be assessed against the person committing such violation. Proceedings under this section shall be expedited by the Secretary and the Commission. Any order issued by the Commission under this paragraph shall be subject to judicial review in accordance with section 816 of this title. Violations by any person of paragraph (1) shall be subject to the provisions of sections 818 and 820(a) of this title.

United States Code
29 U.S.C. § 158(a)(4)
National Labor Relations Act,
Nonretaliation Provision

§ 158. Unfair labor practices

(a) *Unfair labor practices by employer.* It shall be an unfair labor practice for an employer—

(4) to discharge or otherwise discriminate against an employee because he has filed charges or given testimony under this subchapter.

United States Code
18 U.S.C. § 1512(b)(c)(d) and (e)
Obstruction of Justice

§ 1512. Tampering with a witness, victim, or an informant

(b) Whoever knowingly uses intimidation or physical force, threatens, or corruptly persuades another person, or attempts to do so, or engages in misleading conduct toward another person, with intent to—

(1) influence, delay, or prevent the testimony of any person in an official proceeding;

(2) cause or induce any person to—

(A) withhold testimony, or withhold a record, document, or other object, from an official proceeding;

(B) alter, destroy, mutilate, or conceal an object with intent to impair the object's integrity or availability for use in an official proceeding;

(C) evade legal process summoning that person to appear as a witness, or to produce a record, document, or other object, in an official proceeding; or

(D) be absent from an official proceeding to which such person has been summoned by legal process; or

(3) hinder, delay, or prevent the communication to a law enforcement officer or judge of the United States of information relating to the commission or possible commission of a Federal offense or a violation of conditions of probation, parole, or release pending judicial proceedings; shall be fined under this title or imprisoned not more than ten years, or both.

(c) Whoever intentionally harasses another person and thereby hinders, delays, prevents, or dissuades any person from—

(1) attending or testifying in an official proceeding;

(2) reporting to a law enforcement officer or judge of the United States the commission or possible commission of a Federal offense or a violation of conditions of probation, parole, or release pending judicial proceedings;

(3) arresting or seeking the arrest of another person in connection with a Federal offense; or

(4) causing a criminal prosecution, or a parole or probation revocation proceeding, to be sought or instituted, or assisting in such prosecution or proceeding; or attempts to do so, shall be fined under this title or imprisoned not more than one year, or both.

(d) In a prosecution for an offense under this section, it is an affirmative defense, as to which the defendant has the burden of proof by a preponderance of the evidence, that the conduct consisted solely of lawful conduct and that the defendant's sole intention was to encourage, induce, or cause the other person to testify truthfully.

(e) For the purposes of this section—

(1) an official proceeding need not be pending or about to be instituted at the time of the offense; and

(2) the testimony, or the record, document, or other object need not be admissible in evidence or free of a claim of privilege.

United States Code
29 U.S.C. § 660(c)
Occupational Safety and Health Act,
Nonretaliation Provision

§ 660. Judicial review

(c) *Discharge or discrimination against employee for exercise of rights under this chapter; prohibition; procedure for relief.* (1) No person shall discharge or in any manner discriminate against any employee because such employee has filed any complaint or instituted or caused to be instituted any proceeding under or related to this chapter or has testified or is about to testify in any such proceeding or because of the exercise by such employee on behalf of himself or others of any right afforded by this chapter.

(2) Any employee who believes that he has been discharged or otherwise discriminated against by any person in violation of this subsection may, within thirty days after such violation occurs, file a complaint with the Secretary alleging such discrimination. Upon receipt of such complaint, the Secretary shall cause such investigation to be made as he deems appropriate. If upon such investigation, the Secretary determines that the provisions of this subsection have been violated, he shall bring an action in any appropriate United States district court against such person. In any such action the United States district courts shall have jurisdiction, for cause shown to restrain violations of paragraph (1) of this subsection and order all appropriate relief including rehiring or reinstatement of the employee to his former position with back pay.

(3) Within 90 days of the receipt of a complaint filed under this subsection the Secretary shall notify the complainant of his determination under paragraph (2) of this subsection.

United States Code
46 U.S.C. § 1506
Safe Containers for International Cargo Act,
Employee Protection Provision

§ 1506. Employee protection

(a) *Discrimination against a reporting employee prohibited.* No person shall discharge or in any manner discriminate against an employee because the employee has reported the existence of an unsafe container or reported a violation of this chapter to the Secretary or his agents.

(b) *Complaint alleging discrimination.* An employee who believes that he has been discharged or discriminated against in violation of this section may, within 60 days after the violation occurs, file a complaint alleging discrimination with the Secretary of Labor.

(c) *Investigation by Secretary of Labor; judicial relief.* The Secretary of Labor may investigate the complaint and, if he determines that this section has been violated, bring an action in an appropriate United States district court. The district court shall have jurisdiction to restrain violations of subsection (a) of this section and to order appropriate relief, including rehiring and reinstatement of the employee to his former position with back pay.

(d) *Notification to complainant of intended action.* Within 30 days after the receipt of a complaint filed under this section the Secretary of Labor shall notify the complainant of his intended action regarding the complaint.

United States Code
42 U.S.C. § 300j-9(i)
Safe Drinking Water Act,
Employee Protection Provision

§ 300 j-9(i). General Provisions

(i)Discrimination prohibition: filing of complaint: investigation: orders of Secretary: notice and hearing: settlements: attorneys' fees: judicial review: filing of petition: procedural requirements: stay of orders: exclusiveness of remedy: civil actions for enforcement of orders: appropriate relief: mandamus proceedings: prohibition inapplicable to undirected but deliberate violations—

(1) No employer may discharge any employee or otherwise discriminate against any employee with respect to his compensation, terms, conditions, or privileges of employment because the employee (or any person acting pursuant to a request of the employee) has—

(A) commenced, caused to be commenced, or is about to commence or cause to be commenced a proceeding under this subchapter or a proceeding for the administration or enforcement of drinking water regulations or underground injection control programs of a State,

(B) testified or is about to testify in any such proceeding, or

(C) assisted or participated or is about to assist or participate in any manner in such a proceeding or in any other action to carry out the purposes of this subchapter.

(2)(A) Any employee who believes that he has been discharged or otherwise discriminated against by any person in violation of paragraph (1) may, within 30 days after such violation occurs, file (or have any person file on his behalf) a complaint with the Secretary of Labor (hereinafter in this subsection referred to as the "Secretary") alleging such discharge or discrimination. Upon receipt of such a complaint, the Secretary shall notify the person named in the complaint of the filing of the complaint.

(B)(i) Upon receipt of a complaint filed under subparagraph (A), the Secretary shall conduct an investigation of the violation alleged in the complaint. Within 30 days of the receipt of such complaint, the Secretary shall complete such investigation and shall notify in writing the complainant (and any person acting in his behalf) and the person alleged to have committed such violation of the results of the investigation conducted pursuant to this subparagraph. Within 90 days of the receipt of such complaint the Secretary shall, unless the proceeding on the complaint is terminated by the Secretary on the basis of a settlement entered into by the Secretary and the person alleged to have committed such violation, issue an order either providing the relief prescribed by clause (ii) or denying the complaint. An order of the Secretary shall be made on the record after notice and opportunity for agency hearing. The Secretary may not enter into a settlement terminating a proceeding on a complaint without the participation and consent of the complainant.

(ii) If in response to a complaint filed under subparagraph (A) the Secretary determines that a violation of paragraph (1) has occurred, the Secretary shall order

(I) the person who committed such violation to take affirmative action to abate the violation,

(II) such person to reinstate the complainant to his former position together with the compensation (including back pay), terms, conditions, and privileges of his employment,

(III) compensatory damages, and

(IV) where appropriate, exemplary damages. If such an order is issued, the Secretary, at the request of the complainant, shall assess against the person against whom the order is issued a sum equal to the aggregate amount of all costs and expenses (including attorneys' fees) reasonably incurred, as determined by the Secretary, by the complainant for, or in connection with, the bringing of the complaint upon which the order was issued.

(3)(A) Any person adversely affected or aggrieved by an order issued under paragraph (2) may obtain review of the order in the United States Court of Appeals for the circuit in which the violation, with respect to which the order was issued, allegedly occurred. The petition for review must be filed within sixty days from the issuance of the Secretary's order. Review shall conform to chapter 7 of title 5. The commencement of proceedings under this subparagraph shall not, unless ordered by the court, operate as a stay of the Secretary's order.

(B) An order of the Secretary with respect to which review could have been obtained under subparagraph (A) shall not be subject to judicial review in any criminal or other civil proceeding.

(4) Whenever a person has failed to comply with an order issued under paragraph (2)(B), the Secretary shall file a civil action in the United States District Court for the district in which the violation was found to occur to enforce such order. In actions brought under this paragraph, the district courts shall have jurisdiction to grant all appropriate relief including, but not limited to, injunctive relief, compensatory, and exemplary damages.

(5) Any nondiscretionary duty imposed by this section is enforceable in mandamus proceeding brought under section 1361 of title 28.

(6) Paragraph (1) shall not apply with respect to any employee who, acting without direction from his employer (or the employer's agent), deliberately causes a violation of any requirement of this subchapter.

United States Code
42 U.S.C. § 6971
Solid Waste Disposal Act,
Employee Protection Provision

§ 6971. Employee protection

(a) *General.* No person shall fire, or in any other way discriminate against, or cause to be fired or discriminated against, any employee or any authorized representative of employees by reason of the fact that such employee or representative has filed, instituted, or caused to be filed or instituted any proceeding under this chapter or under any applicable implementation plan, or has testified or is about to testify in any proceeding resulting from the administration or enforcement of the provisions of this chapter or of any applicable implementation plan.

(b) *Remedy.* Any employee or a representative of employees who believes that he has been fired or otherwise discriminated against by any person in violation of subsection (a) of this section may, within thirty days after such alleged violation occurs, apply to the Secretary of Labor for a review of such firing or alleged discrimination. A copy of the application shall be sent to such person who shall be the respondent. Upon receipt of such application, the Secretary of Labor shall cause such investigation to be made as he deems appropriate. Such investigation shall provide an opportunity for a public hearing at the request of any party to such review to enable the parties to present information relating to such alleged violation. The parties shall be given written notice of the time and place of the hearing at least five days prior to the hearing. Any such hearing shall be of record and shall be subject to section 554 of title 5. Upon receiving the report of such investigation, the Secretary of Labor shall make findings of fact. If he finds that such violation did occur, he shall issue a decision, incorporating an order therein and his findings, requiring the party committing such violation to take such affirmative action to abate the violation as the Secretary of Labor deems appropriate, including, but not limited to, the rehiring or reinstatement of the employee or representative of employees to his former position with compensation. If he finds that there was no such violation, he shall issue an order denying the application. Such order issued by the Secretary of Labor under this subparagraph shall be subject to judicial review in the same manner as orders and decisions of the Administrator or subject to judicial review under this chapter.

(c) *Costs.* Whenever an order is issued under this section to abate such violation, at the request of the applicant, a sum equal to the aggregate amount of all costs and expenses (including the attorney's fees) as determined by the Secretary of Labor, to have been reasonably incurred by the applicant for, or in connection with, the institution and prosecution of such proceedings, shall be assessed against the person committing such violation.

(d) *Exception.* This section shall have no application to any employee who, acting without direction from his employer (or his agent) deliberately violates any requirement of this chapter.

(e) *Employment shifts and loss.* The Administrator shall conduct continuing evaluations of potential loss or shifts of employment which may result from the administration or enforcement of the provisions of this chapter and applicable implementation plans, including, where appropriate, investigating threatened plant closures or reductions in employment allegedly resulting from such administration or enforcement. Any employee who is discharged, or laid off, threatened with discharge or layoff, or otherwise discriminated against by any person because of the alleged results of such administration or enforcement, or any representative of such employee, may request the Administrator to conduct a full investigation of the matter. The Administrator shall thereupon investigate the matter and, at the request of any party, shall hold public hearings on not less than five days' notice, and shall at such hearings require the parties, including the employer involved, to present information relating to the actual or potential effect of such administration or enforcement on employment and on any alleged discharge, layoff, or other discrimination and the detailed reasons or justification therefor. Any such hearing shall be of record and shall be subject to section 554 of title 5. Upon receiving the report of such investigation, the Administrator shall make findings of fact as to the effect of such administration or enforcement on employment and on the alleged discharge, layoff, or discrimination and shall make such recommendations as he deems appropriate. Such report, findings, and recommendations shall be available to the public. Nothing in this subsection shall be construed to require or authorize the Administrator or any State to modify or withdraw any standard, limitation, or any other requirement of this chapter or any applicable implementation plan.

(f) *Occupational safety and health.* In order to assist the Secretary of Labor and the Director of the National Institute for Occupational Safety and Health in carrying out their duties under the Occupational Safety and Health Act of 1970 (29 U.S.C. 651 et seq.), the Administrator shall—

(1) provide the following information, as such information becomes available, to the Secretary and the Director:

(A) the identity of any hazardous waste generation, treatment, storage, disposal facility or site where cleanup is planned or underway;

(B) information identifying the hazards to which persons working at a hazardous waste generation, treatment, storage, disposal facility or site or otherwise handling hazardous waste may be exposed, the nature and extent of the exposure, and methods to protect workers from such hazards; and

(C) incidents of worker injury or harm at a hazardous waste generation, treatment, storage or disposal facility or site; and

(2) notify the Secretary and the Director of the Administrator's receipt of notifications

under section 6930 or reports under sections 6922, 6923, and 6924 of this title and make such notifications and reports available to the Secretary and the Director.

United States Code
30 U.S.C. § 1293
Surface Mining Act,
Employee Protection Provision

§ 1293. Employee protection

(a) *Retaliatory practices prohibited.* No person shall discharge, or in any other way discriminate against, or cause to be fired or discriminated against, any employee or any authorized representative of employees by reason of the fact that such employee or representative has filed, instituted, or caused to be filed or instituted any proceeding under this chapter, or has testified or is about to testify in any proceeding resulting from the administration or enforcement of the provisions of this chapter.

(b) *Review by Secretary; investigation; notice; hearing; findings of fact; judicial review.* Any employee or a representative of employees who believes that he has been fired or otherwise discriminated against by any person in violation of subsection (a) of this section may, within thirty days after such alleged violation occurs, apply to the Secretary for a review of such firing or alleged discrimination. A copy of the application shall be sent to the person or operator who will be the respondent. Upon receipt of such application, the Secretary shall cause such investigation to be made as he deems appropriate. Such investigation shall provide an opportunity for a public hearing at the request of any party to such review to enable the parties to present information relating to the alleged violation. The parties shall be given written notice of the time and place of the hearing at least five days prior to the hearing. Any such hearing shall be of record and shall be subject to section 554 of title 5. Upon receiving the report of such investigation the Secretary shall make findings of fact. If he finds that a violation did occur, he shall issue a decision incorporating therein his findings and an order requiring the party committing the violation to take such affirmative action to abate the violation as the Secretary deems appropriate, including, but not limited to, the rehiring or reinstatement of the employee or representative of employees to his former position with compensation. If he finds that there was no violation, he will issue a finding. Orders issued by the Secretary under this subsection shall be subject to judicial review in the same manner as orders and decisions of the Secretary are subject to judicial review under this chapter.

(c) *Costs.* Whenever an order is issued under this section to abate any violation, at the request of the applicant a sum equal to the aggregate amount of all costs and expenses (including attorneys' fees) to have been reasonably incurred by the applicant for, or in connection with, the institution and prosecution of such proceedings, shall be assessed against the persons committing the violation.

United States Code
49 U.S.C. §§ 31101, 31105
Surface Transportation Assistance Act

§ 31101. Definitions

In this subchapter —

(1) *"commercial motor vehicle"* means (except in section 31106) a self-propelled or towed vehicle used on the highways in commerce principally to transport passengers or cargo, if the vehicle—

(A) has a gross vehicle weight rating of at least 10,000 pounds;

(B) is designed to transport more than 10 passengers including the driver; or

(C) is used in transporting material found by the Secretary of Transportation to be hazardous under section 5103 of this title.

(2) *"employee"* means a driver of a commercial motor vehicle (including an independent contractor when personally operating a commercial motor vehicle), a mechanic, a freight handler, or an individual not an employer, who—

(A) directly affects commercial motor vehicle safety in the course of employment by a commercial motor carrier; and

(B) is not an employee of the United States Government, a State, or a political subdivision of a State acting in the course of employment.

(3) *"employer"*—

(A) means a person engaged in a business affecting commerce that owns or leases a commercial motor vehicle in connection with that business, or assigns an employee to operate the vehicle in commerce; but

(B) does not include the Government, a State, or a political subdivision of a State.

(4) *"State"* means a State of the United States, the District of Columbia, Puerto Rico, the Virgin Islands, American Samoa, Guam, and the Northern Mariana Islands.

§ 31105. Employee Protections

(a) *Prohibitions.* (1) A person may not discharge an employee, or discipline or discriminate against an employee regarding pay, terms, or privileges of employment, because—

(A) the employee, or another person at the employee's request, has filed a complaint or begun a proceeding related to a violation of a commercial motor vehicle safety regulation, standard, or order, or has testified or will testify in such a proceeding; or

(B) the employee refuses to operate a vehicle because—

(i) the operation violates a regulation, standard, or order of the United States related to commercial motor vehicle safety or health; or

(ii) the employee has a reasonable apprehension of serious injury to the employee or the public because of the vehicle's unsafe condition.

(2) Under paragraph (1)(B)(ii) of this subsection, an employee's apprehension of serious injury is reasonable only if a reasonable individual in the circumstances then confronting the employee would conclude that the unsafe condition establishes a real danger of accident, injury, or serious impairment to health. To qualify for protection, the employee must have sought from the employer, and been unable to obtain, correction of the unsafe condition.

(b) *Filing Complaints and Procedures.* (1) An employee alleging discharge, discipline, or discrimination in violation of subsection (a) of this section, or another person at the employee's request, may file a complaint with the Secretary of Labor not later than 180 days after the alleged violation occurred. On receiving the complaint, the Secretary shall notify the person alleged to have committed the violation of the filing of the complaint.

(2)(A) Not later than 60 days after receiving a complaint, the Secretary shall conduct an investigation, decide whether it is reasonable to believe the complaint has merit, and notify the complainant and the person alleged to have committed the violation of the findings. If the Secretary decides it is reasonable to believe a violation occurred, the Secretary shall include with the decision findings and a preliminary order for the relief provided under paragraph (3) of this subsection.

(B) Not later than 30 days after the notice under subparagraph (A) of this paragraph, the complainant and the person alleged to have committed the violation may file objections to the findings or preliminary order, or both, and request a hearing on the record. The filing of objections does not stay a reinstatement ordered in the preliminary order. If a hearing is not requested within the 30 days, the preliminary order is final and not subject to judicial review.

(C) A hearing shall be conducted expeditiously. Not later than 120 days after the end of the hearing, the Secretary shall issue a final order. Before the final order is issued, the proceeding may be ended by a settlement agreement made by the Secretary, the complainant, and the person alleged to have committed the violation.

(3)(A) If the Secretary decides, on the basis of a complaint, a person violated subsection (a) of this section, the Secretary shall order the person to (i) take affirmative action to abate the violation; (ii) reinstate the complainant to the former position with the same pay and terms and privileges of employment; and (iii) pay compensatory damages, including back pay.

(B) If the Secretary issues an order under subparagraph (A) of this paragraph and the complainant requests, the Secretary may assess against the person against whom the order is issued the costs (including attorney's fees) reasonably incurred by the complainant in bringing the complaint. The Secretary shall determine the costs that reasonably were incurred.

(c) *Judicial Review and Venue.* A person adversely affected by an order issued after a hearing under subsection (b) of this section may file a petition for review, not later than 60 days after the order is issued, in the court of appeals of the United States for the circuit in which the violation occurred or the person resided on the date of the violation. The review shall be heard and decided expeditiously. An order of the Secretary subject to review under this subsection is not subject to judicial review in a criminal or other civil proceeding.

(d) *Civil Actions To Enforce.* If a person fails to comply with an order issued under subsection (b) of this section, the Secretary shall bring a civil action to enforce the order in the district court of the United States for the judicial district in which the violation occurred.

United States Code
15 U.S.C. § 2622
Toxic Substances Control Act,
Employee Protection Provision

§ 2622. Employee protection.

(a) *In general.* No employer may discharge any employee or otherwise discriminate against any employee with respect to the employee's compensation, terms, conditions, or privileges of employment because the employee (or any person acting pursuant to a request of the employee) has—

(1) commenced, caused to be commenced, or is about to commence or cause to be commenced a proceeding under this chapter;

(2) testified or is about to testify in any such proceeding; or

(3) assisted or participated or is about to assist or participate in any manner in such a proceeding or in any other action to carry out the purposes of this chapter.

(b) *Remedy.* (1) Any employee who believes that the employee has been discharged or otherwise discriminated against by any person in violation of subsection (a) of this section may, within 30 days after such alleged violation occurs, file (or have any person file on the employee's behalf) a complaint with the Secretary of Labor (hereinafter in this section referred to as the "Secretary") alleging such discharge or discrimination. Upon receipt of such a complaint, the Secretary shall notify the person named in the complaint of the filing of the complaint.

(2)(A) Upon receipt of a complaint filed under paragraph (1), the Secretary shall conduct an investigation of the violation alleged in the complaint. Within 30 days of the receipt of such complaint, the Secretary shall complete such investigation and shall notify in writing the complainant (and any person acting on behalf of the complainant) and the person alleged to have committed such violation of the results of the investigation conducted pursuant to this paragraph. Within ninety days of the receipt of such complaint the Secretary shall, unless the proceeding on the complaint is terminated by the Secretary on the basis of a settlement entered into by the Secretary and the person alleged to have committed such violation, issue an order either providing the relief prescribed by subparagraph (B) or denying the complaint. An order of the Secretary shall be made on the record after notice and opportunity for agency hearing. The Secretary may not enter into a settlement terminating a proceeding on a complaint without the participation and consent of the complainant.

(B) If in response to a complaint filed under paragraph (1) the Secretary determines that a violation of subsection (a) of this section has occurred, the Secretary shall order

(i) the person who committed such violation to take affirmative action to abate the violation,

(ii) such person to reinstate the complainant to the complainant's former position together with the compensation (including back pay), terms, conditions, and privileges of the complainant's employment,

(iii) compensatory damages, and

(iv) where appropriate, exemplary damages. If such an order issued, the Secretary, at the request of the complainant, shall assess against the person against whom the order is issued a sum equal to the aggregate amount of all costs and expenses (including attorney's fees) reasonably incurred, as determined by the Secretary, by the complainant for, or in connection with, the bringing of the complaint upon which the order was issued.

(c) *Review.* (1) Any employee or employer adversely affected or aggrieved by

an order issued under subsection (b) of this section may obtain review of the order in the United States Court of Appeals for the circuit in which the violation, with respect to which the order was issued, allegedly occurred. The petition for review must be filed within sixty days from the issuance of the Secretary's order. Review shall conform to chapter 7 of title 5.

(2) An order of the Secretary, with respect to which review could have been obtained under paragraph (1), shall not be subject to judicial review in any criminal or other civil proceeding.

(d) *Enforcement.* Whenever a person has failed to comply with an order issued under subsection (b)(2) of this section, the Secretary shall file a civil action in the United States district court for the district in which the violation was found to occur to enforce such order. In actions brought under this subsection, the district courts shall have jurisdiction to grant all appropriate relief, including injunctive relief and compensatory and exemplary damages.

(e) *Exclusion.* Subsection (a) of this section shall not apply with respect to any employee who, acting without direction from the employee's employer (or any agent of the employer), deliberately causes a violation of any requirement of this chapter.

United States Code
33 U.S.C. § 1367
Water Pollution Control Act,
Employee Protection Provision

§ 1367. Employee protection

(a) *Discrimination against persons filing, instituting, or testifying in proceedings under this chapter prohibited.* No person shall fire, or in any other way discriminate against, or cause to be fired or discriminated against, any employee or any authorized representative of employees by reason of the fact that such employee or representative has filed, instituted, or caused to be filed or instituted any proceeding under this chapter, or has testified or is about to testify in any proceeding resulting from the administration or enforcement of the provisions of this chapter.

(b) *Application for review; investigation; hearing; review.* Any employee or a representative of employees who believes that he has been fired or otherwise discriminated against by any person in violation of subsection (a) of this section may, within thirty days after such alleged violation occurs, apply to the Secretary of Labor for a review of such firing or alleged discrimination. A copy of the application shall be sent to such person who shall be the respondent. Upon receipt of such application, the Secretary of Labor shall cause such investigation to be made as he deems appropriate. Such investigation shall provide an opportunity for a public hearing at the request of any party to such review to enable the parties to present information relating to such alleged violation. The parties shall be given written notice of the time and place of the hearing at least five days prior to the hearing. Any such hearing shall be of record and shall be subject to section 554 of title 5. Upon receiving the report of such investigation, the Secretary of Labor shall make findings of fact. If he finds that such violation did occur, he shall issue a decision, incorporating an order therein and his findings, requiring the party committing such violation to take such affirmative action to abate the violation as the Secretary of Labor deems appropriate, including, but not limited to, the rehiring or reinstatement of the employee or representative of employees to his former position with compensation. If he finds that there was no such violation, he shall issue an order denying the application. Such order issued by the Secretary of Labor under this subparagraph shall be subject to judicial review in the same manner as orders and decisions of the Administrator are subject to judicial review under this chapter.

(c) *Costs and expenses.* Whenever an order is issued under this section to abate such violation, at the request of the applicant, a sum equal to the aggregate amount of all costs and expenses (including the attorney's fees), as determined by the Secretary of Labor, to have been reasonably incurred by the applicant for, or in connection with, the institution and prosecution of such proceedings, shall be assessed against the person committing such violation.

(d) *Deliberate violations by employee acting without direction from his employer or his agent.* This section shall have no application to any employee who, acting without direction from his employer (or his agent) deliberately violates any prohibition of effluent limitation or other limitation under section 1311 or 1312 of this title, standards of performance under section 1316 of this title, effluent standard, prohibition or pretreatment standard under section 1317 of this title, or any other prohibition or limitation established under this chapter.

(e) *Investigations of employment reductions.* The Administrator shall conduct continuing evaluations of potential loss or shifts of employment which may result from the issuance of any effluent limitation or order under this chapter, including, where appropriate, investigating threatened plant closures or reductions in employment allegedly resulting from such limitation or order. Any employee who is discharged or laid-off, threatened with discharge or lay-off, or otherwise discriminated against by any person because of the alleged results of any effluent limitation or order issued under this chapter, or any representative of such employee, may request the Administrator to conduct a full investigation of the matter. The Administrator shall thereupon investigate the matter and, at the request of any party, shall hold public hearings on not less than five days notice, and shall at such hearings require the parties, including the employer involved, to present information relating to the actual or potential effect of such limitation or order on employment and on any alleged discharge, lay-off, or other discrimination and the detailed reasons or justification therefor. Any such hearing shall be of record and shall be subject to section 554 of title 5. Upon receiving the report of such investigation, the Administrator shall make findings of fact as to the effect of such effluent limitation or order on employment and on the alleged discharge, lay-off, or discrimination and shall make such recommendations as he deems appropriate. Such report, findings, and recommendations shall be available to the public. Nothing in this subsection shall be construed to require or authorize the Administrator to modify or withdraw any effluent limitation or order issued under this chapter.

APPENDIX C:
FEDERAL REGULATIONS

OFFICE OF THE SECRETARY OF LABOR 29 CFR SUBTITLE A (7-1-98 EDITION) PART 18—RULES OF PRACTICE AND PROCEDURE FOR ADMINISTRATIVE HEARINGS BEFORE THE OFFICE OF ADMINISTRATIVE LAW JUDGES

Subpart A—General

§ 18.1 Scope of rules.

(a) *General application.* These rules of practice are generally applicable to adjudicatory proceedings before the Office of Administrative Law Judges, United States Department of Labor. Such proceedings shall be conducted expeditiously and the parties shall make every effort at each stage of a proceeding to avoid delay. To the extent that these rules may be inconsistent with a rule of special application as provided by statute, executive order, or regulation, the latter is controlling. The Rules of Civil Procedure for the District Courts of the United States shall be applied in any situation not provided for or controlled by these rules, or by any statute, executive order or regulation.

(b) *Waiver, modification, or suspension.* Upon notice to all parties, the administrative law judge may, with respect to matters pending before him or her, modify or waive any rule herein upon a determination that no party will be prejudiced and that the ends of justice will be served thereby. These rules may, from time to time, be suspended, modified or revoked in whole or part.

§ 18.2 Definitions.

For purposes of these rules:

(a) *Adjudicatory proceeding* means a judicial-type proceeding leading to the formulation of a final order;

(b) *Administrative law judge* means an administrative law judge appointed pursuant to the provisions of 5 U.S.C. 3105 (provisions of the rules in this part which refer to administrative law judges may be applicable to other Presiding Officers as well);

(c) *Administrative Procedure Act* means those provisions of the Administrative Procedure Act, as codified, which are contained in 5 U.S.C. 551 through 559;

(d) *Complaint* means any document initiating an

adjudicatory proceeding, whether designated a complaint, appeal or an order for proceeding or otherwise;

(e) *Hearing* means that part of a proceeding which involves the submission of evidence, either by oral presentation or written submission;

(f) *Order* means the whole or any part of a final procedural or substantive disposition of a matter by the administrative law judge in a matter other than rulemaking;

(g) *Party* includes a person or agency named or admitted as a party to a proceeding;

(h) *Person* includes an individual, partnership, corporation, association, exchange or other entity or organization;

(i) *Pleading* means the complaint, the answer to the complaint, any supplement or amendment thereto, and any reply that may be permitted to any answer, supplement or amendment;

(j) *Respondent* means a party to an adjudicatory proceeding against whom findings may be made or who may be required to provide *relief or take remedial action;*

(k) *Secretary* means the Secretary of Labor and includes any administrator, commissioner, appellate body, board, or other official thereunder for purposes of appeal of recommended or final decisions of administrative law judges;

(l) *Complainant* means a person who is seeking relief from any act or omission in violation of a statute, executive order or regulation;

(m) The term *petition* means a written request, made by a person or party, for some affirmative action;

(n) The term *Consent Agreement* means any written document containing a specified proposed remedy or other relief acceptable to all parties;

(o) *Commencement of Proceeding* is the filing of a request for hearing, order of reference, or referral of a claim for hearing.

§ 18.3 Service and filing of documents.

(a) *Generally.* Except as otherwise provided in this part, copies of all documents shall be served on all parties of record. All documents should clearly designate the docket number, if any, and short title of the matter. If the matter involves a program administered by the Office of Workers' Compensation Programs (OWCP), the document should contain the OWCP number in addition to the docket number. All documents to be filed shall be delivered or mailed to the Chief Docket Clerk, Office of Administrative Law Judges (OALJ), 800 K Street, NW., Suite 400, Washington, DC 20001–8002, or to the OALJ Regional Office to which the proceeding may have been transferred for hearing. Each document filed shall be clear and legible.

(b) *How made: by parties.* All documents shall be filed with the Office of Administrative Law Judges, except that notices of deposition, depositions, interrogatories, requests for admissions, and answers and responses thereto, shall not be so filed unless the presiding judge so orders, the document is being offered into evidence, the document is submitted in support of a motion or a response to a motion, filing is required by a specialized rule, or there is some other compelling reason for its submission. Whenever under this part service by a party is required to be made upon a party represented by an attorney or other representative the service shall be made upon the attorney or other representative unless service upon the party is ordered by the presiding administrative law judge. Service of any document upon any party may be made by personal delivery or by mailing a copy to the last known address. The person serving the document shall certify to the manner and date of service.

(c) *By the Office of Administrative Law Judges.* Service of notices, orders, decisions and all other documents, except complaints, shall be made by regular mail to the last known address.

(d) *Service of complaints.* Service of complaints or charges in enforcement proceedings shall be made either: (1) By delivering a copy to the individual, partner, officer of a corporation, or attorney of record; (2) by leaving a copy at the principal office, place of business, or residence; (3) by mailing to the last known address of such individual, partner, officer or attorney. If done by certified mail, service is complete upon mailing. If done by regular mail, service is complete upon receipt by addressee.

(e) *Form of pleadings.* (1) Every pleading shall contain a caption setting forth the name of the agency under which the proceeding is instituted, the title of the proceeding, the docket number assigned by the Office of Administrative Law Judges, and a designation of the type of pleading or paper (e.g., complaint, motion to dismiss, etc.). The pleading or papers shall be signed and shall contain the address and telephone number of the party or person representing the party. Although there are no formal specifications for documents, they should be typewritten when possible on standard size (8 1/2 x 11) paper, legal size (8 1/2 x 14) paper will not be accepted after July 31, 1983.

(2) Illegible documents, whether handwritten,

typewritten, photocopied, or otherwise will not be accepted. Papers may be reproduced by any duplicating process, provided all copies are clear and legible.

(f) *Filing and service by facsimile.*

(1) *Filing by a party: when permitted.*

Filings by a party may be made by facsimile (fax) when explicitly permitted by statute or regulation, or when directed or permitted by the administrative law judge assigned to the case. If prior permission to file by facsimile cannot be obtained because the presiding administrative law judge is not available, a party may file by facsimile and attach a statement of the circumstances requiring that the document be filed by facsimile rather than by regular mail. That statement does not ensure that the filing will be accepted, but will be considered by the presiding judge in determining whether the facsimile will be accepted *nunc pro tunc* as a filing.

(2) *Service by facsimile: when permitted.* Service upon a party by another party or by the administrative law judge may be made by facsimile (fax) when explicitly permitted by statute or regulation, or when the receiving party consents to service by facsimile.

(3) *Service sheet and proof of service.* Documents filed or served by facsimile (fax) shall include a service sheet which states the means by which filing and/or service was made. A facsimile transmission report generated by the sender's facsimile equipment and which indicates that the transmission was successful shall be presumed adequate proof of filing or service.

(4) *Cover sheet.* Filings or service by facsimile (fax) shall include a cover sheet that identifies the sender, the total number of pages transmitted, and the caption and docket number of the case, if known.

(5) *Originals.* Documents filed or served by facsimile (fax) shall be presumed to be accurate reproductions of the original document until proven otherwise. The party proffering the document shall retain the original in the event of a dispute over authenticity or the accuracy of the transmission. The original document need not be submitted unless so ordered by the presiding judge, or unless an original signature is required by statute or regulation. If an original signature is required to be filed, the date of the facsimile transmission shall govern the effective date of the filing provided that the document containing the original signature is filed within ten calendar days of the facsimile transmission.

(6) *Length of document.* Documents filed by facsimile (fax) should not exceed 12 pages including the cover sheet, the service sheet and all accompanying exhibits or appendices, except that this page limitation may be exceeded if prior permission is granted by the presiding judge or if the document's length cannot be conformed because of statutory or regulatory requirements.

(7) *Hours for filing by facsimile.* Filings by facsimile (fax) should normally be made between 8:00 am and 5:00 pm, local time at the receiving location.

(g) *Filing and service by courier service.* Documents transmitted by courier service shall be deemed transmitted by regular mail in proceedings before the Office of Administrative Law Judges.

[48 FR 32538, July 15, 1983, as amended at 56 FR 54708, Oct. 22, 1991; 59 FR 41876, Aug. 15, 1994; 60 FR 26970, May 19, 1995]

§ 18.4 Time computations.

(a) *Generally.* In computing any period of time under these rules or in an order issued hereunder the time begins with the day following the act, event, or default, and includes the last day of the period, unless it is a Saturday, Sunday or legal holiday observed by the Federal Government in which case the time period includes the next business day. When the period of time prescribed is seven (7) days or less, intermediate Saturdays, Sundays, and holidays shall be excluded in the computation.

(b) *Date of entry of orders.* In computing any period of time involving the date of the entry of an order, the date of entry shall be the date the order is served by the Chief Docket Clerk.

(c) *Computation of time for delivery by mail.* (1) Documents are not deemed filed until received by the Chief Clerk at the Office of Administrative Law Judges. However, when documents are filed by mail, five (5) days shall be added to the prescribed period.

(2) Service of all documents other than complaints is deemed effected at the time of mailing.

(3) Whenever a party has the right or is required to take some action within a prescribed period after the service of a pleading, notice, or other document upon said party, and the pleading, notice or document is served upon said party by mail, five (5) days shall be added to the prescribed period.

(d) *Filing or service by facsimile.* Filing or service by facsimile (fax) is effective upon receipt of the entire document by the receiving facsimile machine. For purposes of filings by facsimile the time printed on the transmission by the facsimile equipment constitutes the date stamp of the Chief Docket Clerk.

[48 FR 32538, July 15, 1983, as amended at 59 FR 41877, Aug. 15, 1994]

§ 18.5 Responsive pleadings—answer and request for hearing.

(a) *Time for answer.* Within thirty (30) days after the service of a complaint, each respondent shall file an answer.

(b) *Default.* Failure of the respondent to file an answer within the time provided shall be deemed to constitute a waiver of his right to appear and contest the allegations of the complaint and to authorize the administrative law judge to find the facts as alleged in the complaint and to enter an initial or final decision containing such findings, appropriate conclusions, and order.

(c) *Signature required.* Every answer filed pursuant to these rules shall be signed by the party filing it or by at least one attorney, in his or her individual name, representing such party. The signature constitutes a certificate by the signer that he or she has read the answer; that to the best of his or her knowledge, information and belief there is good ground to support it; and that it is not interposed for delay.

(d) *Content of answer*—(1) *Orders to show cause.* Any person to whom an order to show cause has been directed and served shall respond to the same by filing an answer in writing. Arguments opposing the proposed sanction should be supported by reference to specific circumstances or facts surrounding the basis for the order to show cause.

(2) *Complaints.* Any respondent contesting any material fact alleged in a complaint, or contending that the amount of a proposed penalty or award is excessive or inappropriate or contending that he or she is entitled to judgment as a matter of law, shall file an answer in writing. An answer shall include:

(i) A statement that the respondent admits, denies, or does not have and is unable to obtain sufficient information to admit or deny each allegation; a statement of lack of information shall have the effect of a denial; any allegation not expressly denied shall be deemed to be admitted;

(ii) A statement of the facts supporting each affirmative defense.

(e) *Amendments and supplemental pleadings.* If and whenever determination of a controversy on the merits will be facilitated thereby, the administrative law judge may, upon such conditions as are necessary to avoid prejudicing the public interest and the rights of the parties, allow appropriate amendments to complaints, answers, or other pleadings; provided, however, that a complaint may be amended once as a matter of right prior to the answer, and thereafter if the administrative law judge determines that the amendment is reasonably within the scope of the original complaint. When issues not raised by the pleadings are reasonably within the scope of the original complaint and are tried by express or implied consent of the parties, they shall be treated in all respects as if they had been raised in the pleadings, and such amendments may be made as necessary to make them conform to the evidence. The administrative law judge may, upon reasonable notice and such terms as are just, permit supplemental pleadings setting forth transactions, occurrences or events which have happened since the date of the pleadings and which are relevant to any of the issues involved.

§ 18.6 Motions and requests.

(a) *Generally.* Any application for an order or any other request shall be made by motion which, unless made during a hearing or trial, shall be made in writing unless good cause is established to preclude such submission, shall state with particularity the grounds therefor, and shall set forth the relief or order sought. Motions or requests made during the course of any hearing or appearance before an administrative law judge shall be stated orally and made part of the transcript. Whether made orally or in writing, all parties shall be given reasonable opportunity to state an objection to the motion or request.

(b) *Answers to motions.* Within ten (10) days after a motion is served, or within such other period as the administrative law judge may fix, any party to the proceeding may file an answer in support or in opposition to the motion, accompanied by such affidavits or other evidence as he or she desires to rely upon. Unless the administrative law judge provides otherwise, no reply to an answer, response to a reply, or any further responsive document shall be filed.

(c) *Oral arguments or briefs.* No oral argument will be heard on motions unless the administrative law judge otherwise directs. Written memoranda or briefs may be filed with motions or answers to motions, stating the points and authorities relied upon in support of the position taken.

(d) *Motion for order compelling answer: sanctions.* (1) A party who has requested admissions or who has served interrogatories may move to determine the sufficiency of the answers or objections thereto. Unless the objecting party sustains his or her burden of showing that the objection is justified, the administrative law judge shall order that an answer be served. If the administrative law judge determines that an answer does not comply with the requirements of these rules, he or she may order either that the matter is admitted or that an amended answer be served.

(2) If a party or an officer or agent of a party fails to comply with a subpoena or with an order, including, but not limited to, an order for the taking of a deposition, the production of documents, or the answering of interrogatories, or requests for admissions, or any other order of the administrative law judge, the administrative law judge, for the purpose of permitting resolution of the relevant issues and disposition of the proceeding without unnecessary delay despite such failure, may take such action in regard thereto as is just, including but not limited to the following:

(i) Infer that the admission, testimony, documents or other evidence would have been adverse to the non-complying party;

(ii) Rule that for the purposes of the proceeding the matter or matters concerning which the order or subpoena was issued be taken as established adversely to the non-complying party;

(iii) Rule that the non-complying party may not introduce into evidence or otherwise rely upon testimony by such party, officer or agent, or the documents or other evidence, in support of or in opposition to any claim or defense;

(iv) Rule that the non-complying party may not be heard to object to introduction and use of secondary evidence to show what the withheld admission, testimony, documents, or other evidence should have shown.

(v) Rule that a pleading, or part of a pleading, or a motion or other submission by the non-complying party, concerning which the order or subpoena was issued, be stricken, or that a decision of the proceeding be rendered against the non-complying party, or both.

§ 18.7 Pre-hearing statements.

(a) At any time prior to the commencement of the hearing, the administrative law judge may order any party to file a pre-hearing statement of position.

(b) A pre-hearing statement shall state the name of the party or parties on whose behalf it is presented and shall briefly set forth the following matters, unless otherwise ordered by the administrative law judge:

(1) Issues involved in the proceeding;

(2) Facts stipulated pursuant to the procedures together with a statement that the party or parties have communicated or conferred in a good faith effort to reach stipulation to the fullest extent possible;

(3) Facts in dispute;

(4) Witnesses, except to the extent that disclosure would be privileged, and exhibits by which disputed facts will be litigated;

(5) A brief statement of applicable law;

(6) The conclusion to be drawn;

(7) Suggested time and location of hearing and estimated time required for presentation of the party's or parties' case;

(8) Any appropriate comments, suggestions or information which might assist the parties in preparing for the hearing or otherwise aid in the disposition of the proceeding.

§ 18.8 Pre-hearing conferences.

(a) *Purpose and scope.* (1) Upon motion of a party or upon the administrative law judge's own motion, the judge may direct the parties or their counsel to participate in a conference at any reasonable time, prior to or during the course of the hearing, when the administrative law judge finds that the proceeding would be expedited by a pre-hearing conference. Such conferences normally shall be conducted by conference telephonic communication unless, in the opinion of the administrative law judge, such method would be impractical, or when such conferences can be conducted in a more expeditious or effective manner by correspondence or personal appearance. Reasonable notice of the time, place and manner of the conference shall be given.

(2) At the conference, the following matters shall be considered:

(i) The simplification of issues;

(ii) The necessity of amendments to pleadings;

(iii) The possibility of obtaining stipulations of facts and of the authenticity, accuracy, and admissibility of documents, which will avoid unnecessary proof;

(iv) The limitation of the number of expert or other witnesses;

(v) Negotiation, compromise, or settlement of issues;

(vi) The exchange of copies of proposed exhibits;

(vii) The identification of documents or matters of which official notice may be requested;

(viii) A schedule to be followed by the parties for completion of the actions decided at the conference; and

(ix) Such other matters as may expedite and aid in the disposition of the proceeding.

(b) *Reporting.* A pre-hearing conference will be stenographically reported. unless otherwise directed by the administrative law judge.

(c) *Order.* Actions taken as a result of a conference shall be reduced to a written order, unless the administrative law judge concludes that a stenographic report shall suffice, or, if the conference takes place within 7 days of the beginning of the hearing, the administrative law judge elects to make a statement on the record at the hearing summarizing the actions taken.

§ 18.9 Consent order or settlement; settlement judge procedure.

(a) *Generally.* At any time after the commencement of a proceeding, the parties jointly may move to defer the hearing for a reasonable time to permit negotiation of a settlement or an agreement containing findings and an order disposing of the whole or any part of the proceeding. The allowance of such deferment and the duration thereof shall be in the discretion of the administrative law judge, after consideration of such factors as the nature of the proceeding, the requirements of the public interest, the representations of the parties and the probability of reaching an agreement which will result in a just disposition of the issues involved.

(b) *Content.* Any agreement containing consent findings and an order disposing of a proceeding or any part thereof shall also provide:

(1) That the order shall have the same force and effect as an order made after full hearing;

(2) That the entire record on which any order may be based shall consist solely of the complaint, order of reference or notice of administrative determination (or amended notice, if one is filed), as appropriate, and the agreement;

(3) A waiver of any further procedural steps before the administrative law judge; and

(4) A waiver of any right to challenge or contest the validity of the order entered into in accordance with the agreement.

(c) *Submission.* On or before the expiration of the time granted for negotiations, the parties or their authorized representative or their counsel may:

(1) Submit the proposed agreement containing consent findings and an order for consideration by the administrative law judge, or

(2) Notify the administrative law judge that the parties have reached a full settlement and have agreed to dismissal of the action. or

(3) Inform the administrative law judge that

agreement cannot be reached.

(d) *Disposition.* In the event an agreement containing consent findings and an order is submitted within the time allowed therefor, the administrative law judge, within thirty (30) days thereafter, shall, if satisfied with its form and substance, accept such agreement by issuing a decision based upon the agreed findings.

(e)(1) *Settlement judge procedure: purpose.* This paragraph establishes a voluntary process whereby the parties may use a settlement judge to mediate settlement negotiations. A settlement judge is an active or retired administrative law judge who convenes and presides over settlement conferences and negotiations, confers with the parties jointly and/or individually, and seeks voluntary resolution of issues. Unlike a presiding judge, a settlement judge does not render a formal judgment or decision in the case; his or her role is solely to facilitate fair and equitable solutions and to provide an assessment of the relative merits of the respective positions of the parties.

(2) *How initiated.* A settlement judge may be appointed by the Chief Administrative Law Judge upon a request by a party or the presiding administrative law judge. The Chief Administrative Law Judge has sole discretion to decide whether to appoint a settlement judge, except that a settlement judge shall not be appointed when—

(i) A party objects to referral of the matter to a settlement judge;

(ii) Such appointment is inconsistent with a statute, executive order, or regulation;

(iii) The proceeding arises pursuant to the Longshore and Harbor Workers' Compensation Act, 33 U.S.C. 901 et seq., and associated acts such as the District of Columbia Workmen's Compensation Act, 36 DC Code 501 et seq.; or

(iv) The proceeding arises pursuant to Title IV of the Federal Mine Safety and Health Act, 30 U.S.C. 901 et seq., also known as the Black Lung Benefits Act.

(3) *Selection of settlement judge.* (i) The selection of a settlement judge is at the sole discretion of the Chief Administrative Law Judge, provided that the individual selected—

(A) is an active or retired administrative law judge, and

(B) is not the administrative law judge assigned to hear and decide the case.

(ii) The settlement judge shall not be appointed to hear and decide the case.

(4) *Duration of proceeding.* Unless the Chief Administrative Law Judge directs otherwise, settlement negotiations under this section shall

not exceed thirty days from the date of appointment of the settlement judge, except that with the consent of the parties, the settlement judge may request an extension from the Chief Administrative Law Judge. The negotiations will be terminated immediately if a party unambiguously indicates that it no longer wishes to participate, or if in the judgment of the settlement judge, further negotiations would be fruitless or otherwise inappropriate.

(5) *General powers of the settlement judge.* The settlement judge has the power to convene settlement conferences: to require that parties, or representatives of the parties having the authority to settle, participate in conferences; and to impose other reasonable requirements on the parties to expedite an amicable resolution of the case, provided that all such powers shall terminate immediately if negotiations are terminated pursuant to paragraph (e)(4).

(6) *Suspension of discovery.* Requests for suspension of discovery during the settlement negotiations shall be directed to the presiding administrative law judge who shall have sole discretion in granting or denying such requests.

(7) *Settlement conference.* In general the settlement judge should communicate with the parties by telephone conference call. The settlement judge may, however, schedule a personal conference with the parties when:

(i) The settlement judge is scheduled to preside in other proceedings in a place convenient to all parties and representatives involved;

(ii) The offices of the attorneys or other representatives of the parties,

and the settlement judge, are in the same metropolitan area; or

(iii) The settlement judge, with the concurrence of the Chief Administrative Law Judge, determines that a personal meeting is necessary for a resolution of substantial issues, and represents a prudent use of resources.

(8) *Confidentiality of settlement discussions.* All discussions between the parties and the settlement judge shall be off-the-record. No evidence regarding statements or conduct in the proceedings under this section is admissible in the instant proceeding or any subsequent administrative proceeding before the Department, except by stipulation of the parties. Documents disclosed in the settlement process may not be used in litigation unless obtained through appropriate discovery or subpoena. The settlement judge shall not discuss any aspect of the case with any administrative law judge or other person, nor be subpoe-

naed or called as a witness in any hearing of the case or any subsequent administrative proceedings before the Department with respect to any statement or conduct during the settlement discussions.

(9) *Contents of consent order or settlement agreement.* Any agreement disposing of all or part of the proceeding shall be written and signed by the parties. Such agreement shall conform to the requirements of paragraph (b) of this section.

(10) *Report of the settlement.* If a settlement is reached, the parties shall report to the presiding judge in writing within seven working days of the termination of negotiations. The report shall include a copy of the settlement agreement and/or proposed consent order. If a settlement is not reached, the parties shall report this to the presiding judge without further elaboration.

(11) *Review of agreement by presiding judge.* A settlement agreement arrived at with the help of a settlement judge shall be treated by the presiding judge as would be any other settlement agreement.

(12) *Non-reviewable decisions.* Decisions concerning whether a settlement judge should be appointed, the selection of a particular settlement judge, or the termination of proceedings under this section, are not subject to review by Department officials.

[48 FR 32538, July 15, 1983, as amended at 58 FR 38500, July 16, 1993]

§ 18.10 Parties, how designated.

(a) The term *party* whenever used in these rules shall include any natural person, corporation, association, firm, partnership, trustee, receiver, agency, public or private organization, or governmental agency. A party who seeks relief or other affirmative action shall be designated as *plaintiff, complainant* or *claimant,* as appropriate. A party against whom relief or other affirmative action is sought in any proceeding shall be designated as a *defendant* or *respondent,* as appropriate. When a party to the proceeding, the Department of Labor shall be either a party or party-in-interest.

(b) Other persons or organizations shall have the right to participate as parties if the administrative law judge determines that the final decision could directly and adversely affect them or the class they represent, and if they may contribute materially to the disposition of the proceedings and their interest is not adequately represented by existing parties.

(c) A person or organization wishing to participate as a party under this section shall submit a petition to the administrative law judge within fifteen (15) days after the person or organization has knowledge of or should have known about the proceeding. The petition shall be filed with the administrative law judge and served on each person or organization who has been made a party at the time of filing. Such petition shall concisely state: (1) Petitioner's interest in the proceeding, (2) how his or her participation as a party will contribute materially to the disposition of the proceeding, (3) who will appear for petitioner, (4) the issues on which petitioner wishes to participate, and (5) whether petitioner intends to present witnesses.

(d) If objections to the petition are filed, the administrative law judge shall then determine whether petitioners have the requisite interest to be a party in the proceedings, as defined in paragraphs (a) and (b) of this section, and shall permit or deny participation accordingly. Where petitions to participate as parties are made by individuals or groups with common interests, the administrative law judge may request all such petitioners to designate a single representative, or he or she may recognize one or more of such petitioners. The administrative law judge shall give each such petitioner written notice of the decision on his or her petition. If the petition is denied, he or she shall briefly state the grounds for denial and shall then treat the petition as a request for participation as amicus curiae. The administrative law judge shall give written notice to each party of each petition granted.

§ 18.11 Consolidation of hearings.

When two or more hearings are to be held, and the same or substantially similar evidence is relevant and material to the matters at issue at each such hearing, the Chief Administrative Law Judge or the administrative law judge assigned may, upon motion by any party or on his or her own motion, order that a consolidated hearing be conducted. Where consolidated hearings are held, a single record of the proceedings may be made and the evidence introduced in one matter may be considered as introduced in the others, and a separate or joint decision shall be made, at the discretion of the administrative law judge as appropriate.

§ 18.12 Amicus curiae.

A brief of an amicus curiae may be filed only with the written consent of all parties, or by leave of the administrative law judge granted upon motion, or on the request of the administrative law judge, except that consent or leave shall not be required when the brief is presented by an officer of an agency of the United States, or by a state, territory or commonwealth. The amicus curiae shall not participate in any way in the conduct of the hearing, including the presentation of evidence and the examination of witnesses.

§ 18.13 Discovery methods.

Parties may obtain discovery by one or more of the following methods: Depositions upon oral examination or written questions; written interrogatories; production of documents or other evidence for inspection and other purposes; and requests for admission. Unless the administrative law judge orders otherwise, the frequency or sequence of these methods is not limited.

§ 18.14 Scope of discovery.

(a) Unless otherwise limited by order of the administrative law judge in accordance with these rules, the parties may obtain discovery regarding any matter, not privileged, which is relevant to the subject matter involved in the proceeding, including the existence, description, nature, custody, condition, and location of any books, documents, or other tangible things and the identity and location of persons having knowledge of any discoverable matter.

(b) It is not ground for objection that information sought will not be admissible at the hearing if the information sought appears reasonably calculated to lead to the discovery of admissible evidence.

(c) A party may obtain discovery of documents and tangible things otherwise discoverable under paragraph (a) of this section and prepared in anticipation of or for the hearing by or for another party's representative (including his or her attorney, consultant, surety, indemnitor, insurer, or agent) only upon a showing that the party seeking discovery has substantial need of the materials in the preparation of his or her case and that he or she is unable without undue hardship to obtain the substantial equivalent of the materials by other means. In ordering discovery of such materials when the required showing has been made, the administrative law judge shall protect against disclosure of the mental impressions, conclusions, opinions, or legal theories of an attorney or other representative of a party concerning the proceeding.

§ 18.15 Protective orders.

(a) Upon motion by a party or the person from whom discovery is sought, and for good cause shown, the administrative law judge may make any order which justice requires to protect a party or person from annoyance, embarrassment, oppression, or undue burden or expense, including one or more of the following:

(1) The discovery not be had;

(2) The discovery may be had only on specified terms and conditions, including a designation of the time or place;

(3) The discovery may be had only by a method of discovery other than that selected by the party seeking discovery;

(4) Certain matters not relevant may not be inquired into, or that the scope of discovery be limited to certain matters;

(5) Discovery be conducted with no one present except persons designated by the administrative law judge; or

(6) A trade secret or other confidential research, development or commercial information may not be disclosed or be disclosed only in a designated way.

§ 18.16 Supplementation of responses.

A party who has responded to a request for discovery with a response that was complete when made is under no duty to supplement his response to include information thereafter acquired, except as follows:

(a) A party is under a duty to supplement timely his response with respect to any question directly addressed to:

(1) The identity and location of persons having knowledge of discoverable matters; and

(2) The identity of each person expected to be called as an expert witness at the hearing, the subject matter on which he or she is expected to testify and the substance of his or her testimony.

(b) A party is under a duty to amend timely a prior response if he or she later obtains information upon the basis of which:

(1) He or she knows the response was incorrect when made; or

(2) He or she knows that the response though correct when made is no longer true and the circumstances are such that a failure to amend the response is in substance a knowing concealment.

(c) A duty to supplement responses may be imposed by order of the administrative law judge or agreement of the parties.

§ 18.17 Stipulations regarding discovery.

Unless otherwise ordered, a written stipulation entered into by all the parties and filed with the Chief Administrative Law Judge or the adminis-

trative law judge assigned may: (a) Provide that depositions be taken before any person, at any time or place, upon sufficient notice, and in any manner and when so taken may be used like other depositions, and (b) modify the procedures provided by these rules for other methods of discovery.

§ 18.18 Written interrogatories to parties.

(a) Any party may serve upon any other party written interrogatories to be answered in writing by the party served, or if the party served is a public or private corporation or a partnership or association or governmental agency, by any authorized officer or agent, who shall furnish such information as is available to the party. A copy of the interrogatories, answers, and all related pleadings shall be served on all parties to the proceeding. Copies of interrogatories and responses thereto shall not be filed with the Office of Administrative Law Judges unless the presiding judge so orders, the document is being offered into evidence, the document is submitted in support of a motion or a response to a motion, filing is required by a specialized rule, or there is some other compelling reason for its submission.

(b) Each interrogatory shall be answered separately and fully in writing under oath or affirmation, unless it is objected to, in which event the reasons for objection shall be stated in lieu of an answer. The answers and objections shall be signed by the person making them. The party upon whom the interrogatories were served shall serve a copy of the answer and objections upon all parties to the proceeding within thirty (30) days after service of the interrogatories, or within such shorter or longer period as the administrative law judge may allow.

(c) An interrogatory otherwise proper is not necessarily objectionable merely because an answer to the interrogatory involves an opinion or contention that relates to fact or the application of law to fact, but the administrative law judge may order that such an interrogatory need not be answered until after designated discovery has been completed or until a pre-hearing conference or other later time.

[48 FR 32538, July 15, 1983, as amended at 59 FR 41877, Aug. 15, 1994]

§ 18.19 Production of documents and other evidence; entry upon land for inspection and other purposes; and physical and mental examination.

(a) Any party may serve on any other party a

request to:

(1) Produce and permit the party making the request, or a person acting on his or her behalf, to inspect and copy any designated documents, or to inspect and copy, test, or sample any tangible things which are in the possession, custody, or control of the party upon whom the request is served; or

(2) Permit entry upon designated land or other property in the possession or control of the party upon whom the request is served for the purpose of inspection and measuring, photographing, testing, or for other purposes as stated in paragraph (a)(1) of this section.

(3) Submit to a physical or mental examination by a physician.

(b) The request may be served on any party without leave of the administrative law judge.

(c) The request shall:

(1) Set forth the items to be inspected either by individual item or by category;

(2) Describe each item or category with reasonable particularity;

(3) Specify a reasonable time, place, and manner of making the inspection and performing the related acts;

(4) Specify the time, place, manner, conditions, and scope of the physical or mental examination and the person or persons by whom it is to be made. A report of examining physician shall be made in accordance with Rule 35(b) of the Federal Rules of Civil Procedure, title 28 U.S.C., as amended.

(d) The party upon whom the request is served shall serve on the party submitting the request a written response within thirty (30) days after service of the request.

(e) The response shall state, with respect to each item or category:

(1) That inspection and related activities will be permitted as requested; or

(2) That objection is made in whole or in part, in which case the reasons for objection shall be stated.

(f) A copy of each request for production and each written response shall be served on all parties, but shall not be filed with the Office of Administrative Law Judges unless the presiding judge so orders, the document is being offered into evidence, the document is submitted in support of a motion or a response to a motion, filing is required by a specialized rule, or there is some other compelling reason for its submission. [48 FR 32538, July 15, 1983, as amended at 59 FR 41877, Aug. 15, 1994]

§ 18.20 Admissions.

(a) A party may serve upon any other party a written request for the admission, for purposes of the pending action only, of the genuineness and authenticity of any relevant document described in or attached to the request, or for the admission of the truth of any specified relevant matter of fact.

(b) Each matter of which an admission is requested is admitted unless, within thirty (30) days after service of the request or such shorter or longer time as the administrative law judge may allow, the party to whom the request is directed serves on the requesting party:

(1) A written statement denying specifically the relevant matters of which an admission is requested;

(2) A written statement setting forth in detail the reasons why he or she can neither truthfully admit nor deny them; or

(3) Written objections on the ground that some or all of the matters involved are privileged or irrelevant or that the request is otherwise improper in whole or in part.

(c) An answering party may not give lack of information or knowledge as a reason for failure to admit or deny unless the party states that he or she has made reasonable inquiry and that the information known or readily obtainable by him or her is insufficient to enable the party to admit or deny.

(d) The party who has requested the admissions may move to determine the sufficiency of the answers or objections. Unless the administrative law judge determines that an objection is justified, he or she shall order that an answer be served. If the administrative law judge determines that an answer does not comply with the requirements of this section, he or she may order either that the matter is admitted or that an amended answer be served. The administrative law judge may, in lieu of these orders, determine that final disposition of the request be made at a pre-hearing conference or at a designated time prior to hearing.

(e) Any matter admitted under this section is conclusively established unless the administrative law judge on motion permits withdrawal or amendment of the admission.

(f) Any admission made by a party under this section is for the purpose of the pending action only and is not an admission by him or her for any other purpose nor may it be used against him or her in any other proceeding.

(g) A copy of each request for admission and each written response shall be served on all parties, but shall not be filed with the Office of Administrative Law Judges unless the presiding judge so orders, the document is being offered into evidence, the document is submitted in support of a motion or a response to a motion, filing is required by a specialized rule, or there is some other compelling reason for its submission.

[48 FR 32538, July 15, 1983, as amended at 59 FR 41877, Aug. 15, 1994]

§ 18.21 Motion to compel discovery.

(a) If a deponent fails to answer a question propounded or a party upon whom a request is made pursuant to §§ 18.18 through 18.20, or a party upon whom interrogatories are served fails to respond adequately or objects to the request, or any part thereof, or fails to permit inspection as requested, the discovering party may move the administrative law judge for an order compelling a response or inspection in accordance with the request.

(b) The motion shall set forth:

(1) The nature of the questions or request;

(2) The response or objections of the party upon whom the request was served; and

(3) Arguments in support of the motion.

(c) For purposes of this section, an evasive answer or incomplete answer or response shall be treated as a failure to answer or respond.

(d) In ruling on a motion made pursuant to this section, the administrative law judge may make and enter a protective order such as he or she is authorized to enter on a motion made pursuant to § 18.15(a).

§ 18.22 Depositions.

(a) *When, how, and by whom taken.* The deposition of any witness may be taken at any stage of the proceeding at reasonable times. Depositions may be taken by oral examination or upon written interrogatories before any person having power to administer oaths.

(b) *Application.* Any party desiring to take the deposition of a witness shall indicate to the witness and all other parties the time when, the place where, and the name and post office address of the person before whom the deposition is to be taken; the name and address of each witness; and the subject matter concerning which each such witness is expected to testify.

(c) *Notice.* Notice shall be given for the taking of a deposition, which shall not be less than five (5) days written notice when the deposition is to be taken within the continental United States and not less than twenty (20) days written notice when the

deposition is to be taken elsewhere. A copy of the Notice shall not be filed with the Office of Administrative Law Judges unless the presiding judge so orders, the document is being offered into evidence, the document is submitted in support of a motion or a response to a motion, filing is required by a specialized rule, or there is some other compelling reason for its submission.

(d) *Taking and receiving in evidence.* Each witness testifying upon deposition shall be sworn, and any other party shall have the right to cross-examine. The questions propounded and the answers thereto, together with all objections made, shall be reduced to writing; read by or to, and subscribed by the witness; and certified by the person administering the oath. Subject to such objections to the questions and answers as were noted at the time of taking the deposition and which would have been valid if the witness were personally present and testifying, such deposition may be read and offered in evidence by the party taking it as against any party who was present or represented at the taking of the deposition or who had due notice thereof.

(e) *Motion to terminate or limit examination.* During the taking of a deposition, a party or deponent may request suspension of the deposition on grounds of bad faith in the conduct of the examination, oppression of a deponent or party or improper questions propounded. The deposition will then be adjourned. However, the objecting party or deponent must immediately move the administrative law judge for a ruling on his or her objections to the deposition conduct or proceedings. The administrative law judge may then limit the scope or manner of the taking of the deposition.

[48 FR 32538, July 15, 1983; 49 FR 2739, Jan. 20, 1984; 59 FR 41877, Aug. 15, 1994]

§ 18.23 Use of depositions at hearings.

(a) *Generally.* At the hearing, any part or all of a deposition, so far as admissible under the rules of evidence, may be used against any party who was present or represented at the taking of the deposition or who had due notice thereof in accordance with any one of the following provisions:

(1) Any deposition may be used by any party for the purpose of contradicting or impeaching the testimony of the deponent as a witness.

(2) The deposition of expert witnesses, particularly the deposition of physicians, may be used by any party for any purpose, unless the administrative law judge rules that such use would be unfair or a violation of due process.

(3) The deposition of a party or of anyone who at the time of taking the deposition was an officer, director, or duly authorized agent of a public or private corporation, partnership, or association which is a party, may be used by any other party for any purpose.

(4) The deposition of a witness, whether or not a party, may be used by any party for any purpose if the presiding officer finds:

(i) That the witness is dead; or

(ii) That the witness is out of the United States or more than 100 miles from the place of hearing unless it appears that the absence of the witness was procured by the party offering the deposition; or

(iii) That the witness is unable to attend to testify because of age, sickness, infirmity, or imprisonment; or

(iv) That the party offering the deposition has been unable to procure the attendance of the witness by subpoena; or

(v) Upon application and notice, that such exceptional circumstances exist as to make it desirable, in the interest of justice and with due regard to the importance of presenting the testimony of witnesses orally in open hearing, to allow the deposition to be used.

(5) If only part of a deposition is offered in evidence by a party, any other party may require him or her to introduce all of it which is relevant to the part introduced, and any party may introduce any other parts.

(6) Substitution of parties does not affect the right to use depositions previously taken; and, when a proceeding in any hearing has been dismissed and another proceeding involving the same subject matter is afterward brought between the same parties or their representatives or successors in interest, all depositions lawfully taken and duly filed in the former proceeding may be used in the latter as if originally taken therefor.

(b) *Objections to admissibility.* Except as provided in this paragraph, objection may be made at the hearing to receiving in evidence any deposition or part thereof for any reason which would require the exclusion of the evidence if the witness were then present and testifying.

(1) Objections to the competency of a witness or to the competency, relevancy, or materiality of testimony are not waived by failure to make them before or during the taking of the deposition, unless the ground of the objection is one which might have been obviated or removed if presented at that time.

(2) Errors and irregularities occurring at the oral examination in the manner of taking the deposition, in the form of the questions or answers, in the oath or affirmation, or in the conduct of parties and errors of any kind which might be obviated, removed, or cured if promptly presented, are waived unless reasonable objection thereto is made at the taking of the deposition.

(3) Objections to the form or written interrogatories are waived unless served in writing upon the party propounding them.

(c) *Effect of taking or using depositions.*

A party shall not be deemed to make a person his or her own witness for any purpose by taking his or her deposition. The introduction in evidence of the deposition or any part thereof for any purpose other than that of contradicting or impeaching the deponent makes the deponent the witness of the party introducing the deposition, but this shall not apply to the use by any other party of a deposition as described in paragraph (a)(2) of this section. At the hearing, any party may rebut any relevant evidence contained in a deposition whether introduced by him or her or by any other party.

§ 18.24 Subpoenas.

(a) Except as provided in paragraph

(b) of this section, the Chief Administrative Law Judge or the presiding administrative law judge, as appropriate, may issue subpoenas as authorized by statute or law upon written application of a party requiring attendance of witnesses and production of relevant papers, books, documents, or tangible things in their possession and under their control. A subpoena may be served by certified mail or by any person who is not less than 18 years of age. A witness, other than a witness for the Federal Government, may not be required to attend a deposition or hearing unless the mileage and witness fee applicable to witnesses in courts of the United States for each date of attendance is paid in advance of the date of the proceeding.

(b) If a party's written application for subpoena is submitted three (3) working days or less before the hearing to which it relates, a subpoena shall issue at the discretion of the Chief Administrative Law Judge or presiding administrative law judge, as appropriate.

(c) *Motion to quash or limit subpoena.* Within ten (10) days of receipt of a subpoena but no later than the date of the hearing, the person against whom it is directed may file a motion to quash or limit the subpoena, setting forth the reasons why the subpoena should be withdrawn or why it should by limited in scope. Any such motion shall be answered within ten (10) days of service, and shall be ruled on immediately thereafter. The order shall specify the date, if any, for compliance with the specifications of the subpoena.

(d) *Failure to comply.* Upon the failure of any person to comply with an order to testify or a subpoena, the party adversely affected by such failure to comply may, where authorized by statute or by law, apply to the appropriate district court for enforcement of the order or subpoena.

§ 18.25 Designation of administrative law judge.

Hearings shall be held before an administrative law judge appointed under 5 U.S.C. 3105 and assigned to the Department of Labor. The presiding judge shall be designated by the Chief Administrative Law Judge.

§ 18.26 Conduct of hearings.

Unless otherwise required by statute or regulations, hearings shall be conducted in conformance with the Administrative Procedure Act, 5 U.S.C. 554.

§ 18.27 Notice of hearing.

(a) *Generally.* Except when hearings are scheduled by calendar call, the administrative law judge to whom the matter is referred shall notify the parties by mail of a day, time, and place set for hearing thereon or for a pre-hearing conference, or both. No date earlier than fifteen (15) days after the date of such notice shall be set for such hearing or conference, except by agreement of the parties. Service of such notice shall be made by regular, first-class mail, unless under the circumstances it appears to the administrative law judge that certified mail, mailgram, telephone, or any combination of these methods should be used instead.

(b) *Change of date, time and place.* The Chief Administrative Law Judge or the administrative law judge assigned to the case may change the time, date and place of the hearing, or temporarily adjourn a hearing, on his or her own motion or for good cause shown by a party. The parties shall be given not less than ten (10) days notice of the new hearing date, unless they agree to such change without such notice.

(c) *Place of hearing.* Unless otherwise required by statute or regulation, due regard shall be given to the convenience of the parties and the witnesses in selecting a place for the hearing.

§ 18.28 Continuances.

(a) *When granted.* Continuances will only by granted in cases of prior judicial commitments or undue hardship, or a showing of other good cause.

(b) *Time limit for requesting.* Except for good cause arising thereafter, requests for continuances must be filed within fourteen (14) days prior to the date set for hearing.

(c) *How filed.* Motions for continuances shall be in writing. At least 3" x 3 1/2" of blank space shall be provided on the last page of the motion to permit space for the entry of an order by the administrative law judge. Copies shall be served on all parties. Any motions for continuances made within ten (10) days of the date of the scheduled proceeding shall, in addition to the written request, be telephonically conveyed to the administrative law judge or a member of his or her staff and to all other parties. Motions for continuances, based on reasons not reasonably ascertainable prior thereto, may also be made on the record at calendar calls, pre-hearing conferences or hearings.

(d) *Ruling.* Time permitting, the administrative law judge shall issue a written order in advance of the scheduled proceeding date which either allows or denies the request. Otherwise the ruling may be made orally by telephonic communication to the party requesting same who shall be responsible for telephonically notifying all other parties. Oral orders shall be confirmed in writing. [48 FR 32538, July 15, 1983; 49 FR 2739, Jan. 20, 1984]

§ 18.29 Authority of administrative law judge.

(a) *General powers.* In any proceeding under this part, the administrative law judge shall have all powers necessary to the conduct of fair and impartial hearings, including, but not limited to, the following:

(1) Conduct formal hearings in accordance with the provisions of this part;

(2) Administer oaths and examine witnesses;

(3) Compel the production of documents and appearance of witnesses in control of the parties;

(4) Compel the appearance of witnesses by the issuance of subpoenas as authorized by statute or law;

(5) Issue decisions and orders;

(6) Take any action authorized by the Administrative Procedure Act;

(7) Exercise, for the purpose of the hearing and in regulating the conduct of the proceeding, such powers vested in the Secretary of Labor as are

necessary and appropriate therefor:

(8) Where applicable, take any appropriate action authorized by the Rules of Civil Procedure for the United States District Courts, issued from time to time and amended pursuant to 28 U.S.C. 2072; and

(9) Do all other things necessary to enable him or her to discharge the duties of the office.

(b) *Enforcement.* If any person in proceedings before an adjudication officer disobeys or resists any lawful order or process, or misbehaves during a hearing or so near the place thereof as to obstruct the same, or neglects to produce, after having been ordered to do so, any pertinent book, paper or document, or refuses to appear after having been subpoenaed, or upon appearing refuses to take the oath as a witness, or after having taken the oath refuses to be examined according to law, the administrative law judge responsible for the adjudication, where authorized by statute or law, may certify the facts to the Federal District Court having jurisdiction in the place in which he or she is sitting to request appropriate remedies.

§ 18.30 Unavailability of administrative law judge.

In the event the administrative law judge designated to conduct the hearing becomes unavailable, the Chief Administrative Law Judge may designate another administrative law judge for the purpose of further hearing or other appropriate action.

§ 18.31 Disqualification.

(a) When an administrative law judge deems himself or herself disqualified to preside in a particular proceeding, such judge shall withdraw therefrom by notice on the record directed to the Chief Administrative Law Judge.

(b) Whenever any party shall deem the administrative law judge for any reason to be disqualified to preside, or to continue to preside, in a particular proceeding, that party shall file with the administrative law judge a motion to recuse. The motion shall be supported by an affidavit setting forth the alleged grounds for disqualification. The administrative law judge shall rule upon the motion.

(c) In the event of disqualification or recusal of an administrative law judge as provided in paragraph (a) or (b) of this section, the Chief Administrative Law Judge shall refer the matter to another administrative law judge for further proceedings.

§ 18.32 Separation of functions.

No officer, employee, or agent of the Federal Government engaged in the performance of investigative or prosecutorial functions in connection with any proceeding shall, in that proceeding or a factually related proceeding, participate or advise in the decision of the administrative law judge, except as a witness or counsel in the proceedings.

§ 18.33 Expedition.

Hearings shall proceed with all reasonable speed, insofar as practicable and with due regard to the convenience of the parties.

§ 18.34 Representation.

(a) *Appearances.* Any party shall have the right to appear at a hearing in person, by counsel, or by other representative, to examine and cross-examine witnesses, and to introduce into the record documentary or other relevant evidence, except that the participation of any intervenor shall be limited to the extent prescribed by the administrative law judge.

(b) Each attorney or other representative shall file a notice of appearance. Such notice shall indicate the name of the case or controversy, the docket number if assigned, and the party on whose behalf the appearance is made.

(c) *Rights of parties.* Every party shall have the right of timely notice and all other rights essential to a fair hearing, including, but not limited to, the rights to present evidence, to conduct such cross-examination as may be necessary for a full and complete disclosure of the facts, and to be heard by objection, motion, and argument.

(d) *Rights of participants.* Every participant shall have the right to make a written or oral statement of position. At the discretion of the administrative law judge, participants may file proposed findings of fact, conclusions of law and a post hearing brief. (e) *Rights of witnesses.* Any person compelled to testify in a proceeding in response to a subpoena may be accompanied, represented, and advised by counsel or other representative, and may purchase a transcript of his or her testimony. (f) *Office of the Solicitor.* The Department of Labor shall be represented by the Solicitor of Labor or his or her designee and shall participate to the degree deemed appropriate by the Solicitor. (g) *Qualifications.* (1) *Attorneys.* An attorney at law who is admitted to practice before the Federal courts or before the highest court of any State, the District of Columbia, or any territory or commonwealth of the United States, may practice before the Office of Administrative Law Judges. An attorney's own representation that he or she is in good standing before any of such courts shall be sufficient proof thereof, unless otherwise ordered by the administrative law judge. Any attorney of record must file prior notice in writing of intent to withdraw as counsel.

(2) *Persons not attorneys.* Any citizen of the United States who is not an attorney at law shall be admitted to appear in a representative capacity in an adjudicative proceeding. An application by a person not an attorney at law for admission to appear in a proceeding shall be submitted in writing to the Chief Administrative Law Judge prior to the hearing in the proceedings or to the administrative law judge assigned at the commencement of the hearing. The application shall state generally the applicant's qualifications to appear in the proceedings. The administrative law judge may, at any time, inquire as to the qualification or ability of such person to render legal assistance.

(3) *Denial of authority to appear.* The administrative law judge may deny the privilege of appearing to any person, within applicable statutory constraints, e.g. 5 U.S.C. 555, who he or she finds after notice of and opportunity for hearing in the matter does not possess the requisite qualifications to represent others; or is lacking in character or integrity; has engaged in unethical or improper professional conduct; or has engaged in an act involving moral turpitude. No provision hereof shall apply to any person who appears on his or her own behalf or on behalf of any corporation, partnership, or association of which the person is a partner, officer, or regular employee.

(h) *Authority for representation.* Any individual acting in a representative capacity in any adjudicative proceeding may be required by the administrative law judge to show his or her authority to act in such capacity. A regular employee of a party who appears on behalf of the party may be required by the administrative law judge to show his or her authority to so appear.
[48 FR 32538, July 15, 1983; 49 FR 2739, Jan. 20, 1984]

§ 18.35 Legal assistance.

The Office of Administrative Law Judges does not have authority to appoint counsel, nor does it refer parties to attorneys.

§ 18.36 Standards of conduct.

(a) All persons appearing in proceedings before an administrative law judge are expected to act

with integrity, and in an ethical manner.

(b) The administrative law judge may exclude parties, participants, and their representatives for refusal to comply with directions, continued use of dilatory tactics, refusal to adhere to reasonable standards of orderly and ethical conduct, failure to act in good faith, or violation of the prohibition against ex parte communications. The administrative law judge shall state in the record the cause for suspending or barring an attorney or other representative from participation in a particular proceeding. Any attorney or other representative so suspended or barred may appeal to the Chief Judge but no proceeding shall be delayed or suspended pending disposition of the appeal; provided, however, that the administrative law judge shall suspend the proceeding for a reasonable time for the purpose of enabling the party to obtain another attorney or representative.

§ 18.37 Hearing room conduct.

Proceedings shall be conducted in an orderly manner. The consumption of food or beverage, smoking, or rearranging of courtroom furniture, unless specifically authorized by the administrative law judge, are prohibited.
[48 FR 32538, July 15, 1983; 49 FR 2739, Jan. 20, 1984]

§ 18.38 Ex parte communications.

(a) The administrative law judge shall not consult any person, or party, on any fact in issue unless upon notice and opportunity for all parties to participate. Communications by the Office of Administrative Law Judges, the assigned judge, or any party for the sole purpose of scheduling hearings or requesting extensions of time are not considered ex parte communications, except that all other parties shall be notified of such request by the requesting party and be given an opportunity to respond thereto.

(b) *Sanctions.* A party or participant who makes a prohibited ex parte communication, or who encourages or solicits another to make any such communication, may be subject to any appropriate sanction or sanctions, including, but not limited to, exclusion from the proceedings and adverse ruling on the issue which is the subject of the prohibited communication.

§ 18.39 Waiver of right to appear and failure to participate or to appear.

(a) *Waiver of right to appear.* If all parties waive their right to appear before the administrative law judge or to present evidence or argument personally or by representative, it shall not be necessary for the administrative law judge to give notice of and conduct an oral hearing. A waiver of the right to appear and present evidence and allegations as to facts and law shall be made in writing and filed with the Chief Administrative Law Judge or the administrative law judge. Where such a waiver has been filed by all parties and they do not appear before the administrative law judge personally or by representative, the administrative law judge shall make a record of the relevant written evidence submitted by the parties, together with any pleadings they may submit with respect to the issues in the case. Such documents shall be considered as all of the evidence in the case, and the decision shall be based on them.

(b) *Dismissal—Abandonment by Party.* A request for hearing may be dismissed upon its abandonment or settlement by the party or parties who filed it. A party shall be deemed to have abandoned a request for hearing if neither the party nor his or her representative appears at the time and place fixed for the hearing and either (a) prior to the time for hearing such party does not show good cause as to why neither he or she nor his or her representative can appear or (b) within ten (10) days after the mailing of a notice to him or her by the administrative law judge to show cause, such party does not show good cause for such failure to appear and fails to notify the administrative law judge prior to the time fixed for hearing that he or she cannot appear. A default decision, under § 18.5(b), may be entered against any party failing, without good cause, to appear at a hearing.

§ 18.40 Motion for summary decision.

(a) Any party may, at least twenty (20) days before the date fixed for any hearing, move with or without supporting affidavits for a summary decision on all or any part of the proceeding. Any other party may, within ten (10) days after service of the motion, serve opposing affidavits or countermove for summary decision. The administrative law judge may set the matter for argument and/or call for submission of briefs.

(b) Filing of any documents under paragraph (a) of this section shall be with the administrative law judge, and copies of such documents shall be served on all parties.

(c) Any affidavits submitted with the motion shall set forth such facts as would be admissible in evidence in a proceeding subject to 5 U.S.C. 556 and 557 and shall show affirmatively that the affiant is competent to testify to the matters stated

therein. When a motion for summary decision is made and supported as provided in this section, a party opposing the motion may not rest upon the mere allegations or denials of such pleading. Such response must set forth specific facts showing that there is a genuine issue of fact for the hearing.

(d) The administrative law judge may enter summary judgment for either party if the pleadings, affidavits, material obtained by discovery or otherwise, or matters officially noticed show that there is no genuine issue as to any material fact and that a party is entitled to summary decision. The administrative law judge may deny the motion whenever the moving party denies access to information by means of discovery to a party opposing the motion.

§ 18.41 Summary decision.

(a) *No genuine issue of material fact.* (1) Where no genuine issue of a material fact is found to have been raised, the administrative law judge may issue a decision to become final as provided by the statute or regulations under which the matter is to be heard. Any final decision issued as a summary decision shall conform to the requirements for all final decisions.

(2) An initial decision and a final decision made under this paragraph shall include a statement of:

(i) Findings of fact and conclusions of law, and the reasons therefor, on all issues presented; and

(ii) Any terms and conditions of the rule or order.

(3) A copy of any initial decision and final decision under this paragraph shall be served on each party.

(b) *Hearings on issue of fact.* Where a genuine question of material fact is raised, the administrative law judge shall, and in any other case may, set the case for an evidentiary hearing.

§ 18.42 Expedited proceedings.

(a) When expedited proceedings are required by statute or regulation, or at any time after commencement of a proceeding, any party may move to advance the scheduling of a proceeding.

(b) Except when such proceedings are required or as otherwise directed by the Chief Administrative Law Judge or the administrative law judge assigned, any party filing a motion under this section shall:

(1) Make the motion in writing;

(2) Describe the circumstances justifying advancement;

(3) Describe the irreparable harm that would result if the motion is not granted; and

(4) Incorporate in the motion affidavits to support

any representations of fact.

(c) Service of a motion under this section shall be accomplished by personal delivery or by telephonic or telegraphic communication followed by mail. Service is complete upon personal delivery or mailing.

(d) Except when such proceedings are required, or unless otherwise directed by the Chief Administrative Law Judge or the administrative law judge assigned, all parties to the proceeding in which the motion is filed shall have ten (10) days from the date of service of the motion to file an opposition in response to the motion.

(e) Following the timely receipt by the administrative law judge of statements in response to the motion, the administrative law judge may advance pleading schedules, pre-hearing conferences, and the hearing, as deemed appropriate: provided, however, that a hearing on the merits shall not be scheduled with less than five (5) working days notice to the parties, unless all parties consent to an earlier hearing.

(f) When expedited hearings are required by statute or regulation, such hearing shall be scheduled within sixty (60) days from the receipt of request for hearing or order of reference. The decision of the administrative law judge shall be issued within twenty (20) days after receipt of the transcript of any oral hearing or within twenty (20) days after the filing of all documentary evidence if no oral hearing is conducted.

§ 18.43 Formal hearings.

(a) *Public.* Hearings shall be open to the public. However, in unusual circumstances, the administrative law judge may order a hearing or any part thereof closed, where to do so would be in the best interests of the parties, a witness, the public or other affected persons. Any order closing the hearing shall set forth the reasons for the decision. Any objections thereto shall be made a part of the record.

(b) *Jurisdiction.* The administrative law judge shall have jurisdiction to decide all issues of fact and related issues of law.

(c) *Amendments to conform to the evidence.* When issues not raised by the request for hearing, pre-hearing stipulation, or pre-hearing order are tried by express or implied consent of the parties, they shall be treated in all respects as if they had been raised in the pleadings. Such amendment of the pleadings as may be necessary to cause them to conform to the evidence may be made on motion of any party at any time: but failure to so amend does not affect the result of the hearing of

these issues. The administrative law judge may grant a continuance to enable the objecting party to meet such evidence.

§ 18.44 [Reserved]
§ 18.45 Official notice.

Official notice may be taken of any material fact, not appearing in evidence in the record, which is among the traditional matters of judicial notice: Provided, however, that the parties shall be given adequate notice, at the hearing or by reference in the administrative law judge's decision, of the matters so noticed, and shall be given adequate opportunity to show the contrary.

§ 18.46 In camera and protective orders.

(a) *Privileges.* Upon application of any person the administrative law judge may limit discovery or introduction of evidence or issue such protective or other orders as in his or her judgment may be consistent with the objective of protecting privileged communications.

(b) *Classified or sensitive matter.* (1) Without limiting the discretion of the administrative law judge to give effect to any other applicable privilege, it shall be proper for the administrative law judge to limit discovery or introduction of evidence or to issue such protective or other orders as in his or her judgment may be consistent with the objective of preventing undue disclosure of classified or sensitive matter. Where the administrative law judge determines that information in documents containing sensitive matter should be made available to a respondent, he or she may direct the party to prepare an unclassified or nonsensitive summary or extract of the original. The summary or extract may be admitted as evidence in the record.

(2) If the administrative law judge determines that this procedure is inadequate and that classified or otherwise sensitive matter must form part of the record in order to avoid prejudice to a party, he or she may advise the parties and provide opportunity for arrangements to permit a party or a representative to have access to such matter. Such arrangements may include obtaining security clearances or giving counsel for a party access to sensitive information and documents subject to assurances against further disclosure.

§ 18.47 Exhibits.

(a) *Identification.* All exhibits offered in evidence shall be numbered and marked with a designation identifying the party or intervenor by whom the exhibit is offered. (b) *Exchange of exhibits.* When written exhibits are offered in evidence, one copy must be furnished to each of the parties at the hearing, and one copy to the administrative law judge, unless the parties previously have been furnished with copies or the administrative law judge directs otherwise. If the administrative law judge has not fixed a time for the exchange of exhibits the parties shall exchange copies of exhibits at the earliest practicable time, preferably before the hearing, or at the latest at the commencement of the hearing.

(c) *Substitution of copies for original exhibits.* The administrative law judge may permit a party to withdraw original documents offered in evidence and substitute true copies in lieu thereof.

§ 18.48 Records in other proceedings.

In case any portion of the record in any other proceeding or civil or criminal action is offered in evidence, a true copy of such portion shall be presented for the record in the form of an exhibit unless the administrative law judge directs otherwise.

§ 18.49 Designation of parts of documents.

Where relevant and material matter offered in evidence is embraced in a document containing other matter not material or relevant and not intended to be put in evidence, the participant offering the same shall plainly designate the matter so offered, segregating and excluding insofar as practicable the immaterial or irrelevant parts. If other matter in such document is in such bulk or extent as would necessarily encumber the record, such document will not be received in evidence, but may be marked for identification, and if properly authenticated, the relevant and material parts thereof may be read into the record, or if the administrative law judge so directs, a true copy of such matter in proper form shall be received in evidence as an exhibit, and copies shall be delivered by the participant offering the same to the other parties or their attorneys appearing at the hearing, who shall be afforded an opportunity to examine the entire document and to offer in evidence in like manner other material and relevant portions thereof.

§ 18.50 Authenticity.

The authenticity of all documents submitted as proposed exhibits in advance of the hearing shall be deemed admitted unless written objection thereto is filed prior to the hearing, except that a party will be permitted to challenge such authenticity at a later time upon a clear showing of good

cause for failure to have filed such written objection.

§ 18.51 Stipulations.

The parties may by stipulation in writing at any stage of the proceeding, or orally made at hearing, agree upon any pertinent facts in the proceeding. It is desirable that the facts be thus agreed upon so far as and whenever practicable. Stipulations may be received in evidence at a hearing or prior thereto, and when received in evidence, shall be binding on the parties thereto.

§ 18.52 Record of hearings.

(a) All hearings shall be mechanically or stenographically reported. All evidence upon which the administrative law judge relies for decision shall be contained in the transcript of testimony, either directly or by appropriate reference. All exhibits introduced as evidence shall be marked for identification and incorporated into the record. Transcripts may be obtained by the parties and the public from the official reporter at rates not to exceed the applicable rates fixed by the contract with the reporter.

(b) *Corrections.* Corrections to the official transcript will be permitted upon motion. Motions for correction must be submitted within ten (10) days of the receipt of the transcript unless additional time is permitted by the administrative law judge. Corrections of the official transcript will be permitted only when errors of substance are involved and only upon approval of the administrative law judge.

§ 18.53 Closing of hearings.

The administrative law judge may hear arguments of counsel and may limit the time of such arguments at his or her discretion, and may allow briefs to be filed on behalf of either party but shall closely limit the time within which the briefs for both parties shall be filed, so as to avoid unreasonable delay.

§ 18.54 Closing the record.

(a) When there is a hearing, the record shall be closed at the conclusion of the hearing unless the administrative law judge directs otherwise.

(b) If any party waives a hearing, the record shall be closed on the date set by the administrative law judge as the final date for the receipt of submissions of the parties to the matter.

(c) Once the record is closed, no additional evidence shall be accepted into the record except upon a showing that new and material evidence has become available which was not readily available prior to the closing of the record. However, the administrative law judge shall make part of the record, any motions for attorney fees authorized by statutes, and any supporting documentation, any determinations there-on, and any approved correction to the transcript.

§ 18.55 Receipt of documents after hearing.

Documents submitted for the record after the close of the hearing will not be received in evidence except upon ruling of the administrative law judge. Such documents when submitted shall be accompanied by proof that copies have been served upon all parties, who shall have an opportunity to comment thereon. Copies shall be received not later than twenty (20) days after the close of the hearing except for good cause shown, and not less than ten (10) days prior to the date set for filing briefs. Exhibit numbers should be assigned by counsel or the party.

§ 18.56 Restricted access.

On his or her own motion, or on the motion of any party, the administrative law judge may direct that there be a restricted access portion of the record to contain any material in the record to which public access is restricted by law or by the terms of a protective order entered in the proceedings. This portion of the record shall be placed in a separate file and clearly marked to avoid improper disclosure and to identify it as a portion of the official record in the proceedings.

§ 18.57 Decision of the administrative law judge.

(a) *Proposed findings of fact, conclusions, and order.* Within twenty (20) days of filing of the transcript of the testimony or such additional time as the administrative law judge may allow, each party may file with the administrative law judge, subject to the judge's discretion under § 18.55, proposed findings of fact, conclusions of law, and order together with a supporting brief expressing the reasons for such proposals. Such proposals and brief shall be served on all parties, and shall refer to all portions of the record and to all authorities relied upon in support of each proposal.

(b) *Decision of the administrative law judge.* Within a reasonable time after the time allowed for the filing of the proposed findings of fact, conclusions of law, and order, or within thirty (30) days after receipt of an agreement containing consent findings and order disposing of the disputed matter in whole, the administrative law

judge shall make his or her decision. The decision of the administrative law judge shall include findings of fact and conclusions of law, with reasons therefor, upon each material issue of fact or law presented on the record. The decision of the administrative law judge shall be based upon the whole record. It shall be supported by reliable and probative evidence. Such decision shall be in accordance with the regulations and rulings of the statute or regulation conferring jurisdiction.

§ 18.58 Appeals.

The procedures for appeals shall be as provided by the statute or regulation under which hearing jurisdiction is conferred. If no provision is made therefor, the decision of the administrative law judge shall become the final administrative decision of the Secretary.

§ 18.59 Certification of official record.

Upon timely receipt of either a notice or a petition, the Chief Administrative Law Judge shall promptly certify and file with the reviewing authority, appellate body, or appropriate United States District Court, a full, true, and correct copy of the entire record, including the transcript of proceedings.

Subpart B—Rules of Evidence

SOURCE: 55 FR 13219, Apr. 9, 1990, unless otherwise noted.

GENERAL PROVISIONS
§ 18.101 Scope.

These rules govern formal adversarial adjudications of the United States Department of Labor conducted before a presiding officer.

(a) Which are required by Act of Congress to be determined on the record after opportunity for an administrative agency hearing in accordance with the Administrative Procedure Act, 5 U.S.C. 554, 556 and 557, or

(b) Which by United States Department of Labor regulation are conducted in conformance with the foregoing provisions, to the extent and with the exceptions stated in § 18.1101. *Presiding officer,* referred to in these rules as *the judge,* means an Administrative Law Judge, an agency head, or other officer who presides at the reception of evidence at a hearing in such an adjudication.

§ 18.102 Purpose and construction.

These rules shall be construed to secure fairness in administration, elimination of unjustifiable expense and delay, and promotion of growth and development of the law of evidence to the end that the truth may be ascertained and proceedings justly determined.

§ 18.103 Rulings on evidence.

(a) *Effect of erroneous ruling.* Error may not be predicated upon a ruling which admits or excludes evidence unless a substantial right of the party is affected, and

(1) *Objection.* In case the ruling is one admitting evidence, a timely objection or motion to strike appears of record, stating the specific ground of objection, if the specific ground was not apparent from the context; or

(2) *Offer of proof.* In case the ruling is one excluding evidence, the substance of the evidence was made known to the judge by offer or was apparent from the context within which questions were asked. A substantial right of the party is affected unless it is more probably true than not true that the error did not materially contribute to the decision or order of the judge. Properly objected to evidence admitted in error does not affect a substantial right if explicitly not relied upon by the judge in support of the decision or order.

(b) *Record of offer and ruling.* The judge may add any other or further statement which shows the character of the evidence, the form in which it was offered, the objection made, and the ruling thereon. The judge may direct the making of an offer in question and answer form.

(c) *Plain error.* Nothing in this rule precludes taking notice of plain errors affecting substantial rights although they were not brought to the attention of the judge.

§ 18.104 Preliminary questions.

(a) *Questions of admissibility generally.* Preliminary questions concerning the qualification of a person to be a witness, the existence of a privilege, or the admissibility of evidence shall be determined by the judge, subject to the provisions of paragraph (b) of this section. In making such determination the judge is not bound by the rules of evidence except those with respect to privileges.

(b) *Relevance conditioned on fact.* When the relevancy of evidence depends upon the fulfillment of a condition of fact, the judge shall admit it upon, or subject to, the introduction of evidence sufficient to support a finding of the fulfillment of the condition.

(c) *Weight and credibility.* This rule does not limit the right of a party to introduce evidence relevant to weight or credibility.

§ 18.105 Limited admissibility.

When evidence which is admissible as to one party or for one purpose but not admissible as to another party or for another purpose is admitted, the judge, upon request, shall restrict the evidence to its proper scope.

§ 18.106 Remainder of or related writings or recorded statements.

When a writing or recorded statement or part thereof is introduced by a party, an adverse party may require the introduction at that time of any other part or any other writing or recorded statement which ought in fairness to be considered contemporaneously with it.

OFFICIAL NOTICE

§ 18.201 Official notice of adjudicative facts.

(a) *Scope of rule.* This rule governs only official notice of adjudicative facts.

(b) *Kinds of facts.* An officially noticed fact must be one not subject to reasonable dispute in that it is either:

(1) Generally known within the local area,

(2) Capable of accurate and ready determination by resort to sources whose accuracy cannot reasonably be questioned, or

(3) Derived from a not reasonably questioned scientific, medical or other technical process, technique, principle, or explanatory theory within the administrative agency's specialized field of knowledge.

(c) *When discretionary.* A judge may take official notice, whether requested or not.

(d) *When mandatory.* A judge shall take official notice if requested by a party and supplied with the necessary information.

(e) *Opportunity to be heard.* A party is entitled, upon timely request, to an opportunity to be heard as to the propriety of taking official notice and the tenor of the matter noticed. In the absence of prior notification, the request may be made after official notice has been taken.

(f) *Time of taking notice.* Official notice may be taken at any stage of the proceeding.

(g) *Effect of official notice.* An officially noticed fact is accepted as conclusive.

PRESUMPTIONS

§ 18.301 Presumptions in general.

Except as otherwise provided by Act of Congress, or by rules or regulations prescribed by the administrative agency pursuant to statutory authority, or pursuant to executive order, a presumption imposes on the party against whom it is directed the burden of going forward with evidence to rebut or meet the presumption, but does not shift to such party the burden of proof in the sense of the risk of non-persuasion, which remains throughout the trial upon the party on whom it was originally cast.

§ 18.302 Applicability of state law.

The effect of a presumption respecting a fact which is an element of a claim or defense as to which State law supplies the rule of decision is determined in accordance with State law.

RELEVANCY AND ITS LIMITS
§ 18.401 Definition of *relevant evidence*.

Relevant evidence means evidence having any tendency to make the existence of any fact that is of consequence to the determination of the action more probable or less probable than it would be without the evidence.

§ 18.402 Relevant evidence generally admissible; irrelevant evidence inadmissible.

All relevant evidence is admissible, except as otherwise provided by the Constitution of the United States, by Act of Congress, pursuant to executive order, by these rules, or by other rules or regulations prescribed by the administrative agency pursuant to statutory authority. Evidence which is not relevant is not admissible.

§ 18.403 Exclusion of relevant evidence on grounds of confusion or waste of time.

Although relevant, evidence may be excluded if its probative value is substantially outweighed by the danger of confusion of issues, or misleading the judge as trier of fact, or by considerations of undue delay, waste of time, or needless presentation of cumulative evidence.

§ 18.404 Character evidence not admissible to prove conduct; exceptions; other crimes.

(a) *Character evidence generally.* Evidence of a person's character or a trait of character is not admissible for the purpose of proving action in conformity therewith on a particular occasion, except evidence of the character of a witness, as provided in §§ 18.607, 18.608, and 18.609.

(b) *Other crimes, wrongs, or acts.* Evidence of other crimes, wrongs, or acts is not admissible to prove the character of a person in order to show action in conformity therewith. It may, however,

be admissible for other purposes, such as proof of motive, opportunity, intent, preparation, plan, knowledge, identity, or absence of mistake or accident.

§ 18.405 Methods of proving character.

(a) *Reputation of opinion.* In all cases in which evidence of character or a trait of character of a person is admissible, proof may be made by testimony as to reputation or by testimony in the form of an opinion. On cross-examination, inquiry is allowable into relevant specific instances of conduct.

(b) *Specific instances of conduct.* In cases in which character or a trait of character of a person is an essential element of a claim or defense, proof may also be made of specific instances of that person's conduct.

§ 18.406 Habit; routine practice.

Evidence of the habit of a person or of the routine practice of an organization, whether corroborated or not and regardless of the presence of eyewitnesses, is relevant to prove that the conduct of the person or organization on a particular occasion was in conformity with the habit or routine practice.

§ 18.407 Subsequent remedial measures.

When, after an event, measures are taken which, if taken previously, would have made the event less likely to occur, evidence of the subsequent measures is not admissible to prove negligence or culpable conduct in connection with the event. This rule does not require the exclusion of evidence of subsequent measures when offered for another purpose, such as proving ownership, control, or feasibility of precautionary measures, if controverted, or impeachment.

§ 18.408 Compromise and offers to compromise.

Evidence of furnishing or offering or promising to furnish, or of accepting or offering or promising to accept, a valuable consideration in compromising or attempting to compromise a claim which was disputed as to either validity or amount, is not admissible to prove liability for or invalidity of the claim or its amount. Evidence of conduct or statements made in compromise negotiations is likewise not admissible. This rule does not require the exclusion of any evidence otherwise discoverable merely because it is presented in the course of compromise negotiations. This rule does not require exclusion when the evidence is offered for another purpose, such as proving bias or prejudice of a witness, or negativing a contention of undue delay.

§ 18.409 Payment of medical and similar expenses.

Evidence of furnishing or offering or promising to pay medical, hospital, or similar expenses occasioned by an injury is not admissible to prove liability for the injury.

§ 18.410 Inadmissibility of pleas, plea discussion, and related statements.

Except as otherwise provided in this rule, evidence of the following is not admissible against the defendant who made the plea or was a participant in the plea discussions:

(a) A plea of guilty which was later withdrawn;

(b) A plea of nolo contendere;

(c) Any statement made in the course of any proceedings under Rule 11 of the Federal Rules of Criminal Procedure or comparable state procedure regarding either of the foregoing pleas; or

(d) Any statement made in the course of plea discussions with an attorney for the prosecuting authority which do not result in a plea of guilty or which result in a plea of guilty later withdrawn. However, such a statement is admissible in any proceeding wherein another statement made in the course of the same plea discussions has been introduced and the statement ought in fairness be considered contemporaneously with it.

§ 18.411 Liability insurance.

Evidence that a person was or was not insured against liability is not admissible upon the issue whether the person acted negligently or otherwise wrongfully. This rule does not require the exclusion of evidence of insurance against liability when offered for another purpose, such as proof of agency, ownership, or control, or bias or prejudice of a witness.

PRIVILEGES
§ 18.501 General rule.

Except as otherwise required by the Constitution of the United States, or provided by Act of Congress, or by rules or regulations prescribed by the administrative agency pursuant to statutory authority, or pursuant to executive order, the privilege of a witness, person, government, State, or political subdivision thereof shall be governed by the principles of the common law as they may be interpreted by the courts of the United States in the light of reason and experience. However with respect to an element of a claim or defense as to which State law supplies the rule of decision, the privilege of a witness, person, government, State, or political subdivision thereof shall be determined in accordance with State law.

WITNESSES
§ 18.601 General rule of competency.

Every person is competent to be a witness except as otherwise provided in these rules. However with respect to an element of a claim or defense as to which State law supplies the rule of decision, the competency of a witness shall be determined in accordance with State law.

§ 18.602 Lack of personal knowledge.

A witness may not testify to a matter unless evidence is introduced sufficient to support a finding that the witness has personal knowledge of the matter. Evidence to prove personal knowledge may, but need not, consist of the witness' own testimony. This rule is subject to the provisions of § 18.703, relating to opinion testimony by expert witnesses.

§ 18.603 Oath or affirmation.

Before testifying, every witness shall be required to declare that the witness will testify truthfully, by oath or affirmation administered in a form calculated to awaken the witness' conscience and impress the witness' mind with the duty to do so.

§ 18.604 Interpreters.

An interpreter is subject to the provisions of these rules relating to qualification as an expert and the administration of an oath or affirmation to make a true translation.

§ 18.605 Competency of judge as witness.

The judge presiding at the hearing may not testify in that hearing as a witness. No objection need be made in order to preserve the point.

§ 18.606 [Reserved]
§ 18.607 Who may impeach.

The credibility of a witness may be attacked by any party, including the party calling the witness.

§ 18.608 Evidence of character and conduct of witness.

(a) *Opinion and reputation evidence of character.* The credibility of a witness may be attacked or supported by evidence in the form of opinion or reputation, but subject to these limitations:

(1) The evidence may refer only to character for

truthfulness or untruthfulness, and

(2) Evidence of truthful character is admissible only after the character of the witness for truthfulness has been attacked by opinion or reputation evidence or otherwise.

(b) *Specific instances of conduct.* Specific instances of the conduct of a witness, for the purpose of attacking or supporting the witness' credibility, other than conviction of crime as provided in § 18.609, may not be proved by extrinsic evidence. They may, however, in the discretion of the judge, if probative of truthfulness or untruthfulness, be inquired into on cross-examination of the witness, concerning the witness' character for truthfulness or untruthfulness, or concerning the character for truthfulness or untruthfulness of another witness as to which character the witness being cross-examined has testified. The giving of testimony by any witness does not operate as a waiver of the witness' privilege against self-incrimination when examined with respect to matters which relate only to credibility.

§ 18.609 Impeachment by evidence of conviction of crime.

(a) *General rule.* For the purpose of attacking the credibility of a witness, evidence that the witness has been convicted of a crime shall be admitted if the crime was punishable by death or imprisonment in excess of one year under the law under which the witness was convicted, or involved dishonesty or false statement, regardless of the punishment.

(b) *Time limit.* Evidence of a conviction under this rule is not admissible if a period of more than ten years has elapsed since the date of the conviction or of the release of the witness from the confinement imposed for that conviction, whichever is the later date.

(c) *Effect of pardon, annulment, or certificate of rehabilitation.* Evidence of a conviction is not admissible under this rule if:

(1) The conviction has been the subject of a pardon, annulment, certificate of rehabilitation, or other equivalent procedure based on a finding of the rehabilitation of the person convicted, and that person has not been convicted of a subsequent crime which was punishable by death or imprisonment in excess of one year, or

(2) The conviction has been the subject of a pardon, annulment, or other equivalent procedure based on a finding of innocence.

(d) *Juvenile adjudications.* Evidence of juvenile adjudications is not admissible under this rule.

(e) *Pendency of appeal.* The pendency of an appeal therefrom does not render evidence of a conviction inadmissible. Evidence of the pendency of an appeal is admissible.

[55 FR 13219, Apr. 9, 1990; 55 FR 14033, Apr. 13, 1990]

§ 18.610 Religious beliefs or opinions.

Evidence of the beliefs or opinions of a witness on matters of religion is not admissible for the purpose of showing that by reason of their nature the witness' credibility is impaired or enhanced.

§ 18.611 Mode and order of interrogation and presentation.

(a) *Control by judge.* The judge shall exercise reasonable control over the mode and order of interrogating witnesses and presenting evidence so as to:

(1) Make the interrogation and presentation effective for the ascertainment of the truth,

(2) Avoid needless consumption of time, and

(3) Protect witnesses from harassment or undue embarrassment.

(b) *Scope of cross-examination.* Cross-examination should be limited to the subject matter of the direct examination and matters affecting the credibility of the witness. The judge may, in the exercise of discretion, permit inquiry into additional matters as if on direct examination.

(c) *Leading questions.* Leading questions should not be used on the direct examination of a witness except as may be necessary to develop the witness' testimony. Ordinarily leading questions should be permitted on cross-examination. When a party calls a hostile witness, an adverse party, or a witness identified with an adverse party, interrogation may be by leading questions.

§ 18.612 Writing used to refresh memory.

If a witness uses a writing to refresh memory for the purpose of testifying, either while testifying, or before testifying if the judge in the judge's discretion determines it is necessary in the interest of justice, an adverse party is entitled to have the writing produced at the hearing, to inspect it, to cross-examine the witness thereon, and to introduce in evidence those portions which relate to the testimony of the witness. If it is claimed that the writing contains matters not related to the subject matter of the testimony the judge shall examine the writing in camera, excise any portion not so related, and order delivery of the remainder to the party entitled thereto. Any portion withheld over objections shall be preserved and made available in the event of review. If a writing is not produced or delivered pursuant to order under this rule, the judge shall make any order justice requires.

§ 18.613 Prior statements of witnesses.

(a) *Examining witness concerning prior statement.* In examining a witness concerning a prior statement made by the witness, whether written or not, the statement need not be shown nor its contents disclosed to the witness at that time, but on request the same shall be shown or disclosed to opposing counsel.

(b) *Extrinsic evidence of prior inconsistent statement of witness.* Extrinsic evidence of a prior inconsistent statement by a witness is not admissible unless the witness is afforded an opportunity to explain or deny the same and the opposite party is afforded an opportunity to interrogate the witness thereon, or the interests of justice otherwise require. This provision does not apply to admissions of a party-opponent as defined in § 18.801(d)(2).

§ 18.614 Calling and interrogation of witnesses by judge.

(a) *Calling by the judge.* The judge may, on the judge's own motion or at the suggestion of a party, call witnesses, and all parties are entitled to cross-examine witnesses thus called.

(b) *Interrogation by the judge.* The judge may interrogate witnesses, whether called by the judge or by a party.

(c) *Objections.* Objections to the calling of witnesses by the judge or to interrogation by the judge must be timely.

§ 18.615 Exclusion of witnesses.

At the request of a party the judge shall order witnesses excluded so that they cannot hear the testimony of other witnesses, and the judge may make the order of the judge's own motion. This rule does not authorize exclusion of a party who is a natural person, or an officer or employee of a party which is not a natural person designated as its representative by its attorney, or a person whose presence is shown by a party to be essential to the presentation of the party's cause.

OPINIONS AND EXPERT TESTIMONY
§ 18.701 Opinion testimony by lay witnesses.

If the witness is not testifying as an expert, the witness' testimony in the form of opinions or inferences is limited to those opinions or inferences which are rationally based on the perception of the witness and helpful to a clear understanding of the witness' testimony or the determination of a fact in issue.

§ 18.702 Testimony by experts.

If scientific, technical, or other specialized knowledge will assist the judge as trier of fact to understand the evidence or to determine a fact in issue, a witness qualified as an expert by knowledge, skill, experience, training, or education, may testify thereto in the form of an opinion or otherwise.

§ 18.703 Bases of opinion testimony by experts.

The facts or data in the particular case upon which an expert bases an opinion or inference may be those perceived by or made known to the expert at or before the hearing. If of a type reasonably relied upon by experts in the particular field in forming opinions or inferences upon the subject, the facts or data need not be admissible in evidence.

§ 18.704 Opinion on ultimate issue.

Testimony in the form of an opinion or inference otherwise admissible is not objectionable because it embraces an ultimate issue to be decided by the judge as trier of fact.

§ 18.705 Disclosure of facts or data underlying expert opinion.

The expert may testify in terms of opinion or inference and give reasons therefor without prior disclosure of the underlying facts or data, unless the judge requires otherwise. The expert may in any event be required to disclose the underlying facts or data on cross-examination.

§ 18.706 Judge appointed experts.

(a) *Appointment.* The judge may on the judge's own motion or on the motion of any party enter an order to show cause why expert witnesses should not be appointed, and may request the parties to submit nominations. The judge may appoint any expert witnesses agreed upon by the parties, and may appoint expert witnesses of the judge's own selection. An expert witness shall not be appointed by the judge unless the witness consents to act. A witness so appointed shall be informed of the witness' duties by the judge in writing, a copy of which shall be filed with the clerk, or at a conference in which the parties shall have an opportunity to participate. A witness so appointed shall advise the parties of the witness' findings, if any; the witness' deposition may be taken by any party; and the witness may be called to testify by the judge or any party. The witness shall be subject to cross-examination by each party, including a party calling the witness.

(b) *Compensation.* Expert witnesses so appointed are entitled to reasonable compensation in whatever sum the judge may allow. The compensation thus fixed is payable from funds which may be provided by law in hearings involving just compensation under the fifth amendment. In other hearings the compensation shall be paid by the parties in such proportion and at such time as the judge directs, and thereafter charged in like manner as other costs.

(c) *Parties' experts of own selection.* Nothing in this rule limits the parties in calling expert witnesses of their own selection.

HEARSAY
§ 18.801 Definitions.

(a) *Statement.* A *statement* is (1) an oral or written assertion, or (2) non-verbal conduct of a person, if it is intended by the person as an assertion.

(b) *Declarant.* A *declarant* is a person who makes a statement.

(c) *Hearsay. Hearsay* is a statement, other than one made by the declarant while testifying at the hearing, offered in evidence to prove the truth of the matter asserted.

(d) *Statements which are not hearsay.* A statement is not hearsay if:

(1) *Prior statement by witness.* The declarant testifies at the hearing and is subject to cross-examination concerning the statement, and the statement is—

(i) Inconsistent with the declarant's testimony, or

(ii) Consistent with the declarant's testimony and is offered to rebut an express or implied charge against the declarant of recent fabrication or improper influence or motive, or

(iii) One of identification of a person made after perceiving the person; or

(2) *Admission by party-opponent.* The statement is offered against a party and is—

(i) The party's own statement in either an individual or a representative capacity, or

(ii) A statement of which the party has manifested an adoption or belief in its truth, or

(iii) A statement by a person authorized by the party to make a statement concerning the subject, or

(iv) A statement by the party's agent or servant concerning a matter within the scope of the agency or employment, made during the existence of the relationship, or

(v) A statement by a co-conspirator of a party during the course and in furtherance of the conspiracy.

§ 18.802 Hearsay rule.

Hearsay is not admissible except as provided by these rules, or by rules or regulations of the administrative agency prescribed pursuant to statutory authority, or pursuant to executive order, or by Act of Congress.

§ 18.803 Hearsay exceptions; availability of declarant immaterial.

(a) The following are not excluded by the hearsay rule, even though the declarant is available as a witness:

(1) *Present sense impression.* A statement describing or explaining an event or condition made while the declarant was perceiving the event or condition, or immediately thereafter.

(2) *Excited utterance.* A statement relating to a startling event or condition made while the declarant was under the stress of excitement caused by the event or condition.

(3) *Then existing mental, emotional, or physical condition.* A statement of the declarant's then existing state of mind, emotion, sensation, or physical condition (such as intent, plan, motive, design, mental feeling, pain, and bodily health), but not including a statement of memory or belief to prove the fact remembered or believed unless it relates to the execution, revocation, identification, or terms of declarant's will.

(4) *Statements for purposes of medical diagnosis or treatment.* Statements made for purposes of medical diagnosis or treatment and describing medical history, or past or present symptoms, pain, or sensations or the inception or general character of the cause or external source thereof insofar as reasonably pertinent to diagnosis or treatment.

(5) *Recorded recollection.* A memorandum or record concerning a matter about which a witness once had knowledge but now has insufficient recollection to enable the witness to testify fully and accurately, shown to have been made or adopted by the witness when the matter was fresh in the witness' memory and to reflect that knowledge correctly.

(6) *Records of regularly conducted activity.* A memorandum, report, record, or data compilation, in any form, of acts, events, conditions, opinions, or diagnoses, made at or near the time by, or from information transmitted by, a person with knowledge, if kept in the course of a regularly con-

ducted business activity, and if it was the regular practice of that business activity to make the memorandum, report, record, or data compilation, all as shown by the testimony of the custodian or other qualified witness, unless the source of information or the method or circumstances of preparation indicate lack of trustworthiness. The term *business* as used in this paragraph includes business, institution, association, profession, occupation, and calling of every kind, whether or not conducted for profit.

(7) *Absence of entry in records kept in accordance with the provisions of paragraph (6).* Evidence that a matter is not included in the memoranda reports, records, or data compilations, in any form, kept in accordance with the provisions of paragraph (6), to prove the non-occurrence or non-existence of the matter, if the matter was of a kind of which a memorandum, report, record, or data compilation was regularly made and preserved, unless the sources of information or other circumstances indicate lack of trustworthiness.

(8) *Public records and reports.* Records, reports, statements, or data compilations, in any form, of public offices or agencies, setting forth—

(i) The activities of the office or agency, or

(ii) Matters observed pursuant to duty imposed by law as to which matters there was a duty to report, or

(iii) Factual findings resulting from an investigation made pursuant to authority granted by law, unless the sources of information or other circumstances indicate lack of trust-worthiness.

(9) *Records of vital statistics.* Records or data compilations, in any form, of births, fetal deaths, deaths, or marriages, if the report thereof was made to a public office pursuant to requirements of law.

(10) *Absence of public record or entry.* To prove the absence of a record, report, statement, or data compilation, in any form, or the non-occurrence or non-existence of a matter of which a record, report, statement, or data compilation, in any form, was regularly made and preserved by a public office or agency, evidence in the form of a certification in accordance with § 18.902, or testimony, that diligent search failed to disclose the record, report, statement, or date compilation, or entry.

(11) *Records of religious organizations.* Statements of births, marriages, divorces, deaths, legitimacy, ancestry, relationship by blood or marriage, or other similar facts of personal or family history, contained in a regularly kept record of a religious organization.

(12) *Marriage, baptismal, and similar certificates.* Statements of fact contained in a certificate that the maker performed a marriage or other ceremony or administered a sacrament, made by a clergyman, public official, or other person authorized by the rules or practices of a religious organization or by law to perform the act certified, and purporting to have been issued at the time of the act or within a reasonable time thereafter.

(13) *Family records.* Statements of fact concerning personal or family history contained in family Bibles, genealogies, charts, engravings on rings, inscriptions on family portraits, engravings on urns, crypts, or tombstones, or the like.

(14) *Records of documents affecting an interest in property.* The record of a document purporting to establish or affect an interest in property, as proof of the content of the original recorded document and its execution and delivery by each person by whom it purports to have been executed, if the record is a record of a public office and an applicable statute authorizes the recording of documents of that kind in that office.

(15) *Statements in documents affecting an interest in property.* A statement contained in a document purporting to establish or affect an interest in property if the matter stated was relevant to the purpose of the document, unless dealings with the property since the document was made have been inconsistent with the truth of the statement or the purport of the document.

(16) *Statements in ancient documents.* Statements in a document in existence twenty years or more the authenticity of which is established.

(17) *Market reports, commercial publications.* Market quotations, tabulations, lists, directories, or other published compilations, generally used and relied upon by the public or by persons in particular occupations.

(18) *Learned treatises.* To the extent called to the attention of an expert witness upon cross-examination or relied upon by the expert witness in direct examination, statements contained in published treatises, periodicals, or pamphlets on a subject of history, medicine, or other science or art, established as a reliable authority by the testimony or admission of the witness or by other expert testimony or by official notice.

(19) *Reputation concerning personal or family history.* Reputation among members of a person's family by blood, adoption, or marriage, or among a person's associates, or in the community, concerning a person's birth, adoption, marriage,

divorce, death, legitimacy, relationship by blood, adoption, or marriage, ancestry, or other similar fact of personal or family history.

(20) *Reputation concerning boundaries or general history.* Reputation in a community, arising before the controversy, as to boundaries of or customs affecting lands in the community, and reputation as to events of general history important to the community or State or nation in which located.

(21) *Reputation as to character.* Reputation of a person's character among associates or in the community.

(22) *Judgment of previous conviction.* Evidence of a final judgment, entered after a trial or upon a plea of guilty (but not upon a plea of nolo contendere), adjudging a person guilty of a crime punishable by death or imprisonment in excess of one year, to prove any fact essential to sustain the judgment. The pendency of an appeal may be shown but does not affect admissibility.

(23) *Judgment as to personal, family, or general history, or boundaries.* Judgments as proof of matters of personal, family or general history, or boundaries, essential to the judgment, if the same would be provable by evidence of reputation.

(24) *Other exceptions.* A statement not specifically covered by any of the foregoing exceptions but having equivalent circumstantial guarantees of trust-worthiness to the aforementioned hearsay exceptions, if the judge determines that (i) the statement is offered as evidence of a material fact; (ii) the statement is more probative on the point for which it is offered than any other evidence which the proponent can procure through reasonable efforts; and (iii) the general purposes of these rules and the interests of justice will best be served by admission of the statement into evidence. However, a statement may not be admitted under this exception unless the proponent of it makes known to the adverse party sufficiently in advance of the hearing to provide the adverse party with a fair opportunity to prepare to meet it, the proponent's intention to offer the statement and the particulars of it, including the name and address of the declarant.

(25) *Self-authentication.* The self-authentication of documents and other items as provided in § 18.902.

(26) *Bills, estimates and reports.* In actions involving injury, illness, disease, death, disability, or physical or mental impairment, or damage to property, the following bills, estimates, and reports as relevant to prove the value and reasonableness of the charges for services, labor and materials stated therein and, where applicable, the necessity for furnishing the same, unless the sources of information or other circumstances indicate lack of trust-worthiness, provided that a copy of said bill, estimate, or report has been served upon the adverse party sufficiently in advance of the hearing to provide the adverse party with a fair opportunity to prepare to object or meet it:

(i) Hospital bills on the official letterhead or billhead of the hospital, when dated and itemized.

(ii) Bills of doctors and dentists, when dated and containing a statement showing the date of each visit and the charge therefor.

(iii) Bills of registered nurses, licensed practical nurses and physical therapists, or other licensed health care providers when dated and containing an itemized statement of the days and hours of service and charges therefor.

(iv) Bills for medicine, eyeglasses, prosthetic device, medical belts or similar items, when dated and itemized.

(v) Property repair bills or estimates, when dated and itemized, setting forth the charges for labor and material. In the case of an estimate, the party intending to offer the estimate shall forward with his notice to the adverse party, together with a copy of the estimate, a statement indicating whether or not the property was repaired, and, if so, whether the estimated repairs were made in full or in part and by whom, the cost thereof, together with a copy of the bill therefor.

(vi) Reports of past earnings, or of the rate of earnings and time lost from work or lost compensation, prepared by an employer on official letterhead, when dated and itemized. The adverse party may not dispute the authenticity, the value or reasonableness of such charges, the necessity therefor or the accuracy of the report, unless the adverse party files and serves written objection thereto sufficiently in advance of the hearing stating the objections, and the grounds thereof, that the adverse party will make if the bill, estimate, or reports is offered at the time of the hearing. An adverse party may call the author of the bill, estimate, or report as a witness and examine the witness as if under cross-examination.

(27) *Medical reports.* In actions involving injury, illness, disease, death, disability, or physical or mental impairment, doctor, hospital, laboratory and other medical reports, made for purposes of medical treatment, unless the sources of information or other circumstances indicate lack of trust-worthiness, provided that a copy of the report has been filed and served upon the adverse party

sufficiently in advance of the hearing to provide the adverse party with a fair opportunity to prepare to object or meet it. The adverse party may not object to the admissibility of the report unless the adverse party files and serves written objection thereto sufficiently in advance of the hearing stating the objections, and the grounds therefor, that the adverse party will make if the report is offered at the time of the hearing. An adverse party may call the author of the medical report as a witness and examine the witness as if under cross-examination.

(28) *Written reports of expert witnesses.* Written reports of an expert witness prepared with a view toward litigation, including but not limited to a diagnostic report of a physician, including inferences and opinions, when on official letterhead, when dated, when including a statement of the expert's qualifications, when including a summary of experience as an expert witness in litigation, when including the basic facts, data, and opinions forming the basis of the inferences or opinions, and when including the reasons for or explanation of the inferences and opinions, so far as admissible under rules of evidence applied as though the witness was then present and testifying, unless the sources of information or the method or circumstances of preparation indicate lack of trustworthiness, provided that a copy of the report has been filed and served upon the adverse party sufficiently in advance of the hearing to provide the adverse party with a fair opportunity to prepare to object or meet it. The adverse party may not object to the admissibility of the report unless the adverse party files and serves written objection thereto sufficiently in advance of the hearing stating the objections, and the grounds therefor, that the adverse party will make if the report is offered at the time of the hearing. An adverse party may call the expert as a witness and examine the witness as if under cross-examination.

(29) *Written statements of lay witnesses.* Written statements of a lay witness made under oath or affirmation and subject to the penalty of perjury, so far as admissible under the rules of evidence applied as though the witness was then present and testifying, unless the sources of information or the method or circumstances of preparation indicate lack of trustworthiness provided that (i) a copy of the written statement has been filed and served upon the adverse party sufficiently in advance of the hearing to provide the adverse party with a fair opportunity to prepare to object or meet it, and (ii) if the declarant is reasonably

available as a witness, as determined by the judge, no adverse party has sufficiently in advance of the hearing filed and served upon the noticing party a written demand that the declarant be produced in person to testify at the hearing. An adverse party may call the declarant as a witness and examine the witness as if under cross-examination.

(30) *Deposition testimony.* Testimony given as a witness in a deposition taken in compliance with law in the course of the same proceeding, so far as admissible under the rules of evidence applied as though the witness was then present and testifying, if the party against whom the testimony is now offered had an opportunity and similar motive to develop the testimony by direct, cross, or redirect examination, provided that a notice of intention to offer the deposition in evidence, together with a copy thereof if not otherwise previously provided, has been served upon the adverse party sufficiently in advance of the hearing to provide the adverse party with a fair opportunity to prepare to object or meet it. An adverse party may call the deponent as a witness and examine the witness as if under cross-examination.

(b) [Reserved]

§ 18.804 Hearsay exceptions; declarant unavailable.

(a) *Definition of unavailability. Unavailability as a witness* includes situations in which the declarant:

(1) Is exempted by ruling of the judge on the ground of privilege from testifying concerning the subject matter of the declarant's statement; or

(2) Persists in refusing to testify concerning the subject matter of the declarant's statement despite an order of the judge to do so; or

(3) Testifies to a lack of memory of the subject matter of the declarant's statement; or

(4) Is unable to be present or to testify at the hearing because of death or then existing physical or mental illness or infirmity; or

(5) Is absent from the hearing and the proponent of a statement has been unable to procure the declarant's attendance (or in the case of a hearsay exception under paragraph (b) (2), (3), or (4) of this section, the declarant's attendance or testimony) by process or other reasonable means. A declarant is not unavailable as a witness if exemption, refusal, claim of lack of memory, inability, or absence is due to the procurement or wrongdoing of the proponent of a statement for the purpose of preventing the witness from attending or

testifying.

(b) *Hearsay exceptions.* The following are not excluded by the hearsay rule if the declarant is unavailable as a witness:

(1) *Former testimony.* Testimony given as a witness at another hearing of the same or a different proceeding, or in a deposition taken in compliance with law in the course of the same or another proceeding, if the party against whom the testimony is now offered, or a predecessor in interest, had an opportunity and similar motive to develop the testimony by direct, cross, or redirect examination.

(2) *Statement under belief of impending death*A statement made by a declarant while believing that the declarant's death was imminent, concerning the cause or circumstances of what the declarant believed to be impending death.

(3) *Statement against interest.* A statement which was at the time of its making so far contrary to the declarant's pecuniary or proprietary interest, or so far tended to subject the declarant to civil or criminal liability, or to render invalid a claim by the declarant against another, that a reasonable person in the declarant's position would not have made the statement unless believing it to be true.

(4) *Statement of personal or family history.* (i) A statement concerning the declarant's own birth, adoption, marriage, divorce, legitimacy, relationship by blood, adoption, or marriage, ancestry, or other similar fact of personal or family history, even though declarant had no means of acquiring personal knowledge of the matter stated; or

(ii) A statement concerning the foregoing matters, and death also, of another person, if the declarant was related to the other by blood, adoption, or marriage or was so intimately associated with the other's family as to be likely to have accurate information concerning the matter declared.

(5) *Other exceptions.* A statement not specifically covered by any of the foregoing exceptions but having equivalent circumstantial guarantees of trust-worthiness to the aforementioned hearsay exceptions, if the judge determines that—

(i) The statement is offered as evidence of a material fact;

(ii) The statement is more probative on the point for which it is offered than any other evidence which the proponent can procure through reasonable efforts; and

(iii) The general purposes of these rules and the interests of justice will best be served by admission of the statement into evidence. However, a statement may not be admitted under this exception unless the proponent of it makes known to the adverse party sufficiently in advance of the hearing to provide the adverse party with a fair opportunity to prepare to meet it, the proponent's intention to offer the statement and the particulars of it, including the name and address of the declarant.

§ 18.805 Hearsay within hearsay.

Hearsay included within hearsay is not excluded under the hearsay rule if each part of the combined statements conforms with an exception to the hearsay rule provided in these rules.

§18.806 Attacking and supporting credibility of declarant.

When a hearsay statement, or a statement defined in § 18.801(d)(2), (iii), (iv), or (v), has been admitted in evidence, the credibility of the declarant may be attacked, and if attacked may be supported, by any evidence which would be admissible for those purposes if declarant had testified as a witness. Evidence of a statement or conduct by the declarant at any time, inconsistent with the declarant's hearsay statement, is not subject to any requirement that the declarant may have been afforded an opportunity to deny or explain. If the party against whom a hearsay statement has been admitted calls the declarant as a witness, the party is entitled to examine the declarant on the statement as if under cross-examination.

AUTHENTICATION AND IDENTIFICATION

§ 18.901 Requirement of authentication or identification.

(a) *General provision.* The requirement of authentication or identification as a condition precedent to admissibility is satisfied by evidence sufficient to support a finding that the matter in question is what its proponent claims.

(b) *Illustrations.* By way of illustration only, and not by way of limitation, the following are examples of authentication or identification conforming with the requirements of this rule:

(1) *Testimony of witness with knowledge.* Testimony that a matter is what it is claimed to be.

(2) *Non-expert opinion on handwriting.* Non-expert opinion as to the genuineness of handwriting, based upon familiarity not acquired for purposes of litigation.

(3) *Comparison by judge or expert witness.* Comparison by the judge as trier of fact or by expert witnesses with specimens which have been authenticated.

(4) *Distinctive characteristics and the like.*

Appearance, contents, substance, internal patterns, or other distinctive characteristics, taken in conjunction with circumstances.

(5) *Voice identification.* Identification of a voice, whether heard firsthand or through mechanical or electronic transmission or recording, by opinion based upon hearing the voice at any time under circumstances connecting it with the alleged speaker.

(6) *Telephone conversations.* Telephone conversations, by evidence that a call was made to the number assigned at the time by the telephone company to a particular person or business, if—

(i) In the case of a person, circumstances, including self-identification, show the person answering to be the one called, or

(ii) In the case of a business, the call was made to a place of business and the conversation related to business reasonably transacted over the telephone.

(7) *Public records or reports.* Evidence that a writing authorized by law to be recorded or filed and in fact recorded or filed in a public office, or a purported public record, report, statement, or data compilation, in any form, is from the public office where items of this nature are kept.

(8) *Ancient documents or data compilation.* Evidence that a document or data compilation, in any form,

(i) Is in such condition as to create no suspicion concerning its authenticity,

(ii) Was in a place where it, if authentic, would likely be, and

(iii) Has been in existence 20 years or more at the time it is offered.

(9) *Process or system.* Evidence describing a process or system used to produce a result and showing that the process or system produces an accurate result.

(10) *Methods provided by statute or rule.* Any method of authentication or identification provided by Act of Congress, or by rule or regulation prescribed by the administrative agency pursuant to statutory authority, or pursuant to executive order.

§ 18.902 Self-authentication.

(a) Extrinsic evidence of authenticity as a condition precedent to admissibility is not required with respect to the following:

(1) *Domestic public documents under seal.* A document bearing a seal purporting to be that of the United States, or of any State, district, Commonwealth, territory, or insular possession thereof, or the Panama Canal Zone, or the Trust Territory of the Pacific Islands, or of a political subdivision, department, officer, or agency thereof, and a signature purporting to be an attestation or execution.

(2) *Domestic public documents not under seal.* A document purporting to bear the signature in the official capacity of an officer or employee of any entity included in paragraph (a)(1) of this section, having no seal, if a public officer having a seal and having official duties in the district or political subdivision of the officer or employee certifies under seal that the signer has the official capacity and that the signature is genuine.

(3) *Foreign public documents.* A document purporting to be executed or attested in an official capacity by a person authorized by the laws of a foreign country to make the execution or attestation, and accompanied by a final certification as to the genuineness of the signature and official position—

(i) Of the executing or attesting person, or

(ii) Of any foreign official whose certificate of genuineness of signature and official position relates to the execution or attestation or is in a chain of certificates of genuineness of signature and official position relating to the execution or attestation. A final certification may be made by a secretary of embassy or legation, consul, vice consul, or consular agent of the United States, or a diplomatic or consular official of the foreign country assigned or accredited to the United States. If reasonable opportunity has been given to all parties to investigate the authenticity and accuracy of official documents, the judge may, for good cause shown, order that they be treated as presumptively authentic without final certification or permit them to be evidenced by an attested summary with or without final certification.

(4) *Certified copies of public records.* A copy of an official record or report or entry therein, or of a document authorized by law to be recorded or filed and actually recorded or filed in a public office, including data compilations in any form, certified as correct by the custodian or other person authorized to make the certification, by certificate complying with paragraph (a) (1), (2), or (3) of this section, with any Act of Congress, or with any rule or regulation prescribed by the administrative agency pursuant to statutory authority, or pursuant to executive order.

(5) *Official publications.* Books, pamphlets, or other publications purporting to be issued by public authority.

(6) *Newspapers and periodicals.* Printed materials purporting to be newspapers or periodicals.

(7) *Trade inscriptions and the like.* Inscriptions, signs, tags, or labels purporting to have been affixed in the course of business and indicating ownership, control, or origin.

(8) *Acknowledged documents.* Documents accompanied by a certificate of acknowledgment executed in the manner provided by law by a notary public or other officer authorized by law to take acknowledgments.

(9) *Commercial paper and related documents.* Commercial paper, signatures thereon, and documents relating thereto to the extent provided by general commercial law.

(10) *Presumptions under Acts of Congress or administrative agency rules or regulations.* Any signature, document, or other matter declared by Act of Congress or by rule or regulation prescribed by the administrative agency pursuant to statutory authority or pursuant to executive order to be presumptively or prima facie genuine or authentic.

(11) *Certified records of regularly conducted activity.* The original or a duplicate of a record of regularly conducted activity, within the scope of § 18.803(6), which the custodian thereof or another qualified individual certifies

(i) Was made, at or near the time of the occurrence of the matters set forth, by, or from information transmitted by, a person with knowledge of those matters,

(ii) Is kept in the course of the regularly conducted activity, and

(iii) Was made by the regularly conducted activity as a regular practice, unless the sources of information or the method or circumstances of preparation indicate lack of trustworthiness. A record so certified is not self-authenticating under this paragraph unless the proponent makes an intention to offer it known to the adverse party and makes it available for inspection sufficiently in advance of its offer in evidence to provide the adverse party with a fair opportunity to object or meet it. As used in this subsection, *certifies* means, with respect to a domestic record, a written declaration under oath subject to the penalty of perjury and, with respect to a foreign record, a written declaration signed in a foreign country which, if falsely made, would subject the maker to criminal penalty under the laws of that country.

(12) *Bills, estimates, and reports.* In actions involving injury, illness, disease, death, disability, or physical or mental impairment, or damage to property, the following bills, estimates, and reports provided that a copy of said bill, estimate, or report has been served upon the adverse party

sufficiently in advance of the hearing to provide the adverse party with a fair opportunity to prepare to object or meet it:

(i) Hospital bills on the official letterhead or billhead of the hospital, when dated and itemized.

(ii) Bills of doctors and dentists, when dated and containing a statement showing the date of each visit and the charge therefor.

(iii) Bills of registered nurses, licensed practical nurses and physical therapists or other licensed health care providers, when dated and containing an itemized statement of the days and hours of service and the charges therefor.

(iv) Bills for medicine, eyeglasses, prosthetic devices, medical belts or similar items, when dated and itemized.

(v) Property repair bills or estimates, when dated and itemized, setting forth the charges for labor and material. In the case of an estimate, the party intending to offer the estimate shall forward with his notice to the adverse party, together with a copy of the estimate, a statement indicating whether or not the property was repaired, and, if so, whether the estimated repairs were made in full or in part and by whom, the cost thereof, together with a copy of the bill therefor.

(vi) Reports of past earnings, or of the rate of earnings and time lost from work or lost compensation, prepared by an employer on official letterhead, when dated and itemized. The adverse party may not dispute the authenticity, therefore, unless the adverse party files and serves written objection thereto sufficiently in advance of the hearing stating the objections, and the grounds therefore, the adverse party will make if the bill, estimate, or report is offered at the time of the hearing. An adverse party may call the authors of the bill, estimate, or report as a witness and examine the witness as if under cross-examination.

(13) *Medical reports.* In actions involving injury, illness, disease, death, disability or physical or mental impairment, doctor, hospital, laboratory and other medical reports made for purposes of medical treatment, provided that a copy of the report has been filed and served upon the adverse party sufficiently in advance of the hearing to provide the adverse party with a fair opportunity to prepare to object or meet it. The adverse party may not object to the authenticity of the report unless the adverse party files and serves written objection thereto sufficiently in advance of the hearing stating the objections, and the grounds therefore, that the adverse party will make if the report is offered at the time of the hearing. An adverse party may call the author of the medical

report as a witness and examine the witness as if under cross-examination.

(14) *Written reports of expert witnesses.*Written reports of an expert witness prepared with a view toward litigation including but not limited to a diagnostic report of a physician, including inferences and opinions, when on official letterhead, when dated, when including a statement of the expert's qualifications, when including a summary of experience as an expert witness in litigation, when including the basic facts, data, and opinions forming the basis of the inferences or opinions, and when including the reasons for or explanation of the inferences or opinions, so far as admissible under the rules of evidence applied as though the witness was then present and testifying, provided that a copy of the report has been filed and served upon the adverse party sufficiently in advance of the hearing to provide the adverse party with a fair opportunity to prepare to object or meet it. The adverse party may not object to the authenticity of the report unless the adverse party files and serves written objection thereto sufficiently in advance of the hearing stating the objections, and the grounds therefore, that the adverse party will make if the report is offered at the time of the hearing. An adverse party may call the expert as a witness and examine the witness as if under cross-examination.

(15) *Written statements of lay witnesses.*Written statements of a lay witness made under oath or affirmation and subject to the penalty of perjury, so far as admissible under the rules of evidence applied as though the witness was then present and testifying, provided that:

(i) A copy of the written statement has been filed and served upon the adverse party sufficiently in advance of the hearing to provide the adverse party with a fair opportunity to prepare to object or meet it, and:

(ii) If the declarant is reasonably available as a witness, as determined by the judge, no adverse party has sufficiently in advance of the hearing filed and served upon the noticing party a written demand that the declarant be produced in person to testify at the hearing. An adverse party may call the declarant as a witness and examine the witness as if under cross-examination.

(16) *Deposition testimony.*Testimony given as a witness in a deposition taken in compliance with law in the course of the same proceeding, so far as admissible under the rules of evidence applied as though the witness was then present and testifying, if the party against whom the testimony is now offered had an opportunity and similar motive to develop the testimony by direct, cross, or redirect examination, provided that a notice of intention to offer the deposition in evidence, together with a copy thereof if not otherwise previously provided, has been served upon the adverse party sufficiently in advance of the hearing to provide the adverse party with a fair opportunity to prepare to object or meet it. An adverse party may call the deponent as a witness and examine the witness as if under cross-examination.

(b) [Reserved]

§ 18.903 Subscribing witness' testimony unnecessary.

The testimony of a subscribing witness is not necessary to authenticate a writing unless required by the laws of the jurisdiction whose laws govern the validity of the writing.

CONTENTS OF WRITINGS, RECORDINGS, AND PHOTOGRAPHS

§ 18.1001 Definitions.

(a) For purposes of this article the following definitions are applicable:

(1) *Writings and recordings. Writings*and *recordings* consist of letters, words, or numbers, or their equivalent, set down by handwriting, typewriting, printing, photostating, photographing, magnetic impulse, mechanical or electronic recording, or other form of data compilation.

(2) *Photographs. Photographs*include still photographs, X-ray films, video tapes, and motion pictures.

(3) *Original.* An *original*of a writing or recording is the writing or recording itself or any counterpart intended to have the same effect by a person executing or issuing it. An *original* of a photograph includes the negative or, other than with respect of X-ray films, any print therefrom. If data are stored in a computer or similar device, any printout or other output readable by sight, shown to reflect the data accurately, is an *original*.

(4) *Duplicate.* A *duplicate* is a counterpart produced by the same impression as the original, or from the same matrix, or by means of photography, including enlargements and miniatures, or by mechanical or electronic re-recording, or by chemical reproduction, or by other equivalent techniques which accurately reproduces the original.

(b) [Reserved]

§ 18.1002 Requirement of original.

To prove the content of a writing, recording, or

photograph. the original writing, recording, or photograph is required. except as otherwise provided in these rules. or by rule or regulation prescribed by the administrative agency pursuant to statutory authority. or pursuant to executive order. or by Act of Congress.

§ 18.1003 Admissibility of duplicates.

A duplicate is admissible to the same extent as an original unless a genuine question is raised as to the authenticity of the original. or in the circumstances it would be unfair to admit the duplicate in lieu of the original.

§ 18.1004 Admissibility of other evidence of contents.

(a) The original is not required. and other evidence of the contents of a writing, recording, or photograph is admissible if:

(1) *Originals lost or destroyed.* All originals are lost or have been destroyed. unless the proponent lost or destroyed them in bad faith; or

(2) *Original not obtainable.* No original can be obtained by any available judicial process or procedure; or

(3) *Original in possession of opponent.* At a time when an original was under the control of the party against whom offered. that party was put on notice. by the pleading or otherwise. that the contents would be a subject of proof at the hearing. and that party does not produce the original at the hearing; or

(4) *Collateral matters.* The writing, recording, or photograph is not closely related to a controlling issue.

(b) [Reserved]

§ 18.1005 Public records.

The contents of an official record. or of a document authorized to be recorded or filed and actually recorded or filed. including data compilations in any form. if otherwise admissible, may be proved by copy. certified as correct in accordance with § 18.902 or testified to be correct by a witness who has compared it with the original. If a copy which complies with the foregoing cannot be obtained by the exercise of reasonable diligence. then other evidence of the contents may be given.

§ 18.1006 Summaries.

The contents of voluminous writings, recordings, or photographs which cannot conveniently be examined at the hearing may be presented in the form of a chart. summary, or calculation. The originals. or duplicates. shall be made available for examination or copying. or both. by other parties at reasonable time and place. The judge may order that they be produced at the hearing.

§ 18.1007 Testimony or written admission of party.

Contents of writings, recordings. or photographs may be proved by the testimony or deposition of the party against whom offered or by that party's written admission, without accounting for the non-production of the original.

§ 18.1008 Functions of the judge.

When the admissibility of other evidence of contents of writings, recordings. or photographs under these rules depends upon the fulfillment of a condition of fact. the question whether the condition has been fulfilled is ordinarily for the judge to determine in accordance with the provisions of § 18.104(a). However. when an issue is raised whether the asserted writing ever existed: or whether another writing, recording, or photograph produced at the hearing is the original: or whether other evidence of contents correctly reflects the contents. the issue is for the judge as trier of fact to determine as in the case of other issues of fact.

APPLICABILITY
§ 18.1101 Applicability of rules.

(a) *General provision.* These rules govern formal adversarial adjudications conducted by the United States Department of Labor before a presiding officer.

(1) Which are required by Act of Congress to be determined on the record after opportunity for an administrative agency hearing in accordance with the Administrative Procedure Act, 5 U.S.C. 554, 556 and 557. or

(2) Which by United States Department of Labor regulation are conducted in conformance with the foregoing provisions. *Presiding officer,* referred to in these rules as *the judge,* means an Administrative Law Judge. an agency head, or other officer who presides at the reception of evidence at a hearing in such an adjudication.

(b) *Rules inapplicable.* The rules (other than with respect to privileges) do not apply in the following situations:

(1) *Preliminary questions of fact.* The determination of questions of fact preliminary to admissibility of evidence when the issue is to be determined by the judge under § 18.104.

(2) *Longshore. black lung, and related acts.* Other than with respect to §§ 18.403. 18.611(a).

18.614 and without prejudice to current practice, hearings held pursuant to the Longshore and Harbor Workers' Compensation Act, 33 U.S.C. 901; the Federal Mine Safety and Health Act (formerly the Federal Coal Mine Health and Safety Act) as amended by the Black Lung Benefits Act, 30 U.S.C. 901; and acts such as the Defense Base Act, 42 U.S.C. 1651; the District of Columbia Workmen's Compensation Act, 36 DC Code 501; the Outer Continental Shelf Lands Act, 43 U.S.C. 1331; and the Non-appropriated Fund Instrumentalities Act, 5 U.S.C. 8171, which incorporate section 23(a) of the Longshore and Harbor Workers' Compensation Act by reference.

(c) *Rules inapplicable in part.* These rules do not apply to the extent inconsistent with, in conflict with, or to the extent a matter is otherwise specifically provided by an Act of Congress, or by a rule or regulation of specific application prescribed by the United States Department of Labor pursuant to statutory authority, or pursuant to executive order.

§ 18.1102 [Reserved]
§ 18.1103 Title.
These rules may be known as the United States Department of Labor Rules of Evidence and cited as 29 CFR 18.—— (1989).

§ 18.1104 Effective date.
These rules are effective thirty days after date of publication with respect to formal adversarial adjudications as specified in § 18.1101 except that with respect to hearings held following an investigation conducted by the United States Department of Labor, these rules shall be effective only where the investigation commenced thirty days after publication.

OFFICE OF THE SECRETARY OF LABOR
29 CFR Subtitle A (7–1–98 Edition) Pt. 24
PART 24—PROCEDURES FOR THE HANDLING OF DISCRIMINATION COMPLAINTS UNDER FEDERAL EMPLOYEE PROTECTION STATUTES

24.1	Purpose and scope.
24.2	Obligations and prohibited acts.
24.3	Complaint.
24.4	Investigations.
24.5	Investigations under the Energy Reorganization Act.
24.6	Hearings.
24.7	Recommended decision and order.
24.8	Review by the Administrative Review Board.
24.9	Exception.

APPENDIX A TO PART 24—YOUR RIGHTS UNDER THE ENERGY REORGANIZATION ACT.

AUTHORITY: 15 U.S.C. 2622; 33 U.S.C. 1367; 42 U.S.C. 300j–9(i), 5851, 6971, 7622, 9610.

SOURCE: 63 FR 6621, Feb. 9, 1998, unless otherwise noted.

§ 24.1 Purpose and scope.
(a) This part implements the several employee protection provisions for which the Secretary of Labor has been given responsibility pursuant to the following Federal statutes: Safe Drinking Water Act, 42 U.S.C. 300j–9(i); Water Pollution Control Act, 33 U.S.C. 1367; Toxic Substances Control Act, 15 U.S.C. 2622; Solid Waste Disposal Act, 42 U.S.C. 6971; Clean Air Act, 42 U.S.C. 7622; Energy Reorganization Act of 1974, 42 U.S.C. 5851; and Comprehensive Environmental Response, Compensation and Liability Act of 1980, 42 U.S.C. 9610.

(b) Procedures are established by this part pursuant to the Federal statutory provisions listed in paragraph (a) of this section, for the expeditious handling of complaints by employees, or persons acting on their behalf, of discriminatory action by employers.

(c) Throughout this part, "Secretary" or "Secretary of Labor" shall mean the Secretary of Labor, U.S. Department of Labor, or his or her designee. "Assistant Secretary" shall mean the Assistant Secretary for Occupational Safety and Health, U.S. Department of Labor, or his or her designee.

§ 24.2 Obligations and prohibited acts.
(a) No employer subject to the provisions of any of the Federal statutes listed in § 24.1(a), or to the Atomic Energy Act of 1954 (AEA), 42 U.S.C. 2011 *et seq.*, may discharge any employee or otherwise discriminate against any employee with respect to the employee's compensation, terms, conditions, or privileges of employment because the employee, or any person acting pursuant to the employee's request, engaged in any of the activities specified in this section.

(b) Any employer is deemed to have violated the particular federal law and the regulations in this part if such employer intimidates, threatens, restrains, coerces, blacklists, discharges, or in any other manner discriminates against any employee because the employee has:

(1) Commenced or caused to be commenced, or is about to commence or cause to be commenced, a proceeding under one of the Federal statutes listed in § 24.1(a) or a proceeding for the administration or enforcement of any requirement imposed under such Federal statute;

(2) Testified or is about to testify in any such proceeding; or

(3) Assisted or participated, or is about to assist or participate, in any manner in such a proceeding or in any other action to carry out the purposes of such Federal statute.

(c) Under the Energy Reorganization Act, and by interpretation of the Secretary under any of the other statutes listed in § 24.1(a), any employer is deemed to have violated the particular federal law and these regulations if such employer intimidates, threatens, restrains, coerces, blacklists, discharges, or in any other manner discriminates against any employee because the employee has:

(1) Notified the employer of an alleged violation of such Federal statute or the AEA of 1954;

(2) Refused to engage in any practice made unlawful by such Federal statute or the AEA of 1954, if the employee has identified the alleged illegality to the employer; or

(3) Testified before Congress or at any Federal or State proceeding regarding any provision (or proposed provision) of such Federal statute or the AEA of 1954.

(d)(1) Every employer subject to the Energy Reorganization Act of 1974, as amended, shall prominently post and keep posted in any place of employment to which the employee protection provisions of the Act apply a fully legible copy of the notice prepared by the Occupational Safety and Health Administration, printed as appendix A to this part, or a notice approved by the Assistant Secretary for Occupational Safety and Health that contains substantially the same provisions and explains the employee protection provisions of the Act and the regulations in this part. Copies of the notice prepared by DOL may be obtained from the Assistant Secretary for Occupational Safety and Health, Washington, D.C. 20210, from local offices of the Occupational Safety and Health Administration, or from the Department of Labor's Website at http://www.osha.gov.

(2) Where the notice required by paragraph (d)(1) of this section has not been posted, the requirement in § 24.3(b)(2) that a complaint be filed with the Assistant Secretary within 180 days of an alleged violation shall be inoperative unless the respondent establishes that the complainant had notice of the material provisions of the notice. If it is established that the notice was posted at the employee's place of employment after the alleged discriminatory action occurred or that the complainant later obtained actual notice, the 180 days shall ordinarily run from that date.

§ 24.3 Complaint.

(a) *Who may file.* An employee who believes that he or she has been discriminated against by an employer in violation of any of the statutes listed in § 24.1(a) may file, or have another person file on his or her behalf, a complaint alleging such discrimination.

(b) *Time of filing.* (1) Except as provided in paragraph (b)(2) of this section, any complaint shall be filed within 30 days after the occurrence of the alleged violation. For the purpose of determining timeliness of filing, a complaint filed by mail shall be deemed filed as of the date of mailing.

(2) Under the Energy Reorganization Act of 1974, any complaint shall be filed within 180 days after the occurrence of the alleged violation.

(c) *Form of complaint.* No particular form of complaint is required, except that a complaint must be in writing and should include a full statement of the acts and omissions, with pertinent dates, which are believed to constitute the violation.

(d) *Place of filing.* A complaint may be filed in person or by mail at the nearest local office of the Occupational Safety and Health Administration, listed in most telephone directories under U.S. Government, Department of Labor. A complaint may also be filed with the Office of the Assistant Secretary, Occupational Safety and Health Administration, U.S. Department of Labor, Washington, D.C. 20210.

(Approved by the Office of Management and Budget under control number 1215–0183.)

§ 24.4 Investigations.

(a) Upon receipt of a complaint under this part, the Assistant Secretary shall notify the person named in the complaint, and the appropriate office of the Federal agency charged with the administration of the affected program of its filing.

(b) The Assistant Secretary shall, on a priority basis, investigate and gather data concerning such case, and as part of the investigation may enter and inspect such places and records (and make copies thereof), may question persons being proceeded against and other employees of the charged employer, and may require the production of any documentary or other evidence deemed necessary to determine whether a violation of the law involved has been committed.

(c) Investigations under this part shall be conducted in a manner which protects the confidentiality of any person other than the complainant who provides information on a confidential basis, in accordance with part 70 of this title.

(d)(1) Within 30 days of receipt of a complaint, the Assistant Secretary shall complete the investigation, determine whether the alleged violation has occurred, and give notice of the determination. The notice of determination shall contain a statement of reasons for the findings and conclusions therein and, if the Assistant Secretary determines that the alleged violation has occurred, shall include an appropriate order to abate the violation. Notice of the determination shall be given by certified mail to the complainant, the respondent, and their representatives (if any). At the same time, the Assistant Secretary shall file with the Chief Administrative Law Judge, U.S. Department of Labor, the original complaint and a copy of the notice of determination.

(2) The notice of determination shall include or be accompanied by notice to the complainant and the respondent that any party who desires review of the determination or any part thereof, including judicial review, shall file a request for a hearing with the Chief Administrative Law Judge within five business days of receipt of the determination. The complainant or respondent in turn may request a hearing within five business days of the date of a timely request for a hearing by the other party. If a request for a hearing is timely filed, the notice of determination of the Assistant Secretary shall be inoperative, and shall become operative only if the case is later dismissed. If a request for a hearing is not timely filed, the notice of determination shall become the final order of the Secretary.

(3) A request for a hearing shall be filed with the Chief Administrative Law Judge by facsimile (fax), telegram, hand delivery, or next-day delivery service. A copy of the request for a hearing shall be sent by the party requesting a hearing to the complainant or the respondent (employer), as appropriate, on the same day that the hearing is requested, by facsimile (fax), telegram, hand delivery, or nextday delivery service. A copy of the request for a hearing shall also be sent to the Assistant Secretary for Occupational Safety and Health and to the Associate Solicitor, Division of

Fair Labor Standards, U.S. Department of Labor, Washington, D.C. 20210.

§ 24.5 Investigations under the Energy Reorganization Act.

(a) In addition to the investigation procedures set forth in § 24.4, this section sets forth special procedures applicable only to investigations under the Energy Reorganization Act.

(b)(1) A complaint of alleged violation shall be dismissed unless the complainant has made a *prima facie* showing that protected behavior or conduct as provided in § 24.2(b) was a contributing factor in the unfavorable personnel action alleged in the complaint.

(2) The complaint, supplemented as appropriate by interviews of the complainant, must allege the existence of facts and evidence to meet the required elements of a *prima facie* case, as follows:

(i) The employee engaged in a protected activity or conduct, as set forth in § 24.2;

(ii) The respondent knew that the employee engaged in the protected activity;

(iii) The employee has suffered an unfavorable personnel action; and

(iv) The circumstances were sufficient to raise the inference that the protected activity was likely a contributing factor in the unfavorable action.

(3) For purposes of determining whether to investigate, the complainant will be considered to have met the required burden if the complaint on its face, supplemented as appropriate through interviews of the complainant, alleges the existence of facts and either direct or circumstantial evidence to meet the required elements of a *prima facie* case, *i.e.*, to give rise to an inference that the respondent knew that the employee engaged in protected activity, and that the protected activity was likely a reason for the personnel action. Normally the burden is satisfied, for example, if it is shown that the adverse personnel action took place shortly after the protected activity, giving rise to the inference that it was a factor in the adverse action. If these elements are not substantiated in the investigation, the investigation will cease.

(c)(1) Notwithstanding a finding that a complainant has made a *prima facie* showing required by this section with respect to complaints filed under the Energy Reorganization Act, an investigation of the complainant's complaint under that Act shall be discontinued if the respondent demonstrates by clear and convincing evidence that it would have taken the same unfavorable personnel action in the absence of the complainant's protected behavior or conduct.

(2) Upon receipt of a complaint under the Energy Reorganization Act, the respondent shall be provided with a copy of the complaint (as supplemented by interviews of the complainant, if any) and advised that any evidence it may wish to submit to rebut the allegations in the complaint must be received within five business days from receipt of notification of the complaint. If the respondent fails to make a timely response or if the response does not demonstrate by clear and convincing evidence that the unfavorable action would have occurred absent the protected conduct, the investigation shall proceed. The investigation shall proceed whenever it is necessary or appropriate to confirm or verify the information provided by respondent.

(d) Whenever the Assistant Secretary dismisses a complaint pursuant to this section without completion of an investigation, the Assistant Secretary shall give notice of the dismissal, which shall contain a statement of reasons therefor, by certified mail to the complainant, the respondent, and their representatives. At the same time the Assistant Secretary shall file with the Chief Administrative Law Judge, U.S. Department of Labor, a copy of the complaint and a copy of the notice of dismissal. The notice of dismissal shall constitute a notice of determination within the meaning of § 24.4(d), and any request for a hearing shall be filed and served in accordance with the provisions of § 24.4(d) (2) and (3).

§ 24.6 Hearings.

(a) *Notice of hearing.* The administrative law judge to whom the case is assigned shall, within seven calendar days following receipt of the request for hearing, notify the parties by certified mail, directed to the last known address of the parties, of a day, time and place for hearing. All parties shall be given at least five days notice of such hearing. However, because of the time constraints upon the Secretary by the above statutes, no requests for postponement shall be granted except for compelling reasons or with the consent of all parties.

(b) *Consolidated hearings.* When two or more hearings are to be held, and the same or substantially similar evidence is relevant and material to the matters at issue at each such hearing, the Chief Administrative Law Judge may, upon motion by any party or on his own or her own motion, order that a consolidated hearing be conducted. Where consolidated hearings are held, a single record of the proceedings shall be made and the evidence introduced in one case may be considered as introduced in the others, and a separate or joint decision shall be made, as appropriate.

(c) *Place of hearing.* The hearing shall, where possible, be held at a place within 75 miles of the complainant's residence.

(d) *Right to counsel.* In all proceedings under this part, the parties shall have the right to be represented by counsel.

(e) *Procedures, evidence and record*—(1) *Evidence.* Formal rules of evidence shall not apply, but rules or principles designed to assure production of the most probative evidence available shall be applied. The administrative law judge may exclude evidence which is immaterial, irrelevant, or unduly repetitious.

(2) *Record of hearing.* All hearings shall be open to the public and shall be mechanically or stenographically reported. All evidence upon which the administrative law judge relies for decision shall be contained in the transcript of testimony, either directly or by appropriate reference. All exhibits and other pertinent documents or records, either in whole or in material part, introduced as evidence, shall be marked for identification and incorporated into the record.

(3) *Oral argument; briefs.* Any party, upon request, may be allowed a reasonable time for presentation of oral argument and to file a pre-hearing brief or other written statement of fact or law. A copy of any such pre-hearing brief or other written statement shall be filed with the Chief Administrative Law Judge or the administrative law judge assigned to the case before or during the proceeding at which evidence is submitted to the administrative law judge and shall be served upon each party. Post-hearing briefs will not be permitted except at the request of the administrative law judge. When permitted, any such brief shall be limited to the issue or issues specified by the administrative law judge and shall be due within the time prescribed by the administrative law judge.

(4) *Dismissal for cause.*

(i) The administrative law judge may, at the request of any party, or on his or her own motion, issue a recommended decision and order dismissing a claim:

(A) Upon the failure of the complainant or his or her representative to attend a hearing without good cause; or

(B) Upon the failure of the complainant to comply with a lawful order of the administrative law judge.

(ii) In any case where a dismissal of a claim,

defense. or party is sought. the administrative law judge shall issue an order to show cause why the dismissal should not be granted and afford all parties a reasonable time to respond to such order. After the time for response has expired. the administrative law judge shall take such action as is appropriate to rule on the dismissal, which may include a recommended order dismissing the claim. defense or party.

(f)(1) At the Assistant Secretary's discretion. the Assistant Secretary may participate as a party or participate as *amicus curiae* at any time in the proceedings. This right to participate shall include. but is not limited to. the right to petition for review of a recommended decision of an administrative law judge. including a decision based on a settlement agreement between complainant and respondent. to dismiss a complaint or to issue an order encompassing the terms of the settlement.

(2) Copies of pleadings in all cases. whether or not the Assistant Secretary is participating in the proceeding. shall be sent to the Assistant Secretary, Occupational Safety and Health Administration. and to the Associate Solicitor. Division of Fair Labor Standards. U.S. Department of Labor, Washington. D.C. 20210.

(g)(1) A Federal agency which is interested in a proceeding may participate as *amicus curiae* at any time in the proceedings. at the agency's discretion.

(2) At the request of a Federal agency which is interested in a proceeding, copies of all pleadings in a case shall be served on the Federal agency, whether or not the agency is participating in the proceeding.

§ 24.7 Recommended decision and order.

(a) Unless the parties jointly request or agree to an extension of time. the administrative law judge shall issue a recommended decision within 20 days after the termination of the proceeding at which evidence was submitted. The recommended decision shall contain appropriate findings. conclusions. and a recommended order and be served upon all parties to the proceeding.

(b) In cases under the Energy Reorganization Act, a determination that a violation has occurred may only be made if the complainant has demonstrated that protected behavior or conduct was a contributing factor in the unfavorable personnel action alleged in the complaint. Relief may not be ordered if the respondent demonstrates by clear and convincing evidence that it would have taken the same unfavorable personnel action in the absence of such behavior. The proceeding before the

administrative law judge shall be a proceeding on the merits of the complaint. Neither the Assistant Secretary's determination to dismiss a complaint pursuant to § 24.5 without completing an investigation nor the Assistant Secretary's determination not to dismiss a complaint is subject to review by the administrative law judge. and a complaint may not be remanded for the completion of an investigation on the basis that such a determination to dismiss was made in error.

(c)(1) Upon the conclusion of the hearing and the issuance of a recommended decision that the complaint has merit. and that a violation of the Act has occurred. the administrative law judge shall issue a recommended order that the respondent take appropriate affirmative action to abate the violation. including reinstatement of the complainant to his or her former position. if desired. together with the compensation (including back pay). terms. conditions. and privileges of that employment. and. when appropriate. compensatory damages. In cases arising under the Safe Drinking Water Act or the Toxic Substances Control Act. exemplary damages may also be awarded when appropriate.

(2) In cases brought under the Energy Reorganization Act. when an administrative law judge issues a recommended order that the complaint has merit and containing the relief prescribed in paragraph (c)(1) of this section, the administrative law judge shall also issue a preliminary order providing all of the relief specified in paragraph (c)(1) of this section with the exception of compensatory damages. This preliminary order shall constitute the preliminary order of the Secretary and shall be effective immediately. whether or not a petition for review is filed with the Administrative Review Board. Any award of compensatory damages shall not be effective until the final decision is issued by the Administrative Review Board.

(d) The recommended decision of the administrative law judge shall become the final order of the Secretary unless. pursuant to § 24.8. a petition for review is timely filed with the Administrative Review Board.

§ 24.8 Review by the Administrative Review Board.

(a) Any party desiring to seek review. including judicial review. of a recommended decision of the administrative law judge shall file a petition for review with the Administrative Review Board ("the Board"). which has been delegated the authority to act for the Secretary and issue final decisions under this part. To be effective, such a petition must be received within ten business days of the date of the recommended decision of the administrative law judge, and shall be served on all parties and on the Chief Administrative Law Judge. If a timely petition for review is filed, the recommended decision of the administrative law judge shall be inoperative unless and until the Board issues an order adopting the recommended decision, except that for cases arising under the Energy Reorganization Act of 1974, a preliminary order of relief shall be effective while review is conducted by the Board.

(b) Copies of the petition for review and all briefs shall be served on the Assistant Secretary, Occupational Safety and Health Administration, and on the Associate Solicitor, Division of Fair Labor Standards, U.S. Department of Labor, Washington, D.C. 20210.

(c) The final decision shall be issued within 90 days of the receipt of the complaint and shall be served upon all parties and the Chief Administrative Law Judge by mail to the last known address.

(d)(1) If the Board concludes that the party charged has violated the law, the final order shall order the party charged to take appropriate affirmative action to abate the violation, including reinstatement of the complainant to that person's former or substantially equivalent position, if desired, together with the compensation (including back pay), terms, conditions, and privileges of that employment, and, when appropriate, compensatory damages. In cases arising under the Safe Drinking Water Act or the Toxic Substances Control Act, exemplary damages may also be awarded when appropriate.

(2) If such a final order is issued, the Board, at the request of the complainant, shall assess against the respondent a sum equal to the aggregate amount of all costs and expenses (including attorney and expert witness fees) reasonably incurred by the complainant, as determined by the Board, for, or in connection with, the bringing of the complaint upon which the order was issued.

(e) If the Board determines that the party charged has not violated the law, an order shall be issued denying the complaint.

§ 24.9 Exception.

This part shall have no application to any employee alleging activity prohibited by this part who, acting without direction from his or her employer (or the employer's agent), deliberately causes a violation of any requirement of a Federal statute listed in § 24.1(a).

Bibliography

BOOKS AND REPORTS

Adler, Allan. *Litigation Under the Federal Freedom of Information Act and Privacy.* Washington, D.C.: American Civil Liberties Union Foundation, published annually.

American Bar Association, American Law Institute. *Course of Study Materials— Advanced Labor and Employment Law.* Philadelphia: American Law Institute, 1985.

American Bar Association, Section of Labor and Employment Law. *Committee Reports.* Chicago: ABA Press, 1981.

Balk, Walter L. *Managerial Reform and Professional Empowerment in the Public Service.* Westport, Conn.: Quorum Books, 1996.

Beauchamp, Tom L., and Norman E. Bowie, eds. *Ethical Theory and Business.* Englewood Cliffs, N.J.: Prentice-Hall, 1979.

Bender's Forms of Discovery. "*Employment Suits.*" New York: Matthew Bender, 1980.

Bennett, Mark W. *Employment Relationships: Law & Practice.* New York: Aspen Law & Business, 1998.

Boese, John T. *Civil False Claims and Qui Tam Actions.* New York: Aspen Law & Business, 1998.

Boese, John T. *False Claims Act and Qui Tam Actions.* New York: Aspen, 1998 Supplement.

Bompey, Stuart H. *Wrongful Termination Claims: A Preventive Approach.* New York: Practicing Law Institute, 1991.

Borowsky, Philip, and Lex Larson. *Unjust Dismissal.* New York: Matthew Bender, 1987.

Bowman, James, Frederick Elliston, and Paula Lockhart. *Professional Dissent, An Annotated Bibliography and Resource Guide.* New York: Garland Publishing, 1984.

Broida, Peter. *A Guide to Merit Systems Protection Board Law and Practice.* Arlington, Va.: Dewey Publications, 1998.

Connolly, W. A. *Practical Guide to Equal Opportunity Law, Principles and Practices.* New York: Law Review Press, 1975.

Connolly, W., and D. Crowell. *A Practical Guide to the Occupational Safety and Health Act: Law, Principles and Practices.* New York: Law Journal Press, 1977.

Connolly, W., D. Peterson, and M. Connolly. *Use of Statistics in Equal Employment Opportunity Litigation.* New York: Law Journal Seminars Press, 1987.

Cotine, B., L. Birrel, and R. Jennings. *Winning at the Occupational Safety and Health Commission, Workers Handbook on Enforcing Safety and Health Standards.* Washington, D.C.: Public Citizen Health Research Group, 1975.

Decker, Kurt H. *The Individual Employment Rights Primer.* Amityville, New York : Baywood Publishing Co., 1991.

Dolson, W., ed. *Annual Labor and Employment Law Institute, New Dimensions in Labor and Employment Relations.* Littleton, Colo.: Fred Rothman, 1985.

Donaldson, Thomas. *"Employee Rights." In Corporations and Morality.* Englewood Cliffs, N.J.: Prentice-Hall, 1982.

Elliston, Frederick, John Keenan, Paula Lockhart, and Jane Van Schaick. *Whistleblowing Research: Methodological and Moral Issues.* New York: Praeger, 1985.

Ewing, David W. *Freedom Inside the Organization.* New York: E. P. Dutton, 1977.

Fairweather, Owen. *Practice and Procedure in Labor Arbitration.* Washington, D.C.: Bureau of National Affairs, 1973.

Fidell, Eugene. *Federal Protection of Private Sector Health and Safety Whistleblowers: A Report to the Administrative Conference of the United States.* Washington, D.C.: Administrative Conference of the United States, March 1987.

Fitzgerald, Ernest A. *The High Priests of Waste.* New York: W. W. Norton, 1972.

Franklin, Benjamin. *Debates of the Constitutional Convention, July 26, 1787, Reprinted in 457 Formation of the Union: Documents.* Washington, D.C.: Government Printing Office, 1927.

Glazer, Myron, and Pinina Glazer. *The Whistleblowers: Exposing Corruption in Government and Industry.* New York: Basic Books, 1989.

Goodman, Janice, ed. *Employee Rights Litigation: Pleadings and Practice.* New York: Matthew Bender, 1998.

Green, Ronald Michael. *Employer's Guide to Workplace Torts: Negligent Hiring, Fraud, Defamation, and Other Emerging Areas of Employer Liability.* Washington, D.C.: BNA Books, 1992.

Helmer, James B. *False Claims Act: Whistleblower Litigation.* Charlottesville, Va.: Michie Co., 1994.

Helmer, James B. Jr., Ann Lugbill, and Robert C. Neff, Jr. *False Claims Act: Whistleblower Litigation.* Charlottesville: Lexis, 2nd ed. 1999.

Hill, Andrew D. *"Wrongful Discharge"and the Derogation of the At-Will Employment Doctrine.* Philadelphia: Industrial Research Unit, Wharton School, University of Pennsylvania, 1987.

Holloway, William J. *Employment Termination: Rights and Remedies.* Washington, D.C.: Bureau of National Affairs, 1993.

Hunt, James W. *The Law of the Workplace: Rights of Employers and Employees.* Washington, D.C.: Bureau of National Affairs, 1994.

Jackson, Dudley. *Unfair Dismissal.* London: Cambridge University Press, 1975.

Jackson, G. *Labor and Employment Law Desk Book.* Englewood Cliffs, N.J.: Prentice-Hall, 1986.

Jenkins, J. *Labor Law, Its Evolution and Development from Criminal Conspiracy to Protected Rights and Mandatory Duties for Unions and Management Alike.* Cincinnati, Ohio: W. H. Anderson, 1968.

Kelly, John F., and Phillip K. Wearne. *Tainting Evidence: Inside Scandals at the FBI Crime Lab.* New York: The Free Press, 1998.

Kohn, Stephen M. *Protecting Environmental and Nuclear Whistleblowers: A Litigation Manual.* Washington, D.C.: Nuclear Information and Resource Service, 1985.

Kohn, Stephen M. *The Whistleblower Litigation Handbook: Environmental, Nuclear, Health, and Safety Claims.* New York: Wiley Law Publications, 1991.

Kohn, Stephen M., and Michael D. Kohn. *The Labor Lawyer's Guide to the Rights and Responsibilities of Employee Whistleblowers.* New York: Quorum Books, 1989.

Koven, Adolph M. *Just Cause: the Seven Tests.* Washington, D.C.: Bureau of National Affairs, 1992.

Larsen, Lex. *Unjust Dismissal.* New York: Matthew Bender, 1988.

Larson, A., and L. Larson. *Employment Discrimination.* New York: Matthew Bender, 1987.

Maas, Peter. *Serpico.* New York: Basic Books, 1973.

McGovern, K., ed. *Equal Employment Practice Guide.* Washington, D.C.: Federal Bar Association, 1978.

McLaughlin, D., and A. Schoomaker. *The Landrum-Griffin Act and Union Democracy.* Ann Arbor: University of Michigan Press, 1979.

Mason, A. *Organized Labor and the Law.* Durham, N.C.: Duke University Press, 1925.

Miceli, Marcia P. *Blowing the Whistle: The Organizational and Legal Implications for Companies and Employees.* New York: Lexington Books, 1992.

Miller, Marion M., ed. *Great Debates in American History, Vol. 8.* (Civil Rights: Part Two) New York: Current Literature Publishing Company, 1913, p. 197

Mintz, B. *OSHA, History, Law and Policy.* Washington, DC: Bureau of National Affairs, 1984.

Mitchell, Greg. *Truth and Consequences: Seven Who Would Not Be Silenced.* New York: Dembner Books, 1982.

Modjeska, L. *NLRB Practice.* Rochester, New York: Lawyers Cooperative Publishing, 1983.

Molander, Earl A. *"Case Five: Whistle Blowing at the Trojan Nuclear Plant."* In *Responsive Capitalism: Case Studies in Corporate Social Conduct.* New York: McGraw-Hill, 1980.

Moran, Robert. *How to Avoid OSHA.* Houston, Tex.: Gulf Publishing, 1980.

Nader, Ralph, Peter J. Petkas, and Date Blackwell, eds. *Whistle-Blowing: The Report of the Conference on Professional Responsibility.* New York: Grossman, 1972.

National Labor Law Center of the National Lawyers Guild, Robert Gibbs, and Paul Levey, eds. *Employee and Union Member's Guide to Labor Law: A Manual for Attorneys Representing the Labor Movement.* New York: Clark Boardman, 1987.

Nothstein, Gary. *The Law of Occupational Safety and Health.* New York: Free Press, 1981.

Office of Secretary of Labor (SOL). *Procedures for the Handling of Discrimination Complaints Under Federal Employer Protection Statutes.* 63 Federal Register 6614 (February 9, 1998), codified in 9 C.F.R. § 24 (1999).

Passman & Kaplan, P.C. *Federal Employees Legal Survival Guide.* Cincinnati: NERI, 1999.

Pepe, Stephen, and Scott Dunham. *Avoiding and Defending Wrongful Discharge Claims.* Wilmette, Ill.: Callaghan, 1987.

Perritt, Henry H, Jr. *Employee Dismissal Law and Practice.* New York: John Wiley and Sons, 1985.

Perritt, Henry H., Jr. *Employee Dismissal Law and Practice.* New York: Wiley Law Publications, 1998.

Peters, Charles, and Taylor Branch, eds. *Blowing the Whistle: Dissent in the Public Interest.* New York: Praeger, 1972.

Postic, Lionel J. *Wrongful Termination: A State-by-State Survey.* Washington, D.C.: Bureau of National Affairs, 1994.

Practicing Law Institute. *Occupational Disease Litigation, 1983.* New York: Practicing Law Institute, 1983.

Practicing Law Institute. *Unjust Dismissal and At-Will Employment.* New York: Practicing Law Institute, 1982.

Rapalie, Stewart. *A Treatise on Contempt.* New York: L. K. Strouse & Co., 1884.

Rashke, Richard. *The Killing of Karen Silkwood: The Story Behind the Kerr-McGee Plutonium Case.* Boston, Mass.: Houghton Mifflin Co., 1981.

Redeker, L. *Discipline: Policies and Procedures.* Washington, D.C.: Bureau of National Affairs, 1983.

Richy, Charles R. *Manual on Employment Discrimination and Civil Rights Actions in the Federal Courts.* New York: Kluwer Law Book Publishers, Inc., 1985.

Ruzicho, A., and L. Jacobs. *Litigating Age Discrimination Cases.* Wilmette, Ill.: Callaghan, 1986.

Sayre, Francis Bowes. *A Selection of Cases and Other Authorities on Labor Law.* Austin, Tex.: Book Lab, 1995.

U.S. Comptroller General. *First Year Activities of the Merit Systems Protection Board and the Office of Special Counsel.* Washington, D.C.: General Accounting Office, 1980.

U.S. Comptroller General. *The Office of the Special Counsel Can Improve Its Management of Whistleblower Cases.* Washington, D.C.: General Accounting Office, 1980.

U.S. Congress. House. Committee on Armed Services. Subcommittee on Investigations. *Proposed Legislation Regarding Whistleblower Protection: H.R. 2579 and H.R. 3255.* 101st Cong., 1st sess., 1989.

U.S. Congress. House. Committee on Education and Labor. Subcommittee on Labor-Management Relations. *Hearing on H.R. 3368, Whistleblower Protection Act.* 101st Cong., 1st sess., 1989.

U.S. Congress. House. Committee on Education and Labor. Subcommittee on Labor-Management Relations. *Hearing on H.R. 1664, Corporate Whistleblower Protection.* 102nd Cong., 2nd sess., 1992.

U.S. Congress. House. Committee on Government Operations. Legislation and National Security Subcommittee. *Federal Employee Secrecy Agreements.* 101st Cong., 1st sess., 1989.

U.S. Congress. House. Committee on Interstate and Foreign Commerce. Subcommittee on Transportation and Commerce. *Hazardous Waste Disposal Problems at Federal Facilities.* Hearing. 96th Cong. 2nd sess., 1980.

U.S. Congress. House. Committee on the Judiciary. Subcommittee on Commercial and Administrative Law. *Job Creation and Wage Enhancement Act of 1995, on H.R.9 (Title VI, VII, and VIII).* 104th Cong., 1st sess., 1995.

U.S. Congress. House. Committee on the Judiciary. *Impeachment of William Jefferson Clinton, President of the United States.* H.R. 105-830. 105th Cong., 2nd sess ., 1998.

U.S. Congress. House. Committee on Post Office and Civil Service. *Civil Service Reform Act of 1978.* Reprint. 95th Cong., 2nd sess., 1978.

U.S. Congress. House. Committee on Post Office and Civil Service. *Civil Service Reform Hearings on H.R. 11280.* 95th Cong., 2nd sess., 1978.

U.S. Congress. House. Committee on Post Office and Civil Service. *Hearings on the Whistleblower Protection Provision of the Civil Service Reform Act of 1978.* 96th Cong., 2nd sess., 1980.

U.S. Congress. House. Committee on Post Office and Civil Service. *Hearings on Whistleblower Protection.* 99th Cong., 1st sess., 1985.

U.S. Congress. House. Committee on Post Office and Civil Service. Subcommittee on Civil Service. *Civil Service Reform Oversight, Whistle-blower.*
96th Cong., 2nd sess., 1980.

U.S. Congress. House. Committee on Post Office and Civil Service. Subcommittee on Civil Service. *The Directed Reassignments of John Mumma and
L. Lorraine Mintzmyer: Hearing.* 102nd Cong., 1st sess., 1991.

U.S. Congress. House. Committee on Post Office and Civil Service. Subcommittee on Civil Service. *Federal Productivity and Performance Appraisal.
Hearings.* 96th Cong., 1st sess., 1979.

U.S. Congress. House. Committee on Post Office and Civil Service. *Final Report
on Violations and Abuses of Merit Principles in Federal Employment
Together with Minority Views.* 94th Cong., 2nd sess., 1976. Committee
Print.

U.S. Congress. House. Committee on Post Office and Civil Service. *H.R. 2970,
to Reauthorize the Office of Special Counsel and to Make Amendments
to the Whistleblower Protection Act.* 103rd Cong., 1st sess., 1993.

U.S. Congress. House. Committee on Ways and Means of the House of Representatives on H.R. 3448. *Small Business Job Protection Act of 1996,* pp.
142-44, May 20, 1996.

U.S. Congress. House. Permanent Select Committee on Intelligence. *Community
Whistleblower Protection Act of 1998: Report (to Accompany H.R. 3829)
(Including Cost Estimate of the Congressional Budget Office).* 105th
Cong., 2nd sess., 1998.

U.S. Congress. H.R. 1997. *Civil Rights Tax Fairness Act of 1999.* Introduced by
Representative Deborah Price on May 27, 1999.

U.S. Congress. Joint Economic Committee. *The Dismissal of A. Ernest Fitzgerald by the Department of Defense.* Hearings. 91st Cong., 1st sess.,
1969.

U.S. Congress. Senate. Committee on Environment and Public Works. Subcommittee on Nuclear Regulation. *Hearings on Secret Settlement Agreements Restricting Testimony at Comanche Peak Nuclear Power Plant.*
101st Cong., 2nd sess., May 4, 1989.

U.S. Congress. Senate. Committee on Governmental Affairs. *Civil Service
Reform Act of 1978. Conference Report.* 95th Cong., 2nd sess., 1978.

U.S. Congress. Senate. Committee on Governmental Affairs. *Civil Service
Reform Act of 1978 and Reorganization Plan No. 2 of 1978. Hearings,
on S. 2640, S. 2707, and S. 2830.* 95th Cong., 2nd sess., 1978. 2 vols.

U.S. Congress. Senate. Committee on Governmental Affairs. *The Office of
Special Counsel Reauthorization Act of 1992 to Accompany S. 2853.*
102nd Cong., 2nd sess., 1992.

U.S. Congress. Senate. Committee on Governmental Affairs. *The Whistleblowers: A Report on Federal Employees Who Disclose Acts of Governmental
Waste, Abuse, and Corruption.* 95th Cong., 2nd sess., 1978.

U.S. Congress. Senate. Committee on the Judiciary. *Nomination of Otto F.
Otepka. Hearings.* 91st Cong., 1st sess., 1969. 2 pts.

U.S. Congress. Senate. Committee on Labor and Human Resources. Subcommittee on Labor. *Employee Health and Safety Whistleblower Protection on S. 436.* 101st Cong., 1st sess., 1989.

U.S. Congress. Senate Subcommittee on Nuclear Regulation. *Hearings on Secret Settlement Restricting Testimony at Comanche Peak Nuclear Power Plant, etc.*, pp. 131-34. Senate hearing 101-90 (May 4, 1989).

U.S. General Accounting Office. *Nuclear Employee Safety Concerns: Allegation System Offers Better Protection, but Important Issues Remain.* GAO/HEHS-97-51 (March, 1997).

U.S. General Accounting Office. *Whistleblower Complaints Rarely Qualify for Office of Special Counsel Protection.* Washington, D.C., May 10, 1985.

U.S. Merit Systems Protection Board. *Whistleblowing and the Federal Employee: Blowing the Whistle on Fraud, Waste, and Mismanagement–Who Does It and What Happens.* Washington, D.C.: The Board, 1981.

Vaughn, Robert. *Merit Systems Protection Board: Rights and Remedies.* New York: Law Journal Seminars Press, 1984.

Weiner, P., S. Bompey, and M. Brittan. *Wrongful Discharge Claims, A Preventive Approach.* New York: Practicing Law Institute, 1986.

Westin, Alan F., ed. *Whistle-Blowing! Loyalty and Dissent in the Corporation.* New York: McGraw-Hill, 1980.

Westin, Alan F., and Stephan Salisbury, eds. *Individual Rights in the Corporation: A Reader on Employee Rights.* New York: Pantheon Books, 1980.

Westman, Daniel P. *Whistleblowing: The Law of Retaliatory Discharge.* Washington, D.C.: Bureau of National Affairs, 1991.

Whitaker, L. Paige. *Whistleblower Protection for Federal Employees.* Washington, D.C.: Congressional Research Service, 1990.

Wigmore, J. *Evidence § 285, Vol. 2.* City: Publisher, 3rd ed. 1940.

Yager, Daniel V. *Private Sector Whistleblower Protections: Existing Law and Proposed Expansions.* Washington, D.C.: National Foundation for the Study of Employment Policy, 1989.

ARTICLES

Abbot, R. Taylor. *Remedies for Employees Discharged for Reporting an Employer's Violation of Federal Law.* 12 Washington and Lee Law Review 1383 (Fall 1985).

Abramson, G., and S. Silvestri. *Recognition of a Cause of Action for Abusive Discharge in Maryland.* 10 University of Baltimore Law Review 257 (1981).

Adler, James N. *Managing the Whistleblowing Employee.* 8 The Labor Lawyer 19 (Winter 1992).

Adler, James, and Richard Levey. *Preemption of Workers' Compensation Retaliatory Discharge Laws.* 12 Employee Relations Law Review 630 (1987).

Alberts, Robert J. *The Employment At-Will Doctrine: Nevada's Struggle Demonstrates the Need for Reform.* 10 Labor Law Journal 651 (October 1992).

Allen, R., and P. Linenberger. *The Employee's Rights to Refuse Hazardous Work.* 9 Employee Relations Law Journal 251 (1983).

American Bar Association Section of Labor and Employment Law. *Committee Reports Issue.* 2 Labor Lawyer 351 (1986).

Ames, Eric. *The Fifth Circuit Blows the Whistle on Removal Jurisdiction.* 63 Tulane Law Review 1230 (May 1989).

Anglin, Mary K. *Whistleblowers, Nuclear Plant Safety, and Job Discrimination.* 117 Public Utilities Fortnightly 56(3) (April 17, 1976).

Annotation. *Discharge of Employee as Reprisal or Retaliation for Union Organizational Activities.* 83 American Law Reports, 2d 532 (1962).

Appel, Brent. *Employment At-Will in Iowa: A Journey Forward.* 39 Drake Law Review 67 (Fall 1989).

Archer, Edward. *Employment Contracts in Employment At-Will.* 16 Indiana Law Review 225 (1983).

Armour, Jonathan W. J. *Who's afraid of the Big, Bad Whistler? Minnesota's Recent Trend Toward Limiting Employer Liability Under the Whistleblower Statute.* 19 Hamline Law Review 107 (Fall 1995).

Aronson, Geoffrey. *The Co-opting of CASE.* The Nation 678 (December 4, 1989).

Atkins, Brendan J. *Labor Law Michigan's Whistleblowers Protection Act— WPA Protects from Retaliatory Discharge Employees Who Report Crimes of Co-workers Arising Out of Workplace Disputes Over the Handling of the Employer's Business.* 71 University of Detroit Mercy Law Review 1081 (Summer 1994).

Atkins, Chad A. *The Whistleblower Exception to the At-Will Employment Doctrine: An Economic Analysis of Environmental Policy Enforcement. (Costs and Concerns in Environmental Regulation and Litigation).* 70 Denver University Law Review 537 (Summer 1993).

Bakaly, C. *Erosion of the Employment At-Will Doctrine.* 8 Journal of Contemporary Law 63 (1982).

Baldwin, Charles G. *Meek v. Opp. Cotton Mills: The Alabama Supreme Court Refuses to Modify the Employment At-Will Rule.* 36 Alabama Law Review 1039 (Summer 1985).

Baldwin, S. *Fear of Firing—Is There a Cause of Action for Wrongful Discharge in Texas?* 47 Texas Bar Journal 11 (1984).

Ballam, Deborah A. *The Development of the Employment-At-Will Rule Revisited: A Challenge to Its Origins as Based in the Development of Advanced Capitalism.* 13 Hofstra Labor Law Journal 75 (Fall 1995).

Ballam, Deborah A. *Exploding the Original Myth Regarding Employment-At-Will: The True Origins of the Doctrine.* 17 Berkeley Journal of Employment and Labor Law 91 (Summer 1996).

Baran, Andrew. *Federal Employment—The Civil Service Reform Act of 1978 -*

Removing Incompetents and Protecting Whistle Blowers. Wayne Law Review (26 November 1979): 97.

Barbiere, Janet A. *Conspiracies to Obstruct Justice in the Federal Courts: Defining the Scope of Section 1985 (2).* 50 Fordham Law Review 1210 (1982).

Barna, James. *Keeping the Boss at Bay: Post-Termination Retaliation under Title VII.* 47 Washington University Journal of Urban and Contemporary Law 259 (Winter 1995).

Barnett, Tim. *Overview of State Whistleblower Protection Statutes.* 43 Labor Law Journal 440 (July 1992).

Barton, Eric D. *Comparing Kansas Employment-At-Will Law with the Model Employment Termination Act.* 41 University of Kansas Law Review 169 (Fall 1992).

Bast, Carol M. *At What Price Silence: Are Confidentiality Agreements Enforceable?* 25 William Mitchell Law Review 627, 694-713 (1999).

Baxter, R., and J. Farrell. *Constructive Discharge—When Quitting Means Getting Fired.* 7 Employment Law Journal 346 (1982).

Baxter, R., and J. Wohl. *A Special Update: Wrongful Termination Tort Claims.* 11 Employee Relations Law Journal 124 (1985).

Baxter, R., and J. Wohl. *Wrongful Termination Lawsuits: The Employers Finally Win a Few.* 10 Employee Relations Law Journal 258 (1984).

Becker, Claudia Everett. *The At-Will Doctrine: A Proposal to Modify the Texas Employment Relationship.* 36 Baylor Law Review 667 (1984).

Bell, Troy Nathan. *Employment At-Will: A Proposal to Modify the Employment Relationship in Louisiana.* 16 Southern University Law Review 379 (Fall 1989).

Berkovitz, Dan. *California's Nuclear Power Regulations: Federal Preemption?* 9 Hastings Constitutional Law Quarterly 623 (1982).

Berman, Craig. *South Carolina Whistleblower Protection: the Good, the Bad, and the Ugly.* 43 South Carolina Law Review 415 (Winter 1992).

Bierman, L., and S. Youngblood. *Employment At-Will and the South Carolina Experiment.* 7 Industrial Relations Law Journal 28 (1985).

Blackburn, J. *Restricted Employer Discharge Rights: A Changing Concept of Employment At-Will.* 17 American Business Law Journal 467 (1980).

Blades, Lawrence. *Employment At-Will v. Individual Freedom: On Limiting the Abusive Exercise of Employer Power.* 67 Columbia Law Review 1404 (December 1967).

Blank, Ira. *Wrongful Discharge Litigation and Employment-At-Will Rule in Missouri.* 40 Missouri Bar 161 (1984).

Blodgett, Nancy. *Whistle-Blowers Fight Back: More Are Suing Their Former Employers.* 73 American Bar Association Journal 20(2) (June 1, 1987).

Blumberg, Phillip. *Corporate Responsibility and the Employee's Duty of Loyalty and Obedience: A Preliminary Inquiry.* 24 Oklahoma Law Review 279 (August 1971).

Blumrosen, Alfred. *Worker's Rights Against Employers and Unions: Justice*

Francis—A Judge for Our Season. 24 Rutgers Law Journal 480 (1969-1970).

Bogen, Kenneth T. *Managing Technical Dissent in Private Industry: Societal and Corporate Strategies for Dealing with the Whistle-blowing Professional.* 13 Industrial and Labor Relations Forum 3 (1979).

Bok, Sissela. *Whistleblowing and Professional Responsibility.* 11 New York University Education Quarterly 2 (Summer 1980).

Bowman, James S. *Whistle-Blowing in the Public Service: An Overview of the Issues.* 1 Review of Public Personnel Administration 15 (Fall 1980).

Boyan, A. Stephen, Jr. *Whistleblowers: Auxiliary Precautions' Against Government Abuse.* 2 Ethical Society 5 (Spring 1979).

Boyette, K. *Terminating Employees in Virginia: A Roundup for the Employer, the Employee, and Their Counsel.* 17 University of Richmond Law Review 747 (1983).

Boyle, Robert D. *A Review of Whistle Blower Protections and Suggestion for Change.* 41 Labor Law Journal 821 (December 1990).

Brenner, Marie. *The Man Who Knew Too Much.* Vanity Fair 170 (May, 1996).

Broderick, James A., and Daniel Minahan. *Employment Discrimination under the Federal Mine Safety and Health Act.* 84 West Virginia Law Review 1023 (1982).

Brown, F. *Limiting Your Risks in the New Russian Roulette—Discharging Employees.* 8 Employee Relations Law Review 380 (1983).

Bullock, Joan R. *The Pebble in the Shoe: Making the Case for the Government Employee.* 60 Tennessee Law Review 365 (Winter 1993).

Burke, Maureen H. *The Duty of Confidentiality and Disclosing Corporate Misconduct.* 36 Business Lawyer 239 (January 1981).

Burton, Steven. *Breach of Contract and the Common Law Duty to Perform in Good Faith.* 94 Harvard Law Review 369 (December 1980).

Callahan, Elletta Sangrey. *Do Good and Get Rich: Financial Incentives for Whistleblowing and the False Claims Act.* 37 Villanova Law Review 273 (Apr.1992).

Callahan, Elletta Sangrey. *Employment At-Will: The Relationship Between Societal Expectations and the Law.* 28 American Business Law Journal 455 (Fall 1990).

Callan, J. Michael, and H. David. *Professional Responsibility and the Duty of Confidentiality: Disclosure of Client Misconduct in an Adversary System.* 29 Rutgers Law Review 332 (1976).

Campbell, Donald J. *Retaliatory Discharged Injured Workers.* Trial Magazine (October 1999).

Caples, Michael, and Kenneth Hanko. *The Doctrine of At-Will Employment in the Public Sector.* 13 Seton Hall Law Review 21 (1982-1983).

Carrol, M. *Protecting Private Employee Freedom of Political Speech.* 18 Harvard Journal on Legislation 35 (1981).

Catler, S. *The Case Against Proposals to Eliminate the Employment At-Will Rule.* 5 Industrial Relations Law Journal 471 (1983).

Cavico, Frank J. *Employment At-Will and Public Policy.* 25 Akron Law Review 497 (Winter-Spring 1992).

Cerbone, Richard. *The Res Judicata Effect of State Fair Employment Practice Commission Decisions.* 37 Labor Law Journal 780 (1986).

Chalk, Rosemary, and Frank von Hippel. *Due Process for Dissenting Whistle-blowers.* 81 Technology Review 49 (June/July 1979).

Chalk, Rosemary, and Frank von Hippel. *Due Process for Whistle-Blowers: Part 1—The Professional's Dilemma.* 102 Mechanical Engineering 82 (April 1980).

Chalk, Rosemary, and Frank von Hippel. *Due Process for Whistle-Blowers: Part 2—Who Should Protect Dissenters?* 102 Mechanical Engineering 762 (May 1980): p. 76.

Chapman, J. *Bad Faith Discharge of an Employee under a Contract Terminable At-Will.* 10 Trial Lawyer Guide 5 (1966).

Charlip, David J. *Wrongful Discharge: Proposals for Change (Michigan).* 36 Wayne Law Review 143 (Fall 1989).

Chineson, Joel. *The Fate of Whistleblowers.* 22 Trial 80(3) (December 1986).

Christiansen, Jon P. *A Remedy for the Discharge of Professional Employees Who Refuse to Perform Unethical or Illegal Acts: A Proposal in Aid of Professional Ethics.* 28 Vanderbilt Law Review 805 (May 1975).

Clark, Louis. *Blowing the Whistle on Corruption: How to Kill a Career in Washington.* 5 Barrister 10 (Summer 1978).

Cluff, Thomas L., Jr. *In Defense of a Narrow Public Policy Exception to the Employment At-Will Rule.* 16 Mississippi College Law Review 437 (Spring 1996).

Clutterbuck, David. *Blowing the Whistle on Corporate Misconduct.* 35 International Management 14 (January 1980).

Commander, Kathleen. *The Commonwealth Court Construes the Protection Afforded by the Pennsylvania Whistleblower Law Narrowly. (Annual Survey of Pennsylvania Administrative Law).* 5 Widener Journal of Public Law 781 (June 1996).

Comment. *Employment-at-Will and the Law of Contracts.* 23 Buffalo Law Review 211 (1973).

Comment. *"Just Cause" Termination Rights for At-Will Employees.* Det. C.L.R. 591 (1982).

Comment. *Labor Law Preemption Doctrine—State Trespass Laws—Peaceful Picketing—Sears, Roebuck and Co. v. San Diego County District Council of Carpenters.* New York Law School Law Review 689 (1980).

Comment. *Labor Law Preemption—Supreme Court Approves Unemployment Compensation for the Benefit of Striking Employees—New York Telephone Co. v. New York State Department of Labor.* 99 S. Ct. 1328 (1979), Creighton Law Review 1005 (1980).

Comment. *Limiting the Employer's Absolute Right of Discharge: Can Kansas Courts Meet the Challenge?* 29 University of Kansas Law Review 267 (1981).

Comment. *Termination of the At-Will Employee: The General Rule, and the Wisconsin Rule.* 65 Marquette Law Review 673 (1982).

Comment. *Towards a Property Right in Employment.* 22 Buffalo Law Review 1081(1973).

Connor, Susan Marie. *A Survey of Illinois Employment Discrimination Law.* 31 De Paul Law Review 323 (Winter 1987).

Cook, Daniel D. *Whistle-Blowers Friend or Foe?* 5 Industry Week 50 (October 1981).

Coombe, John. *Employee Handbooks: Asset or Liability.* 12 Employee Relations Law Journal 4 (1986).

Copus, D. and R. Lindsay. *Successfully Defending the Discriminatory/Wrongful Discharge Case.* 10 Employee Relations Law Journal 456 (1984-1985).

Corbo, Joan. *Kraus v. New Rochelle Hosp. Medical Ctr.: Are Whistleblowers Finally Getting the Protection They Need? (New York).* 12 Hofstra Labor Law Journal 141 (Fall 1994).

Cornell, Drucilla. *Dialogic Reciprocity and the Critique of Employment At-Will.* 10 Cardozo Law Review 1575 (March-April 1989).

Coven, Mark. *The First Amendment Rights of Policymaking Public Employees.* 12 Harvard Civil Rights—Civil Liberties Law Review 559 (Summer 1977).

Cox, A. *Recent Developments in Federal Labor Law Preemption.* 41 Ohio State Law Journal 277 (1980).

Crook, Penny Lozon. *Employment At-Will: The "American Rule" and Its Application in Alaska.* 2 Alaska Law Review 23 (1985).

Crow, Gregory L. *Arkansas Adopts the Public-Policy Exception to the Employment-At-Will Doctrine.* 42 Arkansas Law Review 187 (Winter 1989).

Culp, David. *Whistleblowers: Corporate Anarchists or Heroes? Towards a Judicial Perspective.* 13 Hofstra Labor Law Journal 109 (Fall 1995).

Dade, Jay M. *Shackling the Secretary's Hands: Limits to Authorizing Whistleblower Settlements under Section 210 of the Energy Reorganization Act.* 1992 Journal of Dispute Resolution 227 (Spring 1992).

Dawson, John P. *Economic Duress and the Fair Exchange in French and German Law.* 11 Tulane Law Review 345 (1937).

Decker, Kurt. *At-Will Employment: Abolition and Federal Statutory Regulation.* 61 University Detroit Journal Urban Law 351 (1984).

Decker, Kurt. *At-Will Employment in Pennsylvania—A Proposal for Its Abolition and Statutory Regulation.* 87 Dickinson Law Review 477 (Spring 1983).

DeFranko, James. *Modification of the Employee At-Will Doctrine.* 30 Saint Louis University Law Journal 65 (October 1985).

De Giuseppe, Joseph, Jr. *The Effect of the Employment-At-Will Rule on Employee Rights to Job Security and Fringe Benefits.* 10 Fordham Urban Law Journal 1 (1981).

De Giuseppe, Joseph, Jr. *The Recognition of Public Policy Exceptions to the Employment-At-Will Rule: A Legislative Function?* 11 Fordham Urban Law Journal 721 (1983).

Delchamps, Afred F., III. *The Employment-at-Will Rule.* 31 Alabama Law Review 421 (1981).

Devine, Thomas M. *The Whistleblower Protection Act of 1989: Foundation for the Modern Law of Employment Dissent.* 51 Administrative Law Review 531 (1999).

Devine, Thomas M. *Whistleblower Protection—The Gap Between the Law and Reality.* 31 Howard Law Journal 223 (Spring 1988).

Devine, Thomas, and Donald Aplin. *Abuse of Authority: The Office of the Special Counsel and Whistleblower Protection.* 4 Antioch Law Journal 5 (Summer 1986).

Dewitt, Anthony L. *Is the Whistle Clean? An Examination of the Ethical Duties of Attorneys in Investigating and Pursuing False Claims Act Lawsuits.* 25 Northern Kentucky Law Review 715 (Summer 1998).

DiSabatino, Michael A. *Modern Status of Rule That Employer May Discharge at-Will Employee for Any Reason.* 12 American Law Reports, 4th 544 (1982).

Doggett, Lloyd and Michael Mucchetti. *Public Access to Public Courts: Discouraging Secrecy in the Public Interest.* 69 Texas Law Review 643 (1991).

Donovan, Kevin L. *Employment "by the book" in New Jersey: Woolley and Its Progeny (Employment At-Will).* 22 Seton Hall Law Review 814 (Summer 1992).

Dorman, Charles. *Justice Brennan: The Individual and Labor Law.* 59 Chicago-Kent Law Review, 1003 (1982).

Drachaler, David. *Brown & Root v. Donovan: An Exercise in Judicial Myopia.* 38 Labor Law Journal 311 (May 1987).

Drachaler, David. *Burdens of Proof in Retaliatory Adverse Action Cases Under Title VII.* 35 Labor Law Journal 28 (1984).

Duffy, Sennis P. *Intentional Infliction of Emotional Distress and Employment At-Will: The Case Against "Tortification" of Labor and Employment Law.* 74 Boston University Law Review 387 (May 1994).

Dwan and Fiedler. *The Federal Statutes.* 22 Minn. Law Review 1008, 1014 (1938).

Dworkin, Terry Morehead. *Internal Whistleblowing: Protecting the Interests of the Employee, the Organization, and Society.* 29 American Business Law Journal 267 (Summer 1991).

Egan, Thomas E. *Wrongful Discharge and Federal Preemption: Nuclear Whistleblower Protection Under State Law And Section 210 of the Energy Reorganization Act.* 17 Boston College Environmental Affairs Law Review 405 (Winter 1990).

Ehrenkranz, Wendy. *Whistleblowing as a Rule 10b-5 Violation.* 36 University of Miami Law Review 987 (Sept.1982).

Ellis, Howard C. *Employment-At-Will and Contract Principles: The Paradigm of Pennsylvania.* 96 Dickinson Law Review 595 (Summer 1992).

Entzeroth, Suzanne. *Labor Law Preemption: Allis Chalmers Corp. v. Lueck.* 60 Tulane Law Review 1077 (1986).

Epstein, Jon. *Pre-emption by Worker's Compensation Statute of Employee's Remedy Under State Whistleblower Statute.* 20 American Law Reports, 5th 677 (1998).

Epstein, Richard. *In Defense of the Contract At-Will.* 51 University of Chicago Law Review 947 (Fall 1984).

Estreicher, Samuel. *At-Will Employment and the Problem of Unjust Dismissal: The Appropriate Judicial Response.* 54 New York State Bar Journal 146 (April 1982).

Ewing, David. *The Employee's Right to Speak Out: The Management Perspective.* 5 Civil Liberties Review 10 (September/October 1978).

Ewing, David. *What Business Thinks About Employee Rights.* 77 Harvard Business Review 81 (September/October 1977).

False Claims Act and Qui Tam Quarterly Review. Taxpayers Against Fraud, published quarterly.

Feerick, John D. *Toward a Model Whistleblower Law.* 19 Fordham Urban Law Journal 585 (Spring 1992).

Feinman, J. *The Development of the Employment-At-Will Rule.* 20 American Journal of Legal History 118 (1976).

Feinman, J. *The Development of the Employment-At-Will Rule Revisited.* 23 Arizona State Law Journal 733 (Fall 1991).

Feldman, David M. *Employment-At-Will in Texas: When and How Will the Whistle Blow?* 10 Corporate Counsel Review 119 (November 1991).

Feliu, Alfred G. *Whistleblowing While You Work.* 72 Business Society Review 65 (1990).

Fentin, Susan G. *The False Claims Act—Finding Middle Ground Between Opportunity and Opportunism: the "Original Source" Provision of 31 U.S.C. § 3730(e)(4).* 17 Western England Law Review 255 (1995).

Fentonmiller, Keith R. *When Does Retaliation Count Under Title VII?* 23 Employee Relations Law Journal 31 (Fall 1997).

Ferguson, John W., Jr. *Texas Supreme Court Refuses to Recognize a "Whistleblower" Exception to the At-Will Employment Rule For Private Employees.* 22 Texas Tech Law Review 1215 (October 1991).

Finberg, B. *What Constitutes an "Interception" of a Telephone or Similar Communication Forbidden by the Federal Communications Act [47 U.S.C.A. § 605] or Similar State Statutes.* 9 American Law Reports, 3d 423 (1967).

Fish, David. *Article: The Legal Rock and the Economic Hard Place: Remedies of Associate Attorneys Wrongfully Terminated For Refusing to Violate Ethical Rules.* 30 University West Los Angeles Review 61 (1999).

Fisher, Bruce D. *The Whistleblower Protection Act of 1989: A False Hope for Whistleblowers.* 43 Rutgers Law Review 355 (Winter 1991).

Forbes, F., and I. Jones. *A Comparative, Attitudinal and Analytical Study of Dismissal of at-Will Employees Without Cause.* 37 Labor Law Journal 157 (1986).

Freedman, A.M. *The Deposition: Cigarette Defector Says CEO Lied to Congress About View of Nicotine.* Wall Street Journal, A-1 (January 26, 1996).

Furlane, M. *Employment At-Will: An Eroding Doctrine.* 65 Chicago Bar Record 36 (1983).

Galinsky, M. S. *Eavesdropping As Violating Right of Privacy.* 11 American Law Reports, 3d 1296 (1967).

Gates, Sean F. *California Antitrust: Standing Room for the Wrongfully Discharged Employees?* 47 Hastings Law Journal 509 (January 1996).

Gearity, Kimberly Kraly. *At-Will Employment: Time for Good Faith and Fair Dealing Between Employers and Employees.* 28 Willamette Law Review 681 (Summer 1992).

Gibson, David G. *Expanding the Public Policy Exception to the Employment-At-Will Doctrine.* 38 Villanova Law Review 1527 (October 1993).

Gillan, Paul A., Jr. *Miller v. Fairchild Industries: Judiciary ot Justified in Recognizing Cause of Action for Abusive Discharge of Environmental Whistleblowing.* 4 University of Baltimore Journal of Environmental Law 121 (Winter 1994).

Gillette, P. *The Implied Covenant of Good Faith and Fair Dealing: Are Employers the Insurers of the Eighties?* 11 Employee Relations Labor Journal 438 (1985-1986).

Glazer, Myron, and Pinina Glazer. *Whistleblowing.* Psychology Today (August 1986).

Glendon, Mary Ann, and Edward Lev. *Changes in the Bonding of the Employment Relationship.* 20 Boston College Industrial and Commercial Law Review 457 (March 1979).

Goetz, Charles, and Robert Scott. *Principles of Relational Contracts.* 67 Virginia Law Review 1089 (September 1981).

Goger, Thomas. *Workmen's Compensation: Recovery for Discharge in Retaliation for Filing Claim.* 63 American Law Reports, 3d 979 (1975).

Goldsmith, Russell. *Contracting Out of Maine's Employment-At-Will Doctrine.* 42 Maine Law Review 553 (July 1990).

Greenbaum, Marc. *Toward a Common Law of Employment Discrimination.* 58 Temple Law Quarterly 65 (Spring 1985).

Grodin, Maryann Lawrence. *Nuclear Whistleblowers: An Environment of Change. (Shaping theLaw of the Environment).* 41 Federal Bar News & Journal 98 (February 1994).

Grove, Kalvin, and Paul Garry. *Employment-at-Will in Illinois: Implications and Anticipations for the Practitioner.* 31 De Paul Law Review 359 (Winter 1982).

Guarino, Glenn A. *Prohibition of Discrimination Against, of Discharge of, Employee because of Exercise of Right Afforded by OSHA under § 11(c)(1) of the Act.* 66 American Law Reports, Federal 650 (1998).

Halbert, Terry Ann. *The Cost of Scruples: A Call for Common Law Protection for the Professional Whistleblower.* 10 Nova Law Journal 1 (Fall 1985).

Hale, A. Craig. *Employment-At-Will And the Implied Covenant of Good Faith and Fair Dealing.* 1992 Utah Law Review 230 (Winter 1992).

Hannum, Wendy J. *"Good Cause": California's New "Exception" to the At-Will Doctrine.* 23 Santa Clara Law Review 263 (1983).

Harper, C. *Expanding Liability for Employment Termination.* 18 Trial 60 (December 1982).

Harrison, Jeffrey. *The "New" Terminable-At-Will Contract: An Interest and Cost Incidence Analysis.* 69 Iowa Law Review 327 (January 1984).

Harrison, Jeffrey. *Wrongful Discharge: Toward A More Efficient Remedy.* 56 Indiana Law Journal 207 (Winter 1981).

Hassel, Diana. *Beyond Pierce v. Ortho Pharmaceutical Corp., the Termination-at-Will Doctrine in New Jersey.* 37 Rutgers Law Review 137 (1984).

Hayford, Stephen L. *Agreements to Arbitrate Statutory Fair Employment Practices Claim: Unforeseen Consequences for the At-Will Employer.* 46 Labor Law Journal 543 (September 1995).

Heinsz, Timothy. *The Assault on the Employment At-Will Doctrine: Management Considerations.* 48 Missouri Law Review 855 (Fall 1983).

Hellow, John R. and Stacie K. Neroni. *Symposium: The Federal False Claims Act: Can Whistle Blowers Reach State and Local Tax Dollars?* 44 St. Louis Law Journal 133 (Winter 2000).

Hentoff, Nat. *Putting the Gag on CIA Whistle Blowers.* 5 Civil Liberties Review 37 (July/August 1978).

Herman, Donald, and Yvonne Sor. *Property Rights in One's Job.* 24 Arizona Law Review 763 (1982).

Heshizer, B. *The Implied Contract Exception to at-Will Employment.* 35 Labor Law Journal 131 (1984).

Ho, Debbie. *Employment Law—Exceptions to the At-Will Doctrine—the Adoption of the Public Policy Exception in Two Specific Situations Could Signal the Adoption of Additional Exceptions to the Doctrine.* 64 Mississippi Law Journal 257 (1994).

Hockman, Shelby L. *Altering the Employment-At-Will Relationship.* 20 American Journal of Trial Advocacy 181 (Fall 1996).

Hoekstra, Kathlyn B. *Palmateer [Palmateer v. International Harvester Co., 421 N.E.2d 876 (Ill.)]: A Further Extension to Retaliatory Discharge in Illinois.* 71 Illinois Bar Journal 298 (1983).

Hoffman, Goeffrey A. *Whistleblower Protection: Is Retaliatory Discharge Allowed under the Employment-At-Will Doctrine in Admiralty?* 21 Tulane Maritime Law Journal 171 (Winter 1996).

Holland, Jennifer L. *Expansion of Oklahoma's Public Policy Exception to the Employment-At-Will doctrine.* 30 Tulsa Law Journal 525 (Spring 1995).

Holmstrom, Brad E. *Employment At-Will in Iowa: Is It the Rule or the Exception?* 39 Drake Law Review 157 (Fall 1989).

Hopkins, Shelley A., and Donald C. Robinson. *Employment At-Will, Wrongful Discharge, and the Covenant of Good Faith and Fair Dealing in Montana, Past, Present and Future.* 46 Montana Law Review 1 (1985).

Hubbell, James W. *Retaliatory Discharge and the Economics of Deterrence.* 60 University of Colorado Law Review 91 (Winter 1989).

Huffman, Kimberly Anne. *Clarifying the Confusion in North Carolina's Employment-At-Will Doctrine.* 70 North Carolina Law Review 2087 (September 1992).

Hursh, R.D. *Discharge from Private Employment on Ground of Political Views or Conduct.* 51 American Law Reports, 2d 742 (1957).

Ichinose, S. *Hawaii's Supreme Court Recognizes Tort of Retaliatory Discharge of an at-Will Employee.* 17 Hawaii Bar Journal 123 (1982).

Ingram, Timothy. *On Muckrakers and Whistle Blowers.* 1 Business and Society Review 21 (August 1972).

Isbell-Sirotkin, Eric. *Defending the Abusively Discharged Employee: In Search of a judicial Solution.* 12 New Mexico Law Review 711 (Spring 1982).

Israel, Francine C. *Fire At-Will: An Analysis of the Missouri At-Will Employment Doctrine.* 25 St. Louis University Law Journal 845 (1982).

Janack, Laurie H. *Constitutional Law —Freedom of Speech: Public Employee— Can We Talk? The Wyoming Supreme Court Grants Little Protection to Public Employee Whistleblowers.* 27 Land and Water Law Review 625 (Summer 1992).

Jones, Marzetta. *The 1996 Arizona Employment Protection Act: A Return to the Employment-At-Will Doctrine.* 39 Arizona Law Review 1139 (Fall 1997).

Jordan, Michael. *Employment-at-will in Kentucky: There Ought to Be a Law.* 20 Northern Kentucky Law Review 785 (Spring 1993).

Jos, Philip H. *In Praise of Difficult People: A Portrait of the Committed Whistleblower.* 49 Public Administration Review 552 (November-December 1989).

Kaden, L. *Federal Labor Preemption: The Supreme Court Draws the Lines.* 18 The Urban Lawyer 607 (1984).

Kane, Michael. *Whistleblowers: Are They Protected?* 20 Ohio Northern University Law Review 1007 (Spring 1994).

Kaner, Cem. *False Claims Act Bar May Be Overturned by Pending Legislation.* 23 Golden Gate University Law Review 279 (Spring 1993).

Kimball, Karen J. *Case Note: Taliento v. Portland West Neighborhood Council: The At Will Doctrine Continues to Thrive in Maine.* 51 Maine Law Review 211 (1999).

Kinyon, Susan, and Josef Rohlik. *"Deflouring" Lucas Through Labored Characterizations: Tort Actions of Unionized Employees.* 30 Saint Louis University Law Journal 1 (October 1985).

Kirk, Valerie P. *The Texas Whistleblower Act: Tme for a Change.* 26 Texas Tech Law Review 75 (Winter 1995).

Kirschner, R., and M. Walfoort. *The Duty of Fair Representation: Implications of Bowen.* 1 Labor Lawyer 19 (1985).

Kobus, John Jacob Jr. *Establishing Corporate Counsel's Right to Sue for Retaliatory Discharge.* 29 Valparaiso University Law Review 1343 (Summer 1995).

Kobylak, Wesley. *Admiralty: Recovery for Retaliatory Discharge of At-Will Maritime Employee.* 62 American Law Reports, Federal 790 (1983).

Koets, Robert F. *What Constitutes Appropriate Relief for Retaliatory Discharge Under § 11(c) of OSHA.* 134 *American Law Reports, Federal* 629 (1997).

Kohn, Stephen. *The Crisis in Environmental Whistleblower Protection: Deficiencies in the Regulations Protecting Employees Who Disclose Violations of Environmental Laws or Testify in 'Citizen Suits.'* 2 New England Environmental Law Forum, 1 7-8 (N.E. School of Law, 1995).

Kohn, Stephen, and Thomas Carpenter. *Nuclear Whistleblower Protection and the Scope of Protected Activity Under Section 210 of the Energy Reorganization Act.* 4 Antioch Law Journal 75 (Summer 1986).

Kohn, Stephen, and Michael Kohn. *An Overview of Federal and State Whistleblower Protections.* 4 Antioch Law journal 99 (Summer 1986).

Kovacic, William E. *Whistleblower Bounty Lawsuits as Monitoring Devices in Government Contracting.* 29 Loyola of Los Angeles Law Review 1799 (June 1996).

Kramer, Mark R. *The Role of Federal Courts in Changing State Law: The Employment At-Will Doctrine in Pennsylvania.* 133 University of Pennsylvania Law Review 227 (1984).

Kraus, Peter Augustine. *Federal Preemption of State Tort Law Claims in the Nuclear Industry (1990-1991: Annual Survey of Labor and Employment Law).* 33 Boston College Law Review 468 (March 1992).

Krauskopf, Joan. *Employment Discharge: Survey and Critique of the Modern At-Will Rule.* 51 University of Missouri—Kansas City Law Review 189 (Winter 1983).

Krawec, Dolores Jacobs. *The Employment-at-Will Sale: The Development of Exceptions and Pennsylvania's Response.* 21 Duquesne Law Review 477 (Winter 1983).

Kreiswirth, Brian J. *Justifiable Limitations on Title VII Anti-Retaliation Provisions.* 107 Yale Law Journal 2339 (May 1998).

Krohn, Mary Dubois. *The False Claims Act and Managed Care: Blowing the Whistle on Underutilization.* 28 Cumberland Law Review 443 (Winter 1998).

Krupnow, Mary McCrory. *Employee Beware - Relocation Does Not Remove the Presumption of Employment-At-Will (North Carolina) (Survey of Developments in North Carolina Law and the Fourth Circuit).* 76 North Carolina Law Review 2423 (Sept. 1998).

Kuhlmann-Macro, Vanessa F. *Blowing the Whistle on the Employment At-Will Doctrine.* 41 Drake Law Review 339 (Spring 1992).

Kurzman, Dani. *Michigan's Whistleblowers' Protection Act: Job Protection for Citizen Crime Fighters.* 5 Corporation, Finance & Business Law Journal 43 (Summer 1981).

Lauretano, Daniel A. *The Military Whistleblower Protection Act and the Military Mental Health Evaluation Protection Act.* Army Lawyer (October 1998): 1

Le Riche, Jeff. *Protection for Employee Whistleblowers under the Fair Labor Standards Act and Missouri's Public Policy Exception: What Happens if the Employee Never Whistled?* 60 Missouri Law Review 973 (Fall 1995).

Levinson, Rosalie Berger. *Silencing Government Employee Whistleblowers in the Name of "Efficiency."* 23 Ohio Northern University Law Review 17 (October 1996).

Levy, Richard. *Discovery: The Plaintiff's Case.* 287 PLI/Lit 125 (July 1, 1985).

Lindauer, Mitchell. *Government Employee Disclosures of Agency Wrongdoing: Protecting the Right to Blow the Whistle.* 42 University of Chicago Law Review 530 (Spring 1975).

Linzer, Peter. *The Decline of Assent: At-Will Employment as a Case Study of the Breakdown of Private Law Theory.* 20 Georgia Law Review 323 (Winter 1986).

Lofgren, Lois A. *Whistleblower Protection: Should Legislatures and the Courts Provide a Shelter to Public and Private Sector Employees Who Disclose the Wrongdoing of Employers?* 38 South Dakota Law Review 316 (Summer 1993).

Loomis, Lloyd. *Employee Assistance Programs: Their Impact on Arbitration and Litigation of Termination Cases.* 12 Employee Relations Law Journal 275 (1986).

Loscalzo, Theresa E. *RICO Conspiracy: Whistleblowers Coming in Through the Back Door.* 10 Labor Lawyer 679 (Fall 1994).

Love, Jean. *Retaliatory Discharge for Filing a Workers' Compensation Claim: The Development of a Modern Tort Action.* 37 Hastings Law Journal 551 (March 1986).

Love, Lisa A. *Has Ohio Gone Too Far in Creating a Public Policy Exception to the Employment At-Will?* 18 Northern Kentucky Law Review 543 (Spring 1991).

Lowy, Joan. *Constitutional Limitations on the Dismissal of Public Employees.* 43 Brooklyn Law Review 1 (Summer 1976).

Ludington, John. *Employer Discrimination Against Employees for Filing Charges or Giving Testimony Under NLRA.* 35 American Law Reports, Federal 132 (1977, 1999 Supplement).

Lyons, W. *State Regulation of Nuclear Power Production: Facing the Preemption Challenge from a New Perspective.* 76 Northwestern University Law Review 134 (1981).

Maddux, Cortlan H. *Employers Beware! The Emerging Use of Promissory Estoppel as an Exception to Employment At-Will.* 49 Baylor Law Review 197 (Winter 1997).

Madison, J. *The Employee's Emerging Right to Sue for Arbitrary or Unfair Discharge.* 6 Employee Relations Law Journal 422 (1981).

Malin, Martin. *The Distributive and Corrective Justice Concerns in the Debate Over Employment-At-Will: Some Preliminary Thoughts.* 68 Chicago-Kent Law Review 117 (Winter 1992).

Malin, Martin. *Protecting the Whistleblower from Retaliatory Discharge.* 16 University of Michigan Journal of Legal Reform 277 (Winter 1983).

Mallur, Jane. *Punitive Damages for Wrongful Discharge of at-Will Employees.* 26 William and Mary Law Review 449 (1984).

Manelbaum, R. *Whistle-blowers; Brown and Williamson v. Wigard.* American Lawyer p. 115 (March 1996).

Marcotte, Paul. *Blowing Whistle Can Pay Off.* 73 American Bar Association Journal 31(1) (March 1, 1987).

Marrinan, S. *Employment At-Will: Pandora's Box May Have an Attractive Cover.* 7 Hamline Law Review 155 (1984).

Marshall, Gary, and Maris Wicker. *The Status of the At-Will Employment Doctrine in Virginia after Bowman v. State Bank of Keysville.* 20 University of Richmond Law Review 267 (Winter 1986).

Martin, B. Morris. *Contracts.* 34 Mercer Law Review 71 (Fall 1982).

Martin, D., K. Bartol, and M. Levine. *The Legal Ramifications of Performance Appraisal.* 12 Employee Relations Law Journal 370 (1986-1987).

Martin, John. *The Whistleblower Revisited.* 8 George Mason University Law Review 123 (Fall 1985).

Martin, Mark L. *Wrongful Discharge of Employees Terminable At Will—A New Theory of Liability in Arkansas.* 34 Arkansas Law Review 729 (1981).

Martin, Read. *Little Big Man.* Dallas Observer (May 18, 1989).

Martucci, William C, and John L. Utz. *Wrongful Interference with Protected Rights under ERISA.* 2 The Labor Lawyer 251 (1986).

Massenoill, Douglas. *Whistleblowing: Protected Activity Or Not?* 15 Employee Relations Law Journal 49 (Summer 1989).

Massingale, Cheryl S. *At-Will Employment: Going, Going...* 24 University of Richmond Law Review 187 (Winter 1990).

Mauk, William. *Wrongful Discharge: The Erosion of 100 Years of Employer Privilege.* 21 Idaho Law Review 201 (Spring 1985).

Mayer, Stephen. *N.J.'s "Whistleblower Act."* 119New Jersey Law Journal (March 5, 1987).

McClenahan, Keenan. *At-Will Employment Agreements: New Focus on Shielding Employers From Wrongful Termination Suits?* 17 Western State University Law Review 131 (Fall 1989).

McCoy, Kimberly A. *Litigating Under the Florida Private Sector Whistle-Blower's Act: Plaintiff Protection and Good Faith.* 52 University of Miami Law Review 855 (April 1998).

McGowan, William. *The Whistleblowing Game.* New Age (September 1984).

McKinney, Charles. *Fair Representation of Employees in Unionized Firms.* 35 Labor Law Journal 693 (1984).

McMillion, Rhonda. *Aiding Whistle-Blowers: Lawmakers Determined to Enact Bill Despite Veto.* 75 ABA Journal 121 (March 1989).

McNett, Margaret. *Employee Handbooks as a Modification to Employment At-Will.* 60 University of Colorado Law Review 169 (Winter 1989).

McWeeny, R. *Out of the Fog: A Different View on Retaliatory Employee Discharge.* 54 Conn. B.I. 235 (1980).

Meek, Barry T. *Policy - Not Ambiguity - Drives the Supreme Court's Decision to Broaden Title VII's Retaliation Coverage.* 31 University of Richmond Law Review 473 (Mar. 1997).

Mello, Jeffrey A. *In Defense of the HR Manager: Rethinking the Title VII Anti-Retaliation Provision.* 48 Labor Law Journal 403 (July 1997).

Mennemeier, K. *Protection from Unjust Discharges: An Arbitration Scheme.* 19 Harvard Journal on Legis. 49 (1982).

Micell, Marcia P. *Who Blows the Whistle and Why?* 45 Industrial and Labor Relations Review 113 (October 1991).

Miller, Anthony H. and R. Wayne Estes. *Recent Judicial Limitations on the Right to Discharge: A California Trilogy.* 16 University of California, Davis Law Review 65 (1982).

Miller, Eric H. J.D. *Permissable Surveillance, Under State Communications Interception Statute, by Person Other than State or Local Law Enforcement Officer or One Acting in Concert with Officer.* 24 *American Law Reports, 4th* 1208 (1981).

Minda, Gary. *The Common Law of Employment at-Will in New York: The Paralysis of Nineteenth Century Doctrine.* 36 Syracuse Law Review 939 (1985).

Minda, Gary. *Time for an Unjust Dismissal Statue in New York.* 54 Brooklyn Law Review 1137 (Winter 1989).

Moberly, Michael D. *Article: Cranking the Wrongful Discharge Ratchet: Judicial Abrogation of Legislative Limitations on the Public Policy Exception.* 24 Seton Hall Legislative Journal 43 (1999).

Molinari, Brian M. *Conspiracy Theory: The RICO Predicate Act Requirement for Wrongful Discharge Cases Brought under 18 U.S.C. § 1962 (d).* 31 Suffolk University Law Review 481 (December 1997).

Mooney, Thomas, and Jeffrey Pingpank. *Wrongful Discharge: A "New" Cause of Action?* 54 Connecticut Bar Journal 213 (June 1980).

Moore, Patricia A. *Parting is Such Sweet Sorrow: The Application of Title VII to Post-employment Retaliation.* 62 Fordham Law Review 205 (October 1993).

Moore, T. *Individual Rights of Employees with the Corporation.* 6 Corporate Law Review 39 (1983).

Morris, Peggy H. *Missouri's Employment At-Will: Vulnerable to Prima Facie Tort?* 27 St. Louis University Law Journal 1001 (1983).

Morriss, Andrew P. *Developing a Framework for Empirical Research on the Common Law: General Principles and Case Studies of the Decline of Employment-At-Will.* 45 Case Western Reserve Law Review 999 (Summer 1995).

Morriss, Andrew P. *Exploding Myths: An Empirical and Economic Reassessment of the Rise of Employment At-Will.* 59 Missouri Law Review 679 (Summer 1994).

Mullings, Sandra. *Is There Whistleblower Protection for Private Employees in New York?* 69 New York State Bar Journal 36 (February 1997).

Murg, G., and C. Seharman. *Employment At-Will: Do the Exceptions Overwhelm the Rule?* 23 Boston College Law Review 329 (1982).

Nader, Ralph. *No Protection for Outspoken Scientists.* Physics Today (July 1973): 77.

Naylor, Gregory. *Employment At-Will: The Decay of an Anachronistic Shield for Employers.* 33 Drake Law Review 113 (1983-84).

Near, Janet, and Marcia Niceli. *Retaliation Against Whistle Blowers: Predictors and Effects.* 71 Journal of Applied Psychology 137 (1986).

Nickel, Henry. *The First Amendment and Public Employees-An Emerging Constitutional Right to be a Policeman?* 37 George Washington Law Review 409 (December 1968).

Note. *Employment At-Will: A Proposal to Adopt the Public Policy Exception in Florida.* 34 University of Florida Law Review 614 (1982).

Nulton, W., H. Jacobs, and C. Craver. *Duty of Fair Representation in Grievance and Arbitration Procedures.* 1 The Labor Lawyer 321 (1985).

Oianen, I. *Preemption—Atomic Energy.* 24 Natural Resources Journal 761 (1984).

Oliveiri, David J. *Right of Employee, Discharged for Refusal to Participate in Employer's Anticompetitive Practices, to Bring Action under Federal Antitrust Laws Against Employer.* 64 American Law Reports, Federal 825 (1983).

Olsen, Justin R. *The Course of the Employment-At-Will Doctrine in Utah—a Turning of the Tide.* 5 Brigham Young University Journal of Public Law 249 (Spring 1991).

Olsen, Theodore. *Wrongful Discharge Claims Raised by At-Will Employees: A New Legal Concern for Employers.* 32 Labor Law Journal 265 (May 1981).

Olson, Timothy P. *Taking the Fear Out of Being a Tattletale: Whistle Blower Protection under the False Claims Act.* 44 DePaul Law Review 1363 (Summer 1995).

Owens, Thomas P., III. *Employment At-Will in Alaska: The Question of Public Policy Torts.* 6 Alaska Law Review 269 (December 1989).

Parker, J. Wilson. *At-Will Employment and the Common Law: A Modest Proposal to De-Marginalize Employment Law.* 81 Iowa Law Review 347 (December 1995).

Parker, J. Wilson. *The Constitutional Status of Public Employee Speech: A Question for the Jury?* 65 Boston University Law Review 483 (May 1985).

Pasman, Nora J. *The Public Interest Exception to the Employment-At-Will Doctrine: from Crime Victims to Whistleblowers. Will the Real Public Policy Please Stand Up?* 70 University of Detroit Mercy Law Review 559 (Spring 1993).

Peck, Cornelius. *Some Kind of Hearing for Persons Discharged from Private Employment.* 16 San Diego Law Review 313 (1979).

Peck, Cornelius. *Unjust Discharges from Employment: A Necessary Change in the Law.* 40 Ohio State Law Journal 1 (1979).

Perritt, Henry H., Jr. *The Future of Wrongful Dismissal Claims: Where Does Employer Self Interest Lie?* 58 University of Cincinnati Law Review 397 (Fall 1989).

Pfeifle, Jane Wipf. *The Evolving Boundaries of the At-Will Employment Doctrine in South Dakota: Defining the Need for Broader Exceptions.* 38 South Dakota Law Review 273 (Summer 1993).

Phelps, Morgan J. *Comment: The False Claims Act's Public Disclosure Bar: Defining the Line Between Parasitic and Beneficial.* 49 Catholic University Law Review 247 (Fall 1999).

Pickens, Bruce Andrew Jr. *Employment At-Will and the Binding Unilateral Contract.* 40 Alabama Law Review 641 (Winter 1989).

Pickholz, Marvin. *The Victim and Witness Protection Act of 1982— Implications for the In-House Counsel.* 13 Securities Regulation Law Journal 195 (Fall 1985).

Pierce, E., R. Mann, and B. Roberts. *Employee Termination At-Will: A Principled Approach.* 28 Villanova Law Review 1 (November 1982).

Pilon, Roger. *Corporations and Rights: On Treating Corporate People Justly.* 13 Georgia Law Review 1245 (Summer 1979).

Platt, L. Steven. *Rethinking the Right of Employers to Terminate at-Will Employees.* 15 John Marshall Law Review 633 (Summer 1982).

Poon, Peter. *Legal Protections for the Scientific Misconduct Whistleblower.* 23 Journal of Law, Medicine & Ethics 88 (Spring 1995).

Posner, Richard A. *Hegel and Employment At-Will: A Comment.* 10 Cardozo Law Review 1625 (March-April 1989).

Powell, Burnele V. *Whistling in the Dark: the Problem of Federal Whistleblower Protection for In-House Reporters of Corporate Wrongdoing.* 68 Oregon Law Review 569 (Summer 1989).

Power, R. *A Defense of the Employment At-Will Rule.* 27 St. Louis University Law Journal 881 (1983).

Price, Patricia A. *An Overview of the Whistleblower Protection Act.* 2 The Federal Circuit Bar Journal 69 (Spring 1992).

Raspanti, Marc S. *Current Practice and Procedure under the Whistleblower Provisions of the Federal False Claims Act.* 71 Temple Law Review 23 (Spring 1998).

Rath, Manesh K. *How Relocation Affects the Employment At-Will Relationship.* 12 The Labor Lawyer 207 (Summer-Fall 1996).

Raven-Hansen, Peter. *Do's and Don'ts for Whistleblowers: Planning for Trouble.* 82 Technology Review 34 (May 1980).

Ray, Douglas. *Title VII Retaliation Cases: Creating a New Protected Class.* 58 University of Pittsburgh Law Review 405 (Winter 1997).

Raymond, Bradley, and Donna Nuyen. *Labor Law.* 29 Wayne Law Review 841 (1983).

Renz, J. *The Effect of Federal Legislation on Historical State Powers of Pollution Control: Has Congress Muddied State Waters?* 43 Montana Law Review 197 (1982).

Richards, T. and J. De Franco. *Retaliatory Discharge: Its Applicability to Employees Protected by a Just Cause Provision.* 72 Illinois Bar Journal 480 (1984).

Riggs, A. *Legal Principles Applicable to Proper Discharge Procedures.* 37 Labor Law Journal 204 (1986).

Riley, Suzanne. *Employees' Retaliation Claims under 42 U.S.C. 1981: Ramifications of the Civil Rights Act of 1991.* 79 Marquette Law Review 579 (1996).

Rishel, G. *Retaliatory Discharge: A Broadened Tort Through Statutory Analogy.* 70 Illinois Bar Journal 454 (1982).

Rittweger, Thomas Michael. *Nuclear Employers No Longer Shielded from Whistleblower State Tort Claims.* 8 Hofstra Labor Law Journal 493 (Spring 1991).

Robbins, Albert. *Dissent in the Corporate World: When Does an Employee Have the Right to Speak Out?* 5 Civil Liberties Review 6 (September/October 1978).

Robbins, M., N. Norwood, and N. Taldone. *A Symposium: Wrongful Discharge and the Unionized Employee.* 12 Employee Relations Law Journal 19 (1986).

Roberts, Scott. *Developments in the Texas Public Whistleblower Act (Texas Employment Law Symposium).* 47 Baylor Law 867 (Summer 1995).

Rohwer, Claude. *Terminable At-Will Employment: New Theories for Job Security.* 15 Pacific Law Review 766

Rongine, Nicholas. *Toward a Coherent Legal Response to the Public Policy Dilemma Posed by Whistleblowing.* Special Issue—Business and the First Amendment, 23 American Business Law Journal 291 (Summer 1985).

Rosenthal, Sandra J. *Kulch v. Structural Fibers, Inc.: Clarifying the Public Policy Exception (Whistleblowers Legal Remedies-Ohio).* 45 Cleveland State Law Review 681 (Fall 1997).

Ross, Kimberly. *Recent Developments: A Survey of Recent Developments in the Law VII. Employment Law.* 25 William Mitchell Law Review 1109 (1999).

Ross, Robert W. *Nuclear Energy---Federal Preemption---State Moratorium on Nuclear Plant Construction Upheld Against Preemption Challenge: Pacific Gas & Electric Co. v. State Energy Resources Conservation & Dev. Comm'n.* 14 Seton Hall Law Review 1034 (1984).

Rutzel, Stefan. *Snitching for the Common Good: In Search of a Response to the Legal Problems Posed by Environmental Whistleblowing.* 14 Temple Environmental Law and Technology Journal 1 (Spring 1995).

Ryan, T. *Status of Wrongful Discharge in Wisconsin.* 56 Wisconsin Bar Bulletin 22 (April 1983).

Salcido, Robert. *Screening Out Unworthy Whistleblower Actions: An Historical Analysis of the Public Disclosures Jurisdictional Bar to Qui Tam Actions under the False Claims Act.* 24 Public Contract Law Journal 237 (Winter 1995).

Sandler, Debbie Rodman. *Retaliation Claims under the Civil Rights Acts: Treacherous Waters for Employers.* 13 The Labor Lawyer 107 (Summer 1997).

Sarno, Gregory G. *Liability for Retaliation Against At-Will Employee for Public Complaints or Efforts Relating to Health or Safety.* 75 American Law Reports, 4th 13 (1998).

Sauter, Susan. *The Employees Health and Safety Whistleblower Protection Act and the Conscientious Employee: The Potential for Federal Statutory Enforcement of the Public Policy Exception to Employment At-Will.* 59 University of Cincinnati Law Review 513 (Fall 1990).

Schlinker, John C., and Charles F. Szymanski. *Michigan's Whistle-Blowers Protection Act: A Practitioner's Guide.* 74 Michigan Bar Journal 1192 (1995).

Schneier, Mark. *Public Policy Limitations on the Retaliatory Discharge of At-Will Employees in the Private Sector.* 14 University of California, Davis Law Review 811 (1981).

Schreiber, Mark. *Wrongful Termination of At-Will Employees.* 68 Massachusetts Law Review 22 (March 1983).

Schwab, Stewart J. *Employment Life Cycles and the Employment-At-Will Doctrine.* 20 Cornell Law Forum 7 (March 1994).

Schwartz, Martin A. *Admissibility of Investigatory Reports in Section 1983 Civil Rights Actions—A User's Manual.* 79 Marquette Law Review 453 (1996).

Seymour, Sally. *The Case of the Willful Whistleblower.* 65 Business and Society Review 56 (Spring 1988).

Shapiro, S. *Action for Wrongful Discharge of an Employee.* 24 Southern Texas Law Journal 883 (1983).

Shaw, Jerry G., Jr. *Survey of MSPB Cases in 1991-1992: Theoretical Critique and Practical Applications. A Review of Recent Decisions of the United States Court of Appeals for the Federal Circuit.* 42 American University Law Review 869 (Spring 1993).

Shelton, Victoria W. *Will the Public Policy Exception to the Employment-At-Will Doctrine ever be Clear?* 14 Campbell Law Review 123 (Winter 1991).

Short, Jodi L. *Killing the Messenger: The Use of Nondisclosure Agreements to Silence Whistleblowers.* 60 University of Pittsburgh Law Review 1207 (1999).

Shotts, Barry J. *The Scope of Bush v. Lucas: An Examination of Congressional Remedies for Whistleblowers.* 88 Columbia Law Review 587 (April 1988).

Simoff, Laura. *Confusion and Deterrence: The Problems That Arise from a Deficiency in Uniform Laws and Procedures for Environmental Whistleblowers.* 8 Dickinson Journal of Environmental Law and Policy (1999).

Singer, Lucy A. *Employment-At-Will and the Aftermath of Foley v. Interactive Data Corp.* 34 Saint Louis University Law Journal 695 (Spring 1990).

Siniscalco, G. *Reductions in Force: Minimizing Exposure to Contract, Tort and Discrimination Claims.* 9 Employee Relations Law Journal 203 (1983).

Smith, Joel E. *Liability of Employer, Supervisor, or Manager for Intentionally or Recklessly Causing Employee Emotional Distress.* 86 American Law Reports, 3d 454 (1978).

Smith, Kevin M. *The Whistleblowing Era: A Management Perspective.* 19 Employee Relations Law Journal 179 (Fall 1993).

Smith, Monica A. *Silkwood v. Kerr-McGee Corp.: Preemption of State Law for Nuclear Torts?* 12 Environmental Law 1059 (1982).

Smith, Ray, and David Kays. *Preempting State Regulation of Employment Relations: A Model for Analysis.* 20 University of San Francisco Law Review 35 (Fall 1985).

Smith, Stephen E. *Due Process and the Subpoena Power in Federal Environmental, Health, and Safety Whistleblower Proceedings.* 32 University of San Francisco Law Review 533 (Spring 1998).

Smyth, Todd R., J.D. *Eavesdropping On Extension Telephone as Invasion of Privacy.* 49 American Law Reports, 4th 430 (1986).

Sniffen, Michael J. *Government's False Claims Recoveries Rise.* Associated Press (February 24, 2000).

Soeken, Beth and Don Soeken. *A Survey of Whistleblowers: Their Stressors and Coping Strategies.* Senate Committee on Governmental Affairs, Subcommittee on Federal Services, Post Office, and Civil Service, Hearings on S. 508, 100th Cong., 1st sess. (July1987).

Solomon, Lewis D., and Terry D. Garcia. *Protecting the Corporate Whistle Blower under Federal Anti-Retaliation Statutes.* 5 The Journal of Corporation Law 275 (Winter 1980).

Spivey, Gary D. *Libel and Slander: Privileged Nature of Communication to Other Employees or Employees' Union of Reason for Plaintiff's Discharge.* 60 American Law Reports, 3d 1080 (1974).

Sprague, Tim L. *What Kulch Accomplished: What Kulch Left Out (Whistleblowers Legal Remedies—Ohio).* 45 Cleveland State Law Review 667 (Fall 1997).

St. Antoine, Theodore. *Employment-At-Will—is the Model Act the Answer? (Model Employment Termination Act).* 23 Stetson Law Review 179 (Fall 1993).

Steiner, J., and A. Dabrow. *The Questionable Value of Inclusion of Language Confirming Employment At-Will Status in Company Personnel Documents.* 37 Labor Law Journal 639 (1986).

Stevens, Blaine Celone. *Employment At-Will: The Time Has Come for Alabama to Embrace Public Policy as an Exception to the Rule of Employment At-Will.* 19 Cumberland Law Review 373 (Winter 1989).

Strader, Kent D. *Counterclaims Against Whistleblowers: Should Counter claims Against Qui Tam Plaintiffs Be Allowed in False Claims Act Cases?* 62 University of Cincinnati Law Review 713 (Fall 1993).

Sullivan, J. Thomas. *The Arkansas Remedy for Employer Retaliation against Workers Compensation Claimants.* 16 University of Arkansas at Little Rock Law Journal 373 (Summer 1994).

Summers, Clyde. *Individual Protection Against Unjust Dismissal: Time for a Statute.* 62 Virginia Law Review 481 (April 1976).

Summers, Clyde. *Protecting All Employees Against Unjust Dismissal.* 58 Harvard Business Review 132 (January/February 1980).

Summers, Clyde. *The Rights of Individual Workers: The Contract of Employment and the Rights of Individual Employees: Fair Representation and Employment At-Will.* 52 Fordham Law Review 1082 (1984).

Swan, George Steven. *The Economics of the Retaliatory Discharge Public Policy Action.* 9 Saint Louis University Public Law Review 605 (Fall 1990).

Taylor, James W. *The California False Claims Act (State and Local Government Procurement).* 25 Public Contract Law Journal 315 (Winter 1996).

Tepker, Harry. *Oklahoma's at-Will Rule: Heeding the Warning of America's Evolving Employment Law?* 39 Oklahoma Law Review 373 (Fall 1986).

Timm, Walter W. *Employment At-Will in Illinois—Has the Employer Been Forgotten?* 9 Northern Illinois University Law Review 603 (Summer 1989).

Tremblay, Paul R. *Ratting.* 17 The American Journal of Trial Advocacy 49 (Summer 1993).

Vaughn, Robert. *Public Employees and the Right to Disobey.* 29 Hastings Law 9 Journal 261 (November 1977).

Vaughn, Robert. *State Whistleblower Statutes and the Future of Whistleblower Protection.* 51 Administrative Law Review 581 (1999).

Vaughn, Robert. *Statutory Protection of Whistleblowers in the Federal Executive Branch.* 3 University of Illinois Law Review 615 (1982).

Vaughn, Robert G. *State Whistleblower Statutes and the Future of Whistleblower Protection.* 51 Administrative Law Review 581 (1999).

Vickory, Frank. *The Erosion of the Employment-At-Will Doctrine and the Statute of Frauds: Time to Amend the Statute.* 30 American Business Law Journal 97 (May 1992).

Villemez, Jane. *The First Amendment and the Law Enforcement Agency: Protecting the Employee Who Blows the Whistle.* 18 Land and Water Law Review 789 (Fall 1983).

Vogel, Robert L. *The Public Disclosure Bar Against Qui Tam Suits.* 24 Public Contract Law Journal 477 (Summer 1995).

Wakefield, Wanda Ellen. *Liability for Discharging At-Will Employees for Refusing to Partcipate in or for Disclosing Unlawful or Unethical Acts of Employer or Coemployees.* 9 American Law Review 4th 329 (1981).

Wald, M., and D. Wolf. *Recent Developments in the Law of Employment At-Will.* 1 The Labor Lawyer 533 (1985).

Wald, Patricia. *NRC Bars Paying Whistleblowers for Silence.* New York Times (May 4, 1989).

Wall, Richard. *At-Will Employment in Washington: A Review of Thompson v. St. Regis Paper Company and its progeny.* 14 The University of Puget Sound Law Review 71 (Fall 1990).

Walters, Kenneth. *Your Employees' Right to Blow the Whistle.* 53 Harvard Business Review 26 (July/August 1975).

Walterscheid, E. *When Employees Act Contrary to the Interests of Their Employers: Activities Unprotected under Title VII.* 12 Employee Relations Law Journal 609 (1987).

Weeks, Joseph. *NLRA Preemption of State Common Law Wrongful Discharge Claims: The Bhopal Brigade Goes Home.* 13 Pepperdine Law Review 607 (1986).

Weinstein, Brian Stryker. *In Defense of Jeffrey Wigand: A First Amendment Challenge to the Enforcement of Employee Confidentiality Agreements Against Whistleblowers.* 49 South Carolina Law Review 129 (Fall 1997).

Weiser, Benjamin. *Lawsuit Spurs a Debate Over Secrets vs. Safety.* The Washington Post, A-1 (July 26, 1994).

Werner, Tom. *The Common Law Employment-At-Will Doctrine: Current Exceptions for Iowa Employees.* 43 Drake Law Review 291 (Spring 1994).

Zimmerman, D., and J. Howard-Martin. *The Federal Preemption Doctrine Revisited.* 37 Labor Law Journal 223 (1986).

Zolner, M. Derek. *Employment Law: Report a Crime. Lose Your Job: The Oklahoma Supreme Court Reins in the Public Policy Exception in Hayes v. Eateries, Inc.* 50 Oklahoma Law Review 585 (Winter 1997).

Index

About the Author

STEPHEN M. KOHN is a partner in the Washington, D.C., law firm of Kohn, Kohn & Colapinto, P.C. and Chairperson of the Board of Directors of the National Whistleblower Center. Mr. Kohn has taught law at the Antioch School of Law and is former Director of Corporate Litigation for the Government Accountability Project. Nationally recognized for his work on whistleblower law, he has contributed numerous articles to law reviews and is author of several books, including *The Labor Lawyer's Guide to the Rights and Responsibilities of Employee Whistleblowers* (Quorum, 1988).